From the Reviewers

The authors have made an important contribution to the services marketing arena in Asia. The timing is perfect with the transition across many Asian countries from economies dominated by the primary sectors to secondary and tertiary sectors. By combining the best of the academic literatures with the managerial and practice domains, they have a book that will provide food for thought for everyone interested in this vital area (i.e., managers, civil servants, and academics).

Professor Paddy Padmanabhan
The INSEAD Chaired Professor of Marketing, INSEAD

Understanding services marketing in Asia ... extracting meaning from the collective knowledge of the four authors will be a stimulating experience for the marketing student and experienced practitioner alike.

Pratap Nambiar
Regional Executive Partner, Global Markets—KPMG Asia Pacific Ltd.

Services Marketing in Asia *sets cutting-edge services marketing knowledge in an Asian context. It is an exciting read, and I will recommend this book to anyone who either is a service leader or seeks to become one.*

Ye Yigan
Chairman of the Board, China Eastern Airlines Corporation Ltd.

I am most delighted to see this new Asian edition of Services Marketing in Asia. *This book is timely as our Asian economies are rapidly becoming increasingly service-dependent. Most important, it contains the cutting-edge knowledge and best practices that students and executives can learn from. The China component empowers us with the needed knowledge on how to succeed in the world's most populous services market.*

Professor David K. Tse
Professor of International Marketing, The University of Hong Kong

An intriguing quest on Asian perspective in services marketing! This book provides a solid understanding of the latest thinking and concepts in services marketing and offers a rational set of tools and tips for today's leaders. Cases from across Asian economies are well researched and discussed which captures the quintessence of Services Marketing in Asia.

Dr Buck P. Tang
Divisional Director (International Business), Service Quality Centre, Singapore

Services Marketing in Asia fills the gap in the understanding of services in Asia. The knowledge gained from this book is both valuable to professors and students, and it is a must-read for top and middle management in services firms.

Professor Yigang Pan
Scotiabank Professor of International Business, Schulich School of Business,
York University, Canada

This second edition of Services Marketing in Asia continues the excellence of the previous edition. The book communicates its core messages in a powerful manner, and makes it compelling and easy to read. An excellent piece of work!

Professor Vijay Mahajan
Dean, Indian School of Business

Professor Lovelock, the pioneer in services marketing, has a classic text in this book. The Asian adaptation is well done, and it's most relevant to students of marketing in Asia.

Professor Tan Chin Tiong
Provost, Singapore Management University

This book is full of priceless insights and relevant examples. It is a must-read for managers who are interested in services marketing in Asia. It can really help your firm to succeed in the competitive environment in Asia. I highly recommend this book.

Professor Teck H. Ho
William Halford, Jr. Family Professor of Marketing, Haas School of Business,
University of California, Berkeley

This book presents the latest thinking and insights on services marketing in Asia. It is well-structured and filled with many inspiring ideas, relevant, and practical examples. This is an excellent book for anyone interested in understanding services marketing practices in Asia.

Professor Jackie Tam
Department of Management and Marketing, The Hong Kong Polytechnic University

As Asian economies continue to mature and Asian consumers become more sophisticated, products alone can commoditize and the role of brand experience and services becomes ever more important for manufacturing companies. Services Marketing in Asia provides both insight and an essential guide to thinking through and acting on these issues for companies in Asia to build and sustain competitive advantage.

Jeremy Rowe
Program Director, ICI Paints (Asia Pacific), Singapore

Services Marketing in Asia is a contemporary book which provides powerful insights on services marketing that will be meaningful not only to students of marketing but to practitioners as well. It is a dynamic reference for executives who want to perfect their craft in customer intimacy and for academicians who need up-to-date reference material in teaching the subject.

Professor Leonardo R. Garcia Jr.
Dean, School of Professional and Continuing Education,
De La Salle College of St. Benilde, Philippines

In many ways, Asia is the home of outstanding service quality. This book does a fantastic job of putting an integrative theoretical framework around service excellence so that there are clear tools and takeaways for the student and practicing manager. The broad spectrum of case studies nicely complements the concepts, and gives the reader an opportunity to practice, refine, and critique the tools. This is an outstanding resource!

Professor Dilip Soman
Corus Professor of Strategy and Professor of Marketing, Rotman School of Management,
University of Toronto, Canada

Readable and research-based—the two seldom go together. However, Services Marketing in Asia *provides comprehensive advice that is equally applicable to either the academic or the practitioner. The chapter on "Pricing and Revenue Management" alone is worth the price of the book.*

David Shackleton
Senior Vice President, Starwood Asia Pacific, Starwood Hotels & Resorts Worldwide Inc.

I find this to be the most authoritative textbook on Asian Services Marketing. In some magical fashion, the authors have combined high levels of academic rigor with liberal doses of practical relevance to present us a book that is not only very enjoyable to read, but is extremely insightful. The conceptual treatment and the case studies are brilliant. I can't think of a better textbook for my services marketing students.

Professor M. Krishna Erramilli
Associate Professor and Head of Marketing and International Business Division,
Nanyang Technological University, Singapore

On balance, services almost always create more value than the physical process of production itself. In China today, the role and value of services are not well understood, and the challenge of services marketing is immense. Its fast growing economy needs more and better service marketing expertise than ever. The contribution of Services Marketing in Asia *is both timely and much needed, and I am convinced that it will make a valuable contribution to best service practices in China.*

Willie Fung
Senior Vice President and General Manager of Greater China, MasterCard International

A useful and practical guide which will give you the edge in the booming field of services marketing in Asia. The clear, comprehensive approach put forward by the authors has helped differentiate our positioning in Asia and better serve our clients. If you are in a service industry in Asia or are considering entering this field, you will find Services Marketing in Asia *an invaluable resource.*

Jeffrey MacCorkle
Managing Director, Arthur D Little Greater China

SERVICES MARKETING IN ASIA

SECOND EDITION

Christopher Lovelock

Jochen Wirtz

Hean Tat Keh

Xiongwen Lu

MANAGING PEOPLE, TECHNOLOGY, AND STRATEGY

PEARSON

Prentice
Hall

Singapore   London   New York   Toronto   Sydney   Tokyo   Madrid
Mexico City   Munich   Paris   Capetown   Hong Kong   Montreal

Published in 2005 by
Prentice Hall
Pearson Education South Asia Pte Ltd
23/25 First Lok Yang Road, Jurong
Singapore 629733

Pearson Education offices in Asia: *Bangkok, Beijing, Hong Kong, Jakarta, Kuala Lumpur, Manila, New Delhi, Seoul, Singapore, Taipei, Tokyo, Shanghai*

Original edition, Services Marketing, 5th edition (by Christopher Lovelock and Jochen Wirtz), published by Prentice-Hall, Inc. Copyright © 2004 by Christopher H. Lovelock and Jochen Wirtz.

Printed in Singapore

5   4   3   2   1
08   07   06   05

ISBN 0-13-127537-2

PEARSON
Prentice
Hall

To my son, Tim, and my daughter, Liz.
Christopher H. Lovelock

To Jeannette and our children Lorraine, Stefanie, and Alexander, with love.
Jochen Wirtz

To my wife, Karen, and our sons, Sean Rong and Sean Heng. Thank you for your love, support, patience, and putting up with my long hours at work.
Hean Tat Keh

To my wife, Vicky, and my parents.
Xiongwen Lu

Brief Contents

Cases

Contents

Preface

The preparation of the second edition of *Services Marketing in Asia: Managing People, Technology, and Strategy* has been an exciting challenge. Building on the success of the first edition, this second edition offers a unique and truly Asian perspective of services marketing. As far as we are aware, this is still the only textbook on services marketing that has been specifically written with a direct focus on Asian practice, viewed from multiple perspectives.

This book incorporates the latest thinking in services marketing. We have pooled our skills in teaching, consulting, and research to create a versatile, flexible text for instructors teaching in a variety of environments in different parts of Asia. The geographic coverage of the book is very broad, covering all major economies in Asia, including China, Hong Kong, India, Indonesia, Japan, Malaysia, the Philippines, Singapore, South Korea, Taiwan, Thailand, and Vietnam.

As its title implies, the second edition of *Services Marketing in Asia: Managing People, Technology, and Strategy* takes a strongly managerial perspective, but it is also rooted in solid academic research, complemented by memorable concepts and frameworks—all designed to bridge the gap between the real world and academic theory.

Services marketing, once a tiny academic field championed by just a handful of pioneering professors, has become a thriving area of activity in other parts of the world as well as in Asia. Paralleling growth in the service sector is the increasing enrollment in services marketing courses at tertiary institutions. Therefore, a good understanding of the latest thinking and concepts is important, especially as managers often find that manufacturing-based models of business practice are not always useful to the service-specific issues that they face.

Objectives of This Book

The four authors aimed to achieve the following main objectives when writing this second edition:

- To provide an in-depth appreciation and understanding of the unique challenges inherent in managing and delivering service excellence at a profit. Readers will be introduced to, and have the opportunity to work with, tools and strategies that address these challenges.
- To develop an understanding of the "state of the art" of service management principles, combined with local and regional perspectives.

- To promote a customer-service-oriented mindset.
- To help the reader to work more effectively as a manager (or consultant) in service-driven organizations, bringing Asian insights to the global stage.

By the time readers finish this book, we predict that few of them will ever look at the services their company provides, any service firms they interact with, or the services they themselves experience in the same light again!

What's New in the Second Asian Edition?

Responding to the rapid changes in technology and the environment of the service sector in Asia, this second edition has been both streamlined and restructured to sharpen the focus on essentials and add in-depth coverage of new concepts and ideas. It consists of 15 chapters and 17 cases of varying lengths and levels of difficulty. We feature new Asian cases on firms operating across many Asian cultures (e.g., Banyan Tree, DHL, KFC, McDonald's, and Giordano) as well as on organizations operating in specific Asian countries and regions, including in China, Hong Kong, Taiwan, India, Malaysia, Myanmar, the Philippines, and Singapore.

New Topics, New Structure

- The book presents coverage of the latest research and developments in the service sector, ranging from customer relationship management (CRM), customer asset management, and Six Sigma quality to revenue (yield) management and customer feedback systems. In addition, there is substantive coverage of consumer behavior, service staff management issues, branding, business-to-business services, and technology-based services.
- We emphasize that marketing strategy takes place in a highly competitive environment, reflecting our belief that service firms must be competitively positioned as well as customer focused.
- All chapters feature expanded references, with new published research findings being added to every topic.
- The book has been streamlined to avoid unnecessary repetition and restructured to ensure an enhanced sequence of topics. Despite the addition of new material, tighter editing has resulted in a leaner and crisper set of chapters.
- We have reduced the number of chapters to 15 (down from 18 in the previous edition). Every chapter has been revised, and some have been retitled to reflect a more focused emphasis. Material on technology and international strategy will now be found throughout the book rather than being presented in separate chapters. Coverage of demand and capacity management, queuing, and reservations has been consolidated in a single chapter, with material on revenue management being transferred to the pricing chapter.

- Figure A presents the revised four-part structure of the book, showing how chapter topics are sequenced.
- Particular attention has been paid to making this new edition stimulating and highly readable. The result is a text that is clear, focused, and designed to capture student interest. Boxed inserts within each chapter present numerous interesting examples, primarily from Asia, that describe important research findings, illustrate practical applications of important service marketing concepts, and present best practices in services marketing. Many of these inserts are new to this edition.

New Cases

The book features an exceptional selection of up-to-date, classroom-tested cases of varying lengths and levels of difficulty. We prepared or co-authored a majority of the cases, most of which are unavailable elsewhere.

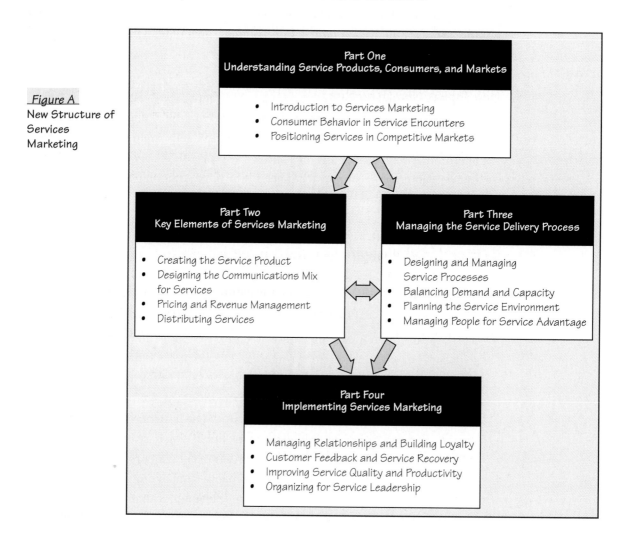

Figure A
New Structure of Services Marketing

- To offer instructors greater choice, the number of cases has been expanded from 13 to 17. The new selection provides a broader coverage of service issues, application areas, and Asian contexts.
- Eleven of the cases are new to this edition. Almost all of the cases carried over from the previous edition have been updated and feature a 2005 copyright date.

Target Audiences and Courses

This text is equally suitable for courses directed at advanced undergraduate or MBA and EMBA students working in an Asian business context. *Services Marketing in Asia*, Second Edition, places marketing issues within a broader management context. Whatever a manager's specific job may be, he or she has to understand and acknowledge the close ties that link the marketing, operations, and human resource functions. With that perspective in mind, this book has been designed so that instructors can make selective use of chapters and cases to teach courses of various lengths and formats in either services marketing or service management.

Distinguishing Features of the Book

Key features of this highly readable book include its strong managerial orientation and strategic focus, use of memorable conceptual frameworks that have been classroom tested for relevance to both undergraduate and MBA students, incorporation of key academic research findings, use of interesting examples to link theory to practice, and inclusion of carefully selected cases to accompany the text chapters.

Services Marketing in Asia is designed to complement the materials found in traditional marketing principles texts. It avoids sweeping and often misleading generalizations about services, recognizing explicitly that the differences between specific categories of services (based on the nature of the underlying service process) may be as important to student understanding as the broader differences between goods marketing and services marketing. It also draws a distinction between the marketing of services and the marketing of goods *through service*.

The book shows how different technologies—and information and communications technology in particular—are changing the nature of service delivery and can offer innovative ways for service providers and customers to relate to each other. Yet many services remain labor intensive, so we devote significant emphasis to the people aspects of service management.

The service sector of the economy can best be characterized by its diversity. No single conceptual model suffices to cover marketing-relevant issues among organizations ranging from huge international corporations (in fields such as airlines, banking, insurance, telecommunications, supply chain management, and professional services) to locally owned and operated small businesses, such as restaurants, laundries, taxis, optometrists, and many business-to-business services. In response, *Services Marketing in Asia* offers a carefully designed "toolbox" for service managers, teaching students how different concepts, frameworks, and analytical procedures can best be used to examine and resolve the varied challenges faced by managers in different situations. Once introduced, many of these tools reappear in subsequent chapters.

Throughout the book, we stress the importance for service marketers of understanding the operational processes underlying service creation and delivery. These processes are grouped into four categories, each of which has distinctive implications for the nature of service encounters, the roles played by customers and service personnel, the strategic application of information and communications technologies to delivery systems, and management practice.

Pedagogical Aids

In response to adopter requests, the following pedagogical enhancements are available for the text:

- An introduction to each chapter highlights key issues and questions to be addressed.
- Four types of boxed inserts accompany many of the chapters:
  - *Best Practice in Action* (demonstrations of the application of best practices)
  - *Research Insights* (summaries of highly relevant rigorous academic research)
  - *Service Perspectives* (in-depth examples that illustrate key concepts)
  - *Management Memo* (reviews of key concepts that apply to service management)
- Interesting graphics, including reproductions of ads and photos, are included to enhance both visual appeal and student learning.
- Review Questions and Application Exercises are located at the end of each chapter.
- Each case includes suggested study questions.
- The *Instructor's Resource Manual for Services Marketing in Asia* includes:
  - Detailed course design and teaching hints, as well as two sample course outlines.
  - Chapter-by-chapter teaching suggestions, along with discussion of learning objectives and sample responses to study questions and exercises.
  - A description of 16 suggested student exercises and five comprehensive projects (designed for either individual or team use).

- Detailed teaching notes for each of the cases, as well as suggestions for possible chapters with which they might be paired.
- CD-ROM with video clips to accompany the text and some of the cases.

New and Improved Teaching Resources at www.prenhall.com/Lovelock

- Revised and enlarged supplements include an excellent online instructor's manual.
- To further enhance the mix of teaching materials, several popular cases from the first edition of the book are being made available on the Web site for *Services Marketing in Asia*. The Web site also includes a "Note on Studying and Learning from Cases" for students.
- Detailed teaching notes are provided for all cases, including teaching objectives, suggested study questions, in-depth analysis of each question, and helpful hints on potential teaching strategies for each case.
- Instructors can now select from more than 400 online PowerPoint slides, keyed to each chapter. These materials include both text slides and graphics. All slides have been designed to be clear, comprehensive, and easily readable. Instructors should contact their local Prentice Hall representative for information on how to access the PowerPoint slides. Additional cases may be downloaded from the Web site (www.prenhall.com/Lovelock) at the discretion of the instructor.

Acknowledgments

Over the years, many colleagues in both the academic and business worlds have provided us with valuable insights into the management and marketing of services, through their writings and in conference or seminar discussions. We have also benefited enormously from in-class and after-class discussions with MBA and executive program participants.

We are pleased to acknowledge the insightful and helpful comments of our editorial advisory board: Bai Changhong of Nankai University, China; Leonardo R. Garcia Jr., De La Salle College of St. Benilde, Philippines; M. Krishna Erramilli of Nanyang Technological University, Singapore; Aliah Hanim M. Salleh of University Kebangsaan Malaysia; and Yigang Pan of the University of Hong Kong. We also express gratitude to Michael Hui of the Chinese University of Hong Kong and Jacob Jou of National Sun Yat-Sen University, Taiwan, for their reviews of the first edition. We are grateful, too, to the many instructors who adopted the book, and suggested improvements to this new edition. They challenged our thinking and, through their critiques and suggestions, encouraged us to include many substantial changes.

Although it's impossible to mention everyone who has influenced our thinking over the years, we particularly want to express our appreciation to the following individuals: John Bateson of SHL Group; Leonard Berry of Texas A&M University; Mary Jo Bitner and Stephen Brown of Arizona State University; David Bowen of the Thunderbird School; Richard Chase of the University of Southern California; Raymond Fisk of the University of New Orleans; Christian Grönroos of the Swedish School of Economics in Finland; Stephen Grove of Clemson University; Evert Gummesson of Stockholm University; James Heskett, Theodore Levitt, Earl Sasser, and Leonard Schlesinger, all currently or formerly of Harvard Business School; Robert Johnston of Warwick Business School; Sheryl Kimes of the Cornell University School of Hotel Administration; David Maister of Maister Associates; Anna Mattila of Pennsylvania State University; "Parsu" Parasuraman of the University of Miami; Javier Reynoso of EGADE, Tec de Monterrey; Roland Rust and Benjamin Schneider of the University of Maryland; Charles Weinberg of the University of British Columbia; Lauren Wright of California State University, Chico; George Yip of London Business School; and Valarie Zeithaml of the University of North Carolina.

We thank, too, the authors (named in the section "About the Contributors") of cases, as well as the copyright holders for permission to reprint these and other materials.

It takes more than authors to create a book and its supplements. Warm thanks are due to our many research assistants who helped us with various aspects of the cases, the text, or the instructor's resource manual. They are: Patricia Y. P. Chew, Ziyun Dai, Seng Lee Lou, Denis C. L. Tan, Shawn T. H. Tay, Wang Bin, Maureen Yong, Joycelin Huang, Elizabeth X. Xie, Ning Cen, and Yingwen Wang. And, of course, we're very appreciative of all the hard work put in by the editing and production team in helping to transform our sometimes messy manuscript into a handsome published text. Thank you for all your enthusiasm and support!

About the Authors

As a team, Christopher Lovelock, Jochen Wirtz, Hean Tat Keh, and Xiongwen Lu possess a blend of skills and experience that is ideally suited to writing an authoritative and engaging services marketing text focusing on Asia.

CHRISTOPHER LOVELOCK is one of the pioneers of services marketing. Based in the United States, he is a frequent visitor to Asia. He consults and gives seminars for managers around the world, with a particular focus on strategic planning in services and managing the customer experience. He is an adjunct professor at the Yale School of Management, where he teaches an MBA services marketing course. Dr Lovelock's distinguished academic career has included 11 years on the faculty of the Harvard Business School and two years as a visiting professor at IMD in Switzerland. He has also held appointments at Berkeley, Stanford, and the Sloan School at MIT, as well as visiting professorships at The University of Queensland in Australia and at both INSEAD and Theseus Institute in France. He obtained a BCom and an MA in economics from the University of Edinburgh, then worked in advertising with the London office of J. Walter Thompson Co. and in corporate planning with Canadian Industries Ltd in Montreal. Later, he obtained an MBA from Harvard and a PhD from Stanford. Author or coauthor of over 60 articles, more than 100 teaching cases, and 26 books, he serves on the editorial review boards of the *International Journal of Service Industry Management, Journal of Service Research, Service Industries Journal, Cornell Hotel and Restaurant Administration Quarterly*, and *Marketing Management*. He is a recipient of the American Marketing Association's Award for Career Contributions to the Services Discipline and of a best article award from the *Journal of Marketing*. Recognized many times for excellence in case writing, he has twice won top honors in the *BusinessWeek* "European Case of the Year" Award.

JOCHEN WIRTZ is one of the leading authorities in services marketing in Asia. He is an Associate Professor at the National University of Singapore, where he teaches services marketing courses in Executive MBA, MBA and undergraduate programs. He is also the codirector of NUS's joint Executive MBA program with UCLA. He received his PhD in services marketing from the London Business School, and holds a BA (Hons) in marketing and accounting and a professional certification in banking from Germany. Dr Wirtz's research focuses on service management and he has published some 50 academic articles in, among others, *Harvard Business Review, Journal of Business Research, Journal of Consumer Psychology, Journal of Retailing, Journal of the Academy of Marketing Science, Journal of Services*

Marketing, Journal of Service Research, Managing Service Quality, and *Psychology and Marketing.* In addition, he has published some 70 conference papers, six books, and some 40 book chapters. He has received six best paper awards, including the "Emerald Literati Club 2003 Award for Excellence" for the most outstanding paper of the year in the *International Journal of Service Industry Management.* In recognition of his teaching excellence, Dr Wirtz has received six awards for outstanding teaching at NUS Business School, including the prestigious universitywide "Outstanding Educator Award" in 2003. Dr Wirtz has also been active as a management consultant, working with both international consulting firms including Accenture, Arthur D. Little, and KPMG, and major service companies in the areas of strategy, business development and service management across Asia. Originally from Germany, Dr Wirtz moved to Asia in 1992 after studying and working in London for seven years.

HEAN TAT KEH is an Associate Professor of Marketing at the Guanghua School of Management, Peking University in Beijing, China. Previously, Dr Keh taught at the National University of Singapore for five years. A Malaysian of Chinese ancestry, he obtained his BBA (Hons) from the University of East Asia, Macau, his MBA from the Hong Kong University of Science and Technology, and his PhD from the University of Washington, Seattle. His corporate experience includes working at the Wharf (Holdings) Limited in Hong Kong. A popular and award-winning educator, Dr Keh has taught widely in undergraduate, MBA, and executive education programs. His research and teaching interests include marketing channels, services marketing, branding, entrepreneurial marketing, and global marketing. A prolific researcher, his research articles appear regularly in prestigious scholarly and managerial journals, including the *European Journal of Operational Research, IEEE Transactions on Engineering Management, Omega, Long Range Planning, Business Horizons,* and *Entrepreneurship Theory and Practice.* Dr Keh is also coauthor of another book, *Strategic Asian Marketing: An Essential Guide for Managers,* published by Prentice Hall in 2004. He has been featured in articles in the *Asian Wall Street Journal,* the *Straits Times* (Singapore), *Today* (Singapore), the *New Straits Times* (Malaysia), and *CEO I.T.* magazine, and has also appeared on Channel News Asia (Singapore) to discuss marketing issues. Dr Keh has consulted for Lundbeck (Denmark), NOL/APL (Singapore), Motorola, Singapore Pools, the Asian Strategy and Leadership Institute (Malaysia), and Rosauer Supermarkets (USA). He is multilingual, and is fluent in English, Mandarin, Cantonese, Fujianese, and Malay.

XIONGWEN LU is Professor of Marketing in the School of Management at Fudan University and Honorary Professor at the University of Hong Kong. Recognized as one of the most distinguished marketing academicians in China, Dr Lu has been elected a Standing Director of the Chinese Marketing Association, Vice Chairman of Shanghai Marketing Association, and Director of the Center for Chinese Marketing Research (cosponsored by the Chinese Marketing Association and Fudan University). He obtained his Bachelor's, Master's and PhD degrees in economics at Fudan University. In the United States, he has been a research fellow at the Tuck School of Business, Dartmouth College, as well as a visiting faculty member at the Sloan School of Management, MIT, and Fisher College of Business, the Ohio State University. An award-winning lecturer, Dr Lu teaches extensively in PhD, Executive MBA and MBA programs in courses on *Current Development of Marketing Theory, Marketing in Immature Markets, International Marketing* and *Services Marketing*. A dedicated and extraordinary researcher, Dr Lu has successfully chaired numerous research projects funded by the National Natural Science Foundation, the State Ministry of Education of China, and Shanghai Municipal Government. His empirical research of immature markets such as China has explored comparative studies on the nature of markets in developed and developing countries. Dr Lu's published works include two research books, one textbook, as well as more than two dozen papers in the leading Chinese journals and international conferences. He is the translator of Dr Lovelock's original *Services Marketing* (3rd edition) in China. He has also been prominent as a consultant to local listed enterprises and multinational companies such as Alcatel, MasterCard, Unilever, Emerson Electric, Bao Steel, and Sunbeam.

About the Contributors

Patricia Chew is a doctoral candidate at NUS Business School, National University of Singapore.

Bhavna Hinduja is an MBA student at the Rotman School of Management, University of Toronto.

Sheryl E. Kimes is a professor at the School of Hotel Administration, Cornell University.

Jill Klein is an associate professor at INSEAD.

Maisy Koh is Corporate Director, Brand Management, at Banyan Tree Hotels and Resorts, and at Angsana Resorts & Spas.

May Lwin is an assistant professor of marketing at NUS Business School, National University of Singapore.

Indranil Sen is research and planning manager at DHL Asia Pacific.

Sanjay Singh is a manager at the Corporate Governance and Reporting Center, NUS Business School, National University of Singapore.

Dilip Soman is a professor of marketing and Corus Entertainment Professor of Communication Strategy at Rotman School of Management, University of Toronto.

Atul Wadhwa is an MBA student at the Rotman School of Management, University of Toronto.

Aliah Hanim M. Salleh Sandhu is an associate professor of marketing, Faculty of Business Management, Universiti Kebangsaan Malaysia.

Understanding Service Products, Consumers, and Markets

PART ONE

CHAPTER ONE

Introduction to Services Marketing

Ours is a service economy and it has been for some time.

KARL ALBRECHT AND RON ZEMKE

The best way to find yourself is to lose yourself in the service of others.

MAHATMA GANDHI

As consumers, we use services every day. Turning on a light, listening to the radio, talking on the telephone, taking a bus, and getting a haircut are all examples of service consumption at the individual level. The institution at which you are studying is itself a complex service organization. Businesses and other organizations are also dependent on a wide array of services, usually purchasing on a much larger scale than individuals or households.

Unfortunately, customers are not always happy with the quality and value of the services they receive. People complain about late deliveries, incompetent personnel, inconvenient service hours, needlessly complicated procedures, long queues, and a host of other problems.

Suppliers of services, who often face stiff competition, sometimes appear to have a very different set of concerns. Many complain about how difficult it is to make a profit, to find skilled and motivated employees, or to please customers.

Fortunately, there are service suppliers who know how to please their customers, while also running a productive, profitable operation, staffed by pleasant and competent employees. In this book, you'll be introduced to innovative organizations, both large and small, from which you can draw important insights on how to get it right.

Although many Asian countries are still best known for manufacturing and agriculture, the role of the service economy continues to increase in importance almost everywhere. In this chapter, we present an overview of today's dynamic service sector in Asia and explore the following questions:

1. How important is the service sector in different Asian countries?
2. What makes services so different from physical goods, and what are the implications for marketing services?
3. What are the important differences between various types of services, and how do these differences impact the way we market them?
4. What are the elements of the services marketing mix?
5. Why do service businesses need to integrate the marketing, operations, and human resource functions?
6. What are the major changes occurring in the service sector, and how are these changes affecting the nature of service competition?

Services Dominate the Modern Economy

The service sector is going through almost revolutionary change, which dramatically affects the way in which we live and work. New services are continually being launched to satisfy our existing needs and to meet needs that we did not even know we had. Just less than ten years ago, few people anticipated a personal need for email, online banking, Web hosting, and many other new services. Today, many people feel they can't do without them. Similar transformations are occurring in business-to-business (B2B) markets.

Service organizations range in size from huge international corporations like airlines, banks, insurance companies, telecommunications companies, and hotel chains to a vast array of locally owned and operated small businesses, including restaurants, laundries, optometrists, and numerous business-to-business services, to name a few.

Structure of the Service Sector

The service sector is remarkably diverse. It comprises a wide array of different industries that sell to individual consumers and business customers, as well as to government agencies and nonprofit organizations. Table 1.1 shows how the service sectors contribute to the economies of more than a dozen Asian countries. Shanghai's striking new skyline (Figure 1.1) dramatizes the growth of financial services, telecommunications, and other service industries in the rapidly expanding Chinese economy.

Services make up the bulk of today's economy and also account for most of the growth in new jobs. Unless you are already predestined for a career in a family manufacturing or agricultural business, the probability is high that you will spend your working life in service organizations. Perhaps you will even start your own service business!

The size of the service sector is increasing in almost all economies around the world. As a national economy develops, the relative share of employment between

Countries	1980[c] (%)	1990 (%)	2002 (%)
East Asia			
China	21.4	31.3	33.7
Hong Kong	63.9	74.4	86.5[d]
South Korea	43.7	48.4	55.1
Taiwan	46.6	54.6	67.1
Southeast Asia			
Indonesia	31.8	41.5	38.1
Malaysia	na	44.2	46.4
Philippines	36.1	43.6	52.8
Singapore	60.6	67.8	66.6
Thailand	48.1	50.3	48.5
Vietnam	26.9	38.6	38.5
South Asia			
India[b]	36.0	39.7	49.2[d]
Pakistan[b]	45.5	48.8	53.4
Sri Lanka[e]	44.0	49.8	53.6

Table 1.1
Share of Service Sector in GDP[a] (percent) for Selected Asian Countries

[a] Unless otherwise stated, GDP data are at current market prices.

[b] Data are based on GDP at current factor cost.

[c] Data for 1980 are based on NMP at current prices.

[d] Refers to 2001.

[e] Data for 2002 are at current factor cost.

Source: Key Indicators 2003: Education for Global Participation, Vol. 34, Asian Development Bank; http://www.adb.org/Documents/Books/KeyIndicators/2003/default.asp, accessed on July 15, 2004.

Figure 1.1
Shanghai, the Rapidly Developing Financial Center in China

agriculture, industry (including manufacturing and mining), and services changes dramatically.[1] Even in emerging economies, service output is growing rapidly and often accounts for half or more of the gross domestic product (GDP).[2] For example, Hong Kong being a major provider of two key services for manufacturers, finance and marine port facilities, has 86.5 percent of its GDP contributed from service sectors.

Figure 1.2 shows how the evolution to a service-dominated economy is likely to take place over time as per capita income rises. Where do you think your country is located on this chart?

Why Is the Service Sector Growing?

In numerous countries, increased productivity and automation in agriculture and industry, combined with growing demand for both new and traditional services, have jointly resulted in a continuing increase over time in the percentage of the labor force that is employed in services. There's a hidden service sector within many large corporations that are classified by government statisticians as being in manufacturing, agricultural, or natural resources industries. These so-called *internal services* cover a wide range of activities, including recruitment, legal and accounting services, payroll administration, office cleaning, landscape maintenance, supply-chain management, advertising, and many other kinds of services. Organizations are increasingly choosing to outsource such internal services that can be performed more efficiently by a specialist provider or a subcontractor. Internal services are also being spun out as separate service operations offered in the wider marketplace. When such tasks are outsourced, they become part of the competitive marketplace and are therefore more easily identifiable as contributing to the services component of the economy.

Figure 1.2
Changing
Structure of
Employment As
an Economy
Develops

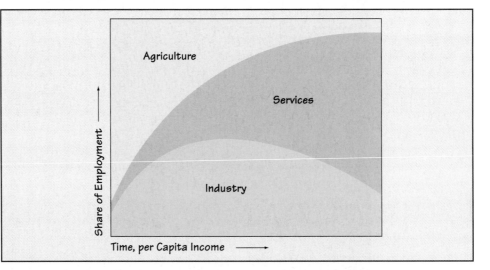

Source: International Monetary Fund, *World Economic Outlook* (Washington, D.C.: International Monetary Fund, May 1997). Reprinted with permission of International Monetary Fund. All rights reserved.

Among the forces that shape service markets are government policies, social changes, business trends, advances in information technology, and internationalization (Figure 1.3). We'll be highlighting the impact of these factors on consumption patterns and competitive strategy throughout the book.

In recent years, the development of technology, especially IT and telecommunication, has become more crucial in services. For instance, the Taiwanese government launched the iAeB Program in 2000 to encourage major foreign and domestic companies as well as domestic suppliers to adopt B2B e-business in the hope of boosting competitiveness and stimulating a trend of B2B e-business. Innovative service providers are interested in applying new technological developments to automate and speed up processes, reduce costs (and perhaps

Figure 1.3
Factors Stimulating the Transformation of the Service Economy

Government Policies	Social Changes	Business Trends	Advances in Information Technology	Internationalization
• Changes in Regulations • Privatization • New Rules to Protect Customers, Employees, and the Environment • New Agreements on Trade in Services	• Rising Consumer Expectations • More Affluence • More People Short of Time • Increased Desire for Buying Experiences versus Things • Rising Ownership of Computers and Mobile Phones • Immigration	• Manufacturers Add Value through Service and Sell Services • More Strategic Alliances • Marketing Emphasis by Nonprofits • Relaxation of Professional Association Standards • Quality Movement • Emphasis on Productivity and Cost Savings • Growth of Franchising • Innovative Hiring Practices	• Convergence of Computers and Telecommunications • Greater Bandwidth • Miniaturization Creates More Compact Mobile Equipment • Wireless Networking • Faster, More Powerful Software • Digitization of Text, Graphics, Audio, and Video • Growth of the Internet	• More Companies Operating on Transnational Basis • Increased International Travel • International Mergers and Alliances

Increased Demand for Services
More Intensive Competition

Service Innovation Stimulated by Application of New and Improved Technologies

Increased Focus on Services Marketing and Management

prices), facilitate service delivery, add appeal to existing products, relate more closely to their customers, and offer them more convenience. The advancement in technology has enabled the creation of an information assembly line—information today can be standardized, built to order, assembled from components, picked, packed, stored, and shipped, all using processes resembling manufacturing's.[3] (See Figure 1.4 for an example of a self-service automated machine that helps to facilitate service delivery and speed up bill payment process.)

What are the implications of these changes? On the positive side, there is likely to be growing demand for many services. The opening up of the service economy means that there will be greater competition.[4] In turn, more competition will stimulate innovation, not least through the application of new and improved technologies. Customer needs and behavior evolve, too, in response to changing demographics and values, as well as new options. Both individually and in combination, these developments will require managers of service organizations to focus more sharply on marketing strategy.

Figure 1.4
Self-service automated machine (SAM), the 24-hour automated post office in Singapore that facilitates a wide range of services from payment of bills, fines and income tax, topping up of pre-paid phone cards, weighing of packages, and buying of postage stamps.

Services Pose Distinctive Marketing Challenges

All *products*—a term that we use in this book to describe the core output of any type of industry—deliver benefits to the customers who purchase and use them. In the case of *goods*, the benefits come from ownership of physical objects or devices, whereas in *services* the benefits are created by actions or performances.[5] (See Service Perspectives 1.1.) The dynamic environment of services today places a premium on effective marketing. Among the keys to competing effectively are skills in marketing strategy and execution, areas in which many service firms have traditionally been weak.

Service Perspectives 1.1

WHAT IS A SERVICE?

Reflecting the physical nature of their activities, manufacturing, mining, and agriculture are easier to describe and define than services, which embrace a huge diversity of activities and often include intangible inputs and outputs. There have been many attempts to define services, including the amusing description of a service as something that can "be bought and sold, but which cannot be dropped on your foot."[6]

Building on previous definitions and our own experience in research and consulting, here is our definition:

Services are economic activities offered by one party to another, most commonly employing time-defined performances to bring about desired results in recipients themselves or in objects or other assets for which purchasers have responsibility. Service customers expect to obtain value from access to labor, professional skills, facilities, networks, systems, and equipment, but do not normally take ownership of any of the physical elements involved.[7]

Marketing can be viewed in several ways. It can be seen as a strategic and competitive thrust pursued by top management, as a set of functional activities performed by line managers (such as product policy, pricing, delivery, and communications), or as a customer-driven orientation for the entire organization. In this book, we seek to integrate all three perspectives. Christian Grönroos argues that the services marketing function is much broader than the activities and output of the traditional marketing department, requiring close cooperation between marketers and those managers responsible for operations and human resources.[8]

Although it's still very important to run an efficient operation, that alone is no longer enough for success. Employees must be customer-service oriented in addition to being concerned about efficiency. The service product must be tailored to customer needs, priced realistically, distributed through convenient channels, and actively promoted to customers. The organization must continuously be aware of trends in the size and structure of each market in which its services compete. And very importantly, it must monitor what its competitors are doing and have a clear strategy for achieving and maintaining competitive advantage. Today, many new market entrants are choosing to avoid head-to-head competition against established firms and positioning their services to appeal to specific market segments.

Are the marketing concepts and practices that have been developed in manufacturing companies directly transferable to service organizations? The answer is often "no," because marketing management tasks in the service sector tend to differ from those in the manufacturing sector in several important respects.

More practical insights are provided in Table 1.2, which lists nine basic differences that can help us to distinguish the tasks associated with services marketing from those involved with marketing physical goods. This table also highlights some key managerial implications that will form the basis for much of our analysis and discussion in this and later chapters.

It's important to recognize that in identifying these differences, we are dealing with generalizations that do not apply equally to all services. Later in this chapter, we will consider how different types of services present somewhat different challenges for marketers and other managers. But first, let's examine each characteristic in more detail and highlight a few fundamental marketing implications.

Customers Do Not Obtain Ownership of Services

Perhaps the key distinction between goods and services lies in the fact that customers usually derive value from services without obtaining ownership of any tangible elements (exceptions include food services, and installation of spare parts during delivery of repair services). In many instances, service marketers offer customers the opportunity to rent the use of a physical object like a rental car or hotel room, to hire the labor and expertise of people, to rent (as a loan) a sum of money, to subscribe to a network, or to pay for admission to a service facility.

A key implication for marketers concerns pricing. When the firm rents out usage of its physical, human, or intangible assets, time becomes an important denominator, and determining the relevant costs requires time-based calculations. Another important issue concerns what criteria drive customer choice behavior for

Table 1.2 Basic Differences between Goods and Services	• Customers do not obtain ownership of services. • Intangible elements dominate value creation. • Customers may be involved in the production process. • Other people may form part of the product. • There is greater variability in operational inputs and outputs. • Many services are difficult for customers to evaluate. • Service products are ephemeral and cannot be inventoried. • The time factor assumes great importance. • Distribution channels take different forms.

a rental, which tends to be short-term in nature. Marketing a car rental service to a customer, for instance, is very different from attempting to sell a car at an automobile dealership to that same person, who may intend keeping it for at least three to five years.

Intangible Elements Dominate Value Creation

Although services often include tangible elements like a hotel bed, food ordered at a restaurant, or equipment in a repair garage, the output of a service business is intangible. Service firms produce performances rather than physical objects, thus, the benefits for services come from the nature of the performance.

An interesting way to distinguish between goods and services, first suggested by Lynn Shostack, is to place them on a scale from tangible-dominant to intangible-dominant.[9] (See Figure 1.5.) One suggested economic test of whether a product is a good or a service is to determine whether more than half the value comes from the service elements.[10] At a full-service restaurant, for example, the cost of the food itself may account for as little as 20–30 percent of the price of the meal. Most of the value added comes from food preparation, cooking, table service, and extras such as parking, toilets, and the nature of the restaurant environment itself.

The notion of service as a performance that cannot be wrapped up and taken away afterwards leads to the use of a theatrical metaphor that likens service delivery to the staging of a play, with service personnel as the actors, the delivery system as the stage, and customers as the audience.[11] Physical images and metaphors may be

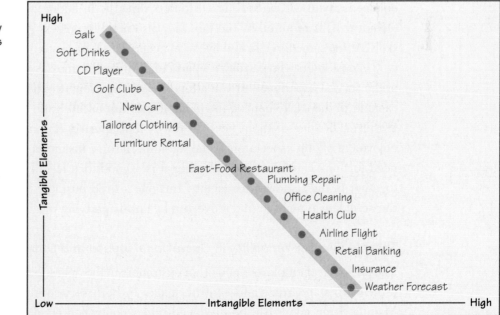

Figure 1.5
Value Added by Tangible versus Intangible Elements in Goods and Services

used to demonstrate the competencies of the service firm and to illustrate the benefits resulting from service delivery.

Customers May Be Involved in the Production Process

Many services require customers to participate in creating the service product.[12] Customer involvement can take the form of self-service, as in using a laundromat or withdrawing money from an automated teller machine (ATM), or cooperation with service personnel in settings such as hairdressers, hotels, colleges, or hospitals. Under such circumstances, customers can be thought of as partial employees and service firms have much to gain from trying to train their customers to make them more competent and productive.[13]

Changing the nature of the production process often affects the role that customers are asked to play in that process. In your own role as a service consumer, you know that while your main interest is in the final output, the way in which you are treated during service delivery can also have an important impact on your satisfaction. When customers are required to visit the service delivery site, that facility should be sited in a convenient location and open at times that suit customers' needs.

People Are Often Part of the Product

The difference between one service and another often lies in the quality of employees who serve the customers. This is especially so in many "high-contact" services. Service firms need to devote special care to selecting, training, and motivating those employees who will be serving customers directly. In addition to possessing the technical skills required by the job, they also need to possess good interpersonal skills. At the same time, firms have to manage and shape customer behavior, as the type of customers who patronize a particular service business can shape the nature of the service experience. If you attend a sporting event, the behavior of the fans can add to the excitement of the game if they are enthusiastic but well-behaved. However, if some of them become rowdy and abusive, it can detract from the enjoyment of other spectators at the stadium. In some instances, service marketers need to think carefully about whether it is a good idea to mix several segments together in the same service facility. Imagine a tired business traveler arriving at the hotel late at night to find it overrun by noisily partying vacationers.

There Is Greater Variability in Operational Inputs and Outputs

The presence of employees and other customers in the operational system makes it difficult to standardize and control quality in both service inputs and outputs. Manufactured goods can be produced under controlled conditions, designed to optimize both productivity and quality, and then checked for conformance with quality standards long before they reach the customer. The same is true for services performed while the customer is absent, such as processing bank checks, repairing cars, or cleaning offices at night. For those services that are consumed as they are produced, however, final "assembly" must take place under real-time conditions, which may vary from customer to customer. Mistakes are more likely to occur, and it is more difficult to shield customers from the results of such service failures. These factors make it difficult for service organizations to improve productivity, control quality, and offer a consistent product. As a former packaged goods marketer observed some years ago after moving to a new position at Holiday Inn:

> We can't control the quality of our product as well as a Procter and Gamble control engineer on a production line can … When you buy a box of Tide, you can reasonably be 99 and 44/100ths percent sure that this stuff will work to get your clothes clean. When you buy a Holiday Inn room, you're sure at some lesser percentage that it will work to give you a good night's sleep without any hassle, or people banging on the walls and all the bad things that can happen in a hotel.[14]

Services Are Often Harder for Customers to Evaluate

Most physical goods tend to be relatively high in "search properties"—those characteristics of the product that a customer can evaluate prior to purchasing it, such as color, shape, price, fit, and feel. Other goods and many services, by contrast, may emphasize "experience properties," that can only be discerned after purchase or during consumption. These include taste, wearability, ease of handling, quietness, and personal treatment. Finally, there are "credence properties," which are characteristics that customers find hard to evaluate even after consumption because they are purchasing expertise in areas where they are not very knowledgeable themselves. Examples include surgery, professional services such as accountancy, and many technical repairs.[15]

Service marketers can reduce customers' perceived risk before a service purchase by helping them to match their needs to specific service features and educating them as to what to expect both during and after service delivery. A firm that develops a reputation for considerate and ethical treatment of its customers will gain the trust of its existing customers and benefit from positive word-of-mouth referrals.

Most Services Are Ephemeral and Cannot Be Inventoried

Because a service is a deed or performance, rather than a tangible item that the customer keeps, it is "perishable" and cannot be stocked as inventory. (Exceptions are found among those service performances that can be recorded for later use in printed or electronic form.) Although the necessary facilities, equipment, and labor can be held in readiness to create the service, these simply represent productive capacity, not the product itself. If there is no demand during a given time period, unused capacity is wasted. During periods when demand exceeds capacity, customers may be sent away disappointed, unless they are prepared to wait.

A key task for service marketers, therefore, is to find ways of smoothing demand levels to match capacity through price incentives, promotions, or other means. Marketers should also be looking for opportunities to manage their productive capacity—in the form of employees, physical space, and equipment—to match predicted fluctuations in demand. If profit maximization is an important goal, then marketers should target the right segments at the right times, focusing on selling during peak periods to those segments that are willing to pay premium prices.

The Time Factor Assumes Great Importance

Many services are delivered in real time while customers are physically present. There are limits as to how long people are willing to spend at the service factory, as customers place a value on their time, and some people are willing to pay more for faster service or priority. Increasingly, busy customers expect service to be available at times when it suits them, rather than when it suits the service company. In response, more and more firms are offering extended hours, with some even staying open 24/7.

Another aspect of the importance of time is elapsed time. Even when customers place an order for a service to be undertaken in their absence, they have expectations about how long a particular task should take to complete, whether it is repairing a machine, completing a research report, cleaning a suit, or preparing a legal document. In general, today's customers are increasingly time sensitive, so speed is often seen as a key element in good service and a way to attract new customers. Service marketers need to understand customers' time constraints and priorities, which may vary from one market segment to another. They also need to look for ways to compete on speed and to minimize waiting times.

Distribution Channels Take Different Forms

Manufacturers usually require physical distribution channels to move goods from factory to customers. Service businesses may choose to combine the service factory, retail outlet, and point of consumption at a single location, or use electronic means to distribute their services, as in broadcasting or electronic funds transfers. Sometimes, as in banking, firms offer customers a choice of distribution channels, ranging from visiting the bank in person to conducting home banking on the Internet.

As a result of advances in computers and telecommunications, especially the growth of the Internet, electronic delivery of services is expanding rapidly. Any information-based component of a service can be delivered instantaneously to anywhere in the world. Thanks to email and Web sites, even small businesses can offer their services inexpensively across vast geographic distances.

In the wired world, the information chain ends in an appliance or tool that directly affects consumer behavior. PDAs, phones, personal computers, and various other boxes will compete for the customer's attention. Customers will expect anywhere, anytime access to information; simple, possibly voice-activated, interfaces; and customization, personalization, responsiveness, and flexibility. As telecommunication providers, operating system companies, and appliance makers intensify their fierce competition for market share, service companies can capitalize on it to dominate the screen and the appliance that are closest to the customers. Ultimately, it would be the design of the interface and service, rather than the appliance or the technology, that determines success.

One company that has captured the strategic ground, at least in one country, is NTT DoCoMo in Japan. NTT DoCoMo understands how to deliver information to the customers in just the right way. Although iMode was introduced using a miserly communication rate of 9kbps, it is more than just another mobile phone service. It offers a range of low-priced services, including Internet access via NTT data network, and hence iMode servers can access a variety of services and content. iMode currently has more than 40 million subscribers and a significant part of iMode's revenue comes from content sold across the iMode platform. For instance, banks and online magazines pay NTT for favorable placement of their content on the iMode screen. NTT DoCoMo uses its appliance to claim a disproportionate degree of power and control over other players in the information chain, just as Microsoft does over the desktop PC operating system.[16]

Important Differences Exist Among Services

Although it's useful to distinguish between goods and services marketing, it's also important to recognize that there are also marketing-relevant differences among services themselves. The traditional way of grouping services is by industry. Service managers may say, "We're in the transportation (or hospitality, or banking, or telecommunications) business." These groupings help us to define the core products offered by the firm and to understand both customer needs and competition. However, this approach can lead to tunnel vision. One hallmark of innovative service firms is that their managers are willing to look outside their own industries for effective strategies that they can adapt for use in their own organizations.

Categorizing Service Processes

Numerous proposals have been made for classifying services.[17] A particularly significant classification is based on the nature of the processes by which services are created and delivered. Marketers don't usually need to know the specifics of how physical goods are manufactured—that's the responsibility of the people who run the factory. However, the situation is different in services. Because customers are often involved in service production, marketers do need to understand the nature of the processes to which their customers may be exposed. A process is a particular method of operation or a series of actions, typically involving multiple steps that often need to take place in a defined sequence. Service processes range from relatively simple procedures involving only a few steps, such as filling a car's tank with fuel, to highly complex activities like transporting passengers on an international flight. Later, we show how these processes can be represented in flowchart diagrams that help us to understand what is going on, and perhaps how a specific process might be improved.

A process implies taking an input and transforming it into output. But if that's the case, then what is each service organization actually processing and how does it perform this task? Two broad categories of things get processed in services: people and objects. In many cases, ranging from passenger transportation to education, customers themselves are the principal input to the service process. In other instances, the key input is an object such as a malfunctioning PC notebook that needs repair or a piece of financial data that needs to be associated with a particular account. In some services, the process is physical and something tangible takes place. In information-based services, however, the process can be intangible.

By looking at service processes from a purely operational perspective, we see that they can be categorized into four broad groups.[18] Figure 1.6 shows a four-way classification scheme based on tangible actions to either customers' bodies or to their physical possessions, and intangible actions to either people's minds or to their intangible assets.

Each category involves fundamentally different processes, with vital implications for marketing, operations, and human resource managers. We will refer to the categories as: *people processing, possession processing, mental stimulus processing,* and *information processing.* Although the industries within each category may appear to be very different, analysis will show that they do, in fact, share important process-related characteristics. As a result, managers from different industries within the same category may obtain useful insights from studying one another, and then create valued innovations for their own organization.

Let's examine why these four different types of processes often have distinctive implications for marketing, operations, and human resource strategies.

PEOPLE PROCESSING   From ancient times, people have sought out services directed at themselves, for example, being transported, fed, lodged, restored to health, or made to look more beautiful. Because they are an integral part of the process, they cannot obtain the benefits they desire by dealing at arm's length with service suppliers and, to receive these types of services, customers must physically enter the service system. They must be prepared to spend time interacting and

Figure 1.6
Understanding
the Nature of the
Service Act

What Is the Nature of the Service Act?	Who or What Is the Direct Recipient of the Service?	
	People	Possessions
Tangible Actions	People processing (services directed at people's bodies):	Possession processing (services directed at physical possessions):
	Passenger transportation Health care Lodging Beauty salons Physical therapy Fitness centers Restaurants/bars Barbers Funeral services	Freight transportation Repair and maintenance Warehousing/storage Office cleaning services Retail distribution Laundry and dry cleaning Refueling Landscaping/gardening Disposal/recycling
Intangible Actions	Mental stimulus processing (services directed at people's minds):	Information processing (services directed at intangible assets):
	Advertising /PR Arts and entertainment Broadcasting/cable Management consulting Education Information services Music concerts Psychotherapy Religion Voice telephone	Accounting Banking Data processing Data transmission Insurance Legal services Programming Research Securities investment Software consulting

actively cooperating with service providers. The level of involvement required of customers may entail anything from boarding a city bus for a five-minute ride, to undergoing a lengthy course of treatments at a hospital. The output from these services is a customer who has reached her destination, or one who is now sporting clean and stylishly cut hair, or one who is now in physically better health.

It's important for managers to think about process and output in terms of what happens to the customer because it helps them to identify what benefits are being created. Reflecting on the service process itself helps to identify some of the non-financial costs, such as time and mental and physical effort, that customers incur in obtaining these benefits.

POSSESSION PROCESSING   Often, customers ask a service organization to provide treatment to some physical possession. This could be anything from a house to a computer, or even a dog. In most possession-processing services, the customer's involvement is usually limited to dropping off the item that needs treatment, requesting the service, explaining the problem, and later returning to pick up the item and pay the bill. If the object to be processed is something that is difficult or impossible to move, like landscaping, heavy equipment, or part of a building, then the "service factory" must go to the customer, with service personnel bringing the tools and materials necessary to complete the job on-site. In all instances, the output should be a satisfactory solution to a customer's problem or some tangible enhancement of the item in question.

MENTAL STIMULUS PROCESSING   Services that interact with people's minds include education, news and information, professional advice, psychotherapy, entertainment, and certain religious practices. Anything touching people's minds has the power to shape attitudes and influence behavior. Thus, if customers are in a position of dependency, or if there is potential for manipulation, strong ethical standards and careful monitoring are required. Receiving these services requires an investment of time on the customer's part. However, recipients do not necessarily have to be physically present in a service factory. They just have to be mentally in communication with the information being presented. There is an interesting contrast here with people-processing services. Although passengers can sleep through a flight and still obtain the benefit of arriving at their desired destination, a student who falls asleep in class will not be any wiser at the end, than at the beginning! Services such as entertainment and education are often created in one place and transmitted by TV or Webcast to individual customers in distant locations. However, they can also be delivered "live and in person" to groups of customers from locations such as theaters or lecture halls.

The core content of all services in this category is information-based, whether it's music, voice, or visual images. Therefore, such services can easily be converted to digital format, recorded, and made available for subsequent replay through electronic channels or transformed into a manufactured product, such as a disk or tape.

INFORMATION PROCESSING   Information is the most intangible form of service output, but it may be transformed into more enduring, tangible forms like letters, reports, books, or disks. Among the services that are highly dependent on effective collection and processing of information are financial and professional services like accounting, law, market research, management consulting, and medical diagnosis.

The extent of customer involvement in information-processing and mental stimulus–processing services is often determined more by tradition and a personal desire to meet the supplier face-to-face, than by the needs of the operational process. Strictly speaking, personal contact is quite unnecessary in industries like banking or insurance. Why should managers subject their firms to all the complexities of managing a people-processing service, when they could deliver the same core product at arm's length? As a customer, why go to the service factory when there's no compelling need to do so?

Habit and tradition often lie at the root of existing service delivery systems and service usage patterns. Professionals and their clients may say they prefer to meet face-to-face because they feel they learn more about each other's needs, capabilities, and personalities that way. However, experience shows that successful personal relationships, built on trust, can be created and maintained purely through telephone, Web sites or email contact. As technology improves and people continue to become more comfortable with videophones or the Internet, we can expect to see a continuing shift to arm's-length transactions.

Designing the Service Factory

The nature of customer involvement often varies sharply among the four categories of service process. Nothing can alter the fact that people-processing services require the customer to be physically present within the service factory. If you're currently in Shanghai and need to be in Kuala Lumpur tomorrow, you simply cannot avoid boarding an international flight and spending time in a jet high above the South China Sea. If you want your hair cut, you cannot delegate this activity to somebody else's head. You have to sit in the hairdresser's chair yourself (Figure 1.7).

Figure 1.7

The hair salon is an example of a service factory that a customer cannot avoid if her hair needs a treat.

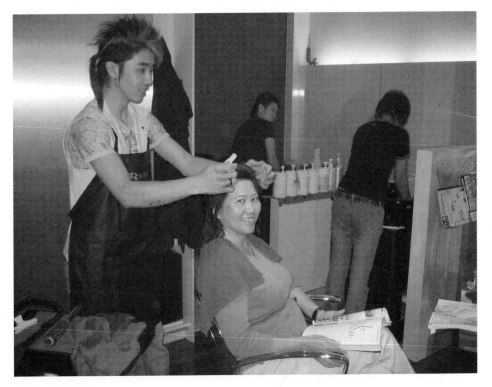

Courtesy of Florence Ang.

When customers visit a service factory, their satisfaction will be influenced by factors such as the exterior and interior appearance and features of service facilities, encounters with service personnel, interactions with self-service equipment, and the characteristics and behavior of other customers. When the nature of the service requires customers to be physically present throughout delivery, the process must be designed with them in mind, from the moment they arrive at the service factory. If the service factory is noisy, confusingly laid out, sited in an inconvenient location, and poorly staffed, customers are likely to be turned off.

Marketing managers need to work closely with their counterparts in operations in order to design facilities that are both pleasing to customers, and efficient to operate. The exterior of a building creates important first impressions, while the interior can be thought of as the "stage" on which the service performance is delivered. The longer customers remain in the factory, and/or the more they expect to spend on purchasing a service, the more important it is to offer facilities that are comfortable and attractive.

Using Alternative Channels for Service Delivery

Unlike the situation in people-processing services, managers responsible for possession-processing, mental stimulus–processing, and information-processing services do not require customers to visit a service factory. Instead, they may be able to offer a choice between one of several alternative delivery channels. Possibilities include (1) letting customers come to a user-friendly factory, (2) limiting contact to a small retail office (or "front office") that is separate from the main factory, (3) coming to the customer's home or office, and (4) conducting business at arm's length via phone, fax, email or a Web site.

Let's take cleaning and pressing of clothes, a possession-processing service, as an example. One approach is to do your laundry at home. If you lack the necessary equipment, then you can pay to use a laundromat, which is essentially a self-service cleaning factory. If you prefer to leave the task of laundry and dry cleaning to professionals, as many people choose to do with their best clothes, you can go to a retail store that serves as a drop-off location for dirty clothes and pick-up point for newly cleaned items. Sometimes, cleaning is conducted in a space behind the store, but at other times, the clothing is transported to an industrial site some distance away. Home pick-up and delivery service is available in many cities, but it tends to be a bit more expensive because of the extra costs involved.

Both physical and electronic channels allow customers and suppliers to conduct service transactions at arm's length. For instance, instead of shopping at a shopping center, you can study a Web site and place an order online for parcel delivery. Information-based items, such as software or research reports, can even be downloaded immediately to your computer.

Today's managers need to be creative, since the combination of information technology and modern package transportation services, like those of DHL, FedEx, national postal services, and other logistics firms, offer many opportunities to rethink the place and time of service delivery (see Figure 1.8). Some manufacturers of small pieces of equipment allow customers to bypass retail dealers when a product needs repair. Instead, a courier will come to pick up the defective item (even supplying appropriate packaging if necessary), ship it to a repair site, and return it a few days later when the problem has been fixed. Electronic distribution channels

Figure 1.8

DHL promotes its innovative supply chain solutions that promise to revolutionize delivery of customers' products.

Reprinted with permission from DHL.

offer even more convenience, since transportation time can be eliminated. For instance, using telecommunication links, engineers in a central facility, which could be located on the other side of the world, may be able to diagnose problems in defective computers and software at distant customer locations and transmit electronic signals to correct the defects.

Rethinking service delivery procedures for all but people-processing services may allow a firm to get customers out of the factory and transform a "high-contact" service into a "low-contact" one. When the nature of the *process* makes it possible to deliver service at arm's length, then the design and location of the factory can focus on purely operational priorities. The chances of success in such an endeavor depend on customer acceptance of the new approach and will be enhanced if the new procedures are user-friendly, cost-effective, and offer customers greater convenience.

Making the Most of Information Technology

It's clear that *information-based services* (a term that covers both mental stimulus–processing and information-processing services) have the most to gain from advances in information technology, as telecommunications and the Internet allow the operation to be physically separated from its customers, without even the need for physical shipments. A growing number of banks are now adding Internet for mobile phone capabilities, so that customers can access their accounts and conduct certain transactions via their mobile phones from wherever they may be.

Today, the Web is having an increasingly significant impact on distribution strategy for a broad array of industries.[19] A distinction needs to be made, however, between marketing the core product, such as insurance coverage or selling and buying shares, and the provision of supplementary services, such as ordering goods from an online retailer or making a reservation for a holiday, to enhance that core product. Much of the discussion surrounding the use of the Internet concerns supplementary services that are based on the transfer of *information relating to the product*, as opposed to downloading the core product itself. Figure 1.9 displays examples of both types of Web sites.

Balancing Supply and Demand

Sharp fluctuations in demand are a bane in the lives of many managers. Manufacturing firms can stock supplies of their product as a hedge against fluctuations in demand. This strategy enables them to enjoy the economies derived from operating factories at steady production levels. However, few service businesses can do this easily. For example, the potential income from an empty seat on an airliner is lost forever once that flight takes off. Hotel room-nights are equally "perishable." Conversely, when demand for service exceeds supply, the excess

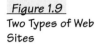

Figure 1.9
Two Types of Web Sites

Web sites can deliver Great Eastern's services directly, but ...

Source: www.lifeisgreat.com.sg, accessed in October 2004.

... Telekom Malaysia requires a physical infrastructure to deliver its mobile and fixed-line telecommunications services. It uses the Web to enhance its core service through its comprehensive and user-friendly Web site.

Source: www.telekom.com.my, accessed in September 2004.

business is usually lost. If someone can't get a seat on one flight, another carrier gets the business, or the trip is canceled. In other situations, customers may be forced to wait in a queue until sufficient productive capacity is available to serve them.

In general, services that process people and physical objects are more likely to face capacity limitations than those that are information-based. Radio and television transmissions, for instance, can reach any number of homes within their receiving areas or cable distribution networks. In recent years, information processing and transmission capacity have been vastly increased by greater computing power, digital switching, and the replacement of coaxial cables with fiber optic ones.

Technology, however, has not found similar ways to increase the capacity of those service operations that process people and their physical possessions without big jumps in costs. Thus, managing demand becomes more essential in improving productivity in those types of services that involve tangible actions. Customers must either be given incentives to use the service outside peak periods, or capacity must be allocated in advance through reservations. For example, a golf course may employ both of these strategies by discounting greens fees during off-peak hours, and requiring reservations for the busier tee times.

The problem for people-processing services is that there are limits to how long customers are willing to wait in line. By contrast, physical possessions rarely suffer if they have to wait, unless they are highly perishable. What is more relevant to customers is the cost and inconvenience associated with delays in waiting to recover the item being serviced. Customers may be inconvenienced, if their clothes or cars are not ready when promised. The issue of demand and capacity management is so central to productive use of assets, and thus profitability, that we'll devote significant coverage to the topic in Chapter 9.

When People Become Part of the Product

In many people-processing services, customers meet a lot of employees and often interact with them for extended periods of time. They are also more likely to run into other customers as many service facilities achieve their operating economies by serving large numbers of customers simultaneously. A bus, college class, restaurant meal, and hairdressing salon all tend to serve many customers simultaneously. When other people become a part of the service experience, their attitudes, behavior, and appearance can enhance it or detract from it.

Direct involvement in service production means that customers evaluate the quality of employees' appearance and social skills, as well as their technical skills. And since customers also make judgments about other customers, managers find themselves trying to manage customer behavior, too. Service businesses of this type tend to be challenging to manage because of the human element.

Marketing Must Be Integrated with Other Functions

In this book, we don't limit our coverage to services marketing. Throughout the chapters, you'll also find continuing reference to two other important functions: service operations and human resource management. Imagine yourself as the manager of a small hotel or think big, if you like, and picture yourself as the CEO of a major bank. In both instances, you need to be concerned about satisfying your customers on a daily basis, about operational systems running smoothly and efficiently, and about making sure that your employees are not only working productively, but also delivering good service. In short, integration of activities between functions is the name of the game. Problems in any one of these three areas can negatively affect execution of tasks in the other functions and result in dissatisfied customers.

The Services Marketing Mix

When discussing strategies to market manufactured goods, marketers usually address four basic strategic elements: product, price, place (or distribution), and promotion (or communication). Collectively, these are often referred to as the *4Ps* of the marketing mix.[20] To capture the distinctive nature of service performances, we will be modifying the terminology and extending the mix by adding three elements associated with service delivery—physical environment, process, and people. Collectively, these seven elements, referred to as the *7Ps* of services marketing, represent a set of interrelated decision variables facing managers of service organizations.[21] Let's look briefly at each in turn.

PRODUCT ELEMENTS   Managers must select the features of both the core product (either a good or service) and the bundle of supplementary service elements surrounding it, with reference to the benefits desired by customers and how well competing products perform. In short, we need to be attentive to all aspects of the service performance that have the potential to create value for customers.

PLACE AND TIME   Delivering product elements to customers involves decisions on the place and time of delivery, as well as the methods and channels employed. Delivery may involve physical or electronic distribution channels (or both), depending on the nature of the service being provided. Use of messaging services and the Internet allows information-based services to be delivered in cyberspace for retrieval, wherever and whenever it suits the customer. Firms may deliver service directly to customers or through intermediary organizations, such as retail outlets that receive a fee or a percentage of the selling price, to perform certain tasks associated with sales, service, and customer contact. Speed and convenience of place and time for the customer are becoming important determinants in service delivery strategy.

PROMOTION AND EDUCATION   No marketing program can succeed without effective communications. This component plays three vital roles: providing needed information and advice, persuading target customers of the merits of a specific product, and encouraging them to take action at specific times. In services marketing, much communication is educational in nature, especially for new customers. Companies may need to teach these customers about the benefits of the service, where and when to obtain it, and provide instructions on how to participate in service processes. Communications can be delivered by individuals, such as salespeople and front-line staff, or through media such as TV, radio, newspapers, magazines, posters, brochures, and Web sites. Promotional activities may influence brand choice and incentives may be used to attract customers to buy.

PRICE AND OTHER COSTS OF SERVICE   This component addresses management of the costs incurred by customers in obtaining benefits from the service product. Service managers not only set the selling price, trade margins, and establish credit terms; they also seek to minimize, where possible, other costs that customers may bear in purchasing and using a service, like related costs (e.g., travel expenses), time, and mental and physical effort.

PHYSICAL ENVIRONMENT   The appearance of buildings, landscaping, vehicles, interior furnishing, equipment, staff members, signs, printed materials, and other visible cues all provide tangible evidence of a firm's service quality. Service firms need to manage physical evidence carefully, since it can have a profound impact on customers' impressions.

PROCESS   Creating and delivering product elements to customers require the design and implementation of effective processes. A process is the method and sequence of actions in the service performance. Badly designed processes like slow, bureaucratic, and ineffective service delivery, commonly annoy customers. Similarly, poor processes make it difficult for front-line staff to do their jobs well, resulting in low productivity and increased likelihood of service failure.

PEOPLE   Many services depend on direct interaction between customers and a firm's employees (like getting a haircut or talking to a call center staff). The nature of these interactions strongly influences the customer's perceptions of service quality.[22] Service quality is often assessed based on customers' interactions with front-line staff, and successful service firms devote significant effort to recruiting, training, and motivating these employees.

Linking the Marketing, Operations, and Human Resources Functions

As shown by the component elements of the 7Ps model, marketing cannot operate successfully in isolation from other functions in a service business. Three management functions play central and interrelated roles in meeting customer needs, namely, marketing, operations, and human resources. Figure 1.10 illustrates this interdependency. In later chapters, we raise the question of how marketers should relate to their colleagues from other functions in planning and implementing marketing strategies.

Service firms must understand the implications of the seven components of integrated service management, as described above, in order to develop effective strategies. Firms whose managers succeed in developing integrated strategies will have a better chance of surviving and prospering.

Marketing Services versus Marketing Goods through Service

With the growth of the service economy, and the increasing emphasis on adding value-enhancing services to manufactured goods,[23] the line between services and manufacturing sometimes become blurred. Theodore Levitt, one of the world's best-known marketing experts, has observed that "There are no such things as service industries. There are only industries whose service components are greater or less than those of other industries. Everybody is in service."[24] More recently, Roland Rust, editor of the *Journal of Service Research*, suggested that manufacturing firms had got this message when he observed that "most goods businesses now view themselves primarily as services."[25] Nevertheless, it's important to clarify the difference between situations in which a service itself is the core product, and those

Figure 1.10
Interdependence of Marketing, Operations, and Human Resource Management

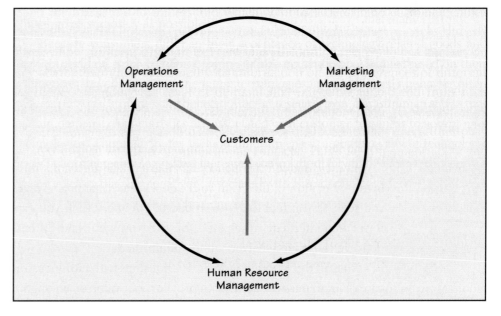

in which manufacturers are adopting service-like strategies to help them market the physical goods that they produce.

In this book, we draw a distinction between *marketing of services*—where a service is the core product—and *marketing through service.* In the latter case, a manufacturing firm may base its marketing strategy on a philosophy of serving customers well and adding supplementary service elements to the core product, but that core product still remains a physical good, and not an intangible performance.

Many of the services that accompany physical products at the time of sale are not charged separately but bundled in with the price of the product itself. Purchasers of a luxury car like the Lexus receive an exceptional level of service from the dealer, based upon the firm's detailed understanding of the benefits that customers seek from owning and driving a prestige brand of car. They also receive excellent warranty coverage. However, the Lexus is still a manufactured product and we still need to distinguish between marketing that product at the time of sale and marketing services that customers will pay for, to maintain their car in good working order for several years after the sale.

Creating Value

By now it should be clear that managers need to be concerned about giving good value to customers and treating them fairly in decisions involving all elements of the 7Ps. Value can be defined as the worth of a specific action or object, relative to an individual's (or organization's) needs at a particular point in time, less the costs involved in obtaining those benefits.

Firms create value by offering the types of services that customers need, at an acceptable price. In return, firms receive value from their customers, primarily in the form of the money paid by the latter to purchase and use the services in question. Such transfers of value illustrate one of the most fundamental concepts in marketing, that of *exchange*, which takes place when one party obtains value from another in return for something else of value. These exchanges aren't limited to buying and selling. An exchange of value also takes place when employees go to work for an organization. The employer gets the benefit of the worker's efforts, while the employee receives wages, benefits, and possibly such valued experiences as training, on-the-job experience, and working with friendly colleagues.

As a customer yourself, you regularly make decisions on whether or not to invest time, money, and effort to obtain a service that promises the specific benefits you seek. If you feel that you've had to pay more than you expected or received fewer benefits than anticipated, or that you were badly treated during service delivery, the value received will be diminished.

No firm that seeks long-term relationships with either customers or employees can afford to mistreat them or to provide poor value on an ongoing basis. Sooner or later, shortchanging or mistreating customers and employees is likely to rebound to the firm's disadvantage. Hence, companies need a set of morally and legally defensible values to guide their actions and to shape their dealings with both employees and customers. A useful way of thinking about "values" is as underlying beliefs about how life should be lived, how people should be treated, and how business should be conducted. To the extent possible, managers would be wise to use their firm's values as a reference point when recruiting and motivating employees. They should also clarify the firm's values and expectations in dealing with prospective customers, as well as make an effort to attract and retain customers who share and appreciate those same values.

More than 30 years ago, Siegmund Warburg of the investment banking house of S. G. Warburg (now part of UBS) remarked that

> a company's reputation for integrity, generosity, and thorough service is its most important asset, more important than any financial item. However, the reputation of a firm is like a very delicate living organism which can easily be damaged and which has to be taken care of incessantly, being mainly a matter of human behavior and human standards.[26]

Today, there is the greater scrutiny given to a firm's business ethics and the presence of tougher legislation designed to protect both customers and employees from abusive treatment. In this book, we will periodically raise ethical issues as they relate to different aspects of service management.

Service Success Requires a Focus on Customers

Recent years have seen much emphasis, especially among American corporations, on the mantra of enhancing shareholder value. However, while profits can certainly be enhanced in the short term by a vigorous effort to reduce expenses, in the long run there can be no creation of value for shareholders unless value is first created for customers. Marketing is the only management function in the firm that is dedicated to generating sales revenues. No business can hope to sustain a revenue stream, unless it is successful in attracting and retaining customers who are willing to keep purchasing its services at prices that collectively cover all costs and leave an appropriate margin for profits and needed reinvestment.

Chapter 2 establishes a theme that will run throughout the book. It is that of being customer focused. This perspective requires understanding customer needs and behavior, and how these are evolving, recognizing how customers fit within different types of service operations, and managing encounters with customers in ways that create satisfaction.

In Chapter 3, we emphasize the importance of being selective in targeting specific types of customers who will value what the firm has to offer relative to competing alternatives and can also be served profitably. Hence the goal should be to develop marketing mix strategies that match customers' needs and purchasing potential to the capabilities of the firm.

Retaining desirable customers in a competitive marketplace requires an understanding of how relationships are created and nurtured. Historically, many service firms were transaction oriented rather than relationship oriented. In operations-oriented firms, one user was seen as good as another, so long as they paid. Today, the emphasis is on developing relationship marketing strategies that will enhance satisfaction among targeted customers and build their loyalty. To achieve this loyalty, savvy service firms know that they must develop a customer-centered understanding of service quality and ensure that everyone in the organization understands his or her role in meeting customer expectations.

The winners in today's highly competitive service markets make progress by continually rethinking the way they do business, looking for innovative ways to serve customers better, and taking advantage of new developments in technology. Consider the six firms profiled in Best Practice in Action 1.1, all leaders in a diverse mix of industries. We'll be meeting some of these companies again at different points in the book.

The marketing tools and strategies that we describe in subsequent chapters emphasize a customer focus and an orientation to competitive dynamics. However, we recognize explicitly that effective integration of marketing activities with those of operations and human resources requires that marketers work closely with their colleagues to ensure that service design and delivery achieve a balance—or even better, a synergy—between quality and productivity.

Best Practice in Action 1.1

SIX CUSTOMER-CENTRIC FIRMS THAT THRIVE ON INNOVATION AND GROWTH

Great Eastern (www.lifeisgreat.com.sg) is the largest insurance company in Singapore and Malaysia, with assets of more than S$35 billion and more than two million policyholders. One of the ways in which the company delivers value-added service to its policyholders is with its comprehensive "Lifeisgreat" portal that provides access to product and policy information. This effective service point enables online transactions and investment planning to be carried out on a 24/7 basis. Great Eastern emphasizes continuous improvements to work processes, focusing on providing quality customer service. For example, the use of technology in its award-winning Call Center allows customer service officers to expeditiously analyze customer information, route calls and walk-in customers, and attend to customer requirements. Recognized for its outstanding customer service and business operations, the company has a reputation for providing value shareholder returns and has been identified as one of "The Most Valuable Brands" in Singapore.

Air Asia (www.airasia.com), Malaysia's budget airline (Figure 1.11), is an Asian clone of the model pioneered by Southwest Airlines in the United States and Ryanair Holdings in Europe. Operating as a low-fare, no-frills airline, Air Asia has expanded

Figure 1.11

Air Asia,
Southeast Asia's
leading low-fare,
no-frills carrier,
has modeled its
operations on
those of innovative
American and
European airlines.

Courtesy of Air Asia's marketing communications team.

to Indonesia and Thailand. Its ingredients of success are low-cost business operations, which include convenient Internet and phone bookings, and affordable daily short-haul flights within the region. The company has set up a Nationwide Call Center in Malaysia, and sells its tickets though Singapore post offices for the convenience of customers. Its low fares give excellent value, especially to those who previously could not afford to fly.

Banyan Tree (www.banyantree.com), one of the world's most lauded luxury resort brands, has managed to find creative ways to grow its revenues and reinforce its brand despite numerous crises that have hit the Asian travel sector. The resort chain has a presence in places like Bangkok, Phuket (Figure 1.12), Bintan, and the Maldives, to name a few. It has spun the hotel's spas and art shops into a separate business line, opening new Banyan Tree branded outlets as stand-alone shops and in other luxury hotels. By selling the tropical luxury experience, Banyan Tree has not only created a niche market, but also a competitive advantage that rivals will find hard to imitate.

Xius (www.xius.org) invents, develops, and delivers innovative products and solutions in wireless technologies to customers across the globe from its headquarters in Hyderabad, India. Its services are designed to maximize revenues and lower operating costs. Xius offers state-of-the-art real-time billing, pre-paid roaming, optimal routing, and mobile commerce applications. A combination of signaling and real-time rating technologies on a single platform allows wireless and other telecommunications carriers to host multiple applications on the same capital infrastructure, saving millions of dollars. Xius has a centralized Network Operations Center that monitors installations across the globe online, with 24-hour support and problem resolution.

Figure 1.12
Luxurious Pool
Villa at the
Banyan Tree
Resort Phuket

Reprinted with permission from Banyan Tree Hotels and Resorts.

eBay (www.ebay.com) defines its mission as "to help people trade practically anything on earth." Founded in 1995, eBay has no physical presence other than its corporate offices in California, which customers never see. Instead, it uses the power of the Web to bring buyers and sellers together, on a regional, national, or even global basis, in a cyberspace auction format. Targeting individual customers—not businesses—the company enables people to offer and bid for items in more than 4,300 categories, including cars, antiques, toys, dolls, jewelry, sports memorabilia, books, pottery, glass, coins, stamps, and much more. Part of eBay's appeal is simply that it is the world's largest person-to-person trading site, offering more new items for sale every day and more potential buyers than any other auction site. eBay has dedicated Web sites and services for many Asian markets, including China (http://www.ebay.com.cn), Hong Kong (http://www.ebay.com.hk/home) and South Korea (http://www.auction.co.kr/). Figure 1.13 shows eBay's home page for China.

Figure 1.13
eBay China's
Homepage

Source: http://www.ebay.com.cn, accessed in June 2004.

SUNDAY (www.sunday.com) is a mobile service operator in Hong Kong. In the telecommunications industry where there is fierce competition, SUNDAY has differentiated itself with a range of innovative services such as Mobile Jukebox and Mobile Boxoffice to encourage its subscribers with WAP-enabled handsets to increase usage. SUNDAY also has a customer-oriented commitment to product innovation and development by cooperating with manufacturers to produce user-friendly devices for GPRS handsets and additional wireless applications and services. The company has been repeatedly rated the highest for overall network performance and voice quality, and has won recognition as a top consumer brand in Hong Kong.

Conclusion

Why study services? Because modern economies are driven by service businesses. Services are responsible for the creation of a substantial majority of new jobs, both skilled and unskilled, around the world. The service sector includes a tremendous variety of different industries, including many activities provided by public and nonprofit organizations. It accounts for over half the economy in most developing countries and for two-thirds or more in many highly developed economies.

As we've shown in this chapter, services differ from manufacturing organizations in many important respects and require a distinctive approach to marketing and other management functions. As a result, managers who want their enterprises to succeed cannot continue to rely solely on tools and concepts developed in the manufacturing sector. However, important differences exist between services. Rather than focusing on broad distinctions between goods and services, it's more useful to identify different categories of services and to study the marketing, operations, and human resource challenges faced within each of these groups.

The four-way classification scheme discussed in this chapter focuses on the implications for customers of different types of service *processes*. Some services require direct physical contact with customers (hairdressing and passenger transport), while others center on contact with people's minds (education and entertainment). Some involve processing of physical objects (cleaning and freight transport), while others process information (accounting and insurance). As you can now appreciate, the operational processes that underlie the creation and delivery of any service have a major impact on marketing and human resource strategies.

The array of strategic tools available to service marketers tends to be broader than commonly found in the marketing of manufacturing products. In addition to making decisions on product elements, pricing, the place and time of service delivery, and promotional strategy, service marketers also find themselves involved with service delivery issues relating to people, processes, and the physical environment. Collectively, we can describe these as the 7Ps of services marketing. In employing these tools, managers need to be aware that they should be selective in choosing which types of customers to serve, and that success requires a continuing focus on achieving customer satisfaction and loyalty.

Review Questions

1. Is it possible for an economy to be entirely based on services? Is it good for an economy to have a large service sector? Discuss.
2. What are the main reasons for the growing share of the service sector in all major economies of the world?
3. What is so distinctive about services marketing that it requires a special approach, set of concepts and body of knowledge?
4. To what extent do you consider the marketing mix, which has been traditionally applied to the goods sector, appropriate for the services sector?
5. Review each of the different ways in which services can be classified. How would you explain the usefulness of each framework to managers?
6. Why is time so important in services?
7. Why do marketing, operations, and human resources have to be more closely linked in services than in manufacturing? Give examples.
8. In what ways does design of the service factory affect (a) customer satisfaction with the service, and (b) employee productivity?
9. What do you see as the major ethical issues facing those responsible for creating and delivering mental stimulus–processing services?

Application Exercises

1. Visit the Web sites of the following national statistical bureaus: National Statistical Office Thailand (www.nso.go.th/eng/); National Bureau of Statistics of China (http://www.stats.gov.cn/english/); Korea National Statistical Office (http://www.nso.go.kr/eng/); National Statistics of Taiwan, the Republic of China (http://www.stat.gov.tw/) and Singapore Department of Statistics (www.singstat.gov.sg). In each instance, obtain data on the latest trends in services as (a) a percentage of gross domestic product, (b) the percentage of employment accounted for by services, (c) breakdowns of these two statistics by type of industry, and (d) service exports and imports.

2. Give examples of how, during the past ten years, Internet and telecommunications technologies (such as interactive voice response systems (IVRs) and mobile commerce (m-Commerce) have changed some of the services that you use.

3. Choose a service company with which you are familiar and show how each of the seven elements (7Ps) of integrated service management applies.

4. Make a list of at least 12 services that you have used during the past month.
   (a) Categorize them by type of process.
   (b) In which instances could you have avoided visiting the service factory and instead obtained service at arm's length? Comment.
   (c) How did other customers affect your own service experiences, either positively or negatively?

5. Visit the facilities of two competing service firms in the same industry (such as two retailers, restaurants, or hotels) that you believe have different approaches to service. Compare and contrast, using one or more of the frameworks in this chapter.

Endnotes

[1]   Organization for Economic Cooperation and Development, *The Service Economy*. Paris: OECD, 2000.

[2]   For comparative data on Latin America in the mid-1990s, see *El Mundo de Trabajo en una Economia Integrada*. Washington, DC: The World Bank, 1996.

[3]   Uday Karmarkar, "Will You Survive the Service Revolution?" *Harvard Business Review* (June 2004): 101–108.

[4]   Michael D. Johnson and Anders Gustafsson, *Competing in a Service Economy* (San Franciso: Jossey-Bass, 2003).

[5]   Leonard L. Berry, "Services Marketing is Different," *Business* (May–June 1980).

[6]   Evert Gummesson, "Lip Service: A Neglected Area in Services Marketing," *Journal of Consumer Services* 1 (Summer 1987): 19–22 (citing an unknown source). For an extended list of definitions, see Christian Grönroos, *Service Management and Marketing*, 2nd ed. (New York: John Wiley & Sons, 2001), 26–27.

[7]   Christopher H. Lovelock and Evert Gummesson, "Whither Services Marketing? In Search of a New Paradigm and Fresh Perspectives," *Journal of Service Research* 7 (August 2004: 20–41). See also the following papers on recent thinking about services and services marketing: Stephen L. Vargo and Robert F. Lusch, "The Four Services Marketing Myths: Remnants of a Goods-Based, Manufacturing Model," *Journal of Service Research* 6, no. 4 (2004): 324–335; Stephen L. Vargo and Robert F. Lusch, "Evolving to a New Dominant Logic for Marketing," *Journal of Marketing* 68 (January 2004): 1–17.

[8]   Christian Grönroos, *op. cit*.

[9]   G. Lynn Shostack, "Breaking Free from Product Marketing," *Journal of Marketing* (April 1977).

[10]   W. Earl Sasser, R. Paul Olsen, and D. Daryl Wyckoff, *Management of Service Operations: Text, Cases, and Readings* (Boston: Allyn & Bacon, 1978).

[11]   Stephen J. Grove, Raymond P. Fisk, and Joby John, "Service as Theater: Guidelines and Implications" in T. A. Schwartz and D. Iacobucci, *Handbook of Services Marketing and Management* (Thousand Oaks, CA: Sage Publications, 2000), 21–36; Richard Harris, Kim Harris, and Steve Baron, "Theatrical Service Experiences: Dramatic Script Development with Employees," *International Journal of Service Industry Management* 14, no. 2 (2003): 184–199.

[12]   Oxana Chervonnaya, "Customer Role and Skill Trajectories in Services," *International Journal of Service Industry Management* 14, no. 3 (2003): 347–363.

[13]   Bonnie Farber Canziani, "Leveraging Customer Competency in Service Firms," *International Journal of Service Industry Management* 8, no. 1 (1997): 5–25.

[14]   Gary Knisely, "Greater Marketing Emphasis by Holiday Inns Breaks Mold," *Advertising Age* (January 15, 1979).

[15]   This section is based on Valarie A. Zeithaml, "How Consumer Evaluation Processes Differ between Goods and Services," in J. A. Donnelly and W. R. George, *Marketing of Services* (Chicago: American Marketing Association, 1981), 186–190.

[16]   Uday Karmarkar, *op.cit.*

[17]   See, for example, Christopher H. Lovelock, "Classifying Services to Gain Strategic Marketing Insights," *Journal of Marketing* 47 (Summer 1983), 9–20; Christian Grönroos, *Service Management and Marketing* (Lexington, Mass.: Lexington Books, 1990), 31–34; John Bowen, "Development of a Taxonomy of Services to Gain Strategic Marketing Insights," *Journal of the Academy of Marketing Science* 18, (Winter 1990), 43–49; Rhian Silvestro, Lyn Fitzgerald, Robert Johnston, and Christopher Voss, "Towards a Classification of Service Processes," *International Journal of Service Industry Management* 3, no. 3, (1992): 62–75; Pratibha A. Dabholkar, "Technology-Based Service Delivery," in T. A. Schwartz, D. E. Bowen, and S. W. Brown, *Advances in Services Marketing and Management*, Volume 3, (Greenwich, CY: JAI Press, 1994): 241–271; and Hans Kasper, Wouter De Vries, and Piet Van Helsdingen, "Classifying Services," Chapter 2 in *Services Marketing Management: An International Perspective* (Chichester, UK: John Wiley & Sons, 1999), 43–70.

[18]   These classifications are derived from Lovelock (1983). For an operations-based discussion of service processes, see "Dealing with Inherent Variability: The Difference between Manufacturing and Service?" *International Journal of Production Management* 7, no. 4 (1987): 13–22.

[19]   Leyland Pitt, Pierre Berthon, and Jean-Paul Berthon, "Changing Channels: The Impact of the Internet on Distribution Strategy," *Business Horizons* (March–April 1999): 19–28.

[20]   The 4Ps classification of marketing decision variables was created by E. Jerome McCarthy, *Basic Marketing: A Managerial Approach* (Homewood, IL: Richard D. Irwin, Inc., 1960.)

[21]   Adapted from Bernard H. Booms and Mary J. Bitner, "Marketing Strategies and Organization Structures for Service Firms," in J. H. Donnelly and W. R. George, *Marketing of Services* (Chicago: American Marketing Association, 1981), 47–51.

[22]   For a review of the literature on this topic, see Michael D. Hartline and O. C. Ferrell, "The Management of Customer Contact Service Employees," *Journal of Marketing* 60, no. 4 (October 1996): 52–70.

[23]   Rogelio Oliva and Robert Kallenberg, "Managing the Transition from Products to Services," *International Journal of Service Industry Management* 14, no. 4 (2003): 160–172.

[24]   Theodore Levitt, *Marketing for Business Growth* (New York: McGraw-Hill, 1974), 5.

[25]   Roland Rust, "What is the Domain of Service Research?" (Editorial), *Journal of Service Research* 1 (November 1998): 107.

[26]   Siegmund Warburg , cited in a presentation by Derek Higgs, London, September 1997.

Consumer Behavior in Service Encounters

All the world's a stage and all the men and women merely players; They have their exits and their entrances and one man in his time plays many parts.

WILLIAM SHAKESPEARE
AS YOU LIKE IT

For companies who want to successfully enter the Indian market, there is no substitute for a deep understanding of the Indian consumer ... Companies doing business in India need to capture the differences in consumers' needs and aspirations and the barriers and triggers to change.

KEKI DADISETH, CHAIRMAN, HINDUSTAN LEVER LTD. INDIA

U nderstanding customer behavior lies at the heart of marketing. An important theme in this chapter is that "high-contact" encounters between customers and service organizations differ sharply from "low-contact" ones. Some services require customers to have active contact with the organization, including visits to its facilities and face-to-face interactions with employees. Examples include restaurants, hospitals, and airlines. In other cases, customers never go near the organization's offices and only need to contact an employee when something goes wrong, in which case they would most likely speak to someone by telephone or send a letter or email. Insurance and broadband services fall into this category.

Customers often find it difficult to evaluate services in advance of purchase but they do form certain expectations. Once a customer has actually purchased a service, marketers need to examine how and when they use it. How does the customer interact with the service facilities, service personnel, and even other customers, especially in the case of high-contact services? Finally, of course, marketers need to know whether the experience of receiving the service and its benefits has met the customer's expectations.

In this chapter, we analyze the nature of service consumption and consider how firms should manage encounters to create satisfied customers and desirable outcomes for the business itself. We'll show how the extent of customer contact affects the nature of the service encounter, shapes customer behavior, and can impact strategies for achieving productivity and quality improvements.

We explore such questions as:

1. Where does the customer fit in a service operation?
2. What perceived risks do customers face in purchasing and using services?
3. How do customers form service expectations, and differentiate between desired and adequate service levels?
4. Why do people often have difficulty in evaluating the services that they use?
5. How does reducing or increasing the level of customer's contact with a service supplier affect the nature of their service experiences?
6. What insights can be gained from viewing service delivery as a form of theater?

Customers Interact with Service Operations

Except for custom-designed products, it's rare for customers to get involved in the actual production of manufactured goods. In services, however, one of the differentiating characteristics is the extent to which customers participate in the process of service creation and delivery. The challenge for service marketers is to understand what that experience is like for customers.

Service Processes Can Be Depicted through Flowcharts

The clearest way to describe a service process is often to chart it in visual form. Using this approach enables us to see how different the customer's involvement with the service organization can be for each of the four categories of services introduced in Chapter 1—people processing, possession processing, mental stimulus processing, and information processing. Let's take one example of each category— staying in a motel, getting a DVD player repaired, obtaining a weather forecast, and purchasing health insurance. Figure 2.1 displays a simple flowchart that demonstrates what's involved in each of four scenarios. Imagine that you are the customer in each instance and think about the extent and nature of your involvement in the service delivery process.

1. *Stay at a motel (people processing).* It's late evening. You're driving on a long trip and are getting tired. You see a motel with a vacancy sign with the price displayed and decide it is time to stop for the night. You park in the lot, noting that the grounds are clean and the buildings seem freshly painted, and enter

Figure 2.1
Simple Flowcharts for Delivery of Various Types of Services

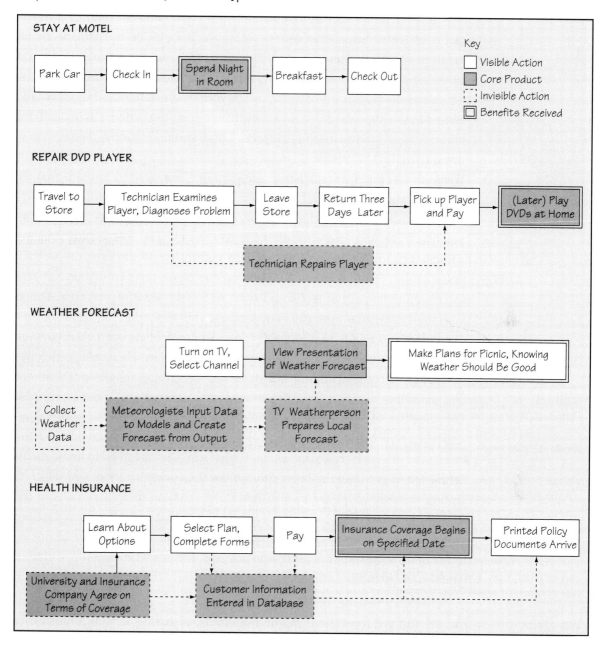

the reception area where a friendly clerk checks you in and gives you the key to your room. You walk across the forecourt to the room with your bag, and let yourself in. After undressing and using the bathroom, you go to bed. Following a good night's sleep, you rise the next morning, shower, dress, and pack, then walk to the lobby, where you take advantage of the free coffee and donuts, return your key to a different clerk, pay, and drive away.

2. *Repair a DVD player (possession processing).* When you use your DVD player, the picture quality on the TV screen is poor. Fed up with the situation, you search the Yellow Pages to find an appliance repair store in your area. At the store, the technician checks your device in the front office and declares that it needs to be adjusted and cleaned. The estimated price seems realistic, so you agree to the work and are told the player will be ready in three days' time. The technician disappears into the back office with your machine and you leave the store. On the appointed day, you return to pick up the product and pay. Back home, you plug in the machine, insert a DVD, and find that the picture is now much improved.

3. *Weather forecast (mental stimulus processing).* You want to arrange a picnic trip to the lake this weekend, three days from now, but one of your friends says she has heard that there is the possibility of a big storm. Back home that evening, you check the long-range weather forecast on TV. The meteorologist shows animated charts indicating the probable path of the storm over the next 72 hours and declares that the latest computer projections from the National Weather Service suggest it is likely to pass well to the south of your area. Armed with this information, you call your friends to tell them that the picnic is on.

4. *Health insurance (information processing).* Your university mails you a package of information before the beginning of the new semester. This package includes a brochure from the student health service describing the several different health insurance options available to students. Although you consider yourself very healthy, except for seasonal allergies, you remember the unfortunate experience of a friend who recently incurred heavy hospital bills for the treatment of a badly fractured ankle. Uninsured, he was forced to liquidate his modest savings to pay the bills. Thus, at the time of registration, you select an option that will cover the cost of hospital treatment, as well as visits to the student health center. You fill in a printed form that includes some standard questions about your medical history, and then sign it. The cost of the insurance is added to your term bill. Subsequently, you receive written confirmation of your coverage in the mail. Now you no longer have to worry about the risk of unexpected medical expenses.

As you can see from these simple flowcharts, your role as a customer varies sharply from one process to another. The first two examples involve physical processes. At the motel, you are actively involved in the service, which is delivered in real time over a period of perhaps eight or nine hours. For a fee, you rent the use of a bedroom, bathroom, and other physical facilities for the night. When you leave, you can't take the service elements with you, but if the bed had been uncomfortable, you might feel tired and physically sore the following day. Your role at the appliance repair store, however, was limited to a few minutes explaining the symptoms, leaving the machine there, and returning several days later to pick it up. You have to trust the technician's competence and honesty in executing the service in your absence, since you are not involved in actual production of the service. If the work has been done well, you will enjoy the benefits later when using the repaired machine. The other two services, weather forecasting and health insurance, involve intangible actions and a relatively passive role for you as a customer.

The Value of Flowcharting

Marketers find flowcharting particularly useful for defining the point(s) in the process at which the customer uses the core service and in identifying the different supplementary services that make up the overall service package.

Although some service encounters are very brief and consist of just a few discrete delivery steps, others may extend over a longer time frame and involve multiple steps. A leisurely restaurant meal might stretch over a couple of hours, while a visit to a theme park might last all day. If you had made a reservation, that first step might have taken place days or even weeks prior to arrival.

It's difficult to improve service quality and productivity without fully understanding the customer's involvement in a given service environment. As customers interact with the service firm—its employees, impersonal delivery systems such as Web sites, physical facilities, and even other customers—they are exposed to information that can influence both their expectations and their evaluations of the service. A key question for managers is whether customers' expectations change during the course of service delivery in light of the perceived quality of sequential steps in the process. Ideally, service firms should try to provide consistently high performance at each step in service delivery. But in reality, many service performances are inconsistent. Richard Chase and Sriram Dasu argue that it's more important to end on a strong note than to begin on one,[1] a principle that applies to low-contact services as well as high-contact ones. They note that many commercial Web sites are designed with attractive home pages that create high expectations, but become progressively less appealing and even problematic to use as customers move toward conclusion of a purchase.

Types of Service Encounters

A service encounter is a period of time during which customers interact directly with a service.[2] As the level of customer contact with the service operation increases, there are likely to be more and longer service encounters. In Figure 2.2, we've grouped services into three levels of customer contact, representing the extent of interaction with service personnel, physical service elements, or both. You'll notice that traditional retail banking, person-to-person telephone banking, and Internet banking are all in different locations on the chart.

Figure 2.2
Levels of
Customer
Contact with
Service
Organizations

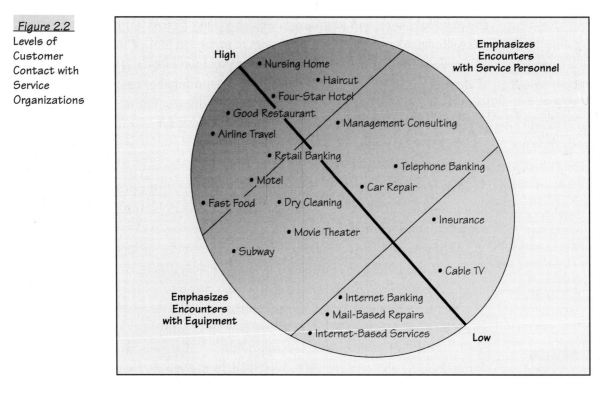

HIGH-CONTACT SERVICES   This group of services tends to be those in which customers visit the service facility in person. Customers are actively involved with the service organization and its personnel throughout service delivery (e.g., hairdressing, lodging, or medical services). All people-processing services (other than those delivered at home) are high contact. Services from the other three process-based categories may also involve high levels of customer contact when, for reasons of tradition, preference, or lack of other alternatives, customers go to the service site and remain there until service delivery is completed. Examples of services that have traditionally been high contact but can be low contact today because of technology include retail banking, purchase of retail goods, and higher education. See Figure 2.3 for an advertisement of a high-contact service.

LOW-CONTACT SERVICES   At the opposite end of the spectrum are services that involve little, if any, physical contact between customers and service providers. Instead, contact takes place at arm's length through the medium of electronic or physical distribution channels—a fast-growing trend in today's convenience-oriented society. Many high-contact and medium-contact services are being transformed into low-contact services as customers engage in home shopping, conduct their insurance and banking transactions by telephone, or research and purchase products through the Internet.[3] See Figure 2.4 for an advertisement by a low-contact service provider, China Unicom.

Figure 2.3

The Executive MBA course offered by the NUS Business School, National University of Singapore, is an example of high-contact service.

Years of experience. Globally exposed. Locally recognized. Highly trained. Highly skilled. Clearly, an expert in his field. Always on strategy. Never on time.

APEX-MBA
(Asia-Pacific Executive MBA)

And he's just the student.

The NUS APEX-MBA focuses on the fastest growing region in the world - the Asia Pacific. It devotes its curriculum to traditional and leading-edge management thinking offered by Western writers, as well as new and emerging body of knowledge on this region.

Program Highlights
Participants
♦ For senior managers with a recognized first degree and minimum 10 years of full-time work experience
♦ Outstanding candidates with 8-9 years of work experience will be considered on a case by case basis

Program Format
♦ 18-month program, consists of six intensive, residential segments. Each segment lasts 2 weeks, during which classes are held from 8am - 7pm, Monday - Saturday
♦ Helps you pursue a reputable MBA without interrupting your career

Rigorous and Relevant Modules
♦ Program consists of 12 modules of study, each entailing 54 hours of instruction (or a total of 648 contact-hours)
♦ Modules have been designed to meet managerial challenges in the global and regional economies

Overseas Campus Design
♦ Two of the six 2-week residential segments will be held in 2 of the largest emerging markets, i.e. China and India

Asian Value-Add
♦ In each country, high-profile guest-speakers from industry, government, think-tanks and consulting firms are invited to address candidates in the evenings

Other Details
Next Intake: July 2002
♦ Application closes 30 March 2002
♦ Please write to us for a complimentary application package OR download the application materials from our website www.apexmba.com

Program Fee
♦ Total fee of S$48,000 on a pay-as-you-go basis
♦ Covers instruction, study materials and meals during residential segments, but excludes accomodation, travel and other (eg insurance, visa) expenses

Contact details

Ms Lily Koh (Program Manager)   or   Ms Mavis Leng (Program Officer)
Tel : (65) 874 3197   Tel : (65) 874 2068/ 6149
Fax : (65) 778 2681   Fax : (65) 778 2681
Email : lily@nus.edu.sg   Email : mavisleng@nus.edu.sg

NUS Business School, a leading business school in Asia with a world-class reputation. We seek to provide a rigorous, relevant and rewarding education for our students. Our diverse degree and non-degree programs are designed to engineer your success in the global economy. A unique learning experience that helps you stay relevant. *NUS Business School. Where it's never business as usual.*

NUS
National University of Singapore

NUS Business School - National University of Singapore
(APEX-MBA Office) 1 Business Link, Biz 2 Building, Level 5, Singapore 117592. Republic of Singapore. Website : www.apexmba.com

Reprinted with permission from NUS Business School, National University of Singapore.

Service Encounters as "Moments of Truth"

Richard Normann borrowed the metaphor *"moment of truth"* from bullfighting to show the importance of contact points with customers. Normann writes:

> [W]e could say that the perceived quality is realized at the moment of truth, when the service provider and the service customer confront one another in the arena.

Figure 2.4

Telecommunication services tend to be low contact because customers often do not need personal contact with the service provider unless they encounter problems or have special requests. Even then, contact is often made via the telephone rather than through face-to-face meetings.

Courtesy of China Unicom Limited.

At that moment they are very much on their own… It is the skill, the motivation, and the tools employed by the firm's representative and the expectations and behavior of the client which together will create the service delivery process.[4]

In bullfighting, what is at stake is the life of either the bull or the matador, or possibly both. The moment of truth is the instant at which the matador deftly slays the bull with his sword—hardly a very comfortable analogy for a service organization intent on building long-term relationships with its customers! Normann's point, of course, is that it's the life of the relationship that is at stake. Contrary to bullfighting, the goal of relationship marketing—which we explore in depth in Chapter 12—is to prevent one unfortunate (mis)encounter from destroying what is already, or has the potential to become, a mutually valued, long-term relationship.

The Purchase Process for Services

When customers decide to buy a service to meet an unfilled need, they go through what is often a complex purchase process. This process has three identifiable stages—the prepurchase stage, the service encounter stage, and the postpurchase stage, each containing two or more steps (see Figure 2.5).

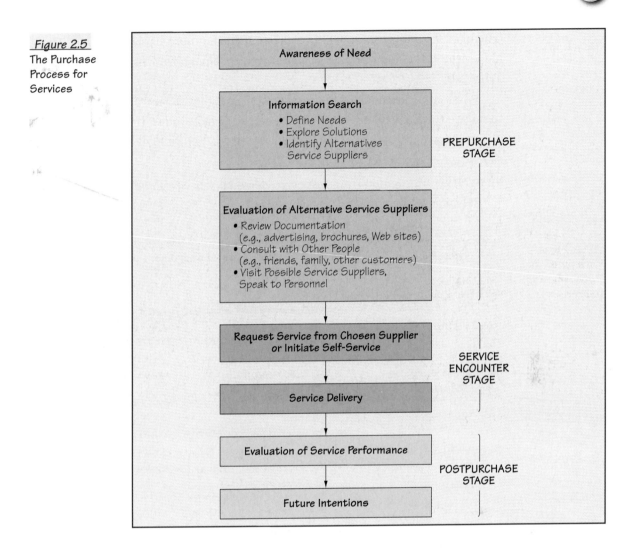

Figure 2.5
The Purchase
Process for
Services

Awareness of Need

Information Search
- Define Needs
- Explore Solutions
- Identify Alternatives
  Service Suppliers

PREPURCHASE
STAGE

Evaluation of Alternative Service Suppliers
- Review Documentation
  (e.g., advertising, brochures, Web sites)
- Consult with Other People
  (e.g., friends, family, other customers)
- Visit Possible Service Suppliers,
  Speak to Personnel

Request Service from Chosen Supplier
or Initiate Self-Service

SERVICE
ENCOUNTER
STAGE

Service Delivery

Evaluation of Service Performance

POSTPURCHASE
STAGE

Future Intentions

Prepurchase Stage

The decision to buy and use a service is made in the prepurchase stage. Individual needs and expectations are very important here, because they influence what alternatives customers will consider. If the purchase is routine and relatively low risk, customers may move quickly to selecting and using a specific service provider. But when more is at stake or a service is about to be used for the first time, they may conduct an intensive information search. (Contrast how you approached the process of applying to university versus buying a pizza!) The next step is to identify potential suppliers and then weigh the benefits and risks of each option before making a final decision.

This element of perceived risk is especially relevant for services that are high in experience or credence attributes and thus difficult to evaluate prior to purchase and consumption. First-time users are especially likely to face greater uncertainty. Risk perceptions reflect customers' judgments of the probability of a negative outcome. The worse the possible outcome and the more likely it is to occur, the higher the perception of risk. Different types of perceived risks are outlined in Table 2.1.

When customers feel uncomfortable with risks, they can use a variety of methods to reduce them during the prepurchase stage. In fact, you've probably tried some of the following risk-reduction strategies yourself before deciding to purchase a service:

- Seeking information from respected personal sources (family, friends, peers)
- Relying on a firm that has a good reputation

Table 2.1 Perceived Risks in Purchasing and Using Services	Type of Risk	Examples of Customer Concerns
	Functional (unsatisfactory performance outcomes)	• Will this training course give me the skill I need to get a better job? • Will this credit card be accepted wherever and whenever I want to make a purchase? • Will the dry cleaner be able to remove the stains from this jacket?
	Financial (monetary loss, unexpected costs)	• Will I lose money if I make the investment recommended by my stockbroker? • Will I incur a lot of unanticipated expenses if I go on this vacation? • Will repairing my car cost more than the original estimate?
	Temporal (wasting time, consequences of delays)	• Will I have to wait in line before entering the exhibition? • Will service at this restaurant be so slow that I will be late for my afternoon meeting? • Will the renovations to our bathroom be completed before our friends come to stay with us?
	Physical (personal injury or damage to possessions)	• Will I get hurt if I go skiing at this resort? • Will the contents of this package get damaged in the mail? • Will I fall sick if I travel abroad on vacation?
	Psychological (personal fears and emotions)	• How can I be sure that this aircraft won't crash? • Will the consultant make me feel stupid? • Will the doctor's diagnosis upset me?
	Social (how others think and react)	• What will my friends think of me if they learn that I stayed at this cheap motel? • Will my relatives approve of the restaurant I have chosen for the family reunion dinner? • Will my business colleagues disapprove of my selection of an unknown law firm?
	Sensory (unwanted impacts on any of the five senses)	• Will I get a view of the parking lot rather than the beach from my room? • Will the bed be uncomfortable? • Will I be kept awake by noise from the guests in the room next door? • Will my room smell of stale cigarette smoke? • Will the coffee at breakfast taste disgusting?

- Looking for guarantees and warranties
- Visiting service facilities or trying aspects of the service before purchasing
- Examining tangible cues or other physical evidence
- Using the Web to compare service offerings.

What can service suppliers do to reduce perceived risk among their customers? In addition to offering guarantees and encouraging prospective customers to visit their facilities (where feasible), it's important to listen to customers and determine their needs and concerns before attempting to recommend a particular solution. It's important to educate customers about the features of a particular service, describe the types of users who can most benefit from it, and offer advice on how to obtain the best results.

Service Encounter Stage

After making a purchase decision, customers experience additional contacts with their chosen service provider. The service encounter stage often begins with submitting an application, requesting a reservation, or placing an order. Contacts may take the form of personal exchanges between customers and service employees, or impersonal interactions with machines or computers. In high-contact services, such as restaurants, health care, hotels, and public transportation, customers may become actively involved in one or more service processes. Often, they experience a variety of elements during service delivery, each of which may provide clues to service.

Postpurchase Stage

During the postpurchase stage, customers continue a process they began in the service encounter stage—evaluating service quality and their satisfaction/dissatisfaction with the service experience. The outcome of this process will affect their future intentions, such as whether or not to return to the provider that delivered service and whether to pass on positive or negative recommendations to family members and other associates.

Customers evaluate service quality by comparing what they expected with what they perceive they received. If their expectations are met or exceeded, they believe they have received high-quality service. If the price/quality relationship is acceptable and other situational and personal factors are positive, then these customers are likely to be satisfied. As a result, they are more likely to make repeat purchases and become loyal customers. However, if the service experience does not meet customers' expectations, they may complain about poor service quality, suffer in silence, or switch providers in the future.[5]

Customer Expectations

Customers buy goods and services to meet specific needs. In many instances, purchase of a good or service may be seen as offering the best solution to meeting a particular need. Subsequently, consumers may compare what they received against what they expected, especially if it cost them money, time, or effort that could have been devoted to obtaining an alternative solution.[6]

In more developed economies, many consumers are reaching the point where they have most of the physical goods they want and are now turning to services to fill new or still unmet needs. Increased spending on more elaborate vacations, sports, entertainment, restaurant meals and other service experiences are assuming greater priority.

According to Daniel Bethamy of American Express, consumers want "memorable experiences, not gadgets."[7] This shift in consumer behavior and attitudes provides opportunities for those service companies that understand and meet changing needs, continuing to adapt their offerings over time as needs evolve. For example, some astute service providers have capitalized on the increased interest in extreme sports by offering services like guided mountain climbs, paragliding, white-water rafting trips and mountain biking adventures.

How Expectations Are Formed

Customers' expectations about what constitutes good service vary from one business to another. For example, although accounting and veterinary surgery are both professional services, the experience of meeting an accountant to talk about your tax returns tends to be very different from visiting a vet to get treatment for your sick pet. Expectations are also likely to vary in relation to differently positioned service providers in the same industry. While travelers expect no-frills service for a short domestic flight on a budget carrier, they would undoubtedly be very dissatisfied with that same level of service on a full-service airline flying from Kuala Lumpur to Hong Kong, or from Seoul to Bangkok, even in economy class. Consequently, it's very important for marketers to understand customer expectations of their own firm's service offerings. Very often, companies also try to shape customers' expectations through promotional tools.

When individual customers or buyers evaluate the quality of a service, they may be judging it against some internal standard that existed prior to the service experience.[8] Perceived service quality results from customers comparing the service they perceive they have received against what they expected to receive. People's expectations about services tend to be strongly influenced by their own prior experience as customers, with a particular service provider, with competing services in the same industry, or with related services in different industries. If they have no relevant prior experience, customers may base their prepurchase expectations on factors like word-of-mouth comments, news stories, or the firm's marketing efforts—all of which may be important factors for a theme park experience such as that provided by Sunway Lagoon (Figure 2.6).

Expectations change over time, influenced by both supplier-controlled factors like advertising, pricing, new technologies, and service innovation as well as social trends, advocacy by consumer organizations, and increased access to information through the media and the Internet. For instance, young Japanese girls are seeking a more participative role in decisions relating to fashion purchases with less regard for their mothers' conservative tastes, due to greater exposure to different media. Service Perspectives 2.1 describes this new assertiveness among this generation of Japanese youths.

The Components of Customer Expectations

Customer expectations embrace several different elements, including desired service, adequate service, predicted service and a zone of tolerance that falls between the desired and adequate service levels.[9] The model shown in Figure 2.7 shows how expectations for desired service and adequate service are formed.

DESIRED AND ADEQUATE SERVICE LEVELS   The type of service customers hope to receive is termed *desired service*. It is a "wished for" level—a combination of

Figure 2.6

The Sunway Lagoon in Malaysia provides an exciting entertainment experience for children, their parents and even grandparents. The expectations of Sunway Lagoon's customers are high!

Courtesy of Joseph Ho, Kuala Lumpur.

Service Perspectives 2.1

YOUNG JAPANESE GIRLS DECIDE THEIR OWN FASHION STYLE

Blue Cross Girls, Daisy Lovers, Angel Blue, and Mezzo Piano are just a few names of fashion stores that cater specifically to young girls aged eight to 14. Run by Narumiya International, these retail stores sell expensive, bright-colored clothing to suit the changing tastes of this target market. Big, garish designs emblazoned with everything from cartoon characters to heart shapes, and bold colors are typical of the outfits Narumiya carries in its stores, and more often than not, these designs are hardly what adults would consider attractive or high-quality. In the past, mothers usually made the purchase decisions for their children. Nowadays, the daughters are taking fashion much more seriously and are taking matters into their own hands.

The mothers may not understand their daughters' taste for such clothes, but are still more than willing to indulge in any interest in fashion. While mothers would go for the classic Burberry and Ralph Lauren, the young girls like loud street fashion, preferably with pink colors and sparkling designs. According to Yuzo Narumiya, the company's president, "the key to luring young girls is to ignore their mothers' tastes altogether." This is just as well since the daughters are becoming more fashion-conscious and more expressive in their preferences. This trend comes as a result of an increasing number of young girls getting more exposure to fashion magazines like *Nicola* and *Pichi Lemon*, which are sponsored by Narumiya. These girls also get invited to marketing events such as fashion shows featuring young models and young celebrities to encourage them to buy new clothes and keep the cash registers ringing. They can take a picture with the models, but only if they first purchase ¥5,000 (US$47) worth of products from any of the Narumiya stores. Such events have been successful because they help to create the excitement and fun children want to experience.

Source: Ichiko Fuyuno, "Pretty in Pink," *Far Eastern Economic Review* (October 13, 2003).

Figure 2.7
Factors That Influence Customer Expectations of Service

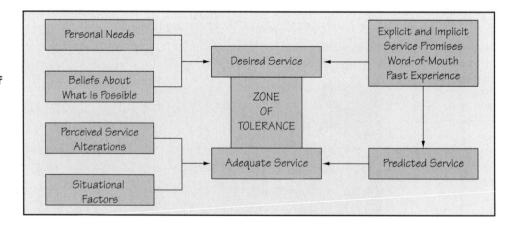

what customers believe can and should be delivered in the context of their personal needs. However, most customers are realistic and understand that companies can't always deliver the level of service they would prefer. Hence, they also have a threshold level of expectations, termed *adequate service*, which is defined as the minimum level of service customers will accept without being dissatisfied. Among the factors that set this expectation are situational factors affecting service performance and the level of service that might be anticipated from alternative suppliers. In highly competitive service markets, customers expect service providers to anticipate their needs and deliver on them more than ever.[10]

PREDICTED SERVICE LEVEL   The level of service that customers actually anticipate receiving is known as *predicted service*, which directly affects how they define "adequate service" on that occasion. If good service is predicted, the adequate level will be higher than if poorer service is predicted. Customer predictions of service may be situation specific. For example, from past experience, customers visiting a museum on a summer day may expect to see larger crowds if the weather is poor than if the sun is shining. So a ten-minute wait to buy tickets on a cool, rainy day in summer might not fall below their adequate service level.

ZONE OF TOLERANCE   The inherent nature of services makes consistent service delivery difficult across employees in the same company and even by the same service employee from one day to another. The extent to which customers are willing to accept this variation is called the *zone of tolerance* (refer to Figure 2.7). A performance that falls below the adequate service level will cause frustration and dissatisfaction, whereas one that exceeds the desired service level will both please and surprise customers. Another way of looking at the zone of tolerance is to think of it as the range of service within which customers don't pay explicit attention to service performance.[11] When service falls outside this range, customers will react either positively or negatively.

The zone of tolerance can increase or decrease for individual customers depending on factors like competition, price, or importance of specific service attributes. These factors most often affect adequate service levels (which may move up or down in response to situational factors), while desired service levels tend to move up very slowly in response to accumulated customer experiences. Consider a small business owner who needs some advice from her accountant. Her ideal level of professional service may be a thoughtful response by the following day. But if she makes the request at the time of year when all accountants are busy preparing corporate and individual tax returns, she will probably know from experience not to expect a fast response. Although her ideal service level probably won't change, her zone of tolerance for response time may be much broader because she has a lower adequate service threshold.

How Customers Evaluate Services

Service performances, especially those that contain few tangible clues, can be difficult for consumers to evaluate, both in advance of purchase and even afterwards. As a result, there is a greater risk of making a purchase that proves to be disappointing. Although some services can be repeated, such as recleaning clothes that have not been satisfactorily laundered, this is not a practical solution in the case of a poorly performed play or a badly taught course.

Product Attributes Affecting Ease of Evaluation

Product attributes can be divided into search, experience, and credence properties. All products can be placed on a continuum ranging from "easy to evaluate" to "difficult to evaluate," depending on whether they are high in search attributes, experience attributes, or credence attributes.

SEARCH ATTRIBUTES   Physical goods tend to emphasize those attributes that allow customers to evaluate a product before purchasing it. Features like style, color, texture, taste, and sound allow prospective consumers to try out, taste test, or "test drive" the product prior to purchase. These tangible attributes help customers understand and evaluate what they will get in exchange for their money and reduces the sense of uncertainty or risk associated with the purchase occasion. Goods such as clothing, furniture, cars, electronic equipment, and foods are high in search attributes.

EXPERIENCE ATTRIBUTES   When attributes can't be evaluated prior to purchase, customers must experience the service to know what they are getting. Holidays, live entertainment performances, sporting events, and restaurants fall into this category. Although people can examine brochures, scroll through Web sites describing the holiday destination, view travel films, or read reviews by travel experts, they can't really evaluate or feel the dramatic beauty associated with hiking in the Nepal Himalayas or the magic of scuba diving in the Philippines until they actually experience these activities.

CREDENCE ATTRIBUTES   Product characteristics that customers find impossible to evaluate confidently even after purchase and consumption are known as credence attributes, because the customer is forced to trust that certain benefits have been delivered, even though it may be hard to document them. Therefore, from the customers' point of view, the relative intangibility of credence services is what causes an increase in perceived risk. For example, patients can't usually evaluate how well their dentists have performed complex dental procedures. This information asymmetry between buyers and sellers potentially creates incentives for sellers of credence goods to act in an unethical manner, and this adds to consumers' risk perceptions.[12]

Strategic Responses to Difficulties in Evaluating Services

The reasons why many services tend to be high in experience and credence attributes relate to the intangible nature of service performances and the variability of inputs and outputs, which often lead to quality control problems. These characteristics

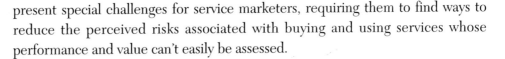

present special challenges for service marketers, requiring them to find ways to reduce the perceived risks associated with buying and using services whose performance and value can't easily be assessed.

INTANGIBILITY OF SERVICE PERFORMANCES   Marketers whose products are high in experience characteristics often try to provide more search attributes for their customers. One approach is to offer free trials or incentives. Some telecommunications companies have adopted this strategy. For example, Netvigator, a wireless broadband service provider in Hong Kong, allows customers to enjoy an installation fee waiver, free decoder, and no monthly fee when they subscribe to Netvigator's Broadband Internet service. This reduces customers' concerns about entering into a paid contract without first being able to test the service. Netvigator hopes that such incentives will entice consumers to sign up for their subscription plans and continue to remain with the company.

Advertising is another way to help customers visualize service benefits. For instance, the only tangible thing credit card customers get directly from the company is a small plastic card, followed by account statements. But that's hardly the essence of the benefits provided by this low-contact service. Think about the credit card advertisements you've seen recently. Did they promote the card itself or did they feature exciting products you could purchase and exotic places to which you could travel by using your card? Such advertisements stimulate consumer interest by showing physical evidence of the benefits of credit card use. The credit card business is emerging in Mainland China and many cardholders are still not used to shopping with their cards. In order to encourage consumers to use their cards, the Industrial and Commercial Bank of China (ICBC), the largest commercial bank in China, launched the campaign "Swiping Your Peony Card for Daily Awards" (Peony is the brand name of bank cards issued by ICBC). It announced in an advertisement (Figure 2.8) that from December 15, 2003 to February 15, 2004, anyone shopping in any of the ten designated stores in Beijing using his or her Peony Card stood the chance of winning RMB2,000 in cash. To win the award, the code "ICBC888888" should appear on the point-of-sale (POS) bill. It was guaranteed that at least one lucky consumer in each store would be picked at random every day. In the Chinese culture, the number 8 means fortune and luck, and six 8's are, therefore, strongly associated with a big fortune.

Besides credit card companies, many tourism boards also advertise frequently to promote their tourism industry, as holidays also fall into the experience attributes category. Figure 2.9 shows one of the advertisements put up by the tourism board in Malaysia.

Providers of services that are high in credence characteristics have an even greater challenge. Their benefits may be so intangible that customers can't evaluate the quality of what they have received even after the service has been purchased

Figure 2.8
ICBC encouraged
customers to
swipe their Peony
credit cards more
often through the
launch of a
campaign that
gave out daily
rewards.

Courtesy of Industrial and Commercial Bank of China.

and consumed. In this case, marketers often try to provide tangible cues to customers about their services. Professionals like doctors, architects, and lawyers often display their degrees and other certifications for the same reason. They want customers to "see" the credentials that qualify them to provide expert service. Many professional firms have developed Web sites to inform prospective clients about their services, highlight their expertise, and even showcase successful past engagements.

Figure 2.9
The Malaysian Tourism Board tries to entice business travelers to integrate pleasure into every business trip, hoping that this would lead to an increase in spending per day, durational stay, and perhaps even the frequency of business trips.

Courtesy of Tourism Malaysia.

VARIABILITY AND QUALITY CONTROL PROBLEMS   Quality control for products is much easier than for services since the elements of production can be more closely monitored and failures spotted before the product reaches the customer. However, quality control for services that fall in the experience and credence ranges is complicated by customer involvement in production.

Evaluations of such services may be affected by customers' interactions with the physical setting of the business, employees, and even other customers. For example, your experience of a haircut may combine your impression of the hair salon; how well you can describe what you want to the stylist; the stylist's ability to understand and do what you've requested; and the appearance of the other customers and employees in the salon. Stylists note that it's difficult for them to do a good job if customers are uncooperative.

Many credence services have few tangible characteristics and rely on the expertise of a professional service provider to provide a quality offering. In this case, providers must be able to interact with customers effectively to produce a satisfactory product. Problems can occur when this interaction doesn't produce an outcome that meets customers' expectations, even though the service provider may not be at fault.

How Confirmation or Disconfirmation of Expectations Relate to Satisfaction

The terms "quality" and "satisfaction" are sometimes used interchangeably. But some researchers believe that perceived service quality is just one component of customer satisfaction, which also reflects price/quality tradeoffs, and personal and situational factors.[13]

Satisfaction can be defined as an attitude-like judgment following a purchase act or a series of consumer product interactions.[14] Most studies are based on the theory that the confirmation/disconfirmation of preconsumption expectations is the essential determinant of satisfaction.[15] This means that customers have certain service standards in mind prior to consumption (their expectations), observe service performance and compare it to their standards, and then form satisfaction judgments based upon this comparison. The resulting judgment is labeled *negative disconfirmation* if the service is worse than expected, *positive disconfirmation* if better than expected, and simple *confirmation* if as expected.[16] When there is substantial positive disconfirmation, along with pleasure and an element of surprise, then customers are likely to be delighted

The results of a research project done by Oliver, Rust, and Varki suggest that delight is a function of three components: unexpectedly high levels of performance, arousal (e.g., surprise, excitement), and positive affect (e.g., pleasure, joy, or happiness).[17] Satisfaction is a function of positively disconfirmed expectations (better than expected) and positive affect. These researchers ask: "If delight is a function of surprisingly unexpected pleasure, is it possible for delight to be manifest in truly mundane services and products, such as newspaper delivery or trash collecting?" See Best Practice in Action 2.1 for an example of how hotels in Asia seek to delight their women guests.

HOTELS IN ASIA SEEK TO DELIGHT THE LADIES

According to official estimates, by the middle of this decade, women would make up half of the world's business travelers. These women are successful professionals with strong purchasing power, who enjoy having fresh flowers and fragrant candles in their rooms.

So how are hotels in Asia responding to the more demanding needs of their "new" female guests? A survey on Asia, conducted by *Asia Inc.*, revealed that big hotel chains have long discovered and developed an interest in this niche market. "Businesswomen are an important target group for us," said Lucinda Semark, sales and marketing vice-president of Singapore-based InterContinental Hotels Group (IHG) Asia Pacific. And Ms Semark is not the only one thinking this way. She also added that IHG recognizes the "unique needs" of women travelers and is responding to them "with alacrity." IHG properties in Shanghai and Yokohama have entire floors with rooms that are reserved exclusively for women, as does the Makati Shangri-La in the Philippines.

Hotel Sheraton Grande Sukhumvit in Bangkok also adopted a similar strategy to provide complimentary packs of everything a busy woman on the move might need—from needles to pins to exclusive beauty products. Hong Kong's Ritz-Carlton has even gone one step further to incorporate all the needs into a special "LADY" package. The LADY package includes "luxury amenities" ranging from nail varnish to pantyhose and sweet-smelling potpourri bags. All these complimentary services have only one aim—to delight the women guests.

When looking for a suitable hotel, women travelers ranked these so-called "conveniences" highly. A survey carried out by America's Businesswomen's Research Institute on 500 women business travelers found that "conveniences, small luxuries, and safety" were top priorities when deciding on a room. Most luxury and prestige hotel chains can provide small luxuries, and convenience for their guests. However, most hotels find it harder to guarantee its women guests' safety.

Despite the hotels' careful and meticulous planning to meet the unique and sophisticated needs of businesswomen, their strategy is not without risk. After all, not all businesswomen are willing to pay for such expensive services.

Source: Adapted from "What Women Want," *Asia Inc.* (September 2003).

However, once customers have been delighted, their expectations are raised. They will be dissatisfied if service levels return to previous levels, and it will take more effort to "delight" them in the future.[18] So achieving delight requires focusing on what is currently unknown or unexpected by the customer. In short, it's more than just avoiding problems—the "zero defects" strategy.

Why is satisfaction important to service managers? There's evidence of strategic links between the level of customer satisfaction and a firm's overall performance. Researchers from the University of Michigan found that on average, every 1 percent increase in customer satisfaction is associated with a 2.37 percent increase in a firm's return on investment (ROI).[19] And Fournier and Mick state:

> Customer satisfaction is central to the marketing concept ... [I]t is now common to find mission statements designed around the satisfaction notion, marketing plans and

incentive programs that target satisfaction as a goal, and consumer communications that trumpet awards for satisfaction achievements in the marketplace.[20]

Determining Consumer Comfort with Service Providers

Important though satisfaction is as a performance measure, it is an evaluation that is normally made after a transaction. Spake *et al.* have developed a methodology for measuring a consumer's comfort level, which can be applied both prior to and following a given service encounter, and is particularly applicable to high-contact services.[21] Prior to an interaction, the customer has only expectations concerning the transaction, and so cannot easily discuss satisfaction at that point. However, the customer's comfort level with the service provider can be ascertained at every stage from prepurchase to postpurchase. In surveying consumers, Spake *et al.* found that respondents associated an increased comfort level with reduced perceived risk. Words and phrases such as safety, security, being worry-free, and having assurance of the quality of the service provided were mentioned, as were having peace of mind, being at ease with the service provider, and trusting them.

It is a mistake for service firms to rely solely on posttransaction satisfaction studies, particularly in extended high-contact encounters, because this approach inevitably misses opportunities to address problems while the customer is still engaged in the process—or before they have even made a decision on usage. If customers are uneasy with the prospect of using a particular service, they may decide against purchasing it. And if they feel uncomfortable with some aspect of a service encounter, they may decide to quit before completing a transaction, especially if they haven't yet had to pay for it.

Although it is not always practical to administer formal surveys in mid-encounter, managers can train service personnel to be more observant, so that they can identify customers who appear to be having difficulties, look frustrated, or seem otherwise ill at ease, and then ask if they need assistance. If experience shows that customers are continually discomforted by a particular aspect of the service encounter, this would indicate a need for redesign and improvement.

Viewing the Service Business As a System

The types of encounters that take place during service delivery depend to a great extent on the level of contact that customers have with the provider. A service business can be viewed as a system, composed of three overlapping elements:

- *Service operations*, where inputs are processed and the elements of the service product are created
- *Service delivery*, where final "assembly" of these elements takes place and the product is delivered to the customer

- *Service marketing*, which embraces all points of contact with customers, including advertising, billing, and market research.

Parts of this system are visible (or otherwise apparent) to customers. Other parts are hidden and the customer may not even know of their existence.[22] Some writers use the terms "front office" and "back office" in referring to the visible and invisible parts of the operation. Others talk about "front stage" and "backstage," using the analogy of theater to dramatize the notion that service is a performance.[23] We like this analogy—sometimes referred to as "dramaturgy"—and will be using it throughout the book.

Service Operations System

Like a play in a theater, the visible components of service operations can be divided into those relating to the actors, or service personnel, and those relating to the stage set, or physical facilities, equipment, and other tangibles. What goes on backstage is of little interest to customers. Like any audience, they evaluate the production on those elements they actually experience during service delivery and on the perceived service outcome. Naturally, if the backstage personnel and systems (e.g., billing, ordering, account keeping) fail to perform their support tasks properly in ways that affect the quality of front stage activities, customers will notice. For instance, restaurant patrons will be disappointed if they order fish from the menu but are told it is unavailable or find that their food is overcooked. Other examples of backstage failures include receiving an incorrect hotel bill due to a keying error, not receiving course grades because of a computer failure in the college registrar's office, or being delayed on a flight because the aircraft has been taken out of service for engine repairs.

The proportion of the overall service operation that is visible to customers varies according to the level of customer contact. Since high-contact services directly involve the physical person of the customer, the visible component of the service operations system tends to be substantial.

Low-contact services usually strive to minimize customer contact with the service provider, so most of the service operations system is confined to a remotely located backstage (sometimes referred to as a technical core). Front stage elements are normally limited to mail and telecommunications contacts. Think for a moment about the telephone company that you use. Do you have any idea where its exchange is located?

Service Delivery System

Service delivery is concerned with where, when, and how the service product is delivered to the customer. It includes not only the visible elements of the service operating system—buildings, equipment, and personnel—but may also involve exposure to other customers.

Using the theatrical analogy, the distinction between high-contact and low-contact services can be likened to the differences between live theater on a stage and a drama created for television. That's because customers of low-contact services normally never see the "factory" where the work is performed. At most, they will talk with a service provider (or problem solver) by telephone. Without buildings and furnishings or even the appearance of employees to provide tangible clues, customers must make judgments about service quality based on the ease of telephone access, followed by the voice and responsiveness of a telephone-based customer service representative.

When service is delivered through impersonal electronic channels, such as self-service machines, automated telephone calls to a central computer, or via the customer's own computer, there is very little traditional "theater" left to the performance. Some firms compensate for this by giving their machines names, playing recorded music, or installing moving color graphics on video screens, adding sounds, and creating computer-based interactive capabilities to give the experience a more human feeling.

Responsibility for designing and managing service delivery systems has traditionally fallen to operations managers. But marketing needs to be involved, too, to research how consumers behave during service delivery and ensure that the system is designed with their needs and concerns in mind.

Service Marketing System

In addition to the service delivery system, other elements also contribute to the customer's overall view of a service business. These include communication efforts by the advertising and sales departments, telephone calls and letters from service personnel, billings from the accounting department, random exposures to service personnel and facilities, news stories and editorials in the mass media, word-of-mouth comments from current or former customers, and even participation in market research studies.

Collectively, the components just cited—along with those in the service delivery system—add up to what we call the service marketing system. The service marketing system represents all the different ways the customer may encounter or learn about the organization in question. Since services are experiential, each of these elements offers clues about the nature and quality of the service product. Inconsistency between different elements may weaken the organization's credibility in the customers' eyes. Figure 2.10 depicts the service system for a high-contact service like a hotel, health club, or full-service restaurant.

As you know from your own experience, the scope and structure of the service marketing system often vary sharply from one type of organization to another. Figure 2.11 shows how things change when we are dealing with a low-contact service, such

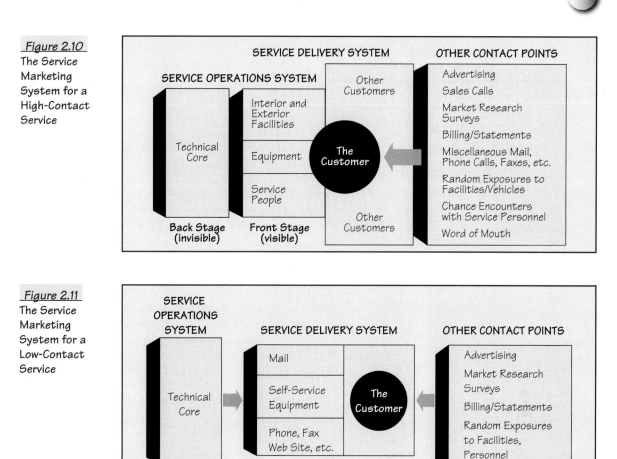

Figure 2.10
The Service
Marketing
System for a
High-Contact
Service

Figure 2.11
The Service
Marketing
System for a
Low-Contact
Service

as a credit card account or Internet-based insurance firm. The significance of this approach to conceptualizing service creation and delivery is that it represents the customer's view, looking at the service business from the outside, as opposed to an internally focused operations perspective.

Theater as a Metaphor for Service Delivery

The theater is a good metaphor for services since service delivery consists of a series of events that customers experience as a *performance*.[24] It is a particularly useful approach for high-contact service providers like physicians, educators, restaurants, and hotels, and for businesses that serve many people simultaneously rather than providing individualized service (like professional sports, hospitals, and entertainment). In practice, the extent to which theatrical elements are present and can be used by marketers to dramatic effect, depends to a large extent on the nature of the service process. Table 2.2 provides a summary of the drama implications for the four categories of service processes identified earlier.

Table 2.2
Theatrical Considerations for Different Types of Services

Service Process Category	Level of Contact	Drama Implications
People processing	High	Because the actors and audience are in close contact, the setting and front-stage performances affect customers' perceptions of service quality. Important theater aspects include design and ambience of the setting, appearance and behavior of the actors, props, costumes, and scripts. Other audience members (customers) can influence one another's service experience and the perceived quality of the service performance.
Mental stimulus processing	High	If actors and audience are in close physical proximity, then many of the drama implications for people-processing services may apply.
	Low	If the performance is conducted at arm's length, audience members do not typically interact with one another. The physical appearances of the actors and setting are less important. Scripts may still be useful in ensuring that actors and audience members play their parts correctly.
Possession processing	Medium	The performance can either take place at the service firm or at the audience members' home or business. Contact between actors and audience may be limited to the start and end of the service. (At these contact points, the drama elements described for people-processing services do apply but on a less substantial level.)
	Low	In some circumstances—for instance, lawn mowing and office janitorial services—the service performance may occur without the audience present. The outcomes of such services are usually tangible and may be used as a proxy for judging the quality of the service performance.
Information processing	Low	There is minimal contact between actors and audience members. Both the act and the recipient (intangible assets) are intangible, and the performance usually occurs in the absence of the customer. Because of these factors, only the outcomes can be assessed, not the process. However, even the outcome may be difficult for customers to evaluate.

Developed from information in Stephen J. Grove, Raymond P. Fisk, and Joby John, "Services as Theater: Guidelines and Implications," in Teresa A. Schwartz and Dawn Iacobucci, *Handbook of Service Marketing and Management* (Thousand Oaks, CA: Sage Publications, 2000), 31.

We can think of service facilities as containing the stage on which the drama unfolds. Sometimes the setting changes from one act to another (for example, when airline passengers move from the entrance, to the terminal, to the check-in stations, and then on to the boarding lounge and finally step inside the aircraft). The stage may have minimal "props," as in a typical post office, or elaborate scenery, as in some modern resort hotels. Many service dramas are tightly scripted (as in the way that service is delivered in a formal restaurant setting), while others are improvisational in nature (like teaching a university class).

Some services are more ritualized than others. In highly structured environments like dental services, "blocking" may define how the actors (in this case, receptionists, dental hygienists, technicians, and dentists) should move relative to the stage (the dentist's office), items of scenery (furniture and equipment), and other actors.

Not all service providers require customers to attend performances at the company's "theater," especially in a business-to-business context. In many instances, the customer's own facilities provide the stage where the service employees perform with their props. For example, outside accountants are often hired to provide specialized services at a client's site. Telecommunication linkages offer an alternative performance environment, allowing customers to be involved in the drama from a remote location.

Front-stage personnel are members of a cast, playing roles as *actors* in a drama, and supported by a backstage production team. In some instances, they are expected to wear special costumes when on stage (like the protective clothing—traditionally white—worn by dental professionals, or the fanciful uniforms often worn by hotel doormen). When service employees wear distinctive apparel, they stand out from personnel at other firms. In this respect, uniform designs can be seen as a form of packaging that provides physical evidence of brand identity.[25] In many service companies, the choice of uniform design and colors is carefully integrated with other corporate design elements. Many front-stage employees must conform to both a dress code and grooming standards (like Disney's rule that employees can't wear beards, except as required in costumed roles).

Depending on the nature of their work, employees may be required to learn and repeat specific lines ranging from announcements in several languages to a sing-song sales spiel (just think of the last telemarketer who called you!) to a parting salutation of "Have a nice day!" And as in the theater, companies often use scripting to define actors' behavior as well as their lines. Eye contact, smiles, and handshakes may be required in addition to a spoken greeting. Other rules of conduct may include bans on smoking, eating and drinking, or gum chewing while on duty.

Role and Script Theories

Role and script theories offer some interesting insights for service providers. If we view service delivery as a theatrical experience, then both employees and customers act out their parts in the performance according to predetermined *roles*. Stephen Grove and Ray Fisk define a role as "a set of behavior patterns learned through experience and communication, to be performed by an individual in a certain social interaction in order to attain maximum effectiveness in goal accomplishment."[26] Roles have also been defined as combinations of social cues, or expectations of society, that guide behavior in a specific setting or context.[27] In service encounters, employees and customers each have roles to play. The satisfaction of both parties depends on role congruence, or the extent to which each person acts out his or her prescribed role during a service encounter. Employees must perform their roles to customer expectations or risk dissatisfying or losing customers altogether. And customers, too, must "play by the rules," or they risk causing problems for the firm, its employees, and even other customers.

Scripts are sequences of behavior that both employees and customers are expected to learn and follow during service delivery. Scripts are learned through experience, education, and communication with others.[28] Much like a movie script, a service script provides detailed actions that customers and employees are expected to perform. The more experience a customer has with a service company, the more familiar the script becomes. Any deviations from this known script may frustrate both customers and employees and can lead to dissatisfaction. If a company decides to change a service script (for example, by using technology to turn a high-contact service into a low-contact one), service personnel and customers should be educated about the new script and the benefits it provides.

Some scripts are highly structured and allow service employees to move through their duties quickly and efficiently (like flight attendants' scripts for economy class). Sales scripts often prescribe specific opening and closing phrases and techniques. However, not all services involve tightly scripted performances. For providers of highly customized services, such as doctors, educators, hair stylists, or consultants, the service script is flexible and may vary by situation and by customer. When customers are new to a service, they may not know what to expect and may be fearful of behaving incorrectly. Organizations should be ready to educate new customers about their roles in service delivery, since inappropriate behaviors can disrupt service delivery and make customers feel embarrassed and uncomfortable.

A flowchart can provide the basis for development of a well-planned script that provides a full description of what should take place during a service encounter, including the roles played by customers and service personnel at different points in the process. Figure 2.12 shows a script for teeth cleaning and a simple dental examination, involving three players—the patient, the receptionist, and the dental hygienist. Each has a specific role to play. In this instance, the script is driven primarily by the need to execute a technical task both proficiently and safely (note the mask and gloves). The core service of examining and cleaning teeth can only be accomplished satisfactorily if the patient cooperates in an experience that is at best neutral and at worst uncomfortable or even painful. Several elements in this script relate to information flows. Confirming and honoring appointments avoids delays for customers and ensures effective use of dental professionals' time. Obtaining patient histories and documenting analysis and treatment are vital for maintaining complete dental records and also for accurate billing. Payment on receipt of treatment improves cash flow and avoids the problem of bad debts. And finally, adding greetings, statements of thanks, and good-byes displays friendly good manners and helps to humanize what most people see as a slightly unpleasant experience.

<u>Figure 2.12</u>
Script for Teeth Cleaning and Simple Dental Examination

Patient	Receptionist	Dental Hygienist
1. Phone for appointment	2. Confirm needs and set date	
3. Arrive at dental office	4. Greet patient; verify purpose; direct to waiting room; notify hygienist of arrival	5. Review notes on patient
6. Sit in waiting room		7. Greet patient and lead way to treatment room
8. Enter room; sit in dental chair		9. Verify medical and dental history; ask about any issues since previous visit
		10. Place protective covers over patient's clothes
		11. Lower dental chair; put on own protective face mask, gloves, and glasses
		12. Inspect patient's teeth (option to ask questions)
		13. Place suction device in patient's mouth
		14. Use high-speed equipment and hand tools to clean teeth in sequence
		15. Remove suction device; complete cleaning process
		16. Raise chair to sitting position; ask patient to rinse
17. Rinse mouth		18. Remove and dispose of mask and gloves; remove glasses
		19. Complete notes on treatment; return patient file to receptionist
		20. Remove covers from patient
		21. Give patient free toothbrush; offer advice on personal dental care for future
22. Rise from chair		23. Thank patient and say good-bye
24. Leave treatment room	25. Greet patient; confirm treatment received; present bill	
26. Pay bill	27. Give receipt; agree on date for next appointment; document agreed-on date	
28. Take appointment card	29. Thank patient and say good-bye	
30. Leave dental office		

Service Firms as Teachers

Although service providers attempt to design the ideal level of customer participation into the service delivery system, in reality it is customers' actions that determine the actual amount of participation. Underparticipation causes customers to experience a decrease in service benefits (a student learning less or a dieter losing less weight). If customers overparticipate, they may cause the firm to spend more resources customizing a service than was originally intended (a request for customization of a hamburger at a fast-food restaurant). Service businesses must

*Service
Perspectives
2.2*

THE USE OF SCRIPT IN ASIAN CONTEXT BY TELEMARKETERS

Multinationals are moving their back-office operations to countries which have large numbers of low-wage, English-speaking workers. Through such a move, also known as "business process outsourcing," multinationals have created a huge number of call centers in India and the Philippines. Employees of these call centers handle credit card enquiries, payroll questions, market research, and customer complaints from European and North American clients.

Naman works in one such call center in New Delhi, India. Naman is known by clients as Norman. He speaks in fluent American or British accent without a hint of "Hinglish," a mix of English and Hindi accent, which he uses when speaking to friends. In order to hide the location of these outsourced back offices, employees like him go through courses to remove their native accents when they speak English. During the one-month training, they learn voice enhancement techniques and cross-cultural communication. Employees are also encouraged to watch productions such as *Friends, Ally McBeal* and *MTV*.

Sales scripts are also customized for each new product Naman telemarkets. The aim of the scripts is to win sales. The script consists of different sections: call-opening, "must say" phrases, and call-closing techniques. His computer screen would flash reminders as he speaks to the clients. A list of "do's" and "don'ts" is also given to the employees.

Naman highlights that one "don't" is to never divulge his true identity. He says, "I don't lie, but if someone asks me 'where are you calling from?', I say 'from an international contact center.' Although most people accept this reply, exceptions do occur. There is always this odd customer who will persist and ask, 'which city?' Then, I have to tell the truth. Some people get angry and bang the phone down. Others are flattered to receive a call from overseas."

Source: Adapted from "When the Sun Sets over the Call Center... Norman Service Resumes," *Asia-Inc.* (January 2003).

teach their customers what roles to play to optimize participation levels during service production and consumption.

The more work that customers are expected to do, the greater their need for information about how to perform for best results. The necessary education can be provided in many different ways. Brochures and posted instructions are two widely used approaches (see Figure 2.13). Thoughtful banks place a telephone beside their ATMs so that customers can call a real person for help and advice at any time if they are confused about the on-screen instructions or if the machine malfunctions. In many businesses, customers look to employees for advice and assistance and are frustrated if they cannot obtain it.

Schneider and Bowen suggest giving customers a realistic service preview in advance of service delivery to provide them with a clear picture of the role they will play in service coproduction.[29] For example, a company might show a video presentation to help customers understand their role in the service encounter. This technique is used by some dentists to help patients understand the surgical processes

Figure 2.13

This Asia Life/Maybank brochure provides comprehensive information for parents who are interested in setting up an education fund for the apple of their eyes.

As a parent, you would want to lay a strong foundation for your child to realize his/her full potential. A vital part of this foundation is education and you want to be sure you'll have the funds to finance your child's studies.

Asia Education Plan
can put your mind at ease.

assured fund
for education

Upon maturity, you're guaranteed the basic sum assured PLUS any declared bonuses. The money will be paid in one lump sum and you can use it to fund your child's tertiary fees. The plan term can range from 10 to 25 years.

That's not all...the plan grows your money too! For instance, a 25-year plan on the life of a 1-year old child could enjoy a projected yield of 4.4%* p.a.

insurance protection
for your child

The plan not only alleviates your worry over the cost of education, it offers Death and Total & Permanent Disability (TPD) coverage for your child as well.

choices for
enhanced flexibility

By adding the following riders to Asia Education Plan, you can mix and match benefits. Pick a combination that's easy on your pockets!

☑ Payer Benefit Rider/ Enhanced Payer Benefit Rider**
With Payer Benefit Rider, the child will still be able to enjoy the plan's features should Death or TPD occur to the assured. To include coverage against any of the 30 Dread Diseases (DD), just opt for Enhanced Payer Benefit Rider.

☑ Enhanced CrisisAssurance Rider**
The addition of Enhanced CrisisAssurance Rider will ensure additional protection for the child should Death, TPD or any of the 30 DD strike. The plan can cover either parent or child or both parties simultaneously.

☑ Family Expense Rider/Enhanced IncomeCare Rider**
Family Expense Rider is payable upon Death or TPD while Enhanced IncomeCare Rider incorporates DD coverage. This plan provides monthly payments to the remaining family members for a specified period of time in the event that the above catastrophes occur.

about Asia Life.

Founded in 1948, Asia Life is one of Singapore's earliest life insurance companies. It holds a strong position in the Singapore life insurance market with a sizeable portfolio of policies. It has total group assets of S$1.8 billion and a network of offices in Malaysia, Brunei and China. As an indicator of its financial stability, Asia Life has one of the highest surplus ratios in the industry. It is also noteworthy to mention that it has not cut its bonus ever since declaring its maiden bonus to its participating policyholders in 1951. Asia Life has been rated 'A+' by Standard & Poor's and attained ISO9001:2000 certification. Furthermore, it has been awarded the 'Singapore 1000' Certificate of Achievement (2002/2003).

For more information, please call us at

1800-MAYBANK (1800-629 2265)

We'll be glad to be of assistance.

* As the bonus rates used for the benefits illustrated above are not guaranteed, the actual benefits payable may vary according to the future experience of the fund.

** Premium rates are not guaranteed. The Society reserves the right to change the premium rate by giving 30 days written notice. The rate may be adjusted based on future experience relating to DD.

NOTE:
Buying a life insurance policy is a long-term commitment. An early termination of the policy usually involves high costs and the surrender value payable may be less than the total premiums paid.

This brochure is for general information only and is not a contract of insurance. The precise terms and conditions of this insurance plan are specified in the policy contract.

The information in this brochure is accurate at the time of printing.

WA/1103/20K

ASIA Life   ◎ **Maybank**

give your child
the right start
Asia Education Plan

Courtesy of The Asia Life Assurance Society Limited.

they are about to experience and indicate how they should cooperate to help make things go as smoothly as possible.

Because consumers differ in their acceptance of technology-related goods and services, marketers have become interested in segmenting customers based on their willingness and ability to use the latest technologies.[30] An individual's behavior often reflects personal attitudes and beliefs.[31] Recent research by A. Parasuraman shows that certain personal characteristics are associated with customer readiness to accept new technologies. These attributes include innovativeness, a positive view of technology, and a belief that technology offers increased control, flexibility, and efficiency in people's lives.[32] Factors that are negatively associated with the adoption of technology include distrust, a perceived lack of control, feelings of being overwhelmed by technology, and skepticism about whether the technology will perform satisfactorily. Service providers must consider these factors before implementing new technologies that may negatively affect customers' evaluations of the service experience.[33]

Conclusion

Services cover a spectrum from high-contact to low-contact operations, reflecting the type of service involved and the nature of the processes used in service creation and delivery. Flowcharting helps us to understand the nature of the customer's involvement.

In all types of services, understanding and managing service encounters between customers and service personnel is central to creating satisfied customers who are willing to enter into long-term relationships with the service firm. Gaining a better understanding of how customers evaluate, select, and use services should lie at the heart of strategies for designing and delivering the service product. It also has implications for choice of service processes, presentation of physical evidence, and use of marketing communications—not least for educational purposes. Several of the distinctive characteristics of services (especially intangibility and quality control problems) result in customer evaluation procedures that differ from those involved in evaluating physical goods.

Service businesses can be divided into three overlapping systems. The operations system consists of the personnel, facilities, and equipment required to run the service operation and create the service product. Only part of this system, called "front stage," is visible to the customer. The delivery system incorporates the visible operations elements and customers themselves, who sometimes take an active role in helping to create the service product as opposed to being passively waited on. The higher the level of contact, the more we can apply theatrical analogies to the process of "staging" service delivery in which employees and customers play roles, often following well-defined scripts. Finally, the marketing system includes not only the delivery system, which is essentially composed of the product and distribution elements of the traditional marketing mix, but also additional components such as billing and payment systems, exposure to advertising and salespeople, and word-of-mouth comments from other people.

Review Questions

1. Clarify the difference between high-contact and low-contact services and explain how the nature of the customer's experience may differ between the two. Give examples.
2. Describe search, experience, and credence attributes, and give examples of each.
3. Explain why services tend to be harder for customers to evaluate than goods.
4. How are customers' expectations formed? Explain the difference between desired service and adequate service with reference to a service experience you've had recently.
5. Choose a service that you are familiar with and create a simple flowchart for it. Define the "front-stage" and "backstage" activities.
6. Describe the relationship between customer expectations and customer satisfaction.
7. Clarify the distinction between the service operations system, the service delivery system, and the service marketing system. Identify key distinctions in these systems between high-contact and low-contact services.

Application Exercises

1. What actions could a bank take to encourage more customers to bank by phone, mail, Internet, or through ATMs rather than visiting a branch?

2. Select three services, one high in search attributes, one high in experience attributes, and one high in credence attributes. Specify what product characteristics make them easy or difficult for consumers to evaluate and suggest specific strategies that marketers can adopt in each case to facilitate evaluation and reduce perceived risk.

3. What are the backstage elements of (a) a car repair facility, (b) an airline, (c) a university, and (d) a consulting firm? Under what circumstances would it be appropriate to allow customers to see some of these backstage elements, and how would you do it?

4. What roles are played by front-stage service personnel in low-contact organizations? Are these roles more or less important to customer satisfaction compared to high-contact services?

5. Describe an unsatisfactory encounter that you have experienced with (a) a high-contact service, and (b) a low-contact, self-service operation. In each instance, what could the service provider have done to improve the situation?

6. Develop two different customer scripts, one for a standardized service and one for a customized service. What are the key differences between the two?

Endnotes

1. Richard B. Chase and Sriram Dasu, "Want to Perfect Your Company's Service? Use Behavioral Science," *Harvard Business Review* 79 (June 2001): 79–84.

2. Lynn Shostack, "Planning the Service Encounter," in *The Service Encounter*, ed. J. A. Czepiel, M. R. Solomon, and C. F. Surprenant (Lexington, MA: Lexington Books, 1985), 243–254.

3. James G. Barnes, Peter A. Dunne, and William J. Glynn, "Self-Service and Technology: Unanticipated and Unintended Effects on Customer Relationships," in Teresa A. Schwartz and Dawn Iacobucci, *Handbook of Service Marketing and Management* (Thousand Oaks, CA: Sage Publications, 2000), 89–102.

4. Normann first used the term "moments of truth" in a Swedish study in 1978. Subsequently, it appeared in English in Richard Normann, *Service Management: Strategy and Leadership in Service Businesses*, 2nd ed. (Chichester, UK: John Wiley & Sons, 1991), 16–17.

5. Jaishankar Ganesh, Mark J. Arnold, and Kristy E. Reynolds, "Understanding the Customer Base of Service Providers: An Examination of the Differences between Switchers and Stayers," *Journal of Marketing* 64, no. 3 (2000): 65–87.

6. For a recent discussion on how expectations are formed, refer to: Ray W. Coye, "Managing Customer Expectations in the Service Encounter," *International Journal of Service Industry Management* 15, no. 4 (2004): 54–71.

7. Stephanie Anderson Forest, Katie Kerwin, and Susan Jackson, "Presents That Won't Fit under the Christmas Tree," *BusinessWeek* (December 1, 1997): 42.

8. See Benjamin Schneider and David E. Bowen, *Winning the Service Game* (Boston, MA: Harvard Business School Press, 1995); and Valarie A. Zeithaml, Leonard L. Berry, and A. Parasuraman, "The Nature and Determinants of Customer Expectations of Services," *Journal of the Academy of Marketing Science* 21 (1993): 1–12

9. Valarie A. Zeithaml, Leonard L. Berry, and A. Parasuraman, "The Behavioral Consequences of Service Quality," *Journal of Marketing* 60 (April 1996): 31–46. For a recent study on the zone of tolerance, refer also to R. Kenneth Teas and Thomas E. DeCarlo, "An Examination and Extension of the Zone-of-Tolerance

Model: A Comparison to Performance-Based Models on Perceived Quality," *Journal of Service Research* 6, no. 3 (2004): 272–286.

10 Uday Karmarkar, "Will You Survive the Service Revolution?" *Harvard Business Review* (June 2004): 101–108.

11 Robert Johnston, "The Zone of Tolerance: Exploring the Relationship between Service Transactions and Satisfaction with the Overall Service," *International Journal of Service Industry Management* 6, no. 5 (1995): 46–61.

12 Y. L. R. Moorthi, "An Approach to Branding Services," *The Journal of Services Marketing* 16, Issue 2, 2002: 159–174.

13 Valarie A. Zeithaml and Mary Jo Bitner, *Services Marketing: Integrating Customer Focus across the Firm,* 3rd ed. (Burr Ridge, IL: Irwin-McGraw-Hill, 2003).

14 Youjae Yi, "A Critical Review of Customer Satisfaction," in *Review of Marketing*, ed. V. A. Zeithaml (Chicago, American Marketing Association, 1990).

15 Richard L. Oliver, "Customer Satisfaction with Service", in Teresa A. Schwartz and Dawn Iacobucci, *Handbook of Service Marketing and Management* (Thousand Oaks, CA: Sage Publications, 2000), 247–254; Jochen Wirtz and Anna S. Mattila, "Exploring the Role of Alternative Perceived Performance Measures and Needs-Congruency in the Consumer Satisfaction Process," *Journal of Consumer Psychology* 11, no. 3 (2001): 181–192.

16 Richard L. Oliver, *Satisfaction: A Behavioral Perspective on the Consumer* (New York: McGraw-Hill, 1997).

17 Richard L. Oliver, Roland T. Rust, and Sajeev Varki, "Customer Delight: Foundations, Findings, and Managerial Insight," *Journal of Retailing* 73 (Fall 1997): 311–336.

18 Roland T. Rust and Richard L. Oliver, "Should We Delight the Customer?" *Journal of the Academy of Marketing Science* 28, no. 1 (2000): 86–94.

19 Eugene W. Anderson and Vikas Mittal, "Strengthening the Satisfaction-Profit Chain," *Journal of Service Research* 3 (November 2000): 107–120.

20 Susan Fournier and David Glen Mick, "Rediscovering Satisfaction," *Journal of Marketing* 63 (October 1999): 5–23.

21 Deborah F. Spake, Sharon E. Beatty, Beverly K. Brockman, and Tammy Neal Crutchfield, "Development of the Consumer Comfort Scale: A Multi-Study Investigation of Service Relationships," *Journal of Service Research* 5, no. 4 (May 2003): 316–332.

22 Richard B. Chase, "Where Does the Customer Fit in a Service Organization?" *Harvard Business Review* 56 (November–December 1978): 137–142.

23 Stephen J. Grove, Raymond P. Fisk, and Mary Jo Bitner, "Dramatizing the Service Experience: A Managerial Approach," in T. A. Schwartz, D. E. Bowen, and S. W. Brown, *Advances in Services Marketing and Management, Vol. I* (Greenwich, CT: JAI Press, 1992), 91–122. See also, B. Joseph Pine II and James H. Gilmore, *The Experience Economy* (Boston: Harvard Business School Press, 1999).

24 Stephen J. Grove, Raymond P. Fisk, and Joby John, "Services as Theater: Guidelines and Implications," in Teresa A. Schwartz and Dawn Iacobucci, *Handbook of Service Marketing and Management* (Thousand Oaks, CA: Sage Publications, 2000), 21–36; Steve Baron, Kim Harris, and Richard Harris, "Retail Theater: The 'Intended Effect' of the Performance," *Journal of Service Research* 2 (November 2001): 102–117; Ken Bates, Kim Harris, and Steve Baron, "Theatrical Service Experiences: Dramatic Script Development with Employees," *International Journal of Service Industry Management* 14, no. 2 (2003): 184–199.

25 Michael R. Solomon, "Packaging the Service Provider," *The Service Industries Journal* (July 1986).

26 Stephen J. Grove and Raymond P. Fisk, "The Dramaturgy of Services Exchange: An Analytical Framework for Services Marketing," in *Emerging Perspectives on Services Marketing*, eds. L. L. Berry, G. L. Shostack, and G. D. Upah (Chicago, IL: The American Marketing Association, 1983), 45–49.

27 Michael R. Solomon, Carol Suprenant, John A. Czepiel, and Evelyn G. Gutman, "A Role Theory Perspective on Dyadic Interactions: The Service Encounter," *Journal of Marketing* 49 (Winter 1985): 99–111.

28 See R. P. Abelson, "Script Processing in Attitude Formation and Decision-Making," in *Cognitive and Social Behavior*, eds. J. S. Carrol and J. W. Payne (Hillsdale, NJ: Erlbaum, 1976), 33–45; and Ronald H. Humphrey and Blake E. Ashforth, "Cognitive Scripts and Prototypes in Service Encounters," in *Advances in Service Marketing and Management* (Greenwich, CT: JAI Press, 1994), 175–199.

29 Benjamin Schneider and David E. Bowen, *Winning the Service Game* (Boston: Harvard Business School Press, 1995), 92.

30 Zafar Iqbal, Rohit Verma, and Roger Baran, "Understanding Consumer Choices and Preferences in Transaction-Based e-Services," *Journal of Service Research* 6, no. 1 (2003): 51–65; Tonita Perea y Monsuwé, Benedict G. C. Dellaert, and Ko de Ruyter, "What Drives Consumers to Shop Online? A Literature Review," *International Journal of Service Industry Management* 15, no. 1 (2004): 102–121.

31 James M. Curran, Matthew L. Meuter, and Carol F. Surprenant, "Intentions to Use Self-Service Technologies: A Confluence of Multiple Attitudes," *Journal of Service Research* 5, no. 3 (2003): 209–224.

32 A. Parasuraman, "Technology Readiness Index [TRI]: A Multiple-Item Scale to Measure Readiness to Embrace New Technologies," *Journal of Service Research* 2 (2000): 307–320.

33 Mitzi M. Montoya-Weiss, Glenn B. Voss, and Dhruv Grewal, "Determinants of Online Channel Use and Overall Satisfaction with a Relational, Multichannel Service Provider," *Journal of the Academy of Marketing Science* 31, no. 4 (2003): 448–458; Devashish Pujari, "Self-Service with a Smile? Self-Service Technology (SST) Encounters among Canadian Business-to-Business," *International Journal of Service Industry Management* 15, no. 2 (2004): 200–219.

CHAPTER THREE

Positioning Services in Competitive Markets

To succeed in our overcommunicated society, a company must create a position in the prospect's mind, a position that takes into consideration not only a company's own strengths and weaknesses, but those of its competitors as well.

AL RIES AND JACK TROUT

A wise commander always ensures that his forces are put in an invincible position and at the same time will be sure to miss no opportunity to defeat the enemy.

SUN TZU, THE ART OF WAR

Ask a group of managers from different service businesses how they compete, and the chances are high that many will say simply, "on service." Press them a little further, and they may add words and phrases like "value for money," "service quality," "our people," or "convenience."

None of this is very helpful to a marketing specialist who is trying to develop strategies to help an organization compete more effectively. One central question is what makes consumers or institutional buyers select—and remain loyal to—one service supplier over another. Terms such as "service" typically subsume a variety of specific characteristics, ranging from the speed with which a service is delivered to the quality of interactions between customers and service personnel, and from avoiding errors to providing desirable "extras" to supplement the core service. Likewise, "convenience" could refer to a service that's delivered at a convenient location, available at convenient times, or easy to use. Without knowing which product features are of specific interest to customers, it's hard for managers to develop an appropriate competitive strategy.

In a highly competitive environment, there's a risk that customers will perceive little real difference between competing alternatives and so make their choices based on price. Positioning strategy is concerned with creating and maintaining distinctive differences that will be noticed and valued by those customers with whom the firm would most like to develop a long-term relationship. Note, for example, DHL's positioning as the largest supply chain and logistics service provider in Asia (see Figure 3.1). Successful positioning requires managers to understand both their target customers' preferences and the characteristics of their competitors' offerings.

In this chapter, we examine the need for focus in a competitive environment, and review the issues involved in developing a positioning strategy. Specifically, we explore the following questions:

1. Why is it so important for service firms to adopt focused strategies in their choice of markets and products?
2. What is the distinction between important and determinant attributes in consumer choice decisions?

Figure 3.1

DHL's positioning strategy emphasizes its in-depth knowledge of Asia and hence, its ability to deliver on time, every time.

Reprinted with permission from DHL.

3. What are the key concepts underlying competitive positioning strategy in services?
4. When is it appropriate to reposition an existing service offering?
5. How can positioning maps help service marketers to better understand and respond to competitive dynamics?

Focus Underlies the Search for Competitive Advantage

As competition intensifies in the service sector, it's becoming ever more important for service organizations to differentiate their products in ways that are meaningful to customers. In highly developed economies, growth is slowing in such mature consumer service industries as banking, insurance, hospitality, and education. Thus, corporate growth will have to be based on taking share from domestic competitors or by expanding into international markets. In each instance, firms should be selective in targeting customers and seek to be distinctive in the way they present themselves. A market niche that may seem too narrow to offer sufficient sales within one country may represent a substantial market when viewed from an international or even global perspective.

Competitive strategy can take many different routes. George Day observes:

> The diversity of ways a business can achieve a competitive advantage quickly defeats any generalizations or facile prescriptions … First and foremost, a business must set itself apart from its competition. To be successful, it must identify and promote itself as the best provider of attributes that are important to target customers.[1]

What this means is that managers need to think systematically about all facets of the service package and to emphasize competitive advantage on those attributes that will be valued by customers in the target segment(s).

Four Focus Strategies

It is usually not realistic for a firm to try to appeal to all potential buyers in a market, because customers are varied in their needs, purchasing behavior, and consumption patterns, and often also too numerous and geographically widely spread. Different service firms also vary widely in their abilities to serve different types of customers. So, rather than attempting to compete in an entire market, each company needs to focus its efforts on those customers it can serve best. In marketing terms, *focus* means providing a relatively narrow product mix for a particular market segment— a group of buyers who share common characteristics, needs, purchasing behavior, or consumption patterns. This concept is at the heart of virtually all successful service firms, who have identified the strategically important elements in their service operations and have concentrated their resources on them.

The extent of a company's focus can be described on two different dimensions—market focus and service focus.[2] *Market focus* is the extent to which a firm serves few or many markets, while service focus describes the extent to which a firm offers few or many services. These two dimensions define the four basic focus strategies shown in Figure 3.2.

A *fully focused* organization provides a very limited range of services (perhaps just a single core product) to a narrow and specific market segment. A *market-focused* company concentrates on a narrow market segment but has a wide range of services. *Service-focused* firms offer a narrow range of services to a fairly broad market. Finally, many service providers fall into the *unfocused* category because they try to serve broad markets and provide a wide range of services.

How should a firm select which of the three alternative "focused" strategies to pursue? Adopting a fully focused strategy presents both risks and opportunities. Developing recognized expertise in a well-defined niche may provide protection against would-be competitors and allow a firm to charge premium prices. The biggest risk is that the market may be too small to generate the volume of business needed for financial success. Other risks include the danger that demand for the service may be displaced by generic competition from alternative products or that purchasers in the chosen segment may be very susceptible to an economic downturn. One reason why firms with a narrow product line elect to serve multiple segments (a service-focused strategy) is to create a portfolio of customers that hedges against such a risk. However, as new segments are added, the firm needs to develop expertise in serving each segment, which may require a broader sales effort and greater investment in marketing communication. The example of Alexander Health Club (see Best Practice in Action 3.1) shows how a service-focused strategy could be successful.

Offering a broad product line to a narrowly defined target segment often looks attractive because it offers the potential of selling multiple services to a single

Figure 3.2
Basic Focus
Strategies for
Services

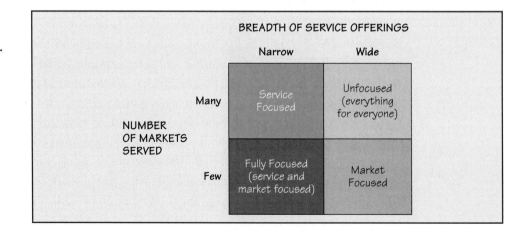

Source: Robert Johnston, "Achieving Focus in Service Organizations," *The Service Industries Journal* 16 (January 1996): 10–20.

ALEXANDER HEALTH CLUB

Alexander Health Club was founded in Taiwan in 1982, and its corporate slogan is "Young, Healthy and Vigorous." At that time, there were only about ten health clubs in Taiwan, and exercising was considered a woman's domain. Thus, Alexander Health Club established "Yazi Rhythm World," which targeted the ladies and children's segments.

With increasing affluence, the Taiwanese were getting more and more westernized. Aware of this trend, Alexander extended its market to professional men, providing them with imported equipment and professional, personal coaches. Many Taiwanese find themselves working very hard at their jobs, and at the same time, having to handle the pressure from family, social relationships, and career development. They thus felt a need to have some form of de-stressing.

Not contented with its development in Taiwan, Alexander Health Club expanded into Mainland China, and established its flagship store, the Shanghai Alexander Club, in Shanghai New World. Like in Taiwan, Shanghai Alexander also used a multibrand strategy to reach its customers.

Tang Yajun, the founder of Alexander Health Club, said, "We do not compete with the existing health clubs, but KTVs, discos, and pubs. Our customers are those who are not satisfied with the existing health clubs and have to go to pubs, discos or KTVs when there is no Alexander [Health] Club. Those customers fall mainly into three types:

1. Gold collar—Shanghai is a fast developing city. Its people are young and one of their desires is to stay in shape, a lifestyle that is supported by their relatively high incomes.
2. White collar—This segment stresses on a healthy lifestyle. They are capable, and as long as they want to be our members, they are welcome.
3. Expatriate business people—This group is accustomed to keeping fit.

In the last 20 years, Alexander Health Club has expanded to more than 20 branches, with nearly 200,000 members all over Taiwan. It is not only the first health club that has attained ISO9001 and 9002 certification—it is the biggest health club chain under direct management in Southeast Asia.

Source: Adapted from http://www.aforme.com/shopping_new/shop_home.asp; and http://tw.people.com.cn/, "Tang YaJun—Flattop in Exercise."

purchaser. Many beauty and slimming centers adopt a market-focused strategy and an example is Marie France Bodyline, which sells a wide variety of slimming and body firming treatments to women who desire a more perfect body.

But before adopting a market-focused strategy, managers need to be sure that their firms have the operational capability to do an excellent job of delivering each of the different services selected. They also need to understand customer purchasing practices and preferences. In a business-to-business context, when trying to cross-sell additional services to the same client, many firms have been disappointed to find that decisions on purchasing the new service are made by an entirely different group within the client company.

Market Segmentation Forms the Basis for Focused Strategies

Different service firms vary widely in their abilities to serve different types of customers. Hence, rather than trying to compete in an entire market, perhaps against superior competitors, each firm should adopt a strategy of market segmentation, identifying those parts, or segments, of the market that it can serve best. Firms that are in tune with customer requirements may choose to employ a needs-based segmentation approach, focusing on those customers identified by research as valuing specific attributes.[3]

The contrast in wealth shown in Figure 3.3 highlights the drastically different requirements among people within the same society. This phenomenon is common in Asia due to the great disparity in income in many of its countries.

Market and Microsegmentation

Because each person or corporate purchaser has distinctive (even unique) characteristics and needs, any prospective buyer is potentially a separate target

Figure 3.3
Disparity in wealth is common in many Asian countries and this leads to equally disparate market segments for Asia's service providers.

© Steve McCurry/Magnum Photos.

segment. Traditionally, firms have sought to achieve economies of scale by marketing to all customers within a specific market segment and serving each in a similar fashion. A strategy of *mass customization*—offering a service with some individualized product elements to a large number of customers at a relatively low price—may be achieved by offering a standardized core product but tailoring supplementary service elements to fit the requirements of individual buyers. The creation of customer databases and sophisticated analytical software makes it possible for firms to adopt *microsegmentation* strategies targeted at small groups of customers that share certain relevant characteristics at a specific point in time. (Note the strategy employed by the Royal Bank of Canada, as described in Best Practice in Action 3.2.)

Best Practice in Action 3.2

CONTINUOUS SEGMENTATION AT THE ROYAL BANK OF CANADA

At least once a month, Toronto-based analysts at the Royal Bank of Canada (the country's largest bank) use data modeling to segment its base of ten million customers. The segmentation variables include credit risk profile, current and projected profitability, life stage, likelihood of leaving the bank, channel preference (i.e., whether customers like to use a branch, self-service machines, the call center, or the Internet), product activation (how quickly customers actually use a product they have bought), and propensity to purchase another product (i.e., cross-selling potential). Says a senior vice president, "Gone are the days when we had mass buckets of customers that would receive the same treatment or same offer on a monthly basis. Our marketing strategy is [now] much more personalized. Of course, it's the technology that allows us to do that."

The main source of data is the marketing information file, which records what products customers hold with the bank, the channels they use, their responses to past campaigns, transactional data, and details of any restrictions on soliciting customers. Another source is the enterprise data warehouse, which stores billing records and information from every document that a new or existing customer fills out.

Royal Bank analysts run models based on complex algorithms that can slice the bank's massive customer database into tightly profiled microsegments that are based on simultaneous use of several variables, including the probability that target customers will respond positively to a particular offer. Customized marketing programs can then be developed for each of these microsegments, giving the appearance of a highly personalized offer. The data can also be used to improve the bank's performance on unprofitable accounts by identifying these customers and offering them incentives to use lower-cost channels.

An important goal of Royal Bank's segmentation analysis is to maintain and enhance profitable relationships. The bank has found that customers who hold packages of several services are more profitable than those who don't. These customers also stay with the bank an average of three years longer. As a result of the sophisticated segmentation practices at Royal Bank, the response rates to its direct marketing programs have jumped from an industry average of only 3 percent to as high as 30 percent.

Source: Meredith Levinson, "Slices of Lives," *CIO Magazine* (August 15, 2000).

Identifying and Selecting Target Segments

A *market segment* is composed of a group of buyers who share common characteristics, needs, purchasing behavior, or consumption patterns. Effective segmentation should group buyers into segments in ways that result in as much similarity as possible on the relevant characteristics within each segment, but dissimilarity on those same characteristics between segments.

A *target segment* is one that a firm has selected from among those in the broader market and may be defined on the basis of several variables. For instance, a department store in a particular city might target residents of the metropolitan area (geographic segmentation), who have incomes within a certain range (demographic segmentation), value personal service from a knowledgeable staff, and are not highly price sensitive (both reflecting segmentation according to expressed attitudes and behavioral intentions). Because competing retailers in the city would probably be targeting the same customers, the department store would have to create a distinctive appeal (appropriate characteristics to highlight might include a wide array of merchandise categories, breadth of selection within each product category, and the availability of such supplementary services as advice and home delivery). Service firms that are developing strategies based on use of technology recognize that customers can also be segmented according to their degree of competence and comfort in using technology-based delivery systems.

An important marketing issue for any business is to accept that some market segments offer better opportunities than others. Target segments should be selected not only on the basis of their sales and profit potential, but also with reference to the firm's ability to match or exceed competing offerings directed at the same segment. Sometimes, research will show that certain market segments are "underserved," meaning that their needs are not well met by existing suppliers. Such markets are often surprisingly large.

For example, there is a trend toward customizing services specially to target young working women, who are becoming more educated and affluent. Taiwanese Shin Kong Life Insurance Company, for instance, developed a specially designed insurance policy that targeted young working women (see Figure 3.4). The insurance policy included some unique features, such as double compensation for the beneficiaries if the insured person loses her life during pregnancy and paying out an annuity to assist the policy holder in the upbringing of her children.

In many emerging-market economies, there are huge numbers of consumers whose incomes are too small to attract the interest of service businesses that are accustomed to focusing on the needs of more affluent customers. Collectively, however, small wage earners represent a very big market and may offer even greater potential for the future as many of them move upward toward middle-class status. Service Perspectives 3.1 describes an innovative approach to providing financial services to rural populations in India.

Figure 3.4
Shin Kong Life
Insurance
Company
Promoting Its
'Specially
Designed for
Women'
Insurance Policy
Targeted at
Young Working
Women

Courtesy of Shin Kong Life Insurance.

Using Research to Develop a Service Concept for a Specific Segment

How can a firm develop the right service concept for a particular target segment? Formal research is often needed to identify what attributes of a given service are important to specific market segments and how well prospective customers perceive competing organizations as performing against these attributes. But it's dangerous to overgeneralize. Strategists should recognize that the same individuals may set different priorities for attributes according to:

*Service
Perspectives
3.1*

ICICI BANK CATERS TO FARMERS IN RURAL INDIA

Kundapur Vaman Kamath, CEO of ICICI Bank, was responsible for the paradigm shift in converting the largest private bank in India from a stodgy, term-lending institution to a consumer-oriented bank. ICICI Bank managed to establish its retail banking business despite mounting competitive pressures in 1997, offering the usual products such as mortgages, auto loans and credit cards. To reach out to the rural masses in India, Kamath described the banking model: "Our paradigm for rural India is that we need to lend money. We don't need to take deposits—not yet. If we provide sustainable credit, rural India develops. Then, when there is surplus cash in the villages, we'll go in and start taking deposits."

ICICI Bank counts 60,000 farmers among its customers, despite having no branches there. Instead, ICICI Bank partners companies such as Cargill and Hindustan Lever who support farmers by providing them with seeds, fertilizers and other inputs, as well as buying back their crop. Farming is getting organized now, and farmers need credit to help them farm. The bank lends through these companies, and when they pay the farmer for his crops, the bank gets paid back. It is a replicable banking model that ICICI Bank has adopted from village to village. The amazing part is that all transactions are done on the Internet, which is how ICICI Bank manages to work with the suppliers, and bypass the need to set up rural branches and sending people on hardship postings.

Source: Vikram Khanna, "Banking on Innovation," *The Business Times* (October 18, 2003).

- The purpose of using the service
- The person who makes the decision
- The timing of use (time of day/week/season)
- Whether the individual is using the service alone or with a group
- The composition of that group.

Consider the criteria that you might use when choosing a restaurant for lunch while on a holiday with friends or family, versus selecting a restaurant for an expense account business lunch at which you were meeting with a prospective client. Given a reasonable selection of alternatives, it's unlikely that you would choose the same type of restaurant in each instance, let alone the same one. It's possible, too, that if you left the decision to another person in the party, he or she would make a different choice.

Important versus Determinant Attributes

Consumers usually make their choices between alternative service offerings on the basis of perceived differences between them. But the attributes that distinguish competing services from one another are not always the most important ones. For instance, many travelers rank "safety" as their number one consideration in air travel. They may avoid traveling on unknown carriers or on an airline that has a poor safety reputation, but after eliminating such alternatives from consideration, a traveler flying on major routes is still likely to have several choices of carriers available, which are perceived as equally safe. Hence, safety is not usually an attribute that influences the customer's choice at this point.

Determinant attributes (i.e., those that actually determine buyers' choices between competing alternatives) are often some way down the list of service characteristics that are important to purchasers, but they are the attributes on which customers see significant differences between competing alternatives. For example, convenience of departure and arrival times, availability of frequent flyer miles and related loyalty privileges, quality of food and drinks service on board the aircraft, or the ease of making reservations, might be examples of determinant characteristics for business travelers when selecting an airline. For budget-conscious holiday-makers, on the other hand, price might assume primary importance.

The marketing researchers' task, of course, is to survey customers in the target segment, identify the relative importance of different attributes and then ask which ones determined recent decisions involving a choice of service suppliers. Researchers also need to be aware of how well each competing service is perceived by customers as performing on these attributes. Findings from such research form the necessary basis for developing a positioning (or repositioning) campaign.[4]

One further issue in evaluating service characteristics and establishing a positioning strategy is that some attributes are easily quantified, whereas others are qualitative and highly judgmental. Price, for instance, is a straightforward quantitative measure. Punctuality of transport services can be expressed in terms of the percentage of trains, buses, or flights arriving within a specified number of minutes from the scheduled time. Both of these measures are easy to understand and therefore generalizable. But characteristics such as the quality of personal service, or a hotel's degree of luxury are more qualitative and therefore subject to individual interpretation—although in the case of hotels, travelers may be prepared to trust the evaluations of independent rating services such as the *Michelin Guide*.

Positioning Distinguishes a Brand from Its Competitors

Competitive positioning strategy is based on establishing and maintaining a distinctive place in the market for an organization and/or its individual product offerings. Jack Trout has distilled the essence of positioning into the following four principles:[5]

1. A company must establish a position in the minds of its targeted customers.
2. The position should be singular, providing one simple and consistent message.
3. The position must set a company apart from its competitors.
4. A company cannot be all things to all people—it must focus its efforts.

These principles apply to any type of organization that competes for customers. Understanding the principles of positioning is key to developing an effective competitive posture. The concept of positioning is certainly not limited to services. Indeed, it had its origins in packaged goods marketing, but it offers valuable insights by forcing service managers to analyze their firm's existing offerings and to provide specific answers to the following questions:

- What does our firm currently stand for in the minds of current and prospective customers?
- What customers do we now serve and which ones would we like to target for the future?
- What are the characteristics of our current service offerings (core products and their accompanying supplementary service elements), and at what market segments is each one targeted?
- In each instance, how do our service offerings differ from those of the competition?
- How well do customers in the chosen target market segments perceive each of our service offerings as meeting their needs?
- What changes do we need to make to our offerings in order to strengthen our competitive position within the market segment(s) of interest to our firm?

Copy Positioning versus Product Positioning

Customers' brand choices reflect which brands they know and remember and then, how each of these brands is positioned within each customer's mind. These positions are perceptual. We need to remember that people make their decisions based on their perceptions of reality, rather than on an expert's definition of that reality.

Many marketers associate positioning primarily with the communication elements of the marketing mix, notably advertising, promotions, and public relations. This view reflects the widespread use of advertising in packaged goods marketing to create images and associations for broadly similar branded products so as to give them a special distinction in the customer's mind—an approach sometimes known as *copy positioning*. Mahajan and Wind maintain that consumers who derive emotional satisfaction from a brand are likely to be less price sensitive.[6]

Examples of how imagery may be used for positioning purposes in the service sector are found in McDonald's efforts to appear kid friendly (including its emphasis on Ronald McDonald, the clown) or humorous advertising by Qoo, a Coca-Cola company beverage featuring a childlike blue creature as its mascot. A brand may develop a reputation over time, reflecting an accumulation of associations. For instance, research has shown that Cathay Pacific, one of Hong Kong's best-known international brand names, is associated with superior customer service, quality, trustworthiness, and value.[7]

Some slogans promise a specific benefit, designed to make the company stand out from its competitors, such as Priceline's "Name Your Own Price," Singapore

Airlines' "A Great Way to Fly," HSBC's "Never Underestimate the Importance of Local Knowledge," (see Figure 3.5) Great Eastern's "Life is Great," Globe Telecom's "Globe, Making Great Things Possible," or South Korea's Incheon International Airport's "The Path Connecting the World."

Figure 3.5

HSBC illustrates the importance of local knowledge by showing the different associations among people from three different countries of the meaning of "bread."

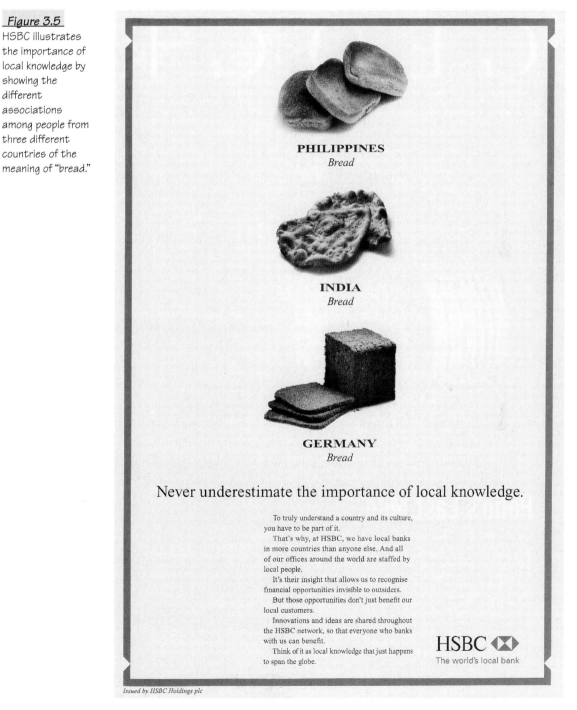

Used by permission of HSBC.

Some companies seek to achieve recognition and differentiation for their products by associating them with a well-known public figure—most commonly a personality from the fields of sports or entertainment. For instance, M-Zone employs the Taiwanese singer Jay Zhou (Best Practice in Action 3.3 and Figure 3.6).

Our primary concern in this chapter is the role of positioning in guiding marketing strategy development for services that compete on more than imagery or vague promises. This entails decisions on substantive attributes that are important to customers, relating to product performance, price, and service availability.

To improve a product's appeal to a specific target segment, it may be necessary to change its performance on certain attributes, to reduce its price, or to alter the times and locations when it is available or the forms of delivery that are offered. In such instances, the primary task of communication—advertising, personal selling, and public relations—is to ensure that prospective customers accurately perceive the position of the service on dimensions that are important to them in making choice decisions. Additional excitement and interest may be created by evoking certain images and associations in the advertising, but these are likely to play only a secondary role in customer choice decisions unless competing services are perceived as virtually identical on performance, price, and availability.

Positioning's Role in Marketing Strategy

Positioning plays a pivotal role in marketing strategy, because it links market analysis and competitive analysis to internal corporate analysis. From these three, a positioning statement can be developed that enables the service organization to answer these questions: What is our product or service concept? What do we want it to become? What actions must we take to get there?" Table 3.1 summarizes the principal uses of positioning analysis as a diagnostic tool, providing input to decisions relating to product development, service delivery, pricing, and communication strategy.

Developing a positioning strategy can take place at several different levels, depending on the nature of the business in question. Among multisite, multiproduct, service businesses, a position might be established for the entire organization, for a given service outlet, or for a specific service offered at that outlet. It is important that there is consistency between the positioning of different services offered at the same location, since the image of one may spill over onto the others. For instance, if a hospital has an excellent reputation for obstetrical services, this may enhance perceptions of its services in gynecology, pediatrics, surgery, and so forth. In contrast, it would be detrimental to both services, if their positioning were conflicting.

Because of the intangible, experiential nature of many services, an explicit positioning strategy is valuable in helping prospective customers to get a mental "fix" on a product that would otherwise be rather amorphous. Failure to select a desired position in the marketplace—and to develop a marketing action plan

Best Practice
in Action 3.3

CHINA MOBILE COMMUNICATION CORPORATION

M-Zone, the mobile communication service brand of China Mobile Communication Corporation (CMCC), was established in March 2003. M-Zone provides many fashionable services including a variety of bargain service packages, high-quality phone-call services, low-priced short message service, personalized rings and pictures download, mobile QQ, mobile games and mobile FLASH, etc.

The target consumers of M-Zone are young people aged 15 to 25. People from that age group tend to be brand sensitive, fashion conscious, and curious about anything new. They emphasize independence, individuality, and freedom. Compared to their peers, they are cool and stand out in a crowd. They create fashion trends and trigger brand worship. With regards to mobile communication services, they favor interactive mobile games and chic ways of communication such as through short messages, color picture messages, mobile QQ, etc.

The Taiwanese singer Jay Zhou, nicknamed "Little King," is regarded by the mass media as the most "hip" star. He sticks to his own styles and the music he believes in. A simple and quiet person, he works diligently and is a productive songwriter who is adored and respected by his fans.

CMCC believes that Jay's public image is suitable for M-Zone's brand image of being "fashionable, interesting, and innovative." Moreover, his intense popularity and influence among young people highly match M-Zone's target clients and its market position (see Figure 3.6).

Figure 3.6
A Series of M-Zone Advertisements Featuring the Highly Popular Jay Zhou Promoting the Various Services That Are Available

Picture 1: Theme Advertisement   Picture 2: Mobile QQ

Picture 3: Ring and Picture Download   Picture 4: Short Message

Table 3.1
Principal Uses of
Positioning
Analysis as a
Diagnostic Tool
	1. Provide a useful diagnostic tool for defining and understanding the relationships between products and markets:
	• How does the product compare with competitive offerings on specific attributes?
	• How well does product performance meet consumer needs and expectations on specific performance criteria?
	• What is the predicted consumption level for a product with a given set of performance characteristics offered at a given price?
	
	2. Identify market opportunities for
	  a. Introducing new products
	    • What segments to target?
	    • What attributes to offer relative to the competition?
	  b. Redesigning (repositioning) existing products
	    • Appeal to the same segments or to new ones?
	    • What attributes to add, drop, or change?
	    • What attributes to emphasize in advertising?
	  c. Eliminating products that
	    • Do not satisfy consumer needs
	    • Face excessive competition
	
	3. Make other marketing mix decisions to preempt or respond to competitive moves:
	  a. Distribution strategies
	    • Where to offer the product (locations, types of outlet)?
	    • When to make the product available?
	  b. Pricing strategies
	    • How much to charge?
	    • What billing and payment procedures to use?
	  c. Communication strategies
	    • What target audience(s) are most easily convinced that the product offers a competitive advantage on attributes that are important to them?
	    • What message(s)? Which attributes should be emphasized and which competitors, if any, should be mentioned as the basis for comparison on those attributes?
	    • Which communication channels: personal selling versus different advertising media? (Selected for their ability to not only convey the chosen message(s) to the target audience(s) but also reinforce the desired image of the product.)

designed to achieve and hold this position—may result in one of several possible outcomes, all undesirable:

1.   The organization (or one of its products) is pushed into a position, where it faces head-on competition from stronger competitors.
2.   The organization (product) is pushed into a position which nobody else wants, because there is little customer demand.
3.   The organization's (product's) position is so blurred that nobody knows what its distinctive competence really is.
4.   The organization (product) has no position at all in the marketplace because nobody has ever heard of it.

Internal, Market, and Competitor Analyses

The research and analysis that underlie development of an effective positioning strategy are designed to highlight both opportunities and threats to the firm in the competitive marketplace, including the presence of generic competition, and competition from substituting products. Figure 3.7 identifies the basic steps involved in identifying a suitable market position and developing a strategy to reach it.

MARKET ANALYSIS This analysis addresses such factors as the overall level and trend of demand, and the geographic location of this demand. Is demand increasing or decreasing for the benefits offered by this type of service? Are there regional or international variations in the level of demand? Alternative ways of segmenting the market should be considered and an appraisal made of the size and potential of different market segments. Research may be needed to gain a better understanding not only of customer needs and preferences within each of the different segments, but also of how each perceives the competition.

INTERNAL CORPORATE ANALYSIS The objective is to identify the organization's resources (financial, human labor and know-how, and physical assets), any limitations or constraints, its goals (profitability, growth, professional preferences, etc.), and how its values shape the way it does business. Using insights from this analysis, management should be able to select a limited number of target market segments which can be served with either new or existing services.

COMPETITOR ANALYSIS Identification and analysis of competitors can provide a marketing strategist with a sense of their strengths and weaknesses, which, in

Figure 3.7
Developing a Market Positioning Strategy

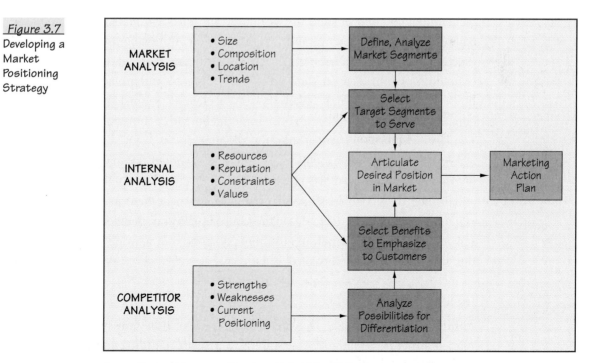

Source: Developed from an earlier schematic by Michael R. Pearce.

turn, may suggest opportunities for differentiation. Relating these insights back to the internal corporate analysis should suggest what might be viable opportunities for differentiation and competitive advantage, and thereby enable managers to decide which benefits should be emphasized to which target segments. This analysis should consider both direct and indirect competition.

POSITION STATEMENT The outcome of integrating these three forms of analysis is a statement that articulates the desired position of the organization in the marketplace (and, if desired, that of each of the component services that it offers). Armed with this understanding, marketers should be able to develop a specific plan of action. The cost of implementing this plan must, of course, be related to the expected payoff.

Anticipating Competitive Response

Before embarking on a specific plan of action, however, management should consider the possibility that one or more competitors might pursue the same market position. Perhaps another service organization has independently conducted the same positioning analysis and arrived at similar conclusions. Or an existing competitor may feel threatened by the new strategy and take steps to reposition its own service so as to compete more effectively. Alternatively, a new entrant to the market may decide to play "follow the leader," yet be able to offer customers a higher service level on one or more attributes and/or a lower price.

The best way to anticipate possible competitive responses is to identify all current or potential competitors and to put oneself in their own management's shoes by conducting an internal corporate analysis for each of these competitors.[8] Coupling the insights from the analysis with data from existing market and competitive analysis (with one's own firm cast in the role of competitor) should provide a good sense of how competitors might be likely to act. If chances seem high that a stronger competitor will move to occupy the same niche with a superior service concept, then it would be wise to reconsider the situation.

Some firms develop sophisticated simulation models to analyze the impact of alternative competitive moves. How would a price cut affect demand, market share, and profits? Based upon past experience, how might customers in different segments respond to increases or decreases in the level of quality on specific service attributes? How long would it take before customers respond to a new advertising campaign designed to change perceptions?

Evolutionary Positioning

Positions are rarely static: They need to evolve over time in response to changing market structures, technology, competitive activity, and the evolution of the firm itself. Many types of business lend themselves to evolutionary repositioning by adding or deleting services and target segments. Some companies have shrunk their offerings and divested certain lines of business in order to be more focused. Others have expanded their offerings in the expectation of increasing sales to existing customers and attracting new ones. Thus, service stations have added small convenience stores offering extended hours of service, while supermarkets and other retailers have added banking services. New developments in technology provide many opportunities for introducing not only new services, but also new delivery systems for existing products. An example of a service firm that capitalized on the development in technology is Reliance India Mobile (see Figure 3.8).

When a company has a trusted and successful brand, it may be possible to extend a position based on perceived quality in one type of service to a variety of related services under the same umbrella brand.

Using Positioning Maps to Plot Competitive Strategy

Developing a positioning "map"—a task sometimes referred to as perceptual mapping—is a useful way of representing consumers' perceptions of alternative products graphically. A map is usually confined to two attributes (although three-dimensional models can be used to portray three of these attributes). When more than three dimensions are needed to describe product performance in a given market, a series of separate charts need to be drawn for visual presentation purposes. A computer model, of course, can handle as many attributes as are relevant.[9]

Information about a product (or company's position relative to any one attribute) can be inferred from market data, derived from ratings by representative consumers, or both. If consumer perceptions of service characteristics differ sharply from "reality" as defined by management, marketing efforts may be needed to change these perceptions.

An Example of Applying Positioning Maps to the Hotel Industry

The hotel business is highly competitive, especially during "low" seasons when the supply of rooms exceeds demand. Within each class of hotels, customers visiting a large city may find that they have several alternatives from which to select a place to stay. The degree of luxury and comfort in physical amenities will be one choice criterion. Research shows that business travelers are concerned not only with the comfort and facilities offered by their rooms (where they may wish to work as well as sleep), but also with other physical spaces, ranging from the reception area, meeting rooms, a business center, to restaurants, swimming pool, and exercise facilities.

The quality and range of services offered by hotel staff is another key criterion: Can a guest get 24-hour room service? Can clothes be laundered and pressed? Is there a knowledgeable concierge on duty? Are staff available to offer professional

Figure 3.8

Reliance India Mobile capitalizes on optic fiber capability to introduce a unique Soft Hand-off technology, which ensures that its customers stay connected even while they are on the move across 700 towns in India.

Courtesy of Reliance Infocomm.

business services? There are other choice criteria, too, perhaps relating to the ambience of the hotel—modern architecture and decor are favored by some customers, whereas others may prefer old-world charm and antique furniture.

Additional attributes include factors such as quietness, safety, cleanliness, and special rewards programs for frequent guests.

Let's look at an example, based on a real-world situation, of how developing a positioning map of its own and competing hotels helped managers of the Palace, a successful four-star hotel, develop a better understanding of future threats to their established market position in a large city that we will call Belleville.

Located on the edge of the booming financial district, the Palace was an elegant old hotel that had been extensively renovated and modernized a few years earlier. Its competitors included eight four-star establishments, and the Grand, one of the city's oldest hotels, which had a five-star rating. The Palace had been very profitable for its owners in recent years and boasted an above-average occupancy rate. For many months of the year, it was sold out on weekdays, reflecting its strong appeal to business travelers, who were very attractive to the hotel, because of their willingness to pay a higher room rate than tourists or congress delegates. But the general manager and his staff saw problems on the horizon. Planning permission had recently been granted for four large new hotels in the city and the Grand had just started a major renovation and expansion project, which included construction of a new wing. There was a risk that customers might see the Palace as falling behind.

To understand better the nature of the competitive threat, the hotel's management team worked with a consultant to prepare charts that displayed the Palace's position in the business traveler market both before and after the advent of new competition. Four attributes were selected for study: room price, level of physical luxury, level of personal service, and location. In this instance, management did not conduct new consumer research. Instead, they inferred customer perceptions based on published information, data from past surveys, and reports from travel agents and knowledgeable hotel staff members who interacted frequently with customers. Information on competing hotels was not difficult to obtain, since the locations were known, the physical structures were relatively easy to visit and evaluate, and the sales staff kept themselves informed on pricing policies and discounts. A convenient surrogate measure for service level was the ratio of rooms per employee, easily calculated from the published number of rooms and employment data provided to the city authorities. Data from surveys of travel agents conducted by the Palace provided additional insights on the quality of personal service at each competitor.

Scales were then created for each attribute. Price was simple, since the average price charged to business travelers for a standard single room at each hotel was already quantified. The rooms per employee ratio formed the basis for a service level scale, with low ratios being equated with high service. This scale was then modified slightly in the light of what was known about the quality of service actually delivered by each major competitor. Level of physical luxury was more subjective.

The management team identified the hotel that members agreed was the most luxurious (the Grand) and then the four-star hotel that they viewed as having the least luxurious physical facilities (the Airport Plaza). All other four-star hotels were then rated on this attribute relative to these two benchmarks.

Location was defined with reference to the stock exchange building in the heart of the financial district, since past research had shown that a majority of the Palace's business guests were visiting destinations in this area. The location scale plotted each hotel in terms of its distance from the stock exchange. The competitive set of ten hotels lay within a four-mile, fan-shaped radius, extending from the exchange through the city's principal retail area (where the convention center was also located) to the inner suburbs and the nearby airport. Two positioning maps were created to portray the existing competitive situation. The first (Figure 3.9) showed the ten hotels on the dimensions of price and service level; the second (Figure 3.10) displayed them on location and degree of physical luxury.

A quick glance at Figure 3.9 shows a clear correlation between the attributes of price and service: Hotels offering higher levels of service are relatively more expensive. The shaded bar running from upper left to lower right highlights this relationship, which is not a surprising one (and can be expected to continue diagonally downwards for three-star and lesser-rated establishments). Further analysis shows that there appears to be three clusters of hotels within what is already an upscale market category. At the top end, the four-star Regency is close to the five-star Grand; in the middle, the Palace is clustered with four other hotels, and at the lower end, there is another cluster of three hotels. One surprising insight from this map is that the Palace appears to be charging significantly more (on a relative basis) than its service level would seem to justify. Since its occupancy rate is very high, guests are evidently willing to pay the going rate.

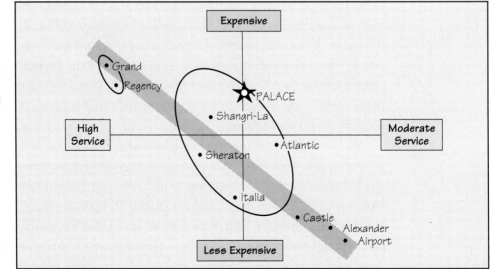

Figure 3.9
Positioning Map of Belleville's Principal Business Hotels: Service Level versus Price Level (Before New Competition)

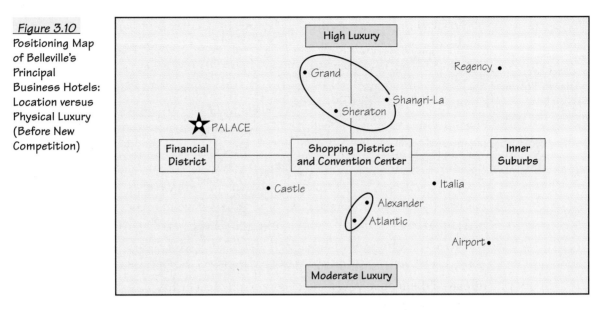

Figure 3.10
Positioning Map of Belleville's Principal Business Hotels: Location versus Physical Luxury (Before New Competition)

In Figure 3.10, we see how the Palace is positioned relative to the competition on location and degree of luxury. We would not expect these two variables to be related and they do not appear to be so. A key insight here is that the Palace occupies a relatively empty portion of the map. It is the only hotel in the financial district—a fact that probably explains its ability to charge more than its service level (or degree of physical luxury) would seem to justify. There are two clusters of hotels in the vicinity of the shopping district and convention center: a relatively luxurious group of three, led by the Grand, and a second group of two offering a moderate level of luxury.

Mapping Future Scenarios to Identify Potential Competitive Responses

What of the future? The Palace's management team next sought to anticipate the positions of the four new hotels being constructed in Belleville, as well as the probable repositioning of the Grand (see Figures 3.11 and 3.12). The construction sites were already known. Two would be in the financial district and two in the vicinity of the convention center, which is also undergoing expansion. Press releases distributed by the Grand had already declared its management's intentions. The "New Grand" would not only be larger but the renovations would also be designed to make it even more luxurious and there were plans to add new service features.

Predicting the positions of the four new hotels was not difficult for experts in the field. However, they recognized that customers might initially have more difficulty in predicting each hotel's level of performance on different attributes, especially if they were unfamiliar with the chain that would be operating the hotel in question. Preliminary details of the new hotels had already been released to city planners and the business community. The owners of two of the hotels had declared their intentions to seek five-star status, although this might take a few years to

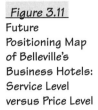

Figure 3.11
Future
Positioning Map
of Belleville's
Business Hotels:
Service Level
versus Price Level

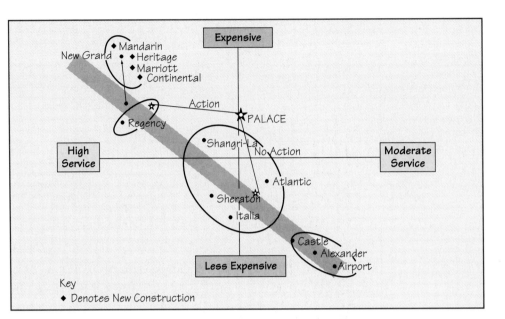

Figure 3.12
Future
Positioning Map
of Belleville's
Business Hotels:
Location versus
Physical Luxury

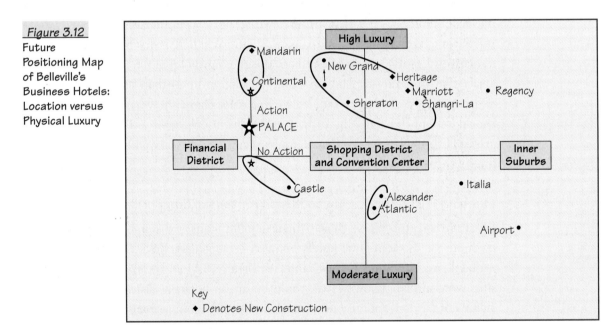

achieve. Three of the newcomers would be affiliated with international chains and their strategies could be guessed by examining recent hotels opened in other cities by these same chains.

Pricing was also easy to project. New hotels use a formula for setting posted room prices (the prices typically charged to individuals staying on a weeknight in high season). This price is linked to the average construction cost per room at the rate of one dollar per night for every thousand dollars of construction costs. Thus, a 200-room hotel that costs US$30 million to build (including land costs) would have an average room cost of US$150,000 and would need to set a price of US$150 per room night. Using this formula, Palace managers concluded that the four new hotels would have to charge significantly more than the Grand or Regency, in effect establishing what marketers call a *price umbrella* above existing price levels and thereby giving competitors the option of raising their own prices. To justify their high prices, the new hotels would have to offer customers very high standards of service and luxury. At the same time, the New Grand would need to raise its own prices to recover the costs of renovation, new construction, and enhanced service offerings (see Figure 3.11).

Assuming no changes by either the Palace or other existing hotels, the impact of the new competition in the market clearly posed a significant threat to the Palace, which would lose its unique locational advantage and in future be one of three hotels in the immediate vicinity of the financial district (Figure 3.12). The sales staff believed that many of the Palace's existing business customers would be attracted to the Continental and the Mandarin and be willing to pay their higher rates in order to obtain the superior benefits offered. The other two newcomers were seen as more of a threat to the Shangri-La, Sheraton, and New Grand in the shopping district/convention center cluster. Meantime, the New Grand and the newcomers would create a high price/high service (and high luxury) cluster at the top end of the market, leaving the Regency in what might prove to be a distinctive—and therefore defensible—space of its own.

Positioning Charts Help Executives Visualize Strategy

The Palace Hotel example demonstrates the insights that come from visualizing competitive situations. One of the challenges that strategic planners face is to ensure that all executives have a clear understanding of the firm's current situation before moving to discuss changes in strategy. Chan Kim and Renée Mauborgne argue that graphic representations of a firm's strategic profile and product positions are much easier to grasp than tables of quantitative data or paragraphs of prose. Charts and maps can facilitate what they call a "visual awakening." By enabling senior managers to compare their business with that of competitors and understand the nature of competitive threats and opportunities, visual presentations can highlight gaps between how customers (or prospects) see the organization and how management sees it, and thus help confirm or dispel beliefs that a service or a firm occupies a unique niche in the marketplace.[10]

By examining how anticipated changes in the competitive environment would literally redraw the current positioning map, the management team at the Palace could see that the hotel could not hope to remain in its current market position once it had lost its locational advantage. Unless they moved proactively to enhance its level of service and physical luxury, raising its prices to pay for such improvements, the hotel was likely to find itself being pushed into a lower price bracket that might even make it difficult to maintain current standards of service and physical upkeep.

Changing Competitive Positioning

Sometimes, firms have to make a significant change in an existing position. Such a strategy, known as *repositioning*, could mean revising service characteristics or redefining target market segments. At the firm level, repositioning may entail abandoning certain products and withdrawing completely from some market segments. For an example of a need to reposition due to changes in environmental conditions, see Best Practice in Action 3.4.

Changing Perceptions through Advertising

Improving negative brand perceptions may require extensive redesign of the core product and/or supplementary services. However, weaknesses are sometimes perceptual rather than real.

Best Practice in Action 3.4

BALI REVIVED BY FINDING A NEW TYPE OF TOURIST

The explosion that took place in October 2002 in Bali has left little trace. The bar where most of the victims died has been torn down. Workers have been busy with the reconstruction of the neighboring buildings and the newly resurfaced road. Surprisingly, tourism is recovering at a fast pace and this recovery, like the bombing, has a profound effect on Bali's tourism industry.

Almost all tourists abandoned Bali within days of the bombing. Airlines had to plan for extra flights to deal with the outgoing tourists and many hotels reported single digit occupancy rates. Indonesia was often viewed as a country with poor security policies, even before the Bali bombing. As a result, the country earned only US$3.8 billion from tourism in 2002, as compared to the official projection of US$5.8 billion.

Fortunately, the government responded to the situation and changed its strategy. Instead of relying heavily on tourists from western countries, who are more vulnerable to terrorist attacks, it started promoting Bali to the locals and Asian tourists from countries such as China, Japan, and South Korea, which were identified as promising markets. Besides that, the government also tried persuading travel associations and donor agencies to hold conferences in Bali as a sign of support.

So far, the results have been encouraging. In December 2003, tourist arrivals in Bali doubled as compared to those in November 2003. Many of the new tourists are Singaporeans and Taiwanese who went to Bali on tour packages. During the Chinese New Year holidays in 2004, Singapore Airlines' flights to Bali received a very positive response and Sheraton Bali was reportedly operating at full occupancy.

However, the new visitors in Bali were mainly attracted by the deep discounts offered, up to 50 percent. And they did not indulge in many of the lucrative activities such as scuba diving, bungee jumping, and bar hopping. The long-term sustainability of the Asian tourist-led recovery is still a question mark.

Source: Adapted from "Indonesia—Lured back to Bali," *The Economist* (February 6, 2004).

Innovation in Positioning

Most companies focus on matching and beating their rivals, with the result that their strategies tend to emphasize the same basic dimensions of competition. However, one way to compete is to introduce new dimensions into the positioning equation that other firms cannot immediately match.

James Heskett frames the issue nicely:

> The most successful service firms separate themselves from "the pack" to achieve a distinctive position in relation to their competition. They differentiate themselves … by altering typical characteristics of their respective industries to their competitive advantage.[11]

In Chapter 7, we look at opportunities for product innovation in services. In later chapters, we consider innovation in delivery systems.

Conclusion

Most service businesses face active competition. Marketers need to find ways of creating meaningful competitive advantages for their products. Ideally, a firm should target segments that it can serve better than other providers, offering a higher level of performance than competitors on those attributes that are particularly valued by the target segment. The nature of services introduces a number of distinctive possibilities for competitive differentiation, including location, scheduling, and speed of service delivery; the caliber of service personnel; and a range of options for customer involvement in the production process.

The concept of positioning is valuable because it forces explicit recognition of the different attributes comprising the overall service concept and emphasizes the need for marketers to understand which attributes determine customer choice behavior. Positioning maps provide a visual way of summarizing research data and display how different firms are perceived as performing relative to one another on key attributes. When combined with information on the preferences of different segments, including the level of demand that might be anticipated from such segments, positioning maps may suggest opportunities for creating new services or repositioning existing ones to take advantage of unserved market needs.

Review Questions

1. Why should service firms focus their efforts? Describe the basic focus options, and illustrate them with examples.
2. What is the distinction between important and determinant attributes in consumer choice decisions? What type of research can help you to understand which is which?
3. Describe what is meant by *positioning* strategy and the marketing concepts that underlie it.
4. Identify the circumstances under which it is appropriate to reposition an existing service offering.
5. How can positioning maps help managers better understand and respond to competitive dynamics?

pplication Exercises

1. Find examples of companies that illustrate each of the four focus strategies discussed in this chapter.
2. Choose an industry you are familiar with (like fast-food restaurants, television networks, or grocery stores) and create a perceptual map showing the competitive positions of different competitors in the industry, using attributes that you consider to represent key consumer choice criteria.
3. The travel agency business is losing business to online bookings offered to passengers by airline Web sites. Identify some possible focus options open to travel agencies wishing to develop new lines of business that would compensate for this loss of airline ticket sales.
4. Imagine that you are a consultant to the Palace Hotel. Consider the options facing the hotel based upon the four attributes appearing in the positioning charts (Figures 3.11 and 3.12). What actions do you recommend that the Palace should take in these circumstances? Justify your recommendations.

Endnotes

1 George S. Day, *Market Driven Strategy* (New York: The Free Press, 1990), 164.
2 Robert Johnston, "Achieving Focus in Service Organizations," *The Service Industries Journal* 16 (January 1996): 10–20.
3 A recent best-practice example in a B2B context is discussed in Ernest Waaser, Marshall Dahneke, Michael Pekkarinen, and Michael Weissel, "How You Slice It: Smarter Segmentation for Your Sales Force," *Harvard Business Review* 82, no. 3 (2004): 105–111.
4 For further insights into multiattribute modeling, see William D. Wells and David Prensky, *Consumer Behavior* (New York: John Wiley & Sons, 1996), 321–325.
5 Jack Trout, *The New Positioning: The Latest on the World's #1 Business Strategy* (New York: McGraw-Hill, 1997).
6 Vijay Mahajan and Yoram (Jerry) Wind, "Got Emotional Product Positioning?" *Marketing Management* (May–June 2002): 36–41.
7 "Cathay Pacific Voted Best Airline," *Worldroom Travel Digest* (April 26, 2002).
8 For a detailed approach, see Michael E. Porter, "A Framework for Competitor Analysis," Chapter 3 in *Competitive Strategy* (New York: The Free Press, 1980), 47–74.
9 For examples of developing research data for perceptual mapping purposes, see Glen L. Urban and John M. Hauser, *Design and Marketing of New Products*, 2nd ed. (Englewood Cliffs, NJ: Prentice Hall, 1993).
10 W. Chan Kim and Renée Mauborgne, "Charting Your Company's Future," *Harvard Business Review* 80 (June 2002): 77–83.
11 James L. Heskett, *Managing in the Service Economy* (Boston: Harvard Business School Press, 1984), 45.

Key Elements of Services Marketing

PART TWO

CHAPTER FOUR

Creating the Service Product

Each and every one of you will make or break the promise that our brand makes to customers.

Since services are intangible, it is difficult not only to persuade local companies to pay for value but to understand and accept that there is value in the services provided.

LISA GIALDINI, MANAGEMENT CONSULTANT WORKING IN KAZAKHSTAN

All service organizations face choices concerning the types of products to offer and the operational procedures to employ in creating them. In a customer-focused organization, these choices are often driven by market factors, with firms seeking to respond to the expressed needs of specific market segments and to differentiate the characteristics of their offerings against those of competitors. The availability of new delivery processes—such as the Internet for information-based services—allows firms to change the nature of the service experience and create new benefits. The growth of Internet banking is a case in point. A more radical form of product innovation involves exploiting technological developments to satisfy latent needs that customers have not previously articulated or even recognized.

A service product typically consists of a core product bundled together with a variety of supplementary service elements. The core elements respond to the customer's need for a basic benefit—such as transportation to a specific location, resolution of a specific health problem, or repair of malfunctioning equipment. Supplementary services are those that facilitate and enhance the use of the core service. They range from provision of needed information, advice, and documentation to problem solving and acts of hospitality.

Designing new services is a challenging task, because it requires thinking about processes, people, and experiences as well as outputs and benefits. Processes can be depicted through blueprints that specify employee tasks and operational sequences, as well as tracking the experience of the customer at each step in service delivery.

In this chapter, we consider the nature of service products, how to add value to them, and how to design them. We explore such questions as:

1. What are the key ingredients in a service product?
2. How might we categorize the supplementary services that surround core products?
3. What are some of the approaches that may be used in designing new services?
4. What is the role of branding for different service products?

Planning and Creating Services

What do we mean by a service "product"? In earlier chapters, we noted that a service is a "performance" rather than a "thing." When customers purchase manufactured goods, they take title to physical objects. But service performances, being intangible and ephemeral, are experienced rather than owned. Even when there are physical elements to which the customer does take title, such as a cooked meal (which is promptly consumed), a gold filling in a tooth, or a replacement part inside a car, a significant portion of the price paid by customers is for the value added by the accompanying service elements, including labor and expertise and the use of specialized equipment.

When customers are required by the nature of the service process to visit the service site—as in people-processing services—or when they choose to do so in other types of services (such as traditional retail bank branches), they may be asked to participate actively in the process of service creation and delivery. In situations where customers perform self-service, their experiences are often shaped by the nature and user-friendliness (or lack thereof!) of the supporting technology. In both instances, evaluations of the service product are likely to be much more closely interwoven with the nature of the delivery process than is the case for manufactured goods.

Key Steps in Service Planning

One of the challenges in services marketing is to ensure that the product management task maintains a strong customer focus at all times. Historically, operations management was often allowed to dominate this task, with the result that customer concerns were sometimes subjugated to operational convenience. On the other hand, marketers cannot work in isolation on new product development, especially when its delivery entails use of new technologies. They need to form a partnership with operations personnel and, in the case of high-contact services, with human resource managers as well. Figure 4.1 outlines the key steps involved

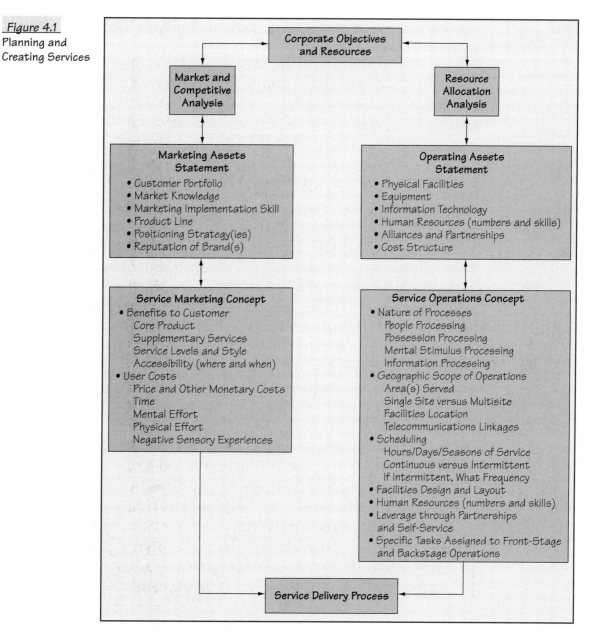

Figure 4.1
Planning and
Creating Services

in planning and creating services, emphasizing the need for managers to relate market opportunities to deployment of their firm's resources—physical, technological, and human.

The task begins at the corporate level with a statement of *objectives*. This statement leads into a detailed *market and competitive analysis*. Paralleling this step is a *resource allocation analysis*, requiring definition and appraisal of the firm's current resources and how they are being allocated, as well as identification of additional resources that might reasonably be obtained. This pair of steps can be thought of collectively as a form of SWOT analysis, identifying strengths, weaknesses, opportunities, and threats on both the marketing and operational/human resources fronts. Each leads to a statement of assets.

The *marketing assets statement* includes details of the firm's existing customer portfolio (including its size, profile, and value), knowledge of the market and competitors, its current product line, the reputation of its brand(s), its marketing implementation skills, and its current positioning strategy or strategies. We saw in Chapter 3 that a positioning statement can be developed for each service that the firm offers to one or more target market segments, indicating the characteristics that distinguish that service from competitive offerings.

The marketing opportunities revealed by this analysis must now be matched against an *operating assets statement.* Can the organization afford to allocate the physical facilities, equipment, information technology, and human resources needed to market existing service products more effectively, add enhancements designed to improve competitive appeal, or create new service offerings? Conversely, does an analysis of these operating assets suggest new opportunities to improve their utilization in the marketplace? If the firm lacks the resources needed for a new marketing initiative, could it leverage its existing assets by partnering with intermediaries or even with customers themselves? Finally, does an identified marketing opportunity promise sufficient profits to yield an acceptable return on the assets employed after deducting all relevant costs?

From a marketing perspective, the next step in transforming an opportunity into reality involves creating a *service marketing concept* to clarify the benefits offered to customers and the costs that they will incur in return. This marketing concept considers both core and supplementary services, the characteristics of these services in terms of both performance level and style, and where, when and how customers will be able to have access to them. The related costs of service include not only money, but also the amount of time, mental hassle, physical effort, and negative sensory experiences likely to be incurred by customers in receiving service.

A parallel step is to establish a *service operations concept*, which stipulates the nature of the processes involved (including use of information technology) and how and when the different types of operating assets should be deployed to perform specific tasks. Hence, there is a need to define the geographic scope and scheduling of operations, describe facilities design and layout, and identify the human resources required. The operations concept also addresses opportunities for leveraging the firm's own resources through the use of intermediaries or the customers themselves. Finally, it clarifies which tasks and resources will be assigned to front-stage and which to backstage operations.

Defining the marketing and operations concepts is necessarily an interactive process, since either or both may have to be modified in order to bring the two into the harmony needed to proceed with a given service offering. The planning task then moves on to a set of choices that management must make in configuring the service delivery process—the topic of Chapter 7.

The Augmented Product

Most manufacturing and service businesses offer their customers a package of benefits, involving delivery of not only the core product but also a variety of service-related activities that we refer to collectively as supplementary services. Increasingly, the latter provide the differentiation that separates successful firms from the others. Among both services and goods, there is a tendency for the core product to become a commodity as competition increases and the industry matures. Although managers continually need to consider opportunities to improve the core product, the search for competitive advantage in a mature industry often emphasizes performance on the supplementary services that are bundled with the core.

The combination of core product and supplementary services is often referred to as the augmented product. Several frameworks can be used to describe augmented products in a services context. Lynn Shostack developed a molecular model (Figure 4.2), which uses a chemical analogy to help marketers visualize and manage what she termed a "total market entity."[1] Her model can be applied to either goods or services. At the center is the core benefit, addressing the basic customer need, linked to a series of other service characteristics. She argues that, as in chemical formulations, a change in one element may completely alter the nature of the entity.

Figure 4.2
Shostack's
Molecular Model:
Passenger Airline
Service

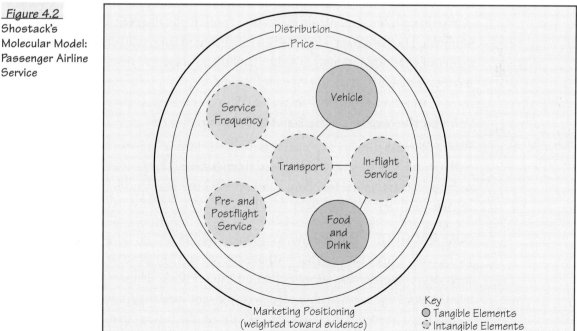

Source: G. Lynn Shostack, "Breaking Free from Product Marketing," *Journal of Marketing* 44 (April 1977), 73–80, published by the American Marketing Association. Reprinted with permission.

Surrounding the molecules are a series of bands representing price, distribution, and market positioning.

The molecular model helps us to identify the tangible and intangible elements involved in service delivery. In an airline, for example, the intangible elements include transportation itself, service frequency, and preflight, in-flight, and postflight service. But the aircraft and the food and drinks that are served are all tangible. By highlighting tangible elements, marketers can determine whether their services are tangible-dominant or intangible-dominant. The greater the proportion of intangible elements, the more necessary it is to provide tangible clues about the features and quality of the service.

Eiglier and Langeard proposed a model in which the core service is surrounded by a circle containing a series of supplementary services that are specific to that particular product.[2] Their approach, like Shostack's, emphasizes the interdependence of the various components. They distinguish between those elements needed to facilitate use of the core service (such as the reception desk at a hotel) and those that enhance the appeal of the core service (such as a fitness center and business services at a hotel).

Both models of the augmented product offer useful insights. Shostack wants us to determine which service elements are tangible and which are intangible in order to help formulate product policy and communication programs. Eiglier and Langeard ask us to think about two issues: First, whether supplementary services are needed to facilitate use of the core service or simply to add extra appeal, and second, whether customers should be charged separately for each service element or whether all elements should be bundled under a single price tag. Further insight is provided by Grönroos, who clarifies the different roles played by supplementary services by describing them as either facilitating services (or goods) or supporting services (or goods).[3]

Defining the Nature of the Service Offering

When designing a service, planners need to take a holistic view of the entire performance that they want customers to experience. The design task must therefore address and integrate four key components: the core product, supplementary services, and delivery processes.

CORE PRODUCT   This central component addresses the questions: What is the buyer really purchasing? What business are we in? The core product supplies the central problem-solving benefits that customers seek. Thus, transport solves the need to move a person or a physical object from one location to another. Management consulting is expected to yield expert advice on the actions that a company should take. Repair services restore a damaged or malfunctioning machine or building to good working order.

SUPPLEMENTARY SERVICES   These elements augment the core product, both facilitating its use and enhancing its value and appeal. The extent and level of supplementary services often play a role in differentiating and positioning the core product. Adding more supplementary elements or increasing the level of performance can serve to add value to the core product and enable the service provider to charge a higher price.

DELIVERY PROCESS   The third component concerns the procedures used to deliver both the core product and each of the supplementary services. In its broadest sense, the design of the service offering must address how the different service components are delivered to the customer, the nature of the customer's role in those processes, how long delivery lasts, and the prescribed level and style of service to be offered. Each of the four categories of processes—people processing, possession processing, mental stimulus processing, and information processing—has different implications for customer involvement, operational procedures, the degree of customer contact with service personnel and facilities, and requirements for supplementary services.

The integration of these three components is captured in Figure 4.3, which illustrates the service offering for an overnight stay at a hotel. The core product—overnight rental of a bedroom—consists of service level, scheduling (how long the room may be used before another payment becomes due), the nature of the process (in this instance, people processing), and the role of the customers in terms of what they are expected to do for themselves and what the hotel will do for them.

Surrounding the core is an array of supplementary services, ranging from reservations to meals to in-room service elements. As with the core product, delivery processes must be specified for each of these elements. The more expensive the hotel, the higher the level of service on each element. Additional services might also be offered, such as a business center, a bar, a pool, and a health club. One of the characteristics of a top-of-the-line hotel is doing things for customers that they might otherwise have to do for themselves and providing an extended schedule for service delivery, including 24-hour room service.

Documenting the Delivery Sequence over Time

A fourth design component that product planners must address is the probable sequence in which customers will use each of the core and supplementary services and the approximate length of time that will be required in each instance. This information, which should reflect a good understanding of customer needs, habits, and expectations, is necessary not only for marketing purposes but also for facilities planning, operations management, and allocation of personnel.

It would be a mistake to assume that the customer consumes all the elements of the augmented product simultaneously. In the hotel industry, neither the core

Figure 4.3
Depicting the
Service Offering
for an Overnight
Hotel Stay

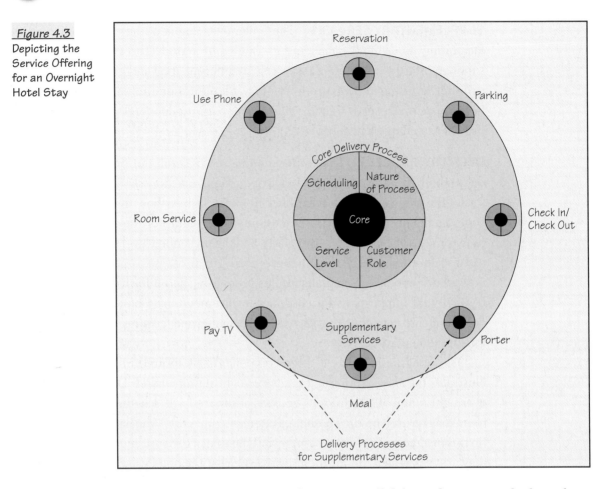

Figure 4.3
Depicting the
Service Offering
for an Overnight
Hotel Stay

service nor its supplementary elements are all delivered continuously throughout the duration of the service performance. Certain services must necessarily be used before others. In many services, in fact, consumption of the core product is sandwiched between the use of supplementary services that are needed earlier or later in the delivery sequence.

Figure 4.4 adds a temporal dimension to the different elements of the augmented hotel product, identifying when and for how long they are consumed. The example illustrated is hotel accommodation, a high-contact, people-processing service. Time plays a key role in services, not only from an operational standpoint as it relates to allocating and scheduling purposes, but also from the perspective of customers themselves.

As suggested in Service Perspectives 4.1, speedy service is often a key product attribute for customers and implementation requires an understanding of both marketing and operational considerations.

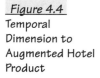

Figure 4.4
Temporal
Dimension to
Augmented Hotel
Product

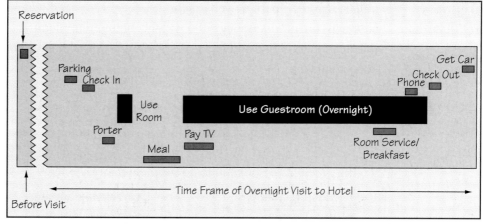

Service
Perspectives
4.1

PLANNING SPEEDY FOOD SERVICE

Restaurant Hospitality, a trade magazine for the restaurant industry, offers the following ten suggestions for serving customers quickly without making them feel like they've been pushed out of the door. As you'll note, some of these tactics involve front-stage processes while others take place backstage—but it is the interaction between operational strategies, marketing insights, and how staff members relate to customers that creates the desired results.

1. Distinguish between patrons in a hurry, and those who are not.
2. Design specials that are quick.
3. Guide hurried customers to those specials.
4. Place the quickest, highest-margin menu items either first or last on the menu.
5. Offer dishes that can be prepared ahead of time.
6. Warn customers when they order menu items that will take a lot of time to prepare.
7. Consider short-line buffets, roving carts, and more sandwiches.
8. Offer "wrap"-style sandwiches, which are a quickly prepared, filling meal.
9. Use equipment built for speed, like combination ovens.
10. Eliminate preparation steps that require cooks to stop cooking.

Source: Adapted from Paul B. Hertneky, "Built for Speed," *Restaurant Hospitality* (January 1997): 58.

Identifying and Classifying Supplementary Services

The more we examine different types of services, the more we find that most of them have many supplementary services in common. Flowcharting (which we introduced in Chapter 2) offers an excellent way to understand the totality of the customer's service experience and identify the many different types of supplementary services accompanying a core product. For instance, at an expensive restaurant, supplementary services include reservations, valet parking, coatrooms, cocktails, being escorted to a table, ordering from the menu, billing, payment, and use of toilets. If you prepare flowcharts for a variety of services, you will soon notice that although core products may differ widely, common supplementary elements—from information to billing and from reservations/order taking to problem resolution—keep recurring.

Facilitating and Enhancing Supplementary Services

There are potentially dozens of different supplementary services, but almost all of them can be classified into one of the following eight clusters. We have listed them as either *facilitating* or *enhancing* supplementary services.

Facilitating Services	Enhancing Services
• Information	• Consultation
• Order taking	• Hospitality
• Billing	• Safekeeping
• Payment	• Exceptions

In Figure 4.5, these eight clusters are displayed as petals surrounding the center of a flower—which we call the *Flower of Service*.[4] We've shown them clockwise in the sequence in which they are often likely to be encountered by customers. In a well-designed and well-managed service organization, the petals and core are fresh and well-formed. A badly designed or poorly executed service is a like a flower with missing, wilted or discolored petals. Even if the core is perfect, the overall impression of the flower is unattractive. Think about your own experiences as a customer (or

<u>Figure 4.5</u>
The Flower of Service: Core Product Surrounded by Cluster of Supplementary Services

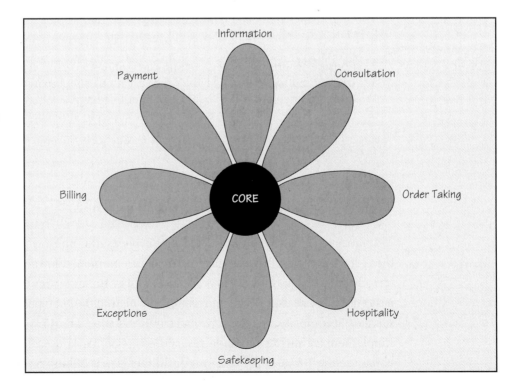

when purchasing on behalf of an organization). When you were dissatisfied with a particular purchase, was it the core that was at fault or was it a problem with one or more of the petals?

Not every core product is surrounded by supplementary elements from all eight clusters. As we'll see, the nature of the product helps to determine which supplementary services must be offered and which might usefully be added to enhance value and make the organization easy to do business with. In general, people-processing and high-contact services tend to be accompanied by more supplementary services than do the other three categories.

A company's market positioning strategy helps to determine which supplementary services should be included (see Chapter 3). A strategy of adding benefits to increase customers' perceptions of quality will probably require more supplementary services (and also a higher level of performance on all such elements) than a strategy of competing on low prices. Firms that offer different grades of service—like first class, business class, and economy class in an airline context—often differentiate them by adding extra supplementary services for each upgrade in service. For example, Entie Commercial Bank in Taiwan offers more privileges to its platinum card holders (see Figure 4.6).

Besides airlines, most luxurious hotel chains also offer different grades of services to their guests according to the type of rooms they check into—deluxe, premier, executive clubroom, and suites. For example, Shangri-La Kuala Lumpur provides a wide array of services ranging from a 24-hour business center to complimentary breakfast and cocktails for business travelers who check into its newly furnished horizon clubrooms (see Figure 4.7).

INFORMATION To obtain full value from any good or service, customers need relevant information (see Table 4.1). New customers and prospects are especially information hungry. Customers' needs may include directions to the site where the product is sold (or details of how to order it), service hours, prices, and usage instructions. Further information, sometimes required by law, could include conditions of sale and use, warnings, reminders, and notification of changes. Finally, customers may want documentation of what has already taken place, such as confirmation of reservations, receipts and tickets, and monthly summaries of account activity.

Companies should make sure that the information they provide is both timely and accurate, since incorrect information can annoy or inconvenience customers. Traditional ways of providing information to customers include using front-line employees (who are not always as well-informed as customers might like), printed notices, brochures, and instruction books. Other information media include videotapes or software-driven tutorials, touch-screen video displays, and menu-driven recorded telephone messages. The most significant recent innovation has

Courtesy of Entie Commercial Bank.

been corporate use of Web sites. Examples of useful applications range from train and airline schedules and hotel details, to assistance in locating specific retail outlets such as restaurants and stores.

ORDER TAKING   Once customers are ready to buy, a key supplementary element comes into play—accepting applications, orders, and reservations (see Table 4.2). The process of order taking should be polite, fast, and accurate so that customers

Figure 4.7
Shangri-La Kuala
Lumpur promotes
its newly furnished
Horizon Club which
provides a wide
variety of
complimentary
services to its
guests.

Courtesy of Shangri-La Hotels and Resorts.

do not waste time and endure unnecessary mental or physical effort. Technology can be used to make order taking easier and faster for both customers and suppliers. The key lies in minimizing the time and effort required of both parties, while also ensuring completeness and accuracy.

Banks, insurance companies, and utilities require prospective customers to go through an application process designed to gather relevant information and to screen out those who do not meet basic enrollment criteria (like a bad credit record or serious health problems). Reservations, including appointments and check-in,

Table 4.1
Examples of Information Elements

Directions to service site

Schedules/service hours

Prices

Instructions on using core product/supplementary services

Reminders

Warnings

Conditions of sale/service

Notification of changes

Documentation

Confirmation of reservations

Summaries of account activity

Receipts and tickets

Table 4.2
Examples of Order-Taking Elements

Applications

- Membership in clubs or programs
- Subscription services (e.g., utilities)
- Prerequisite-based services (e.g., financial credit, college enrollment)

Order Entry

- On-site order fulfillment
- Mail/telephone order placement
- Email/Web site order placement

Reservations and Check-in

- Seats
- Tables
- Rooms
- Vehicles or equipment rental
- Professional appointments
- Admission to restricted facilities (e.g., museums, aquariums)

represent a special type of order taking which entitles customers to a specified unit of service—for example, an airline seat, time with a qualified professional, or admission to a facility such as a theater or sports arena with designated seating.

Ticketless systems, based upon telephone or Web site reservations, provide enormous cost savings for airlines, since there is no travel agent commission and customers can book directly. Ctrip, the largest Internet travel agency in China, also offers telephone order-taking service, but it encourages the customers to book the hotel or flight online with double credits as an incentive. A paper ticket at an airline may be handled 15 times, while an electronic ticket requires just one step. However, some customers are disenchanted by the paperless process. Although they receive a confirmation number by phone when they make the reservations and need only to show identification at the airport to claim their seats, many people feel insecure without tangible proof that they have a seat on a particular flight.[5]

BILLING   Billing is common to almost all services (unless the service is provided free of charge). Inaccurate, illegible, or incomplete bills risk disappointing customers who may, up to that point, have been quite satisfied with their experience. Such failures add insult to injury if the customer is already dissatisfied. Billing should also be timely, because it serves to stimulate faster payment. Procedures range from verbal statements to a machine-displayed price, and from handwritten invoices to elaborate monthly statements of account activity and fees (see Table 4.3). Perhaps the simplest approach is self-billing, when the customer tallies up the amount of an order and either encloses a check or signs a credit card payment authorization. In such instances, billing and payment are combined into a single act, although the seller may still need to check for accuracy.

More and more, billing is being computerized. Despite the potential for productivity improvements, computerized billing has its dark side, as when an innocent customer tries futilely to contest an inaccurate bill and is met by an escalating sequence of ever-larger bills (compounded interest and penalty charges), accompanied by increasingly threatening, computer-generated letters.

Customers usually expect bills to be clear and informative, and itemized in ways that make it clear how the total was computed. American Express (Amex) built its Corporate Card business by offering companies detailed documentation of the spending patterns of individual employees and departments on travel and entertainment. Intelligent thinking about customer needs led Amex to realize that well-organized information has value to a customer, beyond just the basic requirement of knowing how much to pay at the end of each month.

Busy customers hate to be kept waiting for a bill to be prepared in a hotel, restaurant, or rental car lot. Many hotels and rental car firms have now created express check-out options, taking customers' credit card details in advance and documenting charges later by mail. But accuracy is essential. Since customers use the express check-outs to save time, they certainly don't want to waste time later seeking corrections and refunds. An alternative express check-out procedure is used by some car rental companies. An agent meets customers as they return their cars, checks the mileage/kilometrage and fuel gauge readings, and then prints a bill on the spot using a portable wireless terminal. Many hotels push bills under guestroom doors on the morning of departure showing charges to date. Others offer customers the option of previewing their bills before check-out on the TV monitors in their rooms.

Table 4.3
Examples of Billing Elements

- Periodic statements of account activity
- Invoices for individual transactions
- Verbal statements of amount due
- Machine display of amount due
- Self-billing (computed by customer)

PAYMENT   In most cases, a bill requires the customer to take action on payment and such action may be very slow in coming! One exception is bank statements which detail charges that have already been deducted from the customer's account. Increasingly, customers expect ease and convenience of payment, including credit, when they make purchases in their own countries and while traveling abroad.

A variety of options exist to facilitate customer bill-paying (see Table 4.4). Self-service payment systems, for instance, require customers to insert coins, banknotes, tokens, or cards in machines. But equipment breakdowns destroy the whole purpose of such a system, so good maintenance and rapid-response troubleshooting are essential. Understanding the importance of its self-service payment system, Japan Railway's JR East has been upgrading and improving its ticketing machines constantly since their introduction (see Best Practice in Action 4.1).

Much payment still takes place through hand-to-hand transfers of cash and checks, but credit and debit cards are growing in importance as more and more establishments accept them. Other alternatives include tokens, vouchers, coupons, or prepaid tickets. To reinforce good behavior, Dah Sing Bank, one of Hong Kong's local banks, offers an Interest Rate Reduction Reward to its credit card holders who make prompt payments of no less than the minimum payment amount for at least three consecutive months.

To ensure that people actually pay what is due, some service businesses have instituted control systems, such as ticket checks before entering a movie theater or on board a train. However, inspectors and security officers must be trained to

---

Table 4.4
Examples of Payment Elements

Self-Service

- Exact change in machine
- Cash in machine with change returned
- Insert prepayment card
- Insert credit/charge/debit card
- Insert token
- Electronic funds transfer
- Mail a check
- Enter credit card number online

Direct to Payee or Intermediary

- Cash handling and change giving
- Check handling
- Credit/charge/debit card handling
- Coupon redemption
- Tokens, vouchers, etc.

Automatic Deduction from Financial Deposits (e.g., bank charges)
Control and Verification

- Automated systems (e.g., machine-readable tickets that operate entry gates)
- Human systems (e.g., toll collectors, ticket inspectors)

Best Practice
in Action 4.1

EVOLUTION OF RAILWAY TICKET VENDING MACHINES

Presently, JR East, a Japanese railway, sells almost 90 percent of all tickets through its more than 5,000 vending machines. Since the advent of the first ticket vending machine in about 1925, JR East has reached the current model of ticket vending machine after a great deal of modifications and improvements. The following provides brief snapshots to show the transition in JR East railway ticket vending machines.

From Manual to Power-Driven Systems: 1956–1963

In early 1956, a simple machine for issuing platform tickets was developed. Subsequently, a machine that sold a certain type of ticket in response to the insertion of a certain type of coin was developed, as shown in Figure (a). After further improvements, a machine capable of returning 10-yen and 50-yen change in response to the insertion of 10, 50, and 100-yen coins (see Figure (b)) was introduced.

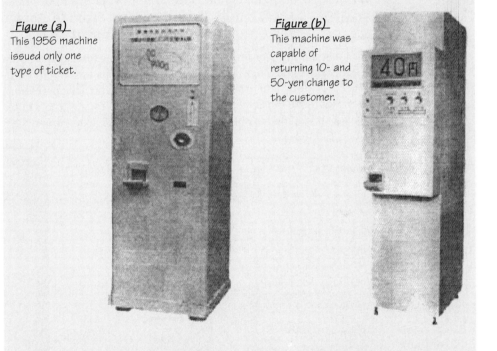

Figure (a)
This 1956 machine issued only one type of ticket.

Figure (b)
This machine was capable of returning 10- and 50-yen change to the customer.

Shift to Systemization: 1987–1993

In 1989, special-purpose machines were developed for selling coupon booklets and map-type Shinkansen non-reserved tickets. In 1991, a prepaid type stored-value fare card system, using the "IO Card," and compatible with automated ticket gates, was launched. To create a totally integrated system, JR East developed an automated commuter pass vending machine, as shown in Figure (c), that sold new passes before old ones expired. A customer-operated ticket reservation terminal "Travel Edie" (see Figure (d)), was introduced in 1993 with a touch screen.

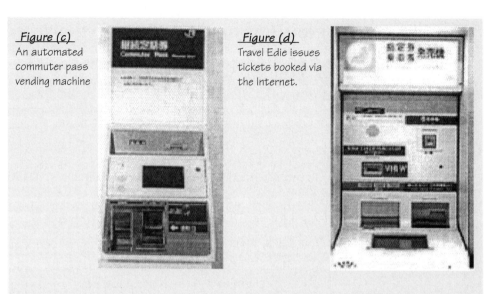

Figure (c)
An automated commuter pass vending machine

Figure (d)
Travel Edie issues tickets booked via the Internet.

User-Friendly Machines that Provide Assistance: 1994 Until Present

To meet a variety of requirements, various types of ticket vending machines have been developed since 1994. The new machines are much more user-friendly and they provide instant assistance for passengers who have problems with the machines (see Figure (e)). An Ekinet vending machine that issued tickets booked via the Internet was also installed at the major stations in 2002 (see Figure (f).)

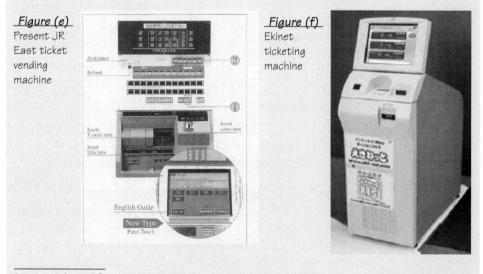

Figure (e)
Present JR East ticket vending machine

Figure (f)
Ekinet ticketing machine

Source: Adapted from Kazuhiro Nakamura, "Transition in Railway Ticket Vending Machines—Greater Convenience to Passengers," *JR East Technical Review* 3; http://www.jreast.co.jp/development/english/paper/index.html (accessed on July 6, 2004).

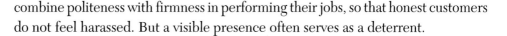

combine politeness with firmness in performing their jobs, so that honest customers do not feel harassed. But a visible presence often serves as a deterrent.

CONSULTATION   Now we move to enhancing supplementary services, led by consultation. In contrast to information, which suggests a simple response to customers' questions (or printed information that anticipates their needs), consultation involves a dialog to probe customer requirements and then develop a tailored solution. Table 4.5 provides examples of several supplementary services in the consultation category. At its simplest, consultation consists of immediate advice from a knowledgeable service person in response to the request: What do you suggest? (For example, you might ask the person who cuts your hair for advice on different hairstyles, colors, and products.) Effective consultation requires an understanding of each customer's current situation, before suggesting a suitable course of action. Good customer records can be a great help in this respect, particularly if relevant data can be retrieved easily from a remote terminal.

Counseling represents a more subtle approach to consultation because it involves helping customers better understand their situations so that they can come up with their own solutions and action programs. This approach can be a particularly valuable supplement to services such as health treatment, when part of the challenge is to get customers to take a long-term view of their personal situation and to adopt more healthful behaviors, often involving some initial sacrifice. For example, the Women's Health and Resource Center in Indonesia provides counseling to help customers with motherhood and general well-being issues and gynecological care, so that the pregnancy and postnatal experience will be easier to manage.

Finally, there are more formalized efforts to provide management and technical consulting for corporate customers, such as the "solution selling" associated with marketing expensive industrial equipment and services. The sales engineer researches the customer's situation and then offers objective advice about what particular package of equipment and systems will yield the best results for the customer. Some consulting services are offered free of charge in the hope of making a sale. However, in other instances, the service is "unbundled" and customers are expected to pay for it. Advice can also be offered through tutorials, group training programs, and public demonstrations.

Table 4.5
Examples of Consultation Elements

- Advice
- Auditing
- Personal counseling
- Tutoring/training in product use
- Management or technical consulting

HOSPITALITY   Hospitality-related services should, ideally, reflect pleasure at meeting new customers and greeting old ones when they return. Well-managed businesses try, at least in small ways, to ensure that their employees treat customers as guests. Courtesy and consideration for customers' needs apply to both face-to-face encounters and telephone interactions (see Table 4.6). Hospitality finds its full expression in face-to-face encounters. In some cases, it starts and ends with an offer of transport to and from the service site, as with courtesy shuttle buses. If customers must wait outdoors before the service can be delivered, a thoughtful service provider will offer weather protection. If indoors, then customers should have a waiting area with seating and even entertainment (TV, newspapers, or magazines) to pass the time. Recruiting employees who are naturally warm, welcoming, and considerate for customer-contact jobs helps to create a hospitable atmosphere.

The quality of the hospitality services offered by a firm can increase or decrease satisfaction with the core product. This is especially true for people-processing services where customers cannot easily leave the service facility. Private hospitals often seek to enhance their appeals by providing the level of room service, including meals, that might be expected in a good hotel. Some airlines seek to differentiate themselves from their competitors with better meals and more attentive cabin crew.

Although preflight and in-flight hospitality is important, an airline journey doesn't really end until passengers reach their final destination. Increasingly, international airports in Asia are building lounges in the airports to cater to the needs of both travelers who are leaving and those who have just arrived. These lounges have entertainment systems (theaters), as well as wireless Internet zones that allow travelers to send urgent email messages. Rooms can also be available for travelers on a short transit or travelers who prefer to freshen up and relax a little before leaving the airport. For example, the Royal Brunei Airline provides a first-class lounge for its First- and Business-class travelers at Brunei International Airport. Royal Brunei introduces its Sky Lounge as an unusual place, as it is well-equipped with comfortable sofas and massage chairs, PC workstations, Internet services, high-

---

Table 4.6 Examples of Hospitality Elements	Greeting
	Food and beverages
	Toilets and washrooms
	Waiting facilities and amenities
	• Lounges, waiting areas, seating
	• Weather protection
	• Magazines, entertainment, newspapers
	Transport
	Security

resolution TV, prayer room, and a comprehensive buffet offering different types of cuisine. At the other extreme are no-frills service environments such as described in Service Perspectives 4.2.

SAFEKEEPING   While visiting a service site, customers often want assistance with their personal possessions. In fact, unless certain safekeeping services are provided (like safe and convenient parking for their cars), some customers may not come at all. The list of potential on-site safekeeping services is long. It includes provision of coatrooms; baggage transport, handling and storage; safekeeping of valuables; and

Service Perspectives 4.2

WAREHOUSE CLUBS IN HONG KONG

Warehouse clubs, also known as wholesale clubs, are large-scale, retail operations that offer a combination of discount retailing and cash-and-carry wholesaling. The clubs are able to offer prices lower than those in competing outlets like supermarkets because they maintain low costs and high turnover. For them, this means a no-frills retail environment, minimal service, and relying on word of mouth for advertising.

The largest, GrandMart, opened its first Hong Kong store in 1993. Value Club, Hong Kong's second-largest warehouse-club chain, began operations in February 1995. Created as a joint venture between U.S.-based Wal-Mart and Thailand-based Charoen Pokphand Agro-Industry Co., an agribusiness firm with interests in dozens of joint ventures across Asia, Value Club is now operated by Charoen Pokphand. Unlike GrandMart, which caters to household consumers, Value Club relies on sales to small businesses. Its product lines resemble those of U.S. warehouse clubs, although some of its prices are slightly lower. Of late, Value Club has been concentrating efforts on expanding into the Chinese market, and recently opened a 100,000-square-foot store in Pudong, Shanghai.

Customers are thought to be willing to give up certain conveniences in order to obtain low prices. However, it is likely that some minimum level of service is necessary in order for the customer to be willing and able to use this retailing form. For example, a study on warehouse clubs in Asia shows that many customers prefer to shop in a comfortable environment with soft lighting, background music and carpeted floors. Most shoppers also expressed a preference for clean retail stores and upkeep of facilities. Wide shopping aisles is another important factor, as they must be wide enough for shopping trolleys to pass and should not be blocked by merchandise. Cooperative salespeople to assist customers are also likely to increase customer value during the shopping experience. Customers also find that neatness of merchandise display is an important contributing factor in store atmospherics.

The study results imply that there definitely is room for improvement to increase customer value in spite of the no-frills concept adopted by warehouse clubs. Retailers could use this information to create more customer-friendly environments that will complement the shopping experience.

Source: Neil C. Herndon, Jr. and Cecilia Chi-Yin Yu, "A New Retail Technology in Asia: Warehouse Clubs," *Management Research News* 19, no.9 (1996): 5–27; http://www.apmforum.com/aplit/mcb11abs.htm (accessed on July 3, 2004); http://www.fas.usda.gov/info/agexporter/1997/January%201997/hongkong.html (modified on February 25, 2003, and accessed on July 3, 2004).

even child care and pet care (see Table 4.7). Responsible businesses also worry about the safety of their customers. These days, many businesses pay close attention to safety and security issues for customers who are visiting their service facilities. This is particularly important for e-commerce sites such as Bank of China's e-banking service (see Figure 4.8). The Web site uses a USB Key IC hardware-based encryption which requires a confidential and secure log-in by the account holder. It has an extensive support system for troubleshooting and a 24-hour hotline for e-banking customers. Bank of China has been awarded the "Best Personal Internet Bank of China" and "Best Corporate/Institutional Internet Bank of China" for its use of new and advanced technology to ensure a safe e-banking environment.

EXCEPTIONS   Exceptions involve supplementary services that fall outside the routine of normal service delivery (see Table 4.8). Astute businesses anticipate exceptions and develop contingency plans and guidelines in advance. That way, employees will not appear helpless and surprised when customers ask for special assistance. Well-defined procedures make it easier for employees to respond promptly and effectively.

There are several different types of exceptions:

1. *Special requests.* There are many circumstances when a customer may request service that requires a departure from normal operating procedures. Advance requests often relate to personal needs, including care of children, dietary requirements, medical needs, religious observance, and personal disabilities. Such special requests are common in the travel and hospitality industries.
2. *Problem solving.* Situations arise when normal service delivery (or product performance) fails to run smoothly as a result of accidents, delays, equipment failures, or customers experiencing difficulty in using the product.
3. *Handling of complaints/suggestions/compliments.* This activity requires well-defined procedures. It should be easy for customers to express dissatisfaction,

Table 4.7 Examples of Safekeeping Elements	Caring for Possessions Customers Bring with Them	Caring for Goods Purchased (or Rented) by Customers
	• Child care • Pet care • Parking facilities for vehicles • Valet parking • Coatrooms • Luggage-handling • Storage space • Safe deposit boxes • Security personnel	• Packaging • Pickup • Transportation • Delivery • Installation • Inspection and diagnosis • Cleaning • Refueling • Preventive maintenance • Repairs and renovation • Upgrade

Figure 4.8
Bank of China's
e-banking Web site
provides
sophisticated
tools and
technologies to
safeguard the
privacy and
security of its
online customers.

Source: https://ibank.bank-of-china.com/, accessed in July 2004.

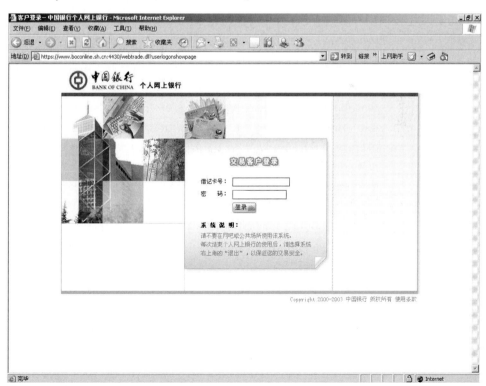

Source: https://www.sh.bank-of-china.com:4430/webtrade.dll?userlogonshowpage, accessed in July 2004.
Courtesy of Bank of China.

Table 4.8	*Special Requests in Advance of Service Delivery*

Table 4.8
Examples of Exceptions Elements

Special Requests in Advance of Service Delivery

- Children's needs
- Dietary requirements
- Medical or disability needs
- Religious observances
- Deviations from standard operating procedures

Handling Special Communications

- Complaints
- Compliments
- Suggestions

Problem Solving

- Warranties and guarantees against product malfunction
- Resolving difficulties that arise from using the product
- Resolving difficulties caused by accidents, service failures, and problems with staff or other customers
- Assisting customers who have suffered an accident or medical emergency

Restitution

- Refunds
- Compensation in kind for unsatisfactory goods and services
- Free repair of defective goods

---

offer suggestions for improvement, or pass on compliments, and service providers should be able to make an appropriate response quickly.

4. *Restitution.* Many customers expect to be compensated for serious performance failures. Compensation may take the form of repairs under warranty, legal settlements, refunds, an offer of free service, or other forms of payment-in-kind.

Managers need to keep an eye on the level of exception requests. Too many requests may indicate that standard procedures need revamping. For instance, if a restaurant constantly receives requests for special vegetarian meals since there are none on the menu, this may indicate that it's time to revise the menu to include at least one or two such dishes. A flexible approach to exceptions is generally a good idea, because it reflects responsiveness to customer needs. On the other hand, too many exceptions may compromise safety, negatively impact other customers, and overburden employees.

Managerial Implications

The eight categories of supplementary services forming the Flower of Service collectively provide many options for enhancing the core product, whether it be a good or a service. Most supplementary services do (or should) represent responses to customer needs. As noted earlier, some are facilitating services—like information and reservations—that enable customers to use the core product more effectively. Others are "extras" that enhance the core or even reduce its nonfinancial costs (for example, meals, magazines, and entertainment are hospitality elements that help pass the time). Some elements—notably billing and payment—are, in effect, imposed by the service provider. But even if not actively desired by the customer, they still form part of the overall service experience. Any badly handled element may negatively affect customers' perceptions of service quality. The "information" and "consultation" petals illustrate the emphasis in this book on the need for education as well as promotion in communicating with service customers.

Not every core product will be surrounded by a large number of supplementary services from all eight petals. People-processing services tend to be the most demanding in terms of supplementary elements. When customers do not visit the service factory, the need for hospitality may be limited to simple courtesies in letters and telecommunications. Possession-processing services sometimes place heavy demands on safekeeping elements, but there may be no need for this particular petal when providing information-processing services in which customers and suppliers deal entirely at arm's length.

Managers face many decisions concerning what types of supplementary services to offer, especially in relation to product-policy and positioning issues. A study of Japanese, American, and European firms serving business-to-business markets found that most companies simply added layer upon layer of services to their core offerings without knowing what customers really valued.[6] Managers surveyed in the study indicated that they did not understand which services should be offered to customers as a standard package accompanying the core, and which could be offered as options for an extra charge. Without this knowledge, developing effective pricing policies can be tricky. There are no simple rules governing pricing decisions for core products and supplementary services. But managers should continually review their own policies and those of competitors to make sure they are in line with both market practice and customer needs. We'll discuss these and other pricing issues in more detail in Chapter 9.

In summary, Tables 4.1–4.8 can serve as a checklist in the continuing search for new ways to augment existing core products and to design new offerings. The lists provided in these eight tables do not claim to be all-encompassing, since some products may require specialized supplementary elements. In general, a firm that competes on a low-cost, no-frills basis will require fewer supplementary elements than one marketing an expensive, high-value-added product. Alternative levels of supplementary services around a common core may offer the basis for a product line of differentiated offerings, similar to the various classes of travel offered by airlines. Regardless of which supplementary services a firm decides to offer, all of the elements in each petal should receive the care and attention needed to consistently meet defined service standards. That way the resulting "flower" will always have a fresh and appealing appearance.

Planning and Branding Service Products

In recent years, more and more service businesses have started talking about their *products*—a term previously associated with manufactured goods. Some will even speak of their "products and services," an expression also used by service-driven manufacturing firms. What is the distinction between these two terms in today's business environment?

A *product* implies a defined and consistent "bundle of output" and also the ability to differentiate one bundle of output from another. In a manufacturing context, the concept is easy to understand and visualize. Service firms can also differentiate their products in similar fashion to the various "models" offered by manufacturers. Quick-service restaurants are sometimes described as "quasi-manufacturing" operations since they produce a physical output combined with value-added service. At each site, they display a menu of their products, which are of course highly tangible—burger connoisseurs can easily distinguish Jollibee's Champ burger from a Regular Yum! burger, as well as a Champ burger from a Big Mac. The service comes from speedy delivery of a freshly prepared food item, the ability (in some instances) to order and pick up freshly cooked food from a drive-in location without leaving one's car, the availability within the restaurant of self-service drinks, condiments and napkins, and the opportunity to sit down and eat one's meal at a table.

But providers of more intangible services also offer a "menu" of products, representing an assembly of carefully prescribed elements that are built around the core product and may bundle in certain value-added supplementary services. Additional supplementary services—often referred to collectively as *customer service*—may be available to facilitate delivery and use of the product, as well as billing and payment.

Product Lines and Brands

Most service organizations offer a line of products rather than just a single product. Within a specific industry, a large firm may choose to offer several, differently positioned entries, each identified by a separate brand name. The Asian region has more than 300 hotel brands competing for business, more than any other product category. Many hotel chains offer a family of brands. For instance, Shangri-La Hotels and Resorts offers several different brands of hotels and resorts under their umbrella brand, including:

- *Shangri-La City Hotels* (big, full-service hotels in cities, offering large public areas, meeting facilities, and access to extensive sporting and recreational amenities)

- *Shangri-La Hotels* (big, full-service hotels in cities, offering meeting facilities and access to business and recreational amenities targeted at business travelers and vacationers)
- *Shangri-La Resorts* (medium-sized hotels in beachfront locations, offering extensive recreational amenities, targeted at vacationers)
- *Traders Hotels* (big, full-service hotels in cities, offering large public areas, meeting facilities, and access to extensive sporting and recreational amenities)
- *Shangri-La Luxury Service Apartments* (residential facilities designed for extended stays, and access to hotel services and amenities).

Each brand promises a distinct mix of benefits, targeted at a different customer segment. The offerings vary by service level (and thus price). There are also different complementary amenities for the various hotel brands. For example, Shangri-La Resorts has a more extensive range of recreational facilities that include water-sports like windsurfing and jet-skiing for holiday-makers, while Shangri-La City Hotels have better-equipped meeting and conference facilities to cater to business travelers.

In some instances, segmentation is situation-based: The same individual may have different needs (and willingness to pay) under differing circumstances. The strategy of brand extension is aimed at encouraging customers to continue patronizing units within the brand family. A study of the brand-switching behavior of some 5,400 hotel customers found that brand extensions do seem to encourage customer retention, but that the strategy may be less effective in discouraging switching when the number of sub-brands reaches four or more.[7]

In other instances, it is unlikely that customers will choose more than a single sub-brand. As an example of branding a high-tech, business-to-business product line, consider Wipro, India's top IT services company. The company offers a comprehensive support program called the Product Support Framework. The framework consists of Help Desk Support, a Technical Assistance Center, and Engineering Support which have been integrated to cater to the needs of every customer. Four levels of customer support are available, from level one to level four, which are displayed in menu form in Figure 4.9. The objective is to give buyers the flexibility to choose a level of support consistent with their own organization's needs (and willingness to pay), ranging from mission-critical support at the enterprise level to assistance with self-service support.

Another example of a service establishment offering a variety of product lines comes from Bumrungrad Hospital in Thailand. Bumrungrad Hospital offers private health care with a complete range of accommodation to meet the needs of all patients. This includes budget four-bedded rooms, two-bedded rooms, single rooms, single deluxe rooms, VIP suites, and Royal suites. The interiors of the single deluxe rooms, and VIP and Royal suites are decorated with carpets and draperies and equipped with private marble bathrooms, television sets, and video cassette

Figure 4.9

Wipro's Product Support Framework enables it to "package," communicate, and price its support service levels.

Level 1	Level 2	Level 3	Level 4
Customer Interaction Services	Technical Help Desk	Technical Assistance, Significant Problems	Engineering Support
Routine Problems, Call Logging	Minor Problems	Engineering Skills, Product Knowledge	Product Problems
Script-Based Solutions	Voice Centric	Accuracy of Solution Critical	Quality of Fix Critical
Voice Centric	Technical Knowledge Important	Code Fixes Limited to Patches	
Language Skills and Interface Skills Critical	Speed of Initial Response Is Critical		
Speed of Initial Response Is Critical			

Reprinted with permission from Wipro Technologies.

recorders; these rooms also have microwave ovens, dishware and glasses, granite dining tables, refrigerators, and cordless phones. These rooms are aimed at wealthy patients who do not want to be reminded that they are in a hospital.

Patients who book a Royal suite have the option of an additional connecting guestroom for their family members. The wide range of in-patient accommodation allows Bumrungrad to attract patients from all income groups. The better-equipped rooms come with better service, which of course comes at a higher price!

Offering a Branded Experience

Branding can be employed at both the corporate and product level by almost any service business. In a well-managed firm, the corporate brand is not only easily recognized but also has meaning for customers. It stands for a particular way of doing business. Some firms choose to associate their corporate brand closely with individual product brands (often referred to as sub-brands). Sub-brands that stand under the umbrella of a corporate brand should reflect the values of the latter. At the same time, the sub-brand should communicate the particular experiences and benefits associated with a given service process. As with corporate brands, sub-branding is an opportunity to establish a mental picture of the service and what it offers to customers.

Globe Telecom, the leading telecommunications company in the Philippines, aims to improve the company's brand value and reward its top customers with its exclusive Globe Platinum membership. Management Memo 4.1 describes Globe Telecom's progress in offering the branded customer experience.

Around the world, many financial service firms continue to create and register brand names to distinguish the different accounts and service packages that they offer. Their objective is to transform a series of service elements and processes into a consistent and recognizable service experience, offering a definable and predictable output at a specified price. Unfortunately, there is often little discernible difference between one bank's branded offering and another's, and the value proposition is unclear. Don Shultz emphasizes that "the brand promise or value proposition is not a tag line, an icon, or a color or a graphic element, although all of these may contribute. It is, instead, the heart and soul of the brand."[8]

An important role for service marketers is to become brand champions, familiar with and responsible for shaping every aspect of the customer's experience. We can relate the notion of a branded service experience to the Flower of Service metaphor by emphasizing the need for consistency in the color and texture of each petal. Unfortunately, many service experiences remain very haphazard and create the impression of a flower stitched together with petals drawn from many different plants!

New Service Development

Competitive intensity and customer expectations are increasing in nearly all service industries. Thus, success lies not only in providing existing services well, but also in creating new approaches to service. Because the outcome and process aspects of a service often combine to create the experience and benefits obtained by customers, both aspects must be addressed in new service development.

Management Memo 4.1

MOVING TOWARD THE BRANDED CUSTOMER EXPERIENCE

A Globe Handyphone subscriber who has been making prompt payments and has an average monthly bill of at least 4,000 pesos (US$72), is likely to be invited to join Globe Telecom's top-caliber subscribers as a member of a club called Globe Platinum. Membership to Globe Platinum is by invitation only. To reward its most profitable customers, it offers an extensive range of benefits such as free use of Japanese, U.S., and Korean handsets, free pick-up and delivery of handsets for repair, a 24-hour dedicated Platinum Hotline, free emergency handset use, and priority handling at the Globe Hub and Business Centers. These customers feel that they are valued at Globe Telecom, and this helps to increase brand loyalty, as well as reduce customer churn rates in a highly competitive industry.

The exclusivity of Globe Platinum contributes to building the branded customer experience. Globe Telecom has been consistently recognized for its dedication to customer satisfaction, and this has been integral in its efforts to improve the brand value of the company.

A Hierarchy of New Service Categories

Below, we identify seven categories of new services, ranging from major innovations to simple style changes.

1. *Major service innovations* are new core products for markets that have not been previously defined. They usually include both new service characteristics and radical new processes. Examples include FedEx's introduction of overnight, nationwide, express package delivery in 1971, the advent of global news service from CNN, and e-Bay's launch of online auction services.

2. *Major process innovations* consist of using new processes to deliver existing core products in new ways with additional benefits. In recent years, the growth of the Internet has led to creation of many new start-up businesses employing new retailing models that exclude use of traditional stores, but save customers time and travel. Often, these models add new, information-based benefits such as greater customization, the opportunity to visit chat rooms with fellow customers, and suggestions for additional products that match well with what has already been purchased. For example, Universitas 21 competes with other institutions of higher learning by delivering Master of Business Administration programs in a non-traditional way. Universitas 21 is an international network of research-intensive universities, with member institutions such as the University of Hong Kong, Fudan University, and Peking University. This academic collaboration is to facilitate communication and cooperation among member institutions and to create global opportunities for students, by taking advantage of strategic alliances.

3. *Product-line extensions* are additions to current product lines by existing firms. The first company in a market to offer such a product may be seen as an innovator. The others are merely followers, often acting defensively. These new services may be targeted at existing customers to serve a broader array of needs or designed to attract new customers with different needs (or both). Airwagon International (Awair) is one of several major carriers to attempt the launch of a separate low-cost operation designed to compete with discount carriers such as Lion Mentari Airlines and Pelita Air Service in Indonesia.

4. *Process-line extensions* are less innovative than process innovations, but often represents distinctive new ways of delivering existing products, either with the intent of offering more convenience and a different experience for existing customers or of attracting new customers who find the traditional approach unappealing. Most commonly, process-line extensions involve adding a lower-contact distribution channel to an existing high-contact channel, such as creating telephone-based or Internet-based banking services. Shanghai Tang, a leading fashion and lifestyle store, allows customers to shop online at their store Web site. Since Shanghai Tang only has stores in Hong Kong, Singapore, and New

York, e-tailing provides customers from all over the world access to its signature "East Meets West" fusion of fashion clothing and lifestyle accessories. Such dual-track approaches are sometimes referred to as "Clicks and Mortar." Creating self-service options to complement delivery by service employees is another form of process-line extension.

5. *Supplementary service innovations* take the form of adding new facilitating or enhancing service elements to an existing core service, or of significantly improving an existing supplementary service. Apart from its core mobile communications services, SmarTone Telecommunications now offers customers broadband Internet access 24/7 in Hong Kong. Low-tech innovations for an existing service can be as simple as adding parking at a retail site or agreeing to accept credit cards for payment. Multiple improvements may have the effect of creating what customers perceive as an altogether new experience, even though it is built around the same core. Theme restaurants like the Rainforest Café enhance the core food service with new experiences. The cafés are designed to keep customers entertained with aquariums, live parrots, waterfalls, fiberglass monkeys, talking trees that spout environmentally related information, and regularly timed thunderstorms, complete with lightning.[9]

6. *Service improvements* are the most common type of innovation. They involve modest changes in the performance of current products, including improvements to either the core product or to existing supplementary services.

7. *Style changes* represent the simplest type of innovation, typically involving no changes in either processes or performance. However, they are often highly visible, create excitement, and may serve to motivate employees. Examples include repainting retail branches and vehicles in new color schemes, outfitting service employees in new uniforms, or introducing a new bank check design.

As the preceding typology suggests, service innovation can occur at many different levels; not every type of innovation has an impact on the characteristics of the service product or is experienced by the customer. Service Perspectives 4.3 tells the story of how a karaoke business remains competitive with its constant innovation.

Physical Goods As a Source of New Service Ideas

Goods and services may be competitive substitutes when they offer the same key benefits. For example, if your lawn needs mowing, you could buy a lawn mower and do it yourself or you could hire a lawn maintenance service to take care of the chore. Such decisions may be shaped by the customer's skills, physical capabilities, time, and budget, as well as such factors as cost comparisons between purchase and use, storage space for purchased products, and anticipated frequency of need. Many services can be built around providing an alternative to owning a physical good and doing the work on one's own. Figure 4.11 shows four possible delivery

Service
Perspectives
4.3

HOLIDAY KTV IN TAIWAN

Founded in 1982, Holiday KTV in Taiwan is now a successful entertainment business, catering mainly to young people. Holiday KTV's unique selling proposition is its innovations in various aspects of the karaoke business.

For singing, Holiday introduced a new machine called "Magic Voice-maker," which can change one's voice into various interesting tones and pitches, such as the tone of a man or a woman, Donald Duck, or even a ghost! This equipment has attracted many customers since its introduction (Figure 4.10). Holiday KTV also invested in V-MIX KTV, which targets heavy and sophisticated users.

To improve the service environment, Holiday KTV has set up many themed rooms. Recently, it redecorated each club in Taiwan with different special themes for its rooms. For instance, it renovated its Party Room (see Figure 4.10) that is highly popular with the young and turned it into a multifunctional area with a platform for individual singing shows, a centrally lit dancing stage, and a special bar. At the same time, it offered unique rooms, including rooms scented with lavender, rooms for lovers, oceanic-style rooms, and Japanese-style rooms, etc. V-MIX-KTV-fitted rooms come with the best audio and video equipment. The chic and outstanding service has consequently attracted celebrities from political and business circles as well as the entertainment industry.

For food and beverages, Holiday KTV was the first to provide a service called "Beverage Bar." During its introduction, drinks were as cheap as NT35 (US$1.05) per person for eight kinds of refillable drinks. After this beverage service turned out to be a success among consumers, Holiday KTV followed up with the introduction of the health beverage series and South Asia-flavored ice series. This was followed by the "Relaxing Bar," which provided hot food, frappe, and a variety of snacks that

Figure 4.10
Anyone can be Jay Chou or Andy Lau at Holiday KTV's Party Room, and enjoy its latest technology which "produces" the ultimate singing experience for its customers.

customers could enjoy. A recent innovation was specialized food prepared by chefs, further differentiating Holiday KTV from its competitors.

Customer feedback is taken seriously. Holiday KTV employs the "Computer-Based Service Evaluation System." Customers can evaluate the service through this system during their stay. If the quality of service is graded low, waiters will approach them and ask for the reasons and implement service recovery immediately. With the Booking Service System, customers are able to use mobile phones to reserve rooms and choose their favorite songs. Facilitated by a simple interface programme based on a Microsoft system and enhanced with the cooperative efforts from I-Mode in Taiwan, this system allows consumers to order everything in advance and enjoy themselves immediately upon arrival at Holiday KTV.

Armed with its formula for success, Holiday KTV has expanded to over 60 clubs across Taiwan by 2004.

Source: http://www.holiday.com.tw/°; http://www.holiday.com.tw/room/ktv_room.aspx? sID=129 accessed on July 5, 2004 and Hung-Chen Huang, *Service Marketing*, Tsang Hai Book Publishing Co. (2003).

Figure 4.11
Services as Substitutes for Owning and/or Using Goods

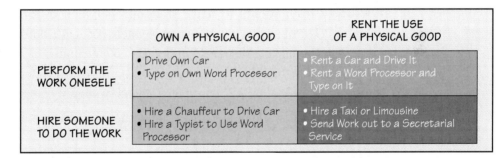

	OWN A PHYSICAL GOOD	RENT THE USE OF A PHYSICAL GOOD
PERFORM THE WORK ONESELF	• Drive Own Car • Type on Own Word Processor	• Rent a Car and Drive It • Rent a Word Processor and Type on It
HIRE SOMEONE TO DO THE WORK	• Hire a Chauffeur to Drive Car • Hire a Typist to Use Word Processor	• Hire a Taxi or Limousine • Send Work out to a Secretarial Service

alternatives each for car travel and word processing, respectively. Three of these alternatives present service opportunities. The alternatives are based on choosing between ownership and rental of the necessary physical goods, and between performing self-service or hiring another person to perform the necessary tasks.

Any new physical product has the potential to create a need for related possession-processing services (particularly if the product is a high-value, durable item.) Industrial equipment may require servicing throughout its lifespan, beginning with shipping and installation and continuing with maintenance, cleaning, consulting advice, problem solving, upgrading, repair, and ultimate disposal. Historically, such after-sales services have generated important revenue streams for many years after the initial sale for products like trucks, factory machinery, locomotives, computers, and jet engines.

Using Research to Design New Services

If a company is designing a new service from scratch, how can it figure out what features and price will create the best value for target customers? It's hard to know without asking these customers—hence the need for research. Let's examine how the Marriott Corporation used market research experts to help with new service development in the hotel industry.

When Marriott was designing a new chain of hotels for business travelers (which eventually became known as Courtyard by Marriott), it hired marketing research experts to help establish an optimal design concept.[10] Since there are limits to how much service and how many amenities can be offered at any given price, Marriott needed to know how customers would make tradeoffs in order to arrive at the most satisfactory compromise in terms of value for money. The intent of the research was to get respondents to trade off different hotel service features to see which ones they valued most. Marriott's goal was to determine if a niche existed between full-service hotels and inexpensive motels, especially in locations where demand was not high enough to justify a large full-service hotel. If such a niche existed, executives wanted to develop a product to fill that gap.

A sample of 601 consumers from four metropolitan areas participated in the study. Researchers used a sophisticated technique known as conjoint analysis, which asks survey respondents to make tradeoffs between different groupings of attributes.[11] The objective is to determine which mix of attributes at specific prices offers them the highest degree of utility. The 50 attributes in the Marriott study were divided into the following seven factors (or sets of attributes), each containing a variety of different features based on detailed studies of competing offerings:

1. *External factors*—building shape, landscaping, pool type and location, hotel size
2. *Room features*—room size and décor, climate control, location and type of bathroom, entertainment systems, other amenities
3. *Food-related services*—type and location of restaurants, menus, room service, vending machines, guest shop, in-room kitchen
4. *Lounge facilities*—location, atmosphere, type of guests
5. *Services*—reservations, registration, check-out, airport limousine, bell desk (baggage service), message center, secretarial services, car rental, laundry, valet
6. *Leisure facilities*—sauna, whirlpool, exercise room, racquetball and tennis courts, game room, children's playground
7. *Security*—guards, smoke detectors, 24-hour video camera

For each of these seven factors, respondents were presented with a series of stimulus cards displaying different levels of performance for each attribute. For instance, the "Rooms" stimulus card displayed nine attributes, each of which had three to five different levels. Thus, *amenities* ranged from "small bar of soap" to "large soap, shampoo packet, shoeshine mitt" to "large soap, bath gel, shower cap, sewing kit, shampoo, special soap" and then to the highest level: "large soap, bath gel, shower cap, sewing kit, special soap, toothpaste, etc."

In the second phase of the analysis, respondents were shown a number of alternative hotel profiles, each featuring different levels of performance on the various attributes contained in the seven factors. They were asked to indicate on a five-point scale how likely they would be to stay at a hotel with these features, given a specific room price per night. Figure 4.12 shows one of the 50 cards that was developed for this research. Each respondent received five cards.

The research yielded detailed guidelines for the selection of almost 200 features and service elements, representing those attributes that provided the highest utility for the customers in the target segments, at prices they were willing to pay. An important aspect of the study was that it focused not only on what business travelers wanted, but also identified what they liked, but weren't prepared to pay for. Using these inputs, the design team was able to meet the specified price while retaining the features most desired by the target market.

Marriott was sufficiently encouraged by the findings to build three Courtyard by Marriott prototype hotels. After testing the concept under real-world conditions and making some refinements, the company subsequently developed a large chain, whose advertising slogan became "Courtyard by Marriott—the hotel designed by business travelers." The new hotel concept filled a gap in the market with a product that represented the best balance between the price customers were prepared to pay and the physical and service features they most desired. The success of this project has led Marriott to develop additional customer-driven products—including Fairfield Inn and SpringHill Suites—using the same research methodology.

Achieving Success in New Service Development

Service firms are not immune to the high failure rates plaguing new manufactured products. The advent of the Internet encouraged entrepreneurs to create numerous new dot.com companies to deliver Internet-based services, but the vast majority failed within just a few years. The reasons for failure ranged widely, including failure to meet a demonstrable consumer need, inability to cover costs from revenues, and poor execution. Storey and Easingwood argue that in developing new services, the product core is of only secondary importance. It is the quality of the total service offering, and also of the marketing support that goes with this, that are of key importance. Underlying success in these areas, they emphasize, is market knowledge: "Without an understanding of the marketplace, knowledge about customers, and knowledge about competitors, it is very unlikely that a new product will be a success."[12]

To what extent can rigorously conducted and controlled development processes for new services enhance their success rate? A study by Edgett and Parkinson focused on discriminating between successful and unsuccessful new financial services.[13] They found that the three factors contributing most to success were, in order of importance:

Figure 4.12

Sample Description of a Hotel Offering

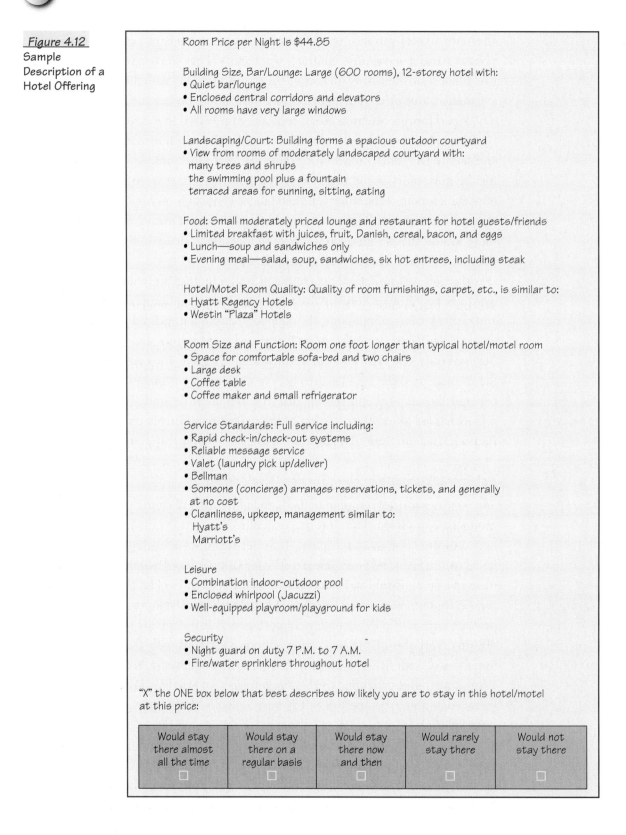

Room Price per Night Is $44.85

Building Size, Bar/Lounge: Large (600 rooms), 12-storey hotel with:
• Quiet bar/lounge
• Enclosed central corridors and elevators
• All rooms have very large windows

Landscaping/Court: Building forms a spacious outdoor courtyard
• View from rooms of moderately landscaped courtyard with:
  many trees and shrubs
  the swimming pool plus a fountain
  terraced areas for sunning, sitting, eating

Food: Small moderately priced lounge and restaurant for hotel guests/friends
• Limited breakfast with juices, fruit, Danish, cereal, bacon, and eggs
• Lunch—soup and sandwiches only
• Evening meal—salad, soup, sandwiches, six hot entrees, including steak

Hotel/Motel Room Quality: Quality of room furnishings, carpet, etc., is similar to:
• Hyatt Regency Hotels
• Westin "Plaza" Hotels

Room Size and Function: Room one foot longer than typical hotel/motel room
• Space for comfortable sofa-bed and two chairs
• Large desk
• Coffee table
• Coffee maker and small refrigerator

Service Standards: Full service including:
• Rapid check-in/check-out systems
• Reliable message service
• Valet (laundry pick up/deliver)
• Bellman
• Someone (concierge) arranges reservations, tickets, and generally
  at no cost
• Cleanliness, upkeep, management similar to:
  Hyatt's
  Marriott's

Leisure
• Combination indoor-outdoor pool
• Enclosed whirlpool (Jacuzzi)
• Well-equipped playroom/playground for kids

Security
• Night guard on duty 7 P.M. to 7 A.M.
• Fire/water sprinklers throughout hotel

"X" the ONE box below that best describes how likely you are to stay in this hotel/motel at this price:

Would stay there almost all the time	Would stay there on a regular basis	Would stay there now and then	Would rarely stay there	Would not stay there
☐	☐	☐	☐	☐

1. *Market synergy*—the new product fit well with the existing image of the firm, provided a superior advantage to competing products in terms of meeting customers' known needs, and received strong support during and after the launch from the firm and its branches. Furthermore, the firm had a good understanding of its customers' purchase decision behavior.
2. *Organizational factors*—there was strong interfunctional cooperation and coordination. Development personnel were fully aware of why they were involved and of the importance of new products to the company.
3. *Market research factors*—detailed and scientifically designed market research studies were conducted early in the development process with a clear idea of the type of information to be obtained. A good definition of the product concept was developed before undertaking field surveys.

Another survey of financial service firms to determine what distinguished successful from unsuccessful products yielded broadly similar findings.[14] In this instance, the key factors underlying success were determined as *synergy* (the fit between the product and the firm in terms of needed expertise and resources being present) and *internal marketing* (the support given to staff prior to launch to help them understand the new product and its underlying systems, as well as details about direct competitors and support).

It is worth noting, however, that there may be limits to the degree of structure that can and should be imposed. Edvardsson, Haglund and Mattsson reviewed new service development in telecommunications, transport, and financial services. They concluded that

> "[C]omplex processes like the development of new services cannot be formally planned altogether. Creativity and innovation cannot only rely on planning and control. There must be some elements of improvization, anarchy, and internal competition in the development of new services … We believe that a contingency approach is needed and that creativity on the one hand and formal planning and control on the other can be balanced, with successful new services as the outcome."[15]

Conclusion

Designing a service product is a complex task that requires an understanding of how the core and supplementary services should be combined, sequenced, and scheduled to create an offering that meets the needs of target market segments. Many firms create an array of offerings with different performance attributes and brand each package with a distinctive name. However, unless each of these sub-brands offers and fulfills a meaningful value proposition, this strategy is likely to be ineffective from a competitive standpoint. In particular, creating a distinctive branded service experience for customers requires consistency across all product elements and at all stages of the service delivery process.

Although innovation is central to effective marketing, major service innovations are relatively rare. More common is the use of new technologies to deliver existing services in new ways. In mature industries, the core service tends to be commoditized. The search for competitive advantage often centers on improvements to the value-creating supplementary services that surround this core. In this chapter, we grouped supplementary services into eight categories, circling the core like the petals of a flower.

A key insight from the Flower of Service concept is that different types of core products often share similar supplementary elements. As a result, customers may make comparisons across industries. For instance, "If my stockbroker can give me a clear documentation of my account activity, why can't the department store where I shop?" Or "If my favorite credit card firm can operate a call center professionally, why can't the hospital downtown?" Questions such as these suggest that managers should be studying businesses outside their own industries in a search for "best-in-class" performers on specific supplementary services.

Review Questions

1. Explain the role of supplementary services. Can they be applied to goods as well as services? If so, how might they relate to marketing strategy?
2. Explain the distinction between enhancing and facilitating supplementary services. Give several examples of each, relative to services that you have used recently.
3. How is branding used in services marketing? What is the distinction between a corporate brand like Shangri-La and the names of its different inn and hotel chains?
4. What does Wipro Technologies gain from using such subsegments for its Customer Support Framework? Why not just use a single customer support division?
5. What is the purpose of techniques such as conjoint analysis in designing new services?

Application Exercises

1. Identify some real-world examples of branding from financial services such as specific types of retail bank accounts or insurance policies, and define their characteristics. How meaningful are these brands likely to be to customers?
2. What service failures have you encountered during the past two weeks? Did they involve the core product or supplementary service elements? Identify possible causes and how such failures might be prevented in the future.

Endnotes

[1]   G. Lynn Shostack, "Breaking Free from Product Marketing," *Journal of Marketing* 44 (April 1977): 73–80.
[2]   Pierre Eiglier and Eric Langeard, "Services As Systems: Marketing Implications," in P. Eiglier, E. Langeard, C. H. Lovelock, J. E. G. Bateson, and R. F. Young, *Marketing Consumer Services: New Insights* (Cambridge,

MA: Marketing Science Institute, 1977), 83–103. Note: An earlier version of this article was published in French in *Révue Française de Gestion* (March–April 1977): 72–84.

3   Christian Grönroos, *Service Management and Marketing*, 2nd ed. (New York: Wiley, 2000), 166.

4   The "Flower of Service" concept presented in this section was first introduced in Christopher H. Lovelock, "Cultivating the Flower of Service: New Ways of Looking at Core and Supplementary Services," in *Marketing, Operations, and Human Resources: Insights into Services,* eds. P. Eiglier and E. Langeard, (Aix-en-Provence, France: IAE, Université d'Aix-Marseille III, 1992), 296–316.

5   Calmetta Coleman, "Fliers Call Electronic Ticketing a Drag," *Wall Street Journal*, January 17, 1997.

6   James C. Anderson and James A. Narus, "Capturing the Value of Supplementary Services," *Harvard Business Review* 73 (January–February 1995): 75–83.

7   Weizhong Jiang, Chekitan S. Dev, and Vithala R. Rao, "Brand Extension and Customer Loyalty: Evidence from the Lodging Industry," *Cornell Hotel and Restaurant Administration Quarterly* (August 2002): 5–16.

8   Don E. Shultz, "Getting to the Heart of the Brand," *Marketing Management* (September–October 2001): 8–9.

9   Chad Rubel, "New Menu for Restaurants: Talking Trees and Blackjack," *Marketing News* (July 29, 1996): 1.

10   Jerry Wind, Paul E. Green, Douglas Shifflet, and Marsha Scarbrough, "Courtyard by Marriott: Designing a Hotel Facility with Consumer-Based Marketing Models," *Interfaces* (January–February 1989): 25–47.

11   Paul E. Green, Abba M. Krieger, and Yoram (Jerry) Wind, "Thirty Years of Conjoint Analysis: Reflections and Prospects," *Interfaces* 31 (May–June 2001): S56–S73.

12   Chris D. Storey and Christopher J. Easingwood, "The Augmented Service Offering: A Conceptualization and Study of Its Impact on New Service Success," *Journal of Product Innovation Management* 15 (1998): 335–351.

13   Scott Edgett and Steven Parkinson, "The Development of New Financial Services: Identifying Determinants of Success and Failure," *International Journal of Service Industry Management* 5, no. 4 (1994): 24–38.

14   Christopher Storey and Christopher Easingwood, "The Impact of the New Product Development Project on the Success of Financial Services," *Service Industries Journal* 13, no. 3 (July 1993): 40–54.

15   Bo Edvardsson, Lars Haglund, and Jan Mattsson, "Analysis, Planning, Improvisation and Control in the Development of New Services," *International Journal of Service Industry Management* 6, no. 2 (1995): 24–35. See also Bo Edvardsson and Jan Olsson, "Key Concepts for New Service Development," *The Service Industries Journal* 16 (April 1996): 140–164.

CHAPTER FIVE

Designing the Communications Mix For Services

Life is for one generation; a good name is forever.

JAPANESE PROVERB

Education costs money, but then so does ignorance.

SIR CLAUS MOSER

Communication is the most visible or audible—some would say intrusive—of marketing activities, but its value is limited unless it is used intelligently in conjunction with other marketing efforts. An old marketing axiom says that the fastest way to kill a poor product is to advertise it heavily. By the same token, an otherwise well-researched and well-planned marketing strategy, designed to deliver, say, new Web-based services at a reasonable price, is likely to fail if people lack knowledge of the service and how to access it.

Through communication, marketers inform existing or prospective customers about service features and benefits, price and other costs, the channels through which service is delivered, and when and where it is available. Where appropriate, persuasive arguments can be marshaled for using a particular service and preference can be created for selecting a specific brand. Both personal instructions and impersonal communications can be employed to help customers become effective participants in service delivery processes.

Much confusion surrounds the scope of marketing communication. Some people still define it narrowly as the use of paid media advertising, public relations, and professional salespeople, failing to recognize the many other ways that a modern organization can communicate with its customers. The location and atmosphere of a service delivery facility, corporate design features such as the consistent use of colors and graphic elements, the appearance and behavior of employees, the design of a Web site—all contribute to an impression in the customer's mind that reinforces or contradicts the specific content of formal communication messages.

In this chapter, we explore the following questions:

1. What is distinctive about the nature of marketing communications for services?
2. What are the elements of the marketing communications mix and what are the strengths and weaknesses of each major element in a services context?
3. How does the level of customer contact affect communication strategy?
4. How should marketing communication objectives be defined?
5. What is the potential value of the Internet as a communication channel?

The Role of Marketing Communication

In a service setting, marketing communications tools are especially important because they help create powerful images and a sense of credibility, confidence, and reassurance. Marketing communications, in one form or another, are essential to a company's success. Without effective communications, prospects may never learn of a service firm's existence, what it has to offer them, or how to use its products to best advantage. Customers might be more easily lured away by competitors and competitive offerings, and there would be no proactive management and control of the firm's identity. Let's look at some specific tasks that can be performed by marketing communication.

Adding Value through Communication Content

Information and consultation represent important ways to add value to a product. Prospective customers may need information and advice about what service options are available to them, where and when these services are available, how much they cost, and what specific features, functions, and service benefits there are. Companies also use marketing communications to persuade target customers that their service product offers the best solution to meet those customers' needs, relative to the offerings of competing firms. See Figure 5.1 for an advertisement on how Citibank conveys this, building on its 100-year experience in Asia.

Communication efforts serve not only to attract new users, but also to maintain contact with an organization's existing customers and build relationships with them. Nurturing customer relationships depends on a comprehensive and up-to-date customer database, and the ability to make use of this in a personalized way.

Techniques for keeping in touch with customers and building their loyalty include direct mail and contacts by telephone or other forms of telecommunication, including faxes, email and Web sites. Doctors, dentists, and household maintenance services often post annual check-up reminders to their customers. Some businesses even send birthday and anniversary cards to valued customers. Banks and utility companies often include a brief newsletter with their account statements or print customized information on each statement in an effort to cross-sell additional

Figure 5.1
Citibank promotes
its pioneering card
services in Asia.

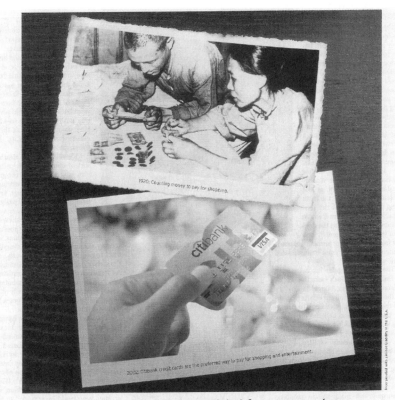

Figure 5.1
Citibank promotes
its pioneering card
services in Asia.

Courtesy of Citibank Global Consumer Bank, Asia Pacific.

services. See Best Practice in Action 5.1, which features a highly targeted campaign by an online broker.

Communicating Services Presents Both Challenges and Opportunities

Traditional marketing communication strategies were largely shaped by the needs and practices associated with marketing manufactured goods. However, several of the differences distinguishing services from goods have a significant impact on the ways we approach the design of marketing communication programs in service businesses.[1] In particular, we need to consider the implications of intangibility in

Best Practice in Action 5.1

REACTIVATING IDLE ACCOUNTS VIA A TARGETED PROMOTION

Well-managed CRM systems give firms an integrated view of the customer that facilitates highly targeted promotions and communications strategies. Consider the following example from Accenture management consultants Kevin Quiring and Nancy Mullen:

> You glance at a message on your pager that has just come in. It is from your online broker. You almost delete it, assuming it's a pedestrian banner ad from its website that has somehow wormed its way into your pager address. Then you noticed that the message is personalized, offering you that the fees for your next trade would be waived. No way that this message was sent to their entire customer base; it would have cost them a bomb! It seems, your online broker has noticed your conspicuous lack of trading activity since your account was opened. The offer makes you want to act immediately. In retrospect, you realize it is not the eight bucks that is spurring you on, but the poignant reminder that your money has been earning zero-point-nothing percent interest for nearly a year in the brokerage account.

This campaign garnered a 30 to 40 percent activation rate, and 20 to 30 percent of those customers repeated transactions after this promotional offer. Note that the majority of those accounts would have been likely candidates for closure without this reactivation campaign. The value and success in terms of increased accuracy and reduced costs are attributed to what is being commonly referred to as an *integrated view of the customer* (or IVoC in CRM language).

Source: Kevin N. Quiring and Nancy K. Mullen, "More Than Data Warehousing: An Integrated View of the Customer," in *The Ultimate CRM Handbook—Strategies and Concepts for Building Enduring Customer Loyalty and Profitability*, ed. John G. Freeland (New York: McGraw-Hill, 2002): 102.

service performances, customer involvement in production, the role of customer contact personnel, the difficulty of evaluating many services, and the need to bring demand and supply into balance.

Overcome the Problems of Intangibility

Since services are performances rather than objects, their benefits can be difficult to communicate to customers. Banwari Mittal suggests that intangibility creates four problems for marketers seeking to promote its attributes or benefits: abstractness, generality, nonsearchability, and mental impalpability.[2] Emphasizing that service marketers need to create messages that clearly communicate intangible service attributes and benefits to potential consumers, he and Julie Baker discuss the implications of each of these problems[3] and propose specific communication strategies for dealing with them (see Table 5.1).

Abstractness. Because abstract concepts such as financial security, expert advice, or safe transportation do not have one-to-one correspondence with physical objects, it can be challenging for marketers to connect their services to those concepts.

Generality. This refers to items that comprise a class of objects, persons, or events—for instance, airline seats, flight attendants, and cabin service. These general

Intangibility Problem	*Advertising Strategy*	*Description*
Incorporeal Existence	**Physical Representation**	**Show Physical Components of Service**
Generality:		
• For objective claims	System documentation	Objectively document physical-system capacity
	Performance documentation	Document and cite past-performance statistics
• For subjective claims	Service-performance episode	Present an actual service-delivery incident
Nonsearchability	Consumption documentation	Obtain and present customer testimonials
	Reputation documentation	Cite independently audited performance
Abstractness	Service-consumption episode	Capture and display typical customers benefiting from the service
Impalpability	Service-process episode	Present a vivid documentary on the step-by-step service process
	Case-history episode	Present an actual case history of what the firm did for a specific client
	Service-consumption episode	An articulate narration or depiction of a customer's subjective experience

Table 5.1
Advertising
Strategies for
Overcoming
Intangibility

Source: Banwari Mittal and Julie Baker, "Advertising Strategies for Hospitality Services," *Cornell Hotel and Restaurant Administration Quarterly* 43 (April 2002): 53. Copyright Cornell University. All rights reserved. Used by permission.

classes do have physical analogues and most consumers of the service know what they are, but a key task for marketers is to communicate what makes a specific offering distinctly different from (and superior to) competing offerings.

Nonsearchability. This refers to the fact that intangibles cannot be searched or inspected before they are purchased. Physical service attributes, such as the appearance of a health club and the type of equipment installed, can be checked in advance, but the experience of working with the trainers can only be determined through experience. And as noted in Chapter 2, credence attributes are those that must be taken on faith, such as a surgeon's expertise.

Mental impalpability. Many services are sufficiently complex, multidimensional, or novel that it is difficult for consumers—especially new prospects—to understand what the experience of using them will be like and what benefits will result.

Commonly used strategies in advertising include the use of tangible cues whenever possible, especially for low-contact services that involve few tangible elements.[4] It's also helpful to include "vivid information" that catches the audience's attention and will produce a strong, clear impression on the senses, especially for services that are complex and highly intangible.[5]

Consider the approach used by Accenture, the global management service and technology consulting company, to dramatize the abstract notion of helping clients capitalize on innovative ideas in a fast-moving world (see Figure 5.2).

Some companies have created metaphors that are tangible in nature to help communicate the benefits of their service offerings. Insurance companies often use this approach to market their highly intangible products, such as the "Trust" campaign launched by AIA in Asia. Examples of the taglines AIA used include: "You put your trust in those you can depend on" and "Trust us for life."

Figure 5.2

Accenture promotes its ability to help clients turn innovative ideas into results.

When possible, advertising metaphors should also include some information about *how* service benefits are actually provided.[6] Consider Taiwan's Trend Micro's problem in advertising its new antivirus monitoring service for corporate networks. Most advertisements for antivirus protection feature devils or evil-looking insects (remember the Millennium Bug that was used to highlight the Y2K problem?). That approach may capture the reader's interest, but it doesn't show how virus protection actually works or how devastating its effects might be. In a technical context like this, explaining the problem and its solution in ways that senior management will understand is not always possible. Trend Micro's clever solution was to use the analogy of airport security to guard against terrorism (see Figure 5.3).

Figure 5.3
Providing Tangible
Metaphors for
Service
Performance

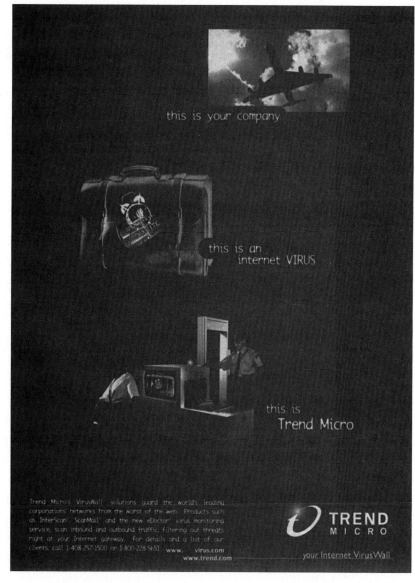

Reproduced with permission from Trend Micro, Inc.

Facilitate Customer Involvement in Production

When customers are actively involved in service production, they need training to help them perform well—just as employees do. Improving productivity often involves innovations in service delivery. However, the desired benefits won't be achieved if customers resist new, technologically based systems or avoid self-service alternatives. One approach recommended by advertising experts is to show service delivery in action.[7] Television is a good medium, because of its ability to engage the viewer as it displays a seamless sequence of events in visual form. Some dentists show their patients videos of surgical procedures before the surgery takes place. This educational technique helps patients prepare mentally for the experience and shows them what role they should play during service delivery.

Advertising and publicity can make customers aware of changes in service features and delivery systems. Marketers often use sales promotions to motivate customers, offering them incentives to make the necessary changes in their behavior. Publicizing price discounts is one way to encourage self-service on an ongoing basis. At self-service gas pumps, for instance, the price difference from full service is often substantial. Other incentives to change include promotions that offer a chance to win a reward. For example, Modern Beauty Salon advertises its free treatment for the first 100 customers to encourage adoption of its beauty services.

Help Customers to Evaluate Service Offerings

Even if customers understand what a service is supposed to do, they may have difficulty distinguishing one firm from another and knowing what level of performance to expect from a particular supplier. Possible solutions include providing tangible clues related to service performance, highlighting the quality of equipment and facilities, and emphasizing employee characteristics such as their qualifications, experience, commitment, and professionalism.

Some performance attributes lend themselves better to advertising than others. When an airline wants to boast about its punctuality, reporting favorable statistics collected by a government agency offers credible support for this claim. However, airlines don't like to talk overtly about safety, because even the admission that things might go wrong makes many passengers nervous. Instead, they approach this ongoing customer concern indirectly, advertising the expertise of their pilots, the newness of their aircraft, and the skills and training of their mechanics. Deer Jet, an Asian business-jet charter operator, approaches safety concerns in its advertisement by listing the safety audit tests it has passed and its experience (see Figure 5.4).

To document the superior quality and reliability of its network coverage and reception, SUNDAY's television commercials in Hong Kong made references to the numerous awards it received for being rated as highest in customer satisfaction for innovative services and quality network coverage from ITU Asia Telecom, an

Figure 5.4
Deer Jet, the largest business air charter fleet in Asia, emphasizes its leadership position in the private charter service industry in Asia.

Courtesy of Deer Jet Co. Ltd.

annual event in the telecommunications industry that recognizes outstanding companies.

In low-contact services, where much of the firm's expertise is hidden, firms may need to illustrate equipment, procedures, and employee activities that are taking place backstage. For example, when the Bangkok Mass Transit System (BTS) first launched its Skytrain, it needed to convince the public of the safety and convenience of using the Skytrain, so its advertisements emphasized the new accessibility from the outskirts to central Bangkok and the efficiently operated trains.

Stimulate or Dampen Demand to Match Capacity

Many live service performances—like a seat at the theater in Singapore for Friday evening's performance, or a haircut at Kamal Salon in Manila on Tuesday morning—are time-specific and can't be stored for resale at a later date. Advertising and sales promotions can help to change the timing of customer use and thus help to match demand with the capacity available at a given time.

Demand management strategies include reducing usage during peak demand periods and stimulating it during off-peak periods. Low demand outside peak periods poses a serious problem for service industries with high fixed costs, like hotels. One strategy is to run promotions that offer extra value—such as a room upgrade and a free breakfast, in an attempt to stimulate demand without decreasing price. When demand increases, the number of promotions can be reduced or eliminated.

Promote the Contribution of Service Personnel

In high-contact services, front-line personnel are central to service delivery. Their presence makes the service more tangible and, in many cases, more personalized. An ad that shows employees at work helps prospective customers understand the nature of the service encounter and implies a promise of the personalized attention that they can expect to receive. See Figure 5.5 for an advertisement by JETRO, a Japanese government organization that provides assistance to companies that are interested in business opportunities in Japan. Businesspeople interested in investing in Japan are concerned about the unique business practices there, and JETRO's employees will help them in this regard.

Advertising and brochures can also show customers the work that goes on behind the scenes to ensure good service delivery. Highlighting the expertise and commitment of employees whom customers normally never encounter may enhance trust in the organization's competence and commitment to service quality.

Advertisers must be reasonably realistic in their depictions of service personnel, since their messages help set customers' expectations. If a firm's brochures and ads show friendly, smiling workers but, in reality, most employees turn out to be glum, frazzled, or rude, customers will most certainly be disappointed. At a minimum, service personnel should be informed about the content of new advertising campaigns or brochures.

Figure 5.5

To instill confidence in potential foreign investors in Japan, JETRO features friendly and welcoming professionals who are ready to help.

Reprinted with permission from JETRO.

Setting Communication Objectives

What role should communication play in helping a service firm achieve its marketing goals? A useful checklist for marketing communications planning is provided by the 5Ws model:

Who is our target audience?

What do we need to communicate and achieve?

How should we communicate this?

Where should we communicate this?

When do the communications need to take place?

Let's consider the issues of defining the target audience and specifying communication objectives. Then we'll review the wide array of communication tools available to service marketers. Issues relating to the location and scheduling of communication activities tend to be situation specific and so we will not address them here.

Target Audience

Target audiences can be broken into three broad categories: prospects, users, and employees. Because marketers of consumer services do not usually know prospects in advance, they usually need to employ a traditional communications mix, comprising such elements as media advertising, public relations, and use of purchased lists for direct mail or telemarketing.

By contrast, more cost-effective channels may be available to reach existing users, including selling efforts by customer contact personnel, point-of-sale promotions, and other information distributed during service encounters. If the firm has a membership relationship with its customers and has a database containing contact information, it can distribute highly targeted information through direct mail, email, or telephone. These channels may serve to complement and reinforce broader communications channels or simply replace them.

Employees serve as a secondary audience for communication campaigns through public media. A well-designed campaign targeted at users, nonusers, or both, can also be motivating for employees, especially those playing front-stage roles. In particular, it may help to shape employees' behavior if the advertising content shows them what is being promised to customers. Advertising by Shangri-La Hotels and Resorts featured a uniformed employee fulfilling the promise of satisfaction with a smile (see Figure 5.6).

However, there's a risk of generating cynicism among employees and actively demotivating them if the communication in question promotes levels of performance that employees regard as unrealistic or even impossible to achieve.

Communications directed specifically at staff are normally part of an internal marketing campaign, using company-specific channels, and so are not accessible to customers. We discussed internal communications earlier in this chapter.

Specifying Communication Objectives

Marketers need to be clear about their goals, otherwise it will be difficult to formulate specific communication objectives and select the most appropriate messages and

Courtesy of Shangri-La Hotels and Resorts.

Figure 5.6
Shangri-La promotes its service promise by featuring an employee in traditional cheongsam with a friendly smile making hotel guests feel welcome and comfortable.

communication tools to achieve them. Table 5.2 presents a list of common educational and promotional objectives for service businesses. Objectives may include shaping and managing customer behavior in any of the three stages of the purchase and consumption process that we discussed in Chapter 2: prepurchase stage, service encounter stage, and postconsumption stage.

Table 5.2
Common
Educational and
Promotional
Objectives in
Service Settings

- Create memorable images of specific companies and their brands.
- Build awareness of and interest in an unfamiliar service or brand.
- Build preference by communicating the strengths and benefits of a specific brand.
- Compare a service with competitors' offerings and counter competitive claims.
- Reposition a service relative to competing offerings.
- Stimulate demand in low-demand periods and discourage demand during peak periods.
- Encourage trial by offering promotional incentives.
- Reduce uncertainty and perceived risk by providing useful information and advice.
- Provide reassurance (e.g., by promoting service guarantees).
- Familiarize customers with service processes in advance of use.
- Teach customers how to use a service to their own best advantage.
- Recognize and reward valued customers and employees.

Key Planning Considerations

Planning a marketing communications campaign should reflect a good understanding of the service product and how well prospective buyers can evaluate its characteristics in advance of purchase. It is essential to understand target market segments and their exposure to different media, as well as consumers' awareness of the product and their attitudes toward it. Decisions include determining the content, structure, and style of the message to be communicated, its manner of presentation, and the media most suited to reaching the intended audience. Additional considerations include the budget available for execution; time frames, as defined by such factors as seasonality, market opportunities, and anticipated competitive activities; and methods of measuring and evaluating performance.

The Marketing Communications Mix

Most service marketers have access to numerous forms of communication, referred to collectively as the *marketing communications mix*. Different communication elements have distinctive capabilities relative to the types of messages that they can convey and the market segments most likely to be exposed to them. As shown in Figure 5.8, the mix includes personal contact, advertising, publicity and public relations, sales promotion, instructional materials, and corporate design.

Communication experts draw a broad division between *personal* communications (those in the left-hand column of boxes in Figure 5.7) which involve personalized messages that move in both directions between the two parties—such as personal selling, telemarketing, customer training, customer service, and word of mouth—and *impersonal* communications, in which messages move in only one direction and are generally targeted at a large group of customers and prospects rather than at a single individual.

Figure 5.7

The Marketing Communications Mix for Services

Personal Communications	Advertising	Sales Promotion	Publicity and Public Relations	Instructional Materials	Corporate Design
Selling	Broadcast	Sampling	Press Releases/Kits	Wed Sites	Signage
Customer Service	Print	Coupons	Press Conferences	Manuals	Interior Decor
Training	Internet	Gifts	Special Events	Brochures	Vehicles
Telemarketing	Outdoor	Sign-up Rebates	Sponsorship	Video/Audio-cassettes	Equipment
* Word of Mouth (other customers)	Direct Mail	Prize Promotions	Trade Shows, Exhibitions	Software CD-ROM	Stationery
			* Media-Initiated Coverage	Voice Mail	Uniforms

* Denotes communications originating from outside the organization

Figure 5.8

Originating Sources of Messages Received by a Target Audience

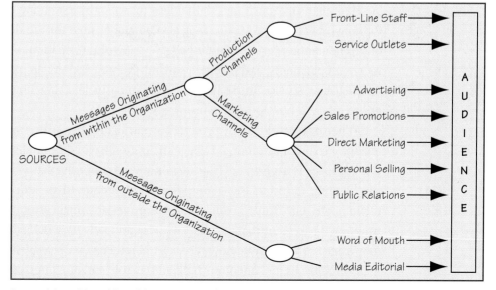

Source: Adapted from Adrian Palmer, *Principles of Services Marketing* (London: McGraw-Hill, 1994), 280.

However, technology has created a gray area between personal and impersonal communications. For instance, firms often combine word processing technology with information from a database to create an impression of personalization. Similarly, interactive software, voice recognition technology, and computer-generated voice prompts and responses can simulate a two-way conversation. A few firms are beginning to experiment with Web-based agents that can move on the screen, speak, and even change expressions.

Communications Originate from Different Sources

It's important to clarify the source from which communications originate. As shown in Figure 5.8, not all communications messages received by the target audience originate from within the service provider's organization. Specifically, word of mouth and media stories or editorials originate from outside the organization and are not under its direct control. Messages from an internal source can be divided into those received through production channels and those that are transmitted through marketing channels. Let's look at the options within each of these three originating sources.

Messages Transmitted through Production Channels

In this category are communications developed within the organization and transmitted through the production channels employed to deliver the service itself, primarily front-line staff and service outlets. A further subdivision is possible within this category if the originating service firm employs intermediaries to deliver service on its behalf.

CUSTOMER SERVICE FROM FRONT-LINE STAFF   Employees in front-line positions may serve customers either face to face or by telephone. Those responsible for delivering the core service may also be responsible for the delivery of a variety of supplementary services, including provision of information, taking reservations, receipt of payments, and problem solving. New customers, in particular, often rely on customer service personnel for assistance in learning how to use a service effectively and how to resolve problems.

When several different products are available from the same supplier, firms encourage their customer service staff to cross-sell additional services. However, this approach is likely to fail if strategies are not properly planned and executed.[8] In the banking industry, for example, a highly competitive marketplace and new technologies have forced banks to add more services in an attempt to increase their profitability. In many banks, tellers who traditionally provided customer service are now expected to promote new services to their customers as well. Despite training, many employees feel uncomfortable in this role and don't perform as effectively as salespeople.

CUSTOMER TRAINING   Some companies, especially those selling complex business-to-business services, offer formal training courses to familiarize their customers with the service product and teach them how to use it to their best advantage. Alternatively (or additionally), this task may be assigned to the same front-line personnel who handle service delivery.

SERVICE OUTLETS   Both planned and unintended messages reach customers through the medium of the service delivery environment itself. Impersonal messages can be distributed in the form of banners, posters, signage, brochures, video screens, and audio. As noted in other chapters, the physical design of the service outlet—what we call the *servicescape*—also sends a message to customers.[9] Corporate design consultants are sometimes asked to advise on servicescape design, to coordinate the visual elements of both interiors and exteriors, so that they may complement and reinforce the positioning of the firm and shape the nature of the customers' service experiences in desired ways.

Messages Transmitted through Marketing Channels

As shown earlier in Figure 5.8, service marketers have a wide array of communication tools at their disposal. We briefly review the principal elements.

PERSONAL SELLING   Interpersonal encounters in which efforts are made to educate customers and promote preference for a particular brand or product are referred to as personal selling. Many firms, especially those marketing business-to-business services, maintain dedicated salesforces or employ agents and distributors to undertake personal selling efforts on their behalf. For infrequently purchased services like property, insurance, and funeral services, the firm's representative may act as a consultant to help buyers make their selections.

Relationship marketing strategies are often based on account management programs, where customers are assigned a designated account manager who acts as an interface between the customer and the supplier.

However, face-to-face selling to new prospects is expensive. A lower-cost alternative is *telemarketing*, involving use of the telephone to reach prospective customers. It's used by about 75 percent of all industrial companies.[10] At the consumer level, there is growing frustration with the intrusive nature of telemarketing, which is often timed to reach people when they are home in the evenings or on weekends.

TRADE SHOWS   In the business-to-business marketplace, trade shows are a popular form of publicity that also combines important personal selling opportunities.[11] In many industries, trade shows stimulate extensive media coverage and offer business customers an opportunity to find out about the latest offerings from a wide array of suppliers in the field. Service vendors provide physical evidence in the form of exhibits, samples and demonstrations, and brochures to educate and impress these potential customers. Trade shows can be very productive promotional tools, since it is one of the few instances in which large numbers of prospective buyers come to the marketer rather than the other way around.

ADVERTISING   As the most dominant form of communication in consumer marketing, advertising is often the first point of contact between service marketers and their customers, serving to build awareness, inform, persuade, and remind. It plays a vital role in providing factual information about services and educating customers about product features and capabilities. To demonstrate this role, Grove, Pickett, and Laband carried out a study comparing newspaper and television advertising for goods and services.[12] Based on a review of some 11,000 television commercials and 31,000 newspaper display advertisements, they found that ads for services were significantly more likely than those for goods to contain factual information on price, guarantees/warranties, documentation of performance, and availability (where, when, and how to acquire products).

One of the challenges facing advertisers is how to get their messages noticed. In general, people are tiring of ads in all their forms. A recent study by Yankelovich Partner, an American marketing-services consultancy firm that provides innovative, solutions-oriented consulting and research across a broad range of industries, says that consumer resistance to the growing intrusiveness of advertising has been pushed to an all-time high. The study found that 65 percent of people feel "constantly bombarded" by ad messages and that 59 percent feel that ads have very little relevance to them.[13] Television and radio broadcasts are cluttered with commercials, while newspapers and magazines sometimes seem to contain more ads than news and features. How can a firm hope to stand out from the crowd? Some advertisers stand out by employing striking designs or a distinctively different format, or an image intended to shock. Service Perspectives 5.1 describes the eye-catching and gut-wrenching advertising employed by the Asian Conservation Awareness Programme (ACAP).

A broad array of paid advertising media is available, including broadcast (TV and radio), print (magazines and newspapers), movie theaters, and many types of outdoor media (posters, billboards, electronic message boards, and the exteriors of buses or cabs). Some media are more focused than others, targeting specific geographic areas or audiences with a particular interest. Advertising messages delivered through mass media are often reinforced by direct marketing.

Despite being the most dominant form of communication in consumer marketing, the effectiveness of advertising remains hugely controversial. Conventional wisdom in the industry is that sales may well increase for a certain period even after the end of the advertising campaign. However, there comes a

*Service
Perspectives
5.1*

ACAP'S ADS SEEK TO SHOCK PEOPLE INTO NEW BEHAVIORS

The Asian Conservation Awareness Programme (ACAP) is a multimedia, international campaign on behalf of WildAid, a nonprofit organization that is working to provide direct protection to endangered wildlife. Working with governments, local groups, and consumers in many different countries, WildAid seeks to curtail illegal trade in wildlife, which Interpol estimates is worth US$6 billion or more a year. Only the illegal trades in drugs and arms are thought to be more profitable.

WildAid's activities address the entire trade cycle, from poaching to smuggling to consumption. Its programs are, therefore, categorized into three areas. *Protecting the Wild* emphasizes such activities as helping to reduce poaching in national parks in several countries—including Thailand, Myanmar and Cambodia—and supporting outreach programs to create economic alternatives for communities surrounding the parks. *Stopping the Illegal Trade* has involved working with national governments to create mobile protection units to recover, care for, and rerelease poached animals before they are killed. Investigative units go undercover to expose participants in illegal trading schemes and the ways in which they circumvent existing rules and regulations.

The third element in the program, *Raising Awareness/Reducing Demand,* targets consumers, seeking to build awareness of the problem of illegal killing and trading of endangered wildlife and its consequences. An important objective is to reduce demand for the end-products, from food products, skins, furs, and tusks to animal by-products that are said to improve virility or have other medicinal qualities. To implement this task and build international awareness, WildAid and its advertising agency, J. Walter Thompson, created ACAP. The campaign uses primarily donated media and has increased its visibility through the use of such high-profile sponsors as the Hong Kong action star, Jackie Chan. If people understand the cruelty, waste, and risk of extinction involved, WildAid is confident that many of them will no longer demand the products that put so many wild animals at risk. And without demand, there will be no trade.

Among some of ACAP's ads are some that employ shocking images to catch the reader's or viewer's attention. Figure 5.9 was one of several ads that employed a black-and-white photograph with blood portrayed in red for dramatic effect, to represent the blood lost by the animals which are killed for their organs. To drive home the suffering of bears whose paws are cut off to be used as cooking ingredient for some Asian cuisines (such as the Chinese Imperial Banquet), ACAP presented mutilated human limbs to represent the nature of the assault on the specific animals—in this case, a bear that had had its paws cut off. ACAP's research showed that increased awareness in markets such as Taiwan and Thailand of how animal parts are obtained has resulted in consumer intentions to cease using the products of endangered species captured in the wild, including decisions to stop eating such delicacies as sharks' fin soup.

Source: www.wildaid.com, www.acapworldwide.com, accessed in June 2004.

point when sales start to decline and it becomes extremely expensive to rebuild the brand. Robert Shaw, a visiting professor at Cranfield School of Management in Britain, runs a forum in which a number of big companies try to monitor the "marketing payback" from advertising. And according to him, the return on

Figure 5.9

The Asian Conservation Awareness Programme (ACAP) uses eye-catching and gut-wrenching advertisements in its information campaign to protect endangered wildlife.

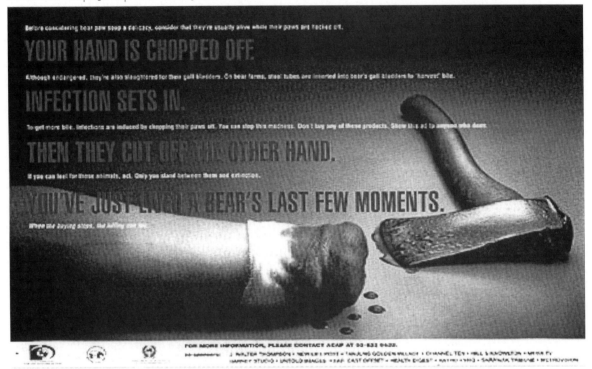

Courtesy of WildAid, Inc.

advertising was "never terribly good," as under half of the ads provide a return on their investment in general.[14]

DIRECT MARKETING   This category embraces such tools as mailings, recorded telephone messages, faxes, and email. These channels offer the potential to send personalized messages to highly targeted microsegments. Direct strategies are most likely to be successful when marketers possess a detailed database of information about customers and prospects.

SALES PROMOTION   A useful way of looking at sales promotions is as a communication attached to an incentive. Sales promotions are usually specific to a time period, price, or customer group—sometimes all three. Typically, the objective is to accelerate the purchasing decision or motivate customers to use a specific service sooner, in greater volume with each purchase, or more frequently. Sales promotions for service firms may take such forms as samples, coupons and other discounts, gifts, and competitions with prizes. Used in these forms, sales promotions add value, provide a "competitive edge," boost sales during periods when demand would otherwise be weak, speed the introduction and acceptance of new services, and generally get customers to act faster than they would in the absence of any promotional incentive.[15]

Hong Kong depends heavily on its service and tourism industries in contributing to the economy. After the Severe Acute Respiratory Syndrome (SARS) outbreak, the Hong Kong Tourism Development Bureau made serious efforts to revive the badly affected tourism sector with a string of promotional activities. In December 2003, the Hong Kong Tourism Development Bureau organized "Hong Kong Colorful Winter Holiday," a celebration fusing western and eastern traditions and festivities, to create an atmosphere of excitement and fun that would draw tourists to visit the city.[16]

PUBLIC RELATIONS   This involves efforts to stimulate positive interest in an organization and its products by sending out news releases, holding press conferences, staging special events, and sponsoring newsworthy activities put on by third parties. A basic element in a public relations (PR) strategy is the preparation and distribution of press releases (including photos and/or videos) that feature stories about the company, its products, and its employees. PR executives also arrange press conferences and distribute press kits when they feel a story is especially newsworthy. A key task performed by corporate PR specialists at many service organizations involves teaching senior managers how to present themselves well at news conferences or in radio and television interviews, especially at times of crisis or when faced with hostile questioning.

Other widely used PR techniques include recognition and reward programs, obtaining testimonials from public figures, community involvement and support, fundraising, and obtaining favorable publicity for the organization through special events. These tools can help a service organization build its reputation and credibility, form strong relationships with its employees, customers, and the community, and secure an image conducive to business success.

Firms can also win wide exposure through sponsorship of sporting events and other high-profile activities where banners, decals, and other visual displays provide continuing repetition of the corporate name and symbol. For example, the Vietnam Mobile Telecom Services Co.'s VMS-Mobifone was a major sponsor for mobile telecommunications in the 22nd Southeast Asian (SEA) Games in 2003. The event provided many PR and advertising opportunities for VMS, including print articles, television news clips, and highly visible banners and posters at competition sites.

Le Tour de Langkawi is one of the most publicized cycling events in Asia. The annual competition relies upon corporate sponsorship to help cover the huge costs of extensive logistics and operations. An event like this typically has several sponsors, whose names or logos appear prominently on the cyclists' jerseys, outdoor banners, and posters. Telekom Malaysia, the title sponsor for the same competition in 2004, also gained tremendous media coverage and publicity. The Telekom Malaysia brand name was closely associated with the established, high-profile sporting event, which was titled "Telekom Malaysia Le Tour de Langkawi." Live telecasts, daily news coverage, highlight segments, and international print media enabled Telekom Malaysia to raise its brand profile significantly (see Figure 5.10).

Unusual activities can present an opportunity to promote a company's expertise. FedEx gained significant favorable publicity when it safely transported two giant pandas from Chengdu, China, to the National Zoo in Washington, DC. The pandas flew in specially designed containers aboard an MD-11 aircraft renamed "FedEx PandaOne." In addition to press releases, the company also featured information about the unusual shipment on a special page on its Web site.

Messages Originating from Outside the Organization

Some of the most powerful messages about a company and its products come from outside the organization and are not controlled by the marketer.

WORD OF MOUTH   Recommendations from other customers are generally viewed as more credible than firm-initiated promotional activities and can have a powerful influence on people's decisions to use (or avoid using) a service. In fact, the greater the risk that customers perceive in purchasing a service, the more actively they will seek and rely on word of mouth (WOM) to guide their decision making.[17] Customers who are less knowledgeable about a service rely more on WOM than expert

Figure 5.10
Telekom Malaysia gained tremendous publicity from its sponsorship of Le Tour de Langkawi 2004.

Courtesy of Telekom Malaysia.

consumers.[18] Interestingly, WOM even happens during the service encounter and can influence their behavior and satisfaction with the service when customers start talking to other customers present in the same setting.[19] Frederick Reichheld even argues that whether or not customers are willing to give positive WOM for a firm is the single most important predictor of top-line growth.[20]

Since WOM can act as such a powerful and highly credible selling agent, some marketers employ a variety of strategies to stimulate positive and persuasive comments from existing customers.[21] These include:

- Referencing other purchasers and knowledgeable individuals, for instance: "We have done a great job for ABC Corp., and if you wish, feel free to talk to Mr Chen, their MIS manager, who oversaw the implementation of our project."
- Creating exciting promotions that get people talking about the great service that the firm provides. Both Cathay Pacific and Singapore Airlines have run many campaigns that successfully stimulated discussions and commentary.
- Developing referral incentive schemes, such as offering an existing customer some units of free or discounted service in return for introducing new customers to the firm.[22]
- Offering promotions that encourage customers to persuade others to join them in using the service, such as "bring two friends, and the third eats for free" or "Subscribe to two mobile service plans, and we'll waive the monthly subscription fee for all subsequent family members."
- Presenting and publicizing testimonials that simulate WOM. Advertising and brochures sometimes feature comments from satisfied customers.

Research shows that the extent and content of word of mouth is related to satisfaction levels. Customers holding strong views are likely to tell more people about their experiences than those with milder views. And extremely dissatisfied customers tell more people than those who are highly satisfied.[23] Noting the important role that service employees play in customer satisfaction, Gremler *et al.* suggest that measures to improve the quality of customer-employee interactions may be an appropriate strategy for stimulating positive WOM.[24] Interestingly, even customers who were initially dissatisfied with a service can end up spreading positive WOM, if they are delighted with the way the firm handled the service recovery.[25]

With the rapid proliferation of the Internet, the spread of personal influence has been accelerated, causing it to evolve into a "viral marketing" phenomena that business cannot afford to ignore.[26] In fact, viral marketing has now become an industry in itself. Dot.com companies like Epinions.com have built their entire businesses and Web sites around customer WOM.[27]

EDITORIAL COVERAGE   Although some media coverage of firms and their services is stimulated by public relations activity, broadcasters and publishers often initiate their own coverage. In addition to news stories about a company and its services, editorial coverage can take several other forms. Investigative reporters may conduct an in-depth study of a company, especially if they believe it is putting customers at risk, cheating them, employing deceptive advertising, or otherwise exploiting them. Some columnists specialize in helping customers who have been unable to get complaints resolved.

Journalists responsible for consumer affairs often contrast and compare service offerings from competing organizations, identifying their strong and weak points, and offering advice on "best buys." In a more specialized context, *ConsumerWise*, the bimonthly publication by The Network for Consumer Protection in Pakistan, periodically evaluates services on a national and global economic basis, voicing the consumer's perspective. The network aims to protect consumer rights and encourage responsible customer behavior.

Ethical Issues in Communication

Few aspects of marketing lend themselves so easily to misuse (and even abuse) as advertising, selling, and sales promotion. The fact that customers often find it hard to evaluate services makes them more dependent on marketing communication for information and advice. Communication messages often include promises about the benefits that customers will receive and the quality of service delivery. When promises are made and then broken, customers are disappointed because their expectations have not been met.[28] Their disappointment and even anger will be even greater if they have wasted money, time, and effort and have no benefits to show in return or have actually suffered a negative impact. Employees, too, may feel disappointed and frustrated as they listen to customers' complaints about unfulfilled expectations.

Some unrealistic service promises result from poor internal communications between operations and marketing personnel concerning the level of service performance that customers can reasonably expect. In other instances, unethical advertisers and salespeople deliberately make exaggerated promises to secure sales. Finally, there are deceptive promotions that lead people to think that they have a much higher chance of winning prizes or awards than is really the case. Fortunately, there are many consumer watchdogs on the lookout for these deceptive marketing practices. They include consumer protection agencies, trade associations within specific industries, and journalists who investigate customer complaints and seek to expose fraud and misrepresentation.

A different type of ethical issue concerns unwanted intrusion by aggressive marketers into people's personal lives. The increase in telemarketing and direct mail is frustrating for those who receive unwanted sales communications. How do you feel if your evening meal at home is interrupted by a telephone call from a stranger trying to interest you in buying services in which you have no interest?

Even if you are interested, you may feel, as many do, that your privacy has been violated. Trade associations like the Direct Marketing of Asia Association (www.dm-asia.org) offer ways for consumers to remove their names from telemarketing and direct mail lists in an attempt to address the growing hostility toward these types of direct marketing techniques.

Branding of Services

Although brand strategy has long been associated primarily with manufactured goods, it is assuming increasing importance in services.[29] "Branding," says Leonard Berry, "plays a special role in service companies because strong brands increase customers' trust of the invisible purchase."[30]

Corporate Brands

Service branding starts with the corporate brand. It's a blend of (1) *the presented brand*, i.e., how the company presents itself through its own controlled communications, (2) *external brand communications*, through nonmarketer controlled channels such as word of mouth and editorial coverage in broadcast and print media, and (3) *brand meaning*, which refers to the customer's perceptions of the brand and the associations that come to mind, not least from personal experience.

Marketing communications plays a key role in creating *brand awareness*, which refers to a consumer's ability to recognize the brand and recall information and associations that distinguish that company from others. A strong and positive brand image is essentially a promise of future satisfaction.

Subbrands

An important trend among many service organizations is to apply branding principles to specific products or processes as a way of both distinguishing a firm's different service offerings and also differentiating each of them from competing alternatives. Typically, the corporate brand serves as an "umbrella" over all the subbrands and is explicitly associated with individual subbrands in advertising or other communications. Singapore Airlines not only brands its business class, which it calls "Raffles Class," but also trademarks such as "SpaceBed," the seat that passengers in that class can transform into a bed when they want to sleep (see Figure 5.11).

The Role of Corporate Design

Many service firms employ a unified and distinctive visual appearance for all tangible elements to facilitate recognition and reinforce a desired brand image. Corporate design strategies are usually created by external consulting firms and include such features as stationery and promotional literature, retail signage, uniforms, and color

Figure 5.11

Singapore Airlines promotes its Raffles Class SpaceBed as "The Biggest Bed in Business Class."

Used by permission of Singapore Airlines.

schemes for painting vehicles, equipment, and building interiors. The objective is to provide a unifying and recognizable theme linking all the firm's operations in a branded service experience through the strategic use of physical evidence.

Corporate design is particularly important for companies operating in competitive markets where it's necessary to stand out from the crowd and to be instantly recognizable in different locations. For example, mobile communications companies in Singapore provide striking contrasts in corporate designs, from SingTel's signature red and white logo, to MobileOne's orange, and StarHub's green hue.

Companies in the highly competitive financial sector tend to use their names as a central element in their corporate designs. When Tai Fook Securities (Hong Kong) wanted to introduce the launch of its new online trading service Taifook.com, the company felt it was essential that the Web site retain the name of the company without any abbreviations. This would allow simplicity and consistency in terms of branding and implementation of marketing efforts so as to avoid confusion among its customers. The launch included a publicity campaign in print, radio, and television advertisements to generate interest. To attract prospects, Tai Fook sent them direct mail packages bearing the logo of the company that carefully explained the mechanics of online trading so that greater brand association could be established.

Many companies use a trademarked symbol, rather than a name, as their primary logo.[31] The United Overseas Bank is instantly recognizable with its distinctive red five-barred logo in Hong Kong, Singapore, Malaysia, and the Philippines (see Figure 5.12). McDonald's "Golden Arches" is said to be the most widely recognized corporate symbol in the world. However, international companies operating in many countries need to select their designs carefully to avoid conveying a culturally inappropriate message through unfortunate choices of names, colors, or images.

At a very basic level, some companies have succeeded in creating tangible, recognizable symbols to associate with their corporate brand names. Animal motifs are common physical symbols for services. Examples include the lion used by Great Eastern in Singapore, the legendary *garuda* (the half-bird, half-man creature in Balinese mythology) by Garuda Indonesia, and the dragon used in the "InvestHK" campaign (see also Service Perspectives 5.2). Easily recognizable corporate symbols are especially important when services are offered in markets where the local language is not written in Roman script or where a significant proportion of the population is functionally illiterate.

Marketing Communications and the Internet

The Internet is playing an increasingly important role in marketing communication. Perhaps the most remarkable aspect of the Internet is its ubiquity: A Web site hosted

Figure 5.12
The United Overseas Bank's logo is instantly recognizable in Hong Kong, Singapore, Malaysia, and the Philippines.

Service Perspectives 5.2

BRANDING HONG KONG

The program to develop a strategic communications platform for Hong Kong arose from a recommendation of the Commission on Strategic Development, set up to advise the Chief Executive on Hong Kong's long-term development.

The positioning for Hong Kong as Asia's world city was developed following extensive research among business and government leaders in Hong Kong and internationally. The research demonstrated that while Hong Kong was held in high regard internationally, not all audiences had a strong grasp of the factors that have made Hong Kong one of the world's most modern and dynamic cities, with a backdrop of beautiful natural assets.

The core values that underpin the program are–progressive, free, stable, opportunity, and high quality. Hong Kong's attributes, reflected in the core values, are–innovative, cosmopolitan, enterprising, a leader, connected.

The visual identity is designed to communicate Hong Kong's link to an historical and cultural icon. The flowing lines of the dragon also mirror Chinese calligraphy. This dual expression symbolizes a fusion of East and West that characterizes Hong Kong. The dragon's fluid shape imparts a sense of movement and speed and its dynamic and contemporary rendering captures Hong Kong's passion to be daring and innovative (see Figure 5.13).

The brand has gained wide international recognition as a model for location branding, and other cities and countries have sought to learn from Hong Kong's branding experience.

Figure 5.13
The flowing lines and fluid shape of the dragon logo symbolizes a dynamic and innovative Hong Kong.

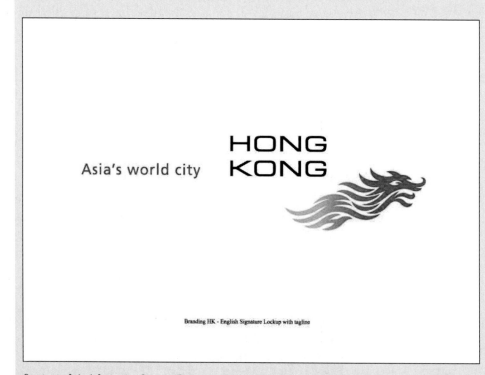

Asia's world city   HONG KONG

Branding HK - English Signature Lockup with tagline

Courtesy of the Information Services Department, Hong Kong Special Administrative Region Government.

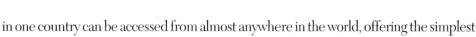

in one country can be accessed from almost anywhere in the world, offering the simplest form of international market entry available. However, creating international access and developing an international strategy are two very different things.

Internet Applications

Marketers use the Internet for a variety of communications tasks. These include promoting consumer awareness and interest, providing information and consultation, facilitating two-way communications with customers through email and chat rooms, stimulating product trial, enabling customers to place orders, and measuring the effectiveness of specific advertising or promotional campaigns.[32] Firms can market through their own Web sites or place advertising on other sites. Advertising on the Web allows companies to supplement conventional communications channels at a reasonable cost. However, like any of the elements of the marketing communications mix, Internet advertising should be part of an integrated, well-designed communications strategy.

The interactive nature of the Internet has the potential to increase customer involvement dramatically, since it enables "self-service" marketing in which individual customers control the nature and extent of their contact with the Web sites they visit. Many banks allow customers to pay bills electronically, apply for loans over the Internet, and check their account balances online. For instance, the Oberoi chain of hotels allows tourists to make online reservations through its Web site (www.oberoihotels.com). The electronic reservation method makes it easier and faster to process requests. The Web site also provides a wealth of information about its locations, facilities, restaurants, and different types of accommodation and rates so that guests can make an informed decision before confirming their stay at the hotel.

Enabling marketers to communicate and establish a rapport with individual customers is one of the Web's greatest strengths. These characteristics lend themselves to a new communication strategy called *permission marketing*,[33] which is based on the idea that traditional advertising doesn't work as well anymore because it fights for attention by interrupting people. For example, a 30-second television spot interrupts a viewer's favorite program, and a telemarketing call interrupts a meal. In the permission marketing model, the goal is to persuade consumers to volunteer their attention. In essence, customers are encouraged to "raise their hands" and agree to learn more about a company and its products in anticipation of receiving information or something else of value to them. This means that customers self-select into the target segment.

Catcha.com and Chinadotcom Corporation agreed to form an email list management alliance based on permission marketing. For an illustration of how this strategy will work effectively for both companies, see Best Practice in Action 5.2.

*Best Practice
in Action 5.2*

PERMISSION MARKETING FOR CHINADOTCOM AND CATCHA.COM

The two companies serve to complement each other's strengths and weaknesses in this e-marketing alliance. Catcha.com is the leading Southeast Asian portal and has an extensive database of diverse users from Singapore, Malaysia, Indonesia, Thailand, and the Philippines. Chinadotcom is an integrated Internet company offering e-business solutions and e-marketing services and it has a new propriety email marketing application called *expresso*. The alliance will enable expresso, whose functions include email fulfillment, tracking, and data mining, to take advantage of Catcha.com's quality database and reach its target audience more effectively.

Expresso will have access to 900,000 permission-based email addresses from the portal's community of users, which allows expresso to target advertisers and marketers with appropriate email marketing campaigns that are adapted to the different languages, cultures, lifestyles, and needs. For Catcha.com, there is the opportunity of enhancing the value of their current list of active Southeast Asian Internet users with expresso's sophisticated profiling and personalization technology.

Source: "Chinadotcom, Catcha.com Form E-Marketing, Sales Alliance," http://in.tech.yahoo.com /010820/8/138fo.html, accessed on May 28, 2004.

Web Site Design Considerations

From a communication standpoint, a Web site should contain information that a company's target customers will find useful and interesting.[34] Internet users expect speedy access, easy navigation, and content that is both relevant and up-to-date.

Service firms should set explicit communication goals for their Web sites. Is the site to be a promotional channel, a self-service option that diverts customers away from contact with service personnel, an automated news room that disseminates information about the company and its products, as well as offering an archive of past press releases, or even all of these? Some firms choose to emphasize promotional content, seeking to present the firm and its products in a favorable light and to stimulate purchase. Others view their sites as educational and encourage visitors to search for needed information, even providing links to related sites.

Innovative companies are continually looking for ways to improve the appeal and usefulness of their sites. The appropriate communication content varies widely from one type of service to another. A business-to-business (B2B) site may offer visitors access to a library of technical information. By contrast, a resort hotel may include attractive photographs featuring the location, the buildings and the guest rooms, and even short videos depicting recreational options.

Marketers must also address other attributes like downloading speed that affect Web site "stickiness."[35] A sticky site is one that encourages repeat visits and purchases by keeping its audience engaged with interactive communication presented in an appealing fashion. A memorable Web address helps to attract visitors to a site. This means displaying the address prominently on business cards, letterhead stationery, catalogs, advertising, promotional materials, and even vehicles.

Internet Advertising

It didn't take long for the Internet to become touted as an important new advertising medium. But after an initial burst of enthusiasm, the volume of online advertising has dropped sharply and so far, the Internet accounts for only a tiny slice of the overall advertising pie. Nevertheless, Web sites can offer advertisers some distinctive advantages.[36]

Many firms pay to place advertising banners and buttons on portals like Yahoo! or Netscape, as well as on other firms' Web sites. The usual goal is to draw online traffic to the advertiser's own site. In many instances, Web sites include advertising messages from other marketers with related but noncompeting services. Yahoo!'s stock quotes page, for example, features a sequence of advertisements for various financial service providers. Similarly, many Web pages devoted to a specific topic feature a small message from Amazon.com, inviting the reader to identify books on these same topics by clicking the accompanying hyperlink button to the Internet retailer's book site. In such instances, it's easy for the advertiser to measure how many visits to its own site are generated by clickthroughs.

However, the Internet has not proven to be as effective an advertising medium as many marketers originally anticipated. Experience shows that simply obtaining a large number of exposures ("eyeballs") to a banner or a skyscraper (a long skinny ad running down one side of a Web site) or a button doesn't necessarily lead to increases in awareness, preference, or sales for the advertiser. One consequence is that the practice of paying a flat monthly rate for banner advertising is falling out of favor. Even when visitors click through to the advertiser's site, this action doesn't necessarily result in sales. Consequently, there's now more emphasis on advertising contracts that tie fees to marketing-relevant behavior by these visitors, such as providing the advertiser with some information about themselves or making a purchase. Today, Internet advertisers usually pay only if a site visitor clicks through on their link. This is the equivalent of paying for the delivery of junk mail only to households that read it.[37]

Some companies use *reciprocal marketing*, where an online retailer allows its paying customers to receive promotions for another online retailer and vice versa, at no up-front cost to either party.[38] In one such promotion, Priceline.com customers received an online coupon offer from Fortress (www.fortress.com.hk), a click-and-mortar electronics store in Hong Kong, when they made a reservation at a specific hotel from their Web site. In exchange, Fortress had a promotional link on its Web site to capture a percentage of that site's customer base.

Conclusion

The marketing communication strategy for services requires a different emphasis from that used to market goods. The communication tasks facing service marketers include emphasizing tangible clues for services that are difficult to evaluate, clarifying the nature and sequence of the service performance, highlighting the performance of customer contact personnel, and educating the customer about how to effectively participate in service delivery.

Many different communication elements are available to help companies create a distinctive position in the market and reach prospective customers. The options in the marketing communications mix include personal communications like personal selling and customer service, as well as impersonal communications like advertising, sales promotions, public relations, corporate design, and the physical evidence offered by the servicescape of the service delivery site. Instructional materials, from brochures to Web sites, often play an important role in educating customers on how to make good choices and obtain the best use from the services they have purchased. Developments in technology, especially the Internet, are changing the face of marketing communications.

Review Questions

1. In what ways do the objectives of services communications differ substantially from those of goods marketing?
2. Which elements of the marketing communications mix would you use for each of the following scenarios? Explain your answers.
   a. A newly established hair salon in a suburban shopping center.
   b. An established restaurant facing declining patronage because of new competitors.
   c. A large, single-office accounting firm in a major city that serves primarily business clients.
3. What roles do personal selling, advertising, and public relations play in (a) attracting new customers to visit a service outlet, and (b) retaining existing customers?
4. Describe the role of personal selling in service communications. Give examples of three different situations where you have encountered this approach.
5. Discuss the relative effectiveness of brochures and Web sites for promoting (a) a ski resort, (b) a business school, (c) a fitness center, and (d) an online broker.
6. Why is word of mouth considered to be so important for the marketing of services? How can a service firm that is the quality leader in its industry induce and manage word of mouth?

Application Exercises

1. Describe four common educational and promotional objectives in service settings, and provide a specific example for each of the objectives you list.
2. Identify one advertisement (or other means of communication) each that aims mainly at managing consumer behavior in the (a) choice, (b) consumption, and (c) postconsumption stage. Explain how they try to achieve their objectives and discuss how effective they may be.
3. Discuss the significance of search, experience, and credence attributes for the communication strategy of a service provider. Assume that the objective of the communication strategy is to attract new customers.
4. Identify an advertisement that runs the risk of attracting mixed segments to a service business. Explain why this may happen, and state what negative consequences, if any, there are likely to be.
5. Analyze several recent public relations efforts made by service firms.

6. What tangible cues could a diving school or a dentist use for up-market positioning?

7. Explore the Web sites of a management consulting firm, an Internet retailer, and an insurance company. Critique them for ease of navigation, content, and visual design. What, if anything, would you change about each site?

Endnotes

1   For a useful review of research on this topic, see Kathleen Mortimer and Brian P. Mathews, "The Advertising of Services: Consumer Views v. Normative Dimensions," *The Service Industries Journal* 18 (July 1998): 14–19.

2   Banwari Mittal, "The Advertising of Services: Meeting the Challenge of Intangibility," *Journal of Service Research* 2 (August 1999): 98–116.

3   Banwari Mittal and Julie Baker, "Advertising Strategies for Hospitality Services," *Cornell Hotel and Restaurant Administration Quarterly* 43 (April 2002): 51–63.

4   William R. George and Leonard L. Berry, "Guidelines for the Advertising of Services," *Business Horizons* (July–August 1981).

5   Donna Legg and Julie Baker, "Advertising Strategies for Service Firms," in *Add Value to Your Service*, ed. C. Surprenant (Chicago: American Marketing Association, 1987), 163–168.

6   Banwari Mittal, "The Advertising of Services: Meeting the Challenge of Intangibility," *Journal of Service Research* 2 (August 1999): 98–116.

7   Legg and Baker, *op. cit*, D.J. Hill and N. Gandhi, "Services Advertising: A Framework for Effectiveness," *Journal of Services Marketing* 3 (Fall 1992): 63–76.

8   David H. Maister, "Why Cross Selling Hasn't Worked," *True Professionalism* (New York: The Free Press, 1997), 178–184.

9   Mary Jo Bitner, "Servicescapes: The Impact of Physical Surroundings on Customers and Employees," *Journal of Marketing* 56 (April 1992): 57–71.

10 Victor L. Hunter and David Tietyen, *Business to Business Marketing: Creating a Community of Customers* (Lincolnwood, IL: NTC Business Books, 1997).

11 Dana James, "Move Cautiously in Trade Show Launch," *Marketing News* (November 20, 2000): 4, 6; Elizabeth Light, "Tradeshows and Expos—Putting Your Business on Show," *Her Business* (March–April 1998): 14–18; and Susan Greco, "Trade Shows versus Face-to-Face Selling," *Inc.* (May 1992): 142.

12 Stephen J. Grove, Gregory M. Pickett, and David N. Laband, "An Empirical Examination of Factual Information Content among Service Advertisements," *The Service Industries Journal* 15 (April 1995): 216–233.

13 "The Future of Advertising: The Harder Hard Sell," *The Economist* (June 24, 2004).

14 *Ibid.*

15 Ken Peattie and Sue Peattie, "Sales Promotion: A Missed Opportunity for Service Marketers," *International Journal of Service Industry Management* 5, no. 1 (1995): 6–21. See also Paul W. Farris and John A. Quelch, "In Defense of Price Promotion," *Sloan Management Review* (Fall 1987): 63–69.

16 "The V-type Recovery of Hong Kong Tourism," *Successful Marketing*, issue 2 (2004).

17 Harvir S. Bansal and Peter A. Voyer, "Word-of-Mouth Processes within a Services Purchase Decision Context," *Journal of Service Research* 3, no. 2 (November 2000): 166–177.

18 Anna S. Mattila and Jochen Wirtz, "The Impact of Knowledge Types on the Consumer Search Process: An Investigation in the Context of Credence Services," *International Journal of Research in Service Industry Management* 13, no. 3 (2002): 214–230.

19 Kim Harris and Steve Baron, "Consumer-to-Consumer Conversations in Service Settings," *Journal of Service Research* 6, no. 3 (2004): 287–303.

[20]   Frederick F. Reichheld, "The One Number You Need to Grow," *Harvard Business Review* 81, no. 12 (2003): 46–55.

[21]   Jochen Wirtz and Patricia Chew, "The Effects of Incentives, Deal Proneness, Satisfaction and Tie Strength on Word-of-Mouth Behavior," *International Journal of Service Industry Management* 13, no. 2 (2002): 141–162.

[22]   Barak Libai, Eyal Biyalogorsky, and Eitan Gerstner, "Setting Referral Fees in Affiliate Marketing," *Journal of Service Research* 5, no. 4 (2003): 303–315.

[23]   Eugene W. Anderson, "Customer Satisfaction and Word of Mouth," *Journal of Service Research* 1 (August 1998): 5–17; Magnus Söderlund, "Customer Satisfaction and Its Consequences on Customer Behaviour Revisited: The Impact of Different Levels of Satisfaction on Word of Mouth, Feedback to the Supplier, and Loyalty, *International Journal of Service Industry Management*, 9, no. 2 (1998): 169–188; Srini S. Srinivasan, Rolph Anderson, and Kishore Ponnavolu, "Customer Loyalty in e-Commerce: An Exploration of Its Antecedents and Consequences," *Journal of Retailing* 78, no. 1 (2002): 41–50.

[24]   Dwayne D. Gremler, Kevin P. Gwinner, and Stephen W. Brown, "Generating Positive Word-of-Mouth Communication through Customer-Employee Relationships," *International Journal of Service Industry Management* 12, no. 1 (2000): 44–59.

[25]   Jeffrey G. Blodgett, Kirk L. Wakefield, and James H. Barnes, "The Effects of Customer Service on Consumers' Complaining Behavior," *Journal of Services Marketing* 9, no. 4 (1995): 31–42; Jeffrey G. Blodgett, and Ronald D. Anderson, "A Bayesian Network Model of the Consumer Complaint Process," *Journal of Service Research* 2, no. 4 (May 2000): 321–338.

[26]   Sandeep Krishnamurthy, "Viral Marketing: What Is It and Why Should Every Service Marketer Care?" *Journal of Services Marketing* 15 (2001):422–424.

[27]   Renee Dye, "The Buzz on Buzz," *Harvard Business Review* (November–December 2000): 139–146.

[28]   Louis Fabien, "Making Promises: The Power of Engagement," *Journal of Services Marketing* 11, no. 3 (1997): 206–214.

[29]   Woo Gon Kim and Hong-Bumm Kim, "Measuring Customer-Based Restaurant Brand Equity: Investigating the Relationship between Brand Equity and Firm's Performance," *Cornell Hotel and Restaurant Administration Quarterly* 45, no. 2 (2004): 115–131.

[30]   Leonard L. Berry, "Cultivating Service Brand Equity," *Journal of the Academy of Marketing Science* 28, no. 1 (2000): 128–137.

[31]   Abbie Griffith, "Product Decisions and Marketing's Role in New Product Development," in *Marketing Best Practices* (Orlando, FL: The Dryden Press, 2000), 253.

[32]   J. William Gurley, "How the Web Will Warp Advertising," *Fortune* (November 9, 1998): 119–120.

[33]   Seth Godin and Don Peppers, *Permission Marketing: Turning Strangers into Friends and Friends into Customers* (New York: Simon & Schuster, 1999).

[34]   Donald Emerick, Kim Round, and Susan Joyce, *Web Marketing and Project Management* (Upper Saddle River, NJ: Prentice Hall, 2000), 27–54.

[35]   Gary A. Poole, "The Riddle of the Abandoned Shopping Cart," *grok* (December 2000–January 2001): 76–82. See also Donald Emerick, Kim Round, and Susan Joyce, *Web Marketing and Project Management*, (Upper Saddle River, NJ: Prentice Hall, 2000), 212-213.

[36]   Heather Green and Ben Elgin, "Do e-Ads Have a Future?" *BusinessWeek E.Biz*, (January 22, 2001): EB44–49.

[37]   "The Future of Advertising: The Harder Hard Sell," *The Economist* (June 24, 2004).

[38]   Dana James, "Don't Wait—Reciprocate," *Marketing News* (November 20, 2000): 13, 17.

CHAPTER SIX

Pricing and Revenue Management

What is a cynic? A man who knows the price of everything and the value of nothing.

OSCAR WILDE

I am waiting for a good price for my talents.

CONFUCIUS, CHINESE ANCIENT PHILOSOPHER

Have you noticed what a wide variety of terms service organizations use to describe the *prices* they set? Universities talk about *tuition*, professional firms collect *fees*, banks charge *interest* and *service charges*, brokers take *commissions*, some expressways impose *tolls*, utilities set *tariffs*, and insurance companies determine *premiums*—the list goes on.

A key goal of an effective pricing strategy is to manage revenues in ways that support the firm's profitability objectives. To do this, a firm has to have a good understanding of its costs, the value created for customers, and competitors' pricing. This sounds straightforward, but is a real challenge for services firms, where unit costs may be difficult to determine and fixed costs difficult to allocate appropriately across multiple service offerings. Value to customers usually varies widely between segments and even within the same segment across time. To complicate matters, demand fluctuates widely, while capacity tends to be relatively fixed. In addition, competitor pricing cannot be compared dollar for dollar with a firm's pricing, as services are often location and time specific.

In this chapter, we review the role of pricing in services marketing and provide some guidelines on how to develop an effective pricing strategy. Specifically, we address the following questions:

1. What are three main approaches to pricing a service?

2. Why is cost-based pricing so challenging for many service firms, and how can activity-based costing improve service costing?
3. What are the key strategies for increasing net value to customers? How are non-monetary costs related to the net value of services?
4. Under what circumstances are service markets less price competitive?
5. How can revenue management drastically improve profitability? And how can we charge different prices to different segments without customers feeling cheated?
6. What are the seven questions marketers need to answer when designing an effective pricing schedule?

Effective Pricing Is Central to Financial Success

Marketing is the only function that brings revenues into the organization. All other management functions incur costs. Pricing is the mechanism by which sales are transformed into revenues. In many service industries, pricing was traditionally driven by a financial and accounting perspective, which often used cost-plus pricing. Price schedules were often tightly constrained by government regulatory agencies—and some still are. Today, however, most service businesses enjoy significant freedom in setting prices and have a good understanding of value-based and competitive pricing. These developments have led to creative pricing schedules and sophisticated yield management systems.

Pricing is typically more complex in services than it is in manufacturing. Because there is no ownership of services, it is usually harder for managers to determine the financial costs of creating a process or performance for a customer, compared to identifying the costs associated with creating and distributing a physical good. The inability to inventory services places a premium on bringing demand and supply into balance, a task in which pricing has a key role to play. The importance of the time factor in service delivery means that speed of delivery and avoidance of waiting time often increase value. With the increase in value, customers are prepared to pay a higher price for the service.

What does a marketing perspective bring to pricing? Effective pricing strategies seek to enhance (or even maximize) the level of revenues, often by discriminating between different market segments based on their value perceptions and ability to pay, and between different time periods based on variations in demand levels over time.

Objectives and Foundations for Setting Prices

Any pricing strategy must be based on a clear understanding of a company's pricing objectives. The most common pricing objectives are related to revenue and profits, and to patronage, market share, and market penetration (see Table 6.1).

Revenue and Profit Objectives

- Seek profit
  - Make the largest possible contribution or profit.
  - Achieve a specific target level, but do not seek to maximize profits.
  - Maximize revenue from a fixed capacity by varying prices and target segments over time, typically using yield or revenue management systems.
- Cover costs
  - Cover fully allocated costs (including institutional overhead).
  - Cover costs of providing one particular service (after deducting any specific uniquely attributable costs to that service).
  - Cover incremental costs of selling one extra unit or to one extra customer.

Patronage and User Base–Related Objectives

- Build demand
  - Maximize demand (when capacity is not a constraint), subject to achieving a certain minimum level of revenues.
  - Achieve full capacity utilization, especially when high capacity utilization adds to the value created for all customers (e.g., a "full-house" adds excitement to a theater play or basketball game).
- Build a user base
  - Stimulate trial and adoption of a service. This is especially important for new services with high infrastructure costs, and for membership-type services that generate significant revenues from their continued usage after adoption (e.g., mobile phone service subscriptions or life insurance plans).
  - Build market share and/or a large user base, especially if there are significant economies of scale that can lead to a competitive cost advantage (e.g., if development or fixed costs are high).

Revenue and Profit Objectives

Within certain limits, profit-seeking firms aim to maximize long-term revenue, contribution, and profits. Perhaps top management is eager to reach a particular landmark financial target or seeks a specific percentage return on investment. Revenue targets may be broken down by division, geographic unit, type of service, and even by key customer segments. This practice requires prices to be set based on a good knowledge of costing, competition, and price elasticity of the market and value perceptions, all of which we will discuss later in this chapter.

In capacity-constrained organizations, financial success is often a function of ensuring optimal use of productive capacity at any given time. Hotels, for instance, seek to fill their rooms, since an empty room is an unproductive asset. Similarly, professional firms want to keep their staff members occupied. Thus, when demand is low, such organizations may offer special discounts to attract additional business. Conversely, when demand exceeds capacity, these types of businesses may increase their prices and focus on segments that are willing to pay higher amounts. We will discuss these practices in detail in the section on revenue management.

Patronage and User Base–Related Objectives

In some instances, maximizing patronage, subject to achieving a certain minimum level of profits, may be more important than profit maximization. Getting a full house in a theater, sports stadium, or race track usually creates excitement that enhances the customer's experience. It also creates an image of success that serves to attract new patrons.

New services, in particular, often have trouble attracting customers. Yet, in order to create the impression of a successful launch and to enhance the image of the firm, it is important that the firm is seen to be attracting a good volume of business from the right types of customers. Introductory price discounts are often used to stimulate trial and sign up customers, sometimes in combination with promotional activities such as contests and giveaways.

In industries with membership relationships and/or where heavy infrastructure investments have to be made (e.g., mobile phone or broadband services), it is often important to get a critical mass of users fast. Market leadership often means low cost per user, and it generates sufficient revenue for future investments like upgrading technology and infrastructure. As a result, penetration pricing is often used in such industries. For example, Hong Kong media network provider Television Broadcast Limited, commonly referred to as TVB, tried to encourage subscription of its sports channel by offering a promotional subscription rate of HK$199 (US$25.50) per month and free gifts for new subscribers (see Figure 6.1) during the UEFA Euro 2004.

Foundations for Setting Prices

The foundations underlying pricing strategy can be described as a tripod, with costs to the provider, competition, and value to the customer as the three legs (see Figure 6.2). The costs that a firm needs to recover usually impose a minimum price, or floor, for a specific service offering, and the customer's perceived value of the offering sets a maximum, or ceiling. The price charged by competitors for similar or substitute services typically determines where, within the floor-to-ceiling range, the price can be set. The pricing objectives of the organization then determine where actual prices should be set given the feasible range provided by the pricing tripod analysis. Let's look at each leg of the pricing tripod in more detail in the next three sections.

Cost-Based Pricing

It's usually harder to establish the costs involved in producing an intangible performance than it is to identify the labor, materials, machine time, storage, and shipping costs associated with producing a physical good. Yet without a good understanding of costs, how can managers price at levels sufficient to yield a desired

Figure 6.1

There is plenty to cheer about for UEFA Euro 2004 besides the hot favorites soccer players, as TVB offers discounted subscription rate for the sports channel and free gifts for everyone to join in the Euro 2004 fever.

profit margin? Because of the labor and infrastructure needed to create performances, many service organizations have a much higher ratio of fixed costs to variable costs than is found in manufacturing firms.

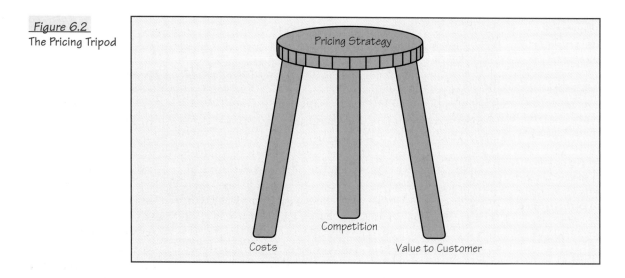

Figure 6.2
The Pricing Tripod

Establishing the Cost of Service

In Management Memo 6.1, we explain how service costs can be estimated, using fixed, semivariable, and variable costs, as well as how the notions of contribution and break-even analysis can help in pricing decisions. These traditional cost-accounting approaches work well for service firms with significant variable costs and/or semivariable costs (e.g., many professional services). For complex product lines with shared infrastructure (e.g., retail banking products), it may be worthwhile considering the more complex activity-based costing (ABC) approach.

ACTIVITY-BASED COSTING A growing number of organizations have reduced their dependence on traditional cost-accounting systems and developed activity-based cost (ABC) management systems, which recognize that virtually all activities taking place within a firm directly or indirectly support the production, marketing, and delivery of goods and services. Moreover, ABC systems link resource expenses to the variety and complexity of products produced, not only to the physical volume. An activity is a set of tasks that combine to compose the processes needed to create and deliver the service. Each step in a flowchart constitutes an activity with which costs can be associated. This approach makes ABC ideally suited for use in a service organization.

If implemented well, the ABC approach yields reasonably accurate cost information about service business activities and processes, and about the costs of creating specific types of services, performing activities in different locations (even different countries), or serving specific customers.[1] The net result is a management tool that can help companies to pinpoint the profitability of different services, channels, market segments, and individual customers.[2]

It is essential to distinguish between those activities that are mandatory for operation within a particular service business and those that are discretionary. The

Management Memo 6.1

UNDERSTANDING COSTS, CONTRIBUTION, AND BREAK-EVEN ANALYSIS

Fixed costs—sometimes referred to as overheads—are those economic costs that a supplier would continue to incur (at least in the short run) even if no services were sold. These costs are likely to include rent, depreciation, utilities, taxes, insurance, salaries and wages for managers and long-term employees, security, and interest payments.

Variable costs refer to the economic costs associated with serving an additional customer, such as making an additional bank transaction, or selling an additional seat on a flight. In many services, such costs are very low. For instance, there is very little labor or fuel cost involved in transporting an extra passenger on a flight. In a theater, the cost of seating an extra patron is close to zero. More significant variable costs are associated with such activities as serving food and beverages, or installing new parts when undertaking repairs, since they include provision of often costly physical products in addition to labor. Just because a firm has sold a service at a price that exceeds its variable cost doesn't mean that the firm is now profitable, for there are still fixed and semivariable costs to be recouped.

Semivariable costs fall in between fixed and variable costs. They represent expenses that rise or fall in a stepwise fashion as the volume of business increases or decreases respectively. Examples include adding an extra flight to meet increased demand on a specific air route or hiring a part-time employee to work in a restaurant on busy weekends.

Contribution is the difference between the variable cost of selling an extra unit of service and the money received from the buyer of that service. It goes to cover fixed and semivariable costs before creating profits.

Determining and allocating economic costs can be a challenging task in some service operations because of the difficulty of deciding how to assign fixed costs in a multiservice facility, such as a hospital. For instance, there are certain fixed costs associated with running the casualty department in a hospital. But beyond that, there are fixed costs for running the hospital of which it is a part. How much of the hospital's fixed costs should be allocated to the casualty department? A hospital manager might use one of several approaches to calculate the casualty department's share of overheads. These could include (1) the percentage of total floor space that it occupies, (2) the percentage of employee hours or payroll that it accounts for, or (3) the percentage of total patient contact hours involved. Each method is likely to yield a totally different fixed-cost allocation. One method might show the casualty ward to be very profitable, while the other might make it seem like a big loss-making operation.

Break-even analysis. Managers need to know at what sales volume a service will become profitable. This is called the break-even point. The necessary analysis involves dividing the total fixed and semivariable costs by the contribution obtained on each unit of service. For instance, if a 100-room hotel needs to cover fixed and semivariable costs of US$2 million a year, and the average contribution per room night is US$100, then the hotel will need to sell 20,000 room nights per year out of a total annual capacity of 36,500. If prices are cut by an average of US$20 per room night (*or* variable costs rise by US$20), then the contribution will drop to US$80 and the hotel's break-even volume will rise to 25,000 room nights. The required sales volume needs to be related to *price sensitivity* (Will customers be willing to pay this much?), *market size* (Is the market large enough to support this level of patronage after taking competition into account?), and *maximum capacity* (the hotel in our example has a capacity of 36,500 room nights per year, assuming no rooms are taken out of service for maintenance or renovation).

traditional approach to cost control often results in a reduction of the value generated for customers, because the activity that is being pruned back is, in fact, mandatory for providing a certain level and quality of service. For instance, many firms have created marketing problems for themselves when they try to save money by firing large numbers of customer service employees. However, this strategy has boomeranged in those situations where it resulted in a rapid decline in service levels that spurred discontented customers to take their business elsewhere. For more details on ABC, see Management Memo 6.2.

Pricing Implications of Cost Analysis

Companies seeking to make a profit must set a price sufficiently high to recover the full costs of producing and marketing a service, and then add a sufficient margin to yield the desired level of profit at the predicted sales volume. Service businesses with high fixed costs include those with expensive physical facilities (such as a hospital or a college), a fleet of vehicles (such as an airline or a trucking company), or a network (such as a telecommunications company, a railroad, or a gas pipeline). For such services, the variable costs of serving one extra customer may be minimal.

Under these conditions, managers may feel that they have tremendous pricing flexibility and it is tempting to set a very low price for a service in order to make an extra sale. Some firms promote *loss leaders*, which are services sold at less than full cost to attract customers, who will then be tempted to buy profitable service offerings from the same organization in the future. However, there will be no profit at the end of the year unless all relevant costs have been recovered. Many service businesses have gone bankrupt because they ignored this fact. Hence, firms that compete on the basis of low prices need to have a very good understanding of their cost structure and of the sales volume needed to break even at particular prices.

Ideally, all activities and costs incurred create value for customers. Managers need to move beyond seeing costs from just an accounting perspective. Rather, they should view costs as an integral part of the company's efforts to create value for its customers. Carù and Cugini clarify the limitations of traditional cost measurement systems, and recommend relating the costs of any given activity to its value generated:

> Costs have nothing to do with value, which is established by the market and, in the final analysis, by the degree of customer acceptance. The customer is not interested a priori in the cost of a product … but in its value and price …
>
> Management control which limits itself to cost monitoring without interesting itself in value is completely one-sided … The problem of businesses is not so much

Management
Memo 6.2

ACTIVITY-BASED COSTING

Traditional cost systems provide useful data for pricing purposes when a single operation creates one homogeneous product for customers who behave in broadly similar ways. However, when service businesses experience considerable variability in both inputs and outputs, it is unrealistic to assign the same proportion of indirect and support costs to each unit of output. Customers, too, often vary in the demands they place upon the firm.

Costs are not intrinsically fixed or variable, argue Cooper and Kaplan:

> Different products, brands, customers, and distribution channels make tremendously different demands on a company's resources .... ABC analysis enables managers to slice the business into many different ways—by product or group of similar products, by individual customer or client group, or by distribution channel—and gives them a close up view of whatever slice they are considering. ABC analysis also illuminates exactly what activities are associated with that part of the business and how those activities are linked to the generation of revenues and the consumption of resources.

Instead of focusing on expense categories, ABC analysis begins with the identification of the different activities being performed and then determines the cost of each activity as it relates to each expense category. When managers segregate activities in this way, a cost hierarchy emerges, reflecting the level at which the cost is incurred. For instance, unit-level activities need to be performed for every unit of service produced (e.g., rotating the tires on a customer's car at a service garage), whereas batch-level activities are those that have to be performed for each batch or setup of work performed (e.g., periodically maintaining the equipment needed for tire rotation).

Other activities provide the overall capability that enables the company to produce a given type of service (e.g., establishing performance standards for tire rotation) to support customers (e.g. account management) and product lines (e.g., advertising), or to sustain facilities (e.g., building maintenance and insurance). Expenses are attached to each activity based on estimates by employees of how they divide up their time among different tasks and what percentage of other resources (e.g., electricity consumption) is being consumed by each activity.

In short, the ABC hierarchy provides a structured way of thinking about the relationship between activities and the resources that they consume. A key question is whether each enumerated activity actually adds customer value to the services that the firm is selling.

Determining customer profitability is a key issue for many businesses. Traditional cost analysis tends to result in loading the same overhead costs on all customers, leading to the assumption that larger purchasers are more profitable. By contrast, ABC analysis can pinpoint differences in the costs of serving different customers, not only by identifying the types of activity associated with each customer, but also by determining the amount of each activity demanded. For instance, a customer who buys in large volumes, but who is extremely demanding in terms of the amount and level of support required may, in fact, prove to be less profitable than a small customer who requires little support.

Sources: Robin Cooper and Robert S. Kaplan, "Profit Priorities from Activity-Based Costing," *Harvard Business Review* (May–June, 1991); Robert S. Kaplan, "Introduction to Activity-Based Costing," Note #9-197-076, (Boston: Harvard Business School Publishing, 1997); and Jerold L. Zimmerman, *Accounting for Decision Making and Control,* 3rd ed. (New York: McGraw-Hill, 2000).

that of cost control as it is the separation of value activities from other activities. The market only pays for the former. Businesses which carry out unnecessary activities are destined to find themselves being overtaken by competitors which have already eliminated these.[3]

Value-Based Pricing

No customer will pay more for a service than he or she thinks it is worth. So marketers need to understand how customers perceive service value in order to set an appropriate price. Smith and Nagle emphasize the importance of understanding the monetary worth of the incremental value created by a service, a task that often requires extensive marketing research, especially in business-to-business markets.[4] For example, in April 2004, MoneyGram Payment Systems Inc. introduced a simple value-pricing system for money transfers sent from Taiwan to China. The new pricing strategy is an extension of MoneyGram's commitment to providing people with affordable, reliable, and convenient money transfer service worldwide. MoneyGram Payment System allows customers to use its services to remit funds to their family and friends in China in about ten minutes for a fee starting from US$30.

Understanding Net Value

When customers purchase a service, they are weighing the perceived benefits obtained from the service against the perceived costs they will incur. Recognizing the different tradeoffs that customers are willing to make between these various costs, service companies sometimes create several levels of service. For example, airlines and hotel chains often provide multiple classes of service, offering customers the option of paying more in exchange for additional benefits. The essential tradeoff for people choosing to stay in a low-price airline such as AirAsia is that they must renounce the greater physical comfort and many value-enhancing supplementary services to be found in, say, Malaysian Airlines that charges a higher price. Similarly, a company purchasing the "silver" level of hardware and software support from Wipro Technologies cannot count on the same speed of response, hours of service, and additional benefits offered to "platinum" customers.

Research by Valarie Zeithaml suggests that customer definitions of value may be highly personal and idiosyncratic. Four broad expressions of value emerged from her study: (1) value is low price, (2) value is whatever I want in a product, (3) value is the quality I get for the price I pay, and (4) value is what I get for what I give.[5] In this book, we base our definition of value on this fourth category and use the term *net value*, which is defined as the sum of all the perceived benefits (gross value) minus the sum of all the perceived costs of service (Figure 6.3). The greater the positive difference between the two, the greater the net value. Economists use the

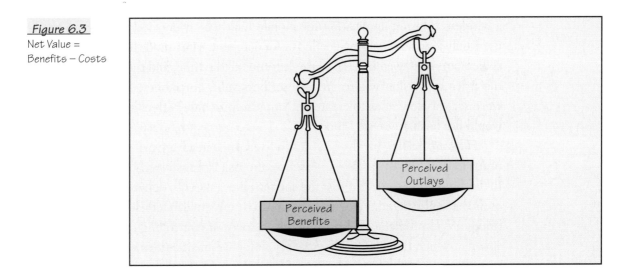

Figure 6.3
Net Value =
Benefits – Costs

term *consumer surplus* to define the difference between the price customers pay and the amount they would actually have been willing to pay to obtain the desired benefits (or "utility") offered by a specific product. When customers evaluate competing services, they are basically comparing the relative net values.

Enhancing Gross Value

Hermann Simon, an international consultant, argues that service pricing strategies are often unsuccessful because they lack any clear association between price and value.[6] As discussed in Chapter 4, a marketer can increase the gross value of a service by adding benefits to the core product and by enhancing supplementary services. There are four distinct but related strategies for capturing and communicating the value of a service: uncertainty reduction, relationship enhancement, low-cost leadership, and value perception management.[7]

PRICING STRATEGIES TO REDUCE UNCERTAINTY   If customers are unsure about how much value they will receive from a particular service, they may remain with a supplier they already know or not purchase at all. Possible ways, individually or in combination, to reduce this uncertainty, include benefit-driven pricing and flat-rate pricing.

Benefit-driven pricing involves pricing that aspect of the service that directly benefits customers (requiring marketers to research what aspects of the service their customers value most and what aspects they value least.) For instance, prices for online information services are often based on log-on time, but what customers really value is the information that is browsed and retrieved. Poorly designed Web sites often waste customers' time because they are difficult to navigate and make it hard for users to find what they are looking for. The result is that pricing and value creation are out of sync. When NTT DoCoMo set the pricing strategy for i-mode, a wireless Internet application for mobile handsets, it decided to charge i-mode users only for what they downloaded or for data sent. The i-mode technology allowed subscribers to stay connected to the Internet all the time, and the rationale behind the pricing decision was to give subscribers value for money. Even then, prices were set very low so as to create an "impulse purchase" effect so that subscribers would not hesitate to use i-mode.

Flat-rate pricing involves quoting a fixed price in advance of service delivery in order to avoid any surprises. In essence, the risk is transferred from the customer to the supplier in the event that the service takes longer to deliver or involves more costs than anticipated. Flat-rate pricing can be effective in industries where service prices are unpredictable and suppliers are poor at controlling their costs and the speed at which they work. They are also effective in situations where competitors make low estimates to win business, but subsequently claim that they were only giving an estimate, not making a firm pricing commitment. See Service Perspectives 6.1 for more information on the flat-rate pricing strategy adopted by Thailand's cellular phone operators.

Service Perspectives 6.1

AIS'S NATIONWIDE FLAT-RATE PROMOTION

Thailand's largest cellular phone operator, Advanced Info Service (AIS), recently launched a nationwide flat-rate promotion, joining the trend started by its rival DTAC. The company aims to increase its market share and encourage adoption through its four flat-rate promotional packages. For the first package, subscribers would only need to pay a monthly fee of Bt300 to enjoy a nationwide flat-rate of Bt3 (US$0.074) per minute on all calls, regardless of which part of Thailand they made the calls from.

For the other three packages, subscribers would pay a monthly fee and receive fixed hours of free airtime. Besides that, the subscribers can enjoy a Bt2 per minute nationwide flat rate for all subsequent calls. The amount of airtime that consumers are entitled to depends on their monthly subscription charges, which ranges from Bt700 to Bt2,000. Under the previous GSM Advanced pricing plan, consumers were charged Bt3, Bt8 and Bt12 per minute, depending on where in the country the calls were made.

AIS also waived the Bt100 subscription charges for its "One Love One Number" promotion that features a Bt1 per minute nationwide flat rate. DTAC, Thailand's second largest cellular phone operator, was the first to introduce the flat-rate charges and newcomer TA Orange also adopts a similar pricing strategy.

Source: Adapted from "AIS Launches Nationwide Flat-Rate Promotion," *The Nation* (Thailand), August 2, 2002.

RELATIONSHIP PRICING   How does pricing strategy relate to developing and maintaining long-term customer relationships? Discounting to win new business is not the best approach if a firm is seeking to attract customers who will remain loyal. Research indicates that those who are attracted by cut-price offers can easily be enticed away by another offer from a competitor.[8] More creative strategies focus on giving customers both price and nonprice incentives to consolidate their business with a single supplier. A strategy of discounting prices for large purchases can often be profitable for both parties, since the customer benefits from lower prices, while the supplier may enjoy lower variable costs resulting from economies of scale. An alternative to volume discounting on a single service is for a firm to offer its customers discounts when two or more services are purchased together. The greater the number of different services a customer purchases from a single supplier, the closer the relationship is likely to be. A close relationship allows the firm to learn more about the customer and improve and customize its service, and it is more inconvenient for the customer to shift its business elsewhere. For example, according to International Data Corp (IDC), broadband service providers in Hong Kong were moving toward more innovative pricing models, such as bundling and cross-selling multiple services, as prices for access services were falling sharply in Hong Kong.[9]

LOW-COST LEADERSHIP   Low-priced services appeal to customers who are on a tight financial budget. They may also lead purchasers to buy in larger volumes. One challenge when pricing low is to convince customers that they should not equate price with quality. Rather, they must feel they are getting good value. A second challenge is to ensure that economic costs are kept low enough to enable the firm to make a profit. Some service businesses have built their entire strategy around being the low-cost leader. An example of a low-cost leader in the airline business is AirAsia, whose low fares compete with the prices of bus, train, or car travel. AirAsia has adopted a similar strategy to Southwest Airlines' low-cost operations strategy which has been studied by airlines all over the world. The other budget airlines in Asia that have imitated this successful formula are Lion Mentari Airlines, Mandala Airlines and ValuAir.

MANAGING THE PERCEPTION OF VALUE   Value is subjective, and few customers are expert enough to truly appreciate and assess the quality and value they receive. This is true in particular for credence services, where customers cannot assess the quality of a service even after consumption.[10] The invisibility of necessary backstage facilities and labor makes it hard for customers to see what they are getting for their money. Consider a homeowner who calls an electrician to repair a defective circuit. The electrician arrives, carrying a small bag of tools. He then disappears into the closet where the circuit board is located, soon locates the problem, replaces a defective circuit breaker, and presto! Everything works. A mere 20 minutes has elapsed. A few days later, the homeowner is horrified to receive a bill for US$90, most of it for labor charges.

Just think what the couple could have bought for that amount of money. What they fail to think of are all the fixed costs that the owner of the business needs to recoup: the office, telephone, insurance, vehicles, tools, fuel, and office support staff. The variable costs of the visit are also higher than they appear. To the 20 minutes spent at the house must be added 15 minutes of driving each way, plus five minutes each to unload and reload needed tools and supplies from the van, thus effectively tripling the labor time to a total of 60 minutes devoted to this call. And, the firm still has to add a margin in order to make a profit.

Not surprisingly, customers are often left feeling that they have been exploited. Hence, effective communications and even personal explanations are needed to help customers recognize and appreciate the value they receive. Similarly, marketers of high-end credence services must find ways to powerfully communicate the time, research, professional expertise, and attention to detail that go into, for example, completing a best-practice consulting project.

Knowing that the definition of value is highly subjective, Priceline introduced the "name your own price" feature. Priceline allows its users to name the price that they are willing to pay for a service (e.g. air tickets, hotel rooms, car rental, and tour packages) that were sold through its Web site. This enables customers to pay a price that matches their perceived value. If the service is more expensive than what the customer is willing to pay, he can choose to increase the price or to forgo the deal (see Figure 6.4).

Reducing Related Monetary and Nonmonetary Costs

From a customer's standpoint, the price charged by a supplier is only part of the costs involved in purchasing and using a service. There are other *costs of service*, which are composed of both financial outlays charged by other parties and *nonmonetary* costs.

Among the financial costs of a service are not only the price paid to the supplier, but also the expenses incurred by the customer in searching for, purchasing, and using the service. To give a simple example, the cost of an evening at the movies for a couple with young children usually far exceeds the price of the two tickets, because it can include expenses such as hiring a babysitter, traveling, parking, food, and beverages.

The nonmonetary costs reflect the time, effort, and discomfort associated with search, purchase, and use of a service. Customers sometimes refer to these costs collectively as "effort" or "hassle." These costs tend to be higher when customers are involved in production (which is particularly important in people-processing services and in self-service), where they have to travel to the service site, wait for service, figure out queuing systems and service process, and so on. Services that are high on experience and credence attributes may also create psychological costs, such as anxiety. Nonmonetary costs of service can be grouped into four distinct categories:

- *Time costs* are inherent in service delivery. There is an opportunity cost to customers for the time they are involved in the service delivery process, since

Figure 6.4
Priceline allows consumers to set the price they are willing to pay for a service.

they could spend that time in other ways. Internet users are often frustrated by the amount of time they waste trying to find some particular information on a Web site. Time spent waiting is usually seen as particularly unpleasant, and carries a high perceived cost, often so high, that the customer would rather not buy! In addition, time costs are often incurred when it is inconvenient—working adults, for example, do not want to have to go to a service branch during working hours.

- *Physical costs* (like fatigue or discomfort) may be incurred in obtaining services, especially if customers must go to the service factory, if queuing is involved, and if delivery entails self-service.

- *Psychological costs* like mental effort, perceived risk, cognitive dissonance, feelings of inadequacy, or fear are sometimes attached to buying and using a particular service.

- *Sensory costs* relate to unpleasant sensations affecting any of the five senses. In a service environment, these costs may include putting up with noise, unpleasant smells, drafts, excessive heat or cold, uncomfortable seating, visually unappealing environments, and even nasty tastes.

As shown in Figure 6.5, consumers can incur costs during any of the three stages of a purchase process, and therefore firms have to consider (1) *search costs*, (2) *purchase and usage costs*, and (3) *postconsumption* or *aftercosts*.

From a managerial perspective, it makes great sense to minimize those nonmonetary and related monetary costs to increase consumer value. Possible approaches include:

- Reducing the time costs involved in service purchase, delivery, and consumption.
- Minimizing unwanted psychological costs of service at each stage by going through the service blueprint and identifying ways to enhance the service experience by cutting or redesigning unpleasant or inconvenient steps in the process.
- Eliminating unwanted physical costs of service that customers may incur, notably during the search and delivery processes.
- Decreasing unpleasant sensory costs of service by creating more attractive visual environments, reducing noise, installing more comfortable furniture and equipment, curtailing offensive smells, and the like.

Figure 6.5
Defining Total
User Costs

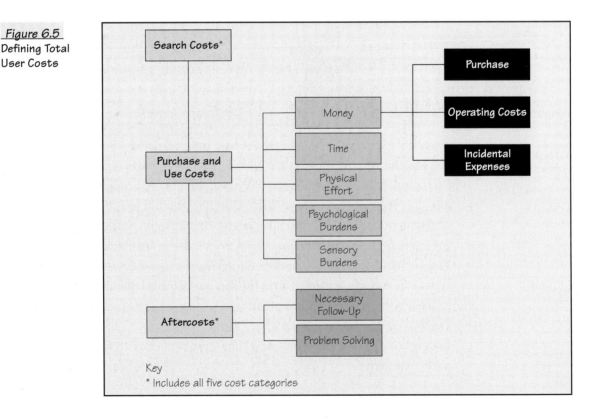

Key
* Includes all five cost categories

- Identifying carefully what other monetary costs consumers incur and specifying ways to reduce them or offering alternatives. For example, banks often require customers to come personally to initiate telegraphic transfers or banker's checks, incurring related travel costs (e.g., transit fares or fuel and parking). Perhaps, the process can be redesigned to be delivered online.

Perceptions of net value may vary widely between customers and from one situation to another for the same customer. One way of segmenting service markets is by sensitivity to time savings and convenience[11] versus sensitivity to price savings. Consider Figure 6.6, which identifies a choice of three clinics available to an individual who needs to obtain a routine chest x-ray. In addition to varying dollar prices for the service, there are different time and effort costs associated with using each service. Depending on the customer's priorities, nonmonetary costs may be as important, or even more important, than the price charged by the service providers.

Competition-Based Pricing

Firms with relatively undifferentiated services need to monitor what competitors are charging and try to price accordingly. When customers see little or no difference between competing offerings, they may just choose what they perceive as the cheapest. In such a situation, the firm with the lowest cost per unit of service enjoys an enviable market advantage and often assumes *price leadership*. Here, one firm acts as the price leader, with others taking their cue from this company. You can sometimes see this phenomenon at the local level when several petrol stations compete within a short distance of one another. As soon as one station raises or lowers its prices, the others follow promptly.

Figure 6.6
Trading Off Monetary and Nonmonetary Costs

Clinic A	Clinic B	Clinic C
• Price $45	• Price $85	• Price $125
• Located one hour away by car or transit	• Located 15 minutes away by car or transit	• Located next to your office building (or college)
• Next available appointment is in three weeks	• Next available appointment is in one week	• Next available appointment is in one day
• Hours: Monday–Friday, 9a.m.–5p.m.	• Hours: Monday–Friday, 8a.m.–10p.m.	• Hours: Monday–Saturday, 8a.m.–10p.m.
• Estimated wait at clinic is about two hours	• Estimated wait at clinic is about 30 to 45 minutes	• By appointment; estimated wait at clinic is about 0 to 15 minutes

Price competition increases with (1) increasing number of competitors, (2) increasing number of substitute offers, (3) wider distribution of competitor and/or substitute offers, and (4) increasing surplus capacity in the industry. Although some service industries can be fiercely competitive (e.g., the airline industry or online banking), many are less so, especially when one or more of the following circumstances reduce price competition:

- *Non-price-related costs of using competing alternatives are high.* When saving time and effort are of equal or greater importance to customers than price in selecting a supplier, the intensity of price competition is reduced.
- *Personalization, customization, and switching costs matter.* In services that are highly personalized and customized, such as hair styling or family medical care, relationships with individual providers are often very important to customers, thus discouraging them from responding to competitive offers. In many other services, switching costs involve time and money, thus reducing the ability of consumers to switch easily between providers and to take advantage of lower-priced competing offers. Cellular phone providers often require one- or two-year contracts from their subscribers, specifying significant financial penalties for early cancellation of service.
- *Time and location specificity reduce choice.* When people want to use a service at a specific location or at a particular time (or perhaps both, simultaneously), they usually find they have fewer options. Many people choose a bank that has an ATM and/or a branch either close to the home or close to the office. How many brands can customers with these preferences choose from? Probably not many. If a business traveler needs to fly from Jakarta direct to Seoul, leaving next Wednesday evening after 8 p.m., then the choice of airlines will be limited. And even then, not all airlines that have suitable flight connections may still have seats available.

Firms that are always reacting to competitors' pricing run the risk of setting prices lower than might really be necessary. Managers should beware of falling into the trap of comparing competitors' prices dollar for dollar, and then seeking to match them. Instead, they should take into account the entire cost to customers of each competitive offering, including all related financial and nonmonetary costs and potential switching costs. They should also assess the impact of distribution, time, and location factors, as well as estimating competitors' available capacity.

Revenue Management

Many service businesses are now focusing on strategies to maximize the revenue (or contribution) that can be derived from available capacity at any given point in time. Revenue management (often also called yield management) is a sophisticated form of supply and demand management. Airlines, hotels, and car rental firms, in particular, have become adept at varying their prices in response to the price sensitivity of different market segments at different times of the day, week, or season. The challenge they face is to capture sufficient customers to fill the available capacity without creating consumer surplus for customers who are willing to pay more.

How Does Revenue Management Work?

RESERVING CAPACITY FOR HIGH-YIELD CUSTOMERS   In practice, revenue management means setting prices according to predicted demand levels among different market segments. The least price-sensitive segment is allocated capacity first at the highest price, followed by the next segment at a lower price, and so on. As higher-paying segments often book closer to the time of actual consumption, firms need a disciplined approach of keeping the capacity free for them instead of simply selling on a first-come-first-serve basis. For example, business travelers often reserve airline seats, hotel rooms, and rental cars at short notice, but vacationers may book leisure travel months in advance. A good revenue management system is able to predict with reasonable accuracy how many customers will want to use a service for a given slot, flight or day at each of several different price levels and "block" the relevant amount of capacity at each level (known as a *price bucket*) in anticipation.

Advanced software has made it possible for firms to use very sophisticated mathematical models in yield management analysis. In the case of an airline, for example, these models integrate massive historical databases on past passenger travel and forecast demand of up to one year in advance for each individual departure. At fixed intervals, the revenue manager will check the actual pace of bookings (i.e., sales at a given time before departure) and compare it with the forecasted pace. Indirectly, this practice picks up competitors' pricing, too. If there are significant deviations between actual and forecasted demand, adjustments to the "price buckets" will be made.

For example, if the booking pace for a higher-paying segment is stronger than expected, additional capacity will be allocated to this segment and taken away from the lowest-paying segment. The objective is to have the flight take off with no seat empty, and each seat sold to the highest-paying segment. Ideally, no higher-paying travelers (e.g., full-fare paying business travelers) are turned away because of "no seats available," and customers are only turned away at the lowest rate on that flight. Best Practice in Action 6.1 illustrates an airline company that has adopted this system.

Revenue management has been most effective when applied to operations that have relatively fixed capacity, a high fixed-cost structure, perishable inventory, demand that is variable and uncertain, and varying customer price sensitivity.

Industries that have successfully implemented revenue management include airlines, car rentals, hotels, and more recently hospitals, restaurants, golf courses, and even nonprofit organizations.[12]

Best Practice in Action 6.1

PRICING SEATS ON FLIGHT AA 2015

Revenue management departments use sophisticated yield management software and powerful computers to forecast, track, and manage each flight on a given date separately. Let's look at American Airlines 2015, a popular flight from Chicago to Phoenix, Arizona, which departs daily at 5:30 p.m. on the 1,370 mile (2,200 km) journey.

The 125 seats in coach (economy class) are divided into seven fare categories, referred to by yield management specialists as "buckets." There is an enormous variation in ticket prices among these seats: round-trip fares range from US$238 for a bargain excursion ticket (with various restrictions and a cancellation penalty attached) all the way up to an unrestricted fare of US$1,404. Seats are also available at an even higher price in the small first-class section. Scott McCartney tells how ongoing analysis by the computer program changes the allocation of seats between each of the seven buckets in economy class:

> In the weeks before each Chicago–Phoenix flight, American's yield management computers constantly adjust the number of seats in each bucket, taking into account tickets sold, historical ridership patterns, and connecting passengers likely to use the route as one leg of a longer trip.
>
> If advance bookings are slim, American adds seats to low-fare buckets. If business customers buy unrestricted fares earlier than expected, the yield management computer takes seats out of the discount buckets and preserves them for last-minute bookings that the database predicts will still show up.
>
> With 69 of 125 coach seats already sold four weeks before one recent departure of Flight 2015, American's computer began to limit the number of seats in lower-priced buckets. A week later, it totally shut off sales for the bottom three buckets, priced US$300 or less. To a Chicago customer looking for a cheap seat, the flight was "sold out" ...
>
> One day before departure, with 130 passengers booked for the 125-seat flight, American still offered five seats at full fare because its computer database indicated ten passengers were likely not to show up or take other flights. Flight 2015 departed full and no one was bumped.

Although AA 2015 for that date is now history, it has not been forgotten. The booking experience for this flight was saved in the memory of the yield management program to help the airline do an even better job of forecasting in the future.

In Asia, most airlines have now implemented revenue management systems. For example, China Southern Airlines implemented the PROS 5 Revenue Optimization System to forecast, manage, and optimize the seating inventory at different fares across its network. As for American Airlines, its system ensures that, with the help of highly trained and experienced analysts, each departure offers the optimal mix of fare class inventory relative to expected demand.

Sources: Scott McCartney, "Ticket Shock: Business Fares Increase Even as Leisure Travel Keeps Getting Cheaper," *Wall Street Journal*, November 3, 1997, A1, A10; *http://www.prosairline.com/news/2001_archive*, accessed in April 2004.

EFFECT OF COMPETITORS' PRICING ON REVENUE MANAGEMENT   Because revenue management systems monitor booking pace, competitor pricing is indirectly picked up. If a firm prices too low, it will experience a higher booking pace, and its cheaper seats fill up quickly. That is generally not good, as it means a higher share of late booking but high-fare-paying customers will not be able to get their seats confirmed, and will therefore fly on competing airlines. If the initial pricing is too high, the firm will get too low a share of early booking segments (which still tend to offer a reasonable yield), and may later have to sell excess capacity last minute at very low prices to still recover some contribution toward its fixed costs.

Price Elasticity

For revenue management to work effectively, we need two or more segments that attach different value to the service and have different price elasticity. To allocate and price capacity effectively, the revenue manager needs to determine how sensitive demand is to price and what net revenues will be generated at different prices for each target segment. The concept of elasticity describes how sensitive demand is to changes in price, and is computed as follows:

$$\text{Price elasticity} = \frac{\text{Percentage change in demand}}{\text{Percentage change in price}}$$

When price elasticity is at "unity," sales of a service rise (or fall) by the same percentage that price falls (or rises). When a small change in price has a big impact on sales, demand for that product is said to be *price elastic*. But when a change in price has little effect on sales, demand is described as *price inelastic*. The concept is illustrated in the simple chart presented in Figure 6.7, which shows the price elasticity for two segments, one with a highly elastic demand (a small change in price results in a big change in the amount demanded), and the other with a highly inelastic demand (even big changes in price have little impact on the amount demanded).

Designing Rate Fences

Inherent in revenue management is the concept of *price customization*—that is, charging different customers different prices for what is, in effect, the same product. As noted by Simon and Dolan,

> The basic idea of price customization is simple: Have people pay prices based on the value they put on the product. Obviously you can't just hang out a sign saying "Pay me what it's worth to you" or "It's $80 if you value it that much but only $40 if you don't." You have to find a way to segment customers by their valuations. In a sense, you have to "build a fence" between high-value customers and low-value customers so the "high" buyers can't take advantage of the low price.[13]

How can a firm ensure that customers for whom the service offers high value are unable to take advantage of lower price buckets? Properly designed rate fences

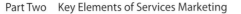

Figure 6.7
Illustrations of
Price Elasticity

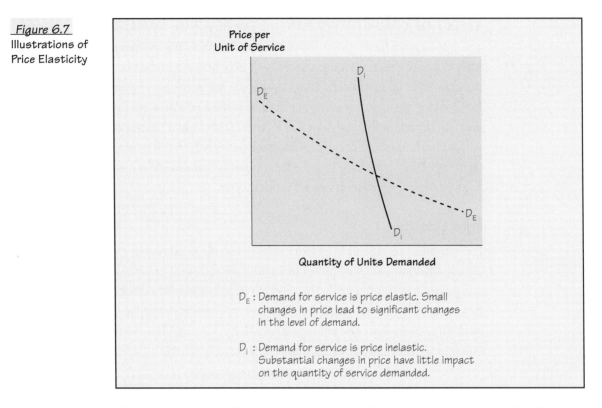

Price per
Unit of Service

Quantity of Units Demanded

D_E : Demand for service is price elastic. Small
changes in price lead to significant changes
in the level of demand.

D_i : Demand for service is price inelastic.
Substantial changes in price have little impact
on the quantity of service demanded.

allow customers to self-segment on the basis of service characteristics and willingness to pay, and help companies to restrict lower prices to customers who are willing to accept certain restrictions on their purchase and consumption experiences.

Fences can be either *physical* or *nonphysical*. Physical fences refer to tangible product differences related to the different prices, such as the seat location in a theater, or the size and furnishing of a hotel room. Nonphysical fences refer to consumption, transaction, or buyer characteristics. For example, they include staying a certain length of time in a hotel, playing golf on a weekday afternoon, cancellation or change penalties, or booking a certain length of time ahead. Examples of common rate fences are shown in Table 6.2.

Physical fences reflect tangible differences in the actual service (e.g., it is a different experience flying first class compared to economy class), whereas nonphysical services actually refer to the same basic service (e.g., there is no difference in service whether a person bought a really cheap economy class ticket over the Internet or whether someone paid full fare for it—both travelers receive the same service product).

In summary, revenue management requires a detailed understanding of customer needs and preferences, and their willingness to pay. With this, the product and revenue manager together can design effective products that consist of the core service, physical product features (physical fences), and nonphysical product features (nonphysical fences). Next, a good understanding of the demand curve is

Rate Fences	Examples
Physical (product-related) Fences	
• Basic product	• Class of travel (business/economy class)
	• Size and furnishing of a hotel room
	• Seat location in a theater
• Amenities	• Free breakfast at a hotel, airport pick up, etc.
	• Free golf cart at a golf course
• Service level	• Priority wait-listing, separate check-in counters with no or only short lines
	• Increase in baggage allowance
	• Dedicated service hotlines
	• Dedicated account management team
Nonphysical Fences	
Transaction Characteristics	
• Time of booking or reservation	• Requirements for advance purchase
	• Must pay full fare two weeks before departure
• Location of booking or reservation	• Passengers booking air tickets for an identical route in different countries are charged different prices
• Flexibility of ticket usage	• Fees/penalties for canceling or changing a reservation (up to loss of entire ticket price)
	• Nonrefundable reservations fees
Consumption Characteristics	
• Time or duration of use	• Early-bird special in a restaurant before 6:00 p.m.
	• Must stay over a Saturday night for an airline, hotel, or car rental booking
	• Must stay for at least five nights
• Location of consumption	• Price depends on departure location, especially in international travel
	• Prices vary by location (between cities, city center versus edges of the city)
Buyer Characteristics	
• Frequency or volume of consumption	• Member of certain loyalty-tier with the firm (e.g., Platinum member) get priority pricing, discounts, or loyalty benefits
• Group membership	• Child, student, senior citizen discounts
	• Affiliation with certain groups (e.g., alumni)
• Size of customer group	• Group discounts based on size of group

Table 6.2
Key Categories of Rate Fences

needed so that "buckets" of inventory can be assigned to the various products and price categories. An example from the airline industry is shown in Figure 6.8.

Ethical Concerns And Perceived Fairness Of Pricing Policies

Customers often have difficulty understanding how much it is going to cost them to use a service, and generally tend to have a bias that selling prices are higher than what would be fair.[14] Moreover, they cannot always be sure in advance what they will receive in return for their payments. Many services are intangible, and it is

Figure 6.8
Relating Price
Buckets to the
Demand Curve

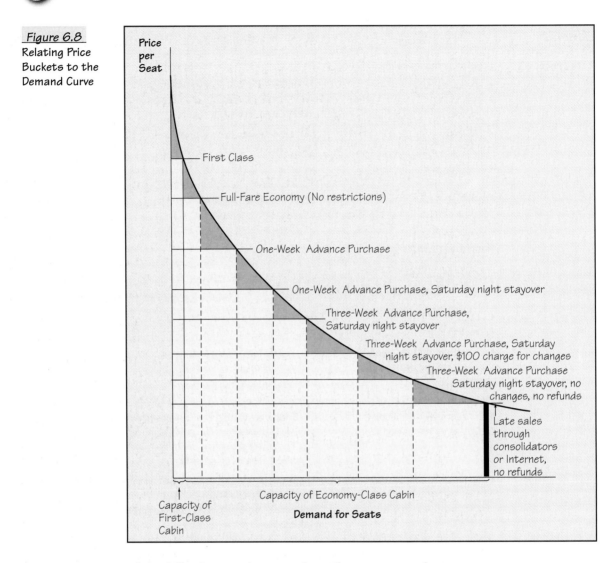

often difficult to evaluate quality. There is an implicit assumption among many customers that a higher-priced service must offer more benefits and greater quality than a lower-priced one. For example, a high-priced professional—say a lawyer—is assumed to be more skilled than one who charges lower fees. Although price can serve as a surrogate for quality, it is sometimes hard to be sure whether the extra value is really there.

Service Pricing Schedules Are Often Complex

Pricing schedules for services tend to be complex, and often cannot be understood and compared across providers without complex spreadsheets or even mathematical formulas. The quoted prices typically used by consumers for price comparisons may be only the first of several expenditures that they will incur. As described in Service Perspectives 6.2, cellular phone service is particularly problematic in this respect.

COMPLEXITY IN CELLULAR PHONE SERVICE PRICING

Deregulation in the Asian telecommunications industry has resulted in a rapid expansion in the availability of mobile communications services. Asia is currently one of the largest mobile markets in the world with over 250 million mobile subscribers in China alone. Research also suggests that the Asia Pacific region will continue to grow, accounting for 60 percent of global growth in mobile telephony over the next six years.

In an effort to tailor their services to the widely varying needs and calling patterns of different market segments, mobile service companies have developed a bewildering array of plans that defy easy comparison across suppliers. Plans can be national, regional, or purely local in scope. Monthly fees also vary according to the number of minutes selected in advance, which typically include separate allowances for peak and off-peak minutes, reflecting the times of day and days of the week when calls are actually made. Overtime minutes and "roaming minutes" on other carriers are charged at higher rates. Some plans allow unlimited off-peak calling, while others allow free incoming calls. Some providers charge calls per second, per six-second blocks or even per minute blocks, resulting in vastly different costs per call. An alternative is prepaid calling, which enables customers to buy a phone and then purchase time as needed.

A study done on the telecommunications industry in Malaysia with respect to the relationship between price, perceived value, and customer satisfaction showed that the lower the perception on value of service, the higher respondents felt the current price was. The perceived value of service also influenced the degree of customer satisfaction to a large extent. Respondents felt that high current prices should go hand in hand with high-service quality, which was not perceived as the case, thus resulting in high levels of customer dissatisfaction. Malaysia's telecommunications service providers can afford to improve service quality, which includes quality of reception, accessible service, comprehensive pricing and billing systems, fewer dropped calls, and better customer service.

Source: Adapted from Hishamudi Ismail and Ali Khatibi, "Study of the Relationship between Perception of Value and Price and Customer Satisfaction: The Case of Malaysian Telecommunications Industry," *Journal of American Academy of Business* 4, issue 1/2 (March 2004): 309.

Many people find it difficult to assess and forecast their own usage profiles accurately, which makes it hard to compute comparative prices when competing suppliers base their fees on a variety of usage-related factors. It is no coincidence that the humorist Scott Adams (best known as the creator of Dilbert) used exclusively service examples when he 'branded' the future of pricing as being "confusopolized." Noting that firms such as telecommunication companies, banks, insurance firms, and other financial service providers offer nearly identical services, he remarks:

> You would think this would create a price war and drive prices down to the cost of providing it (that's what I learned between naps in my economic classes), but it isn't happening. The companies are forming efficient confusopolies so customers can't tell who has the lowest prices. Companies have learned to use the complexities of life as an economic tool.[15]

One of the roles of effective government regulation should be to discourage this tendency for certain service industries to evolve into "confusopolies."

Ethical Concerns, Perceived Fairness, and Trust

Services often invite performance and pricing abuses, especially credence services. When customers don't know what they are getting from the service supplier, aren't present when the work is being performed, and lack the technical skills to know if a good job has been done, they are vulnerable to paying for work that wasn't done, wasn't necessary, or was not well executed.

Complexity of pricing schedules also makes it easy (and perhaps more tempting) for firms to engage in unethical behavior. In Singapore, the proliferation of slimming and beauty salons across the island has resulted in a highly competitive industry. Firms have significantly reduced the prices of beauty treatments, massages, and other services, compared to prices in the past. The price competition has also led to many salons offering price promotions which lead unsuspecting customers to think they are getting a good deal, if they do not clarify the "small print" contract terms. For example, PrettiSlim, a Singapore-based bust enhancement specialist, offers 15 free sessions for *Her World* magazine readers in a special promotion. However, it was stated in a much smaller point size that the free sessions would only be given upon enrollment of ten sessions.[16]

When customers know that they are vulnerable to potential abuse, they tend to become suspicious of both the firm and its employees. This situation complicates the task of promoting and delivering service excellence.

In a revenue management context, the overdependence on the output of computer models can easily lead to pricing strategies that are full of rules and regulations, cancellation penalties, and a cynical strategy of overbooking without thought for disappointed customers who believed they had a firm reservation. Revenue management needs to be implemented whereby the firm can charge different prices without risking customer perceptions of unfairness. For example, higher prices charged during busy periods can easily be seen as price gouging, while the discounts during low-demand periods may reduce customer reference prices which, in turn, make future purchases at regular prices seem less fair.

Designing Fairness into Pricing Strategy

Pricing schedules have to be designed with customer perceptions of fairness in mind. Likewise, a well-implemented revenue management strategy does not mean blind pursuit of short-term yield maximization. The following specific approaches can help to reconcile pricing schedules and yield management practices with customer satisfaction, trust, and goodwill:[17]

- *Design price schedules and fences that are clear, logical and fair.* Firms should proactively spell out all fees and expenses clearly in advance so that there are no surprises. A related approach is to develop a simple fee structure so that customers can more easily understand the financial implications of a specific usage situation. For a rate fence to be perceived as fair, customers must be able to easily understand it (i.e., the fence has to be transparent and upfront), see the logic in it, and be convinced that it is difficult to circumvent and therefore fair.

- *Use high published prices and frame fences as discounts.* Rate fences framed as customer gains (i.e., discounts) are generally perceived as fairer than those framed as customer losses (i.e., surcharges), even if the situations are economically equivalent. For example, a customer who patronizes her hair salon on Saturdays may perceive the salon as profiteering if she finds herself facing a weekend surcharge. However, she is likely to find the higher weekend price more acceptable if the hair salon advertises its peak weekend price as the published price and offers a US$5 discount for weekday haircuts. Furthermore, having a high published price also helps to increase the reference price and potentially quality perceptions, in addition to the feeling of being rewarded for the weekday patronage.

- *Communicate consumer benefits of revenue management.* Marketing communications should position revenue management as a win-win practice. Providing different price and value balances allows a broader spectrum of customers to self-segment and enjoy the service. It allows each customer to find the price and benefits (value) balance that best satisfies his or her needs.

- *Use bundling to "hide" discounts.* Bundling a service into a package effectively obscures the discounted price. When a cruise line includes the price of air travel or ground transportation in the cruise package, the customer only knows the total price, not the cost of the individual components. Bundling usually makes price comparisons between the bundles and its components impossible, and thereby sidesteps potential unfairness perceptions and reductions in reference prices.

- *Take care of loyal customers.* To maintain goodwill and build relationships, a company should build in strategies for retaining valued customer relationships, even to the extent of not charging the maximum feasible amount on a given transaction. After all, customer perceptions of price gouging do not build trust. Also, if implemented indiscriminately, yield management systems allocate capacity during peak times to the highest-paying customers, not necessarily the most loyal customers. An intermittent availability of capacity to regular customers can cause them to become frustrated and angry, and put their loyalty at risk. This is especially so if they feel that their loyalty should be recognized and rewarded. One solution is to program yield management systems to incorporate "loyalty multipliers" for regular customers, so that reservations systems can accord preferred availability, giving them "special treatment" status, even though they may not be paying premium rates.

- *Use service recovery to compensate for overbooking.* As part of their revenue management regime, many service firms overbook to compensate for anticipated cancellations and no-shows. If a firm increases overbooking, the reduced inventory wastage will bring higher revenue. The flip side is that the incidence of not being able to honor reservations would also increase, and customers with bookings or reservations may be "bumped" by their airline, or "walked" by their hotel. This can lead to a loss of customer loyalty and adversely affect a firm's reputation. Here, it is important to back up overbooking programs with well-designed service recovery procedures.

Important guidelines include: (1) giving customers a choice between retaining their reservation and being displaced with compensation for the inconvenience; (2) providing sufficient advance notice so that customers are able to make alternative arrangements; (3) if possible, offer a substitute service that delights customers. A Westin beach resort that has occasional "oversales" has found that it can free up capacity by offering guests who are departing the next day the option of spending their last night in a luxury hotel near the airport or in the city at no cost. Guest feedback on the free room, upgraded service, and a night in the city after a beach holiday has been very positive. From the hotel's perspective, this practice trades the cost of securing a one-night stay in another hotel against that of turning away a multiple-night guest arriving that same day.

Putting Service Pricing Into Practice

Although the main decision in pricing is usually seen as how much to charge, there are other decisions to be made. Table 6.3 summarizes the questions that service marketers need to ask themselves as they prepare to create and implement a well-thought-out pricing strategy. Let's look at each in turn.

How Much to Charge?

Realistic decisions on pricing are critical for financial solvency. The pricing tripod model, discussed earlier (refer to Figure 6.2), provides a useful departure point. The three elements involve determining the relevant economic costs to be recovered at different sales volumes and setting the relevant floor price; assessing the elasticity of demand of the service from both the providers' and customers' perspectives, as it helps to set a "ceiling" price for any given market segment; and analyzing the intensity of price competition among the providers. Finally, a specific figure must

Table 6.3
Some Pricing
Issues

1. How much should be charged for this service?
    - What costs are the organization attempting to recover? Is the organization trying to achieve a specific profit margin or return on investment by selling this service?
    - How sensitive are customers to various prices?
    - What prices are charged by competitors?
    - What discount(s) should be offered from basic prices?
    - Are psychological pricing points (e.g., $4.95 versus $5.00) customarily used?

2. What should be the basis of pricing?
    - Execution of a specific task
    - Admission to a service facility
    - Units of time (hour, week, month, year)
    - Percentage commission on the value of the transaction
    - Physical resources consumed
    - Geographic distance covered
    - Weight or size of object serviced
    - Should each service element be billed independently?
    - Should a single price be charged for a bundled package?

3. Who should collect payment?
    - The organization that provides the service
    - A specialist intermediary (travel or ticket agent, bank, retailer, etc.)
    - How should the intermediary be compensated for this work—flat fee or percentage commission?

4. Where should payment be made?
    - The location at which the service is delivered
    - A convenient retail outlet or financial intermediary (e.g., bank)
    - The purchaser's home (by mail or phone)

5. When should payment be made?
    - Before or after delivery of the service
    - At which times of day
    - On which days of the week

6. How should payment be made?
    - Cash (exact change or not?)
    - Token (where can these be purchased?)
    - Stored value card
    - Check (how to verify?)
    - Electronic funds transfer
    - Charge card (credit or debit)
    - Credit account with service provider
    - Vouchers
    - Third-party payment (e.g., insurance company or government agency)?

7. How should prices be communicated to the target market?
    - Through what communication medium? (advertising, signage, electronic display, salespeople, customer service personnel)
    - What message content (how much emphasis should be placed on price?)

be set for the price that customers will be asked to pay. There are several considerations that the firm should take into account in the setting of the final price. For example, the firm would need to consider the pros and cons of setting a rounded price and the ethical issues involved in setting a price exclusive of taxes, service charges and other extras, as customers might be misled into thinking that the quoted price is final and inclusive of all charges.

What Should Be the Basis for Pricing?

It's not always easy to define a unit of service. Should price be based on completing a specific service task—such as repairing a piece of equipment, cleaning a jacket, or cutting a customer's hair, or based on admission to a service performance—such as an educational program, or a film, concert, or sports event? Should it be time based—for instance, using an hour of a lawyer's time, occupying a hotel room for a night, or subscribing to a satellite TV service for a month, or related to a monetary value associated with service delivery, as when an insurance company scales its premiums to reflect the amount of coverage provided or a realtor takes a commission that is a percentage of the selling price of a house?

Some service prices are tied to the consumption of physical resources, such as food, drinks, water, or natural gas. For example, in the hospitality industry, rather than charging customers an hourly rate for occupying a table and chairs, restaurants put a sizable markup on the food and drink items consumed. Recognizing the fixed cost of table service, such as a clean tablecloth for each party, restaurants in some countries impose a fixed cover charge that is added to the cost of the meal. Transport firms have traditionally charged by distance, with freight companies using a combination of weight or cubic volume and distance to set their rates. Such a policy has the virtue of consistency and reflects calculation of an average cost per mile (or kilometer). However, it ignores relative market strength on different routes, which should be included when a yield management system is used. Simplicity may suggest a flat rate, as with postal charges for domestic letters below a certain weight, or a rate for packages that groups geographic distances into broad zones.

For some services, prices may include separate charges for access and for usage. Recent research suggests that access or subscription fees are an important driver of adoption and customer retention, whereas usage fees are much more important drivers of actual usage.[18]

PRICE BUNDLING   As emphasized throughout this book, many services unite a core product with a variety of supplementary services. Meals and bar service on a cruise ship offer one example, baggage service on a train or aircraft is another. Should such service packages be priced as a whole (referred to as a "bundle"), or should each element be priced separately? To the extent that people prefer to avoid making many small payments, bundled pricing may be preferable, and is certainly simpler to administer. But if customers dislike feeling that they have been charged for product elements they did not use, itemized pricing may be preferable.

Bundled prices offer a service firm certain guaranteed revenue from each customer, while giving the latter a clear idea of how much the bill will be in advance. Unbundled pricing provides customers with flexibility in what they choose to acquire and pay for. However, customers may be angered if they discover that the actual price of what they consume, inflated by all the "extras," is substantially higher than the advertised base price that attracted them in the first place.

DISCOUNTING   As discussed in the context of yield management, selective price discounting targeted at specific market segments can offer important opportunities to attract new customers and fill capacity that would otherwise go unused. However, unless used with effective rate fences that allow a clean targeting of specific segments, a strategy of discounting should be approached cautiously. It reduces the average price and contribution received, and may attract customers whose only loyalty is to the firm that can offer the lowest price on the next transaction. Volume discounts are sometimes used to cement the loyalty of large corporate customers who might otherwise spread their purchases among several different suppliers.

Who Should Collect Payment?

As discussed in Chapter 4, supplementary services include information, order taking, billing, and payment. Customers appreciate it when a firm makes it easy to obtain price information and make reservations. They also expect well-presented billing and convenient procedures for making payment. Sometimes, firms delegate these tasks to intermediaries, such as travel agents who make hotel and transport bookings and collect payment from customers, and ticket agents who sell seats for theaters, concert halls, and sports stadiums. Although the original supplier pays a commission, the intermediary is usually able to offer customers greater convenience in terms of where, when, and how payment can be made. Using intermediaries may also result in a net savings in administrative costs. Nowadays, however, many service firms are promoting their Web sites as direct channels for customer self-service, thus bypassing traditional intermediaries and avoiding payment of commissions.

Where Should Payment Be Made?

Service delivery sites are not always conveniently located. Airports, theaters, and stadiums, for instance, are often situated some distance from where potential patrons live or work. When consumers have to purchase a service before using it, there are obvious benefits to using intermediaries that are more conveniently located, or allowing payment by mail or bank transfer. A growing number of organizations now accept Internet, telephone, and fax bookings with payment by credit card.

When Should Payment Be Made?

Two basic options are to ask customers to pay in advance (as with an admission charge, airline ticket, or postage stamps) or to bill them once service delivery has been completed, as with restaurant bills and repair charges. Occasionally, a service provider may ask for an initial payment in advance of service delivery, with the balance being due later. This approach is quite common with expensive repair and maintenance jobs, when the firm—often a small business with limited working capital—must buy materials up front.

Asking customers to pay in advance means that the buyer is paying before the benefits are received. However, prepayments may be advantageous to the customer as well as to the provider. Sometimes it is inconvenient to pay each time a regularly patronized service—such as the post or public transport—is used. To save time and effort, customers may prefer the convenience of buying a book of stamps or a monthly travel pass. Performing-arts organizations with heavy up-front financing requirements offer discounted subscription tickets in order to bring in money before the season begins.

Finally, it is shown that the timing of payment may determine usage pattern. From an analysis of the payment and attendance records of a Colorado-based health club, John Gourville and Dilip Soman found that members' usage patterns were closely related to their payment schedules. When members made payments, their use of the club was highest during the months immediately following payment and then declined steadily until the next payment. Members with monthly payment plans attended the health club much more consistently and were more likely to renew their membership, perhaps because each month's payment encouraged them to use what they were paying for.

Gourville and Soman conclude that the timing of payment can be used more strategically to manage capacity utilization. For instance, if a golf club wants to reduce the demand during its busiest time, it can bill its fees long before the season begins (e.g., in January rather than in May or June), as the member's pain of payment will have faded by the time the peak summer months come, and thereby reduces the need to get his/her money's worth. A reduction in demand during the peak period would then allow the club to increase its membership.[19]

How Should Payment Be Made?

As shown earlier in Table 6.3, there are many different forms of payment. Cash may appear to be the simplest method, but it raises security problems and is inconvenient when exact change is required to operate machines. Accepting payment by check for all but the smallest purchases is now fairly widespread and offers customer benefits, although it may require controls to discourage bad checks, such as a substantial charge for returned checks (a fee of US$15–20 on top of any bank charges is not uncommon at retail stores).

Credit and debit cards can be used around the world. As their acceptance has become more universal, businesses that refuse to accept them increasingly find themselves at a competitive disadvantage. Many companies also offer customers the convenience of a credit account, which generates a membership relationship between the customer and the firm. Other payment procedures include tokens or vouchers as supplements to (or instead of) cash. Tokens with a predefined value can simplify the process of paying road and bridge tolls or bus and subway fares. Vouchers are sometimes provided by social service agencies to elderly or low-income people. Such a policy achieves the same benefits as discounting, but avoids the need to publicize different prices and to require cashiers to check eligibility.

Now coming into broader usage are prepayment systems based on cards that store value on a magnetic strip or in a microchip embedded within the card. Service firms that want to accept payment in this form, however, must first install card readers. In Hong Kong, for example, a rechargeable and contactless smart card allows customers to pay for a number of products and services, ranging from bus and train trips purchased from vending machines and cafés, to car parks and sporting events. Also in Hong Kong, vending machine operators and mobile service providers offer a service, whereby customers can simply dial a number on their cellular phones and have the purchase amount charged to their monthly phone bills.

Interestingly, Dilip Soman found in a recent study that the payment mechanism has impact on the total spending of customers, especially for discretionary consumption items such as snacks from vending machines and spending in cafés.[20] The less tangible or immediate the payment mechanism, the more consumers tend to spend. Cash is the most tangible (i.e., consumers would be more careful and spend less), followed by credit cards, prepayment cards, and finally more sophisticated and even less tangible and immediate mechanisms such as payment via one's mobile phone bills such as in the Hong Kong example.

Finally, service marketers should remember that the simplicity and speed with which payment is made may influence the customer's perception of overall service quality.

Communicating Prices to the Target Markets

The final task, once each of the other issues has been addressed, is to decide how the organization's pricing policies can best be communicated to the target market(s). People need to know the price for some product offerings well in advance of purchase. They may also need to know how, where, and when that price is payable. This information must be presented in ways that are intelligible and unambiguous, so that customers will not be misled and question the ethical standards of the firm. E-tailers such as NexTag (www.nextag.com) not only has online shopping but also allows Internet users to compare prices across different hotel rates, air fares, etc. Besides travel, NexTag has a variety of other services such as loans, insurance, and Internet services, where most people compare prices first before deciding on their purchase. This enables customers to make a more well-informed decision and increases the incentive of making their purchases with NexTag.

Managers must decide whether or not to include information on pricing in advertising for the service. It may be appropriate to relate the price to the costs of competing products. Certainly, salespeople and customer service representatives should be able to give prompt, accurate responses to customer queries about pricing, payment, and credit. Good signage at retail points of sale will save staff members from having to answer basic questions on prices.

Finally, when the price is presented in the form of an itemized bill, marketers should ensure that it is both accurate and intelligible. Hospital bills, which may run to several pages and contain dozens of items, have been much criticized for inaccuracy.

Conclusion

To determine an effective pricing strategy, a firm has to have a good understanding of its costs, the value created for customers, and competitor pricing. Defining costs tends to be more difficult in a service business than in a manufacturing operation. Without a good understanding of costs, managers cannot be sure that the prices set are, in fact, sufficient to recover all costs.

Another challenge is to relate the value that customers perceive in a service, to the price they are willing to pay for it. This step requires an understanding of other costs that the customer may be incurring in purchase and use, including costs of a nonfinancial nature, such as time and effort. Managers also need to recognize that the same service may not be valued in the same way by all customers, offering the potential to set different prices for different market segments.

Competitor pricing cannot be compared dollar for dollar. Services tend to be location and time specific, and competitor services have their own set of related monetary and nonmonetary costs, sometimes to the extent that the actual prices charged become secondary for competitive comparisons. Competitive pricing needs to take all those factors into account.

Revenue management is a powerful tool that helps to manage demand and price different segments closer to their reservation prices. Well-designed physical and nonphysical rate fences help to define "products" for each target segment. However, great care has to be taken in the way revenue management is implemented so that customer satisfaction and perceived fairness are not compromised.

A pricing strategy must address the central issue of what price to charge for selling a given unit of service at a particular point in time (however that unit may be defined). Because services often combine multiple elements, pricing strategies need to be highly creative. Finally, firms need to be careful lest pricing schedules become so complex and hard to compare that they simply confuse customers. A policy of deliberately creating confusing price schedules, including hiding certain costs that only become apparent to customers after usage, is likely to lead to accusations of unethical behavior, loss of trust and customer dissatisfaction.

Review Questions

1. How can the three main approaches to service pricing be integrated to arrive at a good pricing point for a particular service?
2. How can a service firm compute its unit costs for pricing purposes? How do predicted and actual capacity utilization affect unit costs and profitability?
3. Why is the price charged by the firm only one, and often not the most important, component of the total cost to the consumer? When should we cut non-price-related costs to the bone, even if that incurs higher costs and a higher price to be charged?
4. Why can't we compare competitor prices dollar for dollar in a service context?
5. What type of service operations benefit most from good yield management systems and why?
6. How can we charge different prices to different segments without customers feeling cheated? How can we even charge the same customer different prices at different times, contexts and/or occasions, and at the same time be seen as fair?

Application Exercises

1. From a customer perspective, what serves to define value in the following services:
   a. a hairdressing salon
   b. a legal firm specializing in business and taxation law
   c. a nightclub
2. Select a service organization of your choice and find out what their pricing policies and methods are. In what respects are they similar to or different from what has been discussed in this chapter?
3. Review recent bills that you have received from service businesses, such as those for telephone, car repair, cable TV, credit card, etc. Evaluate each one against the following criteria: (a) general appearance and clarity of presentation, (b) easily understood terms of payment, (c) avoidance of confusing terms and definitions, (d) appropriate level of detail, (e) unanticipated ("hidden") charges, (f) accuracy, (g) ease of access to customer service in case of problems or disputes.
4. How might revenue management be applied to (a) a professional firm (e.g., consulting), (b) a restaurant, and (c) a golf course? What rate fences would you use and why?
5. Collect the pricing schedules of three leading cellular phone service providers. Identify all the pricing dimensions (e.g., air time, subscription fees, free minutes, per second/six seconds/minute billing, air time rollover, etc.) and pricing levels for each dimension (i.e., the range that is offered by the players in the market). Determine the usage profile for a particular target segment (e.g., a young executive who uses the phone mostly for personal calls, or a full-time student). Based on the usage profile, determine the lowest-cost provider. Next, measure the pricing schedule preferences of your target segment (e.g., via conjoint analysis). Finally, advise the smallest of the three providers how to redesign its pricing schedule to make it more attractive to your target segment.
6. What are potential consumer responses to complex pricing schedules? How can we improve the perceived fairness of pricing schedules, and what are the implications of these recommendations?
7. Pick a service of your choice, and develop a comprehensive pricing schedule. Apply the seven questions marketers need to answer for designing an effective pricing schedule.

Endnotes

1. Daniel J. Goebel, Greg W. Marshall, and William B. Locander, "Activity-Based Costing: Accounting for a Marketing Orientation," *Industrial Marketing Management* 27, no. 6 (1998): 497–510; Thomas H. Stevenson and David W.E. Cabell, "Integrating Transfer Pricing Policy and Activity-Based Costing," *Journal of International Marketing* 10, no. 4 (2002): 77–88.

2. Robin Cooper and Robert S. Kaplan, "Profit Priorities from Activity-Based Costing," *Harvard Business Review* 69, no. 3 (May–June 1991): 130–135.

3. Antonella Carù and Antonella Cugini, "Profitability and Customer Satisfaction in Services: An Integrated Perspective between Marketing and Cost Management Analysis," *International Journal of Service Industry Management* 10, no. 2 (1999): 132–156.

4. Gerald E. Smith and Thomas T. Nagle, "How Much Are Customers Willing to Pay?" *Marketing Research* (Winter 2002): 20–25.

5. Valarie A. Zeithaml, "Consumer Perceptions of Price, Quality, and Value: A Means-End Model and Synthesis of Evidence," *Journal of Marketing* 52 (July 1988): 2–21.

6. Hermann Simon, "Pricing Opportunities and How to Exploit Them," *Sloan Management Review* 33 (Winter 1992): 71–84.

7. This discussion is based primarily on Leonard L. Berry and Manjit S. Yadav, "Capture and Communicate Value in the Pricing of Services," *Sloan Management Review* 37 (Summer 1996): 41–51.

8. Frederick F. Reichheld, *The Loyalty Effect* (Boston: Harvard Business School Press, 1996), 82–84.

9. "SAR No 2 in Broadband Penetration," Hong Kong iMail (China), April 10, 2003.

10. Anna S. Mattila and Jochen Wirtz, "The Impact of Knowledge Types on the Consumer Search Process–An Investigation in the Context of Credence Services," *International Journal of Service Industry Management* 13, no. 3 (2002): 214–230.

11. For an excellent review and conceptual framework for understanding service convenience, refer to Leonard L. Berry, Kathleen Seiders, and Dhruv Grewal, "Understanding Service Convenience," *Journal of Marketing* 66 (July 2002): 1–17.

12. For recent work on the application of yield management to industries beyond the traditional airline, hotel, and car rental contexts, see Sheryl E. Kimes, "Revenue Management on the Links: Applying Yield Management to the Golf Industry," *Cornell Hotel and Restaurant Administration Quarterly* 41, no. 1 (2000): 120–127; Sheryl E. Kimes and Jochen Wirtz, "Perceived Fairness of Revenue Management in the U.S. Golf Industry," *Journal of Revenue and Pricing Management* 1, no. 4 (2003): 332–344; Sheryl E. Kimes and Jochen Wirtz, "Has Revenue Management Become Acceptable? Findings from an International Study and the Perceived Fairness of Rate Fences," *Journal of Service Research* 6 (November 2003); Richard Metters and Vicente Vargas, "Yield Management for the Nonprofit Sector," *Journal of Service Research* 1 (February 1999): 215–226; Anthony Ingold, Una McMahon-Beattie, and Ian Yeoman, eds., *Yield Management Strategies for the Service Industries*, 2nd ed. (London: Continuum, 2000); and Alex M. Susskind, Dennis Reynolds, and Eriko Tsuchiya, "An Evaluation of Guests' Preferred Incentives to Shift Time-Variable Demand in Restaurants," *Cornell Hotel and Restaurant Administration Quarterly* 44, no. 1 (2004): 68–84.

13. Hermann Simon and Robert J. Dolan, "Price Customization," *Marketing Management* (Fall 1998): 11–17.

14. Lisa E. Bolton, Luk Warlop, and Joseph W. Alba, "Consumer Perceptions of Price (Un)Fairness," *Journal of Consumer Research* 29, no. 4 (2003): 474–491.

15. Scott Adams, *The Dilbert™ Future—Thriving on Business Stupidities in the 21st Century* (New York: HarperBusiness, 1997), 160.

16. Information is extracted from an advertisement by PrettiSlim in *Her World* magazine (June 2004).

[17]   Parts of this section are based on Jochen Wirtz, Sheryl E. Kimes, Jeannette P. T. Ho, and Paul Patterson, "Revenue Management: Resolving Potential Customer Conflicts," *Journal of Revenue and Pricing Management* 2, no. 3 (2003): 216–228.

[18]   Peter J. Danaher, "Optimal Pricing of New Subscription Services: An Analysis of a Market Experiment," *Marketing Science* 21 (Spring 2002): 119–129; and Gilia E. Fruchter and Ram C. Rao, "Optimal Membership Fee and Usage Price over Time for a Network Service," *Journal of Services Research* 4 (2001): 3–15.

[19]   John Gourville and Dilip Soman, "Pricing and the Psychology of Consumption," *Harvard Business Review* (September 2002): 90–96.

[20]   Dilip Soman, "The Effect of Payment Transparency on Consumption: Quasi-Experiments from the Field," *Marketing Letters* 14, no. 3 (2003): 173–183.

CHAPTER SEVEN

Distributing Services

Companies best equipped for the twenty-first century will consider investment in real time systems as essential to maintaining their competitive edge and keeping their customers.

REGIS McKENNA

Think globally, act locally.

JOHN NAISBITT

Delivering a service to customers involves decisions about where, when, and how. The rapid growth of the Internet and now also broadband mobile communications means that service marketing strategy must address issues of place, cyberspace, and time, paying at least as much attention to speed, scheduling, and electronic access as to the more traditional notion of physical location. Furthermore, with the heat of globalization, important questions are being raised concerning the design and implementation of international service marketing strategies.

In this chapter, we discuss the role delivery plays in service marketing strategy locally and globally, and explore the following questions:

1. How can services be distributed? What are the main modes of distribution?
2. What are the distinctive challenges of distributing people-processing, possession-processing, and information-based services?
3. What are the implications for a firm of delivering through both physical and electronic channels?
4. What roles should intermediaries play in distributing services?
5. What are the drivers of globalization of services and their distribution?

Distribution in a Services Context

Mention distribution, and many people think of moving boxes to retailers and/or other channels for sale to end users. In a services context, we often have nothing to move, as "experiences" are not being shipped and stored, and informational transactions are increasingly conducted via electronic and not physical channels. How then does distribution work in a services context? In a typical sales cycle, distribution embraces three interrelated elements:

1. *Information and promotion flow.* This element refers to the distribution of information and promotion materials relating to the service offer. The objective is to get the customer interested in buying the service.

2. *Negotiation flow.* This element focuses on reaching an agreement on the service features and configuration and the terms of the offer so that a purchase contract can be closed. The objective is to sell the right to use a service (e.g., sell a reservation or a ticket).

3. *Product flow.* Many services, especially those involving people or possession processing, require physical facilities for delivery. Here, distribution strategy requires development of a network of local sites. For information-processing services, such as weather forecasts, Internet banking transactions, distance education by satellite, broadcast news, and entertainment, the product flow can be undertaken via electronic channels, employing one or more centralized sites.

Distinguishing between Distribution of Supplementary and Core Services

Distribution can relate to the core service as well as to supplementary services. That is an important distinction, as many core services require a physical location, which severely restricts distribution. For instance, a tour of the Great Wall of China can only be consumed in China itself, and experiencing the Formula 1 Race in Asia must take place at the stadium in Sepang, Malaysia. However, many of the supplementary services are informational in nature and can be distributed widely and cost-effectively via other means. Prospective tourists can get information and consultation about the Great Wall from a travel agent, either face to face, online, by phone or even by mail, and then make a booking through one of these same channels. Similarly, tickets to the Formula 1 Race can be purchased through a ticketing agency without the need for an advance trip to the physical facility itself.

As we look at the eight petals of the Flower of Service, we can see that no fewer than five supplementary services are information based (see Figure 7.1). Information, consultation, order taking, billing, and payment (e.g., via credit cards or electronic fund transfer) can all be transmitted using the digital language of computers. Even service businesses that involve physical core products, such as retailing and repair, are shifting delivery of many supplementary services to the Internet, closing physical branches, and relying on speedy business logistics to enable a new strategy of arm's-length transactions with their customers.

The distribution of information, consultation, and order taking (or reservations and ticket sales) has reached extremely sophisticated levels in some global service

Figure 7.1
Information and
Physical
Processes of the
Augmented
Service Product

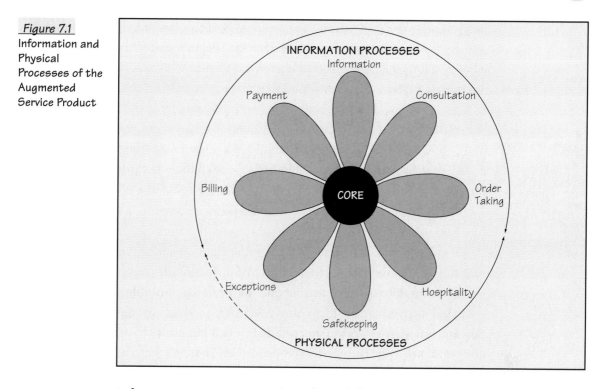

industries, requiring a number of carefully integrated channels targeted at key customer segments. For instance, Starwood Hotels & Resorts Worldwide—whose 725 hotels include such brands as Sheraton, Westin, and St. Regis—has more than 30 global sales offices (GSOs) around the world to manage customer relationships with key global accounts, offering a one-stop solution to corporate travel planners, wholesalers, meeting planners, incentive houses, and major travel organizations.[1] The company has also set up 12 customer servicing centers (CSCs) around the world to provide one-stop customer service for its guests, covering worldwide hotel reservations, enrollment and redemption of Starwood's loyalty program, and general customer service. Guests only need to call one toll-free number to book any Starwood hotel. Reservations can also be made through electronic channels, including the Westin and Sheraton Web sites.

Determining the Type of Contact: Options for Service Delivery

Decisions on where, when, and how to deliver service have an important impact on the nature of customers' service experiences because they determine the types of encounters (if any) with service personnel, and the price and other costs incurred to obtain the service.

Several factors serve to shape distribution and delivery strategies. A key question is: Does the nature of the service or the firm's positioning strategy require customers to be in direct physical contact with its personnel, equipment, and facilities? (As we saw in Chapter 1, this is inevitable for people-processing services but optional for other categories.) If so, do customers have to visit the facilities of the service organization or will the latter send personnel and equipment to customers' own sites? Alternatively, can transactions between provider and customer be completed at arm's length through the use of either telecommunications or physical channels of distribution?

Another issue concerns the firm's strategy in terms of distribution sites: Should it maintain just a single outlet or offer to serve customers through multiple outlets at different locations? The possible options, combining both type of contact and number of sites, can be seen in Table 7.1, which consists of six different cells.

Customers Visit the Service Site

The convenience of service factory locations and operational schedules assumes great importance when a customer has to be physically present—either throughout service delivery or even just to initiate and terminate the transaction. Elaborate statistical analysis, in the form of retail gravity models, is sometimes used to aid decisions on where to locate supermarkets relative to prospective customers' homes and workplaces. Traffic counts and pedestrian counts help to establish how many prospective customers pass by certain locations in a day. Construction of an expressway or the introduction of a new bus or rail service may have a significant effect on travel patterns and, in turn, determine which sites are now more desirable and which, less so.

The tradition of having customers visit the service site for services other than in the people-processing category is now being challenged by advances in telecommunications and business logistics, which are leading to a shift to services delivered at arm's length.

Service Providers Go to Their Customers

For some types of services, the supplier visits the customer. A firm like Daikin, a Japanese firm that sells air-conditioners to both home users as well as industrial

Table 7.1 Method of Service Delivery		Availability of Service Outlets	
	Nature of Interaction between Customer and Service Organization	Single Site	Multiple Sites
	Customer goes to service organization	Theater Barbershop	Bus service Fast-food chain
	Service organization comes to customer	House painting Mobile car wash	Mail delivery Auto club road service
	Customer and service organization transact at arm's length (mail or electronic communications)	Credit card company Local TV station	Broadcast network Telephone company

users, must necessarily bring its machinery, tools, and personnel to the customer's site, because the need is location specific. Going to the customer's site is unavoidable whenever the object of the service is some immovable physical item, such as a tree to be pruned, installed machinery to be repaired, or a house that requires pest-control treatment.

In other instances, going to the customer is optional. Because it's more expensive and time consuming for service personnel and their equipment to travel to the customer than vice versa, the trend has been toward requiring customers to come to the service provider instead (fewer doctors make house calls nowadays!). In countries like Indonesia, which consists of more than 17,000 islands, service providers often fly to visit their customers, because the customers find it so difficult to travel. Australia is famous for its Royal Flying Doctor Service, in which physicians fly to make house calls at farms and stations in the Outback.

In general, service providers are more likely to visit corporate customers at their premises than to visit individuals in their homes, reflecting the larger volume associated with business-to-business transactions. However, there may be a profitable niche in serving individuals who are willing to pay a premium for the convenience of receiving personal visits. One young veterinary doctor has built her business around house calls to sick pets. She has found that customers are glad to pay extra for a service which not only saves them time, but is also less stressful for the pet than waiting in a crowded veterinary clinic, full of other animals and their worried owners. Other consumer services of this nature include mobile car washing, office and in-home catering, and made-to-measure tailoring services for business people.

Service Transaction Is Conducted at Arm's Length

Dealing with a service firm through arm's-length transactions may mean that a customer never sees the service facilities and never meets the service personnel face to face. An important consequence is that the number of service encounters tends to be fewer and those encounters that do take place with service personnel are more likely to be made by telephone or, even more remotely, by mail, fax, or email.

Repair services for small pieces of equipment sometimes require customers to ship the product to a maintenance facility, where it will be serviced and then returned again by parcel service (with the option of paying extra for express shipment). Many service providers have implemented integrated solutions with the help of courier firms, which have developed impressive solutions for their clients. The solutions range from storage and express delivery of spare parts for aircrafts as and when needed (B2B delivery), and pick up of defective mobile phones from customers' homes and delivery of the repaired phone back to the customer (B2C pickup and delivery).

Any information-based product can be delivered almost instantaneously through telecommunication channels to any point in the globe where a suitable reception

220

terminal exists. As a result, physical logistics services now find themselves competing with telecommunications services.

Channel Preferences Vary among Consumers

The use of different channels to deliver the same service—say, banking services delivered via the Internet, mobile phone interface, voice response system, call center, automatic teller machines, and via face to face in a branch, or visits at the customer's home—not only has different cost implications for the bank, but also drastically affects the nature of the service experience for the customer. See Service Perspectives 7.1 for an example on how the use of different channels for cash withdrawal services can affect the banks and the service experience of customers.

Recent research has explored consumer choice of personal, impersonal, and self-service channels and has identified the following key drivers:[2]

- The more complex and the higher the perceived risk associated with a service delivery or purchase, the higher is the reliance on personal channels. For example, customers are happy to apply for credit cards using remote channels, but prefer a face-to-face transaction when obtaining a mortgage.
- Consumers with higher confidence and knowledge about a service and/or the channel are more likely to use impersonal and self-service channels.
- Customers who look for the instrumental aspects of a transaction prefer more convenience, and this often means the use of impersonal and self-service channels. Customers with social motives tend to use personal channels.
- Convenience is a key driver of channel choice for the majority of consumers. Service convenience means saving consumers' time and effort rather than saving them money. A customer's search for convenience is not just confined to the purchase of core products but also includes convenient times and places. People want easy access to supplementary services, too, especially information, reservations, and problem solving.

Service providers have to be careful when channels are priced differently—increasingly, sophisticated consumers arbitrage.[3] For example, they can ask the expensive full-service broker for advice (and perhaps place a small order) and then conduct the bulk of their trades via the much lower-priced discount broker. Effective strategies need to be in place for the service providers to deliver value and capture it at the appropriate channel.

Place and Time Decisions

How should service managers make decisions on the places where service is delivered and the times when it is available? The answer is likely to reflect customer needs and expectations, competitive activity, and the nature of the service operation. As

*Service
Perspectives
7.1*

REVOLUTION OF JAPAN'S RETAIL BANKING SECTOR

For years, Japan's retail banks have been following a strategy of "inconvenience banking," according to a Japanese banker. After the merger wave, numerous branches were closed down. As a result, most banks' customers have to pay at least ¥210 (US$1.90) to use a cash dispenser, if they want to withdraw cash after office hours in a convenience store, for example. For frequent use of machines that exchange notes or coins of bigger denominations for smaller denominations, the Bank of Tokyo-Mitsubishi charges a fee of ¥200.

Fortunately for the customers, banks have decided to change their strategy, in a bid to improve their service levels. On September 24, 2003, UFJ, Japan's fourth-largest bank, became the first big bank to start operating cash dispensers 24 hours a day, charging its customers only ¥105 (US$0.94) per withdrawal after working hours. As a part of its new retail strategy, UFJ would operate one-third of its 6,000 dispensers 24 hours a day and will also offer 24-hour telephone banking service. Besides UFJ, only Shinsei Bank (now owned by an American private-equity firm), Citibank, and a few small regional banks offer cash dispenser service 24 hours a day.

People who are used to 24-hour free banking services in other countries are amused by the practices of Japan's retail banks. Yet, all is not lost for the Japanese who have been the victims of the "inconvenience banking" strategy. The efforts by UFJ and other foreign banks would probably motivate other Japanese banks into offering better services for their customers. New ideas by more adventurous banks, such as Shinsei, which launched PowerFlex in 2001, a customer-friendly account that has helped to win 370,000 new accounts, have also added immense pressure on the other banks to keep up with the trend. There are signs that the Japanese banks are starting to take their retail customers seriously.

As the Japanese stock markets rebounded and the piling of bad debts stopped, Japanese banks can finally focus on business development. The announcement of the winding up of state-subsidized Housing Loan Corporation by 2005 has also caused banks to see their retail customers as not merely a source of cheap funding, but also a source of potential profit. These are additional incentives for the banks to treat retail customers better.

However, Japanese banks still find it hard to make money from retail banking. This is because almost half of the deposits accounts are dormant. If that is the case, wouldn't it make more sense for the banks to make it more convenient for their customers to carry out transactions?

Source: Adapted from "Retail Banking in Japan—At Your Service," *The Economist* (September 25, 2003).

noted earlier, the distribution strategies employed for some of the supplementary service elements may differ from those used to deliver the core product itself. For instance, as a customer, you are probably willing to go to a particular location at a specific time to attend a sporting or entertainment event. However, you probably want greater flexibility and convenience when reserving a seat in advance, so you may expect the reservations service to be open for extended hours, to offer booking and credit card payment by phone or Web, and to deliver tickets through postal or electronic channels.

Where Should Service Be Delivered in a Bricks-and-Mortar Context?

Deciding where to locate a service facility that will be visited by customers involves very different considerations from decisions related to locating the backstage elements, where cost considerations, productivity, and access to labor are often key determinants. In the former case, questions of customer convenience and preference come to the fore. Frequently purchased services that are not easily differentiated from competitors' need to be easily accessible from customers' homes or workplaces.[4] Examples include retail banks and quick-service restaurants. However, customers may be willing to travel further for specialty services that fit their needs well.

LOCATIONAL CONSTRAINTS   Although customer convenience is important, operational requirements set tight constraints for some services. Airports, for instance, are often inconveniently located relative to travelers' homes, offices, or destinations. Because of noise and environmental factors, finding suitable sites for the construction of new airports or expansion of existing ones is a very difficult task. The only way to make them less inconvenient is to install fast rail links, such as the futuristic 420 km/h service to Shanghai's new airport, the first in the world to use magnetic levitation technology. A different type of location constraint is imposed by other geographic factors. See Service Perspectives 7.2 on why the skiing industry booms in Beijing despite its desert-like climate.

People Get Upset When Electronic Distribution Systems Let Them Down
Reprinted from Christopher Lovelock, Product Plus (New York: McGraw-Hill, 1994), 283.
Copyright © Christopher H. Lovelock 1994.

Service Perspectives 7.2

BEIJING'S NEW ENTERTAINMENT—SNOW SKIING

The rapid growth of the snow skiing industry in Beijing shows it does not matter that Beijing's desert-like climate rarely produces snow, as long as the weather is cold enough in winter for snow-making machines to spray the bare hills in the north of the capital with adequate covering. Thousands of residents of the Chinese capital celebrated the start of the Lunar New Year by going to the ski slopes. This snow-skiing fad is a result of the rapidly growing middle class that is increasingly interested in pleasure-seeking activities (Figure 7.2).

The snow skiing industry has enjoyed an astonishing boom since the first ski slope was opened in Beijing five years ago. There are now more than a dozen ski slopes. Most ski resorts are located in remote locations. Fortunately, the surge in private car sales in recent years has helped to fuel the growth of the leisure industry in Beijing's rural suburbs, which were once considered inaccessible to most ordinary residents. Despite the increase in the number of middle-class pleasure seekers, breaking even and making profits remain as tough challenges for the ski resort operators. This is because building a ski slope requires huge investments and competitors usually rush in before a good idea could yield a positive return on its investments for the operators who took the plunge first.

Figure 7.2
Discovering the Thrill of Snow Skiing on the Hills to the North of Beijing

Agence France-Presse

Source: Adapted from "China–Hitting the Slope," *The Economist* (January 22, 2004).

The need for economies of scale is another operational issue that may restrict choice of locations. Major hospitals offer many different health-care services—even a medical school—at a single location, requiring a very large facility. Customers requiring complex, in-patient treatment must go to the service factory, rather than be treated at home. This is particularly necessary in cases where specialized medical and nursing care is only available in a limited number of hospitals possessing the necessary equipment and skills. Medical specialists, as opposed to general practitioners, often find it convenient to locate their offices close to a hospital because it saves them time when they need to use specialized equipment or services in order to operate on their patients.

MINISTORES   An interesting innovation among multisite service firms has been to create service factories on a very small scale in order to maximize coverage within a geographic area. Automation is one approach, as exemplified by the automated teller machines (ATMs), which offer many of the functions of a bank branch within a small, self-service machine that can be located within stores, hospitals, colleges, airports, and office buildings. Another approach to smaller facilities results from rethinking the links between the front- and backstages of the operation. Giordano, a Hong Kong-based clothing retailer, is cited for its innovative use of store space, involving retail outlets with very small storerooms. The firm does not store inventory in stores in order to fully utilize space and reduce rental. The stores are all connected to a central distribution network which will prompt the headquarters to replenish the stock when inventory is running low.

Sometimes, firms purchase space from another provider in a complementary field. For example, in Taiwan, bubble-tea stations rent a corner of shop space within eateries, grocery stores, and even clothing stores, to sell their drinks as takeaway to the customers of these stores.

LOCATING IN MULTIPURPOSE FACILITIES   The most obvious locations for consumer services are close to where customers live or work. Modern buildings are often designed to be multipurpose, featuring not only office or production space, but also such services as a bank (or at least an ATM), a restaurant, a hair salon, several stores, and even a health club. Some companies even include a children's day care facility onsite to make life easier for busy working parents.

Interest is growing in locating retail and other services on transportation routes or even in bus, rail, and air terminals. Major oil companies are developing chains of retail stores to complement the fuel pumps at their service stations, thus offering customers the convenience of one-stop shopping for fuel, car supplies, food, and household products. Truck stops on highways often include laundromats, toilets, ATMs, fax machines, restaurants, and inexpensive hotels, in addition to a variety of vehicle maintenance and repair services for both trucks and cars. In one of the most interesting new retailing developments, airport terminals—designed as part of the infrastructure for air transportation services—are being transformed from nondescript areas where passengers and their bags are processed into vibrant shopping malls. For example, South Korea's Incheon International Airport that opened in 2001 consists of many leisure and shopping facilities that cater to the 60,000 passengers passing through daily and the 20,000 people living nearby. The retail stores at the Incheon International Airport offer a wide variety of products, ranging from internationally well-known brands such as Chanel, Bally, and Gucci to well-packed boxes of Korean *kimchi*. The airport also consists of many fast-food outlets, including Burger King, McDonald's and Korean Lotteria. The Westin Chosun and Sheraton Walkerhill hotels also operate eight restaurants and four food courts.[5]

Besides airports, big railway stations are also being transformed into entertainment centers. Best Practice in Action 7.1 features how Japanese railway company, JR East, revamped its major stations into entertainment malls in an effort to transform the company into a "lifestyle service group." See Figure 7.3 for an advertisement by JR East.

Best Practice in Action 7.1

JR EAST'S NEW FRONTIER PLAN 21

East Japan Railway Company, more commonly known as JR East, transports 16 million people daily through a network of 1,695 stations in the eastern part of Japan. Despite its strong growth, the road ahead is full of challenges for JR East. This is because the transportation market that accounts for 70 percent of JR East's revenues is a highly mature one.

Nevertheless, JR East President and CEO Mutsutake Otsuka still sees potential in one area—the foreign tourists. Statistics show that Japan receives only five million tourists annually, which means that the tourism industry is performing below potential. Therefore, the Ministry of Land Infrastructure and Transport launched a national project called "Visit Japan Campaign," which aims to double the number of tourist arrivals to Japan by 2010. By facilitating travel for foreigners, developing and marketing air and rail tour packages, and distributing information about Japan to the rest of the world, JR East is working hard to fulfill Otsuka's New Frontier Plan 21.

Under the New Frontier Plan 21, JR East is to transform into a "lifestyle services group." The first step for JR East is to transform stations into entertainment malls where people gather, shop, dine and enjoy themselves, instead of merely passing through. The renovation of the Ueno Station—the first major station to be refurnished—was completed in early 2002. Since then, Ueno Station has been very popular with the passengers and local community.

After Ueno Station, JR East also has plans to redevelop the Tokyo Station, which is the most precious jewel in the crown of gateway stations around the capital. The project aims to restore Tokyo Station to its original Free Classic design and redevelop the area into a major business and commercial complex by 2010.

Besides repackaging the stations, Otsuka also plans to capitalize on the success of the "Sucia" (Super Urban Intelligence Card), a smart card that is used as an electronic train pass. Otsuka intends to expand the services provided by JR East by adding new functions that can be performed using the Sucia. Already in circulation, the "View Sucia Card" is a combination of the digital train pass and credit card. Furthermore, JR East has launched a Sucia IC chip for mobile phones, whose functions are shifting lifestyle services for the IT-savvy Japanese consumers to a new paradigm. And by next spring, an e-money function is likely to be added and the service area will expand to retail stores around the stations.

Source: Adapted from "Working on the New Frontier," *Forbes Global*, Japan Special Advertising Section, (January 12, 2004): S24.

Figure 7.3

JR East promotes its wide range of services, ranging from transportation and logistics services to human resource and hospitality services.

Courtesy of East Japan Railway Company.

When Should Service Be Delivered?

In the past, most retail and professional services in industrialized countries followed a traditional and rather restricted schedule that limited service availability to about 40 to 50 hours a week. In large measure, this routine reflected social norms (and even legal requirements or union agreements) as to what were appropriate hours for people to work and for enterprises to sell things. The situation caused a lot of inconvenience for working people who either had to shop during their lunch break or on Saturdays, if the stores operate six days a week. Historically, Sunday was considered a weekend and a rest day for most companies.

Today, the situation is changing fast. For some highly responsive service operations, the standard has become "24/7" service—24 hours a day, 7 days a week, around the world. For an overview of the factors behind the move to more extended hours, see Management Memo 7.1. Nevertheless, some firms resist the trend of seven-day operations. Many religious bookshops will not open on their designated day of rest because it is part of the basis for their religion. For them, the satisfaction they achieve from fulfilling their religious obligations by resting that day is worth more than the potential profits that they might make.

Delivering Services in Cyberspace

Technological developments during the last 20 years have had a remarkable impact on the way in which services are produced and delivered. Developments in telecommunications and computer technology in particular continue to result in many innovations in service delivery. For example, banks in many countries have embarked on programs of closing bank branches and shifting customers on to cheaper, electronic banking channels, in an effort to boost productivity and remain competitive in an increasingly competitive marketplace.

According to a survey done on 528 Internet users in Beijing, Shanghai, and Guangzhou in 2001, more than half were willing to purchase items online. "The proportion of e-shopping supporters is as high as 50.1 percent, much higher than expected. Its development indicates a bright future for China's online business," said Ling Qingxia, an analyst with Horizon.[6] However, not all customers like to use self-service equipment, so migration of customers to new electronic channels may require different strategies for different segments, as well as recognition that some proportion of customers will never voluntarily shift from their preferred high-contact delivery environments. An alternative that appeals to many people, perhaps because it uses a familiar technology, is banking by voice telephone.

Service Delivery Innovations Facilitated by Technology

More recently, entrepreneurs have taken advantage of the Internet to create new services that can be delivered through electronic channels accessed by computers in customers' homes or offices. Four innovations of particular interest are:

- Development of "smart" mobile telephones and personal digital assistants (PDAs) that can link users to the Internet wherever they may be.
- Usage of voice recognition technology, which allows customers to give information and request service simply by speaking into a phone or microphone.

Management Memo 7.1

FACTORS THAT ENCOURAGE EXTENDED OPERATING HOURS

At least five factors are driving the move toward extended operating hours and seven-day operations. The trend has been spreading rapidly to many other countries around Asia.

- *Economic pressure from consumers.* The growing number of two-income families and single wage earners who live alone need time outside normal working hours to shop and use other services. Once one store or firm in any given area extends its hours to meet the needs of these market segments, competitors often feel obliged to follow. Retail chains have often led the way in this respect.
- *Changes in legislation.* A second factor has been the lack of support for the traditional religious view that a specific day should be legislated as a day of rest for one and all, regardless of religious affiliation. Many Asian countries have multicultural societies and it is difficult to choose which day should be designated as special. Although time is set aside for the necessary religious acts like praying during these special days, most retail shops still remain open to serve its customers.
- *Economic incentives to improve asset utilization.* A great deal of capital is often tied up in service facilities. The incremental cost of extending hours is often relatively modest. If extending hours reduces crowding and increases revenues, then it is economically attractive. There are costs involved in shutting down and reopening a facility like a supermarket, yet climate control and some lighting must be left running all night, and security personnel must be paid to keep an eye on the place. Even if the number of extra customers served is minimal, there are both operational and marketing advantages to remaining open 24 hours.
- *Availability of employees to work during "unsocial" hours.* Changing lifestyles and a desire for part-time employment have combined to create a growing labor pool of people who are willing to work evenings and nights. Some of these workers are students looking for part-time work outside their classroom hours, some are "moonlighting," some are parents juggling child care responsibilities, others simply prefer to work by night and relax or sleep by day.
- *Automated self-service facilities.* Self-service equipment has become increasingly reliable and user friendly. Many machines now accept card-based payments in addition to coins and banknotes. Installing unattended machines may be economically feasible in places that cannot support a staffed facility. Unless a machine requires frequent servicing or is particularly vulnerable to vandalism, the incremental cost of going from limited hours to 24-hour operation is minimal. In fact, it may be much simpler to leave machines running all the time than to turn them on and off, especially if they are placed in widely scattered locations.

- Creation of Web sites that can provide information, take orders, and even serve as a delivery channel for information-based services.
- Commercialization of smart cards containing a microchip that can store detailed information about the customer and act as an electronic purse containing digital money. The ultimate in self-service banking will be when you can not only use a smart card as an electronic wallet for a wide array of transactions, but also refill it from a special card reader connected to your computer modem.

Electronic channels offer a complement or alternative to traditional physical channels for delivering information-based services. Best Practice in Action 7.2 describes a multichannel application for electronic banking.

Best Practice in Action 7.2

MULTICHANNEL BANKING AT ICICI BANK, INDIA

The ICICI Bank in India has become famous throughout the country for being the first to introduce multichannel banking to Indian consumers. ICICI serves more than three million customers through the use of its Internet banking Web site, a large call center, 1,700 automated teller machines (ATMs) and only 450 branches. Despite having fewer branches than other commercial banks in India, it is the second largest bank in the market.

It was the first to launch such an initiative in an industry that was relatively new to tele-banking and the use of ATMs. This stimulated an industrywide shift from high-contact bank branches to low-contact banking by telephone and ATMs.

A central element in this strategy is to offer India's most comprehensive mobile phone banking service, and this was done in two phases. In the initial phase, ICICI customers could receive information about their bank balances via the Short Messaging Service (SMS). The next phase was to allow customers to have access to a full range of services like receiving of account statements, ordering of check books and checking the status of payments made.

Now, other financial service firms are following suit, offering similar services at competitive rates. Multichannel banking has become a norm in India, but ICICI Bank seeks to differentiate its services in a number of ways. Call centers are used to enhance the customer's banking experience by customizing the process according to consumer preferences. ATMs are used not only to dispense cash, but also for a variety of other functions like payment of bills, religious donations, and money transfer.

Central to this multichannel approach is to develop a unified approach to reach out to the consumer. There has to be consistency in the level of service that the consumer experiences throughout the different channels. In this case, ICICI Bank relies on Microsoft's EAI Solution Biztalk to help it to effectively transfer information on customers between different delivery channels.

In recognition of the effectiveness of such a system, ICICI Bank was named "Bank of the Year in India 2003" and beat banks from 124 countries to clinch the "Best Multichannel Strategy 2003" award from the *Banker* magazine.

Source: Based on material in *Business Wire Inc.* (October 2002) and *Financial Times Business Limited* (December 2003).

E-Commerce: The Move to Cyberspace

As a distribution channel, the Internet facilitates information flow, negotiation flow, service flow, transaction flow, and promotion flow. Compared to the traditional channels, it is definitely better for conducting research on consumer information-seeking and search behaviors, for getting feedback from consumers in a short period of time, and for creating communities online to market the products and services.[7]

Among the factors luring customers into virtual stores are convenience, ease of research (obtaining information and searching for desired items or services), better prices, and broad selection. Enjoying 24-hour service with prompt delivery is particularly appealing to customers whose busy lives leave them short of time.

Many retailers, such as the giant bookstore chain Kinokuniya (www.kinokuniya. com), have developed a strong Internet presence to complement their physical stores in an effort to counter competition from "cyberspace retailers" such as Amazon.com, which has no stores (see Figure 7.4 for an example of Kinokuniya's Singapore Web site). However, adding an Internet channel to an already established physical channel is a double-edged strategy. It requires high capital setup and no one can be sure if the investment will definitely lead to long-term profits and high growth potential.[8]

Web sites are becoming increasingly sophisticated, but also more user friendly. They often simulate the services of a well-informed sales assistant in steering customers toward items that are likely to be of interest. Some even provide the opportunity for "live" email dialog with helpful customer service personnel. Facilitating searches is another useful service on many sites, ranging from looking at what books by a particular author are currently available, to finding schedules of flights between two cities on a specific date.

Particularly exciting are recent developments that link Web sites, customer relationship management (CRM) systems, and mobile telephony. Integrating mobile devices into the service delivery infrastructure can be used for (1) increasing the

Figure 7.4
Kinokuniya's Singapore Homepage Featuring Its Latest Promotion on the Spider-Man 2 Storybook, One of Its Best Sellers in July 2004, and Many Other Best Sellers and Interesting News

Source: http://www.kinokuniya.com.sg, accessed in July 2004.
Courtesy of Kinokuniya Book Stores of Singapore Pte Ltd.

accessibility of services, (2) delivering the right information or interaction at the right time, and (3) updating to create and maintain up-to-date, real-time information.[9] For example, customers can set stock alerts on their broker's Web site and get an email or SMS-alert when a certain price or transaction has been conducted (alert), or they can obtain real-time information on stock prices (updating). Customers can then respond by directly trading using their mobile phones as interface (accessing).

Almost every business process within an organization involves information in some form. The price of technology has fallen so low and access has become ever wider, that service firms must take advantage of it wherever they can in developing distribution strategy. To be able to do so, argues Frances Cairncross, management editor of *The Economist,* senior managers will have to think differently about their company's structure and be prepared to modify its culture.[10]

The Role of Intermediaries

Many service organizations find it cost-effective to delegate certain tasks. Most frequently, this delegation concerns supplementary service elements. For instance, despite their greater use of telephone call centers and the Internet, cruise lines and resort hotels still rely on travel agents to handle a significant portion of their customer interactions like giving out information, taking reservations, accepting payment, and ticketing. Of course, many manufacturers rely on the services of distributors or retailers to stock and sell their physical products to end users, and also take on responsibility for supplementary services like information, advice, order taking, delivery, installation, billing and payment, and certain types of problem solving. In some cases, they may also handle certain types of repairs and upgrades.

Delegating Specific Service Elements

How should a service provider work in partnership with one or more intermediaries to deliver a complete service package to customers? In Figure 7.5, we use the Flower of Service framework to depict an example in which the core product is delivered by the originating supplier, together with certain supplementary elements in the informational, consultation, and exceptions categories, but delivery of the remaining supplementary services packaged with this offering has been delegated to an intermediary to complete the offering as experienced by the customer. In other instances, several specialist outsourcers might be involved as intermediaries for specific elements. The challenge for the original supplier is to act as guardian of the overall process, ensuring that each element offered by intermediaries fits the overall service concept to create a consistent and seamless branded service experience.

Figure 7.5
Splitting
Responsibilities
for
Supplementary
Service Delivery

Franchising

Even delivery of the core product can be outsourced to an intermediary. Franchising has become a popular way to expand delivery of an effective service concept embracing all 7Ps to multiple sites, without the level of investment capital that would be needed for rapid expansion of company-owned and -managed sites. It is an appealing strategy for growth-oriented service firms because franchisees are highly motivated to ensure customer orientation and high-quality service operations.[11] Although most commonly associated with fast-food outlets, franchising has been applied to a very wide array of both consumer and business-to-business services. New concepts are being created and commercialized all the time in countries around the world.[12] Service Perspectives 7.3 features a Thai enterprise that plans to expand its operations through franchising.

Nevertheless, research by Scott Shane and Chester Spell shows that there is a significant attrition rate among franchisors in the early years of a new franchise system, with one-third of all systems failing within the first four years and no less than three-quarters of all franchisors ceasing to exist after 12 years.[13] They found that among the factors associated with success for franchisors were the ability to achieve a larger size with a more recognizable brand name, offering franchisees fewer supporting services but longer-term contracts, and having fewer headquarters staff per outlet. Since growth is very important to achieve an efficient scale, some franchisors adopt a strategy known as master franchising, which involves delegating the responsibility for recruiting, training, and supporting franchisees within a given geographic area to the master franchisee. Often, master franchisees are individuals who have already succeeded as operators of an individual franchise outlet.

A disadvantage of delegating activities to franchisees is that it results in some loss of control over the delivery system and, thereby, over how customers experience the actual service. Ensuring that an intermediary adopts exactly the same priorities and procedures as prescribed by the franchisor is difficult, yet vital to effective quality control.

Service Perspectives 7.3

FUTURE TREND COMMUNICATION CO. —EXPANSION THROUGH FRANCHISING

Future Trend Communication Co., a Thai-based IT systems consulting firm which develops and provides one-stop services for companies, plans to start franchising under the name of Wanflex in 2004, after developing a wide array of new software solutions. Specifically, Future Trend has decided to start franchising in Asian markets, such as China, Singapore, and Malaysia. It would price its products much lower than those of foreign competitors, said the managing director Attapong Poom.

A small-scale enterprise with a paid-up capital of Bt7 million (US$172,000), Future Trend was set up five years ago with the concept of selling software programs to Thai small- and medium-sized enterprises (SMEs) at affordable prices. It concentrates on developing software programs to help manufacturers manage their operations, from raw materials, inventory, and finished products to customer relationships. In addition, it offers online application, interactive media, and Web site design and support services.

Customer relationship management (CRM), material requirements planning (MRP), and manufacturing resource planning (MRP II) are some services that the company plans to launch. CRM enables corporations to maximize customer satisfaction by storing customer data such as their personalities and buying behavior. MRP facilitates the management of raw materials to provide production-unit sufficiency, while MRP II enables companies to operate an inventory management system efficiently and effectively. MRP and MRP II are mostly for industrial enterprises.

Franchising is one of the alternatives for Future Trend, said a Thai venture firm. Mr Poom estimated that Future Trend's net profit is expected to reach Bt24 million in 2003, and the figure does not include a possible contribution from franchising.

Source: Adapted from "Future Trend Eyes Expansion by Franchising," *The Nation*, February 5, 2003.

An ongoing problem is that as franchisees gain experience, they may start to resent the various fees they pay the franchisor and believe that they can operate the business better without the constraints imposed by the agreement. The resulting disputes often lead to legal fights between the two parties.

An alternative to business format franchising is licensing another supplier to act on the original supplier's behalf to deliver the core product. Trucking companies regularly make use of independent agents, instead of locating company-owned branches in each of the different cities they serve. They may also choose to contract with independent "owner-operators," who drive their own trucks, rather than buy their own trucks and employ full-time drivers. Universities sometimes license another educational institution to deliver courses designed by the former. For example, Singapore-based Informatics Group owns licenses to deliver courses designed by several universities, such as Curtin University and University of Canberra from Australia, and University of Leicester and University of Liverpool from the United Kingdom (see Figure 7.6).

Figure 7.6
Figure 7.6
Informatics Group,
which strives to
deliver high-quality
learning services
and be a global
leader in the
private education
industry, offers a
wide variety of
courses from many
universities from
around the world.

Courtesy of Informatics Group.

The Challenge of National Distribution in Large Markets

There are important differences between marketing services within a compact geographic area and marketing services in a federal nation covering a large geographic area, such as China, India, or Indonesia. Physical logistics immediately become more challenging for many types of services, because of the distances involved and the existence of multiple time zones. Multiculturalism is also an issue, because of the growing proportion of immigrants and the presence of indigenous peoples. In addition, firms marketing across India have to communicate not only in English but also in one of the numerous Indian languages. Although the majority of the Indian population speaks Hindi, there are as many as 18 different official languages included in the Eighth Schedule of the Indian Constitution. Thus one can imagine the challenges involved. Finally, there are differences within each country between the laws and tax rates of the various states or provinces and those of the respective federal governments. In the megaeconomy of China, service marketers also face challenges similar to those they face in India and Indonesia.

First, India and China share numerous similarities. China today is very much like India a decade ago—it presents a huge opportunity for service providers to access new consumer markets as discretionary spending levels increase.[14] And like in India, marketing in China involves dealing with a huge population—over 1.2 billion people—and transcontinental distances that exceed 5,200 km. The different regions in this immense market differ greatly in topography and climate as well. From a logistical standpoint, serving over one billion customers in this market is extremely complex, especially since different parts of the country are developed to different extents. While Shanghai may have a well-developed communications, transportation, and distribution infrastructure, the same cannot be said for a less developed area like Shandong.

The legal system in China is also complex. Because of the size of the country, there exist four levels of legislation—the Constitution, the National People's Congress (NPC), State Council Ministries, and the laws of the local governments. Laws in the Constitution and the NPC are the same throughout China. However, local laws implemented by the State Council Ministries and local governments may differ. In addition to observing Constitutional and NPC laws, service businesses operating nationwide may also need to conform to relevant state and local laws and plan for variations in tax policies from one state to another.

As the Chinese population becomes increasingly mobile and multicultural, market segmentation issues have become more complex for service marketers operating on a national scale. The Chinese people speak numerous dialects, each with its own distinct accent. There is wide disparity between the incomes of different households, especially between urban cities like Shanghai and rural areas like Anhui.

Faced with an enormous and diverse domestic marketplace, most large Chinese service companies simplify their marketing and management tasks by targeting specific market segments. Some firms segment on a geographic basis. Others target certain groups based on demographics, lifestyle, needs, or—in a corporate context—on industry type and company size. Smaller firms wishing to operate nationally usually choose to seek out narrow market niches, a task made easier today by the growing use of Web sites and email. Yet, the largest national service operations face tremendous challenges as they seek to serve multiple segments across the huge geographic area encompassed by China. They must strike a balance between standardization of strategies across all the elements embraced by the 7Ps (see Chapter 1) and adaptation to local market conditions—decisions that are especially challenging when they concern high-contact services.

Distributing Services Internationally

What are the alternative ways for a service company to tap the potential of international markets? It depends in part on the nature of the underlying process and the delivery system. People, possession, and information-based services have vastly different requirements on an international distribution strategy.

How Service Processes Affect International Market Entry

PEOPLE-PROCESSING SERVICES   These services require direct contact with the customer. Three options present themselves:

- *Export the service concept.* Acting alone or in partnership with local suppliers, the firm establishes a service factory in another country. The objective may be to reach out to new customers, or to follow existing corporate or individual customers to new locations (or both). This approach is commonly used by chain restaurants, hotels, car rental firms, and weight-reduction clinics, where a local presence is essential in order to be able to compete. For corporate customers, the industries are likely to be in fields like banking, professional services, and business logistics, among others.

- *Import customers.*[15] Customers from other countries are invited to come to a service factory with distinctive appeal or competencies in the firm's home country. People from abroad will travel to Phuket in Thailand to enjoy the powder-white sand and the glistening clear waters at its beautiful beaches. Foreigners from all over Asia will travel to Singapore to seek specialist medical treatment, including undergoing high-risk medical operations, at famous hospitals such as Raffles Hospital and Mount Elizabeth Hospital.

- *Transport customers to new locations.* In the case of passenger transportation, embarking on international service takes the form of opening new routes to desired destinations. This strategy is generally used to attract new customers, in addition to expanding the choices for existing customers.

Service Perspectives 7.4 describes some of the ways in which a major international hotel chain has developed a global presence. See also Figure 7.8 for a Raffles International Hotels and Resorts advertisement.

POSSESSION-PROCESSING SERVICES   This category involves services to the customer's physical possessions and includes repair and maintenance, freight transport, cleaning, and warehousing. Most services in this category require an ongoing local presence, regardless of whether customers drop off items at a service facility or personnel visit the customer's site. Sometimes, however, expert personnel may be flown in from a base in another country. In a few instances, a transportable item of equipment may be shipped to a foreign service center for repair, maintenance, or upgrade. Like passenger carriers, operators of freight transport services enter new markets by opening new routes.

INFORMATION-BASED SERVICES   This group includes two categories, *mental-processing services* (services to the customer's mind, such as news and entertainment) and *information-processing services* (services to customers' intangible assets, such

Service Perspectives 7.4

RAFFLES AIMS TO BE IN THE TOP TEN

Singapore's Raffles Hotel used to be a single hotel, having been restored to its original 1915 design after a major refurnishing in 1987. But now, Raffles is a worldwide hotel chain with 37 hotels in 32 destinations, including two rebranded properties, Raffles the Plaza and Swissotel the Stamford—located in Raffles City in Singapore.

The original Raffles Hotel was built in 1886 and it was named after the founder of modern Singapore, Sir Stamford Raffles. The hotel was declared a national monument by the Singapore government in 1987, and in 1989, a new company called Raffles International, which served as a platform for Raffles' future expansion into an international chain, was formed. In 2001, Raffles International acquired the Swissotel chain and its portfolio increased by more than 20 properties. The company also merged its second-tier Merchant Court brand into Swissotel.

The rebranding is all part of an aggressive Raffles expansion plan that aims to double its worldwide room inventory by 2005. In Asia, the hotel chain is looking at potential acquisition in Hong Kong, Shanghai, and Tokyo. Managing Director of the two Raffles City properties, T. Markland Blaiklock, said that his hotel company is currently the 60th largest in the world, but it is aiming to be in the top ten by 2005.

One way to achieve the goal is by reaching out to agents in the United States, as U.S. traffic slowed after the September 11 incident. In September 2002, Blaiklock, along with three other representatives of Raffles, crisscrossed the United States, visiting agencies and spreading the news about the new Raffles. There were also road shows and advertising campaigns in consumer and trade magazines to complement Blaiklock's visits to the United States. The ads promote Raffles as a combination of ultimate comfort, business facilities, and recreational facilities—the Raffles service tradition.

Source: Adapted from "Raffles Trumpets Rebranded Singapore Hotels," *Travel Weekly* 61, issue 40 (October 7, 2002): 58–59.

as banking and insurance). Information-based services can be distributed internationally in one of three ways.

- *Export the service to a local service factory.* The service can be made available in a local facility that customers visit. For instance, a film made in Hollywood can be shown in movie theaters around the world, or a college course can be designed in one country and then be offered by approved teachers elsewhere.

- *Import customers.* Customers may travel abroad to visit a specialist facility, in which case the service takes on the characteristics of a people-processing service. For instance, large numbers of foreign students study in Singapore and Hong Kong universities.

- *Export the information via telecommunications and transform it locally.* Rather than ship object-based services from their country of origin, the data can be downloaded from that country for physical production in local markets (even by customers themselves).

Figure 7.8
Raffles
International builds
its brand to stand
for luxury hotels
around the world.

Raffles Brown's Hotel   **Raffles Hotel Vier Jahreszeiten**

FOUR MAGNIFICENT HOTELS

NOW SHARE THE

SAME SUBLIME DETAIL

THE

RAFFLES

NAME

A subtle transformation from the marvellous to the extraordinary. Flawless service, attention to detail, luxury and comfort. Raffles, synonymous around the globe with the best in style and luxury, proudly adds its name to four of the world's most distinguished hotels. As always, they will continue to offer discerning travellers the highest standards of hospitality, in their own inimitable style.

Raffles Grand Hotel d'Angkor   **Raffles Hotel Le Royal**

The ever-growing *Raffles* collection includes:

Raffles Hotel, Singapore	Raffles Grand Hotel d'Angkor Siem Reap, Kingdom of Cambodia	Raffles Hotel Vier Jahreszeiten Hamburg, Germany	Le Montreux Palace Switzerland	Raffles Resort Mallorca* Colinas d'Es Trenc, Spain
Raffles The Plaza, Singapore	Raffles Hotel Le Royal Phnom Penh, Kingdom of Cambodia	Raffles L'Ermitage Beverly Hills, California, USA	Raffles Resort Bali* Jimbaran, Indonesia	Raffles Resort* Bintan, Indonesia
Raffles Brown's Hotel London, United Kingdom				

Raffles   **swissôtel**   **MERCHANT COURT**

Raffles

Raffles
INTERNATIONAL
Hotels & Resorts

RAFFLES INTERNATIONAL MANAGES HOTELS AND RESORTS IN 33 DESTINATIONS ACROSS SIX CONTINENTS
UNDER RAFFLES, SWISSÔTEL AND MERCHANT COURT BRANDS.
Asia • Australia • Europe • Middle East & Mediterranean • North America • South America
www.raffles.com   * under development

By courtesy of Raffles International Limited.

In theory, none of these information-based services require face-to-face contact with customers, since all can potentially be delivered at arm's length through telecommunications or mail. Banking and insurance are good examples of services that can be delivered from other countries, with cash delivery available through global ATM networks. In practice, however, a local presence may be necessary to build personal relationships, conduct on-site research, or even to fulfill legal requirements.

Barriers to International Trade in Services

The marketing of services internationally has been the fastest growth segment of international trade.[16] Transnational strategy involves the integration of strategy formulation and its implementation across all the countries in which the company elects to do business. Barriers to entry, historically a serious problem for foreign firms wishing to do business abroad, are slowly diminishing. The passage of free-trade legislation in recent years has been an important facilitator of transnational operations. Notable developments in Asia include APEC (linking Asia Pacific countries and the United States) and ASEAN (linking Southeast Asian countries such as Malaysia, Brunei, Singapore, the Philippines, and Thailand). See Management Memo 7.2 for the details of the formation of the Asean Economic Community (AEC) by members of the Association of South East Asian Nations (ASEAN).

However, operating successfully in international markets remains difficult for some services. Despite the efforts of the World Trade Organization (WTO) and its predecessor, GATT (General Agreement on Trade and Tariffs), there are many hurdles to overcome. Airline access is a sore point. Many countries require bilateral (two-country) agreements on establishing new routes. If one country is willing to allow entry by a new carrier, but the other is not, then access will be blocked. Compounding government restrictions of this nature are capacity limits at certain major airports that lead to denial of new or additional landing rights for foreign airlines. Both passenger and freight transport are affected by such restrictions.

Other constraints may include administrative delays, refusals by immigration offices to provide work permit applications for foreign managers and workers, heavy taxes on foreign firms, domestic preference policies designed to protect local suppliers, legal restrictions on operational and marketing procedures (including international data flows), and the lack of broadly agreed accounting standards for services. Different languages and cultural norms may require expensive changes in the nature of a service and how it is delivered and promoted. The cultural issue has been particularly significant for the entertainment industry. Many nations are wary of seeing their own culture swamped by American imports.

Factors Favoring Adoption of Transnational Strategies

Several forces or *industry drivers* influence the trend toward globalization and the creation of transnationally integrated strategies.[17] As applied to services, these forces are market drivers, competition drivers, technology drivers, cost drivers, and government drivers. Their relative significance may vary by type of service.

*Management
Memo 7.2*

FORMATION OF THE ASEAN ECONOMIC COMMUNITY

ASEAN (Association of South East Asian Nations) economic ministers have proposed advancing the target date for the formation of the Asean Economic Community (AEC) from 2020 to 2015 in a meeting held in October 2003. The formation of AEC would facilitate the integration of goods, services, investment, and skilled labor throughout the ASEAN region. AEC can be viewed as the Asian version of the European Union (EU) as they both share similar purposes, one of which is to provide seamless trading of goods or services across the borders of their members.

The proposal to accelerate the target date by five years aimed to ensure the competitiveness and mutual benefits for ASEAN members. Since ASEAN members have been negotiating free trade agreements (FTAs) with Asian economic powerhouses such as India, China, and Japan, and these countries have targeted achieving a zero-percent tariff by 2010, 2011, and 2012 respectively, the attractiveness and benefits of the formation of AEC would be greatly reduced if it were to be formed only by 2020, said Thai Commerce Minister Adisai Bodharamik. Therefore, in order for AEC to be more attractive and beneficial for its members, the integration should be created in line with the FTAs that have been formed with other countries, added Adisai.

ASEAN economic ministers have also proposed eliminating tariffs for the 11 AEC sectors by 2010. The sectors are electronics, wood-based products, automotive, agro-based products, fisheries, air travel (open-sky policy), tourism, rubber-based products, textiles, and clothing, "e-ASEAN," and health care. According to Adisai, the purpose of forming AEC was to facilitate the creation of a "single market and single production base" for food and services in the region, which means that ASEAN members would be encouraged to use raw materials supplied by its own members. The AEC service-sector deadline had already been advanced to 2010 from 2015, with priorities given to tourism, air travel, information and communications technology, and health care industries.

Four ASEAN countries, Thailand, Singapore, Brunei, and Cambodia, have already agreed on an open-sky policy and are expected to start negotiations on the matter very soon. The countries should be able to agree on the open-sky policy before the AEC 2010 deadline, according to Adisai. AEC relied on the so-called "Asean minus X" factor, in which members who are ready can immediately join the scheme. Economic ministers also talked about a plan to form an ASEAN-India FTA by 2011 for five ASEAN members, including Thailand, and by 2016 for Cambodia, Laos, Myanmar, Vietnam, and the Philippines.

The ASEAN-India FTA will be implemented from November 2004, focusing on fast-tracking a zero tariff on 105 products by 2007. Cambodia, Laos, Myanmar, and Vietnam will also get to enjoy special relationships with India, with 111 low-tariff products added to their fast-track list. ASEAN leaders and the Indian trade minister signed the agreement to form the ASEAN-India FTA on the second day of the two-day ASEAN leaders' summit. AEC is one of the three pillars contained in the Bali Concord II, the other two being the Asean Security Community and Asean Social and Cultural Community.

Source: Adapted from "Asean Economic Community: 2015 Integration Target on the Cards," *The Nation* (Thailand) (October 7, 2003).

MARKET DRIVERS Market factors that stimulate the move toward transnational strategies include common customer needs across many countries, global customers who demand consistent service from suppliers around the world, and the availability of international channels in the form of efficient physical supply chains or electronic networks. As large corporate customers become global, they often seek to standardize and simplify the suppliers they use in different countries for a wide array of business-to-business services. For instance, companies that operate globally often seek to minimize the number of auditors they use around the world. Similarly, international business travelers and tourists often feel more comfortable with predictable international standards of performance for such travel-related services as airlines and hotels. Also, the development of international logistics capabilities among such firms as DHL, Exel, FedEx, UPS (see Figure 7.9 for an ad of UPS), and Nippon Yusen Kaisha (NYK) Line has encouraged many manufacturers to outsource responsibility for their logistics function to a single firm, which then coordinates transportation and warehousing operations. For example, Japan-based logistics company NYK Line provides customers with comprehensive logistics and supply chain solutions through a synergy of sophisticated distribution systems and sea, air, and overland transport, instead of simply carrying goods between ports. NYK Line provides a full package of supply chain management services that help their clients to reduce their workload and enable them to track stock and flow of goods along the supply train.[18]

COMPETITION DRIVERS The presence of competitors from different countries, the interdependence of countries, and the transnational policies of competitors themselves are among the key competition drivers that exercise a powerful force in many service industries. Firms may be obliged to follow their competitors into new markets in order to protect their positions elsewhere. Similarly, once a major player moves into a new foreign market, a scramble for territory among competing firms may ensue.

TECHNOLOGY DRIVERS These factors tend to center around advances in information technology, such as enhanced performance and capabilities in telecommunications, computerization, and software; miniaturization of equipment; and the digitization of voice, video, and text so that all can be stored and transmitted in the digital language of computers. For information-based services, the growing availability of broadband telecommunication channels, capable of moving vast amounts of data at great speed, is playing a major role in opening up new markets. Access to the Internet, or World Wide Web, is accelerating around the world. Significant economies may be gained by centralizing "information hubs" on a continentwide or even global basis. Firms can take advantage of favorable labor costs and exchange rates by consolidating operations of supplementary services

Figure 7.9
UPS uses a synchronized sushi chain common in Japanese restaurants as a metaphor to communicate the value proposition of its supply chain management services.

Courtesy of UPS.

(such as reservations) or back-office functions (such as accounting) in only one or a few selected countries.[19]

COST DRIVERS   Big is sometimes beautiful from a cost standpoint. There may be economies of scale to be gained from operating on an international or even global basis, as well as sourcing efficiencies as a result of favorable logistics and lower costs in certain countries. Lower operating costs for telecommunications and transportation, accompanied by improved performance, facilitate entry into international markets. The effect of these drivers varies according to the level of fixed costs required to enter an industry and the potential for cost savings. Barriers to entry caused by the up-front cost of equipment and facilities may be reduced by such strategies as equipment leasing (as in airlines), seeking investor-owned facilities such as hotels and then obtaining management contracts, or awarding franchises to local entrepreneurs. However, cost drivers may be less applicable for services that are primarily people-based. When most elements of the service factory have to be replicated in multiple locations, scale economies tend to be lower and experience curves flatter.

GOVERNMENT DRIVERS   Government policies can serve to encourage or discourage development of transnationally integrated strategies. Among these drivers are favorable trade policies, compatible technical standards, and common marketing regulations. For instance, the actions taken by the European Commission to create a single market throughout the EU are a stimulus to the creation of pan-European service strategies in numerous industries.

Furthermore, the World Trade Organization (WTO), with its focus on the internationalization of services, has pushed governments around the world to create more favorable regulatory environments for transnational service strategies. The power of the drivers for internationalization can be seen in the case of the Thai airliner arriving in Hong Kong, described in Service Perspectives 7.5.

Many of the factors driving internationalization and the adoption of transnational strategies also promote the trend to have nationwide operations. The market, cost, technological, and competitive forces that encourage creation of nationwide service businesses or franchise chains are often the same as those that subsequently drive some of the same firms to operate transnationally.

How the Nature of Service Processes Affects Opportunities for Internationalization

Are some types of services easier to internationalize than others? Our analysis suggests that this is indeed the case. Table 7.2 summarizes important variations in the impact of each of the five groups of drivers on three broad categories of services: people-processing services, possession-processing services; and information-based services.

PEOPLE-PROCESSING SERVICES   The service provider needs to maintain a local geographic presence, stationing the necessary personnel, buildings, equipment, vehicles, and supplies within easy reach of target customers. If the customers are themselves mobile, as in the case of business travelers and tourists, then the same customers may patronize a company's offerings in many different locations, and make comparisons between them.

*Service
Perspectives
7.5*

FLIGHT TO HONG KONG: A SNAPSHOT OF GLOBALIZATION

A white and purple Boeing 747, sporting the circular logo of Thai Airways, banks low over Hong Kong's dramatic harbor, crowded with merchant vessels, as it nears the end of its three-hour flight from Bangkok. Once landed, the aircraft taxis past a kaleidoscope of tail fins, representing airlines from more than a dozen different countries on several continents.

The passengers include business travelers and tourists, as well as returning residents. After passing through immigration and customs, most visitors will be heading first for their hotels, many of which belong to global chains (some of them, Hong Kong-based). Some travelers will be picking up cars, reserved earlier from Hertz or one of the other well-known rental car companies with facilities at the airport. Others will take the fast train into the city. Tourists on packaged vacations are actively looking forward to enjoying Hong Kong's renowned Cantonese cuisine. Many of the more affluent tourists are planning to go shopping, not only in distinctive Chinese jewelry and antiques stores, but also in the internationally branded luxury stores that can be found in most world-class cities.

What brings the business travelers to this SAR (Special Administrative Region) of China? Many are negotiating supply contracts for manufactured goods ranging from clothing to toys to computer components, whereas others have come to market their own goods and services. Some are in the shipping or construction businesses, others in an array of service industries ranging from telecommunications to entertainment and international law. More than a few of the passengers either work for international banking and financial service firms or have come to Hong Kong, one of the world's most dynamic financial centers, to seek financing for their own ventures.

In the Boeing's freight hold can be found not only passengers' bags, but also cargo for delivery to Hong Kong and other Chinese destinations. The freight includes mail, some bales of Thai silk, boxes of fruit and flowers native to Thailand, a container full of brochures and display materials about the Thai tourism industry for an upcoming trade promotion, and a variety of other high-value merchandise. Waiting at the airport for the aircraft's arrival are local Thai Airways personnel, baggage handlers, cleaners, mechanics and other technical staff, customs and immigration officials, and, of course, people who have come to greet individual passengers. A few are Thai, but the great majority are local Hong Kong Chinese, many of whom have never traveled very far afield. Yet in their daily lives, they patronize banks, fast-food outlets, retail stores, and insurance companies whose brand names may be equally familiar to their expatriate relatives living in countries such as Australia, Britain, Canada, Singapore, and the United States. They can watch CNN on cable TV, listen to the BBC World Service on the radio, make phone calls through Hong Kong Telecom (itself part of a worldwide operation), and watch movies from Hollywood either in English or dubbed into the Cantonese dialect of Chinese. Welcome to the world of global services marketing!

POSSESSION-PROCESSING SERVICES   These may be geographically constrained in many instances. A local presence is still required when the supplier must come to repair or maintain objects in a fixed location. However, smaller transportable items can be shipped to distant service centers, although transportation costs, customs duties, and government regulations may constrain shipment across large

Table 7.2

Impact of Globalization Drivers on Different Service Categories

Globalization Drivers	People Processing	Possession Processing	Information Based
Competition	Simultaneity of production and consumption limits leverage of foreign-based competitive advantage in front-stage of service factory, but advantage in management systems can be basis for globalization.	Lead role of technology creates driver for globalization of competitors with technical edge (e.g., Singapore Airlines' technical servicing for other carriers' aircraft).	Highly vulnerable to global dominance by competitors with monopoly or competitive advantage in information (e.g., BBC, Hollywood, CNN), unless restricted by governments.
Market	People differ economically and culturally, so needs for service and ability to pay may vary. Culture and education may affect willingness to do self-service.	Less variation for service to corporate possessions, but level of economic development impacts demand for services to individually owned goods.	Demand for many services is derived to a significant degree from economic and educational levels. Cultural issues may affect demand for entertainment.
Technology	Use of IT for delivery of supplementary services may be a function of ownership and familiarity with technology, including telecommunications and intelligent terminals.	Need for technology-based service delivery systems is a function of the types of possessions requiring service and the cost tradeoffs in labor substitution.	Ability to deliver core services through remote terminals may be a function of investments in computerization, quality of telecommunications infrastructure, and education levels.
Cost	Variable labor rates may impact on pricing in labor-intensive services (consider self-service in high-cost locations).	Variable labor rates may favor low-cost locations if not offset by shipment costs. Consider substituting equipment for labor.	Major cost elements can be centralized and minor cost elements localized.
Government	Social policies (e.g., health) vary widely and may affect labor costs, role of women in front-stage jobs, and hours/days on which work can be performed.	Tax laws, environmental regulations, and technical standards may decrease/increase costs and encourage/discourage certain types of activity.	Policies on education, censorship, public ownership of communications, and infrastructure standards may impact demand and supply and distort pricing.

distances or national frontiers. On the other hand, modern technology now allows certain types of service processes to be administered from a distance through electronic diagnostics and transmission of so-called remote fixes.

INFORMATION-BASED SERVICES   They are, perhaps, the most interesting category of services from the standpoint of global strategy development, because they depend on the transmission or manipulation of data in order to create value. The advent of modern global telecommunications, linking intelligent machines to powerful databases, makes it increasingly easy to deliver information-based services around the world. Local presence requirements may be limited to a terminal, ranging from a simple telephone or fax machine to a computer or more specialized equipment such as a bank ATM, connected to a reliable telecommunications infrastructure. If the local infrastructure is not of sufficiently high quality, the use of mobile or satellite communications may solve the problem in some instances.

Conclusion

"Where? When? and How?" Responses to these three questions form the foundation of service delivery strategy. The customer's service experience is a function of both service performance and delivery characteristics.

"Where?" relates, of course, to the places where customers can obtain delivery of the core product, one or more supplementary services, or a complete package. In this chapter, we presented a categorization scheme for thinking about alternative place-related strategies, ranging from customers coming to the service site, to service personnel visiting the customer, and finally a variety of options for arm's-length transactions, including delivery through both physical and electronic channels.

"When?" involves decisions on scheduling of service delivery. Customer demands for greater convenience are leading many firms to extend their hours and days of service, with the ultimate flexibility being offered by 24/7 service every day of the year.

"How?" concerns channels and procedures for delivering the core and supplementary service elements to customers. Advances in technology are having a major impact on the alternatives available and on the economics of those alternatives. Responding to customer needs for flexibility, many firms now offer several alternative choices of delivery channels.

Although service firms are much more likely than a manufacturer to control their own delivery systems, there is also a role for intermediaries to deliver either the core services as is the case for franchisees, or supplementary services such as travel agents.

More and more service firms are marketing across national borders. Stimulating (or constraining) the move to transnational strategies are five key industry drivers: market factors, costs, technology, government policies, and competitive forces. However, significant differences exist in the extent to which the various drivers apply to people-processing, possession-processing, and information-based services.

Review Questions

1. What is meant by "distributing services?" How can an experience or something intangible be distributed?
2. Why is it important to consider the distribution of core and supplementary services separately?
3. What risks and opportunities are present for a retail service firm in adding electronic channels of delivery (a) paralleling a channel involving physical stores, (b) replacing the physical stores with an all-Internet cum call center channel? Give examples.
4. Why should service marketers be concerned with new developments in mobile communications?

5. What can service marketers who are planning transnational strategies learn from studying China?

6. What marketing and management challenges are raised by the use of intermediaries in a service setting?

7. What are the key drivers for increasing globalization of services?

8. How does the nature of the service affect the opportunities for globalization?

Application Exercises

1. Using the same service organization, or another of your choice, examine its use of technology in facilitating service delivery. Might there be other opportunities for technology to be employed beneficially? What are these?

2. Identify three situations in which you use self-service delivery. What is your motivation for using this approach to delivery, rather than having service personnel do it for you?

3. Think of three services which you mostly or exclusively buy or use via the Internet. What is the value proposition of this channel to you over alternative channels (e.g., phone, mail, or branch network)?

4. Select two business format franchises other than food service, choosing one targeted primarily at consumer markets and the other primarily at business-to-business markets. Develop a profile of each, examining their strategy across each of the 7Ps and also evaluating their competitive positioning.

5. Select three different service industries. In each instance, which do you see as the most significant of the five industry drivers as forces for globalization, and why?

6. Obtain recent statistics for international trade in services for India and another country of your choice. What are the dominant categories of service exports and imports? What factors do you think are driving trade in specific service categories? What differences do you see between the countries?

Endnotes

[1] Jochen Wirtz and Jeannette P. T. Ho, "Westin in Asia: Distributing Hotel Rooms Globally," in Christopher H. Lovelock, Jochen Wirtz, and Hean Tat Keh, *Services Marketing in Asia–Managing People, Technology and Strategy* (Singapore: Prentice Hall, 2002), 645–651.

[2] The section was based on the following research: Nancy Jo Black, Andy Lockett, Christine Ennew, Heidi Winklhofer, and Sally McKechnie, "Modelling Consumer Choice of Distribution Channels: An Illustration from Financial Services," *International Journal of Bank Marketing* 20, no. 4 (2002): 161–173; Jinkook Lee, "A Key to Marketing Financial Services: The Right Mix of Products, Services, Channels and Customers," *Journal of Services Marketing* 16, no. 3 (2002): 238–258; and Leonard L Berry, Kathleen Seiders, and Dhruv Grewal, "Understanding Service Convenience," *Journal of Marketing* 66, no. 3 (July 2002): 1–17.

[3] Paul F. Nunes and Frank V. Cespedes, "The Customer has Escaped," *Harvard Business Review* 81, no. 11 (2003): 96–105.

[4] Michael A. Jones, David L. Mothersbaugh, and Sharon E. Beatty, "The Effects of Locational Convenience on Customer Repurchase Intentions across Service Types," *Journal of Services Marketing* 17, no. 7 (2004): 701–712.

[5] "Winging to Success," *Business Traveller Asia-Pacific* (April 2004): 20–21.

[6] "China: City Internet Users Boost e-purchasing," *Asiainfo Daily China News*, May 30, 2001.

[7] P. K. Kannan, "Introduction to the Special Issue: Marketing in the e-Channel," *International Journal of Electronic Commerce* 5, no. 3 (2001): 3–6.

[8] Inge Geyskens, Katrijn Gielens, and Marnik G. Dekimpe, "The Market Valuation of Internet Channel Additions," *Journal of Marketing* 66, no. 2 (April 2002): 102–119.

9   Katherine N. Lemon, Frederick B. Newell, and Loren J. Lemon, "The Wireless Rules for e-Service," in *New Directions in Theory and Practice*, eds. Roland T. Rust and P. K. Kannan (Armonk, New York: M. E. Sharpe, 2002), 200–232.

10 Frances Cairncross, *The Company of the Future* (Boston, MA: Harvard Business School Press, 2002).

11 James Cross and Bruce J. Walker, "Addressing Service Marketing Challenges through Franchising," in *Handbook of Services Marketing & Management*, eds. Teresa A. Swartz and Dawn Iacobucci (Thousand Oaks, CA: Sage Publications, 2000), 473–484.

12 Richard C. Hoffman and John F. Preble, "Global Franchising: Current Status and Future Challenges," *Journal of Services Marketing* 18, no. 2 (2004): 101–113.

13 Scott Shane and Chester Spell, "Factors for New Franchise Success," *Sloan Management Review* (Spring 1998): 43–50.

14 Mark Kennedy, "Brand New Chances Lying in Wait as India Eyes Up World Stage," *Media Asia,* March 26, 2004, 11.

15 This term was coined by Curtis P. McLauglin and James A. Fitzsimmons in "e-Service: Strategies for Globalizing Service Operations," *International Journal of Service Industry Management* 7, no. 4 (1996): 43–57.

16 Rajshkhar G. Javalgi and D. Steven White, "Strategic Challenges for the Marketing of Services Internationally," *International Marketing Review* 19, no. 6 (2002): 563–581.

17 Johny K. Johansson and George S. Yip, "Exploiting Globalization Potential: U.S. and Japanese Strategies," *Strategic Management Journal* (October 1994): 579–601; Christopher H. Lovelock and George S. Yip, "Developing Global Strategies for Service Businesses," *California Management Review* 38 (Winter 1996): 64–86; Rajshkhar G. Javalgi and D. Steven White, "Strategic Challenges for the Marketing of Services Internationally," *International Marketing Review* 19, no. 6 (2002): 563–581; May Aung and Roger Heeler, "Core Competencies of Service Firms: A Framework for Strategic Decisions in International Markets," *Journal of Marketing Management* 17 (2001): 619–643.

18 *Fortune,* Japan Special Advertising Section, no. 15 (August 19, 2002).

19 Frances Cairncross, *The Death of Distance* (Boston, MA: Harvard Business School Press, 1997).

Managing the Service Delivery Process

PART THREE

CHAPTER EIGHT

Designing and Managing Service Processes

Ultimately, only one thing really matters in service encounters—the customer's perceptions of what occurred.

RICHARD B. CHASE AND SRIRAM DASU[1]

Processes are the architecture of services. They describe the method and sequence in which service operating systems work and how they link together to create the service experience and outcome that customers will value. In high-contact services, customers themselves become an integral part of the operation. Badly designed processes are likely to annoy customers because they often result in slow, frustrating, and poor-quality service delivery. Similarly, poor processes make it difficult for front-line staff to do their jobs well, result in low productivity, and increase the risk of service failures.

One of the distinctive characteristics of many services is the way in which the customer is involved in their creation and delivery. But all too often, service design and operational execution seem to ignore the customer perspective, with each step in the process being handled as a discrete event, rather than integrated into a seamless process.

In this chapter, we emphasize the importance for service marketers of understanding how service processes work and where customers fit within the operation. Specifically, we address the following questions:

1. How can service blueprinting be used to design a service and create a satisfying experience for customers?
2. What can be done to reduce the likelihood of failures during service delivery?
3. How can service redesign improve both quality and productivity?
4. Under what circumstances should customers be viewed as coproducers of service and what are the implications?
5. What factors lead customers to embrace or reject new self-service technologies?
6. What should managers do to control uncooperative or abusive customers?

Blueprinting Services to Create Valued Experiences and Productive Operations

It's no easy task to design a service, especially one that must be delivered in real time with customers present in the service factory. To design services that are both satisfying for customers and operationally efficient, marketers and operations specialists need to work together. In high-contact services where employees interact directly with customers (see Figure 8.1), it may also be appropriate to involve human resource experts in the

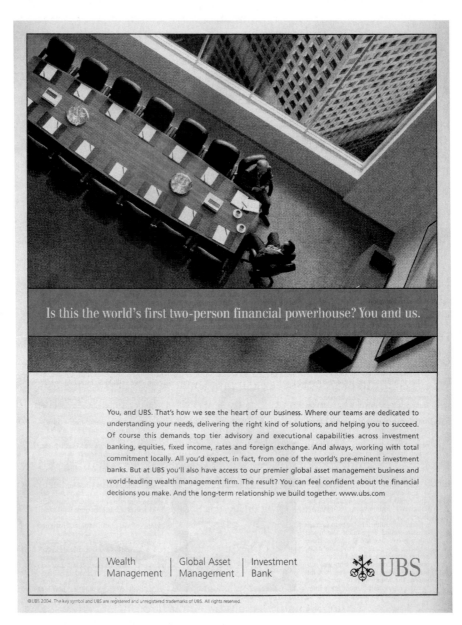

Figure 8.1
UBS financial specialists need extensive interaction with their clients to develop tailored financial solutions.

Courtesy of UBS.
The contents of the publication express the views and opinions of the authors and are not necessarily the views of UBS AG.

design of service processes. A key tool in service design is a more sophisticated version of flowcharting (introduced in Chapter 2) known as blueprinting.

The design for a new building or a ship is usually captured on architectural drawings called blueprints. These blueprints show what the product should look like and detail the specifications to which it should conform. In contrast to the physical architecture of a building, ship, or piece of equipment, service processes have a largely intangible structure. That makes them all the more difficult to visualize. The same is true of processes such as logistics, industrial engineering, decision theory, and computer systems analysis, each of which employs blueprint-like techniques to describe processes involving flows, sequences, relationships, and dependencies.[2]

Developing a Blueprint

How does one get started on developing a service blueprint? First, you need to identify all the key activities involved in creating and delivering the service in question and then you must specify the linkages between these activities.[3] Initially, it is best to keep activities relatively aggregated in order to define the "big picture." Subsequently, any given activity can be refined by "drilling down" to obtain a higher level of detail. In an airline context, for instance, the passenger activity of "boards aircraft" can be decomposed into such steps as "wait for seat rows to be announced, give agent boarding pass for verification, walk down jetway, enter aircraft, let flight attendant verify boarding pass, find seat, stow carry-on bag, sit down."

A key characteristic of service blueprinting is that it distinguishes between what customers experience "front-stage" and the activities of employees and support processes "backstage," where customers can't see them. Between the two lies what is called the line of visibility. Operationally oriented businesses are sometimes so focused on managing backstage activities that they neglect to consider the customer's view of front-stage activities. Accounting firms, for instance, often have elaborately documented procedures and standards for how to conduct an audit properly, but may lack clear standards for when and how to host a meeting with clients or how to answer the telephone when they call.

Service blueprints clarify the interactions between customers and employees and how these are supported by additional activities and systems backstage. Since blueprints show the interrelationships between employee roles, operational processes, information technology, and customer interactions, they can facilitate the integration of marketing, operations, and human resource management within a firm. There is no single, required way to prepare a service blueprint, but it's recommended that a consistent approach be used within any one organization. To illustrate blueprinting later in this chapter, we adapt and simplify an approach proposed by Jane Kingman-Brundage.[4]

Blueprinting also gives managers the opportunity to identify potential *fail points* in the process where there is a significant risk of things going wrong and diminishing service quality. Knowledge of such fail points enables managers to design procedures to avoid their occurrence or to prepare contingency plans (or both). Points in the process where customers commonly have to wait can also be pinpointed. Standards can then be developed for execution of each activity, including times for completion of a task, maximum wait times in between tasks, and scripts to guide interactions between staff members and customers.

Creating a Script for Employees and Customers

A well-planned script should provide a full description of the service encounter and can help identify potential or existing problems in a specific service process. Recall from Chapter 2 the discussion and script for teeth cleaning and a simple dental examination involving three players—the patient, the receptionist, and the dental hygienist. By examining existing scripts, service managers may discover ways to modify the nature of customer and employee roles to improve service delivery, increase productivity, and enhance the nature of the customer's experience. As service delivery procedures evolve in response to new technology or other factors, revised scripts may need to be developed.

Blueprinting the Restaurant Experience: A Three-Act Performance

To illustrate blueprinting of a high-contact, people-processing service, we examine the experience of dinner for two at Chez Jean, an upscale restaurant that enhances its core food service with a variety of other supplementary services (Figure 8.2). A typical rule of thumb in full-service restaurants is that the cost of purchasing the food ingredients represents about 20 to 30 percent of the price of the meal. The balance can be seen as the "fees" that the customer is willing to pay for renting a table and chairs in a pleasant setting, hiring the services of food preparation experts and their kitchen equipment, and providing serving staff to wait on them both inside and outside the dining room.

The key components of the blueprint, reading from top to bottom, are:

1. Definition of standards for each front-stage activity (only a few examples are actually specified in the figure)
2. Physical and other evidence for front-stage activities (specified for all steps)
3. Principal customer actions (illustrated by pictures)
4. Line of interaction
5. Front-stage actions by customer contact personnel
6. Line of visibility
7. Backstage actions by customer contact personnel

8.   Support processes involving other service personnel
9.   Support processes involving information technology

Reading from left to right, the blueprint prescribes the sequence of actions over time. In earlier chapters, we saw that service performances could be likened to theater. To emphasize the involvement of human actors in service delivery, we have followed the practice adopted by some service organizations of using pictures to illustrate each of the 14 principal steps involving our two customers (there are other steps not shown), beginning with making a reservation and concluding with departure from the restaurant after the meal. Like many high-contact services involving discrete transactions, the "restaurant drama" can be divided into three "acts," representing activities that take place before the core product is encountered, delivery of the core product (in this case, the meal), and subsequent activities while still involved with the service provider.

The "stage" or servicescape includes both the exterior and interior of the restaurant. Front-stage actions take place in a very visual environment. Restaurants are often quite theatrical in their use of physical evidence (such as furnishings, décor, uniforms, lighting, and table settings) and may also employ background music in their efforts to create a themed environment that matches their market positioning.

Identifying Fail Points

Running a good restaurant is a complex business and much can go wrong. A good blueprint should draw attention to points in service delivery where things are particularly at risk of going wrong. From a customer perspective, the most serious fail points, marked in our blueprint by **F**, are those that will result in failure to access or enjoy the core product. They involve the reservation (Could the customer get through by phone? Was a table available at the desired time and date? Was the reservation recorded accurately?) and seating (Was a table available when promised?).

Since service delivery takes place over time, there is also the possibility of delays between specific actions, requiring the customers to wait. Common locations for such waits are identified by ⚠W. Excessive waits will annoy customers. In practice, every step in the process, both front-stage and backstage, has some potential for failures and delays. In fact, failures often lead directly to delays, reflecting orders that were never passed on, or time spent correcting mistakes.

David Maister coined the term OTSU ("opportunity to screw up") to highlight the importance of thinking about all the things that might go wrong in delivering a particular type of service.[5] OTSUs are funny when you talk about them. However, customers don't always see the funny side when the joke is on them. It's only by identifying all the possible OTSUs associated with a particular task that service managers can put together a delivery system which is explicitly designed to avoid such problems.

Figure 8.2
Blueprinting a Full-Service Restaurant Experience

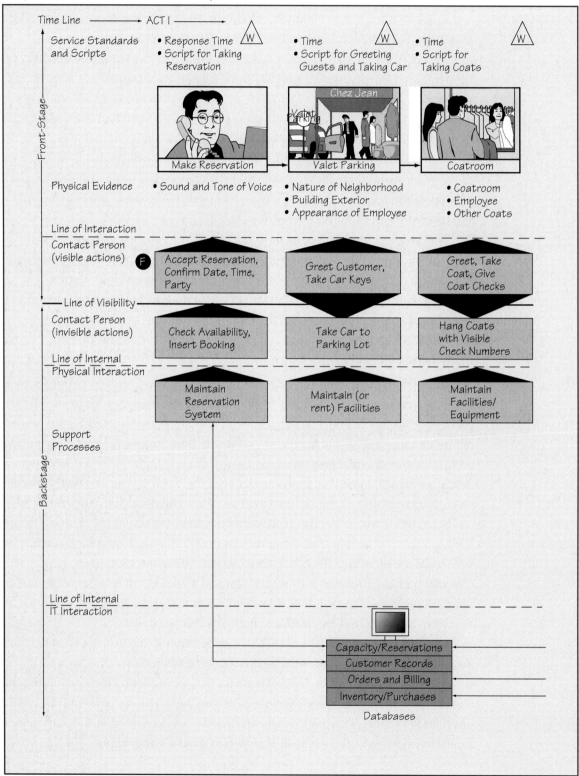

Figure 8.2
(Continued)

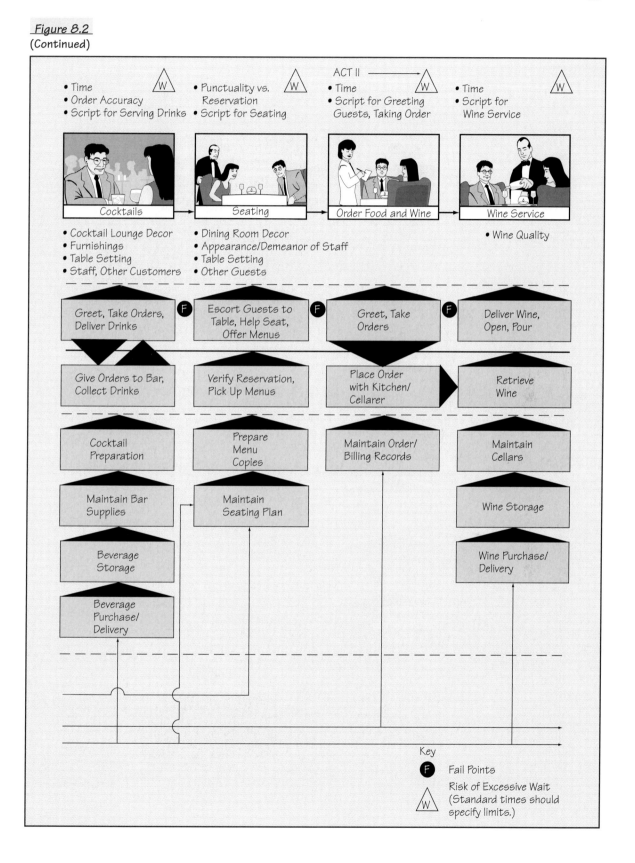

Figure 8.2
(Continued)

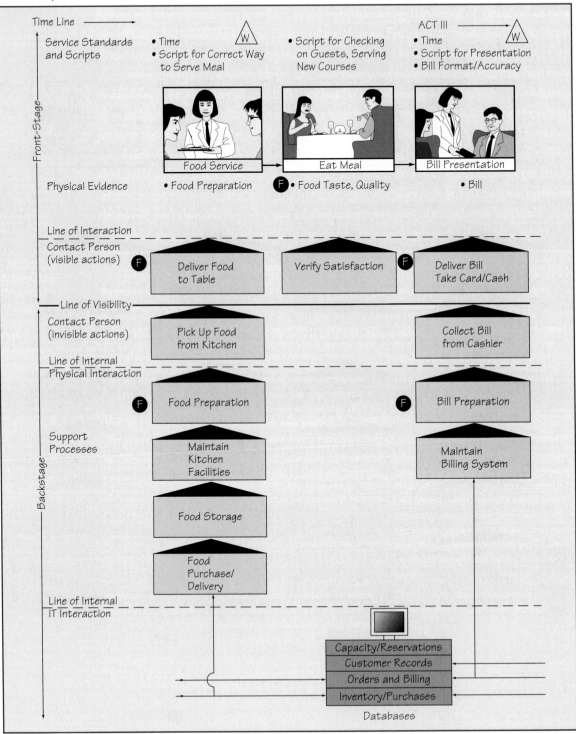

Figure 8.2
(Continued)

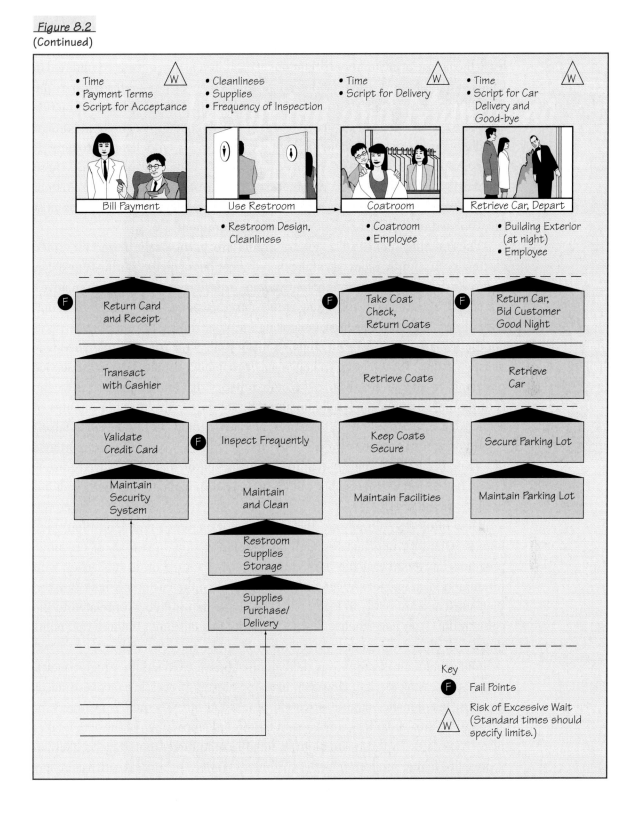

Setting Service Standards

Through both formal research and on-the-job experience, service managers can learn the nature of customer expectations at each step in the process. As outlined in Chapter 2, customers' expectations range across a spectrum—referred to as the zone of tolerance—from desired service (an ideal), to a threshold level of merely adequate service (refer to Figure 2.7 on page 50). Service providers should design standards for each step sufficiently high to satisfy and even delight customers. If that's not possible, then they will need to modify customer expectations. These standards may include time parameters, the script for a technically correct performance, and prescriptions for appropriate style and demeanor. Standards must be expressed in ways that permit objective measurement.

The opening scenes of a service drama are particularly important, since customers' first impressions can affect their evaluations of quality during later stages of service delivery. Perceptions of their service experiences tend to be cumulative.[6] If a couple of things go badly wrong at the outset, customers may simply walk out. Even if they stay, they may now be looking for other things that aren't quite right. On the other hand, if the first steps go really well, their zones of tolerance may increase so that they are more willing to overlook minor mistakes later in the service performance. Research by Marriott Hotels indicates that four of the five top factors contributing to customer loyalty come into play during the first ten minutes of service delivery.[7] However, performance standards should not be allowed to fall off toward the end of service delivery. Other research findings point to the importance of a strong finish and suggest that a service encounter that is perceived to start poorly but then builds in quality will be better rated than one that starts well but declines to end poorly.[8]

How often do failures ruin the customers' experience and spoil their good humor? Our own informal research among participants in dozens of executive programs has found that the most commonly cited source of dissatisfaction with restaurants is an inability to get the bill quickly when the customers have finished their meal and are ready to leave! This seemingly minor failing, unrelated to the core product, can nevertheless leave a bad taste in a customer's mouth that taints the overall dining experience, even if everything else has gone well.

Our restaurant example was deliberately chosen to illustrate a high-contact, people-processing service. However, many possession-processing services such as repair or maintenance, and information-processing services such as insurance or accounting, involve far less contact with customers, since much of the action takes place backstage. In these situations, a failure committed front stage is likely to represent a higher proportion of the customer's service encounters with a company and may therefore be viewed even more seriously, because there are fewer subsequent opportunities to create a favorable impression.

Failure Proofing Can Improve Reliability of Service Processes[9]

Careful analysis of the reasons for failure in service processes often reveals opportunities for failure proofing certain activities in order to reduce or even eliminate the risk of errors.

Fail-safe methods need to be designed not only for employees but also for customers, especially in services where the latter participate actively in creation and delivery processes.

FAIL-SAFE METHODS FOR SERVICE PERSONNEL   The goal of fail-safe procedures is to prevent errors such as performing tasks incorrectly, in the wrong order, or too slowly; or doing work that wasn't requested in the first place. Solutions vary by industry. In hospitals, trays for surgical instruments have indentations for each instrument, and all the instruments employed during an operation are nested in the tray. This not only ensures that a surgeon has all the tools needed for a specific operation, but also highlights any missing instruments that might still be in the patient before the surgeon closes the incision.

Treatment errors are those that occur during the contact between the server and the customer, such as lack of courteous, professional behavior. They may include failure to acknowledge, listen to, or react appropriately to the customer (Figure 8.2).

Tangible errors relate to failures in the physical elements of the service, and preventive measures include standards for cleaning of facilities and uniforms and appropriate control and adjustment of noise, odors, light, and temperature. Mirrors placed in ways that allow a worker to automatically check his or her appearance before greeting a customer foster a neat appearance. Hotels often wrap paper strips around towels to help the housekeeping staff distinguish quickly between those that are clean and those that should be replaced.

FAIL-SAFE METHODS FOR THE CUSTOMER   Customer errors can occur in the preparation stage before a service encounter takes place. Marketing communications can help shape prior expectations and inform the customer on how to access the service correctly. For example, marketers at the service division of one computer manufacturer provide customers with a simple flowchart that clarifies the correct way to place a service call. By guiding them through three "yes" or "no" questions, the firm ensures that customers are ready to supply the necessary information (e.g., their equipment model and registration number) and that they contact the appropriate provider for the type of service required.

Among the physical fail-safe devices used to control customers' behavior are chains to configure waiting lines and height bars at amusement parks to ensure that riders do not fall outside maximum and minimum size limitations.

Customers may also make errors at the resolution stage of the service encounter. Child care centers use toy outlines on walls and floors to show where toys should be placed after use. At a growing number of hotels, the key cards that open the doors to guest rooms must be placed in a wall socket inside the room in order to activate the lights. As a result, when guests take their cards as they leave their rooms, they automatically turn off the lights.

Service Process Redesign

Service process redesign revitalizes processes that have become outdated. This does not necessarily mean that the processes were poorly designed in the first place. Rather, changes in technology, customer needs, added service features, and new offerings have made existing processes crack and creak.[10]

Examining blueprints of existing services may suggest opportunities for product improvement that might be achieved by reconfiguring delivery systems, adding or deleting specific elements, or repositioning the service to appeal to other segments.

Managers in charge of service process redesign projects often do not want to spend more money on better quality. Rather, they aim to achieve a quantum leap in both productivity and service quality at the same time, striving for what is also called the Lean Service Machine,[11] a term borrowed and adopted from lean manufacturing. Restructuring or reengineering the ways in which tasks are performed has significant potential to increase output, especially in many backstage jobs.[12] Redesign efforts typically focus on achieving the following key performance measures: (1) reduced number of service failures, (2) reduced cycle time from customer initiation of a service process to its completion, (3) enhanced productivity, and (4) increased customer satisfaction. Ideally, redesign efforts should achieve all of the four measures simultaneously.

TYPES OF SERVICE PROCESS REDESIGNS[13]   Service process redesign encompasses reconstitution, rearrangement, or substitution of service processes. These efforts can be categorized into a number of types, including:

- *Eliminating non-value adding steps.* Often, activities at the front-end and back-end processes of services can be streamlined with the goal of focusing on the benefit-producing part of the service encounter. For example, a customer wanting to rent a car is not interested in filling out forms or processing payment and check of the returned car. Service redesign streamlines these tasks by trying to eliminate non-value-adding steps.
- *Shifting to self-service.* Significant productivity and sometimes even service quality gains can be achieved by increasing self-service when redesigning services. For example, FedEx succeeded in shifting more than 50 percent of its transactions from its call centers to its Web site, thus reducing the number of employees in its call centers by some 20,000 persons.

- *Delivering direct service.* This type of redesign involves bringing the service to the customer instead of bringing the customer to the service firm. This is often done to improve convenience for the customer, but can also result in productivity gains if companies can do away with high-rent locations.
- *Bundling services.* Bundling services involves bundling, or grouping, multiple services into one offer, focusing on a well-defined customer group. Bundling can help increase productivity, while at the same time adding value to the customer through lower transaction costs. It often has a better fit to the needs of the target segment. For example, it is very common for hotels to bundle several services into one package (e.g., hotels bundle wedding banquets and hotel room services together, as it is easier for them to sell their rooms to couples holding wedding dinners in their hotels).
- *Redesigning the physical aspects of service processes.* Physical service redesign focuses on the tangible elements of a service process and includes changes to the service facilities and equipment to improve the service experience. This leads to convenience and productivity, and often also enhances the satisfaction and productivity of front-line staff.

Table 8.1 summarizes the five redesign types and provides an overview of their potential benefits for the firm and its customers, and also highlights potential challenges or limitations. It is important to note that these redesign types are often used in combination.

The Customer as Co-Producer

Blueprinting helps to specify the role of customers in service delivery and to identify the extent of contact between them and service providers. It also clarifies whether the customer's role in a given service process is primarily that of passive recipient or entails active involvement in creating and producing the service.

Levels of Customer Participation

Customer participation refers to the actions and resources supplied by customers during service production and/or delivery and includes mental, physical, and even emotional inputs.[14] Some degree of customer participation in service delivery is inevitable in people-processing services and in any service involving real-time contact between customers and providers. In many instances, both the experience and the ultimate outcome reflect interactions between customers, facilities, employees, and systems. However, the level of this participation varies widely. Table 8.2 groups customer participation levels into three broad categories.[15]

LOW PARTICIPATION LEVEL   Employees and systems do all the work. Products tend to be standardized and service is provided regardless of any individual purchase.

Table 8.1

Five Types of Service Redesign

Approach and Concept	Potential Company Benefits	Potential Customer Benefits	Challenges/ Limitations
Elimination of non-value-added steps (streamlines all steps involved in a service transaction from purchase to payment)	• Improves efficiency • Increases productivity • Increases ability to customize service • Differentiates company	• Increases speed of service • Improves efficiency • Shifts tasks from customer to service firm • Separates service activation from delivery • Customizes service	• Requires extra customer education and employee training to implement smoothly and effectively
Self-service (customer assumes role of producer)	• Lowers cost • Improves productivity • Enhances technology reputation • Differentiates company	• Increases speed of service • Improves access • Saves money • Increases perception of control	• Requires customer preparation for the role • Limits face-to-face interaction • Creates difficulty in obtaining customer feedback • Creates difficulty in establishing customer loyalty/relationships
Direct service (service delivered to the customer's location)	• Eliminates store location limitations • Expands customer base • Differentiates company	• Increases convenience • Improves access	• Imposes logistical burdens • May require costly investments • Requires credibility and trust
Bundled service (combines multiple services into a package)	• Differentiates company • Aids customer retention • Increases per capita service use	• Increases convenience • Customizes service	• Requires extensive knowledge of targeted customers • May be perceived as wasteful
Physical service (manipulation of tangibles associated with the service)	• Improves employee satisfaction • Increases productivity • Differentiates company	• Increases convenience • Enhances function • Cultivates interest	• Easily imitated • Requires expense to effect and maintain • Raises customer expectations for the industry

Source: Adapted from Leonard L. Berry and Sandra K. Lampo, "Teaching an Old Service New Tricks: The Promise of Service Redesign," *Journal of Service Research* 2, no. 3 (2000): 265–275.

Payment may be the only required customer input. In situations where customers come to the service factory, all that is required is the customers' physical presence. Visiting a movie theater is an example. In possession-processing services such as routine cleaning or maintenance, customers can remain entirely uninvolved with the process other than providing access to service providers and making payment.

MODERATE PARTICIPATION LEVEL   Customer inputs are required to assist the organization in creating and delivering the service and in providing a degree of

Table 8.2
Levels of Customer Participation across Different Services

Low (Customer Presence Required During Service Delivery)	Moderate (Customer Inputs Required for Service Creation)	High (Customer Coproduces the Service Product)
Products are standardized.	Client inputs customize a standard service.	Active client participation guides the customized service.
Service is provided regardless of any individual purchase.	Provision of service requires customer purchase.	Service cannot be created apart from the customer's purchase and active participation.
Payment may be the only required customer input.	Customer inputs (information, materials) are necessary for an adequate outcome; but the service firm provides the service.	Customer inputs are mandatory and coproduce the outcome.
Examples		
Consumer Services		
Bus travel	Haircut	Marriage counseling
Motel stay	Annual physical exam	Personal training
Movie theater	Full-service restaurant	Weight-reduction program
Business-to-Business Services		
Uniform cleaning service	Agency-created advertising campaign	Management consulting
Pest control	Payroll service	Executive management seminar
Interior greenery maintenance	Independent freight transportation	Installation of wide area network (WAN)

Source: Adapted from Mary Jo Bitner, William T. Faranda, Amy R. Hubbert, and Valarie A. Zeithaml, "Customer Contributions and Roles in Service Delivery," *International Journal of Service Industry Management* 8, no. 3 (1997): 193–205.

customization. These inputs may include provision of information, personal effort, or even physical possessions. When getting their hair washed and cut, customers must let the hairdresser know what they want and cooperate during the different steps in the process. If a client wants an accountant to prepare a tax return, she must first pull together information and physical documentation that the accountant can use to prepare the return correctly and then be prepared to respond to any questions that the latter may have.

HIGH PARTICIPATION LEVEL   In these instances, customers work actively with the provider to coproduce the service. Service cannot be created apart from the customer's purchase and active participation. In fact, if customers fail to assume this role effectively and don't perform certain mandatory production tasks, they will jeopardize the quality of the service outcome. Some health-related services fall into this category, especially those related to improvement of the patient's physical condition, such as rehabilitation or weight loss, where customers work under professional supervision. Successful delivery of many business-to-business services requires customers and providers to work closely together as members of a team.

Self-Service Technologies

The ultimate form of involvement in service production is for customers to undertake a specific activity themselves, using facilities or systems provided by the service supplier. In effect, the customer's time and effort replace those of a service employee. In the case of telephone and Internet-based service, customers even provide their own terminals.

The concept of self-service is not new. Perhaps the most radical shift in the history of retailing occurred with the creation of supermarkets in the 1930s. For the first time, customers were required to select their own groceries from the shelves, put them in a trolley, and transport them to the checkout station. Both customers and retailers saw benefits in coproduction and the concept flourished, later spreading to other types of retail operations.

Nevertheless, early attempts to introduce self-service scanning at supermarket checkouts were unsuccessful, being resisted by consumers. It was not until the early 2000s that significant numbers of supermarkets began to give customers the option of completing their visit to the store by using a self-service checkout station, where they could scan and pay for their purchases. This development reflected not only much improved technology and reasonably foolproof processes, but also an economic tradeoff between the declining cost of these self-service systems and the rising cost of labor. Modern supermarket shoppers seem more willing to accept this new approach today, reflecting their greater comfort level with technology.[16]

Today's consumers are faced with an array of self-service technologies (SSTs) that allow them to produce a service independent of direct service employee involvement.[17] SSTs include automated banking terminals and self-service gasoline pumps (both introduced during the 1970s and progressively refined), automated telephone systems such as phone banking, automated hotel checkout, and numerous Internet-based services. Information-based services lend themselves particularly well to use of SSTs and include not only such supplementary services as getting information, placing orders and reservations, and making payment, but also delivery of core products in fields such as banking, research, entertainment, and self-paced education. For example, automated teller machines (ATMs), a form of SST, offer a surprising variety of services in many countries in Asia (see Figure 8.3). In addition to all the standard services such as cash withdrawals and balance checks, the services offered range from fund transfer, purchase of investment funds, applications for initial public offers (IPOs), and payment of bills, to topping up of prepaid phone cards and purchase of travel insurance. Another example is the fast increasing prevalence of government-provided services over the Internet, also called e-Government.[18]

PSYCHOLOGICAL FACTORS IN CUSTOMER COPRODUCTION   The logic of self-service has historically relied on an economic rationale, emphasizing the productivity gains and cost savings that result when customers take over work previously

Figure 8.3
Automated teller machines (ATM), a form of SST, offer a surprising variety of services in many countries in Asia.

performed by employees. In many instances, a portion of the resulting savings is shared with customers in the form of lower prices as an inducement for them to them to change their behavior. However, researchers Bendapudi and Leone argue that customers' psychological responses to participation in production should also be considered in self-service environments, specifically their tendency to take credit for successful outcomes, but not the blame for unsuccessful ones.[19] Their research indicated that this tendency was reduced when customers were given a choice on whether or not to participate in service production.

Given the significant investment in both time and money that is often required for firms to design, implement, and manage SSTs, it's critical for service marketers to understand how consumers decide between using an SST option and relying on a human provider. We need to recognize that SSTs present both advantages and disadvantages. In addition to benefiting from time and cost savings, flexibility, convenience of location, greater control over service delivery, and a higher perceived level of customization, customers may also derive fun, enjoyment, and even spontaneous delight from SST usage.[20] However, there's evidence that some consumers see the introduction of SSTs into the service encounters as something of a threat, causing anxiety and stress among those who are uncomfortable with using them.[21] Research by Curran, Meuter, and Surprenant found that multiple attitudes may drive customer intentions to use a specific SST, including global attitudes toward related service technologies, global attitudes toward the specific service firm, and attitudes toward its employees.[22]

SST CHARACTERISTICS AND CUSTOMER ATTITUDES   Research suggests that customers both love and hate SSTs.[23] They love SSTs when they bail them out of difficult situations, often because SST machines are conveniently located and accessible 24/7. Customers also love SSTs when they perform better than the alternative of being served by a service employee, enabling users to get detailed information and complete transactions faster than they could through face-to-face or telephone contact. Many customers are still in awe of technology and what it can do for them—when it works well.

However, customers hate SSTs when they fail. Users get angry when they find that machines are out of service, their PIN (personal identification numbers) are not accepted, Web sites are down, tracking numbers do not work, or items are not shipped as promised. Even when SSTs do work, customers are frustrated by poorly designed technologies that make service processes difficult to understand and use. Poorly designed navigation is a common complaint about Web sites. Users also get frustrated when they themselves mess up, due to such errors as forgetting their passwords, failing to provide information as requested, or simply hitting the wrong buttons. Self-service logically implies that customers can cause their own dissatisfaction. However, even when it is their own fault, customers may still partially blame the service provider for not providing a simpler and more user-friendly system, and then revert to the traditional human-based system on the next occasion.

Designing a Web site to be virtually failure proof is no easy task and can be very expensive, but it is through such investments that companies create loyal users and active word of mouth. Best Practice in Action 8.1 describes the emphasis on user friendliness at TLContact, a company profiled in depth in the case that appears on pages 666–682.

A key problem with SSTs is that so few of them incorporate service recovery systems. In too many instances, when the process fails, there is no simple way to recover on the spot. Typically, customers are forced to telephone or make a personal visit to resolve the problem, which may be exactly what they were trying to avoid in the first place! Mary Jo Bitner suggests that managers should put their firms' SSTs to the test by asking the following basic questions:[24]

- *Does the SST work reliably?* Firms must ensure that SSTs work as dependably as promised and that the design is user friendly for customers. Southwest Airlines' online ticketing services have set a high standard for simplicity and reliability. It boasts the highest percentage of online ticket sales of any airline—clear evidence of customer acceptance.
- *Is the SST better than the interpersonal alternative?* If it doesn't save time or provide ease of access, cost savings, or some other benefit, customers will continue to use familiar conventional processes. Amazon.com's success reflects its efforts to create a highly personalized, efficient alternative to visiting a retail store.

TLCONTACT.COM CREATES AN EXCEPTIONAL USER EXPERIENCE

When his sister Sharon's five-day-old baby, Matthew, underwent surgery at the University of Michigan Medical Center in early 1998 to correct a life-threatening heart defect, Mark Day was more than a thousand miles away at Stanford, studying for a Ph.D. in engineering. Feeling isolated, knowing nothing about the heart, and wanting to do something useful, Mark turned for medical information to the Internet, which was just beginning to hit its stride. Within a few weeks, he had created a simple Web site that family and friends could access. He edited the information he had gathered and loaded it on the site, together with bulletins on Matthew's condition and how the baby was responding to treatment. "It was a very simple site," Mark declared later. "If I had paid somebody else to do it for me, it probably wouldn't have cost more than a few hundred dollars." To minimize the need for e-mail, Mark added a bulletin board so that people could send messages to Sharon and her husband, Eric.

To everyone's surprise, the site proved exceptionally popular. News spread by word of mouth, and the site recorded numerous daily visitors, with more than 200 people leaving messages for the family. People who confessed that they had never before used the Internet found a way to access the site, follow baby Matthew's progress, and send messages.

Two years and three operations later, Matthew was a happy, healthy toddler. His parents, Eric and Sharon Langshur, decided to create a company, TLContact.com, to commercialize Mark's concept as a service for patients and their families. Eric and Sharon invited Mark to join the company as chief technology officer. To ensure quality control and retain intellectual capital, Mark decided to build the necessary software systems in-house rather than subcontract the task to outside vendors. He hired a skilled technical team, including programmers and graphic designers.

Recognizing that TLC's patient sites, known as CarePages, would be accessed by a wide array of individuals, many of whom would be under stress and even having their first experience using the Internet, Mark and his team placed a premium on ease of use. He commented: "It's very difficult to create a piece of software that's really user friendly. It takes an incredible amount of skill, effort, and time to develop something that's usable, functional, and scalable—meaning that it can be expanded and built upon without failing." The total cost of creating the initial functioning Web site was close to half a million dollars.

As the company grew, continued investments were made to expand the functionality of the service for patients, visitors, and sponsoring hospitals to eliminate any problems that users had reported, and to further improve user friendliness. Enhancements included an option for user feedback, addition of an e-mail notification tool to announce updated news on a CarePage, and the ability to access CarePages through a hospital's own Web site. Receiving feedback that users encountered problems when they mistyped a CarePage name and failed to gain access, TLC added software logic to fix common mistakes, thereby reducing the volume of customer service enquiries. By 2003, TLC had turned the corner financially and was growing rapidly. Heartwarming tributes from satisfied users were pouring in. But work continued to enhance the CarePage experience, with software changes and improvements being made every six to eight weeks. By this point, the firm had invested more than two million dollars in technology.

Source: Christopher Lovelock, "TLContact.com" 2003 (case reproduced on pages 666–682).

- *If it fails, what systems are in place to recover?* It's critical for firms to provide systems, structures, and recovery technologies that will enable prompt service recovery when things go wrong. Some banks have a phone beside each ATM, giving customers direct access to a 24-hour customer service center if they have questions or run into difficulties. Supermarkets that have installed self-service checkout lanes usually assign one employee to monitor the lanes. This practice combines security with customer assistance. In telephone-based service systems, well-designed voice-mail menus include an option for customers to reach a customer service representative.

Service Firms as Teachers

Although service providers attempt to design the ideal level of customer participation into the service delivery system, in reality it is customers' actions that determine the actual amount of participation. *Underparticipation* causes customers to experience a decrease in service benefits (for instance, a dieter who doesn't follow guidelines properly will probably lose less weight). *Overparticipation* by customers may take employees away from other tasks and cause the firm to spend more resources customizing a service than was originally intended (consider the impact on productivity at a fast-food restaurant if every customer insisted on customization of their hamburger orders). Service businesses must teach their customers the roles they are expected to play in order to optimize participation levels during service production and consumption. Adoption of new service devices such as ATMs, or new services such as phone banking and e-banking has been spreading rapidly in the consumer banking sector in emerging economies like China. However, the young, well-educated professionals living in the cities are more likely to use the self-service technology. Those who are middle aged and above, poorly educated and earn low incomes, to say nothing of those from rural areas, are likely to rush to bank counters even for small cash withdrawals or account status check, occupying expensive resources and yet are not profitable customers for the banks. The key problem is that no basic education is delivered to them to convert them to using low-cost, technology-based self-services.

The more work that customers are expected to do, the greater their need for information about how to perform their roles for best results. The necessary education can be provided in many different ways. Brochures and posted instructions are two widely used approaches. Automated machines often contain detailed operating instructions and diagrams. Thoughtful banks place a telephone beside their ATMs so that customers can call a real person for help and advice at any time if they are confused about the on-screen instructions. Advertising for new services often contains significant educational content. Many Web sites include an FAQ (frequently asked questions) section. eBay's Web site provides detailed instructions for getting started, including on how to submit an item for auction and how to bid for items you might want to buy. Its Help Center features an A-Z index of topics, including advice on resolving trading concerns.

In many businesses, customers look to employees for advice and assistance and are frustrated if they can't obtain it. Service providers, ranging from sales assistants and customer service representatives to flight attendants and nurses, must be trained to help them improve their teaching skills. People may also turn to other customers for help. eBay's Help Center includes a section titled "Ask eBay Members" which notes that eBay community members are always happy to help one another. [25]

Researchers Benjamin Schneider and David Bowen suggest giving customers a realistic service preview in advance of service delivery, to provide them with a clear picture of their roles in service coproduction.[26] For example, a company might show a video presentation to help customers understand their role in a specific service encounter. This technique is used by some dentists to familiarize patients with the surgical processes they are about to experience and indicate how they should cooperate so as to help make things go as smoothly as possible.

Customers as Partial Employees

Some researchers argue that firms should view customers as "partial employees" who can influence the productivity and quality of service processes and outputs.[27] This perspective requires a change in management mindset, as Schneider and Bowen make clear:

> If you think of customers as partial employees, you begin to think very differently about what you hope customers will bring to the service encounter. Now they must bring not only expectations and needs but also relevant service production competencies that will enable them to fill the role of partial employees. The service management challenge deepens accordingly.[28]

They suggest that customers who are offered an opportunity to participate at an active level are more likely to be satisfied—regardless of whether or not they actually choose the more active role—because they like to be offered a choice.

Managing customers as partial employees requires using the same human resource strategy as managing a firm's paid employees and should follow these four steps:

1. Conduct a "job analysis" of customers' present roles in the business and compare it against the roles that the firm would like them to play.
2. Determine if customers are aware of how they are expected to perform and have the skills needed to perform as required.
3. Motivate customers by ensuring that they will be rewarded for performing well (e.g., satisfaction from better quality and more customized output, enjoyment of participating in the actual process, a belief that their own productivity speeds the process and keeps costs down.)

4. Regularly appraise customers' performance. If it is unsatisfactory, seek to change their roles and the procedures in which they are involved. Alternatively, consider "terminating" these customers (nicely, of course!) and look for new ones.

Effective human resource management starts with recruitment and selection. The same approach should hold true for "partial employees." Thus, if coproduction requires specific skills, firms should target their marketing efforts to recruit new customers who have the competency to perform the necessary tasks (see Figure 8.4).[29]

The Problem of Customer Misbehavior

Other customers often form an important element in service encounters. In many people-processing services, we expect to find other customers present and to share service facilities with them. Their behavior can contribute positively or negatively to the functioning of specific service delivery processes and may even affect the outcome.

Customers who act in uncooperative or abusive ways are a problem for any organization. However, they have more potential for mischief in service businesses, particularly those in which the customer comes to the service factory. As you know from your own experience, the behavior of other customers can affect your enjoyment of a service. If you like classical music and attend symphony concerts, you expect audience members to keep quiet during the performance, rather than spoil the music by talking loudly. By contrast, a silent audience would be deadly during a rock concert or team sports event, where active audience participation

Figure 8.4

The DBS banking center in Singapore consists of many ATMs and self-service banking machines that operate 24 hours, seven days a week, offering greater convenience for customers who prefer self-service.

adds to the excitement. Firms that fail to deal effectively with customer misbehaviors risk damaging their relationships with all the other customers they would like to keep.

Addressing the Challenge of Jaycustomers[30]

Visitors to North America from other English-speaking countries are often puzzled by the term "jaywalker," that distinctively American word used to describe people who cross streets at unauthorized places or in a dangerous manner. The prefix "jay" comes from a 19th-century slang term for a stupid person. We can create a whole vocabulary of derogatory terms by adding the prefix *jay* to existing nouns and verbs. How about *jaycustomer*, for example, to denote someone who "jayuses" a service or "jayconsumes" a physical product (and then "jaydisposes" of it afterwards)? We define a jaycustomer as one who acts in a thoughtless or abusive way, causing problems for the firm, its employees, and other customers. Every service has its share of jaycustomers.

Six Types of Jaycustomers

Jaycustomers are undesirable. At worst, a firm needs to control or prevent their abusive behavior. At best, it would like to avoid attracting them in the first place. We've identified six broad categories of jaycustomers and given them generic names, but many customer contact personnel have come up with their own special terms. As you reflect on these categories, you may be tempted to add a few more of your own.

THE THIEF This jaycustomer has no intention of paying and sets out to steal goods and services (or to pay less than full price by switching price tickets or contesting bills on baseless grounds). Shoplifting is a major problem in retail stores. What retailers euphemistically call "shrinkage" is estimated to cost them huge sums of money in annual revenues. It is easy to avoid payment for many services. For those with technical skills, it's sometimes possible to by-pass electricity meters, access telephone lines free of charge, or circumvent normal cable TV feeds. Riding free on public transportation, sneaking into movie theaters, or not paying for restaurant meals are also popular. There is also the use of fraudulent forms of payment such as stolen credit cards or checks drawn on accounts without any funds. Finding out how people steal a service is the first step in preventing theft or catching thieves and, where appropriate, prosecuting them. However, managers should try not to alienate honest customers by degrading their service experiences. Also, provision must be made for honest but absent-minded customers who forget to pay.

THE RULEBREAKER Just as highways need safety regulations, many service businesses need to establish rules of behavior for employees and customers to guide them safely through the various steps of the service encounter. Some of these rules are imposed by government agencies for health and safety reasons. The sign found in many restaurants that states "No shirt, no shoes—no service" demonstrates a health-related regulation. Air travel provides one of the best examples of rules designed to ensure safety.

In addition to enforcing government regulations, suppliers often impose their own rules to facilitate smooth operations, avoid unreasonable demands on employees, prevent misuse of products and facilities, protect themselves legally, and discourage individual customers from misbehaving. Ski resorts, for instance, are getting tough on careless skiers who pose risks to both themselves and others.[31] Collisions can cause serious injury and even kill. Thus, ski patrol members must be safety oriented and sometimes take on a policing role. Just as dangerous drivers can lose their licenses, dangerous skiers can lose their lift tickets.

How should a firm deal with rulebreakers? Much depends on which rules have been broken. In the case of legally enforceable ones like theft, bad debts, and trying to take guns on aircraft, the courses of action need to be laid down explicitly to protect employees and to punish or discourage wrongdoing by customers. Company rules are a little more ambiguous. Are they really necessary in the first place? If not, the firm should get rid of them. Do they deal with health and safety? If so, educating customers about the rules should reduce the need for taking corrective action. The same is true for rules designed to protect the comfort and enjoyment of all customers. Other customers can often be relied upon to help service personnel enforce rules that affect everybody else. They may even take the initiative in doing so.

There are risks attached to making lots of rules. They can make an organization appear bureaucratic and overbearing. In addition, they can transform employees, whose orientation should be service to customers, into police officers who see their most important task as enforcing all the rules. The fewer the rules, the more explicit the important ones can be.

THE BELLIGERENT   You've probably seen him (or her) in a store, at the airport, in a hotel or restaurant—red in the face and shouting angrily, or perhaps icily calm and mouthing off insults, threats, and obscenities.[32] Things don't always work as they should. Machines break down, service is clumsy, customers are ignored, a flight is delayed, an order is delivered incorrectly, staff are unhelpful, or a promise is broken. Service personnel are often abused, even when they are not to blame. If an employee lacks authority to resolve the problem, the belligerent may become madder still, even to the point of physical attack. Drunkenness and drug abuse add extra layers of complication (see Service Perspectives 8.1). Organizations that care about their employees go to great efforts to develop skills in dealing with these difficult situations. Training exercises that involve role playing help employees develop the self-confidence and assertiveness that they need to deal with upset,

*Service
Perspectives
8.1*

AIR RAGE: UNRULY PASSENGERS POSE A GROWING PROBLEM

Joining the term "road rage"—coined in 1988 to describe angry, aggressive drivers who threaten other road users—is the newer term "air rage." Perpetrators of air rage are violent, unruly passengers who endanger flight attendants, pilots, and other passengers. Incidents of air rage are perpetrated by only a tiny fraction of all airline passengers—reportedly about 5,000 times a year—but each incident in the air may affect the comfort and safety of hundreds of other people.

Although terrorism is an ongoing concern, out-of-control passengers pose a serious threat to safety, too. On a Singapore Airlines plane, a drunken Swiss man punched a flight attendant and leapt off the plane on the runway at Changi International Airport after his unruly act. This act resulted in the evacuation of passengers off the plane, while the police conducted a security search. The entire ordeal caused the flight to be delayed by a good two and a half hours.

A growing number of carriers, however, are taking air rage perpetrators to court. In one suit, a magistrate ordered a perpetrator to pay Singapore Airlines US$10,200 after he had forced a pilot to make an unscheduled landing in Northern Australia. The Construction and Transport Ministry in Japan, on the other hand, has revised the Civil Aeronautics Law to include a maximum 500,000-yen fine (US$4,600) for passengers who fail to heed warnings by the captain to stop detrimental behavior.

What causes air rage? Researchers suggest that air travel has become increasingly stressful as a result of crowding and longer flights. The airlines themselves may have contributed to the problem by squeezing rows of seats more tightly together and failing to explain delays. Findings suggest that risk factors for air travel stress include anxiety and an anger-prone personality. They also show that traveling on unfamiliar routes is more stressful than on a familiar one. Another factor may be restrictions on smoking, but alcohol abuse underlies a majority of incidents.

Airlines are training their employees to handle violent individuals and to spot problem passengers before they start causing serious problems. Some carriers offer travelers specific suggestions on how to relax during long flights. In addition, some airlines have considered offering nicotine patches to passengers who are desperate for a smoke, but are no longer allowed to light up.

Sources: Based on information from multiple sources, including Daniel Eisenberg, "Acting Up in the Air," *Time,* December 21, 1998; Ben Nadarajan, "Swiss Who Leapt off SIA Plane Faces Ban", *The Straits Times*, May 12, 2004; "Singapore Airlines Air Rage Passenger Ordered to Pay Cost of Diverting Flight", *Associated Press Newswires*, December 12, 2003; "Govt Targets In-Flight Misbehaviour", *The Daily Yomiuri*, January 18, 2003.

belligerent customers (sometimes referred to as "irates"). Employees also need to learn how to defuse anger, calm anxiety, and comfort distress, particularly when there is good reason for the customer to be upset with the organization's performance.

What should an employee do when an aggressive customer brushes off attempts to defuse the situation? In a public environment, one priority should be to move the person away from other customers. Sometimes, supervisors may have to arbitrate disputes between customers and staff members. At other times, they need to stand behind the employee's actions. If a customer has physically assaulted an employee, then it may be necessary to summon security officers or the police. Some firms try to conceal such events, fearing bad publicity. Others, however, feel obliged to make a public stand on behalf of their employees, like the Body Shop manager who ordered an ill-tempered customer out of the store, telling her: "I won't stand for your rudeness to my staff."

Telephone rudeness poses a different challenge. Service personnel have been known to hang up on angry customers, but that action doesn't resolve the problem. Bank customers, for instance, tend to get upset when learning that checks have been returned because they are overdrawn (which means they've broken the rules) or that a request for a loan has been denied. One approach for handling customers who continue to berate a telephone-based employee is for the latter to say firmly: "This conversation isn't getting us anywhere. Why don't I call you back in a few minutes when you've had time to digest the information?" In many cases, a break for reflection is exactly what's needed.

THE FAMILY FEUDERS People who get into arguments (or worse) with other customers—often members of their own family, make up a subcategory of belligerents we call family feuders. Employee intervention may calm the situation or actually make it worse. Some situations require detailed analysis and a carefully measured response. Others, like customers starting a food fight in a nice restaurant, require almost instantaneous response. Service managers in these situations need to be prepared to think on their feet and act fast.

THE VANDAL The level of physical abuse to which service facilities and equipment can be subjected is truly astonishing. Soft drinks are poured into bank cash machines; graffiti is scrawled on both interior and exterior surfaces; burn holes from cigarettes scar carpets, tablecloths, and bedcovers; bus seats are slashed and hotel furniture broken; telephone handsets are torn off; customers' cars are vandalized; glass is smashed and fabrics are torn. The list is endless. Customers don't cause all of the damage, of course. Bored or drunk young people are the source of much exterior vandalism. Disgruntled employees have also been known to commit sabotage. However, much of the problem does originate with paying customers who choose to misbehave. Alcohol and drugs are sometimes the cause, psychological problems may contribute, and carelessness can play a role. There are also occasions when unhappy customers, feeling mistreated by the service provider, try to take revenge in some way.

The best cure for vandalism is prevention. Improved security discourages some vandals. Good lighting helps, as does open design of public areas. Companies can choose pleasing yet vandal-resistant surfaces, protective coverings for equipment, and rugged furnishings. Educating customers on how to use equipment properly and providing warnings about fragile objects can reduce the likelihood of abuse or careless handling. There are also economic sanctions like security deposits or signed agreements in which customers agree to pay for any damage that they cause.

What should managers do if prevention fails and damage is done? If the perpetrator is caught, they should first clarify whether there are any extenuating circumstances, because accidents do happen. Sanctions for deliberate damage can range from a warning to prosecution. As far as the physical damage itself is concerned, it's best to fix it fast. The general manager of a bus company had the right idea when he said: "If one of our buses is vandalized, whether it's a broken window, a slashed seat, or graffiti on the ceiling, we take it out of service immediately, so nobody sees it. Otherwise, you just give the same idea to five other characters who were too dumb to think of it in the first place!"

THE DEADBEAT   Leaving aside those individuals who never intended to pay in the first place, there are many reasons why customers fail to pay for services they have received. Once again, preventive action is better than a cure. A growing number of firms insist on prepayment. Any form of ticket sale is a good example of this. Direct marketing organizations ask for your credit card number as they take your order, as do most hotels when you make a reservation. The next best thing is to present the customer with a bill immediately on completion of service. If the bill is to be sent by mail, the firm should send it fast, while the service is still fresh in the customer's mind.

Not every apparent delinquent is a hopeless deadbeat. Perhaps there's good reason for the delay and acceptable payment arrangements can be worked out. A key question is whether such a personalized approach can be cost justified, relative to the results obtained by purchasing the services of a collection agency. There may be other considerations, too. If the client's problems are only temporary ones, what is the long-term value of maintaining the relationship? Will it create positive goodwill and word of mouth to help the customer work things out? These decisions are judgment calls, but if creating and maintaining long-term relationships is the firm's ultimate goal, they bear exploration.

Conclusion

This chapter emphasized the important of designing and managing service processes, which are the heart of the service product and significantly shape the customer experience. We covered in-depth blueprinting as a powerful tool to understand, make tangible, analyze, and improve service processes. Blueprinting helps to identify and reduce service fail points, and provides important insights for service process redesign.

An important part of process design is to define the roles customers should play in the production of services. Their level of desired participation needs to be determined and customers need to be motivated and taught to play their part in the service delivery.

Review Questions

1. What is the role of blueprinting in designing, managing, and redesigning service processes?
2. How can fail-safe procedures be used to reduce service failures?
3. Describe how blueprinting helps to identify the relationship between core and supplementary services.
4. How do creation and evaluation of a service blueprint help managers understand the role of time in service delivery?
5. Why is periodic process redesign necessary, and what are the main types of service process redesign?
6. Why does the customer's role as a coproducer need to be designed into service processes? What are the implications of considering customers as partial employees?
7. Explain what factors make customers like and dislike self-service technologies.
8. What are the different types of jaycustomers, and how can a service firm deal with the behavior of such customers?

Application Exercises

1. Prepare a script for a basic physical examination at a doctor's office. How much participation is required of the customer for the process to work smoothly? In what ways can insufficient cooperation by the customer derail the process? What can the doctor's office do in advance to achieve the necessary cooperation?
2. Review the blueprint of the restaurant visit in Figure 8.2. Identify several possible OTSUs for each step in the front-stage process. Consider possible causes underlying each potential failure and suggest ways to eliminate or minimize these problems.
3. Prepare a flowchart of a service with which you are familiar.
   (a) What are the tangible cues or indicators of quality from the customers' perspective, considering the line of visibility?
   (b) Are all steps in the process necessary?
   (c) To what extent is standardization possible and advisable throughout the process?
   (d) What are the potential fail points and how could they be designed out of the process, or what service recovery procedures could be introduced?
   (e) What are potential measures of process performance?
4. Observe supermarket shoppers who use self-service checkout lanes and compare them to those who use the services of a checker. What differences do you observe? How many of those conducting self-service scanning appear to run into difficulties and how do they resolve their problems?
5. Identify one Web site that is exceptionally user friendly and another that is not. What are the factors that make for a satisfying user experience in the first instance and a frustrating one in the second? Specify recommendations for improvements in the second Web site.
6. Identify the potential behavior of jaycustomers for a service of your choice. How can the service process be designed to minimize or control the behavior of jaycustomers?

Endnotes

1   Richard B. Chase and Sriram Dasu, "Want to Perfect Your Company's Service? Use Behavioral Science," *Harvard Business Review* 79 (June 2001): 78–85.

2   See G. Lynn Shostack, "Understanding Services through Blueprinting," in T. Schwartz *et al.*, *Advances in Services Marketing and Management,* 1992 (Greenwich, CT: JAI Press, 1992), 75–90.

3   G. Lynn Shostack, "Designing Services That Deliver," *Harvard Business Review* (January–February 1984): 133–139.

4   Jane Kingman-Brundage, "The ABCs of Service System Blueprinting," in *Designing a Winning Service Strategy*, eds. M. J. Bitner and L. A. Crosby, (Chicago: American Marketing Association, 1989).

5   David Maister, now president of Maister Associates, coined the term OTSU while teaching at Harvard Business School in the 1980s.

6   See for example, Eric J. Arnould and Linda L. Price, "River Magic: Extraordinary Experience and the Extended Service Encounter," *Journal of Consumer Research* 20 (June 1993): 24–25; Eric J. Arnould and Linda L. Price, "Collaring the Cheshire Cat: Studying Customers' Services Experience through Metaphors," *The Service Industries Journal* 16 (October 1996): 421–442; and Nick Johns and Phil Tyas, "Customer Perceptions of Service Operations: Gestalt, Incident or Mythology?" *The Service Industries Journal* 17 (July 1997): 474–488.

7   "How Marriott Makes a Great First Impression," *The Service Edge* 6 (May 1993): 5.

8   David E. Hansen and Peter J. Danaher, "Inconsistent Performance during the Service Encounter: What's a Good Start Worth?" *Journal of Service Research* 1 (February 1999): 227–235; Chase and Dasu, 2001, *op. cit.*

9   Based in part on Richard B. Chase and Douglas M. Stewart, "Make Your Service Fail-Safe," *Sloan Management Review* (Spring 1994): 35–44.

10 Jochen Wirtz and Monica Tomlin, "Institutionalizing Customer-Driven Learning through Fully Integrated Customer Feedback Systems," *Managing Service Quality* 10, no. 4 (2000): 205–215.

11 Cynthia Karen Swank, "The Lean Service Machine," *Harvard Business Review* 81, no. 10 (2003): 123-129.

12 See, for example, Michael Hammer and James Champy, *Reengineering the Corporation* (New York: Harper Business, 1993).

13 This section is partially based on Leonard L. Berry and Sandra K. Lampo, "Teaching an Old Service New Tricks—The Promise of Service Redesign," *Journal of Service Research* 2, no. 3 (February 2000): 265–275. Berry and Lampo identified the following five service redesign concepts: self-service, direct service, preservice, bundled service, and physical service. We expanded some of these concepts in this section to embrace more of the productivity-enhancing aspects of process redesign such as eliminating non-value-adding work steps in all stages of service delivery.

14 Amy Risch Rodie and Susan Schultz Klein, "Customer Participation in Services Production and Delivery," in *Handbook of Service Marketing and Management*, eds. T. A. Schwartz and D. Iacobucci (Thousand Oaks, CA: Sage Publications, 2000), 111–125.

15 Mary Jo Bitner, William T. Faranda, Amy R. Hubbert, and Valarie A. Zeitham, "Customer Contributions and Roles in Service Delivery," *International Journal of Service Industry Management* 8, no. 3 (1997): 193–205.

16 Pratibha A. Dabholkar, L. Michelle Bobbitt, and Eun-Ju Lee, "Understanding Consumer Motivation and Behavior Related to Self-Scanning in Retailing," *International Journal of Service Industry Management* 14, no. 1 (2003): 59–95.

17 Matthew L. Meuter, Amy L. Ostrom, Robert I. Roundtree, and Mary Jo Bitner, "Self-Service Technologies: Understanding Customer Satisfaction with Technology-Based Service Encounters," *Journal of Marketing* 64 (July 2000): 50–64.

18 Shirley-Ann Hazlett and Frances Hill, "E-Government: The Realities of Using IT to Transform the Public Sector," *Managing Service Quality* 13, no. 6 (2003): 445–452.

19 Neeli Bendapudi and Robert P. Leone, "Psychological Implications of Customer Participation in Co-Production," *Journal of Marketing* 67 (January 2003): 14–28.

20   Pratibha A. Dabholkar, "Consumer Evaluations of New Technology-Based Self-Service Options: An Investigation of Alternative Models of Service Quality," *International Journal of Research in Marketing* 13 (1996): 29–51; Mary Jo. Bitner, Stephen W. Brown, and Matthew L. Meuter, "Technology Infusion in Service Encounters," *Journal of the Academy of Marketing Science* 28, no. 1 (2000): 138–149; Dabholkar *et al.*, 2003 *op. cit.*

21   David G. Mick and Susan Fournier, "Paradoxes of Technology: Consumer Cognizance, Emotions, and Coping Strategies," *Journal of Consumer Research* 25 (September 1998): 123–143.

22   James M. Curran, Matthew L. Meuter, and Carol G. Surprenant, "Intentions to Use Self-Service Technologies: A Confluence of Multiple Attitudes," *Journal of Service Research* 5 (February 2003): 209–224.

23   Meuter *et al.*, 2000; Mary Jo Bitner, "Self-Service Technologies: What Do Customers Expect?" *Marketing Management* (Spring 2001): 10–11.

24   Bitner, 2001, *op. cit.*

25   www.ebay.com, accessed April 2003.

26   Benjamin Schneider and David E. Bowen, *Winning the Service Game* (Boston: Harvard Business School Press, 1995), 92.

27   David E. Bowen, "Managing Customers as Human Resources in Service Organizations," *Human Resources Management* 25, no.3 (1986): 371–383.

28   Schneider and Bowen, *op. cit.*, 85.

29   Bonnie Farber Canziani, "Leveraging Customer Competency in Service Firms," *International Journal of Service Industry Management* 8, no. 1 (1997): 5–25.

30   This section is adapted from Christopher Lovelock, *Product Plus* (New York: McGraw-Hill, 1994), Chapter 15. See also, Lloyd C. Harris and Kate L. Reynolds, "The Consequences of Disfunctional Customer Behavior," *Journal of Service Research*, November 2003, 144–161.

31   Based on Rob Ortega and Emily Nelson, "Skiing Deaths May Fuel Calls for Helmets," *Wall Street Journal*, January 7, 1998, B-1–B-16.

32   For an amusing and explicit depiction of various types of belligerent customers, see Ron Zemke and Kristin Anderson, "The Customers from Hell," *Training* 26 (February 1990): 25–31 [reprinted in John E. G. Bateson and K. Douglas Hoffman, *Managing Services Marketing, 4th ed.* (Fort Worth, TX: The Dryden Press, 1999), 61–62].

CHAPTER NINE

Balancing Demand and Capacity

*Balancing the supply and demand sides of a service industry is not easy,
and whether a manager does it well or not makes all the difference.*

W. EARL SASSER, JR.

Fluctuating demand is a major challenge for many types of service organizations, including restaurants, vacation resorts, courier services, consulting firms, tax authorities and call centers. These demand fluctuations play havoc with the efficient use of productive assets. By working collaboratively with managers in operations and human resources, service marketers may be able to develop strategies to bring demand and capacity into balance in ways that generate benefits for customers, as well as for service suppliers.

In this chapter, we consider the nature of demand and supply in services and explore the following questions:

1. What is meant by "capacity" in a service context and how is it measured?
2. Can variations in demand be predicted and their causes identified?
3. How can capacity management techniques be employed to match variations in demand?
4. What marketing strategies are available to service firms to smooth out fluctuations in demand?
5. If customers must wait for service, how can this activity be made less burdensome for them?
6. What is involved in designing an effective reservations system?

Fluctuations in Demand Threaten Service Productivity

Unlike manufactured goods, services are perishable and normally cannot be stockpiled for sale at a later date. This is a problem for any capacity-constrained service that faces wide swings in demand. The problem is most commonly found among services that process people or physical possessions—such as transportation, lodging, food service, repair and maintenance, entertainment, and health care. It also affects labor-intensive, information-processing services that face cyclical shifts in demand.

In 1997, there were less than 100 hotels in Kunming, a city in the Yunnan Province in China, and none of them were five-star hotels. However, almost all of them were profitable. The Kunming International Horticultural Exposition held from May 1 to October 31, 1999 stimulated the expansion of the hotel industry in Kunming. Today, there are about 1,286 hotels in that city, including 19 rated four-star and five rated five-star, with an overall daily capacity of 110,000 rooms. However, after the exposition, the tourist volume fell dramatically to only 34,000 per day. The stiff competition that followed also drove down hotel room rates. To survive, these hotels had to cut operating costs to make up for losses resulting from lower room rates. They reduced the variety of breakfasts, turned off air-conditioners, and replaced pure cotton sheets with inferior quality ones. Many of the best employees left and guests began filing more complaints.

Effective use of productive capacity is one of the secrets of success in such businesses. The goal should not be to utilize staff, labor, equipment, and facilities as much as possible, but rather to use them as *productively* as possible. At the same time, the search for productivity must not be allowed to undermine service quality and degrade the customer experience

From Excess Demand to Excess Capacity

The problem is a familiar one. "It's either feast or famine for us!" sighs the manager. "In peak periods, we're disappointing prospective customers by turning them away. And in low periods, our facilities are idle, our employees are standing around looking bored, and we're losing money."

At any given moment, a fixed-capacity service may face one of four conditions (see Figure 9.1):

- *Excess demand.* The level of demand exceeds maximum available capacity, with the result that some customers are denied service and business is lost.
- *Demand exceeds optimum capacity.* No one is actually turned away, but conditions are crowded and customers are likely to perceive a deterioration in quality of service and to feel dissatisfied.
- *Demand and supply are well balanced* at the level of optimum capacity. Staff and facilities are busy without being overworked and customers receive good service without delays.
- *Excess capacity.* Demand is below optimum capacity and productive resources are underutilized, resulting in low productivity. Low usage also poses a risk that customers may find the experience disappointing or have doubts about the viability of the service.

Figure 9.1
Implications of
Variations in
Demand Relative
to Capacity

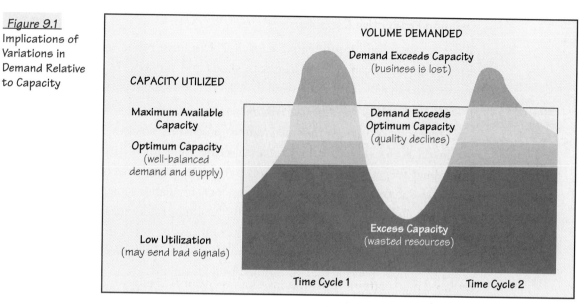

Sometimes optimum and maximum capacities are one and the same. At a live theater or sports performance, a full house is grand, since it stimulates the players and creates a sense of excitement and audience participation. But with most other services, you probably feel that you get better service if the facility is not operating at full capacity. The quality of restaurant service, for instance, often deteriorates when every table is occupied, because staff members are rushed and there is a greater likelihood of errors or delays. When repair and maintenance shops are fully scheduled, delays may result if there is no slack in the system to allow for unexpected problems in completing particular jobs.

There are two basic approaches to the problem of fluctuating demand. One is to adjust the level of capacity to meet variations in demand. This approach requires an understanding of what constitutes productive capacity and how it may be increased or decreased on an incremental basis. The second approach is to manage the level of demand, using marketing strategies to smooth out the peaks and fill in the valleys so as to generate a more consistent flow of requests for service. Many firms use a mix of both approaches.[1]

Many Service Organizations are Capacity-Constrained

There are often limits to a firm's capacity to serve additional customers at a particular point in time. In general, organizations that engage in physical processes, such as people or possession processing, are more likely to face capacity constraints than those that engage in information-based processes. A radio station, for instance, may be constrained in its geographic reach by the strength of its signal, but within that radius, any number of listeners can tune in to a broadcast.

Defining Productive Capacity

What do we mean by productive capacity? The term refers to the resources or assets that a firm can employ to create goods and services. In a service context, productive capacity can take several forms:

1. *Physical facilities designed to contain customers* and used for delivering people-processing services or mental stimulus–processing services. Examples include medical clinics, hotels, passenger aircrafts, and university classrooms. The primary capacity constraint is likely to be defined in terms of furnishings such as beds, rooms, or seats. In some cases, local regulations may set an upper limit to the number of people allowed in for health or safety reasons.

2. *Physical facilities designed for storing or processing goods* that either belong to customers or are being offered to them for sale. Examples include pipelines, warehouses, parking lots, or railroad freight wagons.

3. *Physical equipment used to process people, possessions, or information* may embrace a huge range of items and be very situation specific. Diagnostic equipment, airport security detectors, toll gates, bank ATMs, and "seats" in a call center are among the many items whose absence in sufficient numbers for a given level of demand can bring service to a crawl (or a complete stop).

4. *Labor* is a key element of productive capacity in all high-contact services and many low-contact ones. Staffing levels—whether for restaurant servers or nurses—need to be sufficient to meet anticipated demand, or customers will be kept waiting. Professional services are especially dependent on highly skilled staff to create high-value-added, information-based output. Abraham Lincoln captured it well when he remarked that "A lawyer's time and expertise are his stock in trade."

5. *Infrastructure.* Many organizations are dependent on access to sufficient capacity in the public or private infrastructure to be able to deliver quality service to their own customers. Capacity problems of this nature may include congested airways that lead to air traffic restrictions on flights, traffic jams on major highways, and power failures or "brownouts" caused by reduced voltage.

Measures of capacity utilization include the number of hours (or percentage of total available time) that facilities, labor, and equipment are productively employed in revenue operation, and the units or percentage of available space (e.g., seats, cubic freight capacity, telecommunications bandwidth) that is utilized in revenue operations. Human beings tend to be far more variable than equipment in their ability to sustain consistent levels of output over time. One tired or poorly trained employee staffing a single station in an assembly-line service operation like a cafeteria restaurant or a motor vehicle license bureau can slow the entire service to a crawl.

Many services, such as health care or repair and maintenance, involve multiple actions delivered sequentially. What this means is that a service organization's capacity to satisfy demand is constrained by one or more of its physical facilities, equipment, personnel, and the number and sequence of services provided. In a well-planned, well-managed service operation, the capacity of the facility, supporting equipment, and service personnel will be in balance. Similarly, sequential operations will be designed to minimize the likelihood of bottlenecks at any point in the process. Best Practice in Action 9.1 describes how one airline sought to improve its capacity to serve at the check-in stage.

Financial success in capacity-constrained businesses is, in large measure, a function of management's ability to use productive capacity—staff, labor, equipment, and facilities—as efficiently and as profitably as possible. In practice, however, it is difficult to achieve this ideal all the time. Not only does the level of demand vary over time, often randomly, but the time and effort required to process each person or thing may vary widely at any point in the process. In general, processing times for people are more variable than for objects or things. However, service tasks are not necessarily homogeneous. In both professional services and repair jobs, diagnosis and treatment times vary according to the nature of the customers' problems.

Best Practice in Action 9.1

IMPROVING CHECK-IN SERVICE AT LOGAN AIRPORT

To streamline its check-in service at Boston's Logan International Airport, a major airline turned to MIT Professor Richard Larson, who heads a consulting firm called QED. Technicians from QED installed pressure-sensitive rubber mats on the floor in front of the ticket counters. Pressure from each customer's foot on approaching or leaving the counter recorded the exact time on an electronic device embedded in the mats. From these data, Larson was able to profile the waiting situation at the airline's counters, including average waiting times, how long each transaction took, how many customers waited longer than a given length of time (and at what hours on what days), and even how many bailed out of a long line. Analysis of these data, collected over a long time period, yielded information that helped the airline to plan its staffing levels to match more closely the demand levels projected at different times.

Source: Richard Saltus, "Lines, Lines, Lines, Lines … The Experts Are Trying to Ease the Wait," *Boston Globe*, October 5, 1992.

Capacity Levels Can Sometimes Be Stretched or Shrunk

Some capacity is elastic in its ability to absorb extra demand. A subway car, for instance, may offer 40 seats and allow standing room for another 60 passengers with adequate handrail and floor space for all. Yet at rush hours, perhaps up to 200 standees can be accommodated under sardine-like conditions. Similarly, the capacity of service personnel can be stretched and staff may be able to work at high levels of efficiency for short periods of time. However, they would quickly tire and begin providing inferior service, if they had to work at that pace all day long.

Even where capacity appears fixed, as when it is based on the number of seats, there may still be opportunities to accept extra business at busy times. Some airlines, for instance, increase the capacity of their aircraft by switching to a higher capacity aircraft for a certain route on a busy day. Similarly, a restaurant may add extra tables and chairs. Upper limits to such practices are often set by safety standards or by the capacity of supporting services, such as the kitchen.

Another strategy for stretching capacity within a given time frame is to utilize the facilities for longer periods. Examples of this include restaurants that open for early dinners and late suppers, and universities that offer evening classes and summer semester programs. Alternatively, the average amount of time that customers (or their possessions) spend in process may be reduced. Sometimes, this is achieved by minimizing slack time, as when the bill is presented promptly to a group of diners relaxing at the table after a meal. In other instances, it may be achieved by cutting back the level of service, like offering a simpler menu at busy times of the day.

Adjusting Capacity to Match Demand

Another set of options involves tailoring the overall level of capacity to match variations in demand. This is a strategy also known as *chasing demand*. There are several actions that managers can take to adjust capacity as needed.[2]

- *Schedule downtime during periods of low demand.* To ensure that 100 percent of capacity is available during peak periods, repairs and renovations should be conducted when demand is expected to be low. Employee holidays should also be taken during such periods.

- *Use part-time employees.* Many organizations hire extra workers during their busiest periods. Examples include postal workers and retail shop assistants during Chinese New Year, extra staff in tax preparation service firms at the end of the financial year, and additional hotel employees during holiday periods and major conventions.

- *Rent or share extra facilities and equipment.* To limit investment in fixed assets, a service business may be able to rent extra space or machines at peak times. Firms with complementary demand patterns may enter into formal sharing agreements.

- *Cross-train employees.* Even when the service delivery system appears to be operating at full capacity, certain physical elements—and their attendant employees—may be underutilized. If employees can be cross-trained to perform a variety of tasks, they can be shifted to bottleneck points as needed, thereby increasing total system capacity. In supermarkets, for instance, the manager may call on stockers to operate cash registers when checkout queues start to get too long. Likewise, during slow periods, the cashiers may be asked to help stock shelves.

Sometimes, the problem lies not in the overall capacity but in the mix that's available to serve the needs of different market segments. For instance, on a given flight, an airline may have too few seats in economy class even though there are empty places in the business-class cabin; or a hotel may find itself short of suites one day when standard rooms are still available. One solution lies in designing physical facilities to be flexible. Some hotels build rooms with connecting doors. With the door between two rooms locked, the hotel can sell two bedrooms. With the door unlocked and one of the bedrooms converted into a sitting room, the hotel can now offer a suite.

Facing stiff competition from Airbus Industrie, the Boeing Co. received "outrageous demands" from prospective customers when it was designing its B-777 airliner. The airlines wanted an aircraft in which galleys and lavatories could be relocated, plumbing and all, almost anywhere in the cabin within a matter of hours. Boeing gulped but solved this challenging problem. Airlines can rearrange the passenger cabin of the "Triple Seven" within hours, reconfiguring it with varying numbers of seats allocated among one, two, or three classes.

Not all unsold productive capacity is wasted. Many firms take a strategic approach to disposition of anticipated surplus capacity, allocating it in advance to build relationships with customers, suppliers, employees, and intermediaries.[3] Possible applications include free trials for prospective customers and for intermediaries who sell to end customers, employee rewards, and bartering with the firm's own suppliers. Among the most widely bartered services are advertising space or airtime, airline seats, and hotel rooms.

Patterns and Determinants of Demand

Now let's look at the other side of the equation. To control variations in demand for a particular service, managers need to determine what factors govern that demand.

Understanding Patterns of Demand

Research should begin by getting some answers to a series of important questions about the patterns of demand and their underlying causes (see Table 9.1).

As you think about some of the seemingly "random" causes, consider how rain and cold affect the use of indoor and outdoor recreational or entertainment services. Then reflect on how heart attacks and births affect the demand for hospital services. Finally, consider the impact of natural disasters, such as earthquakes, tornados, tsunamis, and typhoons, not only on emergency services, but also for disaster recovery specialists and insurance firms.

Most periodic cycles influencing demand for a particular service vary in length from one day to 12 months. The impact of seasonal cycles is well known and affects

Table 9.1

Questions About the Patterns of Demand and Their Underlying Causes

1. **Do demand levels follow a predictable cycle?**
    If so, how do you describe the duration of the **demand cycle**?
    - One day (varies by hour)
    - One week (varies by day)
    - One month (varies by day or by week)
    - One year (varies by month or by season, or reflects annual public holidays)
    - Some other period

2. **What are the underlying causes of these cyclical variations?**
    - Employment schedules
    - Billing and tax payment/refund cycles
    - Wage and salary payment dates
    - School hours and vacations
    - Seasonal changes in climate
    - Occurrence of public or religious holidays
    - Natural cycles, such as coastal tides

3. **Do demand levels seem to change randomly?**
    If so, what could the underlying causes be?
    - Day-to-day changes in the weather
    - Health events whose occurrence cannot be pinpointed exactly
    - Accidents, fires, and certain criminal activities
    - Natural disasters, e.g., earthquakes, storms, mudslides, and volcanic eruptions

4. **Can demand for a particular service over time be disaggregated by market segment** to reflect such components as:
    - Using patterns by a particular type of customer or for a particular purpose?
    - Variations in the net profitability of each completed transaction?

demand for a broad array of services. Low demand in the off-season poses significant problems for tourism promoters.

In many instances, multiple cycles may operate simultaneously. For example, demand levels for public transport may vary by time of day (highest during commute hours), day of week (less travel to work on weekends but more leisure travel), and season of year (more travel by tourists in summer). The demand for service during the peak period on a Monday in summer is likely to be very different from that during the peak period on a Saturday in winter, reflecting day-of-week and seasonal variations jointly.

Analyzing Drivers of Demand

No strategy for smoothing demand is likely to succeed unless it is based on an understanding of why customers from a specific market segment choose to use the service when they do. It's difficult for hotels to convince business travelers to remain on Saturday nights since few executives do business over the weekend. Instead, hotel managers may do better to promote weekend use of their facilities for conferences or pleasure travel. Attempts to get commuters to shift their travel to off-peak periods will probably fail, since such travel is determined by people's employment hours. Instead, efforts should be directed at employers to persuade them to adopt flexitime or staggered working hours.

Keeping good records of each transaction helps enormously when it comes to analyzing demand patterns based on past experience. Best-practice queuing systems supported by sophisticated software can track customer consumption patterns by date and time of day automatically. Where relevant, it's also useful to record weather conditions and other special factors (a strike, an accident, a big convention in town, a price change, launch of a competing service, etc.) that might have influenced demand.

Dividing up Demand by Market Segment

Random fluctuations are usually caused by factors beyond management's control. But analysis will sometimes reveal that a predictable demand cycle for one segment is concealed within a broader, seemingly random pattern. This fact illustrates the importance of breaking down demand on a segment-by-segment basis. For instance, a repair and maintenance shop that services industrial electrical equipment may already know that a certain proportion of its work consists of regularly scheduled contracts to perform preventive maintenance. The balance may come from "walk-in" business and emergency repairs. Although it might seem hard to predict or control the timing and volume of such work, further analysis could show that walk-in business was more prevalent on some days of the week than others and that emergency repairs were frequently requested following damage sustained during thunderstorms (which tend to be seasonal in nature and can often be forecast a day or two in advance).

The ease with which total demand can be broken down into smaller components depends on the nature of the records kept by management. If each customer transaction is recorded separately, and backed up by detailed notes (as in a medical or dental visit, or an accountant's audit), then the task of understanding demand is greatly simplified. In subscription and charge account services, when each customer's identity is known and itemized monthly bills are sent, managers can gain some immediate insights into usage patterns. Some services, such as telephone and electrical, even have the ability to track subscriber consumption patterns by time of day. Although these data may not always yield specific information on the purpose for which the service is being used, it is often possible to make informed judgments about the volume of sales generated by different user groups.

Demand Levels Can Be Managed

There are five basic approaches to managing demand. The first, which has the virtue of simplicity but little else, involves *taking no action and leaving demand to find its own levels*. Eventually customers learn from experience or word of mouth when they can expect to stand in line to use the service and when it will be available without delay. The trouble is, they may also learn to find a competitor who is more responsive, and low off-peak utilization cannot be improved unless action is taken. More interventionist approaches involve influencing the level of demand at any given time, by taking active steps to *reduce demand in peak periods* and to *increase demand when there is excess capacity*.

Two more approaches both involve *inventorying demand until capacity becomes available*. A firm can accomplish this either by introducing a booking or *reservations* system that promises customers access to capacity at specified times, or by *creating formalized queuing systems* (or by a combination of the two).

Table 9.2 links these five approaches to the two problem situations of excess demand and excess capacity, and provides a brief strategic commentary on each. Many service businesses face both situations at different points in the cycle of demand, and should consider use of the interventionist strategies described.

Table 9.2
Alternative Demand-Management Strategies for Different Capacity Situations

Approach Used to Manage Demand	Capacity Situation Relative to Demand	
	Insufficient Capacity (excess demand)	Excess Capacity (insufficient demand)
Take no action	Unorganized queuing results (may irritate customers and discourage future use)	Capacity is wasted (customers may have a disappointing experience for services like theater)
Reduce demand	Higher prices will increase profits; communication can encourage use in other time slots (can this effort be focused on less profitable and desirable segments?)	Take no action (but see preceding)
Increase demand	Take no action unless opportunities exist to stimulate (and give priority to) more profitable segments	Lower prices selectively (try to avoid cannibalizing existing business; ensure that all relevant costs are covered); use communications and variation in products and distribution (but recognize extra costs, if any, and make sure that appropriate tradeoffs are made between profitability and use levels)
Inventory demand by reservation system	Consider priority system for most desirable segments; make other customers shift to off-peak period or to future peak	Clarify that space is available and that no reservations are needed
Inventory demand by formalized queuing	Consider override for most desirable segments; try to keep waiting customers occupied and comfortable; try to predict wait period accurately	Not applicable

Marketing Strategies Can Reshape Some Demand Patterns

Several marketing mix variables have roles to play in stimulating demand during periods of excess capacity, and in decreasing or shifting demand during periods of insufficient capacity. Price is often the first variable to be proposed for bringing demand and supply into balance, but changes in product, distribution strategy, and communication efforts can also play an important role. Although each element is discussed separately, effective demand management efforts often require changes in two or more elements jointly.

USE PRICE AND OTHER COSTS TO MANAGE DEMAND   One of the most direct ways of reducing excess demand at peak periods is to charge customers more money to use the service during those periods. Other costs, too, may have a similar effect. For instance, if customers learn that they are likely to face increased time and effort costs during peak periods, this information may lead those who dislike spending time waiting in crowded and unpleasant conditions to try later. Similarly, the lure of cheaper prices and an expectation of no waiting may encourage at least some people to change the timing of their behavior, whether it be shopping, travel, or visiting a museum.

Some firms use pricing strategy in sophisticated ways in order to balance supply and demand. For the monetary price of a service to be effective as a demand management tool, managers must have some sense of the shape and slope of a product's demand curve—that is, how the quantity of service demanded responds to increases or decreases in the price per unit at a particular point in time. (Figure 9.2 shows a sample demand curve.) It's important to determine whether the demand curve for a specific service varies sharply from one time period to another. If so, significantly different pricing schemes may be needed to fill capacity in each time period. To complicate matters further, there may be separate demand curves for

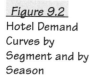

Figure 9.2
Hotel Demand
Curves by
Segment and by
Season

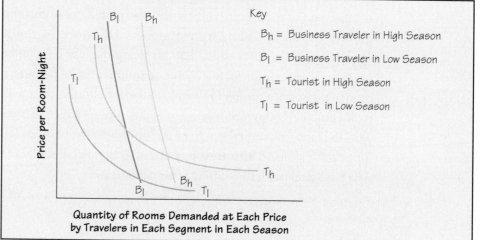

**Quantity of Rooms Demanded at Each Price
by Travelers in Each Segment in Each Season**

different segments within each time period (business travelers are usually less price sensitive than vacationers).

One of the most difficult tasks facing service marketers is to determine the nature of all these different demand curves. Research, trial and error, and analysis of parallel situations in other locations or in comparable services, are all ways of obtaining an understanding of the situation. Many service businesses explicitly recognize the existence of different demand curves by establishing distinct classes of service, each priced at levels appropriate to the demand curve of a particular segment. In essence, each segment receives a variation of the basic product, with value being added to the core service through supplementary services to appeal to higher-paying segments. For instance, in computer and printing service firms, product enhancement takes the form of faster turnaround and more specialized services; and in hotels, a distinction is made between rooms of different size and amenities, and with different views.

In each case, the objective is to maximize the revenues received from each segment. When capacity is constrained, however, the goal in a profit-seeking business should be to ensure that as much capacity as possible is utilized by the most profitable segments available at any given time. Airlines, for instance, hold a certain number of seats for business passengers paying full fare and place restrictive conditions on excursion fares for tourists (such as requiring advance purchase and a Saturday night stay) in order to prevent business travelers from taking advantage of cheap fares designed to attract tourists who can help fill the aircraft. Pricing strategies of this nature are known as *yield management* (see Chapter 6).

CHANGE PRODUCT ELEMENTS   Although pricing is a commonly advocated method of balancing supply and demand, it is not quite as universally feasible for services as for goods. A rather obvious example is provided by the respective problems of a ski manufacturer and a ski slope operator in South Korea during the summer. The former can either produce for inventory or try to sell skis in the summer at a discount. If the skis are sufficiently discounted, some customers will buy before the ski season in order to save money. However, in the absence of skiing opportunities, no skiers would buy lift tickets for use on a midsummer day at any price (see Figure 9.3). So, to encourage summer use of the lifts, the operator has to change the service product offering, and offer alternative activities such as hiking, rock climbing, mountain biking; or build Alpine Slides, curving tracks in which wheeled toboggans could run from the summit to the base, and thus create demand for tickets on the ski lifts. Best Practice in Action 9.2 describes how resort hotels in Asia have dealt with fluctuating seasonal demands.

Best Practice in Action 9.2

RESORTS: HANDLING SEASONAL FLUCTUATIONS

Traditionally, seasonal demand has had a major effect on the profitability of the hospitality industry. Peak season yielded high rates while the lean season meant filling rooms by whatever means possible. To meet target occupancy rates and earnings, resorts generally had to make sacrifices. Success thus depended on how willing resorts were to forego profits in their reach for clients. But the hotel and resort industry has slowly transformed into an all-season business, with seasonal packages playing a less important means of raking in profits. This change occurred with the emergence of "business hotels" that cater not just to leisure travelers, but also to the higher-margin business travelers and corporate clients.

Naturally, when times are lean, price cutting is inevitable as resorts compete for customers. Traditionally, such discounts have been made to boost the sale of rooms. However, hotels with a diversified mix of leisure and corporate clientele now have some insurance against seasonal demand fluctuations. Regardless of season, hotels and resorts can now offer packages and deals for a variety of customers. Seasons have their influence of course, but they no longer intrude on marketing strategy with the tyranny they once did. This has allowed the development of other marketing ideas beside the venerable package deal.

Instead of depending on seasonal packages, resorts are trying to tap new markets and business groups. With an expanding market of foreigners and corporate clients, the gap between the peak and lean periods has lessened significantly.

Figure 9.3
Yongpyong Ski Resort in South Korea has to develop creative service product offerings during the summer months to keep their ski lifts busy.

Reproduced with permission from Yong Pyong Resort.

Source: "Resorts: Beyond Seasonal Packages," accessed online at http://www.yehey.com/on June 11, 2004.

Similar thinking prevails at a variety of other seasonal businesses. Thus, tax preparation firms offer bookkeeping and consulting services to small businesses in slack months, educational institutions offer weekend and summer programs for adults and senior citizens, and small pleasure boats offer cruises in the summer and a dockside venue for private functions in winter months. These firms recognize that no amount of price discounting is likely to develop business out of season and that new value propositions targeted at different segments are needed.

Many service offerings remain unchanged throughout the year, but others undergo significant modifications according to the season. Hospitals, for example, usually offer the same array of services throughout the year. By contrast, resort hotels sharply alter the mix and focus of their peripheral services such as dining, entertainment, and sports to reflect customer preferences in different seasons.

There can be variations in the product offering even during the course of a 24-hour period. Some restaurants provide a good example of this, marking the passage of the hours with changing menus and levels of service, variations in lighting and decor, opening and closing of the bar, and the presence or absence of entertainment. The goal is to appeal to different needs within the same group of customers, to reach out to different customer segments, or to do both, according to the time of day.

In January 2003, Pizza Hut opened its 100th restaurant in China, and started repositioning itself as a "Pleasure Restaurant," a concept that embraces pleasure, relaxation, comfort, sentiment, and taste. When customers enter Pizza Hut, they not only enjoy a choice of fresh cooked pizzas and other good-quality food, but are also exposed to enthusiastic and careful service, and a convivial environment that includes subdued lighting, music, colorful and fashionable decoration, and comfortable, elegant furnishings. To fill capacity during slack hours, Pizza Hut launched services especially for afternoon tea from 2 p.m. to 5 p.m., and supper from 8 p.m. to 10.30 p.m. The menu offered three sets of "Pleasure Refreshments" at prices of 15, 20, and 25 yuan (US$1.80, US$2.40, and US$3.00 respectively), with free refills of all drinks. This strategy helps to explain why almost all Pizza Hut outlets in mainland China are crowded with customers all day long. Most of them are young professionals or college students.

MODIFY THE PLACE AND TIME OF DELIVERY   Rather than seeking to modify demand for a service that continues to be offered at the same time in the same place, some firms respond to market needs by modifying the time and place of delivery. Three basic options are available.

The first represents a strategy of *no change*: regardless of the level of demand, the service continues to be offered in the same location at the same times. By contrast, a second strategy involves *varying the times when the service is available* to reflect changes in customer preference by day of week, by season, and so forth. Theaters and cinema complexes often offer matinees at weekends when people have more leisure time throughout the day. During summer, cafes and restaurants may stay open later because of the general inclination of people to enjoy the longer balmier evenings outdoors.

A third strategy involves *offering the service to customers at a new location*. One approach is to operate mobile units that take the service to customers, rather than requiring them to visit fixed-site service locations. Traveling libraries, mobile car wash services, in-office tailoring services, and home-delivered meals are examples of this. A cleaning and repair firm that wishes to generate business during low demand periods might offer free pickup and delivery of portable items that need servicing. Alternatively, service firms whose productive assets are mobile may choose to follow the market when that, too, is mobile. For instance, in the United States, rental car companies move their fleets around according to the season; when autumn gives way to winter in the Northeast and tourism declines, firms reduce the number of cars there and shift them to warmer locations such as Florida.

PROMOTION AND EDUCATION   Even if the other variables of the marketing mix remain unchanged, communication efforts alone may be able to help smooth demand. Signage, advertising, publicity, and sales messages can be used to educate customers about the timing of peak periods and encourage them to avail themselves of the service at off-peak times when there will be fewer delays. Examples include post office requests to "Mail Early for Christmas," and communications from sales representatives for industrial maintenance firms advising customers of periods when preventive maintenance work can be done quickly. In addition, management can ask service personnel (or intermediaries such as travel agents) to encourage customers with discretionary schedules to favor off-peak periods.

Changes in pricing, product characteristics, and distribution must be communicated clearly. If a firm wants to obtain a specific response to variations in marketing mix elements, it must, of course, inform customers fully about their options. As discussed in Chapter 5, short-term promotions, combining both pricing and communication elements, as well as other incentives, may provide customers with attractive incentives to shift the timing of service usage.

Inventory Demand through Waiting Lines and Reservations

One of the challenges of services is that, being performances, they cannot normally be stored for later use. A hairdresser cannot prepackage a haircut for the following day. It must be done in real time. In an ideal world, nobody would ever have to wait to conduct a service transaction. However, firms cannot afford to provide extensive extra capacity that would go unutilized most of the time. As we have seen, there are a variety of procedures for bringing demand and supply into balance.

In businesses where demand regularly exceeds supply, managers can often take steps to inventory demand. This task can be achieved in one of two ways: (1) by asking customers to wait in line (queuing), usually on a first-come first-served basis, or (2) by offering them the opportunity of reserving or booking space in advance.

Waiting Is a Universal Phenomenon

It is estimated that Americans spend 37 billion hours a year (an average of almost 150 hours per person) waiting in lines, "during which time they fret, fidget, and scowl," according to *The Washington Post*.[4] While we do not have similar figures for Asian countries, we are sure this phenomenon is equally prevalent. Richard Larson suggests that, when everything is added up, the average person may spend as much as 30 minutes per day waiting in line, which would translate to 20 months of waiting in an 80-year lifetime![5]

Nobody likes to be kept waiting. It's boring, time wasting, and sometimes physically uncomfortable, especially if there is nowhere to sit or you are outdoors (see Figure 9.4). Yet, waiting for a service process is an almost universal phenomenon: Almost every organization faces the problem of waiting lines somewhere in its operation.

Even physical and inanimate objects wait for processing, too. Customers' emails sit in customer service staff's in-boxes, appliances wait to be repaired, and checks wait to be cleared at a bank.

Why Waiting Lines Occur

Waiting lines occur whenever the number of arrivals at a facility exceeds the capacity of the system to process them. In a very real sense, queues are basically a symptom of unresolved capacity management problems. Analysis and modeling of queues is

Figure 9.4
Passengers queuing for subway tickets in China do not enjoy having to wait.

a well-established branch of operations management. Queuing theory has been traced back to 1917, when a Danish telephone engineer was charged with determining how large the switching unit in a telephone system had to be to keep the number of busy signals within reason.[6]

As the telephone example suggests, not all queues take the form of a physical waiting line in a single location. When customers deal with a service supplier at arm's length, as in information-processing services, they call from home, office, or college using telecommunication channels such as voice telephone or the Internet. Typically, calls are answered in the order received, often requiring customers to wait their turn in a virtual line. Some physical queues are geographically dispersed. Travelers wait at many different locations for the taxis they have ordered by phone to arrive and pick them up. In an effort to reduce customer waiting time, MK Taxi in Kyoto, Japan, installed a GPS-controlled CTI (Computer Telephony Integration) automatic car allocation system that costs approximately ¥600 million (US$5.5 million). The implementation of the system increased the number of daily taxi bookings from 5,900 to 7,000 and reduced average waiting time by 50 percent to approximately five minutes.[7]

Many Web sites now allow people to do things for themselves, like obtaining information or making reservations, which formerly required making telephone calls or visiting a service facility in person. Although accessing the Web can be slow sometimes, at least the wait is conducted while the customer is comfortably seated and able to attend to other matters while waiting. Best Practice in Action 9.3 features the success of Indian Railways' online booking system that helps customers to save time by allowing them to do the buying and collection of tickets online.

Different Queue Configurations

There are different types of queues and the challenge for managers is to select the most appropriate procedure. Figure 9.6 shows diagrams of several types that you have probably experienced yourself. In *single line sequential stages*, customers proceed through several serving operations, as in a cafeteria. Bottlenecks may occur at any stage where the process takes longer to execute than at previous stages. Many cafeterias have lines at the cash register because the cashier takes longer to calculate how much you owe and to make change than the servers take to slap food on your plate.

Parallel lines to multiple servers offer more than one serving station, allowing customers to select one of several lines in which to wait. Banks and ticket windows are common examples. Fast-food restaurants usually have several serving lines in operation at busy times of day, with each offering the full menu. A parallel system can have either a single stage or multiple stages. The disadvantage of this design is that lines may not move at equal speed. A common solution here is to create a

Best Practice in Action 9.3

INDIAN RAILWAYS' ONLINE BOOKING SYSTEM

Your railway ticket might say "Happy Journey," but you shudder when you think of the hassle of getting it at the station. If this experience rings a bell to you, try Indian Railways' online booking system for easy ticket purchases (see Figure 9.5). Indian Railways is one of the most successful e-commerce companies in India, although few would think of it as a likely candidate. In terms of cash transactions, the online booking facility of the Indian Railway Catering and Tourism Corporation (IRCTC) is the largest in India, far ahead of several high-profile private-sector e-commerce sites.

The success of Indian Railways' online booking system is attributable to its simplicity of usage, nominal charges and effective delivery of tickets, said Amitabh Pandey, Group General Manager for IT services. The registration process at the Web site takes only five minutes, after which users can proceed immediately to a transaction. The service charge for a ticket ranges from 40 to 60 rupees (US$0.10 to US$0.15), and the tickets are delivered via courier within two days.

Sixty percent of Indian Railways' online transactions are made by people aged 30 and above, and that contradicts the popular belief that the younger generation performs online purchases more often. Mr Pandey also added that as long as it was more convenient for people to buy online, people would go for it. The alternative to waiting in a long queue at the railway stations—hassle-free purchase and delivery of tickets—provides a strong incentive for Indian Railways' e-commerce users to switch to the new mode of buying their tickets.

Figure 9.5

Indian Railways' Reservation Web site creates a real "Happy Journey" for its users.

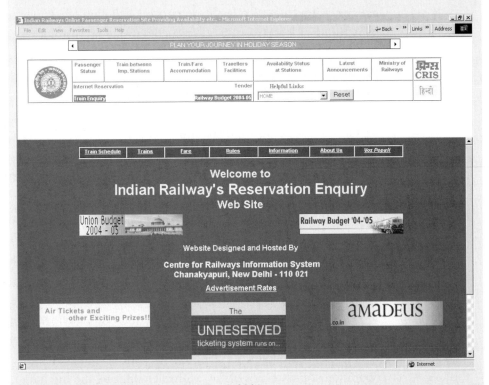

Source: http://www.indianrail.gov.in/, accessed in July 2004.

Source: Adapted from Vipin V. Nair and Gaurav Raghuvanshi, "At Your Door Step," Business Line, *The Hindu*, December 31, 2003.

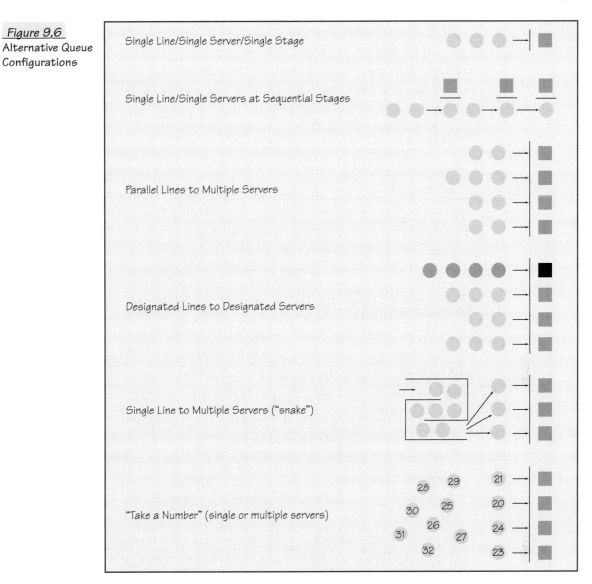

Figure 9.6
Alternative Queue
Configurations

Single Line/Single Server/Single Stage

Single Line/Single Servers at Sequential Stages

Parallel Lines to Multiple Servers

Designated Lines to Designated Servers

Single Line to Multiple Servers ("snake")

"Take a Number" (single or multiple servers)

single line to multiple servers (commonly known as a "snake"). This approach is encountered frequently at post offices and airport check-ins.

Designated lines involve assigning different lines to specific categories of customer. Examples include express lines (for instance, 12 or fewer items) and regular lines at supermarket checkouts, and different check-in stations for first-, business-, and economy-class airline passengers. *Take a number* saves customers the need to stand in a queue, because they know they will be called in sequence. This procedure allows them to sit down and relax (if seating is available) or to guess how long the wait will be and do something else in the meantime, but at the risk of losing their place if earlier customers are served faster than expected. Users of this approach include large travel agents and supermarket departments, such as the butcher or baker.

Hybrid approaches to queue configuration also exist. For instance, a cafeteria with a single serving line might offer two cash register stations at the final stage. Similarly, patients at a small medical clinic might visit a single receptionist for registration, proceed sequentially through multiple channels for testing, diagnosis, and treatment, and conclude by returning to a single line for payment at the receptionist's desk. Research suggests that selecting the most appropriate type of queue is important to customer satisfaction. Rafaeli, Barron, and Haber found that the way a waiting area is structured can produce feelings of injustice and unfairness in customers. Customers who waited in parallel lines to multiple servers reported significantly higher agitation and greater dissatisfaction with the fairness of the service delivery process than customers who waited in a single line ("snake") to access multiple servers, even though both groups of customers waited an identical amount of time and were involved in completely fair service processes.[8]

Queuing Systems Can Be Tailored to Market Segments

Although the basic rule in most queuing systems is "first come, first served," not all queuing systems are organized on this basis. Market segmentation is sometimes used to design queuing strategies that set different priorities for different types of customers. Allocation to separate queuing areas may be based on:

- *Urgency of the job*. At many hospital emergency units, a triage nurse is assigned to greet incoming patients and decide which ones require priority medical treatment and which can safely be asked to register and then sit down while they wait their turn.
- *Duration of service transaction*. Banks, supermarkets, and other retail services often institute "express lanes" for shorter, less complicated tasks.
- *Payment of a premium price*. Airlines usually offer separate check-in lines for first- and economy-class passengers, with a higher ratio of personnel to passengers in the first-class line, resulting in reduced waits for those who have paid more for their tickets.
- *Importance of the customer*. A special area may be reserved for members of frequent user clubs. Airlines often provide lounges, offering newspapers and free refreshments, where frequent flyers can wait for their flights in greater comfort.

Minimize Perceptions of Waiting Time

Research shows that people often think they have waited longer for a service than they actually did. Studies of public transportation use, for instance, have shown that travelers perceive time spent waiting for a bus or train as passing one and a half to seven times more slowly than the time actually spent traveling in the vehicle.[9] People don't like wasting their time on unproductive activities any more than they like wasting money. Customer dissatisfaction with delays in receiving service can often stimulate strong emotions, including anger.[10]

The Psychology of Waiting Time

The noted philosopher William James observed: "Boredom results from being attentive to the passage of time itself." Savvy service marketers recognize that customers experience waiting time in differing ways, depending on the circumstances. Table 9.3 highlights ten propositions on the psychology of waiting lines.

When increasing capacity is simply not feasible, service providers should try to be creative and look for ways to make waiting more palatable for customers. Doctors and dentists stock their waiting rooms with piles of magazines for people to read while waiting. Car repair facilities may have a television for customers to watch. One tire dealer goes even further, providing customers with free popcorn, soft drinks, coffee, and ice cream while they wait for their cars to be returned.

Theme park operators cleverly design their waiting areas to make the wait look shorter than it really is, finding ways to give customers in line the impression of constant progress, and make time seem to pass more quickly by keeping customers amused or diverted while they wait.

Give Customers Information on Waits

Does it help to tell people how long they are likely to have to wait for service? Common sense would suggest that this is useful information for customers, since it allows them to make decisions as to whether they can afford to take the time to wait now or should come back later. It also enables them to plan the use of their time while waiting.

Create an Effective Reservations System

Ask someone what services come to mind when you talk about reservations and most likely they will cite airlines, hotels, restaurants, car rentals, and theater seats. Suggest synonyms like "bookings" or "appointments" and they may add haircuts, visits to professionals such as doctors and consultants, vacation rentals, and service calls to fix anything from a broken refrigerator to a neurotic computer.

Reservations are supposed to guarantee that service will be available when the customer wants it. Systems vary from a simple appointments book for a doctor's office using handwritten entries, to a central computerized data bank for an airline's worldwide operations. When goods require servicing, their owners may not wish to be parted from them for long. Households with only one car, for example, or factories with a vital piece of equipment often cannot afford to be without such items for

Table 9.3

Ten Propositions on the Psychology of Waiting Lines[11]

1. **Unoccupied time feels longer than occupied time.** When you're sitting around with nothing to do, time seems to crawl. The challenge for service organizations is to give customers something to do or to distract them while waiting.

2. **Pre- and postprocess waits feel longer than in-process waits.** Waiting to buy a ticket to enter a theme park is different from waiting to ride on a roller coaster once you're in the park. There's also a difference between waiting for coffee to arrive near the end of a restaurant meal and waiting for the server to bring you the check once you're ready to leave.

3. **Anxiety makes waits seem longer.** Can you remember waiting for someone to show up at a rendezvous and worrying about whether you had got the time or the location correct? While waiting in unfamiliar locations, especially outdoors and after dark, people often worry about their personal safety.

4. **Uncertain waits are longer than known, finite waits.** Although any wait may be frustrating, we can usually adjust mentally to a wait of known length. It's the unknown that keeps us on edge. Imagine waiting for a delayed flight and not being told how long the delay is going to be. You don't know whether you have the time to get up and walk around the terminal or whether to stay at the gate in case the flight is called any minute.

5. **Unexplained waits are longer than explained waits.** Have you ever been in a subway or an elevator which has stopped for no apparent reason without anyone telling you what is going on? Not only is there uncertainty about the length of the wait, there's added worry about what is going to happen. Has there been an accident on the line? Will you have to leave the train in the tunnel? Is the elevator broken? Will you be stuck for hours in close proximity with strangers?

6. **Unfair waits are longer than equitable waits.** Expectations about what is fair or unfair sometimes vary from one culture or country to another. In the United States, Canada, or Britain, for example, people expect everybody to wait their turn in line and are likely to get irritated if they see others jumping ahead or being given priority for no apparent good reason. In Asia, Singaporeans normally keep quiet even if they feel unhappy and irritated, but the often more vocal and outspoken customers in Hong Kong or Taiwan will voice their frustration when irritated.

7. **The more valuable the service, the longer people will wait.** People will queue overnight under uncomfortable conditions to get good seats at a major concert or sports event that is expected to sell out.

8. **Solo waits feel longer than group waits.** Waiting with one or more people you know is reassuring. Conversation with friends can help to pass the time, but not everyone is comfortable talking to a stranger.

9. **Physically uncomfortable waits feel longer than comfortable waits.** "My feet are killing me!" is one of the most frequently heard comments when people are forced to stand in line for a long time. Whether seated or unseated, a wait seems more burdensome if the temperature is too hot or too cold.

10. **Unfamiliar waits seem longer than familiar ones.** Frequent users of a service know what to expect and are less likely to worry while waiting. New or occasional users of a service, by contrast, are often nervous, wondering not only about the probable length of the wait but also about what happens next.

more than a day or two. So a reservations system may be necessary for service businesses in fields such as repair and maintenance. By requiring reservations for routine maintenance, management can ensure that some time will be kept free for handling emergency jobs which, because they carry a premium price, generate a much higher margin. The presence of such reservations systems enables demand to be controlled and smoothed out in a more manageable way. By capturing data, reservation systems also help organizations to prepare financial projections. Best Practice in Action 9.4 features how some Japanese banks work on reducing customer waiting time through an appointment system.

Best Practice in Action 9.4

JAPANESE BANKS—DELIVER FASTER SERVICE THROUGH APPOINTMENT SYSTEM

In an effort to reduce customer waiting time during peak hours, major Japanese banks are introducing appointment systems. For example, in 2004, UFJ Bank, Japan's fourth largest bank, implemented the appointment system at some of its branches. This system allows customers to make appointments through a special phone line. However, appointments have to be made at least one day in advance. This new service was designed to serve clients who are interested in opening new accounts, seeking advice on asset management and other more time-consuming transactions that require advice. UFJ Bank plans to implement the appointment system nationwide at all its approximately 400 branches by the end of September 2004.

Sumitomo Mitsui Banking Corp., one of Japan's largest bank with assets of over ¥94,109 billion (US$870 billion), also plans to introduce an appointment system that will allow customers to make appointments via its Web site. Through the Web site, customers would be able to find out how crowded a specific branch is, and also be able to make an appointment should the need arise. Sumitomo Mitsui will pilot test this new service at two of its busier branches, and based on the feedback and data gathered, decide on the necessary finetuning and the wider implementation of the new service.

Besides UFJ Bank and Sumitomo Mitsui, the Bank of Tokyo-Mitsubishi will also launch an appointment system for customers who need more personal advice as well as information on some of its services. Japanese banks seem determined to deliver faster services to their customers.

Source: Adapted from *Business Custom Wire*, March 13, 2004; http://www.smbc.co.jp.

Taking bookings also serves to presell a service, to inform customers and to educate them about what to expect. Customers who hold reservations should be able to count on avoiding a queue, since they have been guaranteed service at a specific time. A well-organized reservations system allows the organization to deflect demand for service from a first-choice time to earlier or later times, from one class of service to another, and even from first-choice locations to alternative ones. However, problems arise when customers fail to show or when service firms overbook. Marketing strategies for dealing with these operational problems include requiring a deposit, canceling nonpaid bookings after a certain time, and providing compensation to victims of overbooking.

The challenge in designing reservation systems is to make them fast and user friendly for both staff and customers. Many firms now allow customers to make their own reservations on a Web site—a trend that seems certain to grow. Besides Web sites, some creative service providers in Asia also allow customers to make reservations via the short messaging service (SMS). For instance, Malaysian carrier

Air Asia and Holiday Villa Malaysia International have both introduced SMS-based reservation systems, seeking to capitalize on the popularity of SMS in Malaysia. Air Asia has invested three million ringgit (US$790,000) to develop the SMS booking system (see Figure 9.7) jointly with Malaysia's top mobile phone operator, Maxis,

Figure 9.7
Air Asia makes booking truly convenient, allowing travelers to book their flights through Air Asia's call centers, its walk-in sales office, Web site and SMS.

Courtesy of AirAsia's marketing communications team.

and Dutch-based technology firm, Getronics. Holiday Villa Malaysia International's SMS system, called MobileHotel, is the first in the region that targets more casual and less conventional customers who are comfortable with using SMS for making hotel reservations and checking other related information. Senders receive an SMS alert instantly with booking instructions and available room rates. Interested customers can then provide the necessary information to complete the reservation.[12]

Whether customers talk with a reservations agent or make their own bookings, they want quick answers to queries about service availability at a preferred time. They also appreciate it if the system can provide further information about the type of service they are reserving. For instance, can a hotel assign a specific room on request? Or can it assign a room with a view of the lake rather than one with a view of the parking lot and the nearby power station?

Reservations Strategies Should Focus on Yield

Service organizations often use percentage of capacity sold as a measure of operational efficiency. Transport services talk of the "load factor" achieved, hotels of their "occupancy rate," and hospitals of their "census." Similarly, professional firms can calculate what proportion of a partner's or an employee's time is classified as billable hours, and repair shops can look at utilization of both equipment and labor. By themselves, however, these percentage figures tell us little of the relative profitability of the business attracted, since high utilization rates may be obtained at the expense of heavy discounting—or even outright giveaways.

More and more, service firms are looking at their "yield"—that is, the average revenue received per unit of capacity. The aim is to maximize this yield in order to improve profitability. As noted in Chapter 6, pricing strategies designed to achieve this goal are widely used in such capacity-constrained industries as passenger airlines, hotels, and car rentals. Formalized yield management systems, based upon mathematical modeling, are of greatest value for service firms that find it expensive to modify their capacity, but incur relatively low costs when they sell another unit of available capacity.[13] Other characteristics encouraging use of such programs include fluctuating demand levels, ability to segment markets by extent of price sensitivity, and sale of services well in advance of usage.

Yield analysis forces managers to recognize the opportunity cost of allocating capacity to one customer or market segment when another might subsequently yield a higher rate. Consider the following problems facing sales managers for different types of capacity-constrained service organizations.

- Should a hotel accept an advance booking from a tour group of 200 room nights at US$80 each when these same room nights might possibly be sold later at short notice to business travelers at the full posted rate of US$140?

- Should a railway company with 30 empty freight cars at its disposal accept an immediate request for a shipment worth $900 per car or hold the cars idle for a few more days in the hope of getting a priority shipment that would be twice as valuable?
- Should a print shop process all jobs on a first-come first-served basis, with a guaranteed delivery time for each job, or should it charge a premium rate for "rush" work, and tell customers with "standard" jobs to expect some variability in completion dates?

Decisions on such problems deserve to be handled with a little more sophistication than just resorting to the "bird in the hand is worth two in the bush" formula. Thus, managers need a way of figuring out the chances of getting more profitable business if they wait. Good information, based upon detailed record keeping of past usage and supported by current market intelligence and good marketing sense, is the key. The decision to accept or reject business should be based on a realistic estimate of the probabilities of obtaining higher-rated business and awareness of the need to maintain established (and desirable) customer relationships. Managers who decide on the basis of guesswork and "gut feel" are little better than gamblers who bet on rolls of the dice.

There has to be a clear plan, based on analysis of past performance and current market data, that indicates how much capacity should be allocated on specific dates to different types of customers at certain prices. Based on this plan, "selective sell" targets can be assigned to advertising and sales personnel, reflecting allocation of available capacity among different market segments on specific future dates. The last thing a firm wants its sales force to do is to encourage price-sensitive market segments to buy capacity on dates when sales projections predict that there will be strong demand from customers willing to pay full price. Unfortunately, in some industries, the lowest-rated business often books the furthest ahead. Tour groups, which pay much lower room rates than individual travelers, often ask airlines and hotels to block space more than a year in advance.

Figure 9.8 illustrates capacity allocation in a hotel setting, where demand from different types of customers varies not only by day of the week but also by season. These allocation decisions by segment, captured in reservation databases that are accessible worldwide, tell reservations personnel when to stop accepting reservations at certain prices, even though many rooms may still remain unbooked. Loyalty program members, who are primarily business travelers, are obviously a particularly desirable segment.

Similar charts can be constructed for most capacity-constrained businesses. In some instances, capacity is measured in terms of seats for a given performance, seat miles, or room nights. In others, it may be in terms of machine time, labor time, billable professional hours, vehicle miles, or storage volume. Unless it's easy to divert

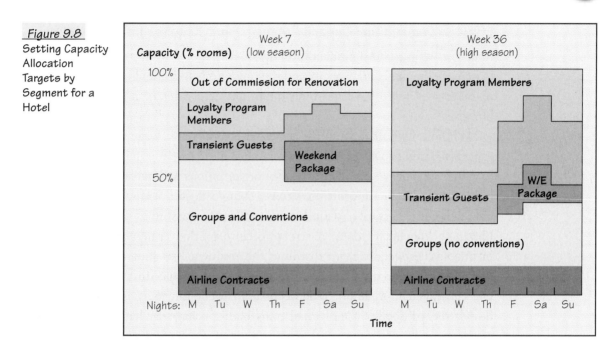

Figure 9.8
Setting Capacity Allocation Targets by Segment for a Hotel

business from one facility to a similar alternative, allocation planning decisions will have to be made at the level of geographic operating units. So each hotel, repair and maintenance center, or computer service bureau may need its own plan. On the other hand, transport vehicles represent a mobile capacity that can be allocated across any geographic area the vehicles are able to serve.

In large organizations, such as major airlines or hotel chains, the market is very dynamic, since the situation is changing all the time. For instance, the demand for both business and pleasure travel reflects current or anticipated economic conditions. Although many business travelers are not price sensitive, some companies insist that employees shop for the best travel bargains they can find within the constraints of their business travel needs. Pleasure travelers, on the other hand, are often very price sensitive. A special promotion, involving discounted fares and room rates, may encourage people to undertake a trip that they would not otherwise have made.

Viewed from the perspective of the individual hotel or airline, competitive activity has the potential to play havoc with patronage forecasts. Imagine that you are a hotel owner and a new hotel opens across the street with a special discount offer. How will it affect you? Alternatively, consider the impact if an existing competitor burns down! The airline business is notoriously changeable. Fares can be slashed overnight. A competitor may introduce a new nonstop service between two cities or cut back its existing schedule on another route. Travel agents and savvy customers watch these movements like hawks and may be quick to cancel one reservation (even if it involves paying a penalty) in order to take advantage of a better price or a more convenient schedule that can be obtained elsewhere.

Effective Demand and Capacity Management Requires Information

Managers require substantial information to help them develop effective strategies to manage demand and capacity and then monitor subsequent performance in the marketplace. Table 9.4 lists some important categories of information for this purpose.

Where might all this information come from? Most large organizations with expensive fixed capacity have professional yield or revenue management systems to gather such data (see Chapter 6). For organizations without such systems, much of the needed data are probably already being collected within the organization—although not necessarily by marketers, and some new studies may be required to obtain the necessary data. A stream of information comes into most service businesses, especially from distilling the multitude of individual transactions conducted. Sales receipts alone often contain vast detail. Most service businesses collect detailed information for operational and accounting purposes. Although some do not record details of individual transactions, a majority have the potential to associate specific customers with specific transactions. Unfortunately, the marketing value of these data is often overlooked and they are not always stored in ways that permit easy retrieval and analysis for marketing purposes. Nevertheless, collection and storage of customer transaction data can often be reformatted to provide marketers with some of the information they require, including how existing segments have responded to past changes in marketing variables.

Other information may have to be collected through special studies, such as customer surveys, or reviews of analogous situations. It may also be necessary to collect information on competitive performance, because changes in the capacity or strategy of competitors may require corrective action.

When new strategies are under consideration, operations researchers can often contribute useful insights by developing simulation models of the impact of changes

Table 9.4 Information Needs for Demand and Capacity Management Strategies	• Historical data on the level and composition of demand over time, including responses to changes in price or other marketing variables • Forecasts of the level of demand for each major segment under specified conditions • Segment-by-segment data to help management evaluate the impact of periodic cycles and random demand fluctuations • Cost data to enable the organization to distinguish between fixed and variable costs and to determine the relative profitability of incremental unit sales to different segments and at different prices • In multisite organizations, *identification of meaningful variations in the levels and composition of demand on a site-by-site basis* • Customer attitudes toward queuing under varying conditions • Customer opinions on whether the quality of service delivered varies with different levels of capacity utilization

in different variables. Such an approach is particularly useful in service "network" environments, such as theme parks and ski resorts, where customers can choose between multiple activities at the same site. Madeleine Pullman and Gary Thompson modeled customer behavior at a ski resort, where skiers can choose between different lifts and ski runs of varying lengths and levels of difficulty. Through analysis, they were able to determine the potential future impact of lift capacity upgrades (bigger or faster chair lifts), capacity expansion in the form of extended skiing terrain, industry growth, day-to-day price variations, customer response to information about wait times at different lifts, and changes in the customer mix.[14]

Conclusion

Because many capacity-constrained service organizations have heavy fixed costs, even modest improvements in capacity utilization can have a significant effect on the bottom line. In this chapter we have also shown how managers can transform fixed costs into variable costs through such strategies as using rented facilities or part-time labor. Creating a more flexible approach to productive capacity allows a firm to adopt strategy to match capacity to demand (also called "chase demand" strategy), thereby improving productivity.

Decisions on *place and time* are closely associated with balancing demand and capacity. Demand is often a function of where the service is located and when it is offered. Marketing strategies involving use of *product elements, price,* and *promotion and education* are often useful in managing the level of demand for a service at a particular place and time.

The time-bound nature of services is a critical management issue today, especially with customers becoming more time sensitive and more conscious of their personal time constraints and availability. People-processing services are particularly likely to impose the burden of unwanted waiting on their customers, since the latter cannot avoid coming to the "factory" for service. Reservations can shape the timing of arrivals, but sometimes queuing is inevitable. Managers who can act to save customers more time (or at least make time pass more pleasantly) than the competition are often able to create a competitive advantage for their organizations.

Review Questions

1. Why is capacity management particularly significant for service firms?
2. What is meant by "chasing demand"?
3. What does "inventory" mean for service firms and why is it perishable?
4. How does optimum capacity utilization differ from maximum capacity utilization? Give examples of situations where the two may be the same and of ones where they differ.

5. Select a service organization of your choice and identify its particular patterns of demand with reference to the checklist provided in Table 9.1.
    (a) What is the nature of this service organization's approach to capacity and demand management?
    (b) What changes would you recommend in relation to its management of capacity and demand, and why?
6. Why should service marketers be concerned about the amount of time that customers spend in (a) preprocess waits, (b) in-process waits, and (c) postprocess waits?
7. What do you see as the advantages and disadvantages of the different types of queues for an organization serving large numbers of customers?

Application Exercises

1. Identify some specific examples of companies in your community (or region) that significantly change their product and/or marketing mix variables in order to encourage patronage during periods of low demand.
2. Give examples, based on your own experience, of a reservation system that worked well, and of one that worked badly. Identify and evaluate the reasons for the success and failure of these two systems. What recommendations would you make to both firms to improve (or further improve in the case of the good example) their reservation systems?
3. Review the ten propositions on the psychology of waiting lines. Which are the most relevant in (a) a city bus stop on a cold, dark evening, (b) check-in for a flight at the airport, (c) a doctor's office where patients are seated, and (d) a ticket line for a football game that is expected to be a sellout.

Endnotes

[1] Kenneth J. Klassen and Thomas R. Rohleder, "Combining Operations and Marketing to Manage Capacity and Demand in Services," *The Service Industries Journal* 21 (April 2001): 1–30.
[2] Based on material in James A. Fitzsimmons and M. J. Fitzsimmons, *Service Management: Operations, Strategy, and Information Technology*, 4th ed. (New York: McGraw-Hill/Irwin, 2004), and W. Earl Sasser, Jr., "Match Supply and Demand in Service Industries," *Harvard Business Review* (November–December 1976).
[3] Irene C. L. Ng, Jochen Wirtz, and Khai Sheang Lee, "The Strategic Role of Unused Service Capacity," *International Journal of Service Industry Management* 10, no. 2 (1999): 211–238.
[4] Malcolm Galdwell, "The Bottom Line for Lots of Time Spent in America," *The Washington Post* syndicated article, February 1993.
[5] Dave Wielenga, "Not So Fine Lines," *Los Angeles Times*, November 28, 1997.
[6] Richard Saltus, "Lines, Lines, Lines, Lines…The Experts Are Trying to Ease the Wait," *The Boston Globe*, October 5, 1992: 39, 42.
[7] Dominic Al-Badri, "Kyoto's MK Taxi Tries to Transform Japan," *Japan Inc.* (July 2003).
[8] Anat Rafaeli, G. Barron, and K. Haber, "The Effects of Queue Structure on Attitudes," *Journal of Service Research* 5 (November 2002): 125–139.
[9] Jay R. Chernow, "Measuring the Values of Travel Time Savings," *Journal of Consumer Research* 7 (March 1981): 360–371. [Note: This entire issue was devoted to the consumption of time.]
[10] Ana B. Casado Diaz and Francisco J. Más Ruiz, "The Consumer's Reaction to Delays in Service," *International Journal of Service Industry Management* 13, no. 2 (2002): 118–140.
[11] Based on David H. Maister, "The Psychology of Waiting Lines," in J. A. Czepiel, M. R. Solomon, and C. F. Surprenant, *The Service Encounter* (Lexington, MA: Lexington Books/D.C. Heath, 1986), 113–123; M. M. Davis and J. Heineke, "Understanding the Roles of the Customer and the Operation for Better Queue

Management," *International Journal of Service Industry Management* 7, no. 5 (1994): 21–34; and Peter Jones and Emma Peppiat, "Managing Perceptions of Waiting Times in Service Queues," *International Journal of Service Industry Management* 7, no. 5 (1996): 47–61.

12   "Making Hotel Reservation through SMS," *New Straits Times*, January 20, 2003.

13   Sheryl E. Kimes and Richard B. Chase, "The Strategic Levers of Yield Management," *Journal of Service Research* 1 (November 1998): 156–166; Anthony Ingold, Una McMahon-Beattie, and Ian Yeoman, eds., *Yield Management Strategies for the Service Industries*, 2nd ed. (London: Continuum, 2000).

14   Madeleine E. Pullman and Gary M. Thompson, "Evaluating Capacity- and Demand-Management Decisions at a Ski Resort," *Cornell Hotel and Restaurant Administration Quarterly* 43 (December 2002): 25–36; and Madeleine E. Pullman and Gary Thompson, "Strategies for Integrating Capacity with Demand in Service Networks," *Journal of Service Research* 5 (February 2003): 169–183.

CHAPTER TEN

Planning the Service Environment

Managers … need to develop a better understanding of the interface between the resources they manipulate in atmospherics and the experience they want to create for the customer.

JEAN-CHARLES CHEBAT AND LAURETTE DUBÉ[1]

Restaurant design has become as compelling an element as menu, food and wine … in determining a restaurant's success.

DANNY MEYER[2]

The physical service environment plays an important role in shaping the service experience and delivering customer satisfaction. Banyan Tree resorts are often cited as vivid examples of service environments that make every customer comfortable and highly satisfied, and leave a long-lasting impression. In fact, organizations from hospitals to hotels and from restaurants to professional firms have come to recognize that the service environment is an important component of their overall value proposition.

In this chapter, which relates back to our earlier discussion in Chapter 2 of the notion of service as a form of theater, we look at the importance of carefully designing service environments that help to engineer customer experiences, convey the target image of the firm, solicit the desired responses from customers and employees, and support service operations and productivity. Specifically, we explore the following questions:

1. What is the purpose of the service environment?
2. What are the various effects that the service environment can have on people?
3. What are the theories behind people's responses?
4. What are the dimensions of the service environment?
5. How can we design a servicescape to achieve the desired effects?

What is the Purpose of Service Environments?

Service environments, also called servicescapes,[3] relate to the style and appearance of the physical surroundings and other experiential elements encountered by customers at service delivery sites. Designing the service environment is an art that takes considerable time and effort, and can be expensive to implement. Once designed and built, service environments are not always easy to change. Let's examine why many service firms take so much trouble to shape the environment in which their customers and service personnel will interact.

Image, Positioning, and Differentiation

For organizations delivering high-contact services, the design of the physical environment and the way in which tasks are performed by customer-contact personnel jointly play a vital role in creating a particular corporate identity and shaping the nature of the customer's experience. The service environment and its accompanying atmosphere impact buyer behavior in three important ways:

1. *As a message-creating medium,* using symbolic cues to communicate to the intended audience about the distinctive nature and quality of the service experience.
2. *As an attention-creating medium,* to make the servicescape stand out from those of competing establishments, and to attract customers from target segments.
3. *As an effect-creating medium,* employing colors, textures, sounds, scents, and spatial design to enhance the desired service experience, and/or to heighten an appetite for certain goods, services, or experiences.

THE SERVICESCAPE AS PART OF THE SERVICE EXPERIENCE   Services are often intangible and customers cannot assess quality well. Here, customers frequently use the service environment as an important quality proxy, and firms take great pains to signal quality and portray the desired image. Think about the reception area of successful professional firms such as investment banks or management consulting firms, where the decor and furnishings tend to be elegant and designed to impress.

Consider Figure 10.1, which shows the lobbies of Big John's Guesthouse and the China World Hotel in Beijing, China, which cater to two very different target segments. One caters to younger guests who love fun and have low budgets, and the other to a more mature, affluent, and more prestigious clientele that includes upscale business travelers. Each servicescape clearly communicates and reinforces its hotel's respective positioning and is particularly important in setting service expectations as guests arrive. In retailing, the store environment affects the perceived quality of the merchandise. Consumers infer higher merchandise quality if the goods

Figure 10.1
The lobbies of Big John's Guesthouse and the China World Hotel send dramatically different messages about the product positioning of each facility.

Courtesy of Big John's Guesthouse.

are displayed in an ambient environment conveying a prestige image than in one that creates a discount image.[4]

Many servicescapes are purely functional. Firms that are trying to convey the impression of low-price service do so by locating in inexpensive neighborhoods, occupying buildings with a simple appearance, minimizing wasteful use of space, and dressing their employees in practical, inexpensive uniforms. However, servicescapes do not always shape customer perceptions and behavior in ways intended by their creators. Veronique Aubert-Gamet notes that customers often make creative use of physical spaces and objects for different purposes. For instance, business people may set aside a restaurant table for use as a temporary office desk, with papers spread around and a laptop computer and mobile phone positioned on its surface, competing for space with the food and beverages.[5] Smart designers keep an eye open for such trends as these may even lead to the creation of a new service concept!

THE SERVICESCAPE AS PART OF THE VALUE PROPOSITION   Physical surroundings help to shape appropriate feelings and reactions in customers and employees. Consider how effectively many amusement parks use the servicescape concept to enhance their service offerings. The clean environment of Hong Kong's Ocean Park or Malaysia's Sunway Lagoon contributes to the sense of fun and excitement that visitors encounter on arrival and throughout their visit.

Actually, in some Asian countries, it is common for people to enjoy the servicescapes more than the services themselves. Take Starbucks Coffee in China for example. Since Starbucks set up their first store in Beijing in 1999, they have rapidly expanded their business into many metropolitan cities in China, reaching a total of 270 stores today. Starbucks' success lies in being able to select high-profile locations on the busiest streets, and designing its stores to feature large glass walls to attract customers who enjoy watching others and being watched themselves (see Figure 10.2).

Resort hotels are another example of using servicescapes and engineered service experiences as a core part of the value proposition. Western resort hotels like Club Med's villages, designed to create a totally carefree atmosphere, may have provided the original inspiration for "get-away" holiday environments. Asian destination resorts, however, are fast catching up in terms of luxury, and in drawing inspiration from theme parks to create fantasy environments, both inside and outside. A good example where the servicescape is carefully engineered is the Keng Tu Yuen Tea Yard Restaurant in Taiwan featured in Best Practice in Action 10.1.

Facilitate the Service Encounter and Enhance Productivity

Service environments are often designed to facilitate the service encounter and to increase productivity. Chase and Stewart highlighted ways in which fail-safe methods embodied in the service environment can help reduce service failures and support a fast and smooth service delivery process.[6] For example, color-coded keys on cash registers allow cashiers to identify the numerical figures and product codes that

Figure 10.2
Starbucks Coffee in Shanghai has become a popular place to hang out and meet friends.

each button stands for. To foster a neat appearance of front-line staff, mirrors can be placed where staff can automatically check their appearance before going "on stage" to meet customers. Child care centers use toy outlines on walls and floors to show where toys should be placed after use. In fast-food restaurants and school canteens, strategically located tray-return stands and notices on walls remind customers to return their trays.

Understanding Consumer Responses to Service Environments

The field of environmental psychology studies how people respond to environments. Services marketing academics have applied the theories from this field to better understand and manage customer responses to service environments.

Feelings Are a Key Driver of Customer Responses to Service Environments

THE MEHRABIAN-RUSSELL STIMULUS-RESPONSE MODEL   Figure 10.3 displays a simple yet fundamental model of how people respond to environments. The model was adopted from environmental psychology and holds that the environment, and its conscious and unconscious perception and interpretation influence how people feel in that environment.[7] People's feelings, in turn, drive their responses to that environment. Feelings are central to the model, which posits that feelings, rather than perceptions or thoughts, drive behavior. For example, we don't avoid an environment simply because there are a lot of people around us. Rather, we are

*Best Practice
in Action 10.1*

KENG TU YUEN TEA YARD RESTAURANT

The first Keng Tu Yuen Tea Yard Restaurant was set up in Taiwan in 1987. With its philosophy of "spreading tea culture and subliming humanity," Keng Tu Yuen tries to fuse the traditional tea culture into the charming and captivating scenery resembling that of Suzhou's China, combining it with professional and friendly service so that customers are able to enjoy tea, food, and conversation in a relaxing place.

The five main parts of the physical environment in Keng Tu Yuen are designed to reflect its business philosophy and to highlight its people-oriented spirit.

1. *Location: Quiet places in the noisy downtown*
   In order to sharpen customers' impressions and produce an effect of contrast, most Keng Tu Yuen restaurants are located downtown. The quietness of the interior contrasts with the noise outside.

2. *Exterior design of the building: Simple and traditional*
   The use of traditional Chinese garden architectural design arouses in customers a feeling of primitive simplicity. Its signboard isn't easily noticeable and might even be overlooked without introduction by frequent visitors.

3. *Visual design: Poetry courtyard*

The visual design of Keng Tu Yuen is a mixture of the style of Suzhou Gardens and that of Minnan architecture. In order to make the whole space design consistent with customers' feelings, and to make customers feel as if they are staying in a courtyard of a poet in ancient times, the whole area in Keng Tu Yuen is decorated with old and tiny designs, and interspersed with rockeries, glides, rearing ponds, and alleys.

4. *Service design: Faint scent of tea and charm of traditional culture*
   The antique furniture and related appliances in Keng Tu Yuen work together to give customers a sense of ultimate indulgence and are tangible cues related to the service offering.

5. *Staff uniforms: Traditional and exquisite clothing*
   To blend in with the ambience of the restaurant, all the serving staff are dressed in the same traditional-styled uniforms. These elegant dresses express simple sincerity to the customers.

Source: http://www.teanet.com.tw/main_2.htm, accessed on July 15, 2004.

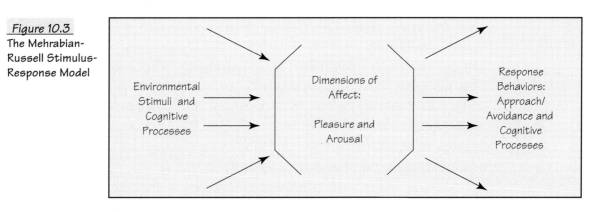

Figure 10.3
The Mehrabian-Russell Stimulus-Response Model

deterred by the unpleasant feeling of crowding, of people being in our way, of lacking perceived control, and of not being able to get what we want as fast as we wish to. If we had all the time in the world, and felt excited about being part of the crowd during seasonal festivities, then exposure to the same number of people might lead to feelings of pleasure and excitement that would lead us to want to stay and explore that environment.

In environmental psychology, the typical outcome variable is *approach* or *avoidance* of an environment. Of course, in services marketing, we can add a long list of additional outcomes that a firm might want to manage, including how much money people spend while on the firm's premises and how satisfied they are with the service experience after they have left the environment.

THE RUSSELL MODEL OF AFFECT   Given that affect, or feelings, are central to how people respond to an environment, we need to understand those feelings better. Russell's model of affect is widely used to help understand feelings in service environments.[8] As shown in Figure 10.4, it suggests that emotional responses to environments can be described along two main dimensions, pleasure and arousal. Pleasure is a direct, subjective response to the environment, depending on how much the individual likes or dislikes the environment. Arousal refers to how

Figure 10.4
The Russell Model of Affect

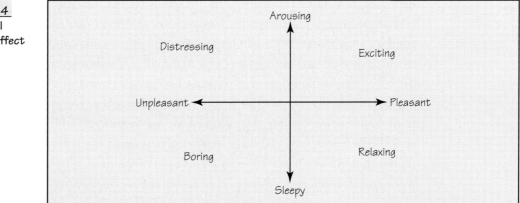

stimulated the individual feels, ranging from deep sleep (very low level of internal activity) to highest levels of adrenaline in the bloodstream, for example, when bungee-jumping (very high level of internal activity). The arousal quality is much less subjective than its pleasure quality. Arousal quality depends largely on the information rate or load of an environment. For example, environments are stimulating (have a high information rate) when they are complex, have motion or change in it, and have novel and surprising elements. A low rate, relaxing environment has the opposite characteristics.

How can all our feelings and emotions be explained by only two dimensions? Russell separated the cognitive or thinking part of emotions from these two basic underlying emotional dimensions. Thus, the emotion of anger about a service failure could be modeled as high arousal and displeasure, which would locate it in the "distressing" region in our model, combined with a cognitive attribution process. When a customer attributes a service failure to the firm (he thinks it is the firm's fault that this has happened, that it is under the firm's control, and that the firm is not doing much to avoid it happening again), then this powerful cognitive attribution process feeds directly into high arousal and displeasure. Similarly, most other emotions can be dissected into their cognitive and affective components.

The advantage of Russell's model of affect is its simplicity as it allows a direct assessment of how customers feel while they are in the service environment. Firms can set targets for affective states. For example, a bungee-jumping business or roller-coaster operator might want its customers to feel aroused (assuming that there is little pleasure when having to gather all one's courage before jumping). A disco or theme park operator may want customers to feel excited. A bank may want its customers to feel confident and so on. Later in this chapter, we discuss how service environments can be designed to deliver the types of service experiences desired by customers.

DRIVERS OF AFFECT   Affect can be caused by perceptions and cognitive processes of any degree of complexity. However, the more complex a cognitive process becomes, the more powerful is its potential impact on affect. For example, a customer's disappointment with service level and food quality in a restaurant (a complex cognitive process, where perceived quality is compared to previously held service expectations) cannot be compensated by a simple cognitive process such as the subconscious perception of pleasant background music.

In practice, the large majority of service encounters are routine, with little high-level cognitive processing. We tend to be on "autopilot" and follow our service scripts when doing routine transactions such as using the subway, entering a fast-food restaurant or a bank. Here, which is most of the time, it is the simple cognitive processes that determine how people feel in the service setting. Those include the conscious and even unconscious perceptions of space, colors, scents, etc. However, should higher levels of cognitive processes be triggered, for instance through something surprising in the service environment, then it is the interpretation of this surprise that determines people's feelings.[9]

BEHAVIORAL CONSEQUENCES OF AFFECT   At the most basic level, pleasant environments result in approach, and unpleasant ones in avoidance behaviors. Arousal acts as an amplifier of the basic effect of pleasure on behavior. If the environment is pleasant, increasing arousal can lead to excitement, leading to a stronger positive consumer response. Conversely, if a service environment is inherently unpleasant, one should avoid increasing arousal levels, as this would move customers into the "distressing" region. For example, loud fast-beat music would increase the stress levels of shoppers trying to do their last-minute shopping in supermarkets on Chinese New Year's Eve. In such situations, the information load of the environment should be lowered.

For some services, customers have strong affective expectations. Think of a romantic candlelight dinner in a restaurant, a relaxing spa visit, or an exciting time at the stadium or the disco. When customers have strong affective expectations, it is important to design the environment to match those expectations.[10] (See Figure 10.5).

Finally, how people feel during the service encounter is an important driver of customer loyalty. For example, positive affect has been shown to drive hedonic shopping value, which in turn increased repeat purchasing behavior, whereas negative affect mostly reduced utilitarian shopping value and thereby lowered customer share.[11]

Figure 10.5
Sheltered by granite boulders, the Banyan Tree Seychelles' spa pavilion uses clear tempered glass walls and elegant woods and natural materials to blur the boundaries of indoors and outdoors.

Reprinted with permission from Banyan Tree Hotels and Resorts.

Linking Theory to Servicescapes

Building on the basic models in environmental psychology, Mary Jo Bitner has developed a comprehensive model that she named the servicescape.[12] Figure 10.6 shows the main dimensions that she identified in service environments, which include ambient conditions, space and functionality, and signs, symbols, and artifacts. Because individuals tend to perceive these dimensions holistically, the key to effective design is how well each individual dimension fits together with everything else.

Next, the model shows that there are customer and employee-response moderators. This means, the same service environment can have different effects on different customers, depending on what they like. Rap music may be sheer pleasure to some customer segments, and sheer torture to others.

One important contribution of Bitner's model was that she included employee responses to the service environment. After all, employees spend much more time there than customers, and it is crucially important that designers become aware of how a particular environment enhances (or at least does not reduce) the productivity of front-line personnel and the quality of service that they deliver.

Figure 10.6
The Servicescape Model

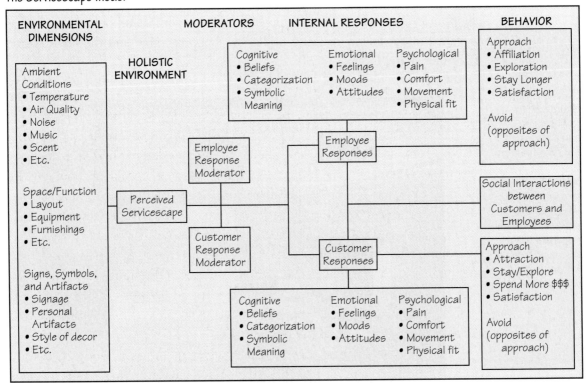

Source: Mary Jo Bitner, "Servicescapes: The Impact of Physical Surroundings on Customers and Employees," *Journal of Marketing 56* (April 1992): 57–71.

Internal customer and employee responses can be categorized into cognitive responses (e.g., quality perceptions and beliefs), emotional responses (e.g., feelings and moods), and psychological responses (e.g., pain and comfort). These internal responses lead to overt behavioral responses such as avoiding a crowded departmental store or responding positively to a relaxing environment by remaining there longer and spending extra money on impulse purchases. It is important to understand that the behavioral responses of customers and employees must be shaped in ways that facilitate production and purchase of high-quality services. Consider how the outcomes of service transactions may differ in situations where both customers and front-line staff feel agitated and stressed rather than relaxed and happy.

Dimensions of the Service Environment

Service environments are complex and have many design elements. In Table 10.1, for example, we can see an overview of all the design elements that might be encountered in a retail outlet. We will focus, in this section, on the main dimensions of the service environment in the servicescape model, which are the ambient conditions, space and functionality, and signs, symbols, and artifacts.[13]

The Impact of Ambient Conditions

Ambient conditions refer to those characteristics of the environment pertaining to our five senses. Even when not consciously noted, they may still affect people's emotional well-being, perceptions, and even attitudes and behaviors. The ambient environment or atmosphere is a gestalt concept, composed of literally hundreds of design elements and details in the service environment that have to work together to create the desired service environment.[14] The resulting atmosphere creates a mood that is perceived and interpreted by the customer.[15] Ambient conditions are perceived both separately and holistically, and include lighting and color schemes, size and shape perceptions, sounds such as noise and music, temperature, and scents. Clever design of these conditions can elicit desired behavioral responses among consumers. Best Practice in Action 10.2 features how a team of Japanese architects created the appropriate ambience when they designed the Kuala Lumpur Stesen Sentral, a building that houses an integrated rail transport system offering one-stop transit service from Kuala Lumpur downtown to the Kuala Lumpur International Airport (KLIA) and beyond (see Figure 10.7).

Also, consider the innovative thinking underlying the new trend to transform shopping centers in Japan into full experiential boutiques. Shopping in Japan is neither utilitarian nor boring, at least not with the new series of stores designed by Masamichi Katayama. These stores cater to the needs of young Japanese consumers

<u>Table 10.1</u>
Design Elements of a Retail Store Environment

Dimensions	Design Elements	
Exterior Facilities	• Architectural style • Height of building • Size of building • Color of building • Exterior walls and exterior signs • Storefront • Marquee • Lawns and gardens	• Display of windows • Entrances • Visibility • Uniqueness • Surrounding stores • Surrounding areas • Parking and accessibility • Congestion
General Interior	• Flooring and carpeting • Color schemes • Lighting • Scents • Odors (e.g., tobacco smoke) • Sounds and music • Fixtures • Wall composition • Wall textures (paint, wall paper) • Ceiling composition	• Temperature • Cleanliness • Width of aisles • Dressing facilities • Vertical transportation • Dead areas • Merchandise layout and displays • Price levels and displays • Cash register placement • Technology/modernization
Store Layout	• Allocation of floor space for selling, merchandise, personnel, and customers • Placement of merchandise • Grouping of merchandise • Workstation placement • Placement of equipment • Placement of cash register	• Waiting areas • Traffic flow • Waiting queues • Furniture • Dead areas • Department locations • Arrangements within departments
Interior Displays	• Point-of-purchase displays • Posters, signs, and cards • Pictures and art work • Wall decorations • Theme setting • Ensemble	• Racks and cases • Product display • Price display • Cut cases and dump bins • Mobiles
Social Dimensions	• Personnel characteristics • Employee uniforms • Crowding	• Customer characteristics • Privacy • Self-service

Sources: Adapted from Barry Berman and Joel R. Evans, *Retail Management—A Strategic Approach*, 8th ed, (Upper Saddle River, NJ: Prentice Hall, 2001), 604; L. W. Turley and Ronald E. Milliman, "Atmospheric Effects on Shopping Behavior: A Review of the Experimental Literature," *Journal of Business Research* 49 (2000): 193–211.

who love to shop. To them, shopping is not merely a physical activity; it is a culture. Katayama's stores are designed to entertain. For instance, one of his stores, Busy Work Lady, is designed to look like a bathroom, complete with small white bathroom tiles, fitting rooms that look like shower stalls and a bathtub that holds sweaters of different colors. Other brands like A Bathing Ape, have US$50 T-shirts individually placed in a flat glass box displayed on racks. The customer flips through this rack of T-shirts to choose his desired design, very much like viewing posters in a museum.[16]

*Best Practice
in Action 10.2*

STESEN SENTRAL TRANSPORTATION HUB

Upon entering Stesen Sentral, a building in Kuala Lumpur that serves as a transportation hub connecting Kuala Lumpur International Airport's (KLIA) express, and its local and national train, bus and taxi connections from KL, one cannot fail to notice that the design of this hub closely resembles that of the KLIA itself. The striking resemblance is not surprising, given that the same Japanese architects designed both structures. However, the similarities in style have a more profound meaning—the architects believe that since Stesen Sentral serves as a link to connect KLIA to the city, its design should also reflect this connection.

In sync with contemporary sensibilities, the architects sought to blend nature and its calming effects. Thus, instead of looking like a boring and busy train station, Stesen Sentral gives people a calm and soothing feeling. For a start, the architects optimized the use of natural light by incorporating glass liberally into the overall design. In addition, paved walkways, courtyards, and green buffer zones were included to create a zen-like peace and tranquility within the building. The building's numerous open areas, both indoors and outdoors, contribute to the sense of lightness.

The result of this well-thought-out and meticulously planned design is a soothing and strangely liberating feeling for all its users. With its universal appeal, the Kuala Lumpur Stesen Sentral is aesthetically pleasing and leaves very favorable impressions on most people who visit it.

Figure 10.7
The Kuala Lumpur
Stesen Sentral
was designed to
optimize the use of
natural light by
incorporating glass
liberally into the
overall design.

Courtesy of Stesen Sentral Kuala Lumpur.

Source: Adapted from "The Future is Sentral," *New Straits Times* (Malaysia), July 9, 2003; http://www.stesensentral.com/gallery.htm (accessed on July 9, 2004); http://www.ktmb.com.my/article.cfm?id=49; http://www.kliaekspres.com (both accessed on July 11, 2004).

The Japanese are taking to this new way of shopping. All the stores in the Harajuku-Aoyama belt are teeming with young shoppers—and it's not only the women. Many men are devoting a whole afternoon to the pursuit of their shopping activities. Overseas customers who have had a glimpse of this innovative way of retailing in their home countries are flocking to Japan to experience it first-hand.

MUSIC   In service settings, music can have a powerful effect on perceptions and behaviors, even if played at barely audible volumes. As shown in the servicescape model in Figure 10.6, the various structural characteristics of music such as tempo, volume, and harmony are perceived holistically, and their effect on internal and behavioral responses is moderated by respondent characteristics (e.g., younger people tend to like different music and therefore respond differently from older people to the same piece of music).[17] Numerous research studies have found that fast-tempo music and high-volume music increases arousal levels,[18] which can then lead people to walk faster and to talk and eat faster in restaurants.[19] People tend to adjust their pace, either voluntarily or involuntarily, to match the tempo of music. This means that restaurants can speed up table turnover by increasing the tempo and volume of the music and serve more diners, or slow diners down with slow beat music and softer volume to keep them longer in the restaurant and increase beverage revenues.

A restaurant study conducted over eight weeks showed that beverage revenue increased by 41 percent and the total gross margin by 15 percent when slow-beat rather than fast-beat music was played (see Table 10.2 for details). Customers dining in a slow-music environment spent an average of 15 minutes longer in the restaurant than did individuals in a fast-music condition.[20] Likewise, shoppers walked less

Table 10.2 Impact of Music on Restaurant Diners	Restaurant Patron Behaviors	Fast-Beat Music Environment	Slow-Beat Music Environment	Difference between Slow- and Fast-Beat Environments	
				Absolute Difference	Percentage Difference
	Customer time spent at the table	45 min	56 min	+ 11 min	+ 24%
	Spending on food	US$55.12	US$55.81	+ US$0.69	+ 1%
	Spending on beverages	US$21.62	US$30.47	+ US$8.85	+ 41%
	Total spending	US$76.74	US$86.28	+ US$9.54	+ 12%
	Estimated gross margin	US$48.62	US$55.82	+ US$7.20	+15%

Source: Ronald E. Milliman, "Using Background Music to Affect the Behavior of Supermarket Shoppers," *Journal of Marketing* 56, no. 3 (1982): 86–91.

rapidly when slow music was played and increased their level of impulse purchases.[21] Playing familiar music in a store was shown to stimulate shoppers, and thereby reduce their browsing time, whereas playing unfamiliar music induced shoppers to spend more time there.[22] In consumer wait situations, music can be used effectively to shorten the perceived waiting time and increase customer satisfaction.[23] Relaxing music proved effective in lowering stress levels in a hospital's surgery waiting room.[24] And pleasant music has even been shown to enhance customers' perception of and attitude toward service personnel.[25] Besides that, music can also help to create the suitable atmosphere and ambience needed for different establishments. For example, when guests enter Hard Rock Hotel in Bali, Indonesia, they feel uplifted instantly because of the "rock-n-roll" music played at the hotel's bar. Service Perspectives 10.1 features how Hard Rock Hotel in Bali uses music and other design elements to create the ultimate "rock-n-roll" environment for the guests.

SCENT   An ambient smell is one that pervades an environment, may or may not be consciously perceived by customers, and is not related to any particular product. We are experiencing the power of smell when we are hungry and get a whiff of freshly baked croissants long before we pass a Delifrance Café. This smell makes us aware of our hunger and points us to the solution (walk into Delifrance and get some food). The same works for bakeries, cafes, pizzerias, and the like. Other examples include the smell of detergent in most hospital lobbies to convey a sense of cleanliness and hygiene, or the smell of candy floss and popcorn at funfairs to make visitors feel relaxed and excited about visiting the fair. The presence of scent can have a strong impact on mood, affective and evaluative responses, and even purchase intentions and in-store behaviors.[26] Table 10.3 shows the effects scent had in a retail environment on the perception of the store, store environment, and merchandise.

Olfaction researcher Alan R. Hirsch, M.D., of the Smell & Taste Treatment and Research Foundation based in Chicago, is convinced that in some ten years, we will understand scents so well that we will be able to use them to effectively manage people's behaviors.[27] Service marketers will be interested in how to make you hungry and thirsty in the restaurant, relax you in a dentist's waiting room and energize you to work out harder in a gym. Scent researcher Bryan Raudenbush has found that sniffing peppermint while exercising will not increase a person's vim and vigor, but the oil from the aromatic plant makes exercising more pleasurable, thus encouraging people to exercise longer.[28] In aromatherapy, it is generally accepted that scents have distinct characteristics and can be used to solicit certain emotional, physiological, and behavioral responses. For example in Tokyo, tired shoppers can step into a booth and inhale a rejuvenating waft of lemonade or peppermint to stimulate their senses.[29]

Table 10.4 shows the generally assumed effects of specific scents on people as prescribed by aromatherapy. In service settings, research has shown that scents can

Service
Perspectives
10.1

TRANSFERRING A SERVICE CONCEPT FROM CAFÉS TO HOTELS

You can feel the pulsating beat the moment you step into the Hard Rock Hotel in Bali, Indonesia. The beat that rocks the mind comes from Centerstage—the large, open-air bar where back-to-back music videos are playing on a huge five-meter video wall. Hard Rock memorabilia occupy all other available wall space, and there is a raised stage for unplugged concerts (see Figure 10.8). In addition to the rock music is the engagingly energetic attitude of the casually attired hotel staff, which further enhances the positive first impression. You know that you couldn't be anywhere else but at the Hard Rock Bali. The brand is best known for its cafes, of which there are more than a hundred around the world. But there are only a handful of Hard Rock Hotels.

Located in the middle of Kuta—the entertainment, shopping, surf-and-sand nerve center of Bali—the Hard Rock Hotel stands next door to a free-standing Hard Rock Café. This hotel is one of the most popular resorts on the island with a clientele consisting mainly of Indonesians from Jakarta, and Japanese, Taiwanese, Korean, and Australian tourists. Most guests are dressed in shorts or swimwear, or simply a T-shirt bearing the words "This Place Rocks!" According to Jamal Hussain, its general manager, Hard Rock Bali has been well received by many locals because the brand name is regarded as a status symbol.

One of the nicest things about the Hard Rock Bali (and other hotels in Bali) is that it is only four-storey high, giving the entire three-hectare resort a lush, warm, and open feel. This is because of the stringent local rule that prohibits man-made structures such as hotels from being built higher than the tallest coconut tree. Coupled with its own in-house radio station, Hard Rock Bali is wired for sound. Music is everywhere and it is like a giant Hard Rock Café—complete with pool, accommodation, spa facilities, and shopping arcade. The spacious guest rooms, decorated in cool colors, are equipped with CD players, TVs, and Internet access.

For guests seeking some rocking entertainment, Centerstage is the right place to go. Most evenings from 6 p.m. to 8 p.m., a classic Hollywood blockbuster is shown on the giant screen. Guests can enjoy the movie while sipping evening cocktails or a light, frothy Indonesian beer. The real fun, however, comes from the resident live bands that change every three months and perform the latest hits and popular requests. Although these bands are mainly Indonesian, the hotel periodically welcomes visiting bands from Australia.

Karaoke is available for guests who want to stage their own live performance. The hotel even has its own recording studio, called the Boom Box, where guests can cut a personal recording for a modest fee. With the assistance of the studio technician, guests are often surprised and delighted to discover how good their singing sounds! Rock star treatment, great food, and high service standards make Bali's Hard Rock Hotel an appealing choice. For foreign visitors who are already familiar with Hard Rock Café, the hotel's design and ambience creates comforting reassurance in a new and exotic location; for Indonesians, it represents novelty and sophistication on home territory.

Sources: "Hard Rock Bali—Rock It!" *New Straits Times* (Malaysia), July 13, 2003; information supplied by Rachel Lovelock, June 2004; http://www.hardrockhotels.net/bali/fnb.htm (accessed on July 10, 2004).

Figure 10.8
Centerstage in Hard Rock Hotel, Bali, features live bands, with an oversized video wall that makes the "rock-n-roll" experience larger than life.

Hard Rock Hotel Bali's Centerstage, courtesy of HPL Hotels & Resorts.

Table 10.3
The Effects of Scents on the Perceptions of Store Environments

Evaluation	Unscented Environment: Mean Ratings	Scented Environment: Mean Ratings	Difference between Unscented and Scented Environments
Store Evaluation			
• Negative/positive	4.65	5.24	+ 0.59
• Outdated/modern image	3.76	4.72	+ 0.96
Store Environment			
• Unattractive/attractive	4.12	4.98	+ 0.86
• Drab/colorful	3.63	4.72	+ 1.09
• Boring/stimulating	3.75	4.40	+ 0.65
Merchandise			
• Outdated/up-to-date style	4.71	5.43	+ 0.72
• Inadequate/adequate range	3.80	4.65	+ 0.85
• Low/high quality	4.81	5.48	+ 0.67
• Low/high price	5.20	4.93	− 0.27

Note: The mean ratings are based on a scale from 1 to 7.
Source: Eric R. Spangenberg, Ayn E. Crowley, and Pamela W. Henderson, "Improving the Store Environment: Do Olfactory Cues Affect Evaluations and Behaviors?" *Journal of Marketing* 60 (April 1996): 67–80.

have significant impact on customer perceptions, attitudes, and behaviors. For example:

• People were more willing to buy Nike sneakers and pay more for them—an average of US$10.33 more per pair—when they tried on the shoes in a floral-

Table 10.4
Aromatherapy: The Effects of Fragrances on People

Fragrance	Aroma Type	Aromatherapy Class	Traditional Use	Potential Psychological Impact on People
Orange	Citrus	Calming	Soothing agent, astringent	Soothes nerves and has a calming and relaxing effect, especially good for nervous or jittery people
Bergamot	Citrus	Calming, balancing	Calming, balancing, antiseptic, deodorant, soothing agent	Has a soothing and calming effect; helps to make people feel comfortable
Mimosa	Floral	Calming, balancing	Muscle relaxant, soothing agent	Helps relaxation and makes people feel comfortable and calm; creates a harmonious and balanced feel
Black pepper	Spicy	Balancing, soothing	Muscle relaxant, aphrodisiac	Helps to balance people's emotions and enables people to feel sexually aroused
Lavender	Herbaceous	Calming, balancing, soothing	Muscle relaxant, soothing agent, astringent, skin conditioner	Relaxing and calming; helps to create a homey and comfortable feel
Jasmine	Floral	Uplifting, balancing	Emollient, soothing agent, aphrodisiac, antiseptic	Helps to make people feel refreshed, joyful, comfortable and sexually aroused
Grapefruit	Citrus	Energizing	Astringent, soothing agent, skin conditioner; helps to keep skin smooth and supple	Stimulating, refreshing, reviving, and improves mental clarity and alertness; can even enhance physical strength and energy
Lemon	Citrus	Energizing, uplifting	Antiseptic, soothing agent	Boosts energy levels and helps to make people feel happy and rejuvenated
Peppermint	Minty	Energizing, stimulating	Insect repellent, antiseptic, and helps to cleanse skin	Increases attention level; boosts energy
Eucalyptus	Camphoraceous	Toning, stimulating	Deodorant, antiseptic, soothing agent; helps remove odor and can be used to cleanse skin	Stimulating and energizing; helps to create balance and the feeling of cleanliness and hygiene

Sources: http://www.fragrant.demon.co.uk, and http://www.naha.org/WhatisAromatherapy; Dana Butcher, "Aromatherapy—Its Past and Future," *Drug and Cosmetic Industry* 16, no. 3 (1998): 22–24; Shirley Price and Len Price, *Aromatherapy For Health Professionals*, 2nd ed. (New York: Churchill Livingstone, 1999), 145–160; Anna S. Mattila and Jochen Wirtz, "Congruency of Scent and Music as a Driver of In-Store Evaluations and Behavior," *Journal of Retailing* 77 (2001): 273–289.

scented room. The same effect was found even when the scent was so faint that people could not detect it (the scent was unconsciously perceived).[30]

- Many restaurants like to serve garlic bread as an appetizer, and research shows they are right to do so. A recent study found that smelling and eating garlic bread during dinner reduced the number of negative interactions by an average of 0.17 incidents or by 23 percent per family member per minute, while at the same time increasing pleasant interactions by 0.25 incidents per family member per minute.[31] This promotes and maintains shared family experiences, and in a restaurant context, makes it a more satisfying dining experience.

Besides having the ability to solicit certain desired emotional, physiological, and behavioral responses among customers, suitable and approximate scents can also be used to enhance the productivity of the employees, which would ultimately contribute to a better service environment. For example, Kaijima Corporation in Japan has installed a Total Environment Perfume Control System in some of its offices to enhance the ambience and boost the moods of its employees. In the morning, the company circulates the scent of lemons through the air conditioner, which would help the employees to stay focused, and it switches to cedar in the afternoon to boost energy.[32]

COLOR   Color "is stimulating, calming, expressive, disturbing, impressional, cultural, exuberant, and symbolic. It pervades every aspect of our lives, embellishes the ordinary, and gives beauty and drama to everyday objects."[33] Researchers have found that colors have a strong impact on people's feelings.[34] The de facto system used in psychological research is the Munsell System, which defines colors in the three dimensions of hue, value, and chroma.[35] *Hue* is the pigment of the color (i.e., the name of the color: red, orange, yellow, green, blue, or violet). *Value* is the degree of lightness or darkness of the color relative to a scale that extends from pure black to pure white. *Chroma* refers to hue intensity, saturation, or brilliance. High chroma colors have a high intensity of pigmentation in them and are perceived as rich and vivid, whereas low chroma colors are perceived as dull.

Hues are classified into *warm* colors (red, orange, and yellow hues) and *cold* colors (blue and green), with orange (a mix of red and yellow) being the warmest, and blue being the coldest of the colors. These colors can be used to manage the warmth of an environment. For example, if a violet is too warm, you can cool it off by reducing the red. Or if a red is too cold, warm it up by giving it a shot of orange.[36] Warm colors are associated with elated mood states and arousal but also heightened anxiety, while cool colors reduce arousal levels and can elicit emotions such as peacefulness, calmness, love, and happiness.[37] Table 10.5 summarizes common associations and responses to colors.

Research in a service environment context has shown that despite differing color preferences, people are generally drawn to warm color environments. However,

<u>Table 10.5</u>
Common Associations and Human Responses to Colors

Color	Degree of Warmth	Nature Symbol	Common Associations and Human Responses to Colors
Red	Warm	Earth	High energy and passion; can excite, stimulate, and increase arousal levels and blood pressure
Orange	Warmest	Sunset	Emotions, expression, and warmth; noted for its ability to encourage verbal expression of emotions
Yellow	Warm	Sun	Optimism, clarity, and intellect; bright yellow often noted for its mood-enhancing ability
Green	Cool	Growth, grass, and trees	Nurturing, healing, and unconditional love
Blue	Coolest	Sky and ocean	Relaxation, serenity, and loyalty; lowers blood pressure; is a healing color for nervous disorders, and for relieving headaches because of its cooling and calming nature
Indigo	Cool	Sunset	Mediation and spirituality
Violet	Cool	Violet flower	Spirituality; reduces stress and can create an inner feeling of calm

Sources: Sara O. Marberry and Laurie Zagon, *The Power of Color—Creating Healthy Interior Spaces* (New York: John Wiley & Sons, 1995), 18; and Sarah Lynch, *Bold Colors for Modern Rooms: Bright Ideas for People Who Love Color*, (Gloucester, MA: Rockport Publishers, 2001), 24–29.

paradoxically, findings show that red-hued retail environments are seen as negative, tense, and less attractive than cool color environments.[38] Warm colors encourage fast decision making and in service situations are best suited for low-involvement decisions or impulse purchases. Cool colors are favored when consumers need time to make high-involvement purchases.[39]

Although we have an understanding of the general impact of colors, their use in any specific context needs to be approached with caution. Most cultures have their own interpretation of what different colors stand for. Some colors are seen as taboo and, hence, inappropriate for joyous events. Other colors are seen as lucky and should be used extensively during a celebration. An example of this is the Malay culture, where green is considered a color of blessing and is worn for happy occasions such as Hari Raya Puasa, but not for a funeral.

Spatial Layout and Functionality

As service environments generally have to fulfill specific purposes and customer needs, spatial layout and functionality are particularly important. Spatial layout refers to the size and shape of furnishings, counters, and potential machinery and equipment, and the ways in which they are arranged. Functionality refers to the ability of those items to facilitate the performance of service transactions. Spatial layout and functionality affect buying behavior, customer satisfaction, and consequently the business performance of the service facility.

Signs, Symbols, and Artifacts

Many things in the service environment act as explicit or implicit signals to communicate the firm's image, help customers find their way (e.g., to certain service counters, departments, or the exit), and to convey the rules of behavior (e.g., smoking/no-smoking areas, or queuing systems). In particular, first-time customers will automatically try to draw meaning from the signs, symbols, and artifacts, and will want to draw cues from the environment to help them form expectations about the type and level of service that is being offered, and to guide them through the service environment and service process.

Customers become disoriented when they cannot derive clear signals from a servicescape, resulting in anxiety and uncertainty about how to proceed and how to obtain the desired service. Inexperienced customers and newcomers can easily feel lost in a confusing environment and experience anger and frustration as a result.

The challenge for servicescape designers is to use signs, symbols, and artifacts to guide customers clearly through the process of service delivery. This task assumes particular importance in situations where there is a high proportion of new or infrequent customers, and/or a high degree of self-service, especially when there are few service staff available to help guide customers through the process. In such situations, signs, symbols, and artifacts have to communicate clearly and teach the service process in as intuitive a manner as possible. For instance, due to the existence of two different subway lines in Central Tokyo, Japan, it is easier for tourists to find the station name on a subway map if they memorized the logos designed for each of the lines (see Figure 10.9).

Figure 10.9
Standardized signs guide passengers through the Tokyo subway system.

Toei Subway   Eidan Subway

At many service facilities, customers' first point of contact is likely to be the location where they park their cars. As emphasized in Best Practice in Action 10.3, the principles of effective environment design apply even in this most mundane environment.

GUIDELINES FOR PARKING DESIGN

Car parks play an important role at many service facilities. Effective use of signs, symbols, and artifacts in a parking lot or garage helps customers find their way, manages their behavior, and portrays a positive image for the sponsoring organization.

- *Friendly warnings.* All warning signs should communicate a customer benefit. For instance, "Fire lane: For everyone's safety, we ask you not to park in the fire lane."
- *Fresh paint.* Curbs, cross walks, and lot lines should be repainted regularly before any cracking, peeling, or disrepair become evident. Proactive and frequent repainting give positive cleanliness cues and projects a positive image.
- *Safety lighting.* Good lighting that penetrates all areas makes life easier for customers and enhances safety. Firms may want to draw attention to this feature with notices stating that "parking lots have been specially lit for your safety."
- *Maternity parking.* A few thoughtful organizations have designated expectant mother parking spaces, painted with a blue/pink stork. This strategy demonstrates a sense of caring and understanding of customer needs.[40]
- *Help customers remember where they left their vehicle.* Forgetting where one left the family car in a huge lot or parking structure can be a nightmare. Many car parks have adopted color-coded floors to help customers remember which level they parked on. Some go a step further. They assign an animal to represent each section of the car park, such as the Monkey, Snake, or Zebra zone. Images of the animals are painted on the walls of the corresponding sections.

People Are Part of the Service Environment, Too

The appearance and behavior of both service personnel and customers can reinforce or detract from the impression created by a service environment. Within the constraints imposed by legal obligations and skill requirements, service firms may seek to recruit staff to fill specific roles, costume them in uniforms that are consistent with the servicescape in which they will be working, and script their speech and movements. Likewise, marketing communications may seek to attract customers who will not only appreciate the ambience created by the service provider but actively enhance it by their appearance and behavior. In hospitality and retail settings, newcomers often survey the array of existing customers before deciding whether to patronize the establishment.

Consider Figure 10.10, which shows the interior of two restaurants. Imagine that you have just entered each of these two dining rooms. How is each positioning itself within the restaurant industry? What sort of meal experience can you expect?

Figure 10.10
Distinctive servicescapes—from table settings and furniture to room design and employee uniforms—create different customer expectations of these two restaurants. Not surprisingly, the dress and demeanor of customers themselves responds to, and reinforces, the overall ambience.

And what are the clues that you employ to make your judgments? In particular, what inferences do you draw from looking at the customers who are already seated in each restaurant?

Putting It All Together

Although individuals often perceive particular aspects or individual design features of an environment, it is the total configuration of all those design features that determines consumer responses. Consumers perceive service environments holistically, and consumer responses to a physical environment depend on ensemble effects or configurations.[41]

Design with a Holistic View

Whether a dark, glossy wooden floor is the perfect flooring depends on everything else in that service environment, including the type, color scheme, and materials of the furniture, the lighting, the promotional materials, to the overall brand perception and positioning of the firm. Servicescapes have to be seen holistically, which means no dimension of the design can be optimized in isolation, because everything depends on everything else. As evidenced in Research Insights 10.1, scents and music must also be matched with other elements.

Research Insights 10.1

MATCH AND MISMATCH OF SCENT AND MUSIC IN THE SERVICESCAPE

Whether a certain type of background enhances consumer responses depends on the ambient scent of the service environment. Using a field experiment, Anna Mattila and Jochen Wirtz manipulated two types of pleasant music and pleasant scent in a gift store that differed in their arousing qualities. Consumer impulse purchasing and satisfaction were measured for the various music and scent conditions.

The experiment used two compact discs from the Tune Your Brain™ series by Elizabeth Miles, an ethnomusicologist. The low-arousal music was the *Relaxing Collection*, featuring slow-tempo music, while the high-arousal music consisted of the *Energizing Collection*, featuring fast-tempo music. Similarly, scent was manipulated to have high- or low-arousal quality. Lavender was used for the low-arousal scent because of its relaxing and calming properties. Grapefruit was used for the high-arousal scent because of its stimulating properties that can refresh, revive, and improve mental clarity and alertness, and can even enhance physical strength and energy.

The results of this experiment show that when the arousal qualities of music and ambient scent were matched, consumers responded more favorably. Figures 10.11(a) and (b) show these effects clearly. For instance, scenting the store with low-arousal scent (lavender) combined with slow-tempo music led to higher satisfaction and impulse purchases than using that scent with high-arousal music. Playing fast-tempo music had a more positive effect when the store was scented with grapefruit (high-arousal scent) rather than with lavender. This study showed that when environmental stimuli act together to provide a coherent atmosphere, consumers in that environment will respond more positively.

These findings suggest that bookstores might induce people to linger longer and buy more by playing slow-tempo music combined with a relaxing scent, or event managers might consider using arousing scents to enhance excitement.

Figure 10.11(a)
The Impact of Scent and Music on Satisfaction

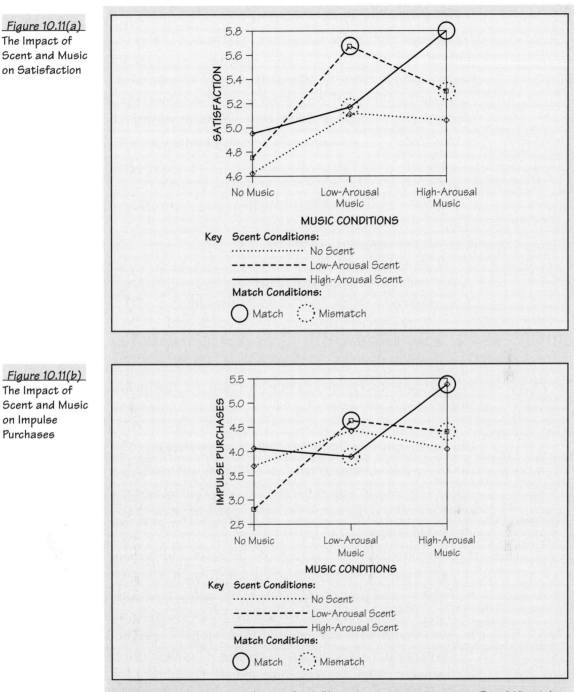

Figure 10.11(b)
The Impact of Scent and Music on Impulse Purchases

Note: Both charts are on a scale from 1 to 7, with 7 being the extreme positive response. The solid-line circles show the match conditions, where both music and scent are either stimulating or relaxing, and the intermitted-line circles show the mismatch conditions, where one stimulus is relaxing and the other stimulating (i.e., relaxing music and stimulating scent, or stimulating music and relaxing scent).

Source: Anna S. Mattila and Jochen Wirtz, "Congruency of Scent and Music As a Driver of In-Store Evaluations and Behavior," *Journal of Retailing* 77 (2001): 273–289.

Design from a Customer's Perspective

Many service environments are built with an emphasis on aesthetic values, and designers sometimes forget the most important factor to consider when designing service environments—the customers who will be using them.

In a recent study, Alain d'Astous explored environmental aspects that irritate shoppers. His findings highlighted the following problems:

- *Ambient conditions* (ordered by severity of irritation):
  - Store is not clean
  - Too hot inside the store or the shopping center
  - Music inside the store is too loud
  - Bad smell in the store
- *Environmental design variables*:
  - No mirror in the dressing room
  - Unable to find what one needs
  - Directions within the store are inadequate
  - Arrangement of store items has been changed
  - Store is too small
  - Finding the way in a large shopping center[42]

Contrast d'Astous' findings with the Disney example in Best Practice in Action 10.4.

Use Tools That Can Guide the Servicescape Design

How do we find out what irritates our customers, and how can we potentially further enhance the good aspects of our servicescape? Among the tools that can be used to better understand the customers' view of and responses to service environments are the following:

- *Keen observation* of customers' behavior and responses to the service environment by management, supervisors, branch managers, and front-line staff.
- *Feedback and ideas from front-line staff and customers* using a broad array of research tools ranging from suggestion boxes to focus groups and surveys.
- *Field experiments* can be used to manipulate specific dimensions in an environment and the effects observed. For instance, one can experiment with the use of various types of music and scents, and then measure the time and money customers spend in the environment, and their level of satisfaction. Laboratory experiments, using slides or videos or other ways to simulate real-world service environments (such as computer-simulated virtual tours), can be used effectively to examine the impact of changes in design elements that cannot easily be manipulated in a field experiment. Examples include testing of alternative color schemes, spatial layouts, or styles of furnishing.

*Best Practice
in Action 10.4*

DESIGN OF DISNEY'S MAGIC KINGDOM

Walt Disney was one of the undisputed champions of designing service environments. His tradition of amazingly careful and detailed planning has become one of his company's hallmarks, and is visible everywhere in its theme parks. For example, Main Street is angled to make it seem longer upon entry into the Magic Kingdom than it actually is. With myriad facilities and attractions strategically inclined and located at each side of the street, people look forward to the relatively long journey to the Castle. However, looking down the slope from the Castle back toward the entrance makes Main Street appear shorter than it really is, relieving exhaustion and rejuvenating guests. It encourages strolling, which minimizes the number of people who take buses and so eliminates the threatening problem of traffic congestion.

Meandering sidewalks with multiple attractions keep guests feeling entertained by both the planned activities and also by watching other guests; rubbish bins are plentiful and always in sight to convey the message that littering is prohibited; and repainting of facilities is a routine procedure that signals a high level of maintenance and cleanliness.

Disney's servicescape design and upkeep help to script customer experiences and create pleasure and satisfaction for guests, not only in its theme parks but also in its cruise ships and hotels.

Disneyland Tokyo celebrates its 20th anniversary on April 15, 2004 with plenty to cheer about. It had successfully transferred the Disney concept from the United States to Japan and reached break-even in only four years.

Sources: Lewis P. Carbone and Stephen H. Haeckel, "Engineering Customer Experiences," *Marketing Management* 3, no. 3 (Winter 1994): 10–11; Kathy Merlock Jackson, *Walt Disney, A Bio-Bibliography* (Westport, CT: Greenwood Press, 1993), 36–39; Andrew Lainsbury, *Once Upon an American Dream: The Story of Euro Disneyland* (Lawrence, KS: University Press of Kansas, 2000), 64–72; "Theme-Parks in Japan," *The Economist,* April 3, 2004.

- *Blueprinting* or service mapping, described in Chapter 8, can be extended to include the physical evidence in the environment. Design elements and tangible cues can be documented as the customer moves through each step of the service delivery process. Photos and videos can supplement the map to make it more vivid.

Table 10.6 shows an analysis of a customer's visit to a movie theater, identifying how different environmental elements at each step exceeded or failed to meet them. The service process was broken up into increments, steps, decisions, duties, and activities, all designed to take the customer through the entire service encounter. The more a service company can see, understand, and experience the same things as its customers, the better equipped it will be to realize errors in the design of its environment, and to further improve upon what is already functioning well.

Table 10.6
A Visit to the Movies: The Service Environment as Perceived by the Customer

Steps in the Service Encounter	Design of the Service Environment	
	Exceeds Expectations	**Fails Expectations**
Locate a parking lot	Ample room in a bright place near to the entrance, with a security officer protecting your valuables	Insufficient parking lots so that patrons have to park in another building
Queuing up to obtain tickets	Strategic placement of mirrors, posters of upcoming movies, and entertainment news to ease perception of long wait, if any; movies and time slots can be easily seen, ticket availability is clearly communicated	A long queue and having to wait for a long while; difficult to see fast what movies are being shown at what time slots, and whether tickets are still available
Checking of tickets to enter the theater	A very well maintained lobby with clear directions to the theater and posters of the movie to enhance patrons' experience	A dirty lobby with rubbish visibly strewn, and unclear or misleading directions to the movie theater
Go to the washroom before the movie starts	Sparkling clean, spacious, brightly lit, dry floors, well-stocked, nice décor, clear mirrors wiped regularly	Dirty, with an unbearable odor; broken toilets; no hand towels, soap, or toilet paper; overcrowded; dusty and dirty mirrors
Enter the theater and locate your seat	Spotless theater; well designed with no bad seats; sufficient lighting to locate your seat; spacious, comfortable chairs, with drink and popcorn holders on each seat; and a suitable temperature	Rubbish strewn on the floor; broken seats; sticky floors; gloomy and insufficient lighting; burnt-out exit signs
Watch the movie	Excellent sound system and film quality; nice audience; an enjoyable and memorable entertainment experience overall	Substandard sound and movie equipment, uncooperative audience that talks and smokes due to lack of "No Smoking" and other signs; a disturbing and unenjoyable entertainment experience overall
Leave the theater and return to the car	Friendly service staff that greet patrons as they leave, an easy exit through a brightly lit and safe parking area back to the car with the help of clear lot signs	A difficult trip, as patrons squeeze through a narrow exit, unable to find the car due to no or insufficient lighting.

Source: Adapted from Steven Albrecht, "See Things from the Customer's Point of View—How to Use the 'Cycles of Service' to Understand What the Customer Goes through to Do Business with You," *World's Executive Digest* (December 1996): 53–58.

Conclusion

The service environment plays a major part in shaping customers' perception of a firm's image and positioning. As service quality is often difficult to assess objectively, customers frequently use the service environment as an important quality signal. Finally, a well-designed service environment makes customers feel good and boosts their satisfaction, and at the same time enhances the productivity of the service operation.

The theoretical underpinnings for understanding the effects of service environments on customers come from the environmental psychology literature. The Mehrabian-Russell Stimulus-Response model holds that environments influence peoples' affective state (or feelings), which in turn drives their behavior in that environment. Affect can be modeled with the two key dimensions of pleasure and arousal, which together determine whether people approach and spend time and money in an environment, or whether they avoid it. The servicescape model built on these theories and developed a comprehensive framework that explains how customers and service staff respond to service environments.

The main dimensions of service environments are ambient conditions (including music, scents, and colors), spatial layout and functionality, and signs, symbols, and artifacts. Each dimension can have important effects on customer responses. For example, the presence or absence of background music—and even type of music, including its tempo and volume—can make significant differences in customer satisfaction, quality perceptions, and even behaviors such as time and money spent in the environment. The other design variables can have similar effects.

Putting it all together is difficult, as environments are perceived holistically. That means no individual aspect of the environment can be optimized without considering everything else in that environment. This makes designing service environments an art, and professional designers focus on the design of specific service environments such as hotel lobbies, restaurants, clubs, cafes and bistros, retail outlets, health care facilities, and so on. Furthermore, apart from an aesthetical perspective, the best service environments are designed with the customer's perspective in mind. The environment needs to facilitate smooth movement through the service process.

Review Questions

1. Compare and contrast the strategic and functional roles of service environments within a service organization.
2. What are affective expectations? What is their role in driving customer satisfaction with service encounters?
3. What is the relationship or link between the Russell Model of Affect and Bitner's servicescape model?
4. Why is it likely that different customers and service staff respond differently to the same service environment?
5. Select a bad and a good waiting experience and contrast the situations with respect to the aesthetics of the surrounding, diversions, people waiting, and attitude of servers.

6. Explain the dimensions of ambient conditions and how each can influence customer responses to the service environment.
7. What are the roles of signs, symbols, and artifacts?
8. What are the implications of the fact that environments are perceived holistically?
9. What tools are available for aiding our understanding of customer responses, and for guiding the design and improvements of service environments?

Application Exercises

1. Identify firms from three different service sectors where the service environment is a crucial part of the overall value proposition. Analyze and explain in detail the value that is being delivered by the service environment.
2. Visit a service environment, and have a detailed look around. Experience the environment and try and feel how the various design parameters shape what you feel and how you behave in that setting.
3. Visit a self-service environment and analyze how the design dimensions guide you thorough the service process. What do you find most effective for you, and what seems least effective? How could that environment be improved to further ease the "way-finding" for self-service customers?

Endnotes

[1] Jean-Charles Chebat and Laurette Dubé, "Evolution and Challenges Facing Retail Atmospherics: The Apprentice Sorcerer Is Dying," *Journal of Business Research* 49 (2000): 89–90.
[2] Danny Meyer, reported in Christine M. Piotrowski and Elizabeth A. Rogers, *Designing Commercial Interiors* (New York: John Wiley & Sons, 1999), 123.
[3] The term was coined by Mary Jo Bitner in her paper "Servicescapes: The Impact of Physical Surroundings on Customers and Employees," *Journal of Marketing* 56 (April 1992): 57–71.
[4] Julie Baker, Dhruv Grewal, and A. Parasuraman, "The Influence of Store Environment on Quality Inferences and Store Image," *Journal of the Academy of Marketing Science* 22, no. 4 (1994): 328–339.
[5] Véronique Aubert-Gamet, "Twisting Servicescapes: Diversion of the Physical Environment in a Reappropriation Process," *International Journal of Service Industry Management* 8, no. 1 (1997): 26–41.
[6] Richard B. Chase and Douglas M. Stewart, "Making Your Service Fail-Safe," *Sloan Management Review* 35 (1994): 35–44.
[7] Robert J. Donovan and John R. Rossiter, "Store Atmosphere: An Environmental Psychology Approach," *Journal of Retailing* 58, no. 1 (1982): 34–57.
[8] James A. Russell, "A Circumplex Model of Affect," *Journal of Personality and Social Psychology* 39, no. 6 (1980): 1161–1178.
[9] Jochen Wirtz and John E. G. Bateson, "Consumer Satisfaction with Services: Integrating the Environmental Perspective in Services Marketing into the Traditional Disconfirmation Paradigm," *Journal of Business Research* 44, no. 1 (1999): 55–66.
[10] Jochen Wirtz, Anna S. Mattila, and Rachel L. P. Tan, "The Moderating Role of Target-Arousal on the Impact of Affect on Satisfaction–An Examination in the Context of Service Experiences," *Journal of Retailing* 76, no. 3 (2000): 347–365.
[11] Barry J. Babin and Jill S. Attaway, "Atmospheric Affect as a Tool for Creating Value and Gaining Share of Customer," *Journal of Business Research* 49 (2000): 91–99.
[12] Mary Jo Bitner, "Servicescapes: The Impact of Physical Surroundings on Customers and Employees," *Journal of Marketing* 56 (April 1992): 57–71.

13 For a comprehensive review of experimental studies on the atmospheric effects, refer to L.W. Turley and Ronald E. Milliman, "Atmospheric Effects on Shopping Behavior: A Review of the Experimental Literature," *Journal of Business Research* 49 (2000): 193–211.

14 Patrick M. Dunne, Robert F. Lusch, and David A. Griffith, *Retailing*, 4th ed. (Orlando, FL: Hartcourt, 2002), 518.

15 Barry Davies and Philippa Ward, *Managing Retail Consumption* (West Sussex, England: John Wiley & Sons, 2002), 179.

16 David Rakoff, "The Economy of Cool," *New York Times*, May 18, 2003.

17 Steve Oakes, "The Influence of the Musicscape within Service Environments," *Journal of Services Marketing* 14, no. 7 (2000): 539–556.

18 Morris B. Holbrook and Punam Anand, "Effects of Tempo and Situational Arousal on the Listener's Perceptual and Affective Responses to Music," *Psychology of Music* 18 (1990): 150–162; and S. J. Rohner and R. Miller, "Degrees of Familiar and Affective Music and Their Effects on State Anxiety," *Journal of Music Therapy* 17, no. 1 (1980): 2–15.

19 Ronald E. Milliman, "The Influence of Background Music on the Behavior of Restaurant Patrons," *Journal of Consumer Research* 13 (1986): 286–289.

20 Clare Caldwell and Sally A. Hibbert, "The Influence of Music Tempo and Musical Preference on Restaurant Patrons' Behavior," *Psychology and Marketing* 19, no. 11 (2002): 895–917.

21 Ronald E. Milliman, "Using Background Music to Affect the Behavior of Supermarket Shoppers," *Journal of Marketing* 56, no. 3 (1982): 86–91.

22 Richard F. Yalch and Eric R. Spangenberg, "The Effects of Music in a Retail Setting on Real and Perceived Shopping Times," *Journal of Business Research* 49 (2000): 139–147.

23 Michael K. Hui, Laurette Dube, and Jean-Charles Chebat, "The Impact of Music on Consumers Reactions to Waiting for Services," *Journal of Retailing* 73, no. 1 (1997): 87–104.

24 David A. Tansik and Robert Routhieaux, "Customer Stress-Relaxation: The Impact of Music in a Hospital Waiting Room," *International Journal of Service Industry Management* 10, no. 1 (1999): 68–81.

25 Laurette Dubé and Sylvie Morin, "Background Music Pleasure and Store Evaluation Intensity Effects and Psychological Mechanisms," *Journal of Business Research* 54 (2001): 107–113.

26 Paula Fitzerald Bone and Pam Scholder Ellen, "Scents in the Marketplace: Explaining a Fraction of Olfaction," *Journal of Retailing* 75, no. 2 (1999): 243–262.

27 Alan R. Hirsch, *Dr. Hirsch's Guide to Scentsational Weight Loss* (UK: Harper Collins, January 1997), 12–15.

28 Mike Fillon, "No Added Pep in Peppermint", *WebMD Feature*, September 22, 2000, *http://mywebmd.com/health_and_wellness/living-better/default.htm* (accessed on February 17, 2003).

29 Manjira Dutta, "Making Sense of Smell," *India Today Plus*, April 1, 2002.

30 Alan R. Hirsch and S.E. Gay, "Effect on Ambient Olfactory Stimuli on the Evaluation of a Common Consumer Product," *Chemical Senses* 16 (1991): 535.

31 Alan R. Hirsch, "Effects of Garlic Bread on Family Interactions," *Journal of American Psychosomatic Society* 62, no. 1 (2000), 1434.

32 Dutta, April 1, 2002, *loc. cit.*

33 Linda Holtzschuhe, *Understanding Color—An Introduction for Designers,* 2nd ed. (New York: John Wiley & Sons, Inc., 2002), 1.

34 Gerald J. Gorn,. Chattopadhyay Amitava, Tracey Yi, and Darren Dahl, "Effects of Color as an Executional Cue in Advertising: They're in the Shade," *Management Science* 43, no. 10 (1997): 1387–1400; Ayn E. Crowley, "The Two-Dimensional Impact of Color on Shopping," *Marketing Letters* 4, no. 1 (1993): 59–69.

35 Albert Henry Munsell, *A Munsell Color Product* (New York: Kollmorgen Corporation 1996).

36 Holtzschuhe, 2002, *op. cit.*

37   Heinrich Zollinger, *Color: A Multidisciplinary Approach* (Zurich: Verlag Helvetica Chimica Acta (VHCA) Weinheim, Wiley-VCH, 1999), 71–79.

38   Joseph A. Bellizzi, Ayn E. Crowley, and Ronald W. Hasty, "The Effects of Color in Store Design," *Journal of Retailing* 59, no. 1 (1983): 21–45.

39   John E.G. Bateson and K. Douglas Hoffman, *Managing Services Marketing*, 4th ed. (Orlando, FL: The Dryden Press, 1999), 143.

40   Lewis P. Carbone and Stephen H. Haeckel, "Engineering Customer Experiences," *Marketing Management* 3, no. 3 (Winter 1994): 9–18.

41   Anna S. Mattila and Jochen Wirtz, "Congruency of Scent and Music as a Driver of In-Store Evaluations and Behavior," *Journal of Retailing* 77 (2001): 273–289.

42   Alan d'Astous, "Irritating Aspects of the Shopping Environment," *Journal of Business Research* 49 (2000): 149–156.

CHAPTER ELEVEN

Managing People for Service Advantage

The old adage "People are your most important asset" is wrong. The right people are your most important asset.

JIM COLLINS

Govern a big family as you would cook a small fish—very gently.

CHINESE PROVERB

Among the most demanding jobs in service businesses are the so-called front-line jobs. Employees are expected to be fast and efficient at executing operational tasks, as well as courteous and helpful in dealing with customers. In fact, front-line employees are a key input for delivering service excellence and competitive advantage. Behind most of today's successful service organizations stands a firm commitment to effective management of human resources (HR), including recruitment, selection, training, motivation, and retention of employees. Organizations that display this commitment are also characterized by a distinctive culture of service leadership and role modeling by top management. It is probably harder for competitors to duplicate high-performance human assets than any other corporate resource.

In this chapter, we focus on the people side of service management and explore the following questions:

1. Why is the front line so crucially important to the success of a service firm?
2. Why is the work of service staff so demanding, challenging, and often difficult?
3. What are the cycles of failure, mediocrity, and success in HR for service firms?
4. How do we get it right? How are we to attract, select, train, motivate, and retain outstanding front-line staff?
5. What is the role of a service culture and service leadership in sustainable service excellence?

Service Staff Are Crucially Important

Almost everybody can recount some horror story of a dreadful experience they have had with a service business. If pressed, many of these same people can also recount a really good service experience. Service personnel usually feature prominently in such dramas. They are either in roles as uncaring, incompetent, mean-spirited villains, or in roles as heroes who went out of their way to help customers by anticipating their needs and resolving problems in a helpful and empathetic manner. From the firm's perspective, service staff are crucially important as they can be a key determinant of customer loyalty (or defections), and therefore play an important role in the service-profit chain. We will discuss both in the following two sections.

Service Personnel As a Source of Customer Loyalty and Competitive Advantage

From a customer's perspective, the encounter with service staff is probably the most important aspect of a service. From the firm's perspective, the service levels and the way service is delivered by the front line can be an important source of differentiation as well as competitive advantage. In addition, the strength of the customer/front-line staff relationship is often an important driver of customer loyalty.[1] Service staff is so important to customers and the firm's competitive positioning because the front line:

- *Is a core part of the product.* Often, it is the most visible element of the service, delivers the service, and significantly determines service quality.
- *Is the service firm.* Front-line staff represent the service firm, and from a customer's perspective, is the firm.
- *Is the brand.* Front-line staff and service are often a core part of the brand. It is the staff that determine whether the brand promise gets delivered or not.

Furthermore, front-line staff play a key role in anticipating customers' needs, customizing the service delivery, and building personalized relationships with customers, which ultimately lead to customer loyalty. Comfort Delgro, the company which operates the Singapore Bus Service (SBS), presents the annual Star Awards in order to recognize DelGro front-line staff who provided excellent customer service. One of the recipients for this award was bus captain Yap Kim San, who has worked for SBS for 22 years. Asked about the challenges he faced at work, Mr Yap said: "We meet all kinds of passengers every day—some are nice, some are moody, and some show their anger. As bus captains, we put up with that all day and make sure we serve them with a smile, so that they are happy with our service."[2] (See Figure 11.1.)

Figure 11.1
Singapore Bus Service (SBS) Star Award Winners for 2004 are honored with a chance to "parade" around Singapore using SBS buses.

Courtesy of SBS Transit Ltd.

This and many other success stories of employees showing discretionary effort that made a difference reinforce the truism that highly motivated people are at the core of service excellence. They are increasingly a key variable for creating and maintaining competitive positioning and advantage.

The intuitive importance of the impact of service staff on customer loyalty was integrated and formalized by Heskett and his colleagues in their research on the service-profit chain.[3] The authors demonstrate the chain of relationships between (1) satisfaction, retention, and productivity; (2) service value; (3) customer satisfaction and loyalty; and (4) revenue growth and profitability. Unlike in manufacturing, our "shop-floor workers" (our front-line staff) are in constant contact with customers, and we have solid evidence that shows that employee satisfaction and customer satisfaction are highly correlated.[4] This chapter focuses on how to get satisfied, loyal, and productive service staff, and the following chapters in Part Four of this book will focus on how to manage customer loyalty.

The Front Line in Low-Contact Services

Most of the published research in service management and many of the best practice examples featured in this chapter relate to high-contact services. This is not entirely surprising, as the people in these jobs are so visible. They are the actors who appear front-stage in the service drama when they serve the customer. Here, it is obvious why the front line is crucially important to customers, and therefore to the competitive positioning of the firm as well. However, there is an increasing trend across virtually all types of services toward low-contact delivery channels such as call centers. Many routine transactions are now being conducted without even involving the front-line staff at all. Some examples include the many types of services that are provided via Web sites, automated teller machines (ATMs) and interactive voice response (IVR) systems. In the light of these trends, is the front line really that important, especially when more and more routine transactions are being shifted to low- or no-contact channels?

Although the quality of the technology and self-service interface is becoming the core engine for service delivery and its importance has been elevated drastically, the quality of front-line staff still remains crucially important. Most people would not have called the service hotline or visited a service center or shop of their mobile operator, or their credit card company more than once or twice in the last 12 months and interacted with front-line staff there. However, it is these one or two service encounters that are critical. These are the "moments of truth" that drive a customer's perceptions of the service firm. A service firm's differentiation rests on these few moments of truth, given that technology is relatively commoditized. Therefore, the service delivered by the front line, whether it is "ear to ear" or via email rather than face to face, is still highly visible and important to the customer, and therefore a critical component of the services strategy and marketing mix of service firms.

Front-Line Work Is Difficult and Stressful

The service-profit chain has high performing, satisfied employees as key requirements for achieving service excellence and customer loyalty. However, these employees work in some of the most demanding jobs in service firms. We will next discuss the main reasons why these jobs are so demanding.

Boundary Spanning

The organizational behavior literature refers to service staff as boundary spanners. Boundary spanners link the inside of an organization to the outside world, operating at the boundary of the company and transferring information between the inside and the outside world. Because of the position they occupy, boundary spanners often have conflicting roles. Customer-contact personnel must attend to both operational and marketing goals. To illustrate, service staff are expected to delight customers, and at the same time be fast and efficient at executing operational tasks. On top of that, they are often expected to do selling and cross-selling as well.

In short, front-line staff may perform triple roles, producing service quality, productivity, and sales. The multiplicity of roles in service jobs often leads to role conflict and role stress among employees.[5]

Sources of Conflict

Three main causes of role stress in front-line positions are person/role, organization/client, and interclient conflicts.

PERSON/ROLE CONFLICT   Service staff feel conflicts between what their job requires and their own personalities, self-perception, and beliefs. For example, the job may require staff to smile and be friendly even to rude customers, when perhaps under other circumstances they would have just given the person a piece of their mind. In order for service staff to provide quality service, it requires an independent, warm, and friendly personality. These traits are more likely to be found in people with higher self-esteem. However, many front-line jobs are often perceived as low-level jobs, which require little education, offer low pay, and often lack future prospects. If an organization is not able to "professionalize" their front-line jobs and move away from such an image, these jobs may be inconsistent with staff's self-perception and lead to person/role conflicts.

ORGANIZATION/CLIENT CONFLICT   Service employees frequently face the dilemma of whether they should follow the company's rules or satisfy customer demands. This conflict is also called the two-bosses dilemma and arises when customers request services, extras, or exceptions that violate the organizational rules. This conflict is especially acute in organizations that are not customer-oriented. Here, staff frequently has to deal with conflicting customer needs and requests, as well as organizational rules, procedures, and productivity requirements.

INTERCLIENT CONFLICT   Conflicts between customers are not uncommon (e.g., smoking in non-smoking sections, jumping queues, speaking on a mobile phone in a cinema, and noisy guests in a restaurant), and it is usually the service staff that are summoned to call the other customer to order. This is a stressful and unpleasant task, as it is difficult and often impossible to satisfy both sides.

Emotional Labor

The term *emotional labor* originated from Arlie Hochschild in her book *The Managed Heart*.[6] Emotional labor arises when there is a discrepancy between the way front-line staff feel inside and the emotions they are expected to portray in front of customers. Front-line staff are expected to have a cheerful disposition, be genial, compassionate, sincere, or even self-effacing—emotions that can be conveyed through facial expressions, gestures, and words. In the event that employees do not feel such emotions, they are required to quell their true feelings in order to conform to customer expectations.

The stress of emotional labor is nicely illustrated in the following: A flight attendant was approached by a passenger with "Let's have a smile." She replied with "Okay. I'll tell you what, first you smile and then I'll smile, okay?" He smiled. "Good," she said. "Now hold that for 15 hours," and walked away.[7]

Emotional labor is a very real problem faced by front-line staff, and companies are now taking steps to help staff to deal with the problem. For example, because of Singapore Airlines' reputation for service excellence, its customers tend to have very high expectations and can be very demanding. This puts considerable pressure on its front-line staff. The Commercial Training Manager of Singapore Airlines (SIA) explained:

> We have recently undertaken an external survey and it appears that more of the "demanding customers" choose to fly with SIA. So the staff are really under a lot of pressure. We have a motto: "If SIA can't do it for you, no other airline can." So we encourage staff to try to sort things out, and to do as much as they can for the customer. Although they are very proud, and indeed protective of the company, we need to help them deal with the emotional turmoil of having to handle their customers well, and at the same time, feel they're not being taking advantage of. The challenge is to help our staff deal with difficult situations and take the brickbats. This will be the next thrust of our training programs."[8]

Firms need to be aware of ongoing emotional stress and to devise ways of alleviating it, including training on how to deal with emotional stress and how to cope with pressure from customers.

Service Sweatshops?

Rapid developments in information technology (IT) are permitting service businesses to make radical improvements in business processes and even completely reengineer their operations. These developments sometimes result in wrenching changes in the nature of work for existing employees. In instances where face-to-face contact has been replaced by use of the Internet or telephone-based services, firms have redefined and relocated jobs, created new employee profiles for recruiting purposes, and sought to hire employees with a different set of qualifications.

As a result of the growing shift from high-contact to low-contact services, a large and increasing number of customer-contact employees work by telephone or email, never meeting customers face to face. For example, an astounding 3 percent plus of the total U.S. workforce is now employed in call centers as so-called customer service representatives (CSRs).[9]

At best, when well designed, such jobs can be rewarding, and often offer mothers and students flexible working hours and part-time jobs (some 50 percent of call center workers are single mothers or students).[10] In fact, recent research has shown that part-time workers are more satisfied with their work as CSRs than full-time staff, and performed just as well.[11] At worst, they place employees in an electronic equivalent of the old-fashioned sweatshop. Even in the best managed call centers, the work is intense, with CSRs expected to deal with up to two calls a minute under a high level of monitoring (including trips to the toilet and breaks). There's a famous (and true) story about a supervisor who offered his staff diapers so that they spent less time in toilets away from their phones.[12]

As we will discuss in this chapter, some of the keys to success in this area involve screening applicants to make sure they already know how to present themselves well on the telephone and that they have the potential to learn additional skills, training them carefully, and giving them a well-designed working environment.

Cycles of Failure, Mediocrity, and Success

All too often, bad working environments translate into dreadful service, with employees treating customers the way their managers treat them. Businesses with high employee turnover are frequently stuck in what has been termed the *"cycle of failure."* Others, which offer job security but little scope for personal initiative, may suffer from an equally undesirable *"cycle of mediocrity."* However, if managed well, there is potential for a virtuous cycle in service employment, termed the *"cycle of success."*[13]

THE CYCLE OF FAILURE   In many service industries, the search for productivity is on with a vengeance. One solution takes the form of simplifying work routines and hiring workers as cheaply as possible to perform repetitive work tasks that require little or no training. Among consumer services, department stores, fast-food restaurants, and call center operations are often cited as examples where this problem abounds. The cycle of failure captures the implications of such a strategy, with its two concentric but interactive cycles: one involving failures with employees; the second, with customers (see Figure 11.2).

The *employee cycle of failure* begins with a narrow design of jobs to accommodate low skill levels, an emphasis on rules rather than service, and the use of technology to control quality. A strategy of low wages is accompanied by minimal effort on selection or training. Consequences include bored employees who lack the ability to respond to customer problems, who become dissatisfied, and who develop a poor service attitude. Outcomes for the firm are low service quality and high employee turnover. Because of weak profit margins, the cycle repeats itself with the hiring of more low-paid employees to work in this unrewarding atmosphere. Some service firms can reach such low levels of employee morale that front-line staff engage in "service sabotage" as featured in Research Insights 11.1, rather than deliver service excellence.[14]

The *customer cycle of failure* begins with repeated emphasis on attracting new customers, who become dissatisfied with employee performance and the lack of continuity implicit in continually changing faces. These customers fail to develop

Figure 11.2
The Cycle of
Failure

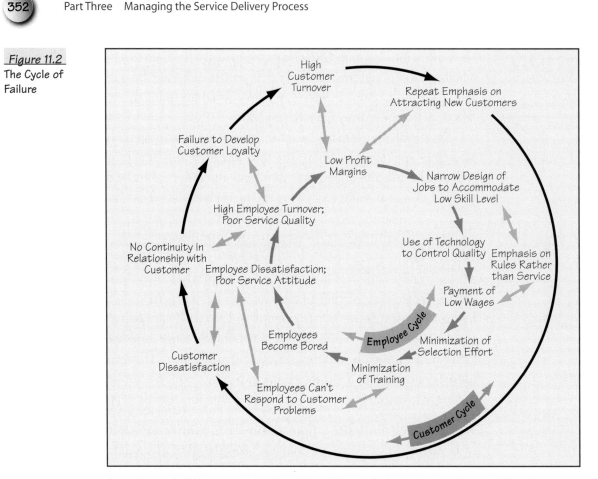

Source: Leonard L. Schlesinger and James L. Heskett, "Breaking the Cycle of Failure in Services," *Sloan Management Review* 31 (Spring 1991): 17–28. Reprinted by permission of publisher. Copyright © 2003 by Massachusetts Institute of Technology. All rights reserved.

Research
Insights 11.1

SERVICE SABOTAGE BY THE FRONT LINE

The next time we are dissatisfied with the service provided by service employees—in a restaurant, for example—it's worth pausing for a moment to think about the consequences of complaining about the service. One might just become the unknowing victim of a malicious case of service sabotage, such as having something unhygienic added to one's food.

Interestingly, there is a relatively high incidence of service sabotage by front-line employees. Lloyd Harris and Emmanuel Ogbonna found in their study of 182 front-line staff that 90 percent of them accepted that front-line behavior with malicious intent to reduce or spoil the service—service sabotage—is an everyday occurrence in their organizations.

They classify service sabotage along two dimensions: covert-overt, and routinized-intermittent behaviors. Covert behaviors are concealed from customers, whereas overt actions are purposefully displayed often to coworkers and also customers. Routinized behaviors are ingrained into the culture, whereas intermittent actions are sporadic and less common. Some true examples of service sabotage classified along the two dimensions are shown in Figure 11.3.

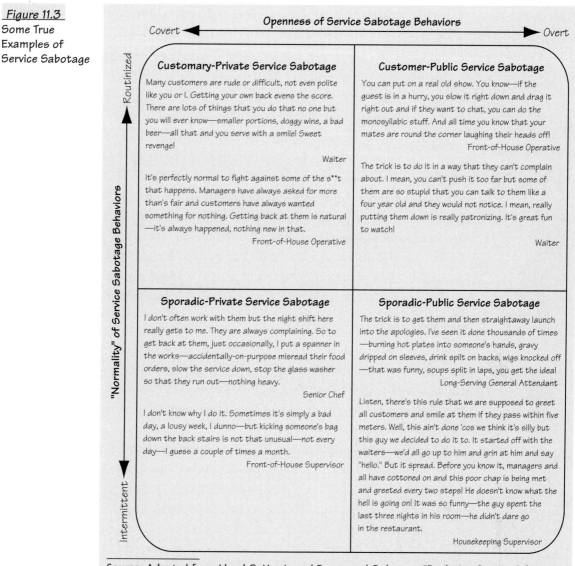

Figure 11.3
Some True
Examples of
Service Sabotage

Openness of Service Sabotage Behaviors

Covert ◄—————————————————————————► Overt

Routinized

"Normality" of Service Sabotage Behaviors

Intermittent

Customary-Private Service Sabotage

Many customers are rude or difficult, not even polite like you or I. Getting your own back evens the score. There are lots of things that you do that no one but you will ever know—smaller portions, doggy wine, a bad beer—all that and you serve with a smile! Sweet revenge!

Waiter

It's perfectly normal to fight against some of the s**t that happens. Managers have always asked for more than's fair and customers have always wanted something for nothing. Getting back at them is natural—it's always happened, nothing new in that.

Front-of-House Operative

Customer-Public Service Sabotage

You can put on a real old show. You know—if the guest is in a hurry, you slow it right down and drag it right out and if they want to chat, you can do the monosyllabic stuff. And all time you know that your mates are round the corner laughing their heads off!

Front-of-House Operative

The trick is to do it in a way that they can't complain about. I mean, you can't push it too far but some of them are so stupid that you can talk to them like a four year old and they would not notice. I mean, really putting them down is really patronizing. It's great fun to watch!

Waiter

Sporadic-Private Service Sabotage

I don't often work with them but the night shift here really gets to me. They are always complaining. So to get back at them, just occasionally, I put a spanner in the works—accidentally-on-purpose misread their food orders, slow the service down, stop the glass washer so that they run out—nothing heavy.

Senior Chef

I don't know why I do it. Sometimes it's simply a bad day, a lousy week, I dunno—but kicking someone's bag down the back stairs is not that unusual—not every day—I guess a couple of times a month.

Front-of-House Supervisor

Sporadic-Public Service Sabotage

The trick is to get them and then straightaway launch into the apologies. I've seen it done thousands of times—burning hot plates into someone's hands, gravy dripped on sleeves, drink spilt on backs, wigs knocked off—that was funny, soups split in laps, you get the idea!

Long-Serving General Attendant

Listen, there's this rule that we are supposed to greet all customers and smile at them if they pass within five meters. Well, this ain't done 'cos we think it's silly but this guy we decided to do it to. It started off with the waiters—we'd all go up to him and grin at him and say "hello." But it spread. Before you know it, managers and all have cottoned on and this poor chap is being met and greeted every two steps! He doesn't know what the hell is going on! It was so funny—the guy spent the last three nights in his room—he didn't dare go in the restaurant.

Housekeeping Supervisor

Source: Adapted from Lloyd C. Harris and Emmanuel Ogbonna, "Exploring Service Sabotage: The Antecedents, Types, and Consequences of Frontline, Deviant, Antiservice Behaviors," *Journal of Service Research* 4, no.3 (2002): 163–183.

any loyalty to the supplier, and turn over as rapidly as the staff. This requires an ongoing search for new customers to maintain sales volume. The departure of discontented customers is especially worrying in the light of what we now know about the greater profitability of a loyal customer base.

Managers have offered excuses and justifications for perpetuating this cycle:

- "You just can't get good people nowadays."
- "People just don't want to work today."
- "To get good people would cost too much and you can't pass on these cost increases to customers."

- "It's not worth training our front-line people when they leave you so quickly."
- "High turnover is simply an inevitable part of our business. You've got to learn to live with it."[15]

Too many managers make shortsighted assumptions about the financial implications of low-pay/high turnover human resource strategies. Part of the problem is the failure to measure all relevant costs. Often omitted are three key cost variables: the cost of constant recruiting, hiring, and training (which is as much a time cost for managers as a financial cost); the lower productivity of inexperienced new workers; and the costs of constantly attracting new customers (requiring extensive advertising and promotional discounts). Also ignored are two revenue variables: future revenue streams that might have continued for years, but are lost when unhappy customers take their business elsewhere; and potential income from prospective customers who are turned off by negative word of mouth. Finally, there are less easily quantifiable costs such as disruptions to service while a job remains unfilled, and loss of the departing employee's knowledge of the business (and its customers).

THE CYCLE OF MEDIOCRITY   Another vicious employment cycle is the "cycle of mediocrity" (Figure 11.4). It is most likely to be found in large, bureaucratic organizations. These are often typified by state monopolies, industrial cartels, or regulated oligopolies, where there is little incentive to improve performance, and where fear of entrenched unions may discourage management from adopting more innovative labor practices.

In such environments, service delivery standards tend to be prescribed by rigid rulebooks, oriented toward standardized service, operational efficiencies, and prevention of both employee fraud and favoritism toward specific customers. Employees are often expected to spend their entire working lives with the organization. Job responsibilities tend to be narrowly and unimaginatively defined, tightly categorized by grade and scope of responsibilities, and further rigidified by union work rules. Salary increases and promotions are based on longevity. Successful performance in a job is often measured by absence of mistakes, rather than by high productivity or outstanding customer service. Training focuses on learning the rules and the technical aspects of the job, and not on improving human interactions with customers and coworkers. Since there are minimal allowances for flexibility or employee initiative, jobs tend to be boring and repetitive. However, in contrast to the cycle of failure, most positions provide adequate pay and often good benefits, combined with high security. Thus, employees are reluctant to leave. This lack of mobility is compounded by an absence of marketable skills that would be valued by organizations in other fields of endeavor.

Customers find such organizations frustrating to deal with. Faced with bureaucratic hassles, lack of service flexibility, and unwillingness of employees to make an effort to serve them well, users of the service may become resentful. What

Figure 11.4
The Cycle of
Mediocrity

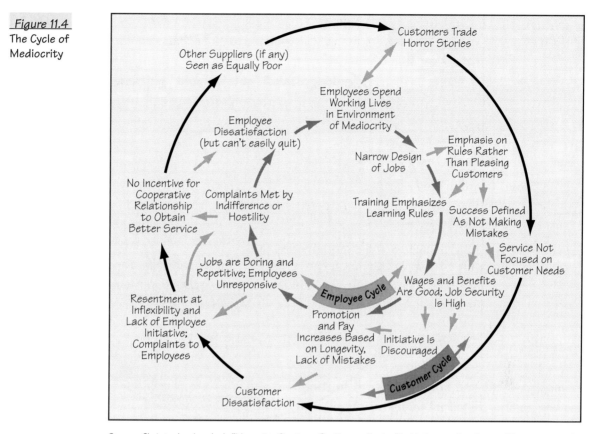

Source: Christopher Lovelock, "Managing Services: The Human Factor," in *Understanding Service Management*, ed.
W. J. Glynn and J. G. Barnes (Chichester, UK: John Wiley, 1995), 228.

happens when there is nowhere else for customers to go, either because the service
provider holds a monopoly, or because all other available players are perceived as
being equally bad or worse?

We should not be surprised if dissatisfied customers display hostility toward
service employees who feel trapped in their jobs and are powerless to improve the
situation. Employees may then protect themselves through such mechanisms as
withdrawal into indifference, playing overtly by the rulebook, or countering rudeness
with rudeness. The net result would be a vicious cycle of mediocrity in which
unhappy customers continually complain to sullen employees about poor service
and bad attitudes, generating greater defensiveness and lack of caring on the part
of the staff. Under such circumstances, there is little incentive for customers to
cooperate with the organization to achieve better service.

THE CYCLE OF SUCCESS   Some firms reject the assumptions underlying the cycles
of failure or mediocrity. Instead, they take a long-term view of financial performance,
seeking to prosper by investing in their people in order to create a "cycle of success"
(Figure 11.5).

Figure 11.5
The Cycle of
Success

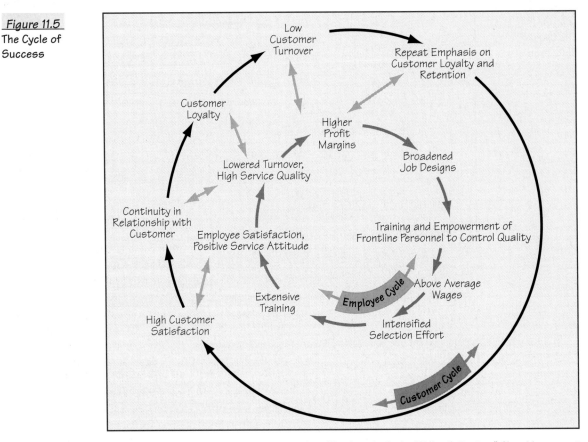

Source: Leonard L. Schlesinger and James L. Heskett, "Breaking the Cycle of Failure in Services," *Sloan Management Review* 31 (Spring 1991): 17–28. Reprinted by permission of publisher. Copyright © 2003 by Massachusetts Institute of Technology. All rights reserved.

As with failure or mediocrity, success applies to both employees and customers. Attractive compensation packages are used to attract good-quality staff. Broadened job designs are accompanied by training and empowerment practices that allow front-line staff to control quality. With more focused recruitment, more intensive training, and better wages, employees are likely to be happier in their work and to provide higher-quality, customer-pleasing service. Regular customers also appreciate the continuity in service relationships resulting from lower turnover, and so are more likely to remain loyal. Profit margins tend to be higher, and the organization is free to focus its marketing efforts on reinforcing customer loyalty through customer-retention strategies. These strategies are usually much more profitable than strategies for attracting new customers. Even public service organizations are increasingly working toward cycles of success and offer their users good-quality service at a lower cost to the public.[16]

A powerful demonstration of a front-line staff member working in the cycle of success is waitress Cora Griffin (featured in Best Practice in Action 11.1). Many of the themes in her nine rules of success are the result of good HR strategies for service firms.

*Best Practice
in Action 11.1*

CORA GRIFFITH: THE OUTSTANDING WAITRESS

Cora Griffith, a waitress for the Orchard Café at the Paper Valley Hotel in Appleton, Wisconsin, is superb in her role, appreciated by first-time customers, famous with her regular customers, and revered by her coworkers. Cora loves her work and it shows. Comfortable in a role that she believes is the right one for her, she implements the following nine rules of success:

1. *Treat customers like family.* First-time customers are not allowed to feel like strangers. Cheerful and proactive, Cora smiles, chats, and includes everyone at the table in the conversation. She is as respectful to children as she is to adults and makes it a point to learn and use everyone's name. "I want people to feel like they're sitting down to dinner right at my house. I want them to feel they're welcome, that they can get comfortable, that they can relax. I don't just serve people, I pamper them."

2. *Listen first.* Cora has developed her listening skills to the point that she rarely writes down customers' orders. She listens carefully and provides a customized service: "Are they in a hurry? Or do they have a special diet or like their selection cooked in a certain way?"

3. *Anticipate customers' wants.* She replenishes beverages and brings extra bread and butter in a timely manner. One regular customer, for example, who likes honey with her coffee gets it without having to ask. "I don't want my customers to have to ask for anything, so I always try to anticipate what they might need."

4. *Simple things make the difference.* She manages the details of her service, monitoring the cleanliness of the utensils and their correct placement. The fold for napkins must be just right. She inspects each plate in the kitchen before taking it to the table. She provides crayons for small children to draw pictures while waiting for the meal. "It's the little things that please the customer."

5. *Work smart.* Cora scans all her tables at once, looking for opportunities to combine tasks. "Never do just one thing at a time. And never go from the kitchen to the dining room empty-handed. Take coffee or iced tea or water with you." When she refills one water glass, she refills others. When clearing one plate, she clears others. "You have to be organized, and you have to keep in touch with the big picture."

6. *Keep learning.* Cora makes it an ongoing effort to improve existing skills and learn new ones.

7. *Success is where you find it.* Cora is contented with her work. She finds satisfaction in pleasing her customers, and she enjoys helping other people enjoy. Her positive attitude is a positive force in the restaurant. She is hard to ignore. "If customers come to the restaurant in a bad mood, I'll try to cheer them up before they leave." Her definition of success: "To be happy in life."

8. *All for one, and one for all.* She has been working with many of the same coworkers for more than eight years. The team supports one another on the crazy days when 300 conventioneers come to the restaurant for breakfast at the same time. Everyone pitches in and helps. The wait staff cover for one another, the managers bus the tables, the chefs garnish the plates. "We are like a little family. We know each other very well and we help each other out. If we have a crazy day, I'll go in the kitchen toward the end of the shift and say, 'Man, I'm just proud of us. We really worked hard today.'"

9. *Take pride in your work.* Cora believes in the importance of her work and in the need to do it well. "I don't think of myself as 'just a waitress'... I've chosen to be

a waitress. I'm doing this to my full potential, and I give it my best. I tell anyone who's starting out: Take pride in what you do. You're never just an anything, no matter what you do. You give it your all … and you do it with pride."

Cora Griffith is a success story. She is loyal to her employer and dedicated to her customers and coworkers. A perfectionist who seeks continuous improvement, Cora's enthusiasm for her work and unflagging spirit create an energy that radiates through the restaurant. She is proud of being a waitress, proud of "touching lives." Says Cora: "I have always wanted to do my best. However, the owners really are the ones who taught me how important it is to take care of the customer and who gave me the freedom to do it. The company always has listened to my concerns and followed up. Had I not worked for the Orchard Café, I would have been a good waitress, but I would not have been the same waitress."

Source: Leonard L. Berry, *Discovering the Soul of Service—The Nine Drivers of Sustainable Business Success* (New York: Free Press, 1999), 156–159.

Human Resources Management: How to Get It Right

Any rational manager would like to operate in the cycle of success. Human resource (HR) strategies can help service firms to move in that direction. Specifically, we discuss how firms will be able to hire, motivate, and retain engaged service employees who are willing and able to perform along the three common dimensions of their jobs—delivering service excellence/customer satisfaction, productivity, and often sales as well.

Also, it is naïve to think that it is sufficient to satisfy employees for them to perform. Employee satisfaction should be seen as necessary, but not sufficient for having high performing staff. For instance, a recent study showed that employee effort was a strong driver of customer satisfaction over and above employee satisfaction.[17] As Jim Collins said, "The old adage 'People are the most important asset' is wrong. The right people are your most important asset." We would like to add to this: "… and the wrong people are a liability." Getting it right starts with hiring the right people.

Hire the Right People

Hiring the right people includes competing for receiving applications from the best employees in the labor market, and then selecting from this wide pool the best candidates for the given jobs to be filled.

BE THE PREFERRED EMPLOYER   To be able to select and hire the best people, they first have to apply for a job with you and then accept your job offer over other potential offers. That means a firm has to first compete for talent market share,[18] or as McKinsey & Company calls it "the war for talent."[19] Competing in the labor market means having an attractive value proposition for prospective employees, and includes factors such having a good image in the community as a place to work for, to delivering high-quality products and services which make employees feel proud to be part of the team.

Furthermore, the compensation package cannot be below average—top people expect above-average packages. In our experience, it takes a salary in the range of the 65th to 80th percentile of the market to attract top performers to top companies. One does not have to be a top paymaster, if other important aspects of the value proposition are attractive. In short, understand the needs of your target employees and get your value proposition right. Figure 11.6 features a pilot recruitment

Figure 11.6

China Airlines promotes career opportunities as pilots to women under the age of 30 who meet the company's requirements of having a good university degree and good eyesight.

Courtesy of China Airlines.

advertisement by China Airlines. The female pilot featured communicates that women are encouraged to apply for the job that is traditionally a male-dominated one throughout the world.

SELECT THE RIGHT PEOPLE   There's no such thing as the perfect employee. Different positions are often best filled by people with different skill sets, styles, and personalities.

What makes outstanding service performers so special? Often it is things that *cannot* be taught. It is the qualities that are intrinsic to the people, and qualities they would bring with them to any employer. As one study of high performers observed:

> Energy ... cannot be taught, it has to be hired. The same is true for charm, for detail orientation, for work ethic, for neatness. Some of these things can be enhanced with on-the-job training ... or incentives ... But by and large, such qualities are instilled early on.[20]

Also, HR managers have discovered that while good manners and the need to smile and make eye contact can be taught, warmth itself cannot. The only realistic solution is to change the organization's recruitment criteria to favor candidates with naturally warm personalities. Jim Collins emphasizes that "The right people are those who would exhibit the desired behaviors anyway, as a natural extension of their character and attitude, regardless of any control and incentive system."[21] The logical conclusion is that service firms should devote great care to attracting and hiring the right candidates.

How to Identify the Best Candidates

There are a number of ways how excellent service firms identify the best candidates in their applicant pool. They include observing behavior, conducting personality tests, interviewing applicants, and providing applicants with a realistic job preview.[22]

OBSERVE BEHAVIOR   Make a decision to hire based on behavior you observe, not words you hear. As John Wooden said: "Show me what you can do, don't tell me what you can do. Too often, the big talkers are the little doers."[23] Behavior can be directly or indirectly observed by using behavioral simulations or assessment center tests that use standardized situations where applicants can be observed to see whether they display the kind of behaviors the firms' clients would expect.

CONDUCT PERSONALITY TESTS   Use personality tests that are relevant for a particular job. For example, traits such as willingness to treat customers and colleagues with courtesy, consideration and tact, perceptiveness of customer needs, and ability to communicate accurately and pleasantly can be measured. Hiring decisions based on such tests tend to be accurate.

For example, the Ritz-Carlton Hotels Group has been using personality profiles on all job applicants for the past ten years. Staff are selected for their natural predisposition for working in a service context. Inherent traits such as a ready smile, a willingness to help others, and an affinity for multitasking enable them to go beyond learned skills. An applicant to Ritz-Carlton shared about her experience of going through the personality test for a job as a junior-level concierge at the Ritz-Carlton Millenia Singapore. Her best advice: Tell the truth. These are experts and they will know if you are lying. "On the big day, they asked if I liked helping people, if I was an organized person and if I liked to smile a lot." Yes, yes, and yes, I said. But I had to support it with real life examples. This, at times, felt rather intrusive. To answer the first question for instance, I had to say a bit about the person I had helped—why she needed help, for example. The test forced me to recall even insignificant things I had done, like learning how to say hello in different languages which helped to get a fix on my character."[24]

Apart from intensive interview-based psychological tests, cost-effective Internet-based testing kits are available. Here, applicants enter their test responses to a Web-based questionnaire, and the prospective employer receives the analysis, the suitability of the candidate and a hiring recommendation. (For a leading global supplier of such tests, see the SHL Group at www.shlgroup.com.) Also, people differ in their disposition to be generally positive and happy versus generally negative and unhappy.[25] It is better to hire upbeat and happy people, because customers report higher satisfaction when being served by more satisfied staff.[26]

EMPLOY MULTIPLE, STRUCTURED INTERVIEWS   To improve hiring decisions, successful recruiters like to employ structured interviews built around job requirements, and to use more than one interviewer. People tend to be more careful in their judgments when they know that another individual is also evaluating the same applicant. Another advantage of using two or more interviewers is that it reduces the risk of "similar to me" biases—we all like people who are similar to ourselves.

GIVE APPLICANTS A REALISTIC PREVIEW OF THE JOB[27]   During the recruitment process, service companies should let the candidates know the reality of the job. This gives candidates a chance to "try on the job" and assess whether it's a fit or not. At the same time, recruiters can observe how candidates respond to the job's realities. This is a way for the company to let some candidates self-select themselves out if they find the job unsuitable for them. At the same time, the company can manage the new employees' expectations of their job. Many service companies adopt this approach.

Train Service Employees Actively

When a firm has good people, investments in training can yield outstanding results. Service champions show a strong commitment in words, dollars, and action to training. As Schneider and Bowen put it: "The combination of attracting a diverse and competent applicant pool, utilizing effective techniques for hiring the most appropriate people from that pool, and then training the heck out of them would be gangbusters in any market."[28] Service employees need to learn:

- *The organizational culture, purpose, and strategy.* Start strong with new hires, and focus on getting emotional commitment to the firm's core strategy, and promote core values such as commitment to service excellence, responsiveness, team spirit, mutual respect, honesty, and integrity. Use managers to teach, and focus on "what", "why," and "how" rather than on the specifics of the job. [29]

- *Interpersonal and technical skills.* Interpersonal skills tend to be generic across service jobs, and include visual communications skills such as making eye contact, attentive listening, body language, and even facial expressions. Technical skills encompass all the required knowledge related to processes (e.g., how to handle a merchandized return), machines (e.g., how to operate the terminal or cash machine), and rules and regulations related to customer service processes. Both technical and interpersonal skills are *necessary* but neither alone is *sufficient* for optimal job performance.[30]

- *Product/service knowledge.* Product knowledge of staff is a key aspect of service quality. Staff have to be able to effectively explain product features and also position it correctly. For instance, see Best Practice in Action 11.2, where Hong Kong Property Services implements measures to ensure that staff are properly trained and are always on their best behavior.

Of course, training has to result in tangible changes in behavior. If staff do not apply what they have learnt, the investment is wasted. Learning is not only about becoming smarter, but about changing behaviors and improving decision making. To achieve this, practice and reinforcement are needed. The role of supervisors in following up on learning objectives is crucial for achieving learning.

Training and learning professionalize the front-line staff, and move them away from the common (self)-image of being in low-end jobs. Well-trained employees are and feel like professionals. A waiter, who knows about food, cooking, wines, dining etiquette, and how to effectively interact with customers (even complaining ones), feels professional, has a higher self-esteem and is respected by his customers. Training is therefore extremely effective in reducing person/role stress.

Empower the Front Line[31]

Virtually all breakthrough service firms have legendary stories of employees who recovered failed service transactions, or walked the extra mile to make a customer's

TRAINING STAFF AT HONG KONG PROPERTY SERVICES

First impressions are lasting impressions, which is why the right training is vital for front-line property consultants. The impression that clients form about a property agency is generally based on the attitude and performance of the front-line staff they first encounter. This is the point at which quality service must begin and training is necessary to ensure consistently professional service.

Caroline Yeung, assistant director of Hong Kong Property Services (Agency) Limited feels strongly that good customer service is important for success in the property service industry. Therefore, HR managers must focus on staff training and performance reviews geared to improving the company's contacts with clients and which promote steady career advancement.

"Training and development are key factors in attracting candidates," says Ms Yeung. "They also show there are good prospects for future career development." She is confident that the comprehensive training offered by her company is among the best in the industry and that it complements the high rates of commission and generous remuneration packages made available for the best recruits.

Keeping track of each branch's performance is a good way to assess the need for training. "The company carries out random branch inspections, arranging for staff to pose as customers," Ms Yeung says. Results are circulated, with both good and bad comments included. "This adds a little extra pressure for the branch management!" Ms Yeung notes. Evaluations and follow-up are the responsibility of the HR department, which will add new elements to the staff orientation program and assessment interviews, if the results indicate such a need.

Individually, front-line staff are interviewed every six months to listen to feedback and assess their performance. Awards are given out to outstanding staff and this is reported in the company's monthly newsletters along with an award for the best branch. The aim is to create a sense of belonging among staff, encourage friendly competition and demonstrate that the company provides an environment which nurtures successful professionals.

Source: Cindy Chan, "Getting It Right from the Start," *Career Times,* May 7, 2004.

day, or avoid some kind of disaster for that client. To allow this to happen, employees have to be empowered. Employee self-direction has become increasingly important, especially in service firms, because front-line staff frequently operate on their own, face to face with their customers, and it tends to be difficult for managers to closely monitor their behavior.[32] Research also linked that high empowerment to higher customer satisfaction.[33]

For many services, providing employees with greater discretion (and training in how to use their judgment) can enable them to provide superior service on the spot. They do not have to take time to seek permission from supervisors. Empowerment looks to front-line staff to find solutions to service problems, and to make appropriate decisions about customizing service delivery.

IS EMPOWERMENT ALWAYS APPROPRIATE?   Advocates claim that the empowerment approach is more likely to yield motivated employees and satisfied customers than the "production-line" alternative, where management designs a relatively standardized system and expects workers to execute tasks within narrow guidelines.

However, David Bowen and Edward Lawler suggest that different situations may require different solutions, declaring that "both the empowerment and production-line approaches have their advantages ... and ... each fits certain situations. The key is to choose the management approach that best meets the needs of both employees and customers." Not all employees are necessarily eager to be empowered, and many employees do not seek personal growth within their jobs, and would prefer to work to specific directions rather than to use their own initiative. Research has shown that a strategy of empowerment is most likely to be appropriate when most of the following factors are present within the organization and its environment:

- The firm's business strategy is based on competitive differentiation and on offering personalized, customized service.
- The approach to customers is based on extended relationships rather than on short-term transactions.
- The organization uses technologies that are complex and nonroutine in nature.
- The business environment is unpredictable and surprises are to be expected.
- Existing managers are comfortable with letting employees work independently for the benefit of both the organization and its customers.
- Employees have a strong need to grow and deepen their skills in the work environment, are interested in working with others, and have good interpersonal and group process skills.[34]

The benefits of a well-conceived empowerment strategy are illustrated in Best Practice in Action 11.3.

CONTROL VERSUS INVOLVEMENT   The production-line approach to managing people is based on the well-established "control" model of organization design and management. There are clearly defined roles, top-down control systems, hierarchical pyramid structures, and an assumption that the management knows best. Empowerment, by contrast, is based upon the "involvement" (or "commitment") model, which assumes that most employees can make good decisions and produce good ideas for operating the business, if they are properly socialized, trained, and informed. It also assumes that employees can be internally motivated to perform effectively and that they are capable of self-control and self-direction. Information technology allows employees to telecommute, working from their homes while linked to a corporate network. New approaches to management and teambuilding are needed for such approaches to succeed.

Schneider and Bowen emphasize that "empowerment isn't just the act of 'setting the front-line free' or 'throwing away the policy manuals.' It requires systematically

EMPOWERMENT AT NOBLE GROUP

At the Noble Group, Asia's largest diversified commodities trading company, the company holds an enviable record of holding on to its employees. "Staff turnover is virtually zero other than at clerical level, where we have a movement of one or two a month in Hong Kong, out of 200 people," says Lydia Law, Noble's human resource manager.

So what is the secret of Noble's low staff turnover? Besides offering recognition through an attractive pay packet, Company CEO Richard Elman also believes that money is seldom the main factor behind staff loyalty. At the heart of Noble's employee-focused philosophy is the concept of employee empowerment. "In a certain sense, we look at our people as a factory would look at its production line," says Ms Law. "We have to work with the people we have, so how [do we] improve efficiency? Very simply, by giving them the authority to excel."

Mr Elman agrees by giving employees the freedom to make decisions on behalf of the company within limits. This gives employees a feeling of self-worth and recognition that they do possess the ability to decide on certain issues and helps them to feel that they are genuinely contributing to the company. It also gives them opportunities to shine and show that they can be responsible for their decisions. "Empowering people means giving them authority, defining well what we expect from them and compensating them accordingly."

Source: Don Gasper , "Empowerment—The Key to Staff Retention," *Career Times*, August 15, 2003.

redistributing four key ingredients throughout the organization, from the top downwards."[35] The four features are:

1. *Power* to make decisions that influence work procedures and organizational direction (e.g., through quality circles and self-managing teams)
2. *Information* about organizational performance (e.g., operating results and measures of competitive performance)
3. *Rewards* based on organizational performance (e.g., bonuses, profit sharing, and stock options)
4. *Knowledge* that enables employees to understand and contribute to organizational performance (e.g., problem-solving skills)

In the control model, the four features are concentrated at the top of the organization, while in the involvement model, these features are pushed down through the organization.

LEVELS OF EMPLOYEE INVOLVEMENT   The empowerment and production-line approaches are at opposite ends of a spectrum that reflects increasing levels of employee involvement as additional knowledge, information, power, and rewards are pushed down to the front line. Empowerment can take place at several levels:

- *Suggestion involvement* empowers employees to make recommendations through formalized programs. McDonald's, often portrayed as an archetype of the production-line approach, listens closely to its front line. Innovations ranging from Egg McMuffin, to methods of wrapping burgers without leaving a thumbprint on the bun, were invented by employees.

- *Job involvement* represents a dramatic opening up of job content. Jobs are redesigned to allow employees to use a wider array of skills. In complex service organizations such as airlines and hospitals, where individual employees cannot offer all facets of a service, job involvement is often accomplished through use of teams. To cope with the added demands accompanying this form of empowerment, employees require training, and supervisors need to be reoriented from directing the group to facilitating its performance in supportive ways.

- *High involvement* gives even the lowest-level employees a sense of involvement in the company's overall performance. Information is shared. Employees develop skills in teamwork, problem solving, and business operations, and they participate in work-unit management decisions. There is profit sharing and often employee ownership of stock or options in the business.

Rosenbluth Travel, a travel company in India, is an illustration of a high-involvement company, promoting common sense and flexibility. The company trusts its employees and gives them the latitude, discretion, and authority they need to do their jobs. For example, one of Rosenbluth's clients had to make an emergency trip at the last minute. When he called to make reservations, he mentioned he was worried about his dogs. Rosenbluth's associates spent the week dog-sitting.

Another incident involved a call at 3 a.m., in a panic, because a client was on the road and his wife was in labor. Rosenbluth's staff chartered him a flight and he made it home in time for the birth of his first child.[36]

Build High-Performance Service Delivery Teams

The nature of many services requires people to work in teams, often across functions, if they want to offer seamless customer service processes. Traditionally, many firms were organized by functional structures. This structure prevents internal service teams from viewing end customers as their own, and this structure can also mean poorer teamwork across functions, slower service, and more errors between functions. When customers have service problems, they easily fall between the cracks.

Empirical research has confirmed that front-line staff themselves regard a lack of interdepartmental support as an important factor in hindering them from satisfying their customers.[37] Because of these problems, we increasingly need cross-functional teams who serve customers from start to finish.

THE POWER OF TEAMWORK IN SERVICES   Katzenbach and Smith define a team as "a small number of people with complementary skills who are committed to a common purpose, set of performance goals, and approach for which they hold themselves mutually accountable."[38] Teams, training, and empowerment go hand in hand. Teams facilitate communication between team members and the sharing of knowledge. By operating like a small, independent unit, service teams take on more responsibility and require less supervision than more traditional functionally organized customer service units. Furthermore, teams often set higher performance targets for themselves than their supervisors would. Pressure to perform is high within a good team.[39]

CREATING SUCCESSFUL SERVICE DELIVERY TEAMS[40]   It's not easy to make teams function well. If people are not prepared for teamwork, and the team structure is not set up right, a firm risks having initially enthusiastic volunteers who lack the competencies that teamwork requires. The skills needed include not only cooperation, listening to others, coaching, and encouraging one another, but also an understanding of how to air differences, tell one another hard truths, and ask tough questions. All these require training.

Management also needs to set up a structure that will steer the teams toward success. A good example is Polaris Software Lab Ltd of India, that developed the following rules for making its teams work:

- Each team has a leader who monitors team progress and team process. Team leaders are selected for their strong business knowledge and people skills.
- Each team has a quality facilitator—someone who knows how to make teams work and who can remove barriers to progress and train others to work together effectively.[41]

Motivate and Energize People[42]

Once a firm has hired the right people, trained them well, empowered them, and organized them in effective service delivery teams, how can it ensure that they will deliver service excellence? Staff performance is a function of ability and motivation. Hiring, training, empowerment, and teams give you able people, and reward systems are the key to motivation. Service staff must get the message that providing quality service holds the key for them being rewarded. Motivating and rewarding strong service performers are some of the most effective ways of retaining them. Staff pick up quickly if those who get promoted are the truly outstanding service providers, and if those who get fired are those that do not deliver at the customer level.

A major way service businesses fail is that they do not utilize the full range of available rewards effectively. Many firms think in terms of money as reward, but it does not pass the test of an effective reward. Receiving a fair salary is a hygiene factor rather than a motivating factor. Paying more than what is seen as fair only has short-term motivating effects, and wears off quickly. On the other hand, bonuses that are contingent on performance have to be earned again and again, and therefore tend to be more lasting in their effectiveness. Other, more lasting rewards are the job content itself, recognition and feedback, and goal accomplishment.

JOB CONTENT   People are motivated and satisfied simply by knowing that they are doing a good job. They feel good about themselves, and like to reinforce that feeling. This is true especially if the job also offers a variety of activities, requires the completion of "whole" and identifiable pieces of work, is seen as significant in the sense that it has an impact on the lives of others, comes with autonomy, and has a source of direct and clear feedback about how well employees did their work (e.g., grateful customers or sales).

FEEDBACK AND RECOGNITION   Humans are social beings, and they derive a sense of identity and belonging to an organization from the recognition and feedback they receive from the people around them, i.e., their customers, colleagues, and bosses. If employees are being recognized and thanked for service excellence, they will desire to deliver it. (We discuss how to measure and use customer feedback in detail in Chapter 13.)

GOAL ACCOMPLISHMENT   Goals focus people's energy. Goals that are specific, difficult but attainable, and accepted by the staff are strong motivators and yield higher performance than no goals or vague goals (e.g., "do your best") or goals that are impossible to achieve.[43] In short, goals are effective motivators.

The following are important points to note for effective goal setting:[44]

- Achieving goals is a reward in itself when those goals are seen as important.
- Goal accomplishment can be used as a basis for giving rewards, including pay, feedback, and recognition. Feedback and recognition from peers can be given faster, more cheaply and effectively than pay, and have the additional benefit of gratifying an employee's self-esteem.
- Service employee goals that are specific and difficult must be set publicly to be accepted. Although goals must be specific, they can be something intangible like improved employee courtesy ratings.
- Progress reports about goal accomplishment (feedback) and goal accomplishment itself must be public events (recognition) if they are to gratify employees' esteem need.
- It is mostly unnecessary to specify the means to achieve goals. Feedback on progress while pursuing the goal serves as a corrective function. As long as the goal is specific, difficult but achievable, and accepted, goal pursuit will result in goal accomplishment, even in the absence of other rewards.

Successful firms recognize that people issues are complex (see Figure 11.7). O'Reilly and Pfeffer conducted in-depth research on why some companies can

Figure 11.7

"People issues are complex. Managing them doesn't have to be." Hewitt Associates, a professional firm delivering human capital management services, captures employees' complexity in its advertising.

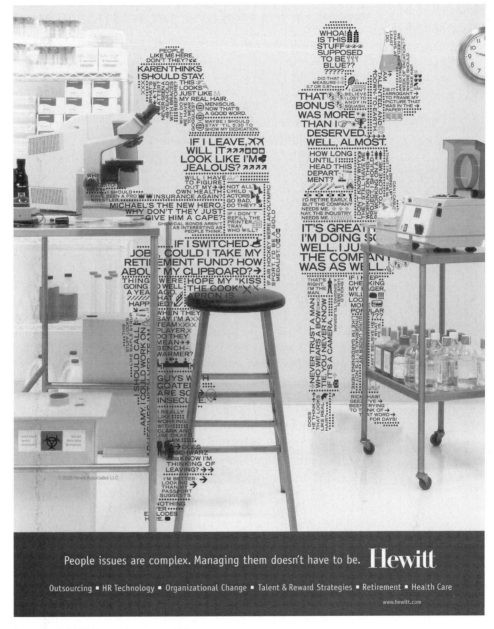

Copyright © 2003 Hewitt Associates LLC.

succeed over long periods of time in highly competitive industries without having the usual sources of competitive advantage such as barriers of entry or proprietary technology. They concluded that these firms did not succeed by winning the war for talent, "but by fully using the talent and unlocking the motivation of the people" they already had in their organizations.[45] Best Practice in Action 11.4 shows how Federal Express creates employee satisfaction in the Philippines.

Best Practice
in Action 11.4

THUMBS UP FOR EMPLOYEE SATISFACTION IN FEDEX PHILIPPINES

In order to push FedEx to greater heights, getting the right people is very important. In order to achieve 100 percent customer satisfaction, FedEx believes that this starts from the employees' attitude toward their work and that is to serve the customers "above and beyond the call of duty." Mr John Allison, vice-president for planning and support and engineering, Asia Pacific, added: "The attitude of doing whatever it takes to serve the customers is reflected from the top to the bottom in the organization's structure. This kind of spirit is integral to FedEx's work culture. This spirit fosters an environment or culture where an employee's performance speaks for himself or herself."

FedEx operating in the Philippines archipelago believes in satisfying not only their customers, but also their employees. All new employees in every department are trained. Employees in certain departments receive special training, while employees dealing with consumers are trained on features of the service with the help of videos and role-playing sessions. With training, employees are educated on their job scope and know very clearly what will be expected of them.

The GOLD (Growth, Opportunity, Leadership, and Development) course gives non-management employees a chance to be promoted into the management. With continuous training of the workforce up to 50 hours per year, employees are developed to their highest potential. 91 percent of people in managerial positions are promoted from non-management employees, and this shows the extent of promotion from within. With career advancement possible for all employees, this becomes a source of motivation. Mr Allison emphasized: "Our promotion from within and career progression policies lay the groundwork for career paths up through top management and laterally into new areas. Career opportunities are posted weekly throughout the company and we're proud to say that our leadership program for developing first-rate managers is a model for other companies."

FedEx also let employees know that they are heard. Using a 360 degree feedback system (known as the "Survey-Feedback-Action" device), the company finds out from the employees how it scores on leadership, pay, job conditions, and general satisfaction. Results are given to managers who will gather all his subordinates to discuss issues and have them taken care of.

Fred Smith, founder of FedEx, has a People-Service-Profit (**PSP**) philosophy. The philosophy means that by treating their employee (**people**) right, they will provide good **service** and satisfy customers, who will in turn become loyal customers to FedEx, and hence reap more **profits** for FedEx.

Source: Adapted from Jude P. Morte, "Special Feature: Best Employers in the Philippines," *Business World*, (Manila), May 29, 2003.

Service Leadership and Culture

So far, we have discussed the key strategies that help to move an organization toward service excellence. However, to truly get there, we need a strong culture that is continuously reinforced and developed by the firm's management. A "charismatic leadership," also called transformational leadership, fundamentally changes the values, goals, and aspirations of the front line to be consistent with the firm's. Here, staff are more likely to perform their best and show performance "above and beyond the call of duty," because it is consistent with their own values, beliefs, and attitudes.[46]

Employees rely heavily on their perceptions of what is important by their perceptions of what the company and their leaders do, not so much what they say. Employees gain their understanding of what is important through the daily experiences they have with the firm's human resource, operations, and marketing practices and procedures.

A strong service culture is one where the entire organization focuses on the front line, and understands that it is the lifeline of the business. The organization understands that today's, as well as tomorrow's, revenues are largely driven by what happens at the service encounter. Figure 11.8 shows the inverted pyramid, which demonstrates the importance of the front line, and shows that the role of top management and middle management is to support the front line in their task of delivering service excellence to their customers.

In firms with a passion for service, top management show by their actions that what happens at the front line is crucially important to them, by being informed and actively involved. They achieve this by regularly talking to and working with front-line staff and customers. Many actually spend significant amounts of time at the front line serving customers.

Service leaders are not only interested in the big picture, but also focus on the details of service. They see opportunities in nuances which competitors might consider trivial, and they believe that the way the firm handles little things sets the tone for how it handles everything else.

Apart from a strong leadership that focuses on the front line, it takes a strong communications effort to shape the culture and get the message to the troops.

Figure 11.8
The Traditional
and Inverted
Organizational
Pyramids

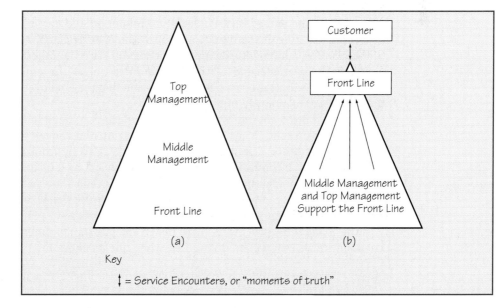

Service leaders use multiple tools to build their service culture, ranging from training, to core principles, to company events and celebrations. Consider the effort by Pearl International Hotel's general manager Jason Bak to launch a courtesy campaign with 12 mottos. The main purpose is to communicate clearly to its employees the kind of service standards that they should provide. See Best Practice in Action 11.5 for more details on Pearl International Hotel's courtesy campaign.

Instead of launching a courtesy campaign, some hotels may choose to communicate to the employees and shape the service culture through other means. For example, Ritz-Carlton translated the key product and service requirements of its customers into the Ritz-Carlton Gold Standards, which include a credo, motto, three steps of service, and 20 "Ritz-Carlton Basics." Tim Kirkpatrick, director of training and development for Ritz-Carlton's Boston Common Hotel, said: "The Gold Standards are part of our uniform, just like your name tag. But remember, it's just a laminated card until you put it into action."[47] To reinforce these standards,

Best Practice in Action 11.5

PEARL INTERNATIONAL HOTEL'S COURTESY CAMPAIGN

Pearl International Hotel in Kuala Lumpur, Malaysia, is no exception when it comes to customer service. The hotel has always believed that quality service is essential in ensuring its success in the highly competitive hospitality industry. With this in mind, hotel general manager Jason Bak launched a hotelwide courtesy campaign, which aimed to improve the service standards provided by the hotel employees.

According to Mr Bak, the campaign also serves as a reevaluation of the training strategies that are employed by the hotel. Mr Bak also added that the hotel hopes to instill the warm Malaysian hospitality and courtesy into the hotel's culture, as it is a vital element in the hospitality industry.

The six-month campaign, from April to September 2004, incorporates 12 mottos. Each motto represents a particular department and will be practiced for two weeks, after which the next motto will take effect. A special committee will conduct an evaluation at the end of each implementation period and an employee who is the best representative of the particular motto would be selected. According to hotel training and development executive Akhtaruddin Hariri, another selection process would be held at the end of the campaign to select the employee who best represented the mottos on an overall basis—and that the employee stands to receive the annual Best Employee of the Year Award.

The 12 mottos are the "Warmest Smile," which is to be practiced by the public relations department; "I Say Thank You" by catering and convention department; "I Care" by front office; "Do It Right the First Time" also by front office; "Malaysian Way of Greeting" by housekeeping; "15-Minute Service" by food and beverage; "Zero Complaint" by engineering; "Malaysian Hospitality Values" by sales and marketing; "Perfect Attendance" by human resources; "I Am Professional" by finance; "Extra-Mile Service" by security; and "Back to Basics" by kitchen.

The evaluation process will be based on guests' comments collated from comment cards that will be distributed when guests check in.

Source: Adapted from "Hotel Launches 12 Mottos to Ensure Best of Services," *New Straits Times* (Malaysia), April 6, 2004.

every morning briefing includes a discussion of one of the standards. The aim of rotating these discussions is to keep the Ritz-Carlton philosophy at the center of its employees' minds.

Conclusion

Successful service organizations are committed to effective management of human resources. Figure 11.9 summarizes our main recommendations for successful HR strategies in service firms. Successful HR strategies start with competing for talent by being the preferred employer, followed by careful hiring, painstaking training, and empowering staff who then have the authority and self-confidence to use their own initiative in delivering service excellence. It also involves effective use of service delivery teams, and energizing and motivating the front line with a full set of rewards: pay, satisfying job content, recognition and feedback, and goal accomplishment. Top and middle management continuously reinforce a strong culture that emphasizes service excellence and productivity. Employees understand and support the goals of an organization, and a value-driven leadership inspires and guides service

Figure 11.9
Wheel of Successful HR in Service Firms

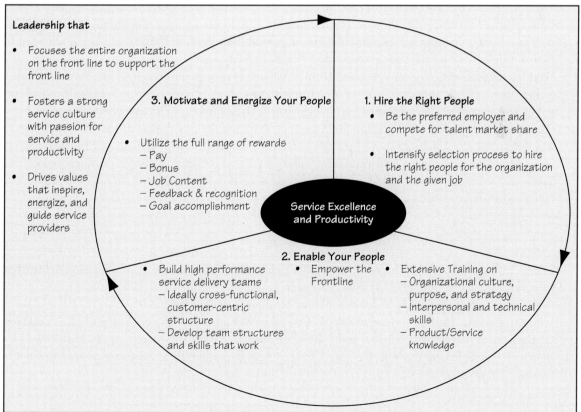

providers, and brings their passion for serving to the full and gives them a fulfilled working life.

The market and financial results can be phenomenal and often lead to a sustainable competitive advantage. It is probably harder to duplicate high-performance human assets than any other corporate resource.

Review Questions

1. Discuss the role service personnel play in creating or destroying customer loyalty.
2. What is emotional labor? Explain the ways in which it may cause stress for employees in specific jobs. Illustrate with suitable examples.
3. What are the key barriers for firms to break the cycle of failure and move into the cycle of success?
4. List five ways in which investment in hiring and selection, training, and ongoing motivation of employees will pay dividends in customer satisfaction for such organizations as (a) a restaurant, (b) an airline, (c) a hospital, and (d) a consulting firm.
5. Identify the factors favoring a strategy of employee empowerment.
6. Define what is meant by the control and involvement models of management.
7. Identify the factors needed to make service teams successful in (a) an airline, (b) a restaurant.
8. How can a service firm build a strong service culture that emphasizes service excellence and productivity?

Application Exercises

1. An airline runs a recruiting advertisement for cabin crew that shows a picture of a small boy sitting in an airline seat and clutching a teddy bear. The headline reads: "His mom told him not to talk to strangers. So what's he having for lunch?" Describe the types of personalities that you think would be (a) attracted to apply for the job by that ad, and (b) discouraged from applying.
2. Consider the following jobs: emergency ward nurse, bill collector, computer repair technician, supermarket cashier, dentist, flight attendant, kindergarten teacher, prosecuting attorney, server in a family restaurant, server in an expensive Chinese restaurant, stockbroker, and undertaker. What type of emotions would you expect each of them to display to customers in the course of doing their job? What drives your expectations?
3. As a human resources manager, which issues do you see as most likely to create boundary spanning problems for customer-contact employees in a customer call center at a major Internet service provider? Select four issues and indicate how you would mediate between operations and marketing to create a satisfactory outcome for all three groups.

Endnotes

[1] Liliana L. Bove and Lester W. Johnson, "Customer Relationships with Service Personnel: Do We Measure Closeness, Quality or Strength?" *Journal of Business Research* 54 (2001): 189–197.
[2] "SBS—Talk to Us over Coffee," *The Straits Times* Singapore, February 12, 2004.
[3] James L. Heskett, Thomas O. Jones, Gary W. Loveman, W. Earl Sasser, Jr., and Leonard A. Schlesinger, "Putting the Service-Profit Chain to Work," *Harvard Business Review* 72 (March–April 1994): 164–174.
[4] Benjamin Schneider and David E. Bowen, "The Service Organization: Human Resources Management Is Crucial," *Organizational Dynamics* 21, no. 4 (Spring 1993): 39–52.

5   David E. Bowen and Benjamin Schneider, "Boundary-Spanning Role Employees and the Service Encounter: Some Guidelines for Management and Research," in J.A. Czepiel, M. R. Solomon, and C.F. Surprenant, *The Service Encounter* (Lexington, MA.: Lexington Books, 1985), 127–148.

6   Arlie R. Hochschild, *The Managed Heart: Commercialization of Human Feeling* (Berkeley: University of California Press, 1983).

7   Arlie Hochschild, "Emotional Labor in the Friendly Skies," *Psychology Today* (June 1982): 13–15. Cited in Valarie A. Zeithaml and Mary Jo Bitner, *Services Marketing: Integrating Customer Focus across the Firm* (New York: McGraw-Hill, 2003), 322.

8   Jochen Wirtz and Robert Johnston, "Singapore Airlines: What It Takes to Sustain Service Excellence—A Senior Management Perspective," *Managing Service Quality* 13, no.1 (2003): 10–19.

9   Call Centre News, "Call Centre Statistics," www.callcentrenews.com, accessed on January 23, 2003.

10   "Call Centres—The Asians Are Coming, Again," *The Economist* (April 28, 2001): 55.

11   Dan Moshavi and James R. Terbord, "The Job Satisfaction and Performance of Contingent and Regular Customer Service Representatives—A Human Capital Perspective," *International Journal of Service Industry Management* 13, no. 4 (2002): 333–347.

12   Knowsley, 2001, *loc. cit.*

13   The terms "cycle of failure" and "cycle of success" were coined by Leonard L. Schlesinger and James L. Heskett, "Breaking the Cycle of Failure in Services," *Sloan Management Review* 42 (Spring 1991): 17–28. The term "cycle of mediocrity" comes from Christopher H. Lovelock, "Managing Services: The Human Factor," in *Understanding Services Management*, eds. W. J. Glynn and J. G. Barnes (Chichester, UK: John Wiley & Sons, 1995), 228.

14   Lloyd C. Harris and Emmanuel Ogbonna, "Exploring Service Sabotage: The Antecedents, Types, and Consequences of Frontline, Deviant, Antiservice Behaviors," *Journal of Service Research* 4, no. 3 (2002): 163–183.

15   Leonard Schlesinger and James L. Heskett, "Breaking the Cycle of Failure," *Sloan Management Review* 42 (Spring 1991): 17–28.

16   Reg Price and Roderick J. Brodie, "Transforming a Public Service Organization from Inside Out to Outside In," *Journal of Service Research* 4, no. 1 (2001): 50–59.

17   Mahn Hee Yoon, "The Effect of Work Climate on Critical Employee and Customer Outcomes," *International Journal of Service Industry Management* 12, no. 5 (2001): 500–521.

18   Leonard L. Berry and A. Parasuraman, *Marketing Services—Competing through Quality* (New York: The Free Press, 1991), 151–152.

19   Charles A. O'Reilly III and Jeffrey Pfeffer, *Hidden Value—How Great Companies Achieve Extraordinary Results with Ordinary People* (Boston, MA: Harvard Business School Press, 2000), 1.

20   Bill Fromm and Len Schlesinger, *The Real Heroes of Business* (New York: Currency Doubleday, 1994), 315–316.

21   Jim Collins, "Turning Goals into Results: The Power of Catalytic Mechanisms," *Harvard Business Review* (July–August 1999): 77.

22   This section was adapted from Benjamin Schneider and David E. Bowen, *Winning the Service Game* (Boston, MA: Harvard Business School Press, 1995), 115–126.

23   John Wooden, *A Lifetime of Observations and Reflections on and off the* Court (Chicago: Lincolnwood, 1997), 66.

24   Serene Goh, "All the Right Staff," and Arlina Arshad, "Putting Your Personality to the Test," *The Straits Times*, September 5, 2001, H1.

25   Timothy A. Judge, "The Dispositional Perspective in Human Resources Research," in *Research in Personnel and Human Resources Management*, 10th ed. Ken Rowland and Gerald Ferris (Greenwich, CT: JAI Press, 1992), 31–72.

[26] For a review of this literature, see Benjamin Schneider, "Service Quality and Profits: Can You Have Your Cake and Eat It, Too?" *Human Resource Planning* 14, no. 2 (1991): 151–157.

[27] This section was adapted from Leonard L. Berry, *On Great Service—A Framework for Action* (New York: The Free Press, 1995), 181–182.

[28] Benjamin Schneider and David E. Bowen, *Winning the Service Game* (Boston, MA: Harvard Business School Press, 1995), 131.

[29] Leonard L. Berry, *Discovering the Soul of Service—The Nine Drivers of Sustainable Business Success* (New York: The Free Press, 1999), 161.

[30] David A. Tansik, "Managing Human Resource Issues for High Contact Service Personnel," in *Service Management Effectiveness*, eds. D.E. Bowen, R. B. Chase, T.G. Cummings, and Associates (San Francisco: Jossey-Bass, 1990), 152–176.

[31] Parts of this section are based on David E. Bowen and Edward E. Lawler, III, "The Empowerment of Service Workers: What, Why, How and When," *Sloan Management Review* (Spring 1992): 32–39.

[32] Dana Yagil, "The Relationship of Customer Satisfaction and Service Workers' Perceived Control—Examination of Three Models," *International Journal of Service Industry Management* 13, no. 4 (2002): 382–398.

[33] Don Gasper,"Empowerment—The Key to Staff Retention," *Career Times*, August 15, 2003.

[34] David E. Bowen and Edward E. Lawler, III, "The Empowerment of Service Workers: What, Why, How and When," *Sloan Management Review* (Spring 1992): 32–39.

[35] Schneider and Bowen, 1995, *op.cit.*, 250.

[36] Hal F. Rosenbluth, CEO of Rosenbluth Travel, "The Customer Comes Second", Copyright 2004 Jobstreet.com.

[37] Andrew Sergeant and Stephen Frenkel, "When Do Customer Contact Employees Satisfy Customers?" *Journal of Service Research* 3, no. 1 (August 2000): 18–34.

[38] Jon R. Katzenbach and Douglas K. Smith, "The Discipline of Teams," *Harvard Business Review* 71 (March–April, 1993): 112. See also on self-managed teams: Ad de Jong, Ko de Ruyter, and Jos Lemmink, "Antecedents and Consequences of the Service Climate in Boundary-Spanning Self-Managing Service Teams," *Journal of Marketing* 68, no. 2 (2004): 18–35.

[39] Leonard L. Berry, *On Great Service—A Framework for Action*, (New York: The Free Press, 1995), 131.

[40] This section is based on Schneider and Bowen, *Winning the Service Game*, 141, and Leonard L. Berry, *On Great Service—A Framework for Action*, 225.

[41] http://www.polaris.co.in/spu/crm/aboutus.htm, accessed on June 1, 2004.

[42] This section is based on Schneider and Bowen, *Winning the Service Game*, 145–173.

[43] A good summary of goal setting and motivation at work can be found in Edwin A. Locke and Gary Latham, *A Theory of Goal Setting and Task Performance* (Englewood Cliffs, NJ: Prentice Hall, 1990).

[44] Schneider and Bowen, 1995, *op.cit.*, 165.

[45] O'Reilly III and Pfeffer, 2000, *op.cit.*, 232.

[46] Scott B. MacKenzie, Philip M. Podsakoff, and Gregory A. Rich, "Transformational and Transactional Leadership and Salesperson Performance," *Journal of the Academy of Marketing Science* 29, no. 2 (2001): 115–134.

[47] Paul Hemp, "My Week as a Room-Service Waiter at the Ritz," *Harvard Business Review* 80 (June 2002): 8–11.

Implementing Services Marketing

PART FOUR

CHAPTER TWELVE

Managing Relationships and Building Loyalty

The first step in managing a loyalty-based business system is finding and acquiring the right customers.

FREDERICK F. REICHHELD

Strategy first, then CRM.

STEVEN S. RAMSEY[1]

Targeting, acquiring, and retaining the "right" customers is at the core of many successful service firms. In this chapter, we emphasize the importance of carefully choosing target segments and taking pains to build and maintain their loyalty through well-conceived relationship marketing strategies. Underlying this strategy is the notion of market segmentation. More and more firms are trying to decide which types of customers they can serve well, rather than try to be all things to all people. Once a firm has won customers whom it sees as desirable, the challenge shifts to building relationships and turning them into loyal customers who will do a growing volume of business with the firm in the future.

Building relationships is a challenge, especially when a firm has many, often millions, of customers who interact with the firm in many different ways (from email to phone calls and face-to-face interactions). When implemented well, customer relationship management (CRM) systems provide managers with the tools to understand their customers and tailor their service, cross-selling, and retention efforts, often on a one-on-one basis.

In this chapter, we explore the following questions:

1. Why is customer loyalty an important driver of profitability for service firms?
2. Why is it so important for service firms to target the "right" customers?
3. How can a firm calculate the life time value (LTV) of its customers?
4. What strategies are associated with the concept of relationship marketing?

5. How can tiering of service, loyalty bonds, and membership programs help in building customer loyalty?

6. What is the role of CRM systems in delivering customized services and building loyalty?

The Search for Customer Loyalty

Loyalty is an old-fashioned word that has traditionally been used to describe fidelity and enthusiastic devotion to a country, cause, or individual. More recently, in a business context, it has been used to describe a customer's willingness to continue patronizing a firm over the long term, and recommending the firm's products to friends and associates. Brand loyalty extends beyond behavior to include preference, liking, and future intentions. Richard Oliver has argued that consumers first become loyal in a cognitive sense, perceiving from brand attribute information that one brand is preferable to its alternatives.[2] At the second stage is affective loyalty, where a consumer develops a liking for the brand based on cumulatively satisfying usage occasions. Such attitudes are not easily dislodged by counter arguments from competitors. At the third stage is conative loyalty, where the consumer is committed to rebuying the same brand. This should lead to the fourth stage, which is action loyalty, where the consumer exhibits consistent repurchase behavior.

"Few companies think of customers as annuities," says Frederick Reichheld, author of *The Loyalty Effect*, and a major researcher in this field.[3] Yet that is precisely what a loyal customer can mean to a firm—a consistent source of revenue over a period of many years. However, this loyalty cannot be taken for granted. It will only continue as long as the customer feels that he or she is receiving better value (including superior quality relative to price) than could be obtained by switching to another supplier. The active management of the customer base and customer loyalty is also referred to as customer asset management.[4]

Defector was a nasty word during the Cold War. It described disloyal people who sold out their own side and went over to the enemy. Even when they defected toward "our" side, rather than away from it, they were still suspect. Today, in a marketing context, the term *defection* is used to describe customers who drop off a company's radar screen and transfer their brand loyalty to another supplier. Reichheld and Sasser popularized the term *zero defections*, which they describe as keeping every customer the company can profitably serve.[5] Not only does a rising defection rate indicate that something is wrong with quality (or that competitors offer better value), it may also signal a coming fall in profits. Large customers don't necessarily disappear overnight. They may signal their mounting dissatisfaction by steadily reducing their purchases and shifting part of their business elsewhere.

Why is Customer Loyalty Important to a Firm's Profitability?

How much is a loyal customer worth in terms of profits? In a classic study, Reichheld and Sasser analyzed the profit per customer in different service businesses, categorized by the number of years that a customer had been with the firm.[6] They found that the longer customers remained with a firm in each of these industries, the more profitable they became to serve. Annual profits per customer, which have been indexed over a five-year period for easier comparison, are summarized in Figure 12.1. The industries studied (with average profits from a first-year customer shown in parentheses) were: Credit cards (US$30), industrial laundry (US$144), industrial distribution (US$45), and automobile servicing (US$25). Similar loyalty effects were also uncovered in the Internet context, where it typically took more than a year to recoup acquisition costs, and profits increased as customers stayed longer with the firm.[7]

Underlying this profit growth, say Reichheld and Sasser, are four factors working to the supplier's advantage to create incremental profits. In order of magnitude at the end of seven years, these factors are:

1. *Profit derived from increased purchases* (or, in a credit card or banking environment, higher account balances). Over time, business customers often grow larger and so need to purchase in greater quantities. Individuals may also purchase more as their families grow or as they become more affluent. Both types of customers may decide to consolidate their purchases with a single supplier who provides high-quality service.

2. *Profit from reduced operating costs*. As customers become more experienced, they make fewer demands on the supplier (for instance, less need for information

Figure 12.1
How Much Profit a Customer Generates over Time

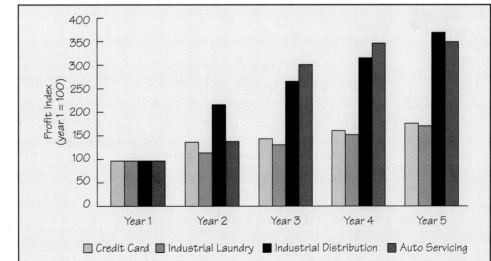

Source: Based on data in Frederick F. Reichheld and W. Earl Sasser, Jr., "Zero Defections: Quality Comes to Services," *Harvard Business Review* 68 (September–October 1990): 105–111.

and assistance). They may also make fewer mistakes when involved in operational processes, thus contributing to greater productivity.

3. *Profit from referrals to other customers.* Positive word-of-mouth recommendations are like free sales and advertising, saving the firm from having to invest as much money in these activities.

4. *Profit from price premium.* New customers often benefit from introductory promotional discounts, whereas long-term customers are more likely to pay regular prices. Moreover, when customers trust a supplier they may be more willing to pay higher prices at peak periods or for express work.

Figure 12.2 shows the relative contribution of each of these different factors over a seven-year period, based on an analysis of 19 different product categories (both goods and services). Reichheld argues that the economic benefits of customer loyalty noted earlier often explain why one firm is more profitable than a competitor. Furthermore, the up-front costs of attracting these buyers can be amortized over many years.

Assessing the Value of a Loyal Customer

It would be a mistake to assume that loyal customers are always more valuable than those making one-time transactions.[8] On the cost side, not all types of services incur heavy promotional expenditures to attract a new customer. Sometimes, it is more important to invest in a good retail location that will attract walk-in traffic. Unlike banks, insurance companies, and other "membership" organizations that require an application process and specific procedures to establish a new account, many service firms face no set-up costs when a new customer first seeks to make a

Figure 12.2
Why Customers
Become More
Profitable over
Time

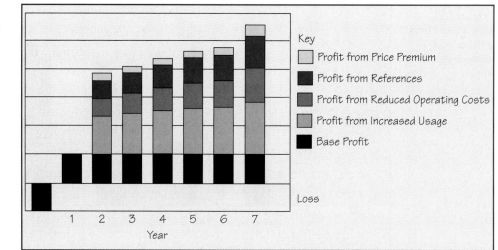

Source: Frederick F. Reichheld and W. Earl Sasser, Jr., "Zero Defections: Quality Comes to Services," *Harvard Business Review* (September–October 1990): 105–111. Reprinted by permission of Harvard Business School.

purchase. On the revenue side, loyal customers may not necessarily spend more than one-time buyers and in some instances, they may even expect price discounts. Finally, revenue does not necessarily increase with time for all types of customers.[9]

Recent work has also shown that the profit impact of a customer can vary dramatically depending on the stage of the product life cycle the service is in. For instance, referrals of satisfied customers and negative word of mouth of defected customers have drastically higher profit impact in the early stages of the product life cycle than in later stages.[10]

The challenge for managers is to investigate the situation and various types of customer segments in their own organizations and determine profitability levels for different types of customers. For insights on how to calculate customer value in any given business, see Management Memo 12.1.[11]

The Gap between Actual and Potential Customer Value

For profit-seeking firms, the potential profitability of a customer should be a key driver in marketing strategy. As Grant and Schlesinger declare: "Achieving the full profit potential of each customer relationship should be the fundamental goal of every business ... Even using conservative estimates, the gap between most companies' current and full potential performance is enormous."[12] They suggest analysis of the following gaps between the actual and potential value of customers:

- What is the current purchasing behavior of customers in each target segment? What would be the impact on sales and profits if they exhibited the ideal behavior profile of (1) buying all services offered by the firm, (2) using these to the exclusion of any purchases from competitors, and (3) paying full price?
- How long, on average, do customers remain with the firm? What impact would it have if they remained customers for life?

As we showed earlier, the profitability of a customer often increases over time. Management's task is to identify the reasons why customers defect and then take corrective action.

Understanding the Customer/Firm Relationship

A fundamental distinction exists between strategies intended to bring about a single transaction and those designed to create extended relationships with customers. The term *relationship marketing* has been widely used to describe the latter type of activity, but until recently it was only loosely defined. Research by Coviello, Brodie, and Munro suggests that there are, in fact, four distinct types of marketing: transactional marketing and three categories of what they call relational marketing, namely, database marketing, interaction marketing, and network marketing.[13]

Management Memo 12.1

WORKSHEET FOR CALCULATING CUSTOMER LIFETIME VALUE

Calculating customer value is an inexact science that is subject to a variety of assumptions. You may want to try varying these assumptions to see how it affects the final figures. Generally speaking, revenues per customer are easier to track on an individualized basis than are the associated costs of serving a customer, unless (1) no individual records are kept and/or (2) the accounts served are very large and all account-related costs are individually documented and assigned.

Acquisition Revenues Less Costs

If individual account records are kept, the initial application fee paid and initial purchase (if relevant) should be found in these records. Costs, by contrast, may have to be based on average data. For instance, the marketing cost of acquiring a new client can be calculated by dividing the total marketing costs (advertising, promotions, selling, etc.) devoted toward acquiring new customers by the total number of new customers acquired during the same period. If each acquisition takes place over an extended period of time, you may want to build in a lagged effect between when marketing expenditures are incurred and when new customers come on board. The cost of credit checks—where relevant—must be divided by the number of new customers, not the total number of applicants, because some applicants will probably fail this hurdle. Account set-up costs will also be an average figure in most organizations.

Annual Revenues and Costs

If annual sales, account fees, and service fees are documented on an individual-account basis, account revenue streams (except referrals) can be easily identified. The first priority is to segment your customer base by the length of its relationship with your firm. Depending on the sophistication and precision of your firm's records, annual costs in each category may be directly assigned to an individual account holder or averaged for all account holders in that age category.

Value of Referrals

Computing the value of referrals requires a variety of assumptions. To get started, you may need to conduct surveys to determine (1) what percentage of new customers claim that they were influenced by a recommendation from another customer and (2) what other marketing activities also drew the firm to that individual's attention. From these two items, estimates can be made of what percentage of the credit for all new customers should be assigned to referrals. Additional research may be needed to clarify whether "older" customers are more likely to be effective recommenders than "younger" ones.

Net Present Value

Calculating net present value (NPV) from a future profit stream will require choice of an appropriate annual discount figure. (This could reflect estimates of future inflation rates.) It also requires assessment of how long the average relationship lasts. The NPV of a customer, then, is the sum of the anticipated annual profit on each customer for the projected relationship lifetime, suitably discounted each year into the future.

Acquisition		Year 1	Year 2	Year 3	Year n
Initial Revenue	Annual Revenues				
Application fee[a] _____	Annual account fee[a]	_____	_____	_____	_____
Initial purchase[a] _____	Sales	_____	_____	_____	_____
	Service fees[a]	_____	_____	_____	_____
	Value of referrals[b]	_____	_____	_____	_____
Total Revenues _____					
Initial Costs	Annual Costs				
Marketing _____	Account management	_____	_____	_____	_____
Credit check[a] _____	Cost of sales	_____	_____	_____	_____
Account setup[a] _____	Write-offs (e.g., bad debts)	_____	_____	_____	_____
Less total costs _____		_____	_____	_____	_____
Net Profit (Loss) _____		_____	_____	_____	_____

[a] If applicable.
[b] Anticipated profits from each new customer referred (could be limited to the first year or expressed as the net present value of the estimated future stream of profits through year n); this value could be negative if an unhappy customer starts to spread negative word of mouth that causes existing customers to defect.

Transactional Marketing

A transaction is an event during which an exchange of value takes place between two parties. One transaction or even a series of transactions doesn't necessarily constitute a relationship, which requires mutual recognition and knowledge between the parties. When each transaction between a customer and a supplier is essentially discrete and anonymous, with no long-term record kept of a customer's purchasing history and little or no mutual recognition between the customer and employees, then no meaningful marketing relationship can be said to exist.

With very few exceptions, consumers buying manufactured goods for household use do so at discrete intervals, paying for each purchase separately and rarely entering into a formal relationship with the original manufacturer. Nevertheless, they may have a relationship with the dealer or retail intermediary that sells the goods. The same is true for many services, ranging from passenger transport to food service or visits to a cinema, where each purchase and use is a discrete event.

Database Marketing

In database marketing, the focus is still on the market transaction, but now includes information exchange. Marketers rely on information technology, usually in the form of a database, to form a relationship with targeted customers and retain their patronage over time. However, the nature of these relationships is often not a close one, with communication being driven and managed by the seller. Technology is used to (1) identify and build a database of current and potential customers, (2) deliver differentiated messages based on consumers' characteristics and preferences, and (3) track each relationship to monitor the cost of acquiring the consumer and the lifetime value of the resulting purchases.[14] Although technology can be used to personalize the relationship, relations remain somewhat distant. Utility services such as electricity, gas, and cable TV are good examples.

Interaction Marketing

A closer relationship exists in situations where there is face-to-face interaction between customers and representatives of the supplier (or "ear-to-ear" interaction by phone). Although the service itself remains important, value is added by people and social processes. Interactions may include negotiations and sharing of insights in both directions. This type of relationship has long existed in many local environments ranging from community banks to dentistry, where buyer and seller know and trust each other. It is also commonly found in many business-to-business services. Both the firm and the customer are prepared to invest resources (including time) to develop a mutually beneficial relationship. This investment may include time spent sharing and recording information.

Network Marketing

We often say that someone is a "good networker" because he or she is able to put individuals in touch with others who have a mutual interest. This type of marketing occurs primarily in a business-to-business context, where firms commit resources to develop positions in a network of relationships with customers, distributors, suppliers, the media, consultants, trade associations, government agencies, competitors, and even the customers of their customers. There is often a team of individuals within the supplier's firm, who must collaborate to provide effective service to a parallel team within the customer's organization. However, the concept of networking is also relevant in consumer marketing environments, where customers are encouraged to refer friends and acquaintances to the service provider.

The four types of marketing described above are not necessarily mutually exclusive. A firm may have transactions with some customers who have neither the desire nor the need to make future purchases, while working hard to serve others whom it is encouraging to climb the loyalty ladder. Evert Gummesson advocates *total relationship marketing,* described as:

> [M]arketing based on relationships, networks, and interaction, recognizing that marketing is embedded in the total management of the networks of the selling organization, the market, and society. It is directed to long-term, win-win relationships with individual customers, and value is jointly created between the parties involved.[15]

He identifies no fewer than 30 types of relationships within the broader context of total relationship marketing.

Creating "Membership" Relationships

Although some services involve discrete transactions, others involve purchasers receiving service on a continuing basis. Even where the transactions are themselves discrete, there may still be an opportunity to create an ongoing relationship. The different nature of the following situations offers an opportunity for categorizing services. First, we can ask: Does the supplier enter into a formal "membership" relationship with customers, as with telephone subscriptions, banking, and the family doctor? Or is there no defined relationship? Second: Is the service delivered on a continuous basis, as in insurance, broadcasting, and police protection? Or is each transaction recorded and charged separately? Table 12.1 shows the matrix resulting from this categorization, with examples in each category.

A *membership relationship* is a formalized relationship between the firm and an identifiable customer, which may offer special benefits to both parties. Services involving discrete transactions can be transformed into membership relationships either by selling the service in bulk (for instance, a theater series subscription or a commuter ticket on public transport) or by offering extra benefits to customers who choose to register with the firm (loyalty programs for hotels, airlines, and car rental firms fall into this category). The advantage to the service organization of having membership relationships is that it knows who its current customers are and, usually, what use they make of the services offered. This can be valuable information for segmentation purposes if good records are kept and the data are

Table 12.1
Relationships
with Customers

Nature of Service Delivery	Type of Relationship between the Service Organization and Its Customers	
	Membership Relationship	No Formal Relationship
Continuous delivery of service	Insurance	Radio station
	Cable TV subscription	Police protection
	College enrollment	Lighthouse
	Banking	Public highway
Discrete transactions	Long-distance calls from subscriber phone	Car rental
		Mail service
	Theater series subscription	Toll highway
	Travel on commuter ticket	Pay phone
	Repair under warranty	Movie theater
	Health treatment for HMO member	Public transportation
		Restaurant

readily accessible for analysis. Knowing the identities and addresses of current customers enables the organization to make effective use of direct mail (including email), telephone selling, and personal sales calls—all highly targeted methods of marketing communication. In turn, members can be given access to special numbers or even designated account managers to facilitate their communications with the firm.

Targeting the Right Customers

Many elements are involved in creating long-term customer relationships and loyalty. The process starts by identifying and targeting the right customers. Customers often differ widely in terms of needs. They also differ in terms of the value that they can contribute to a company. Not all customers offer a good fit with the organization's capabilities, delivery technologies, and strategic direction.

Good Relationships Start with a Good Fit

Companies need to be selective about the segments they target if they want to build successful customer relationships. In this section, we emphasize the importance of choosing to serve a portfolio of several carefully chosen target segments and taking pains to build and maintain their loyalty. (If you have not previously taken a marketing course, you will find it useful to review Management Memo 12.2.)

Matching customers to the firm's capabilities is vital. Managers must think carefully about how customer needs relate to such operational elements as speed and quality, the times when service is available, the firm's capacity to serve many customers simultaneously, and the physical features and appearance of service facilities. They also need to consider how well their service personnel can meet the expectations of specific types of customers, in terms of both personal style and technical competence.[16] Finally, they need to ask themselves whether their company can match or exceed competing services that are directed at the same types of customers.

The result of carefully targeting customers by matching the company capabilities and strengths with customer needs should be a superior service offering in the eyes of those customers, who value what the firm has to offer. As Frederick Reichheld said, "… the result should be a win-win situation, where profits are earned through the success and satisfaction of customers, and not at their expense."[17] See Best Practice in Action 12.1 on Taiwan Cellular Corporation's segmentation strategy.

*Management
Memo 12.2*

IDENTIFYING AND SELECTING TARGET SEGMENTS

Market segmentation is central to almost any professionally planned and executed marketing program. The concept of segmentation recognizes that customers and prospects within a market vary across a variety of dimensions and that not every segment constitutes a desirable target for the firm's marketing efforts.

Market segments. A segment is composed of a group of current and potential customers who share common characteristics, needs, purchasing behavior, or consumption patterns. Effective segmentation should group buyers into segments in ways that result in as much similarity as possible on the relevant characteristics *within* each segment, but dissimilarity on those same characteristics *between* each segment. Two broad categories of variables useful in describing the differences between segments are user characteristics and usage behavior.

User characteristics may vary from one person to another, reflecting *demographic* characteristics (for instance, age, income, and education), *geographic* location, and *psychographics* (the attitudes, values, lifestyles, and opinions of decision makers and users). More recently, marketers have begun to speak of *technographics,* a term trademarked by Forrester Research, that describes the extent to which customers are willing and able to use the latest technology. Another important segmentation variable is user needs and the specific benefits that individuals and corporate purchasers seek from consuming a particular good or service.

Usage behavior relates to how a product is purchased, delivered, and used. Among such variables are when and where purchase and consumption take place, the quantities consumed ("heavy users" are always of particular interest to marketers), the frequency and purpose of use, the occasions when consumption takes place (sometimes referred to as "occasion segmentation"), and sensitivity to marketing variables (e.g., advertising, pricing, speed, and other service features), and availability of alternative delivery systems.

Target segment. After evaluating different segments in the market, a firm should focus its marketing efforts by targeting one or more segments that fit well with the firm's capabilities and goals. Target segments are often defined on the basis of several variables. For instance, a hotel in a particular city might target prospective guests who share user characteristics like (1) traveling on business (demographic segmentation), (2) visiting clients within a defined area around the hotel (geographic segmentation), and (3) willingness to pay a certain daily room rate (user response).

When researching the marketplace, service marketers should be looking for answers to such questions as:

- In what useful ways can the market for our firm's service be segmented?
- What are the needs of the specific segments that we have identified?
- Which of these segments best fits our institution's mission and our current operational capabilities?
- What do customers in each segment see as our firm's competitive advantages and disadvantages? Are the latter correctable?
- In the light of this analysis, which specific segment(s) should we target?
- How should we differentiate our marketing efforts from those of the competition to attract and retain the types of customers that we want?
- What is the long-term financial value of a loyal customer in each of the segments that we currently serve (and those that we would like to serve)?
- How should our firm build long-term relationships with customers from the target segments?
- What strategies are needed to create long-term loyalty?

Best Practice
in Action 12.1

TAIWAN CELLULAR CORPORATION NT$901 SERVICE PACKAGE

In an effort to stand out against its competitor, Chunghwa Telecom, which serves a similar target base, Taiwanese telecommunication provider, Taiwan Cellular Corporation (TCC), created a NT$901 (US$27) service package that targets young couples. TCC marketing communication vice-president, Alex Cheng, explained that the decision to broaden its customer base through segmentation is because Taiwan's mobile market is highly saturated and competitive.

Alex added that NT$901 targets a niche segment, which consists of young couples with very different calling patterns. They usually make calls to each other frequently, so the NT$901 service package that allows the subscribers to make free calls to one selected number appeals to them. The free calls are viewed as a bonus to them. As a result of its effective segmentation strategy, TCC's "Love 901" Valentine-timed TV spot managed to garner a 91 percent recall rate among its niche segment, which is those aged between 15 and 24 years.

TCC also launched another marketing campaign in May 2004 that targets a different market segment. With almost every Taiwanese holding at least one mobile SIM card, and Taiwan's mobile market inching toward saturation, crafting out further campaigns to target different segments with differentiated value propositions seems to be the most feasible way for TCC to gain an edge over its competitors.

Source: Adapted from Janis Tse, "'Mobile Marketer Rides on Valentine's Day to Lead in Recall," *Media Asia*, March 26, 2004: 20.

Searching for Value, Not Just Numbers

Too many service firms still focus on the *number* of customers they serve without giving sufficient attention to the *value* of each customer. Generally speaking, heavy users who buy more frequently and in larger volumes are more profitable than occasional users. Roger Hallowell, a Harvard Business School professor, makes this point nicely in a discussion of banking:

> A bank's population of customers undoubtedly contains individuals who either cannot be satisfied, given the service levels and pricing the bank is capable of offering, or will never be profitable, given their banking activity (their use of resources relative to the revenue they supply). Any bank would be wise to target and serve only those customers whose needs it can meet better than its competitors in a profitable manner. These are the customers who are most likely to remain with that bank for long periods, who will purchase multiple products and services, who will recommend that bank to their friends and relations, and who may be the source of superior returns to the bank's shareholders.[18]

Relationship customers are by definition not buying commodity services. Service customers who strictly buy based on lowest price (a minority in most markets) are not good target customers for relationship marketing in the first place. They are deal-prone, and continuously seek the lowest price on offer.[19]

You shouldn't assume that the "right customers" are always high spenders. Depending on the service business model, the right customers can come from a large group of people that no other supplier is doing a good job of serving. Many firms have successfully built strategies serving customer segments that were neglected by established players that didn't perceive them as sufficiently "valuable."

Finally, however, marketers need to recognize that there are some customers who are just not worth serving because they are too difficult to please or unable to decide on what they want. Loyalty leaders are picky about acquiring only the right customers, which are those for whom their firms have been designed to deliver truly special value. Acquiring the right customers can bring in long-term revenues, continued growth from referrals, and enhanced satisfaction from employees whose daily jobs are improved when they can deal with appreciative customers. Attracting the wrong customers typically results in costly churn, a diminished company reputation, and disillusioned employees. Ironically, it is often the firms that are highly focused and selective in their acquisition, rather than those that focus on unbridled acquisition, that are growing fast over long periods.[20] Best Practice in Action 12.2 shows how Vanguard designed its products and pricing to attract and retain the right customers for its business model.

Selecting an Appropriate Customer Portfolio

Different segments offer different value for a service firm. Like investments, some types of customers may be more profitable than others in the short term, but others may have greater potential for long-term growth. Similarly, the spending patterns of some customers may be stable over time, while others may be more cyclical, spending heavily in boom times but cutting back sharply in recessions. A wise firm may seek a mix of such segments in order to reduce the risks associated with market or macroeconomic forces.

As David Maister emphasizes, marketing is about getting *better* business, not just *more* business.[21] The caliber of a professional firm is measured by the type of clients it serves and the nature of the tasks on which it works. Volume alone is no measure of excellence, sustainability, or profitability. In professional services, such as consulting firms or legal partnerships, the mix of business attracted may play an important role in both defining the firm and providing a suitable mix of assignments for staff members at different levels in the organization.

Analyzing and Managing the Customer Base

Marketers should adopt a strategic approach to retaining, upgrading, and even terminating customers. Customer retention involves developing long-term, cost-effective links with customers for the mutual benefit of both parties, but these efforts need not necessarily target all the customers in a firm with the same level of intensity. Recent research has confirmed that most firms have different tiers of

VANGUARD DISCOURAGES THE ACQUISITION OF "WRONG" CUSTOMERS

The Vanguard Group is a growth leader in the mutual fund industry and built its US$550 billion in managed assets by painstakingly targeting the right customers for its business model. Its share of new sales, which was around 25 percent, reflected its share of assets, or market share. However, it had a far lower share of redemptions, which gave it a market share of net cash flows of 55 percent (new sales minus redemptions), and made it the fastest growing mutual fund in its industry.

How did Vanguard achieve such low redemption rates? The secret was in its careful acquisition, and its product and pricing strategies, which encouraged the acquisition of the "right" customers.

John Bogle, Vanguard's founder, believed in the superiority of index funds and that their lower management fees would lead to higher returns over the long run. He offered Vanguard's clients unparalleled low management fees through a policy of not trading (its index funds hold the market they are designed to track), not having a sales force, and spending only a fraction of what its competitors did on advertising. Another important part of keeping the costs low has been to discourage the acquisition of customers who are not long-term index holders.

John Bogle attributes the high level of customer loyalty Vanguard achieved to a great deal of focus on customer defections, which are redemption rates in the fund context. "I watched them like a hawk," he explained, and analyzed them more carefully than new sales to ensure that Vanguard's customer acquisition strategy was on course. Low redemption rates meant that the firm was attracting the right kind of loyal, long-term investors. The inherent stability of its loyal customer base has been key to Vanguard's cost advantage. Bogle's pickiness became legendary. He scrutinized individual redemptions with a fine-tooth comb to see who let the wrong kind of customers on board. When an institutional investor redeemed US$25 million from an index fund bought only nine months earlier, he regarded the acquisition of this customer a failure of the system. He explained, "We don't want short-term investors. They muck up the game at the expense of the long-term investor." At the end of his chairman's letter to the Vanguard Index Trust, Bogle reiterated: "We urge them [short-term investors] to look elsewhere for their investment opportunities."

This care and attention to acquiring the right customers became legendary. For example, Vanguard turned away an institutional investor who wanted to invest US$40 million because Vanguard suspected that the customer would churn the investment within the next few weeks, creating extra costs for existing customers. The potential customer complained to Vanguard's CEO, who not only supported the decision, but also used it as an opportunity to reinforce to his teams why they needed to be selective about the customers they accept.

Furthermore, Vanguard introduced a number of changes to industry practices which discouraged active traders from buying its funds. For example, Vanguard did not allow telephone transfers for index funds, redemption fees were added to some funds, and the standard practice of subsidizing new accounts at the expense of existing customers was rejected as such a practice was considered as disloyal to its core investor base. These product and pricing policies in effect turned away heavy traders, but made the fund uniquely attractive for the long-term investor.

Finally, Vanguard's pricing was set up to reward loyal customers. For many of its funds, investors pay a one-time up-front fee, which goes into the funds themselves to compensate all current investors for the administrative costs of selling new shares. In essence, this fee subsidizes long-term investors, and penalizes short-term investors. Another novel pricing approach was the creation of its Admiral shares for loyal investors, which carried an expense fee of one-third below ordinary shares (0.12 percent per year instead of 0.18 percent).

Source: Frederick F. Reichheld, *Loyalty Rules! How Today's Leaders Build Lasting Relationships* (Boston: MA, Harvard Business School Press, 2001), 24–29, 84–87, 144–145.

customers in terms of profitability, and that these tiers often have quite different service expectations and needs. According to Zeithaml, Rust, and Lemon, it's critical that service firms should understand the needs of customers within different profitability tiers and adjust their service levels accordingly.[22]

Tiering the Customer Base

Customer tiers can be developed around different levels of profit contribution, needs (including sensitivities to variables such as price, comfort, and speed), and identifiable personal profiles such as demographics. (Service Perspectives 12.1 describes the various customer tiers from the perspective of a market research agency.) Zeithaml, Rust, and Lemon illustrated this principle through a four-level pyramid, as shown in Figure 12.3.[23]

PLATINUM These customers constitute a very small percentage of a firm's customer base. They are heavy users and contribute a large share of the profits generated. Typically, this segment is less price sensitive, but expects highest service levels in return, and is likely to be willing to invest in and try new services.

Figure 12.3
The Customer Pyramid

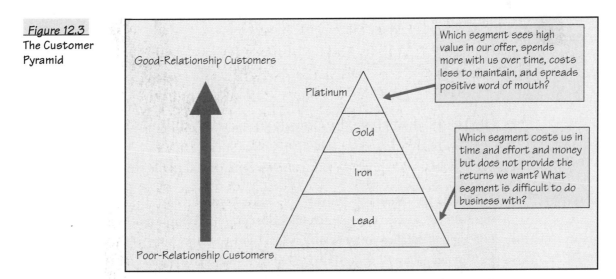

Source: Valarie A. Zeithaml, Roland T. Rust, and Katharine N. Lemon, "The Customer Pyramid: Creating and Serving Profitable Customers," *California Management Review* 43, no. 4 (Summer 2001): 118. Copyright © 2001 by The Regents of the University of California. Reprinted by permission of The Regents.

TIERING THE CUSTOMERS OF A MARKET RESEARCH AGENCY

Tiering its clients helped a leading U.S. market research agency to better understand its customers. The agency defined *platinum clients* as large accounts that were not only willing to plan a certain amount of research work during the year but also able to commit to the timing, scope, and nature of their projects, which made capacity management and project planning much easier for the research firm. The acquisition costs for projects sold to these clients were only between 2 and 5 percent of project values (as compared to as much as 25 percent for clients that required extensive proposal work and project-by-project bidding). Platinum accounts were also more willing to try new services and to buy a wider range of services from their preferred provider. These customers were generally very satisfied with the research agency's work and were willing to act as references to potential new clients.

Gold accounts had a similar profile to platinum clients but were more price sensitive and more inclined to spread their budgets across several firms. Although these accounts had been clients for many years, they were not willing to commit their research work for a year in advance, even though the research firm would have been able to offer them better quality and priority in capacity allocation.

Iron accounts spent moderate amounts on research and commissioned work on a project basis. Selling costs were high, as these firms tended to send out requests for proposals (RFPs) to a number of firms for all their projects. These firms sought the lowest price and often did not give the research firm sufficient time to perform a good-quality job.

Lead accounts conducted only isolated, low-cost, "quick-and-dirty" projects, with little opportunity for the research firm to add value or to apply its skill sets appropriately. Sales costs were high, as the client typically invited several firms to quote. Furthermore, because these firms were inexperienced in conducting research and in working with research agencies, selling a project often took several meetings and required multiple revisions to the proposal. Lead accounts also tended to be high maintenance, as they did not understand research work well; they often changed project parameters, scope, and deliverables midstream and then expected the research agency to absorb the cost of any rework, thus further reducing the profitability of the engagement.

Source: Valarie A Zeithaml, Roland T. Rust, and Katharine N. Lemon, "The Customer Pyramid: Creating and Serving Profitable Customers," *California Management Review* 43, no. 4 (Summer 2001): 127–128.

GOLD   The gold tier forms a larger percentage of customers than the platinum, but individual customers contribute less profit than platinum customers. They tend to be slightly more price sensitive and less committed to the firm.

IRON   These customers provide the bulk of customer base. Their numbers give the firm economies of scale. Hence, they are often important so that a firm can build and maintain a certain capacity level and infrastructure, which is often needed for serving gold and platinum customers. However, iron customers in themselves are often only marginally profitable. Their level of business is not sufficiently substantial for special treatment.

LEAD   Lead-tier customers tend to generate low revenues for a firm, but often still require the same level of service as iron customers, which turns them into a loss-making segment from a firm's perspective.

Building Customer Loyalty

What makes customers loyal to a firm, and how can marketers increase their loyalty? In this section, we first review the common loyalty drivers for customers and then explore the foundations of loyalty and how firms can build or enhance such loyalty drivers further.

How Do Customers See Relational Benefits?

Research by Gwinner, Gremler, and Bitner suggests that relationships create value for individual consumers through such factors as inspiring greater confidence, offering social benefits, and providing special treatment (see Research Insights 12.1). Kumar emphasizes that relationships in a business-to-business service are largely dependent on the quality of the interactions between individuals at each of the partnering firms.[24] "As relationships strengthen over a period of time," he observes, "the service provider's personnel often assume the role of outsourced departments and make critical decisions on behalf of their clients."

The Foundations of Customer Loyalty

The foundation for true loyalty lies in customer satisfaction. Highly satisfied or even delighted customers are more likely to become loyal apostles of a firm,[25] consolidate their buying with one supplier, and spread positive word of mouth. In contrast, dissatisfaction drives customers away and is a key factor in switching behavior.

Figure 12.4 divides the satisfaction/loyalty relationship into three main zones. First, the *zone of defection* is at low satisfaction levels. Customers will switch unless switching costs are high or there are no viable or convenient alternatives. Extremely dissatisfied customers can turn into "terrorists," providing an abundance of negative word of mouth for the service provider. Second, the *zone of indifference* is at intermediate satisfaction levels. Here, customers are willing to switch if they find a better alternative. Third, the *zone of affection* is at very high satisfaction levels, and customers can have such high attitudinal loyalty that they do not look for alternative service providers. Customers who praise the firm in public and refer others to the firm are described as "apostles."

Creating Bonds with Customers

Having the right portfolio of customer segments, attracting the right customers, tiering the service and delivering high levels of satisfaction are a solid foundation

Research Insights 12.1

HOW CUSTOMERS SEE RELATIONAL BENEFITS IN SERVICE INDUSTRIES

What benefits do customers see themselves receiving from an extended relationship with a service firm? Researchers seeking answers to this question conducted two studies. The first consisted of in-depth interviews in their own homes with 21 respondents from a broad cross-section of backgrounds. These interviews averaged 48 minutes in length. Respondents were asked to identify service providers that they used on a regular basis and invited to identify and discuss any benefits they received as a result of being a regular customer. Among some of the verbatim comments were:

- "I like him [hair stylist]...He's really funny and always has lots of good jokes. He's kind of like a friend now."
- "I know what I'm getting—I know that if I go to a restaurant that I regularly go to, rather than taking a chance on all of the new restaurants, the food will be good."
- "I often get price breaks. The little bakery that I go to in the morning, every once in a while, they'll give me a free muffin and say, 'You're a good customer, it's on us today.'"
- "You can get better service than drop-in customers ... We continue to go to the same automobile repair shop because we have gotten to know the owner on a kind of personal basis, and he...can always work us in."
- "Once people feel comfortable, they don't want to switch to another dentist. They don't want to train or break a new dentist in."

After evaluating and categorizing the comments, the researchers designed a second study in which some survey questionnaires were distributed to a convenience sample of about 400 people. The subjects were told to select a specific service provider with whom they had a strong, established relationship. Then the questionnaire asked them to assess the extent to which they received each of 21 benefits (derived from analysis of the first study) as a result of their relationship with the specific provider they had identified. Finally, they were asked to assess the importance of these benefits for them.

A total of 299 usable surveys were returned. A factor analysis of the results showed that most of the benefits that customers derived from relationships could be grouped into three clusters. The first, and most important, group concerned what the researchers labeled confidence benefits, followed by social benefits and special treatment.

Confidence benefits included feelings by customers that in an established relationship, there was less risk of something going wrong, confidence in correct performance, ability to trust the provider, lowered anxiety when purchasing, knowing what to expect, and receipt of the firm's highest level of service.

Social benefits embraced mutual recognition between customers and employees, being known by name, friendship with the service provider, and enjoyment of certain social aspects of the relationship.

Special treatment benefits included better prices, discounts on special deals that were unavailable to most customers, extra services, higher priority when there was a wait, and faster service than most customers received.

Source: Kevin P. Gwinner, Dwayne D. Gremler, and Mary Jo Bitner, "Relational Benefits in Services Industries: The Customer's Perspective," *Journal of the Academy of Marketing Science* 26, no. 2 (1998): 101–114.

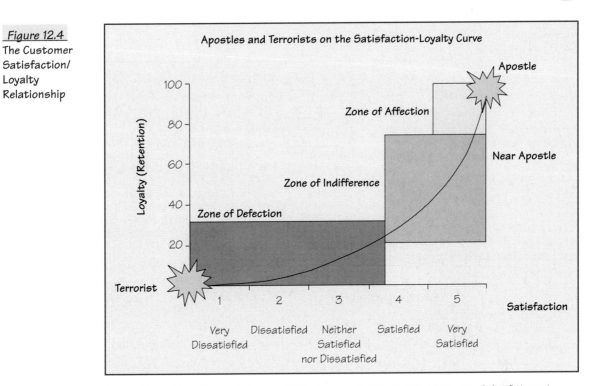

for creating customer loyalty, as shown in Figure 12.5. However, there is more that firms can do to "bond" closer with their customers and specific strategies for loyalty bonds are summarized in item 2 in this figure.[26] At the same time, service marketers should be working to identify and eliminate the factors that result in "churn," or the loss of existing customers and the need to replace them with new ones.

DEEPENING THE RELATIONSHIP   To tie customers closer to the firm, deepening the relationship via bundling and/or cross-selling services is an effective strategy. For example, banks like to sell as many financial products into an account or household as possible. Once a family has its current account, credit card, savings account, safe deposit box, car loan, mortgage, etc. with the same bank, the relationship is so deep that switching becomes a major exercise and is unlikely unless, of course, customers are extremely dissatisfied with the bank.

Another way is to provide exclusive benefits for one's customers that deepen the relationship. For example, HSBC launched a "Home and Away" Privilege Program for its credit card holders, which provides shopping, dining, entertainment and travel discounts across many countries in Asia.

REWARD-BASED BONDS   Within any competitive product category, managers recognize that few customers consistently buy only one brand, especially in situations where service delivery involves a discrete transaction (such as a car rental), rather

Figure 12.5
The Wheel of Loyalty

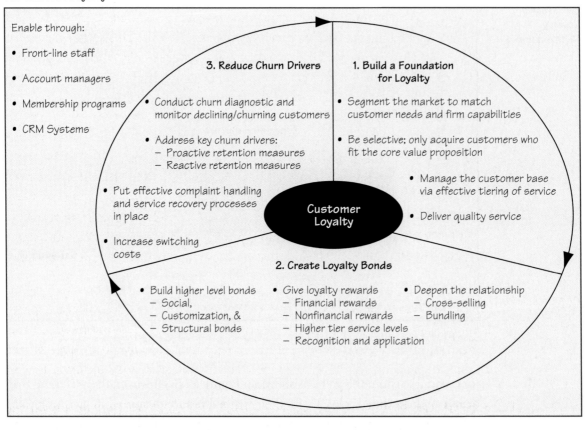

than being continuous in nature (as with insurance coverage). In many instances, consumers are loyal to several brands while spurning others. In such instances, the marketing goal becomes one of strengthening the customer's preference for one brand over the others.

Incentives that offer rewards based on the frequency of purchase, value of purchase, or a combination of both represent a basic level of customer bonds. Reward-based bonds can be financial or nonfinancial in nature. Financial bonds are built when loyal customers are rewarded with incentives that have a financial value, such as discounts on purchases and loyalty program rewards such as frequent flyer miles or the cash-back programs provided by some credit card issuers based on the level of spending charged by card members.

Nonfinancial rewards provide customers with benefits or value that cannot be translated directly into monetary terms. Examples include giving priority to loyalty program members for waitlists and queues in call centers, and access to special services. In the business-to-business (B2B) context, offering service extras often plays a key role in building and sustaining relationships between vendors and purchasers of industrial goods.[27] Informal loyalty rewards, sometimes found in small businesses, may take the form of periodically giving regular customers a small treat as a way of thanking them for their custom.

Even national tourism boards try to use reward-based bonds to make travelers feel more welcome and loyal to their country. For example, Thailand launched the "Thailand Elite" membership in an effort to attract more elite business travelers. This program is the world's first country membership club for friends of Thailand who are entitled to mostly nonfinancial benefits and privileges throughout the Kingdom of Thailand. The benefits cover the whole spectrum of living in Thailand, from leisure, eating, and travel, to immigration and health care.[28] (See Figure 12.6.)

Important intangible rewards include special recognition and appreciation. Customers tend to value the extra attention given to their needs. They also appreciate the implicit service guarantee offered by high-tier memberships, including efforts to meet special requests. However, reward-based loyalty programs are relatively easy for other suppliers to copy and rarely provide a sustained competitive advantage. By contrast, the higher-level bonds that we discuss next tend to be more sustainable.

SOCIAL BONDS Social bonds are typically based on personal relationships between providers and customers. Alternatively, they may reflect pride or satisfaction in holding membership in an organization. Although social bonds are more difficult to build than financial bonds and may require considerable time to achieve, for that same reason they are also harder for other suppliers to replicate for that same

Figure 12.6

Thailand promotes the benefits and privileges of its exclusive "Thailand Elite" membership, which is by invitation only.

customer. A firm that has created social bonds with its customers has a better chance of retaining them for the long term.

CUSTOMIZATION BONDS   These bonds are built when the service provider succeeds in providing customized service to its loyal customers. One-to-one marketing is a more specialized form of customization where each individual is treated as a segment by itself.[29] Many large hotel chains capture the preferences of their customers through their loyalty program databases, so that when customers arrive at their hotel, they find that their individual needs have already been anticipated, from preferred drinks and snacks in the room refrigerator to the kind of pillow they like and the newspaper they want to receive in the morning. When a customer becomes used to this special service, he or she may find it difficult to adjust to another service provider who is not able to customize the service (at least immediately, as it takes time for the new provider to learn about someone's needs).

STRUCTURAL BONDS   Structural bonds are mostly seen in B2B settings and aim to stimulate loyalty through structural relationships between the provider and the customer. Examples include joint investments in projects and sharing of information, processes, and equipment. Structural bonds can be created in a business-to-consumer (B2C) environment, too. For instance, some car rental companies offer travelers the opportunity to create customized pages on the firm's Web site where they can retrieve details of past trips including the types of cars, insurance coverage, and so forth. This simplifies and speeds the task of making new bookings. Once customers have integrated their way of doing things with the firm's processes, structural bonds are created that link the customers to the firm and make it more difficult for competition to draw them away.

TRANSFORMING DISCRETE TRANSACTIONS TO MEMBERSHIP RELATIONSHIPS
Discrete transactions, when each usage involves a payment to the service supplier by an essentially "anonymous" consumer, are typical of services like transport, restaurants, cinemas, and shoe repairs. The problem for marketers of such services is that they tend to be less informed about who their customers are and what use each customer makes of the service, than their counterparts in membership-type organizations. Managers in businesses that sell discrete transactions have to work a little harder to establish relationships. In small businesses such as hairdressers, frequent customers are (or should be) welcomed as "regulars" whose needs and preferences are remembered. Keeping formal records of customers' needs, preferences, and purchasing behavior is useful even in small firms, as it helps employees avoid having to ask repetitive questions on each service occasion, allows them to personalize the service given to each customer, and also enables the firm to anticipate future needs.

In large companies with substantial customer bases, transactions can still be transformed into relationships by implementing loyalty-reward programs, which require customers to apply for membership cards with which transactions can be captured and customers' preferences communicated to the front line.

A number of other service businesses have sought to copy the airline industry, with loyalty programs of their own. Although some provide their own rewards—such as free merchandise, class of vehicle upgrades, or free hotel rooms in vacation resorts—many firms denominate their awards in miles that can be credited to a selected frequent flyer program. In short, air miles have become a form of promotional currency in the service sector. Best Practice in Action 12.3 features Emirates' Skywards frequent flyer program, which was voted Program of the Year in 2003 by the *InsiderFlyer* magazine. Besides airlines and hotels, more and more service firms ranging from retailers (such as department stores, supermarkets, book shops, and petrol stations), telecommunications providers, cafe chains, courier services, and cinema chains have or are also launching similar reward programs in response to the increasing competitiveness of their markets.

Of course, rewards alone will not suffice to retain a firm's most desirable customers. If customers are dissatisfied with the quality of service they receive, or believe that they can obtain better value from a less expensive service, they may quickly become disloyal. Neither Emirates nor any other service business which has instituted an awards program for frequent users can ever afford to lose sight of its broader goals of offering high-quality service and good value relative to the price and other costs incurred by customers.

HOW CUSTOMERS PERCEIVE LOYALTY REWARD PROGRAMS   Recent research in the credit card industry suggests that loyalty programs strengthen the customers' perception of the value proposition, and lead to increased revenues due to fewer defections and higher usage levels.[30] To assess the potential of a loyalty program to alter normal patterns of behavior, Dowling and Uncles argue that marketers need to examine three psychological effects.[31]

1. *Brand loyalty versus deal loyalty*. To what extent are customers loyal to the core service (or brand) rather than to the loyalty program itself? Marketers should focus on loyalty programs that directly support the value proposition and positioning of the product in question.

2. *How buyers value rewards*. Several elements determine a loyalty program's value to customers: (1) the cash value of the redemption rewards (if customers had to purchase them); (2) the range of choice among rewards—for instance a selection of gifts rather than just a single gift; (3) the aspirational value of the rewards—something exotic that the consumer would not normally purchase may have greater appeal than a cash-back offer; (4) whether the amount of usage required to obtain an award places it within the realm of possibility for

Best Practice in Action 12.3

PROGRAM OF THE YEAR 2003: EMIRATES' SKYWARDS

The frequent flyer program of Dubai-based Emirates, Skywards, continues to outpace the industry. Skywards finished first in six categories at *InsiderFlyer* magazine's 15th Annual Freddie Awards in 2003, including the most prestigious international Program of the Year award. Skywards, being only a three-year-old program, has finished well against the world's leading frequent flyer programs. It even managed to beat the six-time "Program of the Year" winner, SAS EuroBonus.

Besides bagging the "Program of the Year" award, the airline also won "Best Elite Level", "Best Consumer Service," "Best Award Redemption," "Best Web Site," and "Best Affinity Card—the Skywards-Citibank credit card." It also came in second in the "Best Newsletter" category. The Freddies competition allows consumers to rank the programs through "value voting" (a system that balances the most popular vote with the overall merit and quality of the program), and is considered the most prestigious loyalty award in its industry.

In an effort to show its appreciation for their customers' loyalty, Skywards is designed as an exclusive club for frequent flyers with Emirates (see Figure 12.7) and Sri Lankan Airlines, offering benefits over and above what customers would usually expect. For every trip, whether for business or pleasure, members can accumulate Skywards Miles for redemption of a variety of inspiring rewards such as free travel, upgrades, and other benefits with Emirates, Sri Lankan Airlines, or their alliances. Collected miles can be redeemed for many attractive prices, including:

- *Flights*: Fly free with Emirates or Sri Lankan Airlines to over 72 destinations worldwide. Factor in the partner airlines and the destination list expands to hundreds of destinations worldwide, with reward flights starting from as little as 10,000 Skywards Miles.
- *Upgrades*: Starting from just 5,000 Skywards Miles, passengers can upgrade their flight with Emirates or Sri Lankan Airlines from economy to business class and travel in comfort and style. They may also upgrade their flight from Business to First Class where available.

Figure 12.7
Emirates Airplane on the Ground at Dubai International Airport

Reproduced with permission from Emirates Singapore.

- *Hotels*: Exotic Arabian nights beckon with a choice of 18 Marriott or Renaissance hotels throughout the Middle East.
- *Leisure and lifestyle rewards*: Passengers can experience the beauty of the desert at Al Maha Desert Resort, an exclusive eco-tourism resort, or immerse themselves in a cultural excursion in the United Arab Emirates with Arabian Adventures. In Dubai, passengers can unwind with a relaxing Danat Dubai Cruise, make a splash at Wild Wadi Water Park, or shop at Magrudy's from a wide range of books and toys.

Besides rewards, Skywards members also get to enjoy additional airline services. For example, members flying Emirates or Sri Lankan Airlines will have access to additional passenger privileges offered by the airlines themselves, including the Dubai visa service, chauffeured transport to and from designated airports, special meal considerations, fast track at the airport, and stopover packages at selected destinations. Members boarding Emirates and Sri Lankan Airlines would also get to enjoy special meals tailored to their medical, religious, or dietary menu requirements.

There are three tiers of membership for Skywards—Skywards Blue, Skywards Silver and Skywards Gold—each offering a greater degree of privilege, reward and recognition. When members advance from Skywards Blue to Skywards Silver or Gold membership, they can gain access to Skywards exclusive and innovative business club, Alumnus, instantly. Alumnus allows members to communicate and network with other dedicated professionals through forums and special events. Skywards Silver members are also entitled to extra travel privileges, including free excess baggage allowances, exclusive lounge access in Dubai and Colombo, and the ability to nominate their own travel coordinator.

Skywards Gold members are entitled to a premium level of service and privileges. Gold members will get to enjoy all the benefits of Skywards Silver, in addition to Gold-only privileges. These benefits include guaranteed reservations on fully booked flights, exclusive lounge access throughout the Emirates and Sri Lankan Airlines network, access to Opening Doors—Skywards' concierge service and premium service package.

Sources: "Emirates' Skywards wins 'Programme of the Year' award," *The Independent* (Bangladesh), May 9, 2003; www.emirates.com and www.skywards.com (accessed on July 10, 2004).

any given consumer; (5) the ease of using the program and making claims for redemption; and (6) the psychological benefits of belonging to the program and accumulating points. In this regard, The Westin Shanghai gives a very good example of how to help the patrons value and redeem the rewards and hence enhance their satisfaction as well as loyalty to the hotel (see Best Practice in Action 12.4).

3. *Timing.* How soon can benefits from participating in the rewards program be obtained by customers? Deferred gratification tends to weaken the appeal of a loyalty program. One solution is to send customers periodic statements of their account status, indicating progress toward reaching a particular milestone and promoting the rewards that might be forthcoming when that point is reached.

Best Practice in Action 12.4

REDEMPTION INITIATIVE FOR THE STARWOOD PREFERRED GUEST PROGRAM AT THE WESTIN SHANGHAI

Starwood Preferred Guest (SPG) is the hotel industry's most rewarding frequent travel program offered by Starwood Hotels and Resorts Worldwide, Inc. SPG members earn two Starpoints for each U.S. dollar or equivalent of all the eligible charges by participating hotels. The guests may redeem their Starpoints for various awards such as free nights, room upgrades, airport transfers, and many more.

Since the start of the program in September 2002, the number of members at the Westin Shanghai has grown from 29 percent to 65 percent. However, there are many SPG guests who have not taken advantage of the Instant Award Redemption benefits available to them during their stay.

To increase program awareness, the hotel conducted a survey, in the middle of 2003, among its SPG members. An email survey was sent to members who had previously stayed at The Westin Shanghai, asking why they had not taken advantage of their accrued Starpoints for complimentary services, and under what circumstance they would like to redeem their Starpoints. The feedback indicated that most of them were elite people in fairly high-level positions and their reservations were often made by personal assistants. This meant that members were not aware of their current point balances upon arrival at the hotel, nor were they familiar with the redemption program. In the same survey, more than 70 percent of the guests said that they would welcome information on their Starpoint balance and what they can redeem in the hotel.

With this finding, The Westin Shanghai created some special programs for redemption of Starpoints. Upon check-in, the SPG member is presented with an Instant Award Redemption leaflet containing information about their Starpoints balance and a list of redemption choices throughout the hotel. For example, a member can upgrade their room type from a deluxe room to an executive suite with 1,500 Starpoints, or they may use 6,000 Starpoints for a 90-minute oil massage at the Banyan Tree Spa, or use another 4,500 Starpoints for their Pudong Airport transfer. In this way, SPG members are able to make their visit more memorable with the assistance of the SPG Instant Award Redemption Program. (See Figure 12.8 for the change in SPG members' behavior.)

Figure 12.8
Redemption Dollars Increased Significantly After Introduction of the New Process

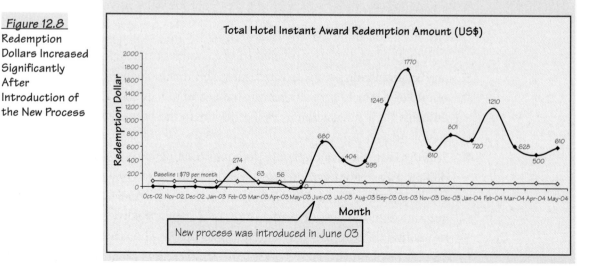

> Before the process change, the average Starpoints redemption was US$79 per month. After the SPG Instant Award Redemption leaflet was introduced, SPG members redeemed an equivalent of US$720 per month from their Starpoints (see Figure 12.8). Although not a great revenue project, reminding guests of their special privileges and encouraging them to take advantage of the extra services provided by the hotel with their Starpoints have significantly enhanced customer satisfaction and loyalty. This improvement was clearly indicated in the Monthly Guest Satisfaction Index question on "Satisfaction with SPG Benefits," where the index has increased significantly from 7.00 out of 10 in December 2002 to 8.58 in July 2004.
>
> Source: Based on an interview conducted by Professor Xiongwen Lu with the management of The Westin Shanghai, June 2004.

Managing and Curtailing Drivers of Customer Defections

So far, we have discussed drivers of loyalty and strategies to tie customers closer to the firm. An alternative approach is to understand drivers of customer defections or churn, and work on eliminating or reducing those drivers. For example, in the cellular phone industry, players regularly conduct what is called churn diagnostics. It includes the analysis of data warehouse information on churned and declining customers, exit interviews (call center staff often have a short set of questions they ask when a customer cancels an account to gain a better understanding of why customers defect), and in-depth interviews of former customers by a third-party research agency, which typically yield a more detailed understanding of churn drivers.[32]

COMMON CHURN DRIVERS   Susan Keaveney conducted a large-scale study across a range of services and found several key reasons for why customers switch to another provider.[33] (See Figure 12.9.) Core service failures were mentioned by 44 percent of respondents as a reason for switching; unsatisfactory service encounters by 34 percent; high, deceptive, or unfair pricing by 30 percent; inconvenience in terms of time, location, or delays by 21 percent; and poor response to service failure by 17 percent. Many respondents described a decision to switch as resulting from interrelated incidents, such as a service failure followed by an unsatisfactory service recovery.

STRATEGIES TO REDUCE CHURN   Keaveney's findings underscore the importance of delivering service quality (see Chapter 14), effective complaint handling and service recovery (see Chapter 13), minimizing inconvenience and other nonmonetary costs, and fair and transparent pricing (see Chapter 6).

In addition to these generic churn drivers, firms may encounter churn drivers that are specific to their own industries. For example, in cellular phone services, handset replacement needs are a common reason for subscribers to discontinue an existing subscription plan and subscribe to a new plan that typically comes with a heavily subsidized new handset. Mobile phone service providers typically provide handset subsidies ranging from US$50 to US$200 per unit, depending on the value

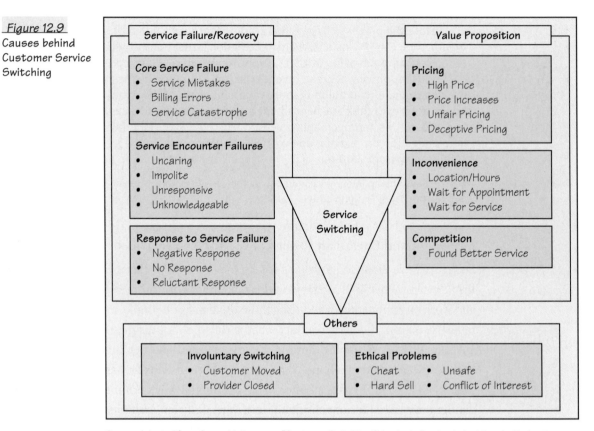

Source: Adapted from Susan M. Keaveney, "Customer Switching Behavior in Service Industries: An Exploratory Study," *Journal of Marketing* 59 (April 1995), 71–82.

Figure 12.9
Causes behind
Customer Service
Switching

of the subscription fee and the length of the contract. To prevent handset-related churn, many providers offer proactive handset replacement programs, where current subscribers can buy subsidized handsets from their providers at regular intervals, or even receive them for free when redeeming loyalty points earned on their mobile usage. Reactive retention measures include specially trained call center staff, so-called "save teams," which deal with customers who intend to cancel their accounts. Their main job is to listen to customer needs and issues, and try to address these with the key focus of retaining the customer.

So-called "churn alert systems" monitor the usage of individual customers and flag and trigger proactive retention efforts such as sending a voucher and/or having a customer service representative call the customer to check on the health of the customer relationship and initiate corrective action if needed.

Another way to reduce churn is to increase switching barriers.[34] Many services have natural switching costs (e.g., it is a lot of work for customers to change their primary banking account, especially when many direct debits, credits, and other related banking services are tied to that account).[35] However, some switching costs can be created by instituting contractual penalties for switching, such as the transfer fees levied by some brokerage firms for moving shares and bonds to another financial institution. However, firms need to be cautious so that they are not perceived as holding their customers hostage. A firm with high switching barriers and poor service quality is likely to generate negative attitudes and bad word of mouth.

Customer Relationship Management (CRM) Systems

Service marketers have understood for some time the power of relationship management, and certain industries have applied it for decades. Examples include the corner grocery store, the neighborhood car repair shop, and providers of banking services to high-net-worth clients.

Mention customer relationship management (CRM), and immediately costly and complex information technology (IT) systems and infrastructure, and CRM vendors such as SAP, Siebel Systems, PeopleSoft, and Oracle come to mind. However, CRM actually signifies the whole process by which relations with the customers are built and maintained.

Objectives of CRM Systems

Many firms have large numbers of customers (often millions), many different touch points (for instance, tellers, call center staff, self-service machines, and Web sites), at multiple geographic locations. At a single large facility, it's unlikely that a customer will be served by the same front-line staff on two consecutive visits. In such situations, managers historically lacked the tools to practice relationship marketing. Today however, CRM systems act as an enabler, capturing customer information, and delivering it to the various touch points.

From a customer perspective, well-implemented CRM systems can offer a "unified customer interface," which means that at each transaction, the relevant account details, knowledge of customer preferences and past transactions, or history of a service problem are at the fingertips of the person serving the customer. This can result in a vast service improvement.

From a company perspective, CRM systems allow the company to better understand, segment, and tier its customer base, better target promotions and cross-selling, and even implement churn-alert systems that signal if a customer was in danger of defecting.[36] Management Memo 12.3 highlights some common CRM applications.

Designing a CRM Strategy

Unfortunately, the majority of CRM implementations fail. According to the Gartner Group, the implementation failure rate is 55 percent and Accenture claims it to be around 60 percent. A key reason for this high failure rate is that firms often equate installing CRM systems with having a customer relationship strategy. They forget that the system is just a tool to enhance the firm's customer servicing capabilities,

Management
Memo 12.3

> ## COMMON CRM APPLICATIONS
>
> - *Data collection.* The system captures customer data such as contact details, demographics, purchasing history, service preferences, and the like.
> - *Data analysis.* The data captured is analyzed and categorized by the system according to criteria set by the firm. This is used to tier the customer base and tailor service delivery accordingly.
> - *Sales force automation.* Sales leads, cross-sell and up-sell opportunities can be effectively identified and processed, and the entire sales cycle from lead generation to close of sales and after-sales service can be tracked and facilitated through the CRM system.
> - *Marketing automation.* Mining of customer data enables the firm to target its market. A good CRM system enables the firm to achieve one-to-one marketing and cost savings. This results in increasing the return on investment (ROI) on its marketing expenditure. CRM systems also enable the assessment of the effectiveness of marketing campaigns through the analysis of responses.
> - *Call center automation.* Call center staff have customer information at their fingertips and can improve their service levels to all customers. Furthermore, caller ID and account numbers allow call centers to identify the customer tier the caller belongs to, and to tailor the service accordingly. For example, platinum callers get priority in waiting loops.

and is not the strategy itself. Seasoned McKinsey consultants believe that even CRM systems that have been implemented and have not yet been showing results can be well positioned for future success. They recommend taking a step back and focusing on how to build customer loyalty, rather than focusing on the technology itself.[37] Similarly, Rigby, Reichheld, and Schefter recommend focusing on the customer strategy and not the technology, posing the question:

> If your best customers knew that you planned to invest [US]$130 million to increase their loyalty …, how would they tell you to spend it? Would they want you to create a loyalty card or would they ask you to open more cash registers and keep enough milk in stock. The answer depends on the kind of company you are and the kinds of relationships you and your customers want to have with one another.[38]

Among the key questions managers should debate when defining their customer relationship strategy for a potential CRM system implementation are:

- How should our value proposition change to increase customer loyalty?
- How much customization or one-to-one marketing and service delivery is appropriate and profitable?
- What is the incremental profit potential of increasing the share of wallet with our current customers? How much does this vary by customer tier and/or segment?
- How much time and resources can we allocate to CRM right now?

- If we believe in customer relationship management, why haven't we taken more steps in that direction in the past? What can we do today to develop customer relationships without spending on technology?[39]

Answering these questions may lead to the conclusion that a CRM system may currently not be the best investment or highest priority, or that a scaled-down version may suffice to deliver the intended customer strategy. In any case, we emphasize that the system is merely a tool to drive the strategy, and must thus be tailored to deliver that strategy. See Management Memo 12.4 on ten steps to successful CRM strategy.

Management Memo 12.4

TEN STEPS TO SUCCESSFUL CRM STRATEGY

There are increasing numbers of organizations in Asia turning to CRM solutions to generate revenue growth, productivity, and customer satisfaction. So far, numerous organizations have achieved desirable results, for example, Genting Group, Hong Leong Bank, and Malaysia National Insurance. However, not all organizations reap the full benefits of the CRM strategies they have rolled out. Some encountered a drastic increase in costs, while others met integration difficulties and low acceptance level. Fortunately, these problems can be avoided if the CRM implementation is well designed and executed.

Here is a list of ten critical success factors to follow for effective design and implementation of CRM systems:

1. Establish measurable business goals, and clarify the exact objectives to be achieved with the CRM solution. This is important because there are different CRM solutions for different objectives, and hence companies must prioritize what they want and choose their CRM technology accordingly.
2. Technology is only a means to achieve the desired goals. Therefore, in order to implement CRM successfully, both the business sponsors and technical personnel must share the responsibility of designing and implementing the system.
3. Get executive support up-front, as CRM projects are strategic initiatives. Therefore, they must get active support from top management. Employees can view a CRM implementation as a fad if top management, including the CEO, does not deliver the message personally and forcefully.
4. Let business goals drive functionality. If a feature of the CRM system does not generate obvious and direct benefits to the company, e.g., helping the company to serve its customers better, do not include such a feature in the configuration decision. Always insist on functionalities that enhance the employees' ability to serve their customers.
5. Minimize customizations, as they are often costly and time consuming, and are a complex component of a CRM implementation.
6. Use trained and experienced consultants who are well-trained and certified by the software providers, as this will help to save time and money.
7. Actively involve end users in the solution design to reduce the possibility of confusion and alienation with the CRM system. The end users are the only people who can tell the engineering department the features of a user-friendly and helpful CRM system.

8. Invest in training to empower end users, as providing sufficient and necessary training is critical to success in CRM implementation. The training should not only focus on demonstrating the features and functionality of the CRM systems, but also on how to effectively execute business processes enabled by the CRM system. Since the implementation of a CRM system also represents a change in operation procedures, training should include "change management" and adaptation to new procedures.

9. Use a phased roll-out schedule, as it enables users to learn step by step. Most successful CRM projects follow a deployment schedule, and each phase is focused on a specific CRM objective or function, and is designed to obtain certain desirable outcomes in a reasonable amount of time.

10. Measure, monitor, and track the system's effectiveness with the thought of increasing its performance continuously. Companies that benefit the most from CRM applications usually set benchmarks for their business processes, identify the performance metrics against those processes and measure the effect of the CRM application on the metrics. It is also important for companies to survey their customers periodically to determine the impact of the CRM solution on customers' attitudes, behavior, and satisfaction.

Source: Adapted from Terrance Chan, Siebel System Inc's Regional Managing Director for East Asia, "10 Steps to CRM Success," *New Straits Times* (Malaysia), May 7, 2003.

Conclusion

Many elements are involved in gaining market share and increasing share of wallet, cross-selling other products and services to existing customers, and creating long-term loyalty. The process starts by identifying and targeting the right customers, then learning about their needs, including their preferences for different forms of service delivery. Translating this knowledge into service delivery, tiered service levels, and customer relationship strategies are the key steps toward achieving customer loyalty.

Marketers need to pay special attention to those customers who offer the firm the greatest value since they purchase its products with the greatest frequency and spend the most on premium services. Programs to reward frequent users—of which the most highly developed are the frequent flyer clubs created by the airlines—identify and provide rewards for high-value customers and facilitate tiered service delivery. They also enable marketers to track the behavior of high-value customers in terms of where and when they use the service, what service classes or types of product they buy, and how much they spend.

Review Questions

1. Why is targeting the "right customers" so important for successful customer relationship management?
2. How can you estimate a customer's life time value (LTV)?

3. Explain what is meant by a customer portfolio. How should a firm decide what is the most appropriate mix of customers to have?

4. What criteria should a marketing manager use to decide which of several possible segments should be targeted by the firm?

5. What is tiering of services?

6. Identify some key measures that can be used to create customer bonds and encourage long-term relationships with customers.

7. What are the arguments for spending money to keep existing customers loyal?

8. What is the role of CRM in delivering a customer relationship strategy?

Application Exercises

1. Identify three service businesses that you patronize on a regular basis. Now, for each business, complete the following sentence: "I am loyal to this business because _____."

2. What conclusions do you draw about (a) yourself as a consumer, and (b) the performance of each of the businesses? Assess whether any of these businesses managed to develop a sustainable competitive advantage through the way it won your loyalty.

3. Identify two service businesses that you used several times but have now ceased to patronize (or plan to stop patronizing soon) because you were dissatisfied. Complete the sentence: "I stopped using (or will soon stop using) this organization as a customer because _____."

4. Again, what conclusions do you draw about yourself and the firms in question? How could each of these firms potentially avoid your defection? What could each of these firms do to avoid defection of customers with a similar profile to yours?

5. Evaluate the strengths and weaknesses of frequent user programs in different service industries.

6. Design a questionnaire and conduct a survey asking about two loyalty programs. The first is about a membership/loyalty program your classmates or their families like best and which makes them loyal to that firm. The second is about a loyalty program that is not well perceived, and does not seem to add value to the customer. Use open-ended questions, such as "What motivated you to sign up in the first place?" "Why are you using this program?" "Has participating in the program changed your purchasing/usage behavior in any way?" "Has it made you less likely to use competing suppliers?" "What do you think of the rewards available?" "Did membership in the program lead to any immediate benefits in the use of the service?", "What role does the loyalty program play in making you loyal?" "What are the three things you like best about this loyalty/membership program?" "What are the three things you like least about this loyalty/ membership program?" and "Suggest improvements to the service." Analyze what features make loyalty/ membership programs successful, and what features do not achieve the desired results. Use frameworks such as the Wheel of Loyalty to guide your analysis and presentation.

Endnotes

1   Steven S. Ramsey, "Introduction: Strategy First, then CRM," in *The Ultimate CRM Handbook—Strategies and Concepts for Building Enduring Customer Loyalty and Profitability*, ed. John G. Freeland (New York: McGraw-Hill, 2002), 13.

2   Richard L. Oliver, "Whence Consumer Loyalty?" *Journal of Marketing* 63 (Special issue, 1999): 33–44.

3   Frederick F. Reichheld and Thomas Teal, *The Loyalty Effect* (Boston, MA: Harvard Business School Press, 1996).

4   Ruth Bolton, Katherine N. Lemon, and Peter C. Verhoef, "The Theoretical Underpinnings of Customer Asset Management: A Framework and Propositions for Future Research," *Journal of the Academy of Marketing Science* 32, no. 3 (2004): 271–292.

5   Frederick F. Reichheld and W. Earl Sasser, Jr., "Zero Defections: Quality Comes to Services," *Harvard Business Review* (October 1990): 105–111.

6   *Ibid.*

7   Frederick F. Reichheld and Phil Schefter, "E-Loyalty—Your Secret Weapon on the Web," *Harvard Business Review* (July–August, 2002): 105–113.

8   Grahame R. Dowling and Mark Uncles, "Do Customer Loyalty Programmes Really Work?' *Sloan Management Review* (Summer 1997): 71–81; Werner Reinartz and V. Kumar, "The Mismanagement of Customer Loyalty," *Harvard Business Review* (July 2002): 86–94.

9   Werner J. Reinartz and V. Kumar, "On the Profitability of Long-Life Customers in a Noncontractual Setting: An Empirical Investigation and Implications for Marketing," *Journal of Marketing* 64 (October 2000): 17–35.

10   John E. Hogan, Katherine N. Lemon, and Barak Libai, "What is the True Cost of a Lost Customer?" *Journal of Services Research* 5, no. 3 (2003): 196–208.

11   For a discussion on how to evaluate the customer base of a firm, see Sunil Gupta, Donald R. Lehmann, and Jennifer Ames Stuart, "Valuing Customers," *Journal of Marketing Research* XLI, no.1 (2004): 7–18.

12   Alan W. H. Grant and Leonard H. Schlesinger, "Realize Your Customer's Full Profit Potential," *Harvard Business Review* 73 (September–October, 1995): 59–75.

13   Nicole E. Coviello, Roderick J. Brodie, and Hugh J. Munro, "Understanding Contemporary Marketing: Development of a Classification Scheme," *Journal of Marketing Management* 13, no. 6 (1995): 501–522.

14   J. R. Copulsky and M. J. Wolf, "Relationship Marketing: Positioning for the Future," *Journal of Business Strategy* 11, no. 4 (1990): 16–20.

15   Evert Gummesson, *Total Relationship Marketing* (Oxford: Butterworth-Heinemann, 1999), 24.

16   It has even been suggested to let "chronically dissatisfied customer go to allow front-line staff to focus on satisfying the 'right' customers," see Ka-shing Woo and Henry K. Y. Fock, "Retaining and Divesting Customers: An Exploratory Study of Right Customers, 'At-Risk' Right Customers, and Wrong Customers," *Journal of Services Marketing* 18, no. 3 (2004): 187–197.

17   Frederick F. Reichheld, *Loyalty Rules—How Today's Leaders Build Lasting Relationships* (Boston, MA: Harvard Business School Press, 2001), 45.

18   Roger Hallowell, "The Relationships of Customer Satisfaction, Customer Loyalty, and Profitability: An Empirical Study," *International Journal of Service Industry Management* 7, no. 4 (1996): 27–42.

19   Leonard L. Berry, *Discovering the Soul of Service—The Nine Drivers of Sustainable Success* (New York: The Free Press, 1999), 148–149.

20   Reichheld, 2001, *op.cit.*, 43, 84–85.

21   David H. Maister, *True Professionalism* (New York: The Free Press, 1997). (See especially Chapter 20.)

22   Valarie A. Zeithaml, Roland T. Rust, and Katharine N. Lemon, "The Customer Pyramid: Creating and Serving Profitable Customers," *California Management Review* 43, no. 4 (Summer 2001):118.

23   *Ibid.*

24   Piyush Kumar, "The Impact of Long-Term Client Relationships on the Performance of Business Service Firms," *Journal of Service Research* 2 (August 1999): 4–18.

25   Not only is there a positive relationship between satisfaction and share of wallet, but the greatest positive impact is seen at the upper extreme levels of satisfaction. For details, refer to Timothy L. Keinngham and Tiffany Perkins-Munn, "The Impact of Customer Satisfaction on Share of Wallet in a Business-to-Business Environment," *Journal of Service Research* 6, no. 1 (2003): 37–50.

26   Valarie A. Zeithaml and Mary Jo Bitner, *Services Marketing*. 3rd ed. (New York: McGraw-Hill, 2003), 175; Leonard L. Berry and A. Parasuraman, "Three Levels of Relationship Marketing," in *Marketing Service—Competing through Quality* (New York: The Free Press, 1991), 136–142.

27   Barbara Bund Jackson, "Build Relationships that Last," *Harvard Business Review* (November–December 1985):120–128.

28   http://www.thailandelite.com (accessed on July 11, 2004).

29   Don Peppers and Martha Rogers, *The One-to-One Manager* (New York: Currency Doubleday, 1999).

30   Ruth N. Bolton, P. K. Kannan, and Matthew D. Bramlett, "Implications of Loyalty Program Membership and Service Experience for Customer Retention and Value," *Journal of the Academy of Marketing Science* 28, no. 1 (2000): 95–108. For a recent study on how reward schemes affect customer perceptions and loyalty, also see Youjae Yi and Hoseong Jeon, "Effects of Loyalty Programs on Value Perception, Program Loyalty, and Brand Loyalty," *Journal of the Academy of Marketing Science* 31, no. 3 (2003): 229–240.

31   Dowling and Uncles, 1997, *loc. cit.*, 74.

32   For a more detailed discussion of situation-specific switching behavior, refer to Inger Roos, Bo Edvardsson, and Anders Gustafsson, "Customer Switching Patterns in Competitive and Noncompetitive Service Industries," *Journal of Service Research* 6, no. 3 (2004): 256–271.

33   Susan M. Keaveney, "Customer Switching Behavior in Service Industries: An Exploratory Study," *Journal of Marketing* 59 (April 1995): 71–82.

34   Jonathan Lee, Janghyuk Lee, and Lawrence Feick, "The Impact of Switching Costs on the Consumer Satisfaction-Loyalty Link: Mobile Phone Service in France," *Journal of Services Marketing* 15, no. 1 (2001): 35–48.

35   Moonkyu Lee and Lawrence F. Cunningham, "A Cost/Benefit Approach to Understanding Loyalty," *Journal of Services Marketing* 15, no. 2 (2001): 113–130.

36   Kevin N. Quiring and Nancy K. Mullen, "More Than Data Warehousing: An Integrated View of the Customer," in *The Ultimate CRM Handbook—Strategies and Concepts for Building Enduring Customer Loyalty and Profitability*, ed. John G. Freeland (New York: McGraw-Hill, 2002), 102–108.

37   Manuel Ebner, Arthur Hu, Daniel Levitt, and Jim McCrory, "How to Rescue CRM?" *The McKinsey Quarterly* 4, (Technology, 2002).

38   Darrell K. Rigby, Frederick F. Reichheld, and Phil Schefter, "Avoid the Four Perils of CRM," *Harvard Business Review* 80 (February 2002): 108.

39   Rigby, Reichheld, and Schefter, "Avoid the Four Perils of CRM," 103.

CHAPTER THIRTEEN

Customer Feedback and Service Recovery

One of the surest signs of a bad or declining relationship is the absence of complaints from the customer. Nobody is ever that satisfied, especially not over an extended period of time.

THEODORE LEVITT

To err is human; to recover, divine.

CHRISTOPHER W. L. HART, JAMES L. HESKETT
AND W. EARL SASSER JR.

The first law of service productivity and quality might be: "Do it right the first time," but we cannot ignore the fact that failures continue to occur, sometimes for reasons outside the organization's control. Various "moments of truth" in service encounters are vulnerable to breakdowns. Such distinctive service characteristics as real-time performance, customer involvement, and people as part of the product greatly increase the chance of service failures. How well a firm handles complaints and resolves problems may determine whether it builds customer loyalty or watches former customers take their business elsewhere.

In this chapter, we explore the following questions:

1. Why do customers complain and what do they expect from the firm?
2. How should an effective service recovery strategy be designed?
3. Under what circumstances should firms offer service guarantees, and is it wise to make them unconditional?
4. How should firms and their front-line staff respond to abusive and/or opportunistic customers?
5. How can organizations institutionalize systematic and continuous learning from customer feedback?

Customer Complaining Behavior

Chances are that you will not be satisfied with at least some of the services you receive. How do you respond to your dissatisfaction with this service? Do you complain informally to an employee, ask to speak to the manager, or file a complaint? If not, perhaps you just mutter darkly to yourself, grumble to your friends and family, and the next time you need a similar type of service, choose an alternative supplier.

If you are among those who do not complain about poor service, then you are not alone. Research around the globe has shown that most people will not complain, especially if they think it will do no good.

Customer Response Options to Service Failures

Figure 13.1 depicts the courses of action a customer may take in response to a service failure. This model suggests at least three major courses of action:

1. Take some form of public action (including complaining to the firm or to a third party such as a customer advocacy group, customer affairs or regulatory agency, or even civil or criminal courts).
2. Take some form of private action (including abandoning the supplier).
3. Take no action.

Figure 13.1
Customer Response Categories to Service Failures

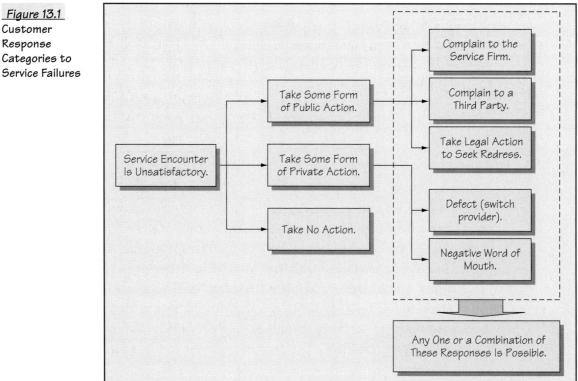

It is important to remember that any one or a combination of any of the alternatives may be pursued by the customer. Managers need to be aware that the impact of a defection can go far beyond the loss of that person's future revenue stream. Angry customers often tell many other people about their problems.[1] The Internet allows unhappy customers to reach thousands of people by posting complaints on bulletin boards or setting up Web sites to publicize their bad experiences with specific organizations.[2]

Understanding Customer Responses to Service Failures

To be able to effectively deal with dissatisfied and complaining customers, managers need to understand key aspects of complaining behavior, starting with the questions posed below.

WHY DO CUSTOMERS COMPLAIN?   In general, studies of consumer complaining behavior have identified four main purposes for complaining.

- *Obtain restitution or compensation.* Often, consumers complain to recover some economic loss by seeking a refund, compensation, and/or have the service performed again.
- *Vent their anger.* Some customers complain to rebuild self-esteem and/or to vent their anger and frustration. When service processes are bureaucratic and unreasonable, or when employees are rude, deliberately intimidating, or apparently uncaring, the customers' self-esteem, self-worth, or sense of fairness can be negatively affected. They may become angry and emotional.
- *Help to improve the service.* When customers are highly involved with a service (e.g., at a college, an alumni association, or their main banking connection), they give feedback to try and contribute toward service improvements.
- *For altruistic reasons.* Finally, some customers are motivated by altruistic reasons. They want to spare other customers from experiencing the same problems, and they might feel bad if a problem is not highlighted.

WHAT PROPORTION OF UNHAPPY CUSTOMERS COMPLAIN?   Research shows that on average, only 5 to 10 percent of customers who have been unhappy with a service actually complain.[3] Sometimes the percentage is far lower. One of the authors of this book analyzed the complaints received by a public bus company in an Asian country, which occurred at the rate of about three complaints for every million passenger trips. Assuming two trips a day, it would take a person 1,370 years (roughly 27 lifetimes) to make a million trips. In other words, the rate of complaints was incredibly low, given that public bus companies are usually not known for good service. However, although generally only a minority of dissatisfied customers complain, there is evidence that consumers across the world are becoming better informed, more self-confident, and more assertive about seeking satisfactory outcomes for their complaints.

WHY DON'T UNHAPPY CUSTOMERS COMPLAIN?   TARP, a customer satisfaction and measurement firm, has identified a number of reasons why customers don't complain.[4] They don't wish to take the time to write a letter, fill out a form, or make a phone call, especially if they don't see the service as sufficiently important to merit the effort. Many customers see the payoff as uncertain and believe that no one would be concerned about their problem or be willing to resolve it. In some situations, people simply do not know where to go or what to do. Additionally, many people feel that complaining is unpleasant. They may be afraid of confrontation, especially if the complaint involves someone whom the customer knows and may have to deal with again.

Complaining behavior can be influenced by role perceptions and social norms. In services where customers have "low power" (defined as the perceived ability to influence or control the transaction), they are less likely to voice complaints.[5] This is particularly true when the problem involves professional service providers, such as doctors, lawyers, or architects (see Figure 13.2). Social norms tend to discourage customer criticism of such individuals, because of their perceived expertise.

Figure 13.2

Patients often hesitate to complain about professional service providers.

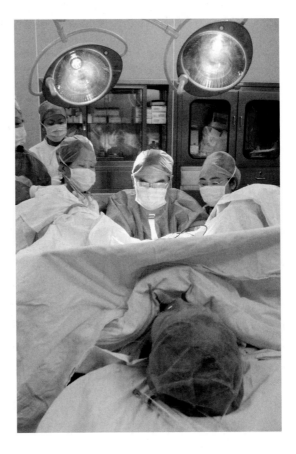

WHO IS MOST LIKELY TO COMPLAIN?   Research findings consistently show that people in higher socioeconomic levels are more likely to complain than those in lower levels. Their better education, higher income, and greater social involvement give them the confidence, knowledge, and motivation to speak up when they encounter problems.[6] Also, those who complain tend to be more knowledgeable about the products in question.

WHERE DO CUSTOMERS COMPLAIN?   Studies show that the majority of complaints are made at the place where the service was received. One of the authors of this book has just completed a consulting project developing and implementing a customer feedback system and found that, astoundingly, 99 percent plus of customer feedback was given face to face or over the phone to customer service representatives. Only less than 1 percent of all complaints were submitted via email, letters, faxes, or customer feedback cards. A survey of airline passengers found that only 3 percent of respondents who were unhappy with their meal actually complained about it, and they all complained to the flight attendant! None complained to the company's headquarters or to a consumer affairs office.[7] Also, customers tend to use noninteractive channels to complain (e.g., email or letters) when they mainly want to vent their anger and frustration, but resort to interactive channels such as face to face or the telephone when they want a problem to be fixed or redressed.[8]

In practice, even when customers do complain, managers often do not hear about the complaints made to front-line staff, and less than 5 percent of the complaints reach corporate headquarters.[9]

What Do Customers Expect Once They Have Made a Complaint?

Whenever there is a service failure, people expect that they be adequately compensated in a fair manner. However, recent studies have shown that many customers feel that they were not treated fairly and did not receive adequate justice. When this happens, customer reactions tend to be immediate, emotional, and enduring.[10]

Tax and Brown found that as much as 85 percent of the variation in the satisfaction with a service recovery was determined by three dimensions of fairness shown in Figure 13.3.[11]

Procedural justice concerns the policies and rules that any customer will have to go through in order to seek fairness. Here, customers expect the firm to assume responsibility, which is the key to the start of a fair procedure, followed by a convenient and responsive recovery process. That includes flexibility of the system, and consideration of customer inputs into the recovery process.

Interactional justice involves the employees of the firm who provide the service recovery and their behavior toward the customer. Providing an explanation for the

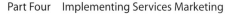

Figure 13.3

Three Dimensions of Perceived Fairness in Service Recovery Processes

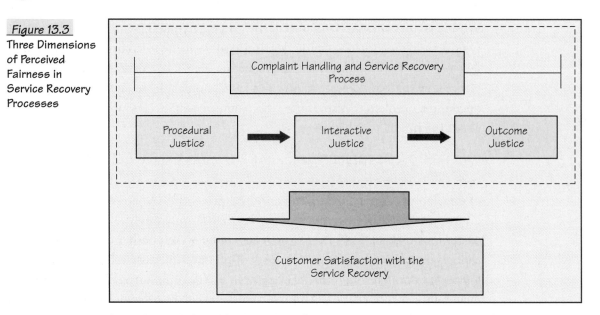

Source: Stephen S. Tax and Stephen W. Brown, "Recovering and Learning from Service Failure," *Sloan Management Review* 49, no. 1 (Fall 1998): 75–88. Reprinted by permission of publisher. Copyright © 2003 by Massachusetts Institute of Technology. All rights reserved.

failure and making effort to resolve the problem are very important. However, the recovery effort must be perceived as genuine, honest, and polite.

Outcome justice concerns the compensation that a customer receives as a result of the losses and inconveniences incurred due to the service failure. This includes compensation not only for the service failure, but also for the time, effort, and energy spent during the process of service recovery.[12]

Customer Responses to Effective Service Recovery

"Thank Heavens for Complainers" was the provocative title of an article about customer complaining behavior, which also featured a successful manager exclaiming, "Thank goodness I've got a dissatisfied customer on the phone! The ones I worry about are the ones I never hear from."[13] Customers who do complain give a firm the chance to correct problems (including some the firm may not even know it has), restore relationships with the complainer, and improve future satisfaction for all.

Service recovery is an umbrella term for systematic efforts by a firm to correct a problem following a service failure and to retain a customer's goodwill. Service recovery efforts play a crucial role in achieving (or restoring) customer satisfaction.[14] In every organization, things may occur that have a negative impact on its relationships with customers. The true test of a firm's commitment to satisfaction and service *quality* isn't in the advertising promises, but in the way it responds when things go wrong for the customer.

Effective service recovery requires thoughtful procedures for resolving problems and handling disgruntled customers. It is critical for firms to have effective recovery strategies, because even a single service problem can destroy a customer's confidence in a firm under the following conditions:

- The failure is totally outrageous (for instance, blatant dishonesty on the part of the supplier).
- The problem fits a pattern of failure, rather than being an isolated incident.
- The recovery efforts are weak, serving to compound the original problem rather than correct it.[15]

The risk of defection is high, especially when there are a variety of competing alternatives available. One study of customer switching behavior in service industries found that close to 60 percent of all respondents who reported changing suppliers did so because of a service failure: 25 percent cited failures in the core service, 19 percent reported an unsatisfactory encounter with an employee, 10 percent reported an unsatisfactory response to a prior service failure, and 4 percent described unethical behavior on the part of the provider.[16]

Impact of Effective Service Recovery on Customer Loyalty

When complaints are satisfactorily resolved, there is a much higher chance that the customers involved will remain loyal. TARP research found that intentions to repurchase for different types of products ranged from 9 percent to 37 percent when customers were dissatisfied but did not complain. For a major complaint, the retention rate increased from 9 percent to 19 percent if customers complained and the company offered a sympathetic ear, but was unable to resolve the complaint to the satisfaction of the customer. If the complaint could be resolved to the satisfaction of the customer, retention rate jumped to 54 percent. The highest retention rate of 82 percent was achieved when problems were fixed quickly, typically on the spot.

The conclusion to be drawn is that complaint handling should be seen as a profit center and not a cost center. When a dissatisfied customer defects, the firm loses more than just the value of the next transaction. It may also lose a long-term stream of profits from that customer, and from anyone else who switches suppliers or is deterred from doing business with that firm, because of negative comments from an unhappy friend. However, as can be seen in Management Memo 13.1, there are managers who have not bought into the concept that it pays to invest in service recovery designed to protect those long-term profits.

The Service Recovery Paradox

The service recovery paradox refers to the sometimes observed effect that customers who experience a service failure and then have it resolved to their full satisfaction are more likely to make future purchases than customers who have no problem in the first place.[17] A study of repeated service failures in a retail banking context

*Management
Memo 13.1*

COMMON SERVICE RECOVERY MISTAKES

Here are some typical service recovery mistakes made by many organizations:

- *Managers disregard evidence that shows that service recovery provides a significant financial return.* In recent years, many organizations have focused on cost cutting, and only paid lip service to retaining their most profitable customers. On top of that, they also lost sight of the need to respect all their customers.
- *Companies do not invest enough in actions that would prevent service issues.* Ideally, service planners address potential problems before they become customer problems. Although preventive measures do not eliminate the need for good service recovery systems, they greatly reduce the burden on front-line staff and the service recovery systems.
- *Customer service staff fail to display good attitudes.* The three most important things in service recovery are attitude, attitude, and attitude. No matter how well designed and well-planned the service recovery system is, it will not work without the friendly and proverbial smile-in-the-voice attitude from front-line staff.
- *Organizations fail to make it easy for customers to complain or give feedback.* Although some improvement can be seen, such as hotels and restaurants offering comment cards, little is done to communicate their simplicity and value to customers. Research shows that a large proportion of customers complain that they are unaware of the existence of a proper feedback system that could help them get their problems solved.

Source: Adapted from Rod Stiefbold, "Dissatisfied Customers Require Service Recovery Plans," *Marketing News* 37, issue 22 (October 27, 2003): 44–45.

showed that the service recovery paradox held for the first service failure that was recovered to customers' full satisfaction.[18] However, when a second service failure occurred, the paradox disappeared. It seems that customers may forgive a firm once, but get disillusioned if failures recur. Furthermore, the study also showed that customers' expectations were raised after they experienced a very good recovery, with the result that the excellent recovery becomes the standard they expect for dealing with future failures.

Some recent studies have challenged the existence of the service recovery paradox. For example, Andreassen conducted a major study with some 8,600 telephone interviews across a wide range of consumer services. The findings showed that after a service recovery, customers' intention to repurchase, and their perceptions of and attitudes toward the company never surpassed the ratings of satisfied customers who did not experience a service problem in the first place. This was true even when the service recovery had gone very well and the customer expressed full satisfaction with the recovery.[19]

Whether a customer comes out delighted from a service recovery probably also depends on the severity and "recoverability" of the failure—no one can replace spoilt wedding photos, a ruined holiday, or an injury caused by some service equipment. In such situations, it is hard to imagine anyone being truly delighted even when a most professional service recovery is conducted. The best strategy is to do it right the first time. As Michael Hargrove puts it: "Service recovery is turning a service failure into an opportunity you wish you never had." It is critical that service recovery is well executed, but failures cannot be tolerated. Unfortunately, empirical evidence shows that a large proportion of customers are dissatisfied with the outcome of their complaints. In recent studies, some 40 to 60 percent of customers reported dissatisfaction with the service recovery process.[20]

Principles of Effective Service Recovery Systems

Recognizing that current customers are a valuable asset base, managers need to develop effective procedures for service recovery from unsatisfactory experiences. We discuss three guiding principles for how to do this well: Make it easy for customers to give feedback, enable effective service recovery, and establish appropriate compensation levels. Figure 13.4 displays the components of an effective service recovery system.

Make It Easy for Customers to Give Feedback

How can managers overcome unhappy customers' reluctance to complain about service failures? The best way is to directly address the reasons for their reluctance. Table 13.1 provides an overview of potential measures that can be taken to overcome

Figure 13.4
Components of an Effective Service Recovery System

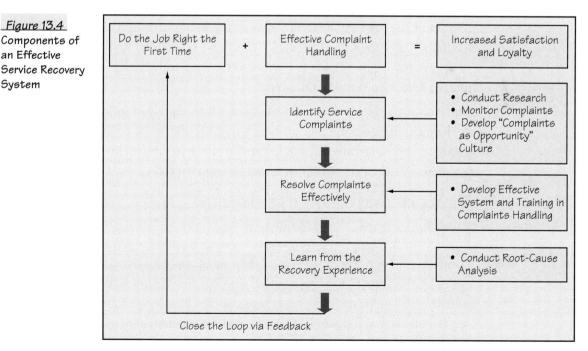

Source: Adapted from Christopher H. Lovelock, Paul G. Patterson, and Rhett Walker, *Services Marketing: Australia and New Zealand* (Sydney: Prentice Hall Australia, 1998), 455.

Table 13.1
Strategies to Reduce Customer Complaint Barriers

Complaint Barriers for Dissatisfied Customers	Strategies to Reduce These Barriers
Inconvenience • Difficult to find the right complaint procedure. • Effort, e.g., writing and mailing a letter.	Make feedback easy and convenient: • Print customer service hotline numbers, and email and postal addresses on all customer communications materials (letters, faxes, bills, brochures, phone book listing, yellow pages, etc.).
Doubtful Payoff • Uncertain whether any or what action will be taken by the firm to address the issue the customer is unhappy with.	Reassure customers that their feedback will be taken seriously and will pay off: • Have service recovery procedures in place and communicate this to customers, e.g., in customer newsletter and Web site. • Feature service improvements that resulted from customer feedback.
Unpleasantness • Fear of being treated rudely. • Fear of being hassled. • Feeling embarrassed.	Make providing feedback a positive experience: • Thank customers for their feedback (can be done publicly and in general by addressing the entire customer base). • Train the front line not to hassle and make customers feel comfortable. • Allow for anonymous feedback.

the reasons we had identified earlier in this chapter. Many companies have improved their complaint collection procedures by adding special toll-free phone lines, links on their Web sites, prominently displayed customer comment cards in their branches, and even providing video terminals for recording complaints. In their customer newsletter, they feature service improvements that were the direct result of customer feedback under the motto "you told us, and we responded."

Enable Effective Service Recovery

Recovering from service failures takes more than just pious expressions of determination to resolve any problems that may occur. It requires commitment, planning, and clear guidelines. Specifically, effective service recovery should be (1) proactive, (2) planned, (3) trained, and (4) empowered.

SERVICE RECOVERY SHOULD BE PROACTIVE   Service recovery needs to be initiated on the spot, ideally before customers have a chance to complain (see Best Practice in Action 13.1). Service personnel should be sensitized to signs of dissatisfaction and ask customers if they might be experiencing a problem. For example, the waiter may ask a guest who has only eaten half of his dinner, "Is everything all right, sir?" The guest may say, "Yes, thank you, I am not very hungry." or "The steak is well done, but I had asked for medium-rare, plus it is very salty." The latter response then gives the waiter a chance to recover the service, rather than have an unhappy diner leave the restaurant and potentially not return.

EFFECTIVE SERVICE RECOVERY IN ACTION

The lobby is deserted. It is not hard to overhear the conversation between the night manager at the Marriott Long Wharf Hotel in Boston and the late arriving guest.

"Yes, Dr Jones, we've been expecting you. I know you are scheduled to be here three nights. I'm sorry to tell you, sir, but we are booked solid tonight. A large number of guests we assumed were checking out did not. Where is your meeting tomorrow, sir?"

The doctor told the clerk where it was.

"That's near the Omni Parker House! That's not very far from here. Let me call them and get you a room for the evening. I'll be right back."

A few minutes later the desk clerk returned with the good news.

"They're holding a room for you at the Omni Parker House, sir. And, of course, we'll pick up the tab. I'll forward any phone calls that come here for you. Here's a letter that will explain the situation and expedite your check-in, along with my business card so you can call me directly here at the front desk if you have any problems."

The doctor's mood was moving from exasperation toward calm. But the desk clerk was not finished with the encounter. He reached into the cash drawer. "Here are two US$5 bills. That should more than cover your cab fare from here to the Parker House and back again in the morning. We don't have a problem tomorrow night, just tonight. And here's a coupon that will get you complimentary continental breakfast on our concierge level on the fifth floor tomorrow morning … and again, I am so sorry this happened."

As the doctor walks away, the night manager turns to the desk clerk, "Give him about 15 minutes and then call to make sure everything went okay."

A week later when it was still a peak period for hotels in that city, the same guest who had overheard the exchange is in a taxi, en route to the same hotel. Along the way, he tells about the great service recovery episode he had witnessed the week before. The pair arrived at the hotel and made their way to the front desk, ready to check in.

They are greeted with unexpected news: "I am so sorry gentlemen. I know you were scheduled here for two nights. But we are booked solid tonight. Where is your meeting scheduled tomorrow?"

The would-be guests exchange a rueful glance as they give the desk clerk their future plans. "That's near the Meridian. Let me call over there and see if I can get you a room. It won't but take a minute." As the clerk walks away, the tale teller says, "I'll bet he comes back with a letter and a business card."

Sure enough, the desk clerk returns to deliver the solution; not a robotic script but all the elements from the previous week's show were on display. What the tale teller thought he witnessed the previous week was pure desk-clerk initiative, he now realized was planned, a spontaneous-feeling yet predetermined response to a specific category of customer problem.

Source: Ron Zemke and Chip R. Bell, *Knock Your Socks off Service Recovery* (New York: AMACOM, 2000), 59–60.

RECOVERY PROCEDURES NEED TO BE PLANNED   Contingency plans have to be developed for service failures, especially for those that can occur regularly and cannot be designed out of the system. Revenue management practices in the travel and hospitality industries often result in overbooking. To simplify the task of front-line staff, firms should identify the most common service problems and develop predetermined solution sets for employees to follow.

RECOVERY SKILLS MUST BE TAUGHT   Customers feel insecure easily at the point of service failure because things are not turning out as anticipated. Effective training arms front-line staff with the confidence and competence to turn distress into delight.[21]

RECOVERY REQUIRES EMPOWERED EMPLOYEES   Service recovery efforts should be flexible and employees should be empowered to use their judgment and communication skills to develop solutions that will satisfy complaining customers.[22] This is especially true for out-of-the-ordinary failures where a firm may not have developed and trained potential solution sets. Employees need to have the authority to make decisions and spend money in order to resolve service problems promptly and recover customer goodwill.

How Generous Should Compensation Be?

Clearly, there are vastly different costs associated with possible recovery strategies. How much compensation should a firm offer when there has been a service failure? Or would an apology be sufficient instead? The following rules of thumb can help to answer these questions:

- *What is the positioning of your firm?* If a firm is known for service excellence, and charges a high premium for quality, then customers will expect service failures to be rare, so the firm should make a demonstrable effort to recover the few failures that do occur and be prepared to offer something of significant value. However, in a more downscale, mass-market business, customers are likely to consider something quite modest, such as a free coffee or dessert as fair compensation.

- *How severe was the service failure?* The general guideline is "let the punishment fit the crime." Customers expect less for minor inconveniences, and a much more significant compensation if major damage in terms of time, effort, annoyance, anxiety, etc., was caused on the customer's side.

- *Who is the affected customer?* Long-term customers and those who spend heavily at a service provider expect more and it is worth making an effort to save their business. Once-off customers tend to be less demanding, and have less economic importance to the firm. Hence, compensation can be less, but should still be fair. There is always the possibility that a first-time user will become a repeat customer if treated fairly. The overall rule of thumb for compensation at service failures should be "well-dosed generosity." Being perceived as stingy adds insult to injury, and the firm would probably be better off just apologizing than offering a minimal compensation.

Overly generous compensation is not only expensive but may even be negatively interpreted by customers.[23] It may raise questions about the soundness of the business and lead customers to become suspicious about the underlying motives. Customers may worry about the implications for the employee as well as for the business. Also, overgenerosity does not seem to result in higher repeat purchase rates than simply offering a fair compensation.[24] There is also the risk that a reputation for overgenerosity might encourage dishonest customers to "seek" service failures.

Guidelines for Employees on Dealing with Complaining Customers

Both managers and front-line employees must be prepared to deal with angry customers who are confrontational and sometimes behave in insulting ways toward service personnel who aren't at fault in any way. Management Memo 13.2 provides specific guidelines for effective problem resolution, designed to help calm upset customers and to deliver a resolution that they will see as fair and satisfying.

Service Guarantees

A growing number of companies offer customers a satisfaction guarantee, promising that if service delivery fails to meet predefined standards, the customer is entitled to one or more forms of compensation, such as an easy-to-claim replacement, refund, or credit. Some firms place conditions on these guarantees, while others offer them unconditionally.

The Power of Service Guarantees

Christopher Hart argues that service guarantees are powerful tools for both promoting and achieving service quality for the following reasons:[25]

1. Guarantees force firms to focus on what their customers want and expect in each element of the service.
2. Guarantees set clear standards, telling customers and employees alike what the company stands for. Payouts to compensate customers for poor service cause managers to take guarantees seriously, because they highlight the financial costs of quality failures.
3. Guarantees require the development of systems for generating meaningful customer feedback and acting on it.

Management
Memo 13.2

GUIDELINES FOR THE FRONT LINE:
HOW TO HANDLE CUSTOMER COMPLAINTS

1. *Act fast.* If the complaint is made during service delivery, then time is of the essence to achieve a full recovery. When complaints are made after the fact, many companies have established policies of responding within 24 hours, or sooner. Even when full resolution is likely to take longer, fast acknowledgment remains very important.

2. *Acknowledge the customer's feelings*, either tacitly or explicitly (for example, "I can understand why you're upset"). This action helps to build rapport, the first step in rebuilding a bruised relationship.

3. *Don't argue with customers.* The goal should be to gather facts to reach a mutually acceptable solution, not to win a debate or prove that the customer is an idiot. Arguing gets in the way of listening and seldom diffuses anger.

4. *Show that you understand the problem from each customer's point of view.* Seeing situations through the customers' eyes is the only way to understand what they think has gone wrong and why they are upset. Service personnel should avoid jumping to conclusions with their own interpretations.

5. *Clarify the truth and sort out the cause.* A failure may result from inefficiency of service, misunderstanding by customers, or the misbehavior of a third party. If you have done wrong, apologize immediately in order to win the understanding and trust of the customer. The more the customer can forgive you, the less he or she expects to be compensated. Do not be defensive. Acting defensively may suggest that the organization has something to hide or is reluctant to fully explore the situation.

6. *Consider compensation.* When customers do not receive the service outcomes that they have paid for or have suffered serious inconvenience and/or loss of time and money because the service failed, either a monetary payment or an offer of equivalent service in kind is appropriate. This type of recovery strategy may also reduce the risk of legal action by an angry customer. Service guarantees often lay out in advance what such compensation will be, and the firm should ensure that all guarantees are met.

7. *Give customers the benefit of the doubt.* Not all customers are truthful and not all complaints are justified. However, customers should be treated as though they have a valid complaint until clear evidence to the contrary emerges. If a lot of money is at stake (as in insurance claims or potential lawsuits), careful investigation is warranted. If the amount involved is small, it may not be worth haggling over a refund or other compensation. However, it's still a good idea to check records to see if there is a past history of dubious complaints by the same customer.

8. *Propose the steps needed to solve the problem.* When instant solutions aren't possible, telling customers how the organization plans to proceed shows that corrective action is being taken. It also sets expectations about the time involved (so firms should be careful not to overpromise!).

9. *Keep customers informed of progress.* Nobody likes being left in the dark. Uncertainty breeds anxiety and stress. People tend to be more accepting of disruptions if they know what is going on and receive periodic progress reports.

10. *Persevere to regain customer goodwill.* When customers have been disappointed, one of the biggest challenges is to restore their confidence and preserve the relationship for the future. Perseverance may be required to

> defuse customers' anger and to convince them that actions are being taken to avoid a recurrence of the problem. Truly exceptional recovery efforts can be extremely effective in building loyalty and referrals. As for the complaint triggered by a fault which does not lie with your company, you still should not only tell them the truth and give an explanation, but also could offer appeasement and acknowledgement. Some gifts can bring about customer surprise and positive word of mouth.
>
> 11. *Self-check the system and pursue eminence.* After seeing the customers off, you must turn around to check whether the service inefficiency is caused by accidental mistakes or system defects. Take advantage of every complaint to perfect the whole service system. Even if the complaint is disclosed to be a misunderstanding by customers, it also implies the ineffectiveness of a certain part of your communication system.

4. Guarantees force service organizations to understand why they fail and encourage them to identify and overcome potential fail points.

5. Guarantees build "marketing muscle" by reducing the risk of the purchase decision and building long-term loyalty.

How to Design Service Guarantees

Some guarantees are simple and unconditional. Others appear to have been written by lawyers and contain many restrictions. Compare the examples in Service Perspectives 13.1 and ask yourself which guarantees instill trust and confidence in you, and would make you like to do business with that supplier.

Christopher Hart also argues that service guarantees should be designed to meet the following criteria.:[26]

1. *Unconditional.* Whatever is promised in the guarantee must be totally unconditional, and there should not be any element of surprise for customers.

2. *Easy to understand and communicate* to customers so they are clearly aware of the benefits that can be gained from the guarantee.

3. *Meaningful to customers* in that the guarantee is on something important to customers and compensation should be more than adequate to cover the service failure.

4. *Easy to invoke.* Less of the guarantee should be dependent on the customer and more on the service provider.

5. *Easy to collect.* If a service failure occurs, customers should be able to collect on the guarantee without any problems.

6. *Credible.* The guarantee should be credible.

Is Full Satisfaction the Best You Can Guarantee?

Full satisfaction guarantees have generally been considered the best possible design. However, recently it has been suggested that the ambiguity often associated with

*Service
Perspectives
13.1*

EXAMPLES OF SERVICE GUARANTEES

NTT-ME's Service Guarantee:
We guarantee XePhion uptime at 99.99 percent per year. When a network service is not available and it's not the customer's fault, we will pay back the fee to the customer, according to the length of the time the network stays down.

Source: NTT-ME, http://www.asiatele.com, accessed on July 14, 2004.

Service Guarantee in The Eaton Hotel, Hong Kong:
This four-star hotel in Hong Kong has a unique series of "guaranteed service" initiatives to ensure its in-house guests receive the best possible service.

- If a guest is not registered within three minutes of approaching the reception desk (not including waiting time for long queues), the first night of accommodation is free.
- Luggage will be delivered to the room within eight minutes of the guest arriving there.
- Hotel guests checking into the smart Executive Wing receive a "guarantee of cleanliness." If a guestroom is unclean in any way, Eaton will refund the first night's stay.
- The hotel also guarantees to facilitate all prior requests it receives via its Online Concierge system (contained in the hotel Web site). These may include transportation, ticket bookings, etc., all of which will be ready for the guests on their arrival.
- If the guarantees are not met, the hotel will pick up the tab.

Source: http://www.worldroom.com, accessed on July 14, 2004.

L.L. Bean's Guarantee:
Our products are guaranteed to give you 100 percent satisfaction in every way. Return anything purchased from us at any time if it proves otherwise. We do not want you to have anything from L.L. Bean that is not completely satisfactory.

Source: Printed in all L.L. Bean catalogs and on the company's Web site, www.llbean.com/customerService/aboutLLBean/guarantee.html, accessed on July 2004.

such guarantees can lead to discounting of their perceived value. Customers may raise questions such as "What does full satisfaction mean?" or "Can I invoke a guarantee when I am dissatisfied, although the fault does not lie with the service firm?"[27]

In a recent study, Wirtz and Kum introduced a new guarantee they called the "combined guarantee."[28] This guarantee combines the wide scope of a full satisfaction guarantee with the low uncertainty of specific performance standards. The combined guarantee was shown to be superior to the pure full satisfaction or attribute-specific guarantee designs. Should the consumer be dissatisfied with any element of the service, the full satisfaction coverage of the combined guarantee applies. Table 13.2 shows examples of the various types of guarantees.

Table 13.2
Different Types of Service Guarantees

Term	Guarantee Scope	Examples
Single attribute-specific guarantee	One key attribute of the service is covered by the guarantee.	"Any of three specified popular pizzas is guaranteed to be served within ten minutes of ordering on working days between 12 a.m. and 2 p.m. If the pizza is late, the customer's next order is free."[29]
Multi-attribute specific guarantee	A few important attributes of the service are covered by the guarantee.	Minneapolis Marriot's Guarantee: "Our quality commitment to you is to provide: • A friendly, efficient check-in • A clean, comfortable room, where everything works • A friendly efficient check-out If we, in your opinion, do not deliver on this commitment, we will give you $20 in cash. No questions asked. It is your interpretation."[30]
Full-satisfaction guarantee	All aspects of the service are covered by the guarantee. There are no exceptions.	Lands' End's Guarantee: "If you are not completely satisfied with any item you buy from us, at any time during your use of it, return it and we will refund your full purchase price. We mean every word of it. Whatever. Whenever. Always. But to make sure this is perfectly clear, we've decided to simplify it further. GUARANTEED. Period."
Combined guarantee	All aspects of the service are covered by the full satisfaction promise of the guarantee. Explicit minimum-performance standards on important attributes are included in the guarantee to reduce uncertainty.	Datapro Information Services guarantees "to deliver the report on time, to high quality standards, and to the contents outlined in this proposal. Should we fail to deliver according to this guarantee, or should you be dissatisfied with any aspect of our work, you can deduct any amount from the final payment which is deemed as fair."[31]

Adapted from Jochen Wirtz and Doreen Kum, "Designing Service Guarantees—Is Full Satisfaction the Best You Can Guarantee?" *Journal of Services Marketing* 15, no. 4 (2001): 282–299.

Guarantees in an Asian Context[32]

In the executive development and MBA programs from Southeast Asia, participants who have been presented with almost exclusively North American examples of successful service guarantees in their Service Marketing sessions have been skeptical of whether guarantees would work in Asia. Their concerns center on their perceptions that Asian customers are much more likely to show opportunistic behavior than, for example, American customers. The reasons for their beliefs seem to be based on lower household incomes and education levels in comparison to North America. As a consequence, two main questions need to be addressed when considering introducing a guarantee in Asia: (1) Are there any firms who have successfully implemented service guarantees in Asia? (2) Do these firms experience a lot of customer cheating on guarantees or, in the eyes of management, unreasonable invocations of their guarantees?

The answer to question one is simply "yes." Research has shown that service guarantees can be successfully implemented in an Asian business environment.[33]

In fact, as service guarantees are still the exception, opportunities for achieving significant marketing impact and service differentiation may exist in a large number of service markets in Asia. Responding to question two, none of the companies studied reported excessive opportunistic behavior, although all admitted that a minority of their customers does take undue advantage of their guarantees. For example, a pizza restaurant reported that groups of students changed the clocks between two tables so that one of the tables would be able to invoke the ten-minute guarantee. However, all firms reported that unreasonable invocations or opportunistic behavior are exceptions and by no means numerous enough for revoking their guarantees. In conclusion, the fear of excessive opportunistic behavior of Asian customers can be managed, and therefore seems unfounded.

It has frequently been proposed that Asians are more trust- and relationship-oriented than, for example, North Americans. However, much of the data these assumptions are based on are old (e.g., Hofstede's classic work on cultural differences[34]), and do not control for other potentially important variables but culture, partly because of the assumption of parity within communities and cultures.[35] For example, Zhang and Bond[36] have argued that the degree of industrialization serves as the critical factor, with people in Hong Kong and the United States (both highly industrialized societies) demonstrating lower trust toward strangers than those in the developing People's Republic of China.

Furthermore, it may be that customer demographics (income and education) and psychographics (e.g., attitude toward nonmonetary costs, such lost effort, going through a repeat service production, etc. related to service failure), or poor process quality (e.g., long waiting times) may be stronger determinants of the perceived value of a guarantee and potential opportunistic behavior than culture or nationality itself. Should this be the case, service firms in any country may be able to implement service guarantees targeted at those customers that value high service quality, and perceive high disutility of nonmonetary costs.

Is It Always Appropriate to Introduce a Service Guarantee?

Managers should think carefully about their firm's strengths and weaknesses before deciding to introduce a service guarantee. Hart and Ostrom suggest that in many instances, it may be inappropriate to do so.[37]

A guarantee may add no value for a service company whose name alone ensures very high quality, and may even confuse the market.[38] By contrast, a firm whose service is currently poor must first work to improve quality to a level above that at which the guarantee might be invoked on a regular basis by most of their customers. Service firms whose quality is truly uncontrollable due to external forces would be foolish to consider a guarantee.

In a market where consumers see little financial, personal, or physiological risk associated with purchasing and using a service, a guarantee adds little value but still costs money to design, implement, and manage. Where little perceived difference in service quality among competing firms exists, the first company to institute a guarantee may be able to obtain a first mover advantage and create a valued differentiation for its services. If more than one competitor already has a guarantee in place, offering a guarantee may become a qualifier for the industry and the only real way to make an impact is to launch a highly distinctive guarantee beyond that already offered by competitors.

Discouraging Abuse and Opportunistic Behavior

Throughout this chapter, we advocate that firms should welcome complaints and invocations of service guarantees, and even encourage them. How can this be done without inviting potential abuse by customers?

Dealing with Consumer Fraud

Dishonest customers can take advantage of generous service recovery strategies, service guarantees, or simply a strong customer orientation in a number of ways. For example, they may steal from the firm, refuse to pay for the service, fake dissatisfaction, purposefully cause service failures to occur, or overstate losses at the time of genuine service failures. What steps can a firm take to protect itself against opportunistic customer behavior?

Treating customers with suspicion is likely to alienate them, especially in situations of service failure. The president of TARP notes:

> Our research has found that premeditated rip-offs represent 1 to 2 percent of the customer base in most organizations. However, most organisations defend themselves against unscrupulous customers by ... treating the 98 percent of honest customers like crooks to catch the 2 percent who *are* crooks.[39]

Using this knowledge, the working assumptions should be "if in doubt, believe the customer." However, as Service Perspectives 13.2 shows, it is crucial to monitor the invocations of service guarantees, or payments compensating for service failure, maintain databases of all such cases, and monitor repeated service payouts to the same customer. For example, one Asian airline found that the same customer lost his suitcase on three consecutive flights. The chances of this truly happening are probably lower than winning in the national lottery, so front-line staff were made aware of this individual. The next time this passenger checked in his suitcase, the check-in staff videotaped the suitcase almost from check-in to pickup in the baggage claim at the destination. It turned out that a companion collected the suitcase and took it through while the traveler again made his way to the lost baggage counter to report his missing suitcase. This time, the police were waiting for him and his friend.

Recent research in Singapore shows that the amount of a guarantee payout (e.g., whether it is a 10 percent or 100 percent money-back guarantee) had no effect on consumer cheating. However, repeat purchase intention significantly reduced cheating intent. These findings suggest important managerial implications: (1) managers can implement and thus reap the bigger marketing benefits of 100 percent money-back guarantees without worrying that the large payouts would increase cheating; and (2) guarantees can be offered to regular customers or as part of a membership program, since repeat customers are unlikely to cheat on service guarantees. A further finding was that customers were also reluctant to cheat if the service quality provided was truly high than when it was just satisfactory. This implied that truly excellent services firms have less to worry about than the average service provider.[40]

Service Perspectives 13.2

CUSTOMERS WHO CHEATED A REFUND SCHEME

A subsidiary store of Seiyu in Sapporo, Japan, had a messy situation on its hands when it offered refunds for Canadian pork and tongue that it had falsely labeled as domestic meat. It had been overcharging its customers for over a year. When this was found out, the store offered refunds to these customers and the refund period was to last for three days, from Friday to Sunday.

However, they did not require receipts and this was the root of their problems. For the next three days, the store was swamped with customers who demanded refunds, claiming that they had purchased the meat during the specified dates. One brazen customer walked away with 100,000 yen (US$930)) in refunds.

On Friday morning, a queue of shoppers formed even before the store opened for business. On Friday night, news of this deal spread over the Internet and on Saturday, the store was full of young people coming for refunds. On Sunday, the crowd of customers swelled to a point where police had to be called in to control the crowd. In the end, the store had to be closed on Monday "in order to reduce confusion," according to the store's management.

At the end of the refund period, the store had handed out 49.28 million yen (US$470,000) in refunds when it had only sold 13.8 million yen (US$130,000) worth of domestic pork and tongue during the designated period.

Source: *The Asahi Shimbun*, October 1, 2002.

Learning from Customer Feedback[41]

There are two ways of looking at complaints: first, as individual customer problems, each of which requires a resolution, and second, as a stream of information that can be used to measure quality and suggest improvements. So far in this chapter, we have taken the former perspective of the individual customer. In this section, we discuss how customer feedback can be systematically collected, analyzed, and disseminated via an institutionalized customer feedback system (CFS) to achieve customer-driven learning.

Key Objectives of Effective Customer Feedback Systems

"It is not the strongest species that survive, nor the most intelligent, but the ones most responsive to change," wrote Charles Darwin. Similarly, many strategists have concluded that in increasingly competitive markets, the ultimate competitive advantage for a firm is to learn and change faster than the competition.[42] Shanghai is not only the economic center, but also an important train hub in China. During the 2004 Spring Festival, the passenger flow into Shanghai Railway Station reached a peak of more than ten million passengers, averaging 250,000 people a day. Ten years ago, mainly due to its monopoly status, no one in Shanghai Railway Station had any concept of customer service. Passengers could not get access to assistance when the station was inundated with crowds. In recent years, fierce competition with the airlines and highway bus carriers compelled the station to improve its service quality. In 2003, Shanghai Railway Station introduced the "duty manager." Passengers can meet an experienced duty manager in a suit sitting in the lobby of the terminal, ready to help. The manager's duties include answering passengers' questions and inquiries, receiving complaints and executing service recovery immediately, and supervising and controlling service quality. Duty managers were warmly welcomed by passengers and their satisfaction has been obviously enhanced.

Specific objectives of effective customer feedback systems typically fall into three main categories.

ASSESSMENT AND BENCHMARKING OF SERVICE QUALITY AND PERFORMANCE The objective is to answer the question, "How satisfied are our customers?" It includes learning about how well a firm performed in comparison to its main competitor(s), how it performed in comparison to the previous year, whether investments in certain service aspects have paid off in terms of customer satisfaction, and where the firm wants to be the following year.

Often, a key objective of comparison against other units (branches, teams, competitors) is to motivate managers and service staff to improve performance, especially when the results are linked to compensation.

CUSTOMER-DRIVEN LEARNING AND IMPROVEMENTS   Here, the objective is to answer the questions, "Why are our customers unhappy?" and "Where and how can we improve?" For this, more specific or detailed information on processes and products is required to guide a firm's service improvement efforts, and to pinpoint areas with potentially high returns for quality investment. It is also about gaining an understanding of the things that other suppliers do well and those that make customers happy.

CREATING A CUSTOMER-ORIENTED SERVICE CULTURE   This objective is concerned with focusing the organization on customer needs and customer satisfaction, and rallying the entire organization toward a service quality culture.

Use a Mix of Customer Feedback Collection Tools

Table 13.3 gives an overview of typically used feedback tools and their ability to meet various requirements. Recognizing that different tools have different strengths and weaknesses, service marketers should select a mix of customer feedback collection tools that jointly deliver the needed information. As Berry and Parasuraman observe: "Combining approaches enables a firm to tap the strengths of each and compensate for weaknesses."[43]

TOTAL MARKET SURVEYS, ANNUAL SURVEYS, AND TRANSACTIONAL SURVEYS *Total market surveys* and *annual surveys* typically measure satisfaction[44] with all major customer service processes and products. The level of measurement is usually at a high level with the objective of obtaining a global index or indicator of overall service satisfaction for the entire firm. This could be based on indexed (e.g., using various attribute ratings) and/or weighted data (e.g., weighted by core segments and/or products).

Table 13.3

Strengths and Weaknesses of Key Customer Feedback Collection Tools (meets requirements fully, ●; moderately, ◐; hardly/not at all, ○)

Collection Tools	Level of Measurement							
	Firm	Process	Transaction specific	Actionable	Representative, Reliable	Potential for Service Recovery	First-Hand Learning	Cost-Effectiveness
Total market survey (including competitors)	●	○	○	○	●	○	○	○
Annual survey on overall satisfaction	●	◐	○	○	●	○	○	○
Transactional survey	●	●	◐	◐	●	○	○	○
Service feedback cards	◐	●	●	◐	◐	●	◐	●
Mystery shopping	○	◐	●	●	○	○	◐	○
Unsolicited feedback (e.g., complaints)	○	◐	●	●	○	●	◐	●
Focus group discussions	○	◐	●	●	○	◐	●	◐
Service reviews	○	◐	●	●	○	●	●	◐

Source: Adapted from Jochen Wirtz and Monica Tomlin, "Institutionalizing Customer-Driven Learning through Fully Integrated Customer Feedback Systems," *Managing Service Quality* 10, no. 4 (2000): 210.

Overall indices such as these tell how satisfied customers are, but not why they are happy or unhappy. There are limits to the number of questions that can be asked about each individual process or product. For example, a typical retail bank has some 30 to 50 key customer service processes (e.g., from car loan applications to cash deposits at the teller). Because of the sheer number of processes, many surveys only have room for one or two questions per process (e.g., how satisfied are you with our ATM services?), and cannot address issues in greater detail.

In contrast, *transactional surveys* are typically conducted after customers have completed a specific transaction, and then they are queried about this process in some depth. At this point, all key attributes and aspects of ATM services could be included in the survey, including some open-ended questions, such as "liked best," "liked least," and "suggested improvements." Such feedback is more actionable, can tell the firm why customers are happy or unhappy with the process, and may yield specific insights on how to improve customer satisfaction.

SERVICE FEEDBACK CARDS   This powerful and inexpensive tool involves giving customers a feedback card following completion of each major service process and inviting them to return it by mail or other means to a central customer feedback unit. For example, a feedback card can be attached to each housing loan approval letter, or to each hospital invoice. Although these cards are a good indicator of process quality and yield specific feedback on what works well and what doesn't, the respondents tend not to be representative, being biased toward customers who are either very satisfied or very dissatisfied.

MYSTERY SHOPPING   Service businesses often use this method to determine if front-line staff are displaying desired behaviors. Banks, retailers, car rental firms, and hotels are among the industries making active use of mystery shoppers. Mystery shopping gives highly actionable and in-depth insights for coaching, training, and performance evaluation. Because the number of mystery calls or visits is typically small, no individual survey is reliable or representative. However, if a particular staff member performs well (or poorly) month after month, managers can infer with reasonable confidence that this person's performance is good (or poor).

UNSOLICITED CUSTOMER FEEDBACK   Customer complaints, compliments, and suggestions can be transformed into a stream of information that can be used to help monitor quality and highlight improvements needed to the service design and delivery. Complaints and compliments are rich sources of detailed feedback on what drives customers nuts and what delights them.

Similar to feedback cards, unsolicited feedback is not a reliable measure of overall customer satisfaction, but it is a good source of improvement ideas. If the objective of collecting feedback is mainly to get feedback on what to improve (rather than for benchmarking and/or assessing staff), then reliability and representativeness are not needed and more qualitative tools such as complaints/compliments or focus groups generally suffice.

Detailed customer complaint and compliment letters, recorded telephone conversations, and direct feedback from employees can serve as an excellent tool for communicating internally what customers want and enable employees and managers at all levels to "listen" to customers first hand. This first-hand learning is much more powerful for shaping the thinking and customer orientation of service staff than using "clinical" statistics and reports.

FOCUS GROUP DISCUSSIONS AND SERVICE REVIEWS   Both tools give great specific insights on potential service improvements and ideas. Typically, focus groups are organized by key customer segments or user groups to drill down on the needs of these users.

Service reviews are in-depth one-on-one interviews, usually conducted once a year with a firm's most valuable customers. Usually, a senior executive of the firm visits the customers and discusses issues like how well the firm did the previous year, and what should be maintained or what should be changed. That senior person then goes back to the organization and discusses the customer's feedback with his/ her account manager, and then both write a letter back to the customer detailing how the firm will respond to that customer's service needs and how the account will be managed the next year.

Apart from providing an excellent learning opportunity (especially when the reviews across all customers are compiled and analyzed), service reviews focus on retention of the most valuable customers and get high marks for service recovery potential.

As we noted earlier, there are advantages to using a mix of feedback tools. Best Practice in Action 13.2 features FedEx's excellent customer feedback system that combines various customer feedback collection tools with a detailed process performance measurement system.

Capturing Unsolicited Customer Feedback

For complaints, suggestions, and inquiries to be useful as research input, they have to be funneled into a central collection point, logged, categorized, and analyzed.[45] That requires a system for capturing customer feedback where it is made, and then reporting it to a central unit. Some firms use a simple Intranet site to record all feedback received by any staff member. Coordinating such activities is not a simple matter, because there are many different entry points, including:

- The firm's own employees at the front line, who may be in contact with customers face to face, by telephone or email.
- Intermediary organizations acting on behalf of the original supplier.

*Best Practice
in Action 13.2*

THE FEDEX CORPORATION'S APPROACH TO LISTENING TO THE VOICE OF THE CUSTOMER

"We believe that service quality must be mathematically measured," declares Frederick W. Smith, Chairman, President and CEO of FedEx Corporation. The company has a commitment to clear, frequently repeated quality goals, followed up with continuous measurement of progress against those goals. This practice forms the foundation for its approach to quality.

FedEx initially set two ambitious quality goals: 100 percent customer satisfaction for every interaction and transaction, and 100 percent service performance on every package handled. Customer satisfaction was measured by the percentage of on-time deliveries, which referred to the number of packages delivered on time as a percentage of total package volume. However, as things turned out, percentage of on-time delivery was an internal standard that was not synonymous with customer satisfaction.

Since FedEx had systematically cataloged customer complaints, FedEx was able to develop what CEO Smith calls the "Hierarchy of Horrors," which referred to the eight most common complaints by customers: (1) wrong day delivery, (2) right day, late delivery, (3) pick-up not made, (4) lost package, (5) customer misinformed by Federal Express, (6) billing and paper work mistakes, (7) employee performance failures, and (8) damaged packages. This list was the foundation on which FedEx built its customer feedback system.

FedEx refined the list of "horrors" and developed the Service Quality Indicator (SQI), a 12-item measure of satisfaction and service quality from the customers' viewpoint. Weights have been assigned to each item based on its relative importance in determining overall customer satisfaction. All items are tracked daily, so that a continuous index may be computed.

In addition to the SQI, which has been modified over time to reflect changes in procedures, services, and customer priorities, FedEx uses a variety of other ways to capture feedback.

- *Customer Satisfaction Survey.* This is a telephone survey conducted on a quarterly basis with several thousand randomly selected customers, stratified by its key segments. The results are relayed to senior management on a quarterly basis.
- *Targeted Customer Satisfaction Survey.* This survey covers specific customer service processes and is conducted on a semiannual basis with clients who have experienced one of the specific FedEx processes within the last three months.
- *FedEx Center Comment Cards.* Comment cards are collected from each FedEx store-front business center. The results are tabulated twice a year and relayed to managers in charge of the centers.
- *Online Customer Feedback Surveys.* FedEx has commissioned regular studies to get feedback for its online services (e.g., package tracking) as well as ad hoc studies on new products.

The information from these various customer feedback measures has helped FedEx to maintain a leadership role in its industry and has played an important role in enabling it to receive the prestigious Malcolm Baldridge National Quality Award.

Sources: "Blueprints for Service Quality: The Federal Express Approach," *AMA Management Briefing*, New York: American Management Association, 1991, 51–64; Linda Rosencrance, "BetaSphere Delivers FedEx Some Customer Feedback," *Computerworld* 14, no.14 (2000): 36.

- Managers who normally work backstage, but who are contacted by a customer seeking higher authority.
- Suggestion or complaint cards mailed, emailed, pasted on the firm's Web site, or placed in a special box.
- Complaints to third parties—consumer advocate groups, legislative agencies, trade organizations, and other customers.

Analysis, Reporting, and Dissemination of Customer Feedback

Choosing the relevant feedback tools and collecting customer feedback are meaningless if the company is unable to disseminate the information to the relevant parties to take action. Hence, to drive continuous improvement and learning, a reporting system needs to deliver feedback and its analysis to front-line staff, process owners, branch or department managers, and top management.

The feedback loop to the front line should be immediate for complaints and compliments, as is practiced in a number of service businesses where complaints, compliments, and suggestions are discussed with staff during a daily morning briefing. In addition, we recommend three types of service performance reports to provide the information necessary for service management and team learning.

1. A monthly Service Performance Update provides process owners with timely feedback on customer comments and operational process performance. Here, the verbatim feedback is provided to the process manager, who can in turn discuss them with his service staff.
2. A quarterly Service Performance Review provides process owners and branch or department managers with trends in process performance and service quality.
3. An annual Service Performance Report gives top management a representative assessment of the status and long-term trends relating to customer satisfaction with the firm's services.

The reports should be short and reader-friendly, focusing on key indicators and providing an easily understood commentary.

Conclusion

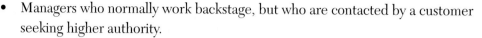

Collecting customer feedback via complaints, suggestions, and compliments provides a means of increasing customer satisfaction. It is an opportunity to get into the hearts and minds of the customer. In all but the worst instances, complaining customers are indicating that they want to continue their relationship with the firm, but they are also indicating that all is not well and that they expect the company to make things right.

Service firms need to develop effective strategies to recover from service failures so that they can maintain customer goodwill. That is vital for the long-term success of the company. Even the best recovery strategy is not as good as being treated right the first time. Well-designed unconditional service guarantees have proven to be a powerful vehicle for identifying and justifying needed improvements, as well as creating a culture in which staff members take proactive steps to ensure that the guests will be satisfied.

Finally, a service firm and its staff must also learn from their mistakes, and try to ensure that problems are being eliminated. Customer feedback systems should ensure that information originating from complaints, compliments, and other feedback tools is systematically collected, analyzed, and disseminated to drive service improvements. The ultimate objective of an effective customer feedback system is to institutionalize systematic and continuous customer-driven learning.

Review Questions

1. Why don't unhappy customers complain? What do customers expect the firm to do once they have filed a complaint?
2. Why would a firm prefer its unhappy customers to come forward and complain?
3. What is the service recovery paradox? Under what conditions is this paradox most likely to hold? Why is it best to deliver the service as planned, even should the paradox hold in a specific context?
4. What could a firm do to make it easy for dissatisfied customers to complain?
5. Why should a service recovery strategy be proactive, planned, trained, and empowered?
6. How generous should compensations related to service recovery be? What are the economic costs to the firm of the typical types of compensation firms offer?
7. How should service guarantees be designed? What are the benefits of service guarantees over and above a good complaint handling and service recovery system?
8. What are the main objectives of customer feedback systems?
9. What customer feedback collection tools do you know, and what are the strengths and weaknesses of each of these tools?

Application Exercises

1. Think about the last time you experienced a less than satisfactory service experience. Did you complain? Why? If you did not complain, explain why not.
2. When was the last time you were truly satisfied with an organization's response to your complaint? Describe in detail what happened and what made you satisfied.
3. What would be an appropriate service recovery policy for a wrongly bounced check for (a) your local savings bank, (b) a major national bank, and (c) a high-end private bank for high-net-worth individuals. Explain your rationale, and also compute the economic costs of the alternative service recovery policies.
4. Design a highly effective service guarantee for a service with high perceived risk. Explain why and how your guarantee would reduce perceived risk of potential customers, and why current customers would appreciate being offered this guarantee although they are already a customer of that firm and therefore are likely to perceive lower levels of risk.
5. Collect a few customer feedback forms and tools (e.g., customer feedback cards, questionnaires, and online forms) and assess how the information gathered in those tools can be used to achieve the three main objectives of effective customer feedback systems.

6. How generous should compensation be? Review the following incident and comment. Then evaluate the available options, comment on each, select the one you recommend, and defend your decision.

    "The shrimp cocktail was half frozen. The waitress apologized, and didn't charge me for any of my dinner," was the response of a very satisfied customer about the service recovery he received.[46] Consider the following range of service recovery policies a restaurant chain could set:

    - Option 1: Smile and apologize, defrost the prawn cocktail, then return it, and smile and apologize again.
    - Option 2: Smile and apologize, replace the prawn cocktail with a new one, and smile and apologize again.
    - Option 3: Smile, apologize, replace the prawn cocktail, and offer a free coffee or dessert.
    - Option 4: Smile, apologize, replace the prawn cocktail, and waive the bill of US$80 for the entire dinner.
    - Option 5: Smile, apologize, replace the prawn cocktail, waive the bill for the entire dinner, and offer a free bottle of champagne.
    - Option 6: Smile, apologize, waive the bill for the entire dinner, offer a free bottle of champagne, and give a voucher valid for another dinner (to be redeemed within three months).

    Try to establish the costs for each policy—some answers are in this chapter's Endnote 47. Before peeking, try first to think about the costs yourself.

 Endnotes

1   Roger Bougie, Rik Pieters, and Marcel Zeelenberg, "Angry Customers Don't Come Back, They Get Back: The Experience and Behavioral Implications of Anger and Dissatisfaction in Service," *Journal of the Academy of Marketing Science* 31, no. 4 (2003): 377–393.

2   Bernd Stauss, "Global Word of Mouth," *Marketing Management* (Fall 1997): 28–30.

3   Stephen S. Tax and Stephen W. Brown, "Recovering and Learning from Service Failure", *Sloan Management Review* 49, no. 1 (Fall 1998): 75–88.

4   Technical Assistance Research Programs Institute (TARP), *Consumer Complaint Handling in America; An Update Study, Part II* (Washington DC: TARP and U.S. Office of Consumer Affairs, April 1986); Nancy Stephens and Kevin P. Gwinner, "Why Don't Some People Complain? A Cognitive-Emotive Process Model of Consumer Complaining Behavior," *Journal of the Academy of Marketing Science* 26, no. 3 (1998): 172–189.

5   Cathy Goodwin and B. J. Verhage, "Role Perceptions of Services: A Cross-Cultural Comparison with Behavioral Implications," *Journal of Economic Psychology* 10 (1990): 543–558.

6   Nancy Stephens, "Complaining," in *Handbook of Services Marketing and Management*, eds. Teresa A. Swartz and Dawn Iacobucci (Thousand Oaks, CA: Sage Publications, 2000), 291.

7   John Goodman, "Basic Facts on Customer Complaint Behavior and the Impact of Service on the Bottom Line," *Competitive Advantage* (June 1999): 1–5.

8   Anna Mattila and Jochen Wirtz, "Consumer Complaining to Firms: The Determinants of Channel Choice," *Journal of Services Marketing* 18, no 2 (2004): 147–155.

9   Technical Assistance Research Programs Institute (TARP), *Consumer Complaint Handling in America; An Update Study, Part II.*

10 Kathleen Seiders and Leonard L Berry, "Service Fairness: What It Is and Why It Matters," *Academy of Management Executive* 12, no. 2 (1990): 8–20.

11 Tax and Brown (1998), *loc.cit.*

12 The following papers explored the role of perceived fairness in customer responses to service recovery efforts: Stephen S. Tax and Stephen W. Brown, "Service Recovery: Research, Insight and Practice," in

Handbook of Services Marketing and Management, eds. Teresa A. Swartz and Dawn Iacobucci, (Thousand Oaks, CA: Sage Publications, 2000), 277; Tor Wallin Andreassen, "Antecedents of Service Recovery," *European Journal of Marketing* 34, no. 1 and 2 (2000): 156–175; Ko de Ruyter and Martin Wetzel, "Customer Equity Considerations in Service Recovery," *International Journal of Service Industry Management* 11, no. 1 (2002): 91–108; Janet R. McColl-Kennedy and Beverley A. Sparks, "Application of Fairness Theory to Service Failures and Service Recovery," *Journal of Service Research* 5, no. 3 (2003): 251–266; Jochen Wirtz and Anna S. Mattila, "Consumer Responses to Compensation, Speed of Recovery and Apology after a Service Failure," *International Journal of Service Industry Management* 15, no. 2 (2004): 150–166.

13   Oren Harari, "Thank Heavens for Complainers," *Management Review* (March 1997): 25–29.

14   For recent work on responses to service recovery in an Asian context, see Clyde A. Warden, Tsung-Chi Liu, Chi-Tsun Huang, and Chi-Hsun Lee, "Service Failures Away from Home: Benefits in Intercultural Service Encounters," *International Journal of Service Industry* Management 14, no. 4 (2003): 436–457; Anna S. Mattila and Paul G. Patterson, "Service Recovery and Fairness Perceptions in Collectivist and Individualist Contexts," *Journal of Service Research* 6, no. 4 (2004): 336–346.

15   Leonard L. Berry, *On Great Service: A Framework for Action* (New York: The Free Press, 1995), 94.

16   Susan M. Keveaney, "Customer Switching Behavior in Service Industries: An Exploratory Study," *Journal of Marketing* 59 (April 1995): 71–82.

17   Stefan Michel, "Analyzing Service Failures and Recoveries: A Process Approach," *International Journal of Service Industry Management* 12, no. 1 (2001): 20–33.

18   James G. Maxham III and Richard G. Netemeyer, "A Longitudinal Study of Complaining Customers' Evaluations of Multiple Service Failures and Recovery Efforts," *Journal of Marketing* 66, no. 4 (2002): 57–72.

19   Tor Wallin Andreassen, "From Disgust to Delight: Do Customers Hold a Grudge?" *Journal of Service Research* 4, no. 1 (2001): 39–49. Other recent studies also confirmed that the service recovery paradox does not hold universally; e.g., Michael A. McCollough, Leonard L. Berry, and Manjit S. Yadav, "An Empirical Investigation of Customer Satisfaction after Service Failure and Recovery," *Journal of Service Research* 3, no. 2 (2000): 121–137; and James G. Maxham III, "Service Recovery's Influence on Consumer Satisfaction, Positive Word-of-Mouth, and Purchase Intentions," *Journal of Business Research* 54 (2001): 11–24.

20   Steven S. Tax and Steven W. Brown, "Recovering and Learning from Service Failure"; Stephen S. Tax, Stephen W. Brown, and Murali Chandrashekaran, "Customer Evaluation of Service Complaint Experiences: Implications for Relationship Marketing," *Journal of Marketing* 62, no. 2 (Spring 1998): 60–76.

21   Ron Zemke and Chip R. Bell, *Knock Your Socks off Service Recovery* (New York: AMACOM, 2000), 60.

22   Barbara R. Lewis, "Customer Care in Services," in *Understanding Services Management*, eds. W. J. Glynn and J. G. Barnes (Chichester, UK: Wiley 1995), 57–89.

23   Hooman Estelami and Peter De Maeyer, "Customer Reactions to Service Provider Overgenerosity," *Journal of Service Research* 4, no. 3 (2002): 205–217.

24   Rhonda Mack, Rene Mueller, John Crotts, and Amanda Broderick, "Perceptions, Corrections and Defections: Implications for Service Recovery in the Restaurant Industry," *Managing Service Quality* 10, no. 6 (2000): 339–346.

25   Christopher W. L Hart, "The Power of Unconditional Service Guarantees," *Harvard Business Review* 68 (July–August 1990): 54–62.

26   *Ibid*.

27   Gordon H. McDougall, Terence Levesque and Peter VanderPlaat, "Designing the Service Guarantee: Unconditional or Specific?" *The Journal of Services Marketing* 12, no. 4 (1998): 278–293; Jochen Wirtz, "Development of a Service Guarantee Model," *Asia Pacific Journal of Management* 15, no. 1 (1998): 51–75.

28   Jochen Wirtz and Doreen Kum, "Designing Service Guarantees—Is Full Satisfaction the Best You Can Guarantee?" *Journal of Services Marketing* 15, no. 4 (2001): 282–299.

29   Jochen Wirtz, "Development of a Service Guarantee Model," *Asia Pacific Journal of Management* 15, no. 1 (1998): 51–75.

30   Christopher W. L. Hart, *Extraordinary Guarantees: A New Way to Build Quality throughout Your Company and Ensure Satisfaction for Your Customers* (New York: AMACOM, 1993).

31   Jochen Wirtz, "Service Guarantee-Datapro Singapore," in *Services Marketing—Integrating Customer Focus across the Firm*, by Valarie A. Zeithaml and Mary Jo Bitner, 3rd ed. (New York: McGraw Hill/Irwin, 2003), 208.

32   Wirtz (1998), *loc. cit.*

33   Wirtz (1998), *loc. cit.*

34   G. H. Hofstede, *Culture's Consequences: International Differences in Work-Related Values* (Beverly Hills: Sage, 1980).

35   Robin Goodwin and Catherine So-kum Tang, "Chinese Personal Relationships," in *Chinese Psychology*, ed. Michael Harris Bond (Hong Kong: Oxford University Press, 1996), 294–308.

36   Zhang J. X. and M. H. Bond, "Target-Based Interpersonal Trust: Cross-Cultural Comparison and Its Cognitive Model (in Chinese)," *Acta Psychologica Sinica* 2 (1993): 164–172.

37   Amy L. Ostrom and Christopher Hart, "Service Guarantee: Research and Practice," in *Handbook of Services Marketing and Management*, eds. T. Schwartz and D. Iacobucci (Thousand Oaks, CA; Sage Publications, 2000), 299–316.

38   Jochen Wirtz, Doreen Kum, and Khai Sheang Lee, "Should a Firm with a Reputation for Outstanding Service Quality Offer a Service Guarantee?" *Journal of Services Marketing* 14, no. 6 (2000): 502–512.

39   John Goodman, quoted in "Improving Service Doesn't Always Require Big Investment," *The Service Edge* (July–August, 1990): 3

40   Jochen Wirtz and Doreen Kum, "Consumer Cheating on Service Guarantees," *Journal of the Academy of Marketing Science* 32, no. 2 (2004): 159–175.

41   This section is based partially on Jochen Wirtz and Monica Tomlin, "Institutionalizing Customer-Driven Learning through Fully Integrated Customer Feedback Systems," *Managing Service Quality* 10, no. 4 (2000): 205–215. For a recent survey of determinants of customer listing practices, see William J. Glynn, Sean de Burca, Teresa Brannick, Brian Fynes, and Sean Ennis, "Listening Practices and Performance in Service Organizations," *International Journal of Service Industry Management* 14, no. 3 (2003): 310–330.

42   W. E. Baker and J. M. Sinkula, "The Synergistic Effect of Market Orientation and Learning Orientation on Organisational Performance", *Journal of the Academy of Marketing Science* 27, no. 4 (1999): 411–427.

43   Leonard L. Berry and A. Parasuraman provide an excellent overview of all key research approaches discussed in this section and a number of other tools in their paper, "Listening to the Customer—The Concept of a Service Quality Information System," *Sloan Management Review* 48 (Spring 1997): 65–76.

44   For a discussion on suitable satisfaction measures, see Jochen Wirtz and Lee Meng Chung, "An Examination of the Quality and Context-Specific Applicability of Commonly Used Customer Satisfaction Measures," *Journal of Service Research* 5 (May 2003): 345–355.

45   Robert Johnston and Sandy Mehra, "Best-Practice Complaint Management," *Academy of Management Executive* 16, no. 4 (2002): 145–154.

46   Mary Jo Bitner, Bernard H. Booms, and Mary Stanfield Tetreault, "The Service Encounter: Diagnosing Favorable and Unfavorable Incidents," *Journal of Marketing* 54 (January 1990): 71–84.

47   Data for calculation of recovery costs in Application Exercise #6:
- *Option 1.* There are no direct costs to this recovery strategy beyond the time needed for the additional workstep.

- *Option 2*. Costs are as for Option 1, plus the material costs of the shrimp cocktail, which typically would be at around ⅓ of the price charged in a restaurant, i.e., perhaps around $3 to $6.
- *Option 3*. Costs are as for Option 2, plus the extra costs incurred by the free coffee or desert. These extra costs are dependent on whether they constitute incremental consumption (i.e., the diner would not have had a coffee or a desert) or whether they substitute consumption. In the former case, the costs are only the material costs, in the latter this recovery strategy replaces revenue, and the cost is the replaced revenue (e.g., $4 for the revenue forgone due to one cup of coffee sold less). The costs of the recovery policy of a free coffee could be computed as follows: Probability of incremental consumption × costs of incremental consumption, plus probability of substitution consumption × menu price for that item.
- *Option 4*. Costs are as for Option 1 plus the full $80, as this is the revenue that is forgone. It is irrelevant here that the food costs may have been only one-third of the revenue lost.
- *Option 5*. As for Option 4, plus the costs for the bottle of champagne, which again needs to be computed using the probabilities of incremental and substitution consumption and their respective costs.
- *Option 6*. As for Option 5, plus the costs of the voucher. The voucher costs again depend on whether it substitutes consumption or whether it is incremental.

CHAPTER FOURTEEN

Improving Service Quality and Productivity

Not everything that counts can be counted, and not everything that can be counted, counts.

ALBERT EINSTEIN

Our mission remains inviolable: Offer the customer the best service we can provide; cut our costs to the bone; and generate a surplus to continue the unending process of renewal.

JOSEPH PILLAY, FORMER CHAIRMAN, SINGAPORE AIRLINES

Productivity was one of the key managerial imperatives of the 1970s. During the 1980s and early 1990s, improving quality became a major priority. In a service context, this strategy entails creating better service processes and outcomes to improve customer satisfaction. At the beginning of the 21st century, we're seeing growing emphasis on linking these two strategies in order to create better value for both customers and the firm.

Both quality and productivity have historically been seen as issues for operations managers. When improvements in these areas required better employee selection, training, and supervision, then human resource managers were expected to get involved too. It was not until service quality was explicitly linked to customer satisfaction that marketers, too, were seen as having an important role to play.

Broadly defined, the task of value enhancement requires quality improvement programs to deliver and continuously enhance the benefits desired by customers. At the same time, productivity improvement efforts must seek to reduce the associated costs. The challenge is to ensure that these two programs are mutually reinforcing in achieving common goals, rather than operating at loggerheads with one another in pursuit of conflicting goals.

In this chapter, we review the challenges involved in improving both productivity and quality in service organizations and explore the following questions:

1. What is meant by *quality* and *productivity* in a service context and why should they be linked when formulating marketing strategy?
2. How can we diagnose and address service quality problems?
3. What are the key tools for improving service productivity?
4. How do concepts like TQM, ISO 9000, Malcolm-Baldrige Approach, and Six Sigma relate to managing and improving productivity and service quality?

Integrating Service Quality and Productivity Strategies

A key theme running through this book is that, where services are concerned, marketing cannot operate in isolation from other functional areas. Tasks that might be considered the sole preserve of operations in a manufacturing environment need to involve marketers, because customers are often exposed to, or even actively involved in service processes. Making service processes more efficient does not necessarily result in a better-quality experience for customers, nor does it always lead to improved benefits for them. Likewise, getting service employees to work faster may sometimes be welcomed by customers, but at other times it may make customers feel rushed and unwanted. Thus, marketing, operations, and human resource managers need to communicate with one another to ensure that they can deliver quality experiences more efficiently.

Similarly, implementing marketing strategies to improve customer satisfaction with services can prove costly and disruptive for an organization if the implications for operations and human resources have not been carefully thought through. Hence, there is a need to consider quality and productivity improvement strategies jointly rather than in isolation.

Service Quality, Productivity, and Marketing

Marketing's interest in service quality is obvious when one thinks about it: Poor quality places a firm at a competitive disadvantage. If customers perceive quality as unsatisfactory, they may be quick to take their business elsewhere. Recent years have witnessed a veritable explosion of discontent with service quality at a time when the quality of many manufactured goods seems to have improved significantly.

Improving productivity is important to marketers for several reasons. First, it helps to keep costs down. Lower costs mean either higher profits or the ability to hold down prices. The company with the lowest costs in an industry has the option to position itself as the low-price leader—usually a significant advantage among price-sensitive market segments. Second, firms with lower costs also generate higher margins, giving them the option of spending more than the competition in marketing activities, improved customer service, and supplementary services. They may also be able to offer higher margins to attract and reward the best distributors and intermediaries. Third is the opportunity to secure the firm's long-term future through investments in new service technologies and in research to create superior new services, improved features, and innovative delivery systems. Finally, efforts to improve productivity often have an impact on customers. Marketers are responsible for ensuring that negative impacts are avoided or minimized and that new procedures are carefully presented to customers. Positive impacts can be promoted as a new advantage.

Quality and productivity are twin paths to creating value for both customers and companies. In broad terms, quality focuses on the benefits created for the customer's side of the equation and productivity is the financial costs incurred by the firm. Carefully integrating quality and productivity improvement programs will improve the long-term profitability of the firm.

What Is Service Quality?

What do we mean when we speak of service quality? Company personnel need a common understanding in order to be able to address issues such as the measurement of service quality, the identification of causes of service quality shortfalls, and the design and implementation of corrective actions.

Different Perspectives of Service Quality

The word *quality* means different things to people according to the context. Garvin identifies five perspectives on quality.[1]

- *The transcendent view* of quality is synonymous with innate excellence—a mark of uncompromising standards and high achievement. This viewpoint is often applied to the performing and visual arts. It argues that people learn to recognize quality only through the experience gained from repeated exposure. However, from a practical standpoint, suggesting that managers or customers will know quality when they see it is not very helpful.
- *The product-based approach* sees quality as a precise and measurable variable. Differences in quality, it argues, reflect differences in the amount of some ingredient or attribute possessed by the product. Because this view is totally objective, it fails to account for differences in the tastes, needs, and preferences of individual customers (or even entire market segments).
- *User-based definitions* start with the premise that quality lies in the eyes of the beholder. These definitions equate quality with maximum satisfaction. This subjective, demand-oriented perspective recognizes that different customers have different wants and needs.

- *The manufacturing-based approach* is supply based, and is primarily concerned with engineering and manufacturing practices. (In services, we would say that quality is operations driven.) It focuses on conformance to internally developed specifications, which are often driven by productivity and cost-containment goals.
- *Value-based definitions* define quality in terms of value and price. By considering the tradeoff between performance (or conformance) and price, quality comes to be defined as "affordable excellence."

Garvin suggests that these alternative views of quality help to explain the conflicts that sometimes arise between managers in different functional departments.

MANUFACTURING-BASED COMPONENTS OF QUALITY   To incorporate the different perspectives, Garvin developed the following components of quality that could be useful as a framework for analysis and strategic planning. These are: (1) performance (primary operating characteristics), (2) features (bells and whistles), (3) reliability (probability of malfunction or failure), (4) conformance (ability to meet specifications), (5) durability (how long the product continues to provide value to the customer), (6) serviceability (speed, courtesy, competence, and ease of having problems fixed), (7) aesthetics (how the product appeals to any or all of the user's five senses), and (8) perceived quality (associations such as the reputation of the company or brand name). Note that these categories were developed from a manufacturing perspective, but they do address the notion of "serviceability" of a physical good. Figure 14.1 shows an advertisement by Hewlett-Packard (HP) that promotes its ability to provide effective solutions to its corporate clients.

SERVICE-BASED COMPONENTS OF QUALITY   Researchers argue that the distinctive nature of services requires a distinctive approach to defining and measuring service quality. Because of the intangible, multifaceted nature of many services, it may be harder to evaluate the quality of a service compared to a good. Since customers are often involved in service production—particularly in people-processing services—a distinction needs to be drawn between the *process* of service delivery (what Grönroos calls functional quality) and the actual *output* of the service (what he calls technical quality).[2] Grönroos and others also suggest that the perceived quality of a service is the result of an evaluation process in which customers compare their perceptions of service delivery and its outcome against what they expect.

The most extensive research into service quality is strongly user oriented. From focus group research, Zeithaml, Berry, and Parasuraman identified ten criteria used by consumers in evaluating service quality (Table 14.1). In subsequent research, they found a high degree of correlation between several of these variables and so consolidated them into five broad dimensions:

- *Tangibles* (appearance of physical elements)
- *Reliability* (dependable, accurate performance)

Figure 14.1
HP implements
leading-edge
infrastructure
solutions for
Orient Overseas
Container Line
(OOCL), allowing it
to adapt to
market-driven
changes at a
faster rate than
its competitors.

Courtesy of Hewlett-Packard.

- *Responsiveness* (promptness and helpfulness)
- *Assurance* (competence, courtesy, credibility, and security)
- *Empathy* (easy access, good communications, and customer understanding)[3]

Only one of these five dimensions, reliability, has a direct parallel to findings from Garvin's research on manufacturing quality.

Table 14.1
Generic Dimensions Customers Use to Evaluate Service Quality

Dimension	Definition	Examples of Customers' Questions
Credibility	Trustworthiness, believability, honesty of the service provider	Does the hospital have a good reputation? Does my stockbroker refrain from pressuring me to buy? Does the repair firm guarantee its work?
Security	Freedom from danger, risk, or doubt	Is it safe for me to use the bank's ATMs at night? Is my credit card protected against unauthorized use? Can I be sure that my insurance policy provides complete coverage?
Access	Approachability and ease of contact	How easy is it for me to talk to a supervisor when I have a problem? Does the airline have a 24-hour toll-free phone number? Is the hotel conveniently located?
Communication	Listening to customers and keeping them informed in language they can understand	When I have a complaint, is the manager willing to listen to me? Does my doctor avoid using technical jargon? Does the electrician call when unable to keep a scheduled appointment?
Understanding the customer	Making the effort to know customers and their needs	Does someone in the hotel recognize me as a regular customer? Does my stockbroker try to determine my specific financial objectives? Is the moving company willing to accommodate my schedule?
Tangibles	Appearance of physical facilities, equipment, personnel, and communication materials	Are the hotel's facilities attractive? Is my accountant dressed appropriately? Is my bank statement easy to understand?
Reliability	Ability to perform the promised service dependably and accurately	Does my lawyer call me back when promised? Is my telephone bill free of errors? Is my television repaired right the first time?
Responsiveness	Willingness to help customers and provide prompt service	When there's a problem, does the firm resolve it quickly? Is my stockbroker willing to answer my questions? Is the cable TV company willing to give me a specific time when the installer will show up?
Competence	Possession of the skills and knowledge required to perform the service	Can the bank teller process my transaction without fumbling around? Is my travel agent able to obtain the information I need when I call? Does the dentist appear competent?
Courtesy	Politeness, respect, consideration, and friendliness of contact personnel	Does the flight attendant have a pleasant demeanor? Are the telephone operators consistently polite when answering my calls? Does the plumber take off muddy shoes before stepping on my carpet?

Source: Adapted from Valarie A. Zeithaml, A. Parasuraman, and Leonard L. Berry, *Delivering Quality Service: Balancing Customer Perceptions and Expectations* (New York: The Free Press, 1990).

Capturing the Customer's Perspective of Service Quality

To measure customer satisfaction with different aspects of service quality, Zeithaml and her colleagues developed a survey research instrument called SERVQUAL.[4] It is based on the premise that customers can evaluate a firm's service quality by comparing their perceptions of its service with their own expectations. SERVQUAL is seen as a generic measurement tool that can be applied across a broad spectrum of service industries. In its basic form, the scale contains 22 perception items and a series of expectation items, reflecting the five dimensions of service quality described earlier (see Table 14.2). Respondents complete a series of scales which measure their expectations of companies in a particular industry on a wide array of specific service characteristics. Subsequently, they are asked to record their perceptions of a specific company whose services they have used, on those same characteristics. When perceived performance ratings are lower than expectations, this is a sign of poor quality. The reverse indicates good quality.

Although SERVQUAL has been widely used by service companies, doubts have been expressed with regard to both its conceptual foundation and methodological limitations.[5] To evaluate the stability of the five underlying dimensions when applied to a variety of different service industries, Mels, Boshoff, and Nel analyzed data sets from banks, insurance brokers, vehicle repairs, electrical repairs, and life insurance.[6] Their findings suggest that, in reality, SERVQUAL scores only measure two factors: intrinsic service quality (resembling what Grönroos termed functional quality) and extrinsic service quality (which refers to the tangible aspects of service delivery and *"resembles to some extent* what Grönroos refers to as technical quality").

These findings do not undermine the value of Zeithaml, Berry, and Parasuraman's achievement in identifying some of the key underlying constructs in service quality, but they do highlight the difficulty of measuring customer perceptions of quality. Smith notes that the majority of researchers using SERVQUAL have omitted from, added to, or altered the list of statements purporting to measure service quality.[7]

Comparing performance to expectations works well in reasonably competitive markets where customers have sufficient knowledge to purposefully choose a service that meets their needs and wants. However, in uncompetitive markets or in situations where customers do not have free choice (e.g., because switching costs would be prohibitive, or because of time or location constraints), there are risks to defining service quality primarily in terms of customers' satisfaction with outcomes relative to their prior expectations. If customers' expectations are low and actual service delivery proves to be marginally better than the dismal level that had been expected, we can hardly claim that customers are receiving good quality service! In such situations, it is better to use needs or wants as comparison standards, and define good service quality as meeting or exceeding customer wants and needs rather than expectations.[8]

Table 14.2
The SERVQUAL Scale

The SERVQUAL scale includes five dimensions: tangibles, reliability, responsiveness, assurance, and empathy. Within each dimension are several items measured on a seven-point scale from strongly agree to strongly disagree, for a total of 21 items.

SERVQUAL Questions

Note: For actual survey respondents, instructions are also included, and each statement is accompanied by a seven-point scale ranging from "strongly agree = 7" to "strongly disagree = 1." Only the end points of the scale are labeled; there are no words above the numbers 2 through 6.

Tangibles

- Excellent banks (refer to cable TV companies, hospitals, or the appropriate service business throughout the questionnaire) will have modern-looking equipment.
- The physical facilities at excellent banks will be visually appealing.
- Employees at excellent banks will be neat in appearance.
- Materials (e.g., brochures or statements) associated with the service will be visually appealing in an excellent bank.

Reliability

- When excellent banks promise to do something by a certain time, they will do so.
- When customers have a problem, excellent banks will show a sincere interest in solving it.
- Excellent banks will perform the service right the first time.
- Excellent banks will provide their services at the time they promise to do so.
- Excellent banks will insist on error-free records.

Responsiveness

- Employees of excellent banks will tell customers exactly when service will be performed.
- Employees of excellent banks will give prompt service to customers.
- Employees of excellent banks will always be willing to help customers.
- Employees of excellent banks will never be too busy to respond to customer requests.

Assurance

- The behavior of employees of excellent banks will instill confidence in customers.
- Customers of excellent banks will feel safe in their transactions.
- Employees of excellent banks will be consistently courteous with customers.
- Employees of excellent banks will have the knowledge to answer customer questions.

Empathy

- Excellent banks will give customers individual attention.
- Excellent banks will have operating hours convenient to all their customers.
- Excellent banks will have employees who give customers personal attention.
- The employees of excellent banks will understand the specific needs of their customers.

Source: Adapted from A. Parasuraman, Valarie A. Zeithaml, and Leonard Berry, "SERVQUAL: A Multiple Item Scale for Measuring Consumer Perceptions of Service Quality," *Journal of Retailing* 64 (1988): 12–40.

Satisfaction-based research into quality assumes that customers are dealing with services that are high in search or experience characteristics (see Chapter 2). A problem arises when they are asked to evaluate the quality of those services that are high in *credence* characteristics, such as complex legal cases or medical treatments, which they find hard to evaluate even after delivery is completed. In short, the customers may not be sure what to expect in advance and they may not know for years, if ever, how good a job the professional actually did. A natural tendency in such situations is for clients or patients to use process factors and tangible cues as proxies to evaluate quality.

Process factors include customers' feelings about the providers' personal style and satisfaction levels with those supplementary elements that they are competent to evaluate (for example, the tastiness of hospital meals or the clarity of bills for legal services). As a result, customer's perceptions of core service quality may be strongly influenced by their evaluation of process attributes and tangible elements of the service—a halo effect.[9] In order to obtain credible measures of professional performance quality, it may be necessary to include peer reviews of both process and outcomes as these relate to service execution on the core product.

Devlin and Dong offer guidelines on how to measure service quality across every aspect of the business in a real-world setting.[10] To help customers recall and evaluate their service experiences, these authors suggest taking them through each step of their service encounters (this approach is sometimes referred to as a walk-through audit). See Service Perspectives 14.1 for a definition of service excellence in Asian restaurants.

Service Perspectives 14.1

SERVICE EXCELLENCE IN BEIJING'S XIAO WANG RESTAURANTS

Joseph Cinque, the president of New York-based American Academy of Hospitality Sciences, an organization with an international award program that honors excellence in the worldwide travel industry, certainly knows what excellent service is. He travels the world to experience excellent service and when he finds it, he lavishes compliments.

The Star Diamond Award, an international honor awarded by the Academy of Hospitality Science, usually goes to upscale businesses like five-star hotels and top-notch airlines. Therefore, it was quite a surprise for a restaurant to win such an award, and it really goes to show how outstanding that restaurant is. Cinque explained that they are looking for things beyond marble floors and crystal chandeliers. It is about the overall package.

According to Cinque, it is the "uniqueness of the dining environment and the level of service" that made Xiao Wang the winner and the first restaurant in China to receive the honor. Cinque is also full of praises for Xiao Wang's Beijing *siheyuan* architecture, as it conveys a friendly formality. In addition, Xiao Wang's head waiter could converse well in English, making it easy for non-Chinese-speaking diners.

Commenting on the culture differences in Asia, Cinque said that the introduction of outdated practices such as having waiters and waitresses kneeling to present customers with so-called ultimate luxury in some restaurants in China, or the practice of serving cold food on top of naked female bodies in Japan would not increase the restaurants' chances of winning the Star Diamond Award. He added that he find those practices unacceptable and simply distasteful.

Source: Adapted from Raymond Zhou, "Service with Chinese Characteristics Wows International Expert," *China Daily*, February 4, 2004, 5.

The Gap Model: A Conceptual tool to Identify and Correct Service Quality Problems

If one accepts the view that quality entails consistently meeting or exceeding customers' expectations, then the manager's task is to balance customer expectations and perceptions and to close any gaps between the two.

Gaps in Service Design and Delivery

Zeithaml, Berry, and Parasuraman identify four potential shortfalls, or gaps, within the service organization that may lead to a final and most serious gap—the difference between what customers expected and what they perceived was delivered.[11] Figure 14.2 extends and refines their framework to identify a total of seven types of gaps that can occur at different points during the design and delivery of a service performance.

1. *The knowledge gap* is the difference between what service providers believe customers expect and customers' actual needs and expectations.
2. *The standards gap* is the difference between management's perceptions of customer expectations and the quality standards established for service delivery.

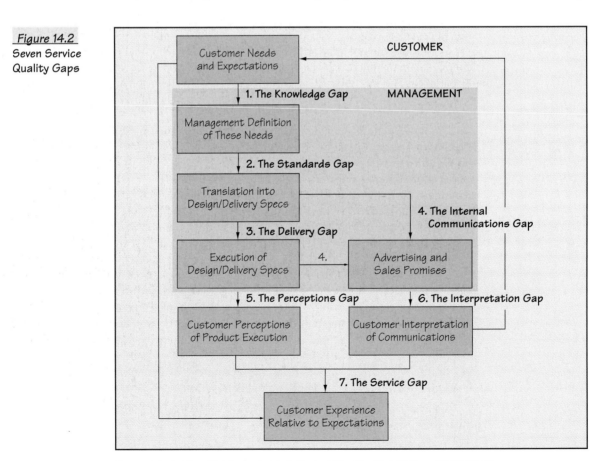

Figure 14.2
Seven Service Quality Gaps

Source: Adapted from Christopher Lovelock, *Product Plus* (New York: McGraw-Hill, 1994): 112.

3. *The delivery gap* is the difference between specified delivery standards and the service provider's actual performance on these standards.

4. *The internal communications gap* is the difference between what the company's advertising and sales personnel think are the product's features, performance, and service quality level and what the company is actually able to deliver.

5. *The perceptions gap* is the difference between what is actually delivered and what customers perceive they have received (because they are unable to accurately evaluate service quality).

6. *The interpretation gap* is the difference between what a service provider's communication efforts (in advance of service delivery) actually promise and what a customer thinks was promised by these communications.

7. *The service gap* is the difference between what customers expect to receive and their perceptions of the service that is actually delivered.

Gaps 1, 5, 6, and 7 represent external gaps between the customer and the organization. Gaps 2, 3, and 4 are internal gaps occurring between different functions and departments within the organization.

Gaps at any point in service design and delivery can damage relationships with customers. The service gap is the most critical. Hence, the ultimate goal in improving service quality is to close or narrow this gap as much as possible. However, to achieve this, service organizations may need to work on one or more of the other six other gaps depicted in Figure 14.2. Improving service quality requires identifying the specific causes of each gap and then developing strategies to close them.

Core Strategies to Address Service Quality Gaps

Zeithaml, Berry, and Parasuraman propose a series of generic steps for closing gaps 1 to 4.[12] Their prescriptions (relabeled to conform to the terminology of Figure 14.2), are summarized in Table 14.3.

What about gaps 5 and 6? Gap 5—the perceptions gap—recognizes that customers do not always correctly understand what the service has done for them. This situation is particularly likely to occur with credence services, where it is hard to judge performance even after delivery. Some service personnel make it a point not only to keep customers informed during service delivery, but also debrief them at the end and, sometimes, offer tangible evidence. For instance, a doctor may explain to a patient what took place during a medical procedure such as surgery, what was found—if anything—that differed from what was expected, and what the patient can expect for the future. To explain the nature of a complex repair, a technician may give a similar debriefing to the customer who commissioned it and provide physical evidence in the form of showing the damaged components that had to be replaced.

To reduce gap 6—the interpretation gap—communication specialists in the firm need to pretest all advertising, brochures, telephone scripts, and Web site

Table 14.3
Prescriptions for Closing Service Gaps

Gap 1   Prescription: Learn What Customers Expect

Understand customer expectations through research, complaint analysis, customer panels, etc.

Increase direct interactions between managers and customers to improve understanding.

Improve upward communication from contact personnel to management.

Turn information and insights into action.

Gap 2   Prescription: Establish the Right Service Quality Standards

---

Ensure that top management displays ongoing commitment to quality as defined by customers.

Set, communicate, and reinforce customer-oriented service standards for all work units.

Train managers in the skills needed to lead employees to deliver quality service.

Become receptive to new ways of doing business that overcome barriers to delivering quality service.

Standardize repetitive work tasks to ensure consistency and reliability by substituting hard technology for human contact and improving work methods (soft technology).

Establish clear service quality goals that are challenging, realistic, and explicitly designed to meet customer expectations.

Clarify which job tasks have the biggest impact on quality and should receive the highest priority.

Ensure that employees understand and accept goals and priorities.

Measure performance and provide regular feedback.

Reward managers and employees for attaining quality goals.

Gap 3   Prescription: Ensure That Service Performance Meets Standards

---

Clarify employee roles.

Ensure that all employees understand how their jobs contribute to customer satisfaction.

Match employees to jobs by selecting for the abilities and skills needed to perform each job well.

Provide employees with the technical training needed to perform their assigned tasks effectively.

Develop innovative recruitment and retention methods to attract the best people and build loyalty.

Enhance performance by selecting the most appropriate and reliable technology and equipment.

Teach employees about customer expectations, perceptions, and problems.

Train employees in interpersonal skills, especially for dealing with customers under stressful conditions.

Eliminate role conflict among employees by involving them in the process of setting standards.

Train employees in priority setting and time management.

Measure employee performance and tie compensation and recognition to delivery of quality service.

Develop reward systems that are meaningful, timely, simple, accurate, and fair.

Empower managers and employees in the field by pushing decision-making power down the organization; allow them greater discretion in the methods they use to reach goals.

Ensure that employees working at internal support jobs provide good service to customer-contact personnel.

Build teamwork so that employees work well together, and use team rewards as incentives.

Treat customers as partial employees; clarify their roles in service delivery; and train and motivate them to perform well in their roles as coproducers.

Gap 4   Prescription: Ensure That Communication Promises Are Realistic

---

Seek inputs from operations personnel when new advertising programs are being created.

Develop advertising that features real employees performing their jobs.

Allow service providers to preview advertisements before customers are exposed to them.

Get sales staff to involve operations staff in face-to-face meetings with customers.

Develop internal educational, motivational, and advertising campaigns to strengthen links among marketing, operations, and human resource departments.

Ensure that consistent standards of service are delivered across multiple locations.

Ensure that advertising content accurately reflects those service characteristics that are most important to customers in their encounters with the organization.

Manage customers' expectations by letting them know what is and is not possible—and the reasons why.

Identify and explain uncontrollable reasons for shortcomings in service performance.

Offer customers different levels of service at different prices, explaining the distinctions.

Source: Distilled from chapters 4, 5, 6, and 7 of Valarie A. Zeithaml, A. Parasuraman, and Leonard L. Berry, _Delivering Quality Service: Balancing Customer Perceptions and Expectations_ (New York: The Free Press, 1990).

content *before* they are published. Pretesting, widely used by advertising agencies, involves presenting communication materials to a sample of customers in advance of publication. Those participating in the pretest can be asked their opinion of the communications in question and what they interpret the specific or implied promises to mean. If their interpretation is not what the firm intended, then changes to text copy or images will be needed.

The strength of the gap methodology is that it offers generic insights and solutions that can be applied across different industries. What it doesn't attempt, of course, is to identify specific quality failures that may occur in particular service businesses. Each firm must develop its own customized approach to ensure that service quality becomes and remains a key objective.

Measuring and Improving Service Quality

It is commonly said that "what is not measured is not managed." Without measurement, managers can't be sure whether service quality gaps exist, let alone what types of gaps, where they exist, and what potential corrective actions should be taken. Of course, measurement is needed to determine whether goals for improvement are being met after changes have been implemented.

The Need for Soft and Hard Service Quality Measures

Customer-defined standards and measures of service quality can be grouped into two broad categories: "soft" and "hard." Soft measures are those that cannot easily be observed and must be collected by talking to customers, employees, or others. As noted by Zeithaml and Bitner, "Soft standards provide direction, guidance, and feedback to employees on ways to achieve customer satisfaction and can be quantified by measuring customer perceptions and beliefs."[13] SERVQUAL is an example of a sophisticated soft measurement system.

By contrast, hard standards and measures relate to those characteristics and activities that can be counted, timed, or measured through audits. Measures may include such things as how many telephone calls were abandoned while the customer was on hold, how many minutes customers had to wait in line at a particular stage in the service delivery, the time required to complete a specific task, the temperature of a particular food item, how many trains arrived late, how many bags were lost, how many patients made a complete recovery following a specific type of operation, and how many orders were filled correctly. Standards are often set with reference to the percentage of occasions on which a particular measure is achieved. The challenge for service marketers is to ensure that operational measures of service quality reflect customer input.

Organizations that are known for excellent service make use of both soft and hard measures. Among other things, they are good at listening to both their customers and their customer-contact employees. The larger the organization, the more important it is to create formalized feedback programs using a variety of professionally designed and implemented research procedures.

Soft Measures of Service Quality

How can companies measure their performance against soft standards of service quality? Berry and Parasuraman argue that:

> [C]ompanies need to establish ongoing listening systems using multiple methods among different customer groups. A single service quality study is a snapshot taken at a point in time and from a particular angle Deeper insight and more informed decision making come from a continuing series of snapshots taken from various angles and through different lenses, which form the essence of systematic listening.[14]

They recommend that ongoing research should be conducted through a portfolio of research approaches. Key customer-centric service quality measures (which we review in Chapter 12) include total market surveys, annual surveys, transactional surveys, service feedback cards, mystery shopping, analysis of unsolicited feedback such as complaints and compliments, focus group discussions, and service reviews. Mystery shopping is widely used in chain service firms such as Starbucks and Shell petrol stations across many Asian countries. It helps those big brands to monitor the service quality of the franchisees' stores from the view of the customers. Among other soft measures are the following:

- *Ongoing surveys of account holders* by telephone or post, using scientific sampling procedures to determine customers' satisfaction in terms of broader relationship issues.
- *Customer advisory panels* to offer feedback and advice on service performance.
- *Employee surveys and panels* to determine perceptions of the quality of service delivered to customers on specific dimensions, barriers to better service, and suggestions for improvement.

Designing and implementing a large-scale customer survey to measure service across a wide array of attributes is no simple task. Line managers sometimes view the findings as threatening when direct comparisons are made of the performance of different departments or branches.

Hard Measures of Service Quality

Hard measures typically refer to operational processes or outcomes. They include data such as uptime, service response times, failure rates, and delivery costs. In a complex service operation, multiple measures of service quality will be recorded at many different points. In low-contact services, where customers are not deeply involved in the service delivery process, many operational measures apply to backstage activities that have only a second-order effect on customers.

FedEx was one of the first service companies to understand the need for a firmwide index of service quality that embraced all the key activities that had an impact on customers. By publishing a single, composite index on a frequent basis, senior managers hoped that all FedEx employees would work toward improving quality. The firm recognized the danger of using percentages as targets, because they might lead to complacency. In an organization as large as FedEx, which ships millions of packages a day, even delivering 99 percent of packages on time or having 99.9 percent of flights arrive safely would lead to horrendous problems. Instead, it was decided to approach quality measurement from the baseline of zero failures.

The design of this "hard" index reflected the findings of extensive "soft" customer research (and has been periodically modified in the light of new research insights). Looking at service failures from the customer's perspective, the Service Quality Index (SQI) measures daily the occurrence of 12 different activities that are likely to lead to customer dissatisfaction. The index is composed by taking the raw number of each event and multiplying it by a weighting—that highlights the seriousness of that event for customers—to give a point score for each item. The points are then totaled to provide an overall index (see Table 14.4). Like a golf score, the lower the index, the better the performance. However, unlike golf, the SQI involves substantial numbers—typically six figures—reflecting the huge number of packages shipped daily. An annual goal is set for the average daily SQI, based on reducing the occurrence of failures over the previous year's total.

Control charts offer a simple method of displaying performance over time against specific quality standards. They can be used to monitor and communicate individual

Table 14.4
Composition of FedEx's Service Quality Index (SQI)

Failure Type	Weighting Factor	× No. of Incidents	= Daily Points
Late delivery—right day	1		
Late delivery—wrong day	5		
Tracing requests unanswered	1		
Complaints reopened	5		
Missing proofs of delivery	1		
Invoice adjustments	1		
Missed pickups	10		
Lost packages	10		
Damaged packages	10		
Aircraft delays (minutes)	5		
Overgoods (packages missing labels)	5		
Abandoned calls	1		
Total Failure Points (SQI)	XXX,XXX		

Source: Christopher Lovelock, *Product Plus* (New York: McGraw-Hill, 1994), 131.

variables or an overall index. Since they are visual, trends are easily identified. Figure 14.3 shows an airline's performance on the important hard standard of on-time departures. The trends displayed suggest that this issue needs to be addressed by management, since performance is erratic and not very satisfactory. Of course, control charts are only as good as the data on which they are based.

Tools to Analyze and Address Service Quality Problems

When a problem is caused by controllable, internal forces, there's no excuse for allowing it to recur. In fact, maintaining customers' goodwill after a service failure depends on keeping promises made to the effect that "we're taking steps to ensure it doesn't happen again!" With prevention in mind, let's look briefly at some tools for determining the root causes of specific service quality problems.

ROOT CAUSE ANALYSIS: THE FISHBONE DIAGRAM   Cause-and-effect analysis employs a technique first developed by the Japanese quality expert Kaoru Ishikawa. Groups of managers and staff brainstorm all the possible reasons that might cause a specific problem. The resulting factors are then categorized into one of five groupings—equipment, manpower (or people), material, procedures, and other—on a cause-and-effect chart, popularly known as a fishbone diagram because of its shape. This technique has been used for many years in manufacturing and, more recently, also in services.

To sharpen the value of the analysis for use in service organizations, we show an extended framework that comprises eight rather than five groupings.[15] "People" has been broken into front-stage personnel and backstage personnel, to highlight the fact that front-stage service problems are often experienced directly by customers, whereas backstage failures tend to show up more obliquely through a

Figure 14.3
Control Chart for Departure Delays Showing Percentage of Flights Departing within 15 Minutes of Schedule

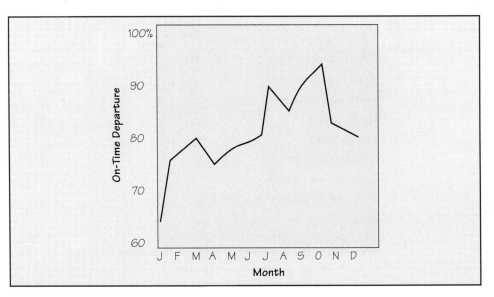

ripple effect. "Information" has been split out from "procedures," recognizing that many service problems result from information failures, especially failures by front-stage personnel to tell customers what to do and when. In manufacturing, customers have little impact on day-to-day operational processes, but in high-contact services, they are involved in front-stage operations. If they don't play their own roles correctly, they may reduce service productivity and cause quality problems for themselves and other customers. For instance, an aircraft can be delayed if a passenger tries to board at the last minute with an oversized suitcase which then has to be loaded into the cargo hold. An example of the extended fishbone is shown in Figure 14.4, displaying 27 possible reasons for late departures of passenger aircraft.[16] Once all the main potential causes for flight delays have been identified, it's necessary to assess how much impact each cause has on actual delays.

Pareto analysis (named after the Italian economist who first developed it) seeks to identify the principal causes of observed outcomes. This type of analysis underlies the so-called 80/20 rule, because it often reveals that around 80 percent of the value of one variable (in this instance, number of service failures) is accounted for by only 20 percent of the causal variable (i.e., number of possible causes).

Figure 14.4
Cause-and-Effect Chart for Flight Departure Delays

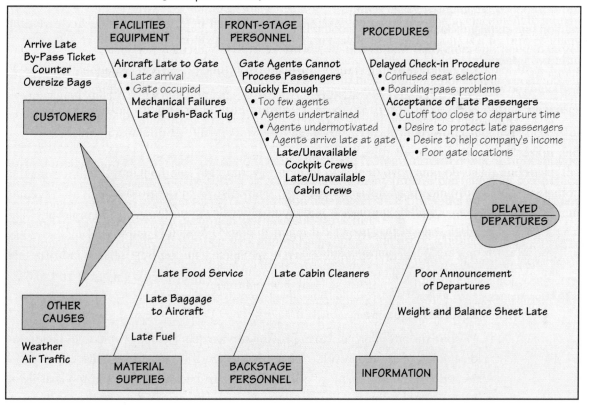

In the airline example, findings showed that 88 percent of the company's late departing flights from the airports that it served were caused by only four (15 percent) of all the possible factors. In fact, more than half the delays were caused by a single factor: acceptance of late passengers (situations when the staff held a flight for one more passenger who was checking in after the official cutoff time).

BLUEPRINTING: A POWERFUL TOOL FOR IDENTIFYING FAIL POINTS   As described in Chapter 8, a well-constructed blueprint enables us to visualize the process of service delivery by depicting the sequence of front-stage interactions that customers experience as they encounter service providers, facilities, and equipment, together with supporting backstage activities, which are hidden from the customers and are not part of the actual service experience.

Blueprints can be used to identify potential *fail points* where failures are most likely to occur. They help us to understand how failures at one point may have a ripple effect later in the process. Using frequency counts, managers can identify the specific types of failures that occur most frequently and thus need urgent attention. One desirable solution is to design fail points out of the system (see Management Memo 14.1 for a review of the poka-yokes technique). In the case of failures that cannot easily be designed out of a process or are not easily prevented (such as problems related to weather or the public infrastructure), solutions may revolve around development of contingency plans and service recovery guidelines. Knowing what can go wrong and where is an important first step in preventing service quality problems.

SIX SIGMA: FROM A DEFECT-REDUCTION APPROACH TO AN OVERALL BUSINESS-IMPROVEMENT APPROACH   The Six Sigma approach was a quality management program originally developed by Motorola in the 1980s, which employs statistical measure to evaluate, control, and improve quality of the business processes (see Appendix).

Starwood Hotel and Resorts Worldwide, Inc. was the first hospitality company in the world to introduce Six Sigma into the hotel industry to increase revenue, reduce cost, and improve the satisfaction of both customers and employees. The Westin Shanghai's Breakage Control Project, which was initiated in mid-2003, represents a good example of what Six Sigma can do in the service industry (see Best Practice in Action 14.1).

Return on Quality

Despite the attention paid to improving service quality, many companies have been disappointed by the results. Firms recognized for service quality efforts have sometimes run into financial difficulties, in part because they spent too lavishly on quality improvements. In some instances, such outcomes reflect poor or incomplete

Management Memo 14.1

POKA-YOKES: AN EFFECTIVE TOOL TO DESIGN FAIL POINTS OUT OF SERVICE PROCESSES

One of the most useful Total Quality Management (TQM) methods in manufacturing is the application of poka-yoke, or fail-safe methods to prevent errors in manufacturing processes. Richard Chase and Douglas Steward introduced this concept to fail-safe service processes.

Part of the challenge of implementing poka-yokes in a service context is the need to address not only server errors, but also customer errors. Server poka-yokes ensure that service staff do things correctly, as requested, in the right order and at the right speed. Examples include surgeons whose surgical instrument trays have indentations for each instrument. For a given operation, all of the instruments are nested in the tray so it is clear if the surgeon has not removed all instruments from the patient before closing the incision.

Some service firms use poka-yokes to ensure that certain steps or standards in the customer-staff interaction are adhered to. A bank ensures eye contact by requiring tellers to record the customer's eye color on a checklist at the start of a transaction. A Korean theme park sews the pockets of its new employees' trousers closed to ensure that they maintain a formal decorum and get used to not putting their hands in the pockets. Some firms place mirrors at the exits of staff areas to foster a neat appearance. Front-line staff can then automatically check their appearance before greeting a customer.

Customer poka-yokes usually focus on preparing the customer for the encounter (including getting them to bring the right materials for the transaction, and to arrive on time, if applicable), understanding and anticipating their role in the service transaction, and selecting the correct service or transaction. Examples that prepare the customer for the encounter include printing dress code requests on invitations, sending reminders of dental appointments, and printing guidelines on customer cards (e.g., "please have your account and pin number ready before calling our service reps"). Poka-yokes that address customer errors during the encounter include beepers at automated teller machines (ATMs) so that customers do not forget to take their card, and locks on aircraft lavatory doors that must be closed to switch on the lights.

Designing poka-yokes is part art and part science. Most of the procedures seem trivial, but this is actually a key advantage of this method. It can be used to design frequently occurring service failures out of service processes, and to ensure adherence to certain service standards or service steps.

Source: Richard B. Chase and Douglas M. Stewart, "Make Your Service Fail-Safe," *Sloan Management Review* (Spring 1994): 35–44.

execution of the quality program itself. In other instances, improved measures of service quality do not seem to translate into bigger profits, increased market share, or higher sales.

ASSESS COSTS AND BENEFITS OF QUALITY INITIATIVES Rust, Zahonik, and Keiningham argue for a "return on quality" (ROQ) approach, based on the assumptions that (1) quality is an investment, (2) quality efforts must be financially accountable, (3) it is possible to spend too much on quality, and (4) not all quality

Best Practice in Action 14.1

THE WESTIN SHANGHAI'S BREAKAGE CONTROL PROJECT

Breakage in the food and beverage world is inevitable, but at what point does it become too much? Jean Hsu, director of Six Sigma at the Westin Shanghai, started the project by conducting a survey with the hotel's sister properties within Starwood, comparing breakage per cover (number of dining guests). After realizing that breakages were higher than the chain's average, she conducted an employee survey. Among the initial feedback received were the following comments:

- "The marble floor is too slippery."
- "Shoes are of poor quality."
- "When the restaurant has more covers, we break more."

Initial improvement suggestions from employees included roughening the marble floor wherever necessary, and providing antislip shoes.

Ms Hsu set about collecting data, through observation and investigation. She developed a data collection form and requested all food and beverage employees in the restaurants and kitchen to fill it in on a daily basis whenever a breakage incident occurred. Data collected included how items were broken, where, when and how many, as well as how many restaurant covers there were for that period. After two months of data collection, analysis of the results showed that 65 percent of the breakage accidents were attributed to human behavior, mostly by poor handling, while "the slippery marble" accounted for only 9 percent of total breakages.

As part of the improvement process, the project team developed a two-hour training program on equipment handling, with the use of pictures for better understanding. Disciplinary action was put in place to correct wrong behaviors, and some hardware was either modified or purchased to help reduce breakage incidents, e.g., by adding rubber cushions to the trolleys.

Immediately following the completion of the breakage project, the overall number of breakage incidents decreased dramatically. Specifically, the breakage costs reduction, which is a direct measure of a Six Sigma project benefit, amounted to US$6,000 within the first three months across the hotel's food and beverage outlets (see Figure 14.5).

Figure 14.5
The chart illustrates the breakage reduction in Prego Restaurant, one of the restaurants in the Westin Shanghai.

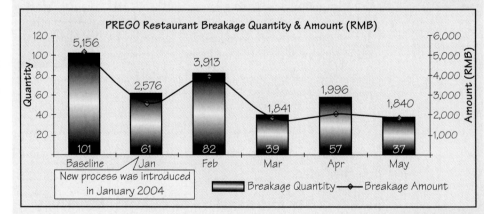

Source: Based on interviews with the management of The Westin Shanghai by Professor Lu Xiongwen, June 2004.

expenditures are equally valid.[17] An important implication of the ROQ perspective is that quality improvement efforts may benefit from being related to productivity improvement programs.

To determine the feasibility of new quality improvement efforts, they must be carefully costed in advance and then related to anticipated customer response. Will the program enable the firm to increase customer loyalty (reduce defections), increase share of wallet, and/or attract more customers (e.g., through word of mouth of current customers), and if so, how much additional net income will be generated? With good documentation, it is sometimes possible for a firm that operates in multiple locations to examine past experience and determine if a relationship exists between service quality and revenues.

DETERMINE THE OPTIMAL LEVEL OF RELIABILITY   A company with poor service quality can often achieve big jumps in reliability with relatively modest investments in improvements. As illustrated in Figure 14.6, initial investments in reducing service failure often bring dramatic results, but at some point, diminishing returns set in as further improvements require increasing levels of investment, even becoming prohibitively expensive. What level of reliability should we target?

Typically, the cost of service recovery is lower than the cost of an unhappy customer. This suggests a strategy of increasing reliability up to the point that the incremental improvement equals the cost of service recovery or the cost of failure. Although this strategy results in a service that is less than 100 percent failure free,

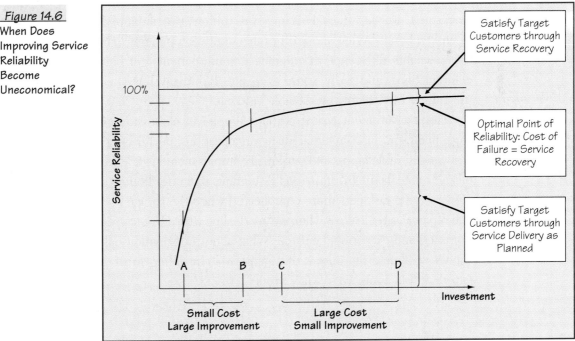

Figure 14.6
When Does Improving Service Reliability Become Uneconomical?

the firm can still aim to satisfy 100 percent of its target customers by ensuring that either they receive the service as planned or, if a failure occurs, they obtain a satisfying service recovery (see Chapter 13).

Defining and Measuring Productivity

Simply defined, productivity measures the amount of output produced relative to the amount of inputs used. Hence, improvements in productivity require an increase in the ratio of outputs to inputs. An improvement in this ratio might be achieved by cutting the resources required to create a given volume of output or by increasing the output obtained from a given level of inputs.

Defining Productivity in a Service Context

What do we mean by "input" in a service context? Input varies according to the nature of the business, but may include labor (both physical and intellectual), materials, energy, and capital (consisting of land, buildings, equipment, information systems, and financial assets). The intangible nature of service performances makes it more difficult to measure the productivity of service industries than that of manufacturing. The problem is especially acute for information-based services.

Measuring productivity is also difficult in services when the output is hard to define. In a people-processing service, such as a hospital, we can look at the number of patients treated in the course of a year and at the hospital's "census" or average bed occupancy. However, how do we account for the different types of interventions performed, such as removal of cancerous tumors, treatment of diabetes, or setting of broken bones? What about differences between patients? How do we evaluate the inevitable difference in outcomes? Some patients get better, some develop complications, and sadly, some even die. Relatively few standardized medical procedures offer highly predictable outcomes.

The measurement task is perhaps simpler in possession-processing services, since many are quasi-manufacturing organizations, performing routine tasks with easily measurable inputs and outputs. Examples include garages that change a car's oil and rotate its tires, or fast-food restaurants that offer limited and simple menus. However, the task gets more complicated when the garage mechanic has to find and repair a water leak, or when we are dealing with a French restaurant known for its varied and exceptional cuisine. What about information-based services? How should we define the output of a bank or a consulting firm? And how does the latter's output compare to a law firm's?

Service Efficiency, Productivity, and Effectiveness

We need to distinguish between efficiency, productivity, and effectiveness.[18] *Efficiency* involves comparison to a standard which is usually time-based, such as how long it takes for an employee to perform a particular task relative to a predefined standard. *Productivity*, however, involves financial valuation of outputs to inputs. *Effectiveness*, by contrast, can be defined as the degree to which an organization is meeting its goals.

A major problem in measuring service productivity concerns variability. As Heskett points out, traditional measures of service output tend to ignore variations in the quality or value of service. In freight transport, for instance, a ton-mile of output for freight that is delivered late is treated the same for productivity purposes as a similar shipment delivered on time.[19]

Another approach—counting the number of customers served per unit of time— suffers from the same shortcoming. What happens when an increase in customer throughput is achieved at the expense of perceived service quality? Suppose a hairdresser serves three customers per hour and finds she can increase her output to one every 15 minutes. Even if the haircut itself is just as good, the delivery process may be perceived as functionally inferior, leading customers to rate the overall service experience less positively.

Classical techniques of productivity measurement focus on outputs rather than *outcomes*, stressing efficiency but neglecting *effectiveness*. In the long run, organizations that are more effective in consistently delivering outcomes desired by customers should be able to command higher prices for their output. The need to emphasize effectiveness and outcomes suggests that issues of productivity cannot be divorced from those of quality and value. Loyal customers who remain with a firm tend to become more profitable over time, an indication of the payback to be obtained from providing quality service.

Improving Service Productivity

Intensive competition in many service sectors pushes firms to constantly seek ways to improve their productivity.[20] This section discusses various potential approaches to and sources of productivity gains.

Generic Productivity Improvement Strategies

The task of improving service productivity has traditionally been assigned to operations managers, whose approach has typically centered on such actions as:

- Careful control of costs at every step in the process.
- Efforts to reduce wasteful use of materials or labor.
- Matching productive capacity to average levels of demand rather than peak

levels, so that workers and equipment are not underemployed for extended periods.

- Replacement of workers by automated machines.

- Providing employees with equipment and databases that enable them to work faster or to a higher level of quality.

- Teaching employees how to work more productively (faster is not necessarily better if it leads to mistakes or unsatisfactory work that has to be redone).

- Broadening the array of tasks that a service worker can perform (which may require revised labor agreements) so as to eliminate bottlenecks and wasteful downtime by allowing managers to deploy workers wherever they are most needed.

- Installing expert systems that allow paraprofessionals to take on work previously performed by more experienced individuals earning higher salaries.

Although improving productivity can be approached in an incremental way, major gains often require reengineering of customer service processes, also known as service process redesign, as discussed in Chapter 8 (see Figure 14.7).

Figure 14.7
It is time for service process redesign when poor processes and low productivity result in unbearably long waiting time for patients in this hospital.

Customer-Driven Approaches to Improve Productivity

In situations where customers are deeply involved in the service production process (typically, people-processing services), operations managers should examine how customers' inputs can be made more productive. Marketing managers should think about what marketing strategies should be employed to influence customers to behave in more productive ways. We review three strategies: Changing the timing of customer demand, involving customers more actively in the production process, and asking customers to use third parties.

CHANGING THE TIMING OF CUSTOMER DEMAND Managing demand in capacity-constrained service businesses has been a recurring theme in this book (see especially Chapters 6 and 9). Customers often complain that the services they use are crowded and congested, reflecting time-of-day, seasonal, or other cyclical peaks in demand. During the off-peak periods in those same cycles, managers often worry that there are too few customers and that their facilities and staff are not fully productive. By shifting demand away from peaks, managers can make better use of their productive assets and provide better service. Post office advertising campaigns to encourage people to "post early for Chinese New Year" have had some success in getting people to plan ahead, rather than leave it until a few days before the holiday to post their cards and packages.

However, some demand cannot be shifted easily without the cooperation of third parties such as employers and schools, who control working hours and holiday schedules. To fill idle capacity during off-peak hours, marketers may need to target new market segments with different needs and schedules, rather than focus exclusively on current segments. If the peaks and valleys of demand can be smoothed and capacity utilization improved, productivity will increase as output increases with constant inputs (assuming negligible variable costs).

INVOLVE CUSTOMERS MORE IN PRODUCTION Customers who assume a more active role in the service production and delivery process can take over some labor tasks from the service organization (see Figure 14.8). Benefits for both parties may result when customers perform self-service.

- Many technological innovations are designed to get customers to perform tasks previously undertaken by service employees. Today, many companies are trying to encourage customers who have access to the Internet to obtain information from the firm's corporate Web sites and even to place orders through the Web, rather than telephone employees at the company's offices. For instance, the Bank of Japan offers very comprehensive information on its Web site for people who are interested to know more about the bank and its services (see Best Practice in Action 14.2 on HSBC's effort to move to the self-service channel).

Figure 14.8

Self-service pumps
have increased
petrol station
productivity.

*Best Practice
in Action 14.2*

HSBC'S SHIFT TO SELF-SERVICE

HSBC Bank Malaysia Bhd would be able to save RM15 million (US$3.9 million) a year in processing costs as a result of an investment of RM10 million over three years to boost financial services. The bank witnessed a decrease of 68 percent in branch headcount and experienced sales growth of between 200 and 400 percent. According to the bank's general manager, Rohit Bharagava, the cost savings and higher sales were achieved following the bank's strategies to raise the service standard and increase customer retention by increasing the level of satisfaction and convenience.

The main objective of HSBC's strategy was to move the mass-customer market to lower-costs channels (e.g., automated teller machines), thereby freeing up employees' time to focus on sales and relationship management. Mr Bharagava said that the increase in sales force and incentive schemes has led to a sales increase of almost 300 percent for some products. He also added that customers are adapting well to the bank's shift to self-service, and that the RM15 million savings in processing costs and 80 percent growth in transaction volume were achieved simultaneously without trading off quality of service.

Despite the growth in transactions by 80 percent, the shift to self-service and more remote channels has reduced the number of tellers needed by 30 percent, changed the front line to backroom ratio to 60:40 from 20:80, and reduced the overall staff strength at the branches by 68 percent, said Mr Bharagava. Now self-service has become the most popular channel among HSBC's customers, as it accounts for 73 percent of all HSBC's transactions.

On average, the bank witnessed a 15 percent increase in income with a 26 percent drop in costs. Some branches have even managed to decrease the cost/income ratio from 53 percent to 34 percent. It seems the RM10 million investment in self-service is a worthwhile one.

Source: Adapted from Hamisah Hamid "HSBC Sees Sales Surge with Shift to Self-Service," *Business Times* (Malaysia), May 5, 2003.

For such changes to succeed, Web sites must be made user friendly and easy to "navigate," and customers must be convinced that it is safe to provide credit card information over the Web. Some companies have been offering promotional incentives to encourage customers to make an initial order on the Web.

Some customers may be more willing than others to serve themselves. In fact, research suggests that this may be a useful segmentation variable. A large-scale study presented respondents with the choice of a do-it-yourself option versus traditional delivery systems at gas stations, banks, restaurants, hotels, airports, and travel services.[21] For each service, a particular scenario was outlined, since earlier interviews had determined that decisions to choose self-service options were very situation specific, depending on such factors as time of day, weather conditions, presence or absence of others in the party, and the perceived time and costs involved.

The results showed that in each instance, a sizable proportion of respondents would select the self-service option—even in the absence of time or monetary savings. When these monetary saving or other benefits were added, the proportions choosing self-service increased. Further analysis showed some overlap between different services. If respondents didn't pump their own fuel, for instance, they were less likely to use an ATM and more likely to prefer being served by a bank clerk.

Quality and productivity improvements often depend on customers' willingness to learn new procedures, follow instructions, and interact cooperatively with employees and other people. Customers who arrive at the service encounter with a set of preexisting norms, values, and role definitions may resist change. Goodwin suggests that insights from research on socialization can help service marketers redesign the nature of the service encounter in ways that increase the chances of gaining customer cooperation.[22] In particular, she argues that customers will need help to learn new skills, form a new self-image ("I can do it myself"), develop new relationships with providers and fellow customers, and acquire new values.

ASK CUSTOMERS TO USE THIRD PARTIES   In some instances, managers may be able to improve service productivity by delegating one or more marketing support functions to third parties. The purchase process often breaks down into four components: information, reservation, payment, and consumption. When consumption of the core product takes place at a location not easily accessible from customers' homes or workplaces (for instance, an airport, theater, stadium, or a hotel in a distant city), it makes sense to delegate delivery of supplementary service elements to intermediary organizations.

Specialist intermediaries may enjoy economies of scale, enabling them to perform the task cheaper than the core service provider, allowing the latter to focus on quality and productivity in its own area of expertise. Some intermediaries are identifiable local organizations, like travel agencies, which customers can visit in person. Others, like hotel reservations centers, often subjugate their own identity to that of the client service company. When intermediaries offer service 24 hours a day nationwide, customer calls can be spread over a broader time base. The peaks and valleys of call demand are further smoothed when the call center serves an entire continent such as Asia, which has multiple time zones, since busy times in (say) New Delhi may be quiet periods in Tokyo.

A growing number of call centers are now being established in India to serve global clients. An Indian-based operation offers facility in English at much lower cost. International call centers, with provision for different languages, are increasing rapidly in number. As with any change in procedures, a move to employ intermediaries to provide supplementary services will only succeed if customers know how to use them and are willing to do so. At a minimum, a promotional and educational campaign may be needed to launch such a change.

How Productivity Improvements Impact Quality and Value

Managers would do well to examine productivity from the broader perspective of the business processes used to transform resource inputs into the outcomes desired by customers—processes that not only cross departmental and sometimes geographic boundaries, but also link the backstage and front-stage areas of the service operation.

HOW BACKSTAGE CHANGES MAY IMPACT CUSTOMERS   The marketing implications of backstage changes depend on whether or not they affect or are noticed by customers. If airline mechanics develop a procedure for servicing jet engines more quickly, without incurring increased wage rates or material costs, then the airline has obtained a productivity improvement that has no impact on the customer's service experience.

Other backstage changes, however, may have a ripple effect that extends front stage and affects customers. Marketers should keep abreast of proposed backstage changes, not only to identify such ripples but also to prepare customers for them. At a bank, for instance, the decision to install new computers and printer peripherals may be driven by plans to improve internal quality controls and reduce the cost of preparing monthly statements. However, this new equipment may change the appearance of bank statements and the time of the month when they are posted. If customers are likely to notice such changes, an explanation may be warranted. If the new statements are easier to read and understand, then the change may be worth promoting as a service enhancement.

FRONT-STAGE EFFORTS TO IMPROVE PRODUCTIVITY   In high-contact services, many productivity enhancements are quite visible. Some changes simply require passive acceptance by customers, while others require customers to adopt new patterns of behavior in their dealings with the organization. If substantial changes are proposed, then it makes sense to conduct market research first to determine how customers may respond. Failure to think through impacts on customers may result in a loss of business and cancel out anticipated productivity gains. Management Memo 14.2 identifies ways of addressing customer resistance to change, particularly when the innovation is a radical one. Once the nature of the changes has been decided, marketing communication can help prepare customers for the change, explaining the rationale, the benefits, and what customers will need to do differently in the future.

A CAUTION ON COST REDUCTION STRATEGIES   In the absence of new technology, most attempts to improve service productivity tend to center on efforts to eliminate waste and reduce labor costs. Skinner sounds a note of caution:

> Resolutely chipping away at waste and inefficiency—the heart of most productivity programs—is not enough to restore competitive health. Indeed, a focus on cost reductions (that is, on raising labor output while holding the amount of labor constant or, better, reducing it) is proving harmful.[23]

Skinner was writing about manufacturing, but he might just as well have been writing about services. Cutbacks in front-stage staffing either mean that the remaining employees have to work harder and faster or that there are insufficient personnel to serve customers promptly at busy times. Although employees may be able to work faster for a brief period of time, few can maintain a rapid pace for extended periods. Workers who are trying to do two or three things at once—serving a customer face to face while simultaneously answering the telephone and sorting papers, for example—may do a poor job of each task. Excessive pressure breeds discontent and frustration, especially among customer-contact personnel who are caught between trying to meet customer needs and attempting to achieve management's productivity goals.

Conclusion

Enhancing service quality and improving service productivity are often two sides of the same coin, offering powerful potential to improve value for both customers and the firm. A key challenge for any service business is to deliver satisfactory outcomes to its customers in ways that are cost effective for the company. If customers are dissatisfied with the quality of a service, they won't be willing to pay very much for it, or even to buy it at all if competitors offer better quality. Low sales volumes and/or low prices mean less productive assets.

The notion that customers are the best judges of the quality of a service process and its outcome is now widely accepted. When the customer is seen as the final arbiter of quality, then marketing managers come to play a key role in defining

Management
Memo 14.2

MANAGING CUSTOMERS' RELUCTANCE TO CHANGE

Customer resistance to changes in familiar environments and long-established behavior patterns can thwart attempts to improve productivity and even quality. Failure to examine proposed changes from the customer's perspective may spur resistance. The following six steps can help smooth the path of change.

1. *Develop customer trust.* It's harder to introduce productivity-related changes when people are basically distrustful of the initiator, as they often are in the case of large, seemingly impersonal institutions. Customers' willingness to accept change may be closely related to the degree of goodwill they bear toward the organization.

2. *Understand customers' habits and expectations.* People often get into a routine around the use of a particular service, with certain steps being taken in a specific sequence. In effect, they have their own individual flowchart in mind. Innovations that disrupt ingrained routines are likely to face resistance unless consumers are carefully briefed as to what changes to expect.

3. *Pretest new procedures and equipment.* To determine probable customer response to new procedures and equipment, marketing researchers can employ concept and laboratory testing and/or field testing. If service personnel are going to be replaced by automatic equipment, it's essential to create designs that customers of almost all types and backgrounds will find easy to use. Even the phrasing of instructions needs careful thought. Ambiguous, complex, or authoritarian instructions may discourage customers with poor reading skills, as well as those used to personal courtesies from the service personnel whom the machine replaces.

4. *Publicize the benefits.* Introduction of self-service equipment or procedures requires consumers to perform part of the task themselves. Although this additional "work" may be associated with such benefits as extended service hours, time savings, and (in some instances) monetary savings, these benefits are not necessarily obvious. They have to be promoted. Useful strategies may include use of mass media advertising, on-site posters and signage, and personal communications to inform people of the innovation, arouse their interest in it, and clarify the specific benefits to customers of changing behavior and using new delivery systems.

5. *Teach customers to use innovations and promote trial.* Assigning service personnel to demonstrate new equipment and answer questions—providing reassurance as well as educational assistance—is a key element in gaining acceptance of new procedures and technology. The costs of such demonstration programs can be spread across multiple outlets by moving staff members from one site to another if the innovation is rolled out sequentially across the various locations. For Web-based innovations, it's important to provide access to telephone-based assistance. Promotional incentives and price discounts may also serve to stimulate initial trial. Once customers have actually tried a self-service option (particularly an electronically based one) and found that it works well, they will be more likely to use it regularly in the future.

6. *Monitor performance and continue to seek improvements.* Introducing quality and productivity improvements is an ongoing process. The competitive edge provided by productivity improvements may quickly be erased as other firms adopt similar or better procedures. Service managers have to work hard to keep up the momentum so that programs achieve their full potential and are

> not allowed to flag. If customers are displeased by new procedures, they may revert to their previous behavior, so it's important to continue monitoring utilization over time.

expectations and in measuring customer satisfaction. However, service marketers need to work closely with other management functions in service design and implementation.

This chapter presented a number of frameworks and tools for defining, measuring, managing, and improving service quality, including research programs to identify quality gaps, and various analytical tools to identify and improve fail points.

Service process redesign was presented as an important tool increasing service productivity. Marketing managers should be included in productivity improvement programs whenever these efforts are likely to have an impact on customers. Because customers are often involved in the service production process, marketers should keep their eyes open for opportunities to reshape customer behavior in ways that may help the service firm to become more productive. Possibilities for cooperative behavior include adopting self-service options, changing the timing of customer demand to less busy periods, and making use of third-party suppliers of supplementary services.

In summary, value, quality, and productivity are all of great concern to senior management, since they relate directly to an organization's profitability and survival in the competitive marketplace. Strategies designed to enhance value are dependent in large measure on continuous improvement in service quality (as defined by customers) and productivity that reinforce rather than counteract customer satisfaction. The marketing function has much to offer in reshaping our thinking about these issues, as well as in helping to achieve significant improvements in all of them.

Review Questions

1. Explain the relationship between service quality, productivity, and marketing.
2. Identify the gaps that can occur in service quality and the steps that service marketers can take to prevent them.
3. Why are both "soft" and "hard" measures of service quality needed?
4. What are the main tools service firms can use to analyze and address service quality problems?
5. Why is productivity a more difficult issue for service firms than for manufacturers?
6. What are the key tools for improving service productivity?
7. (Refer to Appendix.) How do concepts like TQM, ISO 9000, Malcolm-Baldrige Approach, and Six Sigma relate to managing and improving productivity and service quality?

Application Exercises

1. Review the five dimensions of service quality. What do the five dimensions mean in the context of (a) an industrial repair shop, (b) a retail bank, and (c) a Big 4 accounting firm?

2. How would you define "excellent service quality" for an enquiry/information service provided by your phone or electricity company? Call a service organization and go through a service experience and evaluate it against your definition of "excellence."

3. Consider your own recent experiences as a service consumer. On which dimensions of service quality have you most often experienced a large gap between your expectations and your perceptions of the actual service performance? What do you think the underlying causes might be? What steps should management take to improve quality?

4. In what ways can you, as a consumer, help to improve productivity for at least five service organizations that you patronize? What distinctive characteristics of each service make some of these actions possible?

5. What key measures could be used for monitoring service quality, productivity, and profitability for a large pizza restaurant chain? Specifically, what measures would you recommend to such a firm to use, taking administration costs into consideration? Who should receive what type of feedback on the results and why? On which measures would you base a part of the salary scheme of branch level staff and why?

6. (Refer to Appendix.) Conduct research and identify the critical factors for a successful implementation of ISO 9000, the Malcolm-Baldrige Model, and Six Sigma in service firms. Contrast the success factors suggested in the literature.

APPENDIX

Systematic Approaches to Productivity, Quality Improvement, and Process Standardization

Many of the thinking, tools and concepts introduced in this chapter originate from Total Quality Management (TQM), ISO 9000, Six Sigma and the Malcom-Baldrige Model. This appendix provides a brief overview of each approach.

Total Quality Management

TQM concepts, originally developed in Japan, are widely used in manufacturing, and more recently also in service firms. Some concepts and tools of TQM can be directly applied to services. TQM tools such as control charts, flowcharts, fishbone diagrams, etc. are being used by service firms with great results for monitoring service quality and determining the root causes of specific problems. Sureshchandar *et al.* identified 12 critical dimensions for the successful implementation of TQM in a service context: (1) top-management commitment and visionary leadership, (2) human resource management, (3) technical system, including service process design and process management, (4) information and analysis system, (5) benchmarking, (6) continuous improvement, (7) customer focus, (8) employee satisfaction, (9) union intervention and employee relations, (10) social responsibility, (11) servicescapes, and (12) service culture.[24]

ISO 9000 Certification

More than 90 countries are members of the International Organization for Standardization (ISO), based in Geneva, Switzerland. The ISO promotes standardization and quality to facilitate international trade. ISO 9000 comprises requirements, definitions, guidelines, and related standards to provide an independent assessment and certification of a firm's quality management system. The official ISO 9000 definition of quality is: "The totality of features and characteristics of a product or service that bear on its ability to satisfy a stated or implied need. Simply stated, quality is about meeting or exceeding your customer's needs and requirements." To ensure quality, ISO 9000 uses many TQM tools and routinizes their use in participating firms.

As with other quality initiatives, such as TQM and Six Sigma, service firms were late in adopting the ISO 9000 standards, and the majority (around two-thirds) of the total 510,616 organizations that had been certified by ISO 9000 by the end of year 2001 were in manufacturing industries.[25] Major service sectors that have adopted ISO 9000 certification include wholesale and retail firms, IT service providers, health care providers, consultancy firms, and educational institutions.

By adopting ISO 9000 standards, service firms, especially small ones, can not only ensure that their services conform to customer expectations, but also achieve improvements in internal productivity. An example of a small company that adopts the ISO 9000 standard is Singapore-based STA Inspection Pte Ltd (see Figure 14.9 for STA Inspection's advertisement).

Figure 14.9
STA Inspection Pte Ltd has achieved ISO 9000 standards and communicates its pursuit of service excellence in its advertisements.

Image courtesy of STA Inspection Pte Ltd.

Malcolm-Baldrige Model Applied to Services

The Malcolm-Baldrige National Quality Award (MBNQA) was developed by the National Institute of Standards and Technology (NIST) with the goal of promoting best practices in quality management, and recognizing and publicizing quality achievements among U.S. firms.

While the framework is generic and does not distinguish between manufacturing and service organizations, the award has a specific service category, and the model can be used to create a culture of ongoing service improvements. Major services firms that have won the award include Ritz-Carlton,

FedEx, and AT&T. Research has confirmed that employing this framework can improve organizational performance.[26]

The Baldrige Model assesses firms on seven areas: (1) leadership commitment to a service quality culture; (2) planning priorities for improvement, including service standards, performance targets, and measurement of customer satisfaction, defects, cycle time and productivity; (3) information and analysis that will aid the organization to collect, measure, analyze, and report strategic and operational indicators; (4) human resources management that enables the firm to deliver service excellence, ranging from hiring the right people, to involvement, empowerment, and motivation; (5) process management, including monitoring, continuous improvement, and process redesign; (6) customer and market focus that allows the firm to determine customer requirements and expectations; and finally (7) business results.[27]

Six Sigma Applied to Service Organizations

The Six Sigma approach was originally developed by Motorola engineers in the mid-1980s to address the issue of increasing numbers of complaints from its field sales force regarding warranty claims. It was soon adopted by other manufacturing firms to reduce defects in a variety of areas.

Subsequently, service firms embraced various Six Sigma strategies to reduce defects, reduce cycle times, and improve productivity.[28] A classic example of a business that has reinvented the Six Sigma method is the Mumbai "tiffinwallas." Tiffinwallas are men who deliver 175,000 lunches (or "tiffins") each day to offices and schools throughout Mumbai, the business capital of India.

The meals are picked up by 5,000 tiffinwallas from commuters' homes in suburbs around central Mumbai long after the commuters have left for work, delivered to them on time, then picked up and delivered home before the commuters return. The amazing part is that the 5,000 tiffinwallas make a mistake only about once every two months, according to Ragunath Medge, president of the Mumbai Tiffinmen's Association, which means there is only one error for every 16 million transactions. Most of these men are illiterate, yet they are able to run operations efficiently with the use of symbols to represent the originating and destination railway stations, and the building where the addressees are.[29]

Statistically, six sigma means achieving a quality level of only 3.4 defects per million opportunities (DPMO). To understand how stringent this target is, consider mail deliveries. If a mail service delivers with 99 percent accuracy, it misses 3,000 items out of 300,000 deliveries. But if it achieves a six-sigma performance level, only one item out of this total will go astray!

Over time, Six Sigma has evolved from a defect reduction approach to an overall business improvement approach. As defined by Pande, Neuman, and Cavanagh;

> "Six sigma is a comprehensive and flexible system for achieving, sustaining, and maximizing business success. Six sigma is uniquely driven by close understanding of customer needs, disciplined use of facts, data and statistical analysis, and diligent attention to managing, improving, and reinventing business processes."[30]

Two strategies—process improvement and process design/redesign—form the cornerstone of the Six Sigma approach. Process-improvement strategies aim at identifying and eliminating the root causes of the service delivery problems, and thereby improving service quality. Process design/redesign strategies act as a supplementary strategy to improvement strategy. If a root cause can't be identified or effectively eliminated within the existing processes, either new processes are *designed* or existing process are *redesigned* to fully or partially address the problem.

The most popular Six Sigma improvement model used for analyzing and improving business processes is the DMAIC model, shown in Table 14.5. DMAIC stands for **D**efine the opportunities, **M**easure key steps/inputs, **A**nalyze to identify root causes, **I**mprove performance, and **C**ontrol to maintain performance.

Which Methodology Should We Adopt?

As there are various approaches to systematically improving a service firm's service quality and productivity, the question arises with regard to which approach to adopt—TQM, ISO 9000, the Malcolm-Baldrige Model, or Six Sigma? Some firms have even implemented more than one program. In terms of complexity, it seems that TQM can be applied at differing levels of sophistication and basic tools such as flowcharting, frequency charts, and fishbone diagrams probably should be adopted by any type of service firm. ISO 9000 seems the next level of commitment and complexity, followed by the Malcolm-Baldrige Model and, finally, Six Sigma.

Table 14.5

Applying the DMAIC Model to Process Improvement and Redesign

Six Sigma Methodology to Improve and Redesign Processes	
Process Improvement	**Process Design/Redesign**
Define	<ul><li>Identify the problem</li><li>Define requirements</li><li>Set goals</li></ul>	<ul><li>Identify specific or broad problems</li><li>Define goal/change vision</li><li>Clarify scope and customer requirements</li></ul>
Measure	<ul><li>Validate problem/process</li><li>Refine problem/goal</li><li>Measure key steps/inputs</li></ul>	<ul><li>Measure performance to requirements</li><li>Gather process efficiency data</li></ul>
Analyze	<ul><li>Develop causal hypothesis</li><li>Identify "vital few" root causes</li><li>Validate hypothesis</li></ul>	<ul><li>Identify best practices</li><li>Assess process design<ul><li>– Value /non-value-adding</li><li>– Bottlenecks/disconnects</li><li>– Alternative paths</li></ul></li><li>Refine requirements</li></ul>
Improve	<ul><li>Develop ideas to remove root causes</li><li>Test solutions</li><li>Standardize solution / measure results</li></ul>	<ul><li>Design new process<ul><li>– Challenge assumptions</li><li>– Apply creativity</li><li>– Workflow principles</li></ul></li><li>Implement new process, structures, systems</li></ul>
Control	<ul><li>Establish standard measures to maintain performance</li><li>Correct problems as needed</li></ul>	<ul><li>Establish measures and reviews to maintain performance</li><li>Correct problems as needed</li></ul>

Source: Reproduced from Peter Pande, Robert P. Neuman, and Ronald R. Cavanagh, *The Six Sigma Way* (New York: McGraw-Hill, 2000).

By reviewing the various approaches, it becomes clear that, in fact, any one of them can be a useful framework for understanding customer needs, analyzing processes, and improving service quality and productivity. Firms can choose a particular program, depending on their own needs and desired level of sophistication. Each program has its own merits, and firms can adopt more than one program to supplement each other. For example, the ISO 9000 program can be used for standardizing the procedures and process documentation, which can lead to reduction in variability. Six Sigma and Malcolm-Baldrige programs can be used to improve processes and to focus on performance improvement across the organization.

A key success factor of any of these programs depends on how well the particular quality improvement program is integrated with the overall business strategy. Firms that adopt one of these programs due to peer pressure or simply as a marketing tool will be less likely to succeed than firms who view these programs as useful development tools.[31] Service champions make best practices in service quality management a core part of their organizational culture.[32]

The National Institute of Standards and Technology (NIST), which organizes the Malcolm-Baldrige Award program, tracked a hypothetical stock index called the "Baldrige-Index" of Malcolm-Baldrige Award winners and observed that winners consistently outperformed the S&P 500 index.[33] Ironically, the two-time winner of the award and Six Sigma pioneer, Motorola, has been suffering recently financially and losing market share to its main rivals, in part through failure to keep up with new technology. Success cannot be taken for granted, and implementation, commitment, and continual adaptation to changing markets, technologies, and environments are keys for sustained success.

Endnotes

1   David A. Garvin, *Managing Quality* (New York: The Free Press, 1988), especially Chapter 3.
2   Christian Grönroos, *Service Management and Marketing* (Lexington, MA: Lexington Books, 1990), Chapter 2.
3   Valarie A. Zeithaml, A. Parasuraman, and Leonard L. Berry, *Delivering Quality Service* (New York: The Free Press, 1990).
4   A. Parasuraman, Valarie A. Zeithaml, and Leonard Berry, "SERVQUAL: A Multiple Item Scale for Measuring Consumer Perceptions of Service Quality," *Journal of Retailing* 64 (1988): 12–40.
5   See, for instance, Francis Buttle, "SERVQUAL: Review, Critique, Research Agenda," *European Journal of Marketing* 30, no. 1 (1996): 8–32; Simon S. K. Lam and Ka Shing Woo, "Measuring Service Quality: A Test-Retest Reliability Investigation of SERVQUAL," *Journal of the Market Research Society* 39 (April 1997): 381–393; Terrence H. Witkowski and Mary F. Wolfinbarger, "Comparative Service Quality: German and American Ratings across Service Settings," *Journal of Business Research* 55 (2002): 875–881.
6   Gerhard Mels, Christo Boshoff, and Denon Nel, "The Dimensions of Service Quality: The Original European Perspective Revisited," *The Service Industries Journal* 17 (January 1997): 173–189.
7   Anne M. Smith, "Measuring Service Quality: Is SERVQUAL Now Redundant?" *Journal of Marketing Management* 11 (January/February/April 1995): 257–276.
8   Jochen Wirtz and Anna S. Mattila, "Exploring the Role of Alternative Perceived Performance Measures and Needs-Congruency in the Consumer Satisfaction Process," *Journal of Consumer Psychology* 11, no. 3 (2001): 181–192.

9   Jochen Wirtz, "Halo in Customer Satisfaction Measures—The Role of Purpose of Rating, Number of Attributes, and Customer Involvement," *International Journal of Service Industry Management* 14, no. 1 (2003): 96–119.

10   Susan J. Devlin and H. K. Dong, "Service Quality from the Customers' Perspective," *Marketing Research* 6, no. 1 (1994): 5–13.

11   Valarie A. Zeithaml, Leonard L. Berry, and A. Parasuraman, "Communication and Control Processes in the Delivery of Services," *Journal of Marketing* 52 (April 1988): 36–58.

12   Zeithaml *et al.* (1990), *op. cit.*

13   Valarie A. Zeithaml and Mary Jo Bitner, *Services Marketing*, 3rd ed. (New York: McGraw-Hill, 2003), 261.

14   Leonard L. Berry and A. Parasuraman, "Listening to the Customer—The Concept of a Service Quality Information System," *Sloan Management Review* (Spring 1997): 65–76.

15   Christopher Lovelock, *Product Plus: How Product + Service = Competitive Advantage* (New York: McGraw-Hill, 1994), 218.

16   These categories and the research data that follow have been adapted from information in D. Daryl Wyckoff, "New Tools for Achieving Service Quality," *Cornell Hotel and Restaurant Administration Quarterly* (August–September 2001): 25–38.

17   Roland T. Rust, Anthony J. Zahonik, and Timothy L. Keiningham, "Return on Quality (ROQ): Making Service Quality Financially Accountable," *Journal of Marketing* 59 (April 1995): 58–70.

18   See Hean Tat Keh, Singfat Chu, and Jiye Xu, "Efficiency, Effectiveness and Productivity of Marketing in Services," *European Journal of Operational Research*, forthcoming; and Kenneth J. Klassen, Randolph M. Russell, and James J. Chrisman, "Efficiency and Productivity Measures for High Contact Services," *The Service Industries Journal* 18 (October 1998): 1–18.

19   James L. Heskett, *Managing in the Service Economy* (New York: The Free Press, 1986).

20   For a more in-depth discussion on service productivity, refer to Cynthia Karen Swank, "The Lean Service Machine," *Harvard Business Review* 81, no. 10 (2003): 123–129.

21   Eric Langeard, John E. G. Bateson, Christopher H. Lovelock, and Pierre Eiglier, *Services Marketing: New Insights from Consumers and Managers* (Cambridge, MA: Marketing Science Institute, 1981), especially Chapter 2. A good summary of this research is provided in J. E. G. Bateson, "Self-Service Consumer: An Exploratory Study," *Journal of Retailing* 51 (Fall 1985): 49–76.

22   Cathy Goodwin, "I Can Do It Myself: Training the Service Consumer to Contribute to Service Productivity," *Journal of Services Marketing* 2 (Fall 1988): 71–78.

23   Wickham Skinner, "The Productivity Paradox," *McKinsey Quarterly* (Winter 1987): 36–45.

24   G. S. Sureshchandar, Chandrasekharan Rajendran, and R. N. Anantharaman, "A Holistic Model for Total Service Quality," *International Journal of Service Industry Management* 12, no. 4 (2001): 378–412.

25   ISO (2001), The ISO survey of ISO 9000 and ISO 14000 certificates (Eleventh cycle), International Organization for Standards, Geneva, 2001.

26   Susan Meyer Goldstein and Sharon B. Schweikhart, "Empirical Support for the Baldrige Award Framework in U.S. Hospitals," *Health Care Management Review* 27, no. 1 (2002): 62–75.

27   Allan Shirks, William B. Weeks, and Annie Stein, "Baldrige-Based Quality Awards: Veterans Health Administration's 3-Year Experience," *Quality Management in Health Care* 10, no. 3 (2002): 47–54; and National Institute of Standards and Technology, "Baldrige FAQs," http:www.nist.gov./public_affairs/factsheet/baldfaqs.htm (accessed in April 2003).

28   Jim Biolos, "Six Sigma Meets the Service Economy," *Harvard Business Review* (November 2002): 3–5.

29   *Six Sigma to Bombay Tiffinwallas*, http://www.suryakumari.com/articles/sigma.html.

30   Peter S. Pande, Robert P. Neuman, and Ronald R. Cavanagh, *The Six Sigma Way: How GE, Motorola, and Other Top Companies Are Honing Their Performance* (New York: McGraw-Hill, 2000).

[31]   Gavin Dick, Kevin Gallimore, and Jane C. Brown, "ISO 9000 and Quality Emphasis: An Empirical Study of Front-Room and Back-Room Dominated Service Industries," *International Journal of Service Industry Management* 12, no. 2 (2001): 114–136; and Adrian Hughes and David N. Halsall, "Comparison of the 14 Deadly Diseases and the Business Excellence Model," *Total Quality Management* 13, no. 2 (2002): 255–263.

[32]   Cathy A. Enz and Judy A. Siguaw, "Best Practices in Service Quality," *Cornell Hotel and Restaurant Administration Quarterly* (October 2000): 20–29.

[33]   Eight NIST Stock Investment Study (Gaithersburg, MD: National Institute of Standards and Technology, March 2002).

CHAPTER FIFTEEN

Organizing for Service Leadership

*Marketing is so basic that it cannot be considered a separate function ...
It is the whole business seen from the point of view of its final result, that
is, from the customer's point of view. Concern and responsibility for
marketing must, therefore, permeate all areas of the enterprise.*

PETER DRUCKER

Vision without action is a daydream. Action without vision is a nightmare.

JAPANESE PROVERB

What comes to mind when you hear the term "service leadership"? Do you think in terms of market leadership, focusing on those companies that are viewed as leaders in a particular service industry? Alternatively, do you associate leadership with individuals, thinking of the role of the chief executive in leading the organization or of leadership positions at different levels in a service business? In practice, service leadership embraces all these perspectives.

Realistically, it is very difficult for a firm to achieve and maintain leadership in an industry if it lacks human leaders who can articulate a vision and help to bring it about. The emphasis could be setting the standards for service quality, initiating important innovations, using new technologies for competitive advantage, defining the terms on which the company seeks to compete, and creating an outstanding place to work.

This chapter recognizes that marketing activities in service organizations extend beyond the responsibilities assigned to a traditional marketing department. We examine the challenging task of leading a market-oriented service business and raise such questions as:

1. What are the implications of the service-profit chain for service management?

2. What actions are required to move a service firm from a reactive position of merely being available for service, toward the status of world-class service delivery?

3. Why do the marketing, operations, and human resource management functions need to be closely coordinated and integrated in service businesses?

4. What are the causes of interfunctional tensions and how can they be avoided?

5. What role do service leaders play in fostering success within their organizations?

The Search for Synergy in Service Management

A service leader offers services that are known for superior value and quality. It has marketing strategies that beat the competition, yet is viewed as a trustworthy organization that does business in ethical ways. The company should be seen as a leader in operations, too—respected for its superior operational processes and innovative use of technology. Finally, it should be recognized as an outstanding place to work, leading its industry in human resource management practices and creating loyal, productive, and customer-oriented employees. Infosys Technologies has achieved all these criteria (see Best Practice in Action 15.1).

Attaining service leadership requires a coherent vision of what it takes to succeed, defined and driven by a strong, effective leadership team. And implementation involves careful coordination between marketing (which includes customer service), operations (which includes management of technology), and human resources. As emphasized throughout this book, the marketing function in service businesses cannot easily be separated from other management activities.

Although there's a long tradition of functional specialization in business, such a narrow perspective tends to get in the way of effective service management. One of the challenges facing senior managers in any type of organization is to avoid creating what are sometimes referred to as "functional silos" in which each function exists in isolation from the others, jealously guarding its independence. Ideally, service firms should be organized in ways that enable the three functions of marketing, operations, and human resources to work closely together if a service organization is to be responsive to its different stakeholders.

Integrating Marketing, Operations, and Human Resources

Using the concept of what they call the *service-profit chain*, Heskett *et al.* laid out a series of hypothesized links in achieving success in service businesses.[1] (See Figure 15.3.) The themes and relationships underlying the service-profit chain illustrate the mutual dependency that exists between marketing, operations, and human resources (HR). Although managers within each function may have specific responsibilities, effective coordination is the name of the game. They all must participate in strategic

Best Practice in Action 15.1

INFOSYS TECHNOLOGIES: AN INSPIRATIONAL SERVICE LEADER

Infosys Technologies was created by a group of seven entrepreneurs in India in 1981. Today, the company has grown to become one of India's premier software houses with a global presence. Over the years, Infosys has won many awards and prestigious company rankings for its performance quality, excellence in technology enterprise, customer orientation, and management practices (see Figure 15.1).

Infosys provides consulting and information technology services, partnering with its clients to conceptualize and realize technology-driven business transformation initiatives. Its services address specific needs of enterprise IT programs, or communications and Internet technology product development, and also engineering product design and data management.

The company believes in investing in development center campuses, so as to provide a world-class work environment, where its professionals provide high-quality solutions to clients (see Figure 15.2). The development center campuses enhance work productivity and maintain a young and collegial culture for the organization. They are equipped with the latest technologies and solutions for enterprise networking, office productivity, collaborative software engineering, and distributed project management.

Infosys' dedication to innovation extends beyond its business operations—to its clients, employees, investors, and society at large. There are groups of employees responsible for thought leadership to spur the organizational impetus to innovate.

Infosys has also been recognized for its financial performance and corporate governance. Its corporate transparency, well-formed stakeholder objectives and strong organizational commitment to ethics and values have won for Infosys a place in the list of "Top Brands with a Conscience." *Far Eastern Economic Review* rated Infosys the best company in India for the sixth consecutive year, while *Asia Money* voted Infosys the best managed company in India. Imbibed with the company's motto "Powered by

Figure 15.1

The Corporate Block, also called the Customer Care Center, houses conference rooms for customers to use and features the largest video wall in Asia.

Courtesy of Infosys Technologies Ltd.

Figure 15.2
Infosys's Well-
equipped
Development
Center Campus in
Bangalore, India

Courtesy of Infosys Technologies Ltd.

Intellect, Driven by Values," the corporate culture at Infosys is an articulation of how a strong brand value can resonate with the entire organization and its services.

Infosys was rated as the "Best Employer in India" for two consecutive years in a survey conducted by Hewitt Associates, and it also topped the Dataquest "Employee Perception Survey" carried out among the top Indian software companies. To maintain its high standards of human resource capabilities and talent, Infosys is highly selective when it comes to hiring people to join the company. Creating wealth is also a corporate objective of Infosys. Besides offering competitive salaries, the company has an Employee Stock Offer Plan, a first for any Indian software company. Also in place are partnerships with universities to offer exclusive distance learning programs for employees who wish to further their studies without interrupting their careers.

Infosys' internal communications program creates a network for employees to update themselves on the latest corporate and business developments—through workshops, monthly newsletters, articles, daily cartoons, and brainteasers to align themselves with the values and goals of the organization. Employees even call themselves "Infoscions" which helps to create a sense of identity and belonging. As S. Gopalakrishnan, co-founder and board member said:

> We believe in an organization with less hierarchy, and faster decision making. In order to make that happen, every Infoscion needs to know how the organization works, how decisions are made, and what drives us. So it is important for us to communicate this to everyone.

The underlying success factors for Infosys are its consistent focus and commitment to stakeholders, clients, and employees, and a never ending pursuit of innovative solutions. Infosys has finely tuned operations strategies, and global and strategic initiatives that have led to its dominance in the Indian software industry and a worldwide presence.

Sources: http://www.inf.com; www.infosysinbanking.com/No1_employer.htm; www.geocities.com/ypmishra/infy.htm, accessed on July 2004.

Figure 15.3
The Service-Profit Chain

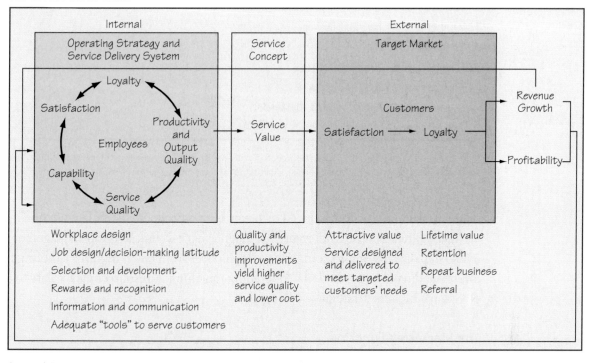

planning, and the execution of specific tasks must be well coordinated. Responsibility for the tasks assigned to each function may be present entirely within one firm or distributed between the originating service organization and its subcontractors, who must work in close partnership if the desired results are to be achieved. Other functions, such as accounting or finance, present less need for close integration because they're less involved in the ongoing processes of service creation and delivery.

The service-profit chain highlights the behaviors required of service leaders in order to manage their organizations effectively (see Table 15.1). Links 1 and 2 focus on customers and include an emphasis on identifying and understanding customer needs, investments to ensure customer retention, and a commitment to adopting new performance measures that track such variables as satisfaction and loyalty among both customers and employees.[2] Link 3 focuses on the value for customers created by the service concept and highlights the need for investments to create higher service quality and productivity improvements to reduce costs.

Another set of service leadership behaviors (links 4–7) relate to employees and include spending time on the front line, investing in the development of promising managers, and supporting the design of jobs that offer greater latitude for employees. Also included in this category is the concept that paying higher wages actually

Table 15.1
Links in the
Service-Profit
Chain

1. Customer loyalty drives profitability and growth.
2. Customer satisfaction drives customer loyalty.
3. Value drives customer satisfaction.
4. Employee productivity drives value.
5. Employee loyalty drives productivity.
6. Employee satisfaction drives loyalty.
7. Internal quality drives employee satisfaction.
8. Top management leadership underlies the chain's success.

Source: James L. Heskett et al., "Putting the Service Profit Chain to Work," *Harvard Business Review* (March–April 1994); James L. Heskett, W. Earl Sasser, and Leonard L. Schlesinger, *The Service Profit Chain* (Boston, MA: Harvard Business School Press, 1997).

decreases labor costs after reduced turnover, higher productivity, and higher quality are taken into account. Underlying the chain's success (link 8) is top-management leadership. Clearly, implementation of the service-profit chain requires a thorough understanding of how marketing, operations, and human resources each relate to a company's broader strategic concerns.

The Marketing Function

As we've noted before, production and consumption are usually clearly separated in manufacturing firms. It's not normally necessary for production personnel to have direct involvement with customers where consumer goods are concerned. In such firms, marketing acts as a link between producers and consumers, providing the manufacturing division with guidelines for product specifications that reflect consumer needs, as well as projections of market demand, information on competitive activity, and feedback on performance in the marketplace. Marketing personnel also work with logistics and transportation specialists to develop distribution strategies.

In service firms, things are different. Many service operations—especially those involving people-processing services—are literally "factories in the field" that customers enter whenever they need the service in question. In a large chain, the company's service delivery sites may be located across a country, a continent, or even the entire world. When customers are actively involved in production and the service output is consumed as it is produced, direct contact between production (operations) and consumers is mandatory. Even in services like repair and maintenance, where customers don't get actively involved in production, they may still have contact with service employees at the beginning and end of the service delivery process. In some cases, of course, there's no contact with personnel since customers are expected to serve themselves independently or communicate through more impersonal media like mail, email, or Web sites.

In manufacturing firms, marketers assume full responsibility for the product once it leaves the production line, often working closely with channel intermediaries such as retailers. In many services, by contrast, operations management is responsible for running service distribution systems, including retail outlets. Moreover, contact between operations personnel and customers is the rule rather than the exception—although the extent of this contact varies according to the nature of the service. Yet, as we have seen in the course of this book, there remains a need in service businesses for a strong, efficient marketing organization to perform the following tasks:

- Evaluate and select the market segments to serve.
- Research customer needs and preferences within each segment.
- Monitor competitive offerings, identifying their principal characteristics, quality levels, and the strategies used to bring them to the market.
- Design the core product to meet the needs of the chosen market segments and ensure that they match or exceed those of competitive offerings.
- Select and establish service levels for supplementary elements needed to enhance the value and appeal of the core product or to facilitate its purchase and use.
- Collaborate with operations personnel in designing the entire service process to ensure that it is "user friendly" and reflects customer needs and preferences.
- Set prices that reflect costs, competitive strategies, and consumer sensitivity to different price levels.
- Tailor location and scheduling of service availability to customers' needs and preferences.
- Develop appropriate communications strategies to transmit messages informing prospective customers about the service and promoting its advantages, without overpromising.
- Develop performance standards, based on customer needs and expectations, for establishing and measuring service quality levels.
- Ensure that all customer-contact personnel understand the firm's desired market position and customer expectations of their own performance.
- Create programs for rewarding and reinforcing customer loyalty.
- Conduct research to evaluate customer satisfaction following service delivery and identify any aspects requiring changes or improvements.

The net result of these requirements is that the services marketing function is closely interrelated with, and dependent on, the procedures, personnel, and facilities managed by the operations function, as well as on the quality of the service personnel recruited and trained by the human resources function. Although initially seen as a poor sister by many operations managers, marketing now possesses significant management clout in many service businesses, with important implications for strategy, organizational design, and assignment of responsibilities.

The Operations Function

Although marketing's importance has increased, the operations function still dominates line management in most service businesses. This is hardly surprising, because operations—typically the largest functional group—remains responsible for most of the processes involved in creating and delivering the service product. It must obtain the necessary resources, maintain operating equipment and facilities, manage the level of capacity over time, and transform inputs into outputs efficiently. When service delivery is halted for any reason, it is up to operations to restore service as quickly as possible.

Unlike marketing, the operations function is responsible for activities taking place both backstage and front stage. Operations managers are usually responsible for maintaining buildings and equipment, including company-owned retail outlets and other customer facilities. In high-contact, labor-intensive services, operations managers may direct the work of large numbers of employees, including many who serve customers directly in widely dispersed locations. The ongoing push for cost savings and higher productivity in the service sector requires a continuing effort by all operations personnel to achieve greater efficiency in service delivery.

An increasingly important role—often assigned to a separate department—is management of the firm's information technology infrastructure. In technology-driven firms, operations managers with the appropriate technical skills work with research and development specialists to design and introduce innovative delivery systems, including use of the Internet. However, it's essential that they understand the implications of such innovations for both employees and customers.

The Human Resources Function

Few service organizations are so technologically advanced that they can be operated without front-line staff. Indeed, many service industries remain highly labor intensive, although the need for technical skills is increasing. People are required to perform operational tasks (either front stage or backstage), to execute a wide array of marketing tasks, and to provide administrative support.

Historically, responsibility for matters relating to employees was often divided among a number of different departments, such as personnel, compensation, industrial relations, and organization development (or training). But during the 1980s, human resources emerged as a separate management function. As defined by academic specialists, "Human resource management (HRM) involves all managerial decisions and actions that affect the nature of the relationship between the organization and its employees—its human resources."[3]

Just as some forward-looking service businesses have developed an expanded vision of marketing, viewing it from a strategic perspective rather than a narrow functional and tactical one, so is HRM coming to be seen as a key element in business strategy. People-related activities in a modern service corporation can be subsumed under four broad policy areas.[4]

1. *Human resource flow* is concerned with ensuring that the right number of people and mix of competencies are available to meet the firm's long-term strategic requirements. Issues include recruitment, training, career development, and promotions.

2. *Work systems* involve all tasks associated with arranging people, information, facilities, and technology to create (or support) the services produced by the organization.

3. *Reward systems* send powerful messages to all employees about what kind of organization management seeks to create and maintain, especially regarding desired attitudes and behavior. Not all rewards are financial in nature. Recognition can be a powerful motivator.

4. *Employee influence* relates to employee inputs concerning business goals, pay, working conditions, career progression, employment security, and the design and implementation of work tasks. The movement toward greater empowerment of employees represents a shift in the nature and extent of employee influence.[5]

In many service businesses, the caliber and commitment of the labor force have become a major source of competitive advantage. This is especially true in high-contact services where customers can discern differences between the employees of competing firms.[6] A strong commitment by top management to human resources (like that exhibited by Infosys' management team) is a feature of many successful service firms.[7] To the extent that employees understand and support the goals of their organization, have the skills and training needed to succeed in their jobs, and recognize the importance of creating and maintaining customer satisfaction, both marketing and operations activities should be easier to manage.

To adopt an increasingly strategic role, HR needs to shift its emphasis away from many of the routine, bureaucratic tasks like payroll and benefits administration that previously consumed much of management's time. Investments in technology can reduce some of the burden, but progressive firms are going even further, outsourcing many noncore administrative tasks.

For HRM to succeed, argues Kabachnick, "it must be a business-driven function with a thorough understanding of the organization's big picture. It must be viewed as a strategic consulting partner, providing innovative solutions and influencing key decisions and policies."[8] Among the tasks that she believes that HRM should perform are:

•   Installing systems that measure an applicant's beliefs and values for comparison to the company's beliefs and values, in order to replace "gut instinct" hiring decisions that often result in rapid turnover.

•   Studying similar industries and identifying what lessons can be learned from their HRM policies.

- Challenging corporate personnel policies if they no longer make sense in today's environment and describing how proposed changes (e.g., job sharing) will affect the bottom line.
- Demonstrating that HRM is in the business of developing and retaining productive workers, rather than just being a training department.

Reducing Interfunctional Conflict

As service firms place more emphasis on developing a strong market orientation and serving customers well, there's increased potential for conflict among the three functions, especially between marketing and operations. How comfortably can the three functions coexist in a service business, and how are their relative roles perceived? Vandermerwe makes the point that high-value-creating enterprises should be thinking in term of *activities*, not functions.[9] Yet in many firms, we still find individuals from marketing and operations backgrounds at odds with one another. For instance, marketers may see their role as one of constantly adding value to the product offering in order to enhance its appeal to customers and thereby increase sales. Operations managers, by contrast, often take the view that their job is to pare back these elements to reflect the reality of service constraints—like staff and equipment—and the accompanying need for cost containment. Conflicts may also occur between human resources and the other two functions, especially where employees are in boundary-spanning roles that require them to balance the seemingly conflicting goals imposed by marketing and operations.

Marketers who want to avoid conflicts with operations should familiarize themselves with the issues that typically provide the foundation for operations strategy. Changing traditional organizational perspectives doesn't come readily to managers who have been comfortable with established approaches. It's easy for them to become obsessed with their own functional tasks, forgetting that all areas of the company must pull together to create a customer-driven organization. As long as a service business continues to be organized along functional lines (and many are), achieving the necessary coordination and strategic synergy requires that top management establish clear imperatives for each function.

Each imperative should relate to customers and define how a specific function contributes to the overall mission. Part of the challenge of service management is to ensure that each of these three functional imperatives is compatible with the others and that all are mutually reinforcing. Although a firm will need to phrase each imperative in ways that are specific to its own business, we can express them generically as follows:

- *The marketing imperative*: To target specific types of customers whom the firm is well equipped to serve and create ongoing relationships with them by delivering a carefully defined service product package in return for a price that offers value to customers and the potential for profits to the firm. Customers will recognize this package as being one of consistent quality that delivers solutions to their needs and is superior to competing alternatives.

- *The operations imperative*: To create and deliver the specified service package to targeted customers by selecting those operational techniques that allow it to consistently meet customer-driven cost, schedule, and quality goals, and also enable the business to reduce its costs through continuing improvements in productivity. The chosen operational methods will match skills that employees and intermediaries or contractors currently possess or can be trained to develop. The firm will have the resources to support these operations with the necessary facilities, equipment, and technology, while avoiding negative impacts on employees and the broader community.

- *The human resources imperative*: To recruit, train, and motivate managers, supervisors, and employees who can work well together for a realistic compensation package to balance the twin goals of customer satisfaction and operational effectiveness. Employees will want to stay with the firm and to enhance their own skills because they value the working environment, appreciate the opportunities that it presents, and take pride in the services they help to create and deliver.

Creating a Leading Service Organization

In your own life as a consumer, you have probably encountered an assortment of service performances ranging from extremely satisfying to infuriatingly bad. You may know some organizations that you can always trust to deliver good service, whereas others are rather unpredictable, offering good service one day and indifferent service the next. Perhaps you even know of a few businesses that consistently deliver bad service and mistreat their customers.

From Losers to Leaders: Four Levels of Service Performance

Service leadership is not based on outstanding performance within a single dimension. Rather, it reflects excellence across multiple dimensions. In an effort to capture this performance spectrum, we need to evaluate the organization within each of the three functional areas described earlier—marketing, operations, and human resources. Table 15.2 modifies and extends an operations-oriented framework proposed by Professor Richard Chase of the University of Southern California and Professor Robert Hayes of Harvard.[10] The service performance framework categorizes service performers into four levels: loser, nonentity, professional, and leader. At each level, there is a brief description of a typical organization across 12 dimensions.

Table 15.2
Four Levels of Service Performance

Level	1. Loser	2. Nonentity
Marketing Function		
Role of marketing	Tactical role only; advertising and promotions lack focus; no involvement in product or pricing decision	Uses mix of selling and mass communication, using simple segmentation strategy; makes selective use of price discounts and promotions; conducts and tabulates basic satisfaction surveys
Competitive appeal	Customers patronize firm for reasons other than performance	Customers neither seek out nor avoid the firm
Customer profile	Unspecified; a mass market to be served at a minimum cost	One or more segments whose basic needs are understood
Service quality	Highly variable, usually unsatisfactory Subservient to operations priorities	Meets some customer expectations; consistent on one or two key dimensions, but not all
Operations Function		
Role of operations	Reactive; cost oriented	The principal line management function: Creates and delivers product, focuses on standardization as key to productivity, defines quality from internal perspective
Service delivery (front stage)	A necessary evil. Locations and schedules are unrelated to preferences of customers, who are routinely ignored	Sticklers for tradition; "If it ain't broke, don't fix it;" tight rules for customers; each step in delivery run independently
Backstage operations	Divorced from front-stage; cogs in a machine	Contributes to individual front-stage delivery steps but organized separately; unfamiliar with customers
Productivity	Undefined; managers are punished for failing to stick within budget	Based on standardization; rewarded for keeping costs below budget
Introduction of new technology	Late adopter, under duress, when necessary for survival	Follows the crowd when justified by cost savings
Human Resources Function		
Role of human resources	Supplies low-cost employees who meet minimum skill requirements for the job	Recruits and trains employees who can perform competently
Workforce	Negative constraint: poor performers, don't care, disloyal	Adequate resource, follows procedures but uninspired; turnover often high
Front-line management	Controls workers	Controls the process

Note: This framework was inspired by—and expands upon—work in service operations management by Richard Chase and Robert Hayes.

Table 15-2
Continued

3. Professional	4. Leader
Marketing Function	
Has clear positioning strategy against competition; uses focused communications with distinctive appeals to clarify promises and educate customers; pricing is based on value; monitors customer usage and operates loyalty programs; uses a variety of research techniques to measure customer satisfaction and obtain ideas for service enhancements; works with operations to introduce new delivery systems	Innovative leader in chosen segments, known for marketing skills; brands at product/process level; conducts sophisticated analysis of relational databases as inputs to one-to-one marketing and proactive account management; uses state-of-the art research techniques; uses concept testing, observation, and use of lead customers as inputs to new-product development; close to operations/HR
Customers seek out the firm, based on its sustained reputation for meeting customer expectations	Company name is synonymous with service excellence; its ability to delight customers raises expectations to levels that competitors can't meet
Groups of individuals whose variation in needs and value to the firm are clearly understood	Individuals are selected and retained based on their future value to the firm, including their potential for new service opportunities and their ability to stimulate innovation
Consistently meets or exceeds customer expectations across multiple dimensions	Raises customer expectations to new levels; improves continuously
Operations Function	
Plays a strategic role in competitive strategy; recognizes tradeoff between productivity and customer-defined quality; willing to outsource; monitors competing operations for ideas, threats	Recognized for innovation, focus, and excellence; an equal partner with marketing and HR management; has in-house research capability and academic contacts; continually experimenting
Driven by customer satisfaction, not tradition; willing to customize, embrace new approaches; emphasis on speed, convenience, and comfort	Delivery is a seamless process organized around the customer; employees know whom they are serving; focuses on continuous improvement
Process is explicitly linked to front-stage activities; sees role as serving "internal customers," who in turn serve external customers	Closely integrated with front-stage delivery, even when geographically far apart; understands how own role relates to overall process of serving external customers; continuing dialogue
Focuses on reengineering backstage processes; avoids productivity improvements that will degrade customers' service experience; continually refining processes for efficiency	Understands concept of return on quality; actively seeks customer involvement in productivity improvement; ongoing testing of new processes and technologies
An early adopter when IT promises to enhance service for customers and provide a competitive edge	Works with technology leaders to develop new applications that create first-mover advantage; seeks to perform at levels competitors can't match
Human Resources Function	
Invests in selective recruiting, ongoing training; keeps close to employees, promotes upward mobility; strives to enhance quality of working life	Sees quality of employees as strategic advantage; firm is recognized as outstanding place to work; HR helps top management to nurture culture
Motivated, hard working, allowed some discretion in choice of procedures, offers suggestions	Innovative and empowered; very loyal, committed to firm's values and goals; creates procedures
Listens to customers; coaches and facilitates workers	Source of new ideas for top management; mentors workers to enhance career growth, value to firm

Under the marketing function, we look at the role of marketing, competitive appeal, customer profile, and service quality. Under the operations function, we consider the role of operations, service delivery (front stage), backstage operations, productivity, and introduction of new technology. Finally, under the human resources function, we consider the role of HRM, the workforce, and front-line management. Obviously, there are overlaps between these dimensions and across functions. Additionally, there may be variations in the relative importance of some dimensions between industries. However, the goal is to obtain some insights into what needs to be changed in organizations that are not performing as well as they might.

SERVICE LOSERS   These are organizations at the bottom of the barrel from both customer and managerial perspectives. They get failing grades in marketing, operations, and human resource management alike. Customers patronize them for reasons other than performance. Typically, there is no viable alternative, which is one reason why service losers continue to survive. Such organizations see service delivery as a necessary evil. New technology is introduced only under duress, and the uncaring workforce is a negative constraint on performance. The cycles of failure and mediocrity presented in Figures 11.2 and 11.4 describe how such organizations behave and what the consequences are.

SERVICE NONENTITIES   Although their performance still leaves much to be desired, nonentities have eliminated the worst features of losers. As shown in Table 15.2, they are dominated by a traditional operations mindset, typically based on achieving cost savings through standardization. They employ unsophisticated marketing strategies, and the roles of human resources and operations might be summed up, respectively, by the philosophies "adequate is good enough" and "if it ain't broke, don't fix it." Consumers neither seek out nor avoid such organizations. There are often several such firms competing in lackluster fashion within a given marketplace, and each one may be almost indistinguishable from the others. Periodic price discounts tend to be the primary means of trying to attract new customers.

SERVICE PROFESSIONALS   These organizations are in a different league from nonentities and have a clear market positioning strategy. Customers within the target segments seek out these firms based on their sustained reputation for meeting expectations. Marketing is more sophisticated, using targeted communications and pricing based on value to the customer. Research is used to measure customer satisfaction and obtain ideas for service enhancement. Operations and marketing work together to introduce new delivery systems and recognize the tradeoff between productivity and customer-defined quality. There are explicit links between backstage and front-stage activities and a much more proactive, investment-oriented approach to human resource management than is found among nonentities.

SERVICE LEADERS These organizations are the *crème de la crème* of their respective industries. While service professionals are good, service leaders are outstanding. Their company names are synonymous with service excellence and an ability to delight customers. They are recognized for their innovation in each functional area of management, as well as for their excellent internal communications and coordination between these three functions—often the result of a relatively flat organizational structure and extensive use of teams. As a result, service delivery is a seamless process organized around the customer.

Marketing efforts by service leaders make extensive use of relational databases that offer strategic insights about customers, who are often addressed on a one-to-one basis. Concept testing, observation, and contacts with lead customers are employed in the development of new, breakthrough services that respond to previously unrecognized needs. Operations specialists work with technology leaders around the world to develop new applications that will create a first-mover advantage and enable the firm to perform at levels that competitors cannot hope to reach for a long period of time. Senior executives see quality of employees as a strategic advantage. HRM works with them to develop and maintain a service-oriented culture and to create an outstanding working environment that simplifies the task of attracting and retaining the best people.[11] The employees themselves are committed to the firm's values and goals. Since they are empowered and quick to embrace change, they are an ongoing source of new ideas.

Let us take a look at how foreign banks in India attempt to be leading service organizations through inculcating a customer service culture within the organization (see Service Perspectives 15.1).

Moving to a Higher Level of Performance

Firms can move either up or down the performance ladder. Once-stellar performers can become complacent and sluggish. Organizations that are devoted to satisfying their current customers may miss important shifts in the marketplace and find themselves turning into has-beens. These businesses may continue to serve a loyal but dwindling band of conservative customers, but they are unable to attract demanding new consumers with different expectations. Companies whose original success was based on mastery of a specific technological process may find that, in defending their control of that process, they have encouraged competitors to find higher-performing alternatives. Organizations whose management has worked for years to build up a loyal workforce with a strong service ethic may find that such a culture can be quickly destroyed as a result of a merger or acquisition that brings in new leaders who emphasize short-term profits. Unfortunately, senior managers sometimes delude themselves into thinking that their company has achieved a

Service Perspectives 15.1

BANKS IN INDIA: INCULCATING A CUSTOMER SERVICE CULTURE

Is high pay enough to motivate one's employees to come singing to work every morning? The answer is no, according to human resource (HR) chiefs in Indian banks.

"Beyond a certain time, money ceases to be the prime motivation," says Jagjit Singh, research and developing manager of HSBC India. Therefore, the responsibility to energize the work environment and bring out the optimum performance from employees falls on the organization. Liberalization in the banking industry has increased the number of private Indian banks that compete in the same segment, making it more difficult for HSBC to excel in India. With many more banks for customers to put their money, wooing new customers and keeping old ones happy is a stressful job for any bank employee.

Besides HSBC, Standard Chartered Bank is also very proactive in trying to inculcate a customer service culture within the company. Standard Chartered Bank started by conducting a survey across the board to find out how to make their employees perform at optimum levels. This was particularly necessary after their merger with ANZ Grindlays when the bank needed to reorganize. The employee dipstick poll developed with the help of the international research agency Gallup, along with an employee strength finder tool, enabled the bank to enhance employees' performance.

A routine question in the survey on recognition by the boss highlighted a very interesting discovery. According to Chandrashekhar Pingali, Standard Chartered Bank's regional head of human resources for India and Nepal, the practice of recognizing an employee's effort for a job well done did not exist in the bank's culture. "We don't appreciate people and this is a cultural shortcoming. So we started making a conscious effort. Just simple things like, 'Thank you for a job well done' gives people motivation to work better," said Mr Pingali.

Other banks organized in-house trekking clubs for their employees and encouraged interbranch cricket matches. While all this seems like fun, it plays an important role in networking for the employees, who otherwise don't normally interact with colleagues from other branches. The main objective of all these practices is to inculcate the customer service culture among all the employees in the bank, which, ultimately, would be reflected in the balance sheet. Most banks in India are trying to achieve this in an aggressive manner.

Source: Adapted from Vidya Srinivas, "Foreign Banks Keep Their Staff Happy to Make Their Customers Smile," *Business India*, July 22, 2002.

superior level of performance when, in fact, the foundations of that success are actually crumbling.

In most markets, we can also find companies that are moving up the performance ladder through conscious efforts to coordinate their marketing, operations, and human resource management functions in order to establish more favorable competitive positions and better satisfy their customers.

In Search of Leadership

Service leaders are those firms that stand out in their respective markets and industries. However, it still requires human leaders to take them in the right direction, set the right strategic priorities, and ensure that the relevant strategies are implemented throughout the organization. Much of the literature on leadership is concerned with turnarounds and transformation. It is easy to see why poorly performing organizations may require a major transformation of their culture and operating procedures in order to make them more competitive. However, in times of rapid change, even high-performing firms need to evolve on a continuing basis, transforming themselves in evolutionary fashion.

Leading a Service Organization

John Kotter, perhaps the best-known authority on leadership, argues that in most successful change management processes, people need to move through eight complicated and often time-consuming stages:[12]

- Creating a sense of urgency to develop the impetus for change
- Putting together a strong enough team to direct the process
- Creating an appropriate vision of where the organization needs to go
- Communicating that new vision broadly
- Empowering employees to act on that vision
- Producing sufficient short-term results to create credibility and counter cynicism
- Building momentum and using that to tackle the tougher change problems
- Anchoring the new behaviors in the organizational culture

LEADERSHIP VERSUS MANAGEMENT   The primary force behind successful change is *leadership*, which is concerned with the development of vision and strategies, and the empowerment of people to overcome obstacles and make the vision happen. *Management*, by contrast, involves keeping the current situation operating through planning, budgeting, organizing, staffing, controlling, and problem solving. Bennis and Nanus distinguish between leaders who emphasize the emotional and even spiritual resources of an organization and managers who stress its physical resources, such as raw materials, technology and capital.[13] Says Kotter:

> Leadership works through people and culture. It's soft and hot. Management works through hierarchy and systems. It's harder and cooler … The fundamental purpose of management is to keep the current system functioning. The fundamental purpose of leadership is to produce useful change, especially nonincremental change. It's possible to have too much or too little of either. Strong leadership with no management risks chaos; the organization might walk right off a cliff. Strong

management with no leadership tends to entrench an organization in deadly bureaucracy.[14]

However, leadership is an essential and growing aspect of managerial work because the rate of change has been increasing. Reflecting the stimulus of both intense competition and technological advances, new services or service features are being introduced at a faster rate and tend to have shorter life cycles (if, indeed, they even survive the introductory phase). Meantime, the competitive environment shifts constantly as a result of international firms entering new geographic markets, mergers and acquisitions, and the exit of former competitors. The process of service delivery itself has sped up, with customers demanding faster service and faster responses when things go wrong. As a result, declares Kotter, effective top executives may now spend up to 80 percent of their time leading, double the figure required not that long ago. Even those at the bottom of the management hierarchy may spend at least 20 percent of their time on leadership.

SETTING DIRECTION VERSUS PLANNING   People often confuse these two activities. Planning, according to Kotter, is a management process, designed to produce orderly results, not change. Setting a direction, by contrast, is more inductive than deductive. Leaders look for patterns, relationships, and linkages that help to explain things and suggest future trends. Direction setting creates visions and strategies that describe a business, technology, or corporate culture in terms of what it should become over the long term and that articulate a feasible way of achieving this goal. Effective leaders have a talent for simplicity in communicating with others who may not share their background or knowledge. They know their audiences and are able to distill their messages, conveying even complicated concepts in just a few phrases.[15] Consider All Nippon Airways (ANA) CEO and President Yoji Ohashi's favorite phrase: "Actions Speak Louder Than Words." It seems just like any other commonly heard and used phrases on the surface but it means so much more in the eyes of Ohashi and ANA's employees (see Best Practice in Action 15.2).

Many of the best visions and strategies are not brilliantly innovative. Rather, they combine some basic insights and translate them into a realistic competitive strategy that serves the interests of customers, employees, and stockholders. Some visions, however, fall into the category that Hamel and Pralahad describe as "stretch"—a challenge to attain new levels of performance and competitive advantage that might, at first sight, seem to be beyond the organization's reach.[16] Stretching to achieve such bold goals requires creative reappraisal of traditional ways of doing business and leverage of existing resources through partnerships. It also requires creating the energy and the will among managers and employees alike to perform at higher levels than they believe themselves able to do.

ALL NIPPON AIRWAYS: ACTIONS ALWAYS SPEAK LOUDER THAN WORDS

Unlike many other CEOs, Yoji Ohashi, CEO and president of All Nippon Airways Co. Ltd (ANA), actually practices the "open door" policy that he preaches. He works in an open office with a huge sliding door that is never closed. He believes that such practices would improve interaction with his employees.

Like most airlines, ANA has been working hard to bring the airline back to profitability. Currently, ANA operates 850 flights daily to 67 destinations, carrying more than 50 million passengers annually. However, problems started to surface for ANA in 2002, when Japan Airlines (JAL) merged with Japan's No. 3 carrier, Japan Air System (JAS). The merger formed a new powerful rival that ANA knew they could not outdo in terms of volume. Therefore, ANA's main focus turned to service quality. To enhance its service level, ANA listens to its customers constantly, and after listening, ANA responds.

ANA receives approximately 40,000 requests, claims, and suggestions every year. Every piece of feedback is processed carefully, and each customer receives an individual reply. By listening attentively to his customers, Ohashi is confident that he can deliver services that are superior to his rivals'.

Ohashi is aware that he needs commitment from all his employees in order to achieve this goal. Therefore, he launched the "Direct Talk" campaign two years ago in an effort to motivate and energize his employees. "Direct Talk" consisted of a series of meetings at every level of the organization. It is designed to encourage every employee to take personal responsibility for customer satisfaction, and be involved in the idea generation processes that aim to better address customer needs. "Direct Talk" also consisted of a card that was created by the employees, which outlines ANA's philosophy. Every employee, including Ohashi, has to carry the card at all times.

The main aim of the "Direct Talk" campaign was to reinforce ANA's customer-focused culture by outlining commitment and course of actions, as Ohashi always believes that actions speak louder than words. Such commitment and effort have started to pay off—ANA turned profitable again in the first half of fiscal 2003. It was also voted as one of the top ten airlines worldwide for "Best Cabin Staff" in a survey conducted by Skytrax Research.

However, Ohashi is far from being satisfied because he knows that there is still room for improvement. He is also confident that ANA will soar higher with its strategies that focus on growth opportunities, efficiency gains, and further increasing customer satisfaction (see Figure 15.4).

Source: Adapted from "Where Actions Speak Louder Than Words," *Forbes Global,* January 12, 2004: S48 (Japan Special Advertising Section).

Planning follows and complements direction setting, serving as a useful reality check and a road map for strategic execution. A good plan provides an action agenda for accomplishing the mission, using existing resources or identifying potential new sources.

Ad reproduced with permission from ANA Japan.

Leadership Qualities

Many commentators have written on the topic of leadership. It has even been described as a service in its own right.[17] The qualities that are often ascribed to leaders include vision, charisma, persistence, high expectations, expertise, empathy, persuasiveness, and integrity. Typical prescriptions for leader behavior stress the importance of establishing (or preserving) a culture that is relevant to corporate success, putting in place an effective strategic planning process, instilling a sense of cohesion in the organization, and providing continuing examples of desired behaviors. Collins concluded that a leader does not require a larger-than-life personality. Rather, he considers it important that a leader has personal humility blended with intensive professional will, ferocious resolve, and the tendency to give credit to others while taking the blame to themselves.[18]

Berry argues that service leadership requires a special perspective. "Regardless of the target markets, the specific services, or the pricing strategy, service leaders visualize quality of service as the foundation for competing."[19] Recognizing the key role of employees in delivering service, he emphasizes that service leaders need to believe in the people who work for them and make communicating with employees a priority. Love of the business is another service leadership characteristic he highlights, to the extent that it combines natural enthusiasm with the right setting in which to express it. Such enthusiasm motivates individuals to teach the business to others and to pass on to them the nuances, secrets, and craft of operating it. Berry also stresses the importance for leaders of being driven by a set of core values which they infuse into the organization, arguing: "A critical role of values-driven leaders is cultivating the leadership qualities of others in the organization." And he notes that "values-driven leaders rely on their values to navigate their companies through difficult periods."[20]

Recent research suggests that a transformational leadership is the preferred style in achieving work outcomes. Transformational leaders operate on the basis of deeply held personal values, change their followers' goals and beliefs, and develop their followers' capacity to look beyond their self-interests by using:

- *Charisma*, providing vision and a sense of mission, instilling pride in employees, and gaining respect and trust
- *Inspirational motivation*, communicating high expectations and expressing important purposes in simple ways
- *Intellectual stimulation*, promoting rationality, logic, and careful problem solving
- *Individual consideration*, paying close attention to individual differences among employees, and coaching and advising staff through personal attention[21]

However, Khurana warns against excessive emphasis on charisma in selecting CEOs, arguing that it leads to unrealistic expectations.[22] He also highlights the problems that may occur when charismatic but unprincipled leaders induce blind obedience in their followers.

In hierarchical organizations, structured on a military model, it's often assumed that leadership at the top is sufficient. However, as Vandermerwe points out, forward-looking service businesses need to be more flexible. Today's greater emphasis on using teams within service businesses means, she argues, that:

[L]eaders are everywhere, disseminated throughout the teams. They are found especially in the customer facing and interfacing jobs in order that decision-making will lead to long-lasting relationships with customers … leaders are customer and project champions who energize the group by virtue of their enthusiasm, interest, and know-how.[23]

Leadership in Different Contexts

There are important distinctions between leading a successful organization that is functioning well, redirecting a firm into new areas of activity, and trying to turn around a dysfunctional organization. In the case of Wal-Mart, Sam Walton created both the company and the culture, so his task was to preserve that culture as the company grew, and to select a successor who would maintain an appropriate culture as the company continued to grow. Herb Kelleher was one of the founders of Southwest Airlines, using his legal skills in his initial role as the company's general counsel; later, he came to deploy his considerable human-relations skills as CEO.

Transformation can take place in two different ways. One involves Darwinian-style evolution—constant mutations designed to ensure the survival of the fittest. Evolution means top management evolves the focus and strategy of the firm to take advantage of changing conditions and the advent of new technologies. Without a continuing series of mutations, it is unlikely a firm can remain successful in a dynamic marketplace.

A different type of transformation occurs in turnaround situations. Li & Fung is a Hong Kong-based company that has transformed itself from a traditional trading house to a technology-based supply chain manager, with the help of Fung Pak-liu's two sons, Victor and William. Victor is the visionary and William, the group's managing director. Together, the brothers make a formidable team. When they first joined the company, Li & Fung's main role was as a sourcing agent for neighboring countries like Singapore, Taiwan, and Korea. The brothers recognized a need to develop more customer-oriented operations and relationships with international clients.

Li & Fung took advantage of the growing opportunity in China to move labor-intensive operations across the border into southern China. After the labor-intensive work was completed, the finished goods came back to Hong Kong for final testing and inspection. This new process of manufacturing led to another major transformation in the company. Victor Fung said:

Dispersed manufacturing forced us to get smart not only about logistics and transportation, but also about dissecting the value chain. Once we figured out how to do it, it became clear that our reach should extend beyond southern China. And so we began what has turned into a constant search for new and better sources of supply.

The series of transformations has propelled Li & Fung into one of the most successful trading companies in Asia.[24] Victor Fung added:

> We deliver a new type of value added, a truly global product that has never been seen before. We're pulling apart the value chain and optimizing each step—and we're doing it globally.

One of the traits of successful leaders is their ability to role model the behavior they expect of managers and other employees. Often, this requires the approach known as "management by wandering around," popularized by Peters and Waterman in their book *In Search of Excellence*.[25] Wandering around involves regular visits, sometimes unannounced, to different areas of the company's operation. It provides insights into both backstage and front-stage operations, the ability to observe and meet both employees and customers, and to see how corporate strategy is implemented at the front line. Periodically, it may lead to the recognition that changes are needed in that strategy. It can also be motivating for service personnel. Taiwan Semiconductor Manufacturing Company Limited (TSMC), ranked one of the "Best Employers in Asia 2003" in a survey conducted by Hewitt Associates, is one of Taiwan's most preferred employers and attracts some of the best talents in the semiconductor industry. TSMC has a rewarding human resource policy. Employees are given stock options, as well as an individual development plan, which is reviewed throughout the employee's career at TSMC to see how the employee is progressing with his career development goals. This plan also takes into account the individual's needs, background, interests, and skills. [26]

In addition to internal leadership, many chief executives have also assumed external leadership roles, serving as ambassadors for their companies in the public arena and promoting the quality and value of their firms' services. There is a risk, of course, that prominent leaders may become too externally focused at the risk of their internal effectiveness. A CEO who enjoys an enormous income, maintains a princely lifestyle, and basks in widespread publicity may even turn off low-paid service workers at the bottom of the organization. Another risk is that a leadership style and focus which has served the company well in the past may become inappropriate for a changing environment.

Evaluating Leadership Potential

The need for leadership is not confined to chief executives or other top managers. Leadership traits are needed of everyone in a supervisory or managerial position, including those heading teams. FedEx believes this so strongly that it requires all employees interested in entering the ranks of first-line management to participate in its Leadership Evaluation and Awareness Process (LEAP).[27]

LEAP's first step involves participation in an introductory, one-day class that familiarizes candidates with managerial responsibilities. About one candidate in five concludes at this point that "management is not for me." The next step is a three-to-six-month period during which the candidate's manager coaches him or her based on a series of leadership attributes identified by the company. A third step involves peer assessment by a number of the candidate's coworkers (selected by the manager). Finally, the candidate must present written and oral arguments regarding specific leadership scenarios to a group of managers trained in LEAP assessment. This panel compares its findings with those from the other sources.

FedEx emphasizes leadership at every level through its "Survey Feedback Action" surveys, including the Leadership Index in which subordinates rate their managers along ten dimensions. Unfortunately, not every company is equally thorough in addressing the role of leadership at all levels in the organization. In many firms, promotional decisions often appear haphazard or based on such criteria as duration of tenure in a previous position.

Leadership, Culture, and Climate[28]

To close this chapter, we take a brief look at a theme that runs throughout this chapter and, indeed, the book: the leader's role in nurturing an effective culture within the firm. *Organizational culture* can be defined as including:

- Shared perceptions or themes regarding what is important in the organization
- Shared values about what is right and wrong
- Shared understanding about what works and what doesn't work
- Shared beliefs, and assumptions about *why* these things are important
- Shared styles of working and relating to others.

Organizational climate represents the tangible surface layer on top of the organization's underlying culture. Among six key factors that influence an organization's working environment are its *flexibility*—how free employees feel to innovate; their sense of *responsibility* to the organization; the level of *standards* that people set; the perceived aptness of *rewards*; the *clarity* people have about mission and values; and the level of *commitment* to a common purpose.[29] From an employee perspective, this climate is directly related to managerial policies and procedures, especially those associated with human resource management. In short, climate represents the shared perceptions of employees concerning the practices, procedures, and types of behaviors that get rewarded and supported in a particular setting.

Because multiple climates often exist simultaneously within a single organization, a climate must relate to something specific, for instance, service, support, innovation, or safety. A climate for service refers to employee perceptions of those practices, procedures, and behaviors that are expected with regard to customer service and service quality, and that get rewarded when performed well. Essential features of a service-oriented culture include clear marketing goals and a strong drive to be the best in delivering superior value or service quality.[30]

Leaders are responsible for creating cultures and the service climates that go along with them. Transformational leadership may require changing a culture that has become dysfunctional in the context of what it takes to be successful. Why are some leaders more effective than others in bringing about a desired change in climate? As presented in Research Insights 15.1, research suggests that it may be a matter of style.

Creating a new climate for service, based upon an understanding of what is needed for market success, may require a radical rethink of human resource management activities, operational procedures, and the firm's reward and recognition policies. Newcomers to an organization must quickly familiarize themselves with the existing culture; otherwise they will find themselves being led by it, rather than leading through it and, if necessary, changing it.

Research Insights 15.1

THE IMPACT OF LEADERSHIP STYLES ON CLIMATE

Daniel Goleman, an applied psychologist at Rutgers University, is known for his work on emotional intelligence—the ability to manage ourselves and our relationships effectively. Having earlier identified six different styles of leadership, he investigated how successful each style has proven to be in affecting climate or working atmosphere, based on a major study of the behavior and impact on their organizations of thousands of executives.

Coercive leaders demand immediate compliance ("Do what I tell you") and were found to have a negative impact on climate. Goleman comments that this controlling style, often highly confrontational, only has value in a crisis or in dealing with problem employees. *Pace-setting leaders* set high standards for performance and exemplify these through their own energetic behavior. This style can be summarized as "Do as I do, now." Somewhat surprisingly, it, too, was found to have a negative impact on climate. In practice, the pace-setting leader may destroy morale by assuming too much, too soon, of subordinates—expecting them to know already what to do and how to do it. Finding others to be less capable than expected, the leader may lapse into obsessing over details and micromanaging. This style is only likely to work when seeking to get quick results from a highly motivated and competent team.

The research found that the most effective style for achieving a positive change in climate came from *authoritative leaders* who have the skills and personality to mobilize people toward a vision, building confidence and using a "Come with me" approach. The research also found that three other styles had quite positive impacts on climate: *affiliative leaders* who believe that "People come first," seeking to create harmony and build emotional bonds; *democratic leaders* who forge consensus through participation ("What do you think?"); and *coaching leaders* who work to develop people for the future and whose style might be summarized as "Try this."

Source: Daniel Goleman, "Leadership That Gets Results," *Harvard Business Review 78* (March–April 2000): 78–93.

Conclusion

No organization can hope to achieve and maintain market leadership without human leaders who articulate and communicate a vision and are backed by individuals with the management skills to make it happen. Service leadership in an industry requires high performance across a number of dimensions that fall within the scope of the marketing, operations, and HRM functions.

Within any given service organization, marketing has to coexist with operations—traditionally the dominant function—whose concerns centered on cost and efficiency rather than on customers. Marketing must also coexist with human resource management, which usually recruits and trains service personnel, including those who have direct contact with the customers. An ongoing challenge is to balance the concerns of each function, not only at the head office but also in the field. Ultimately, a company's ability to effectively integrate marketing, operations, and human resource management will determine whether it is classified as a service loser, a service nonentity, a service professional, or a service leader.

Review Questions

1. Identify the nature of the tasks that are traditionally assigned to (a) marketing, (b) operations, and (c) human resource management.
2. Describe the causes of tension between the marketing, operations, and human resource functions. Provide specific examples of how these tensions might vary from one service industry to another.
3. Briefly define the four levels of service performance. Based on your own service experiences, provide an example of a company for each category.
4. Which level of service performance do you think best describes Infosys? Explain your answer using specific examples from Best Practice in Action 15.1 at the beginning of this chapter.
5. What is the difference between leadership and management?
6. What is the relationship between leadership, climate, and culture?

Application Exercises

1. Contrast the roles of marketing, operations, and human resources in (1) a gas station chain, (2) a Web-based brokerage firm, and (3) an insurance company.
2. Select a company that you know well and obtain additional information from a literature review, Web site, company publications, etc. Evaluate it on as many dimensions of service performance as you can, identifying where you believe it fits on the service performance spectrum shown in Table 15.2.
3. Profile an individual whose leadership skills have played a significant role in the success of a service organization.

Endnotes

[1] James L. Heskett., Thomas O. Jones, Gary W. Loveman, W. Earl Sasser, Jr., and Leonard A. Schlesinger, "Putting the Service Profit Chain to Work," *Harvard Business Review* (March–April 1994); and James L.

Heskett, W. Earl Sasser, Jr., and Leonard A. Schlesinger, *The Service Profit Chain* (New York: The Free Press, 1997).

2   Note that a relationship between employee satisfaction and customer satisfaction may be more likely in high-contact situations where employee behavior is an important aspect of the customers' experience. For an examination of the service-profit link in various types of organizations, see Rhian Silvestro and Stuart Cross, "Applying the Service Profit Chain in a Retail Environment: Challenging the "Satisfaction Mirror," *International Journal of Service Industry Management* 11, no. 3 (2000): 244–268; see also Ken Bates, Hilary Bates, and Robert Johnstion, "Linking Service to Profit: The Business Case for Service Excellence," *International Journal of Service Industry Management* 14, no. 2 (2003): 173–183. The service-profit chain has also been researched in developing countries; see: Daniel Maranto and Javier Reynoso, "Understanding the Service Profit Chain in Latin America: Managerial Perspective from Mexico," *Managing Service Quality* 13, no. 2 (2003): 134–147.

3   M. Beer, B. Spector, P. R. Lawrence, D. Q. Mills, and R. E. Walton, *Human Resource Management: A General Manager's Perspective* (New York: The Free Press, 1985).

4   *Ibid.*

5   David E. Bowen and Edward T. Lawler, III, "The Empowerment of Service Workers: What, Why, How and When," *Sloan Management Review* 70 (Spring 1992): 31–39.

6   See, for example, Jeffrey Pfeffer, *Competitive Advantage through People* (Boston: Harvard Business School Press, 1994).

7   See, for example, Benjamin Schneider and David E. Bowen, *Winning the Service Game* (Boston: Harvard Business School Press, 1995) and Leonard L. Berry, *On Great Service: A Framework for Action* (New York: The Free Press, 1995), Chapters 8–10.

8   Terri Kabachnick, "The Strategic Role of Human Resources," *Arthur Andersen Retailing Issues Letter* 11, no. 1 (January 1999): 3.

9   Sandra Vandermerwe, *From Tin Soldiers to Russian Dolls* (Oxford: Butterworth-Heinemann, 1993), 82.

10   Richard B. Chase and Robert H. Hayes, "Beefing Up Operations in Service Firms," *Sloan Management Review* 43 (Fall 1991): 15–26.

11   Claudia H. Deutsch, "Management: Companies Scramble to Fill Shoes at the Top," *nytimes.com*, November 1, 2000.

12   John P. Kotter, *What Leaders Really Do* (Boston: Harvard Business School Press, 1999), 10–11.

13   Warren Bennis and Burt Nanus, *Leaders: The Strategies for Taking Charge* (New York: Harper and Row, 1985), 92.

14   Kotter (1999), *op. cit.*

15   Deborah Blagg and Susan Young, "What Makes a Leader?" *Harvard Business School Bulletin* (February 2001): 31–36.

16   Gary Hamel and C. K. Prahlahad, *Competing for the Future* (Boston: Harvard Business School Press, 1994).

17   See, for instance, the special issue on "Leadership as a Service" (Celeste Wilderom, guest editor), *International Journal of Service Industry Management* 3, no. 2 (1992).

18   Jim Collins, "Level 5 Leadership: The Triumph of Humility and Fierce Resolve," *Harvard Business Review* 79 (January 2001): 66–76.

19   Berry (1995), *op. cit.*, 9.

20   Leonard L. Berry, *Discovering the Soul of Service* (New York: The Free Press, 1999), 44, 47. See also D. Micheal Abrashoff, "Retention through Redemption," *Harvard Business Review* 79, no. 2 (February 2001): 136–141, which provides a fascinating example on successful leadership in the U.S. Navy.

21   John H. Humphreys, "Transformational Leader Behavior, Proximity and Successful Services Marketing," *Journal of Services Marketing* 16, no. 6 (2002): 487–502.

22   Rakesh Khurana, "The Curse of the Superstar CEO," *Harvard Business Review* 80 (September 2002): 60–66.

23   Vandermerwe (1993), *op. cit.*, 129.

24   *Winning at a Global Game: Part Five of an Eleven-Part Series*, *Asia Business Today*, April 9, 2004, www.asiabusinesstoday.org/briefings/index.cfm?id=32931.

25   Thomas J. Peters and Robert H. Waterman, *In Search of Excellence* (New York: Harper & Row, 1982), 122.

26   www.hewittasia.com/hewitt/ap/resource/rptspubs/hewittquart/issue8/articles/_apr2003_6b.htm.

27   Christopher Lovelock, "Federal Express: Quality Improvement Program," IMD case (Cranfield, UK: European Case Clearing House, 1990).

28   This section is based, in part, on Benjamin Schneider and David E. Bowen, *Winning the Service Game* (Boston: Harvard Business School Press, 1995); and David E. Bowen, Benjamin Schneider, and Sandra S. Kim, "Shaping Service Cultures through Strategic Human Resource Management," in *Handbook of Services Marketing and Management*, ed. T. Schwartz and D. Iacobucci (Thousand Oaks, CA: Sage Publications, 2000), 439–454.

29   Daniel Goleman, "Leadership That Gets Results," *Harvard Business Review* 78 (March–April, 2000): 78–93.

30   Hans Kasper, "Culture and Leadership in Market-Oriented Service Organisations," *European Journal of Marketing* 36, no. 9/10 (2002): 1047–1057.

Cases

Susan Lee, Service Consumer

CHRISTOPHER LOVELOCK

In the course of a single day, a busy young woman makes use of a wide array of services.

Susan Lee, a final-year business student, had breakfast and then clicked onto the Internet to check the local weather forecast. It predicted rain, so she grabbed an umbrella before leaving the apartment and walking to the bus stop for her daily ride to the university. On the way, she dropped a letter in a mailbox. The bus arrived on schedule. It was the usual driver, who recognized her and gave a cheerful greeting as she showed her monthly pass. The bus was quite full, carrying a mix of students and office workers, so she had to stand.

Arriving at her destination, Susan left the bus and walked to the College of Business. Joining a crowd of other students, she took a seat in the large classroom where her finance class was held. The professor lectured in a near monotone for 75 minutes, occasionally projecting charts on a large screen to illustrate certain calculations. Susan reflected that it would be just as effective, and far more convenient, if the course were transmitted over the Web, or recorded on CDs or videotapes that students could watch at their leisure. She much preferred the marketing course that followed because this professor was

a very dynamic individual who believed in having an active dialogue with the students. Susan made several contributions to the discussion and felt that she learned a lot from listening to the analyses and opinions of her fellow students.

She and three friends ate lunch at the recently renovated Student Union. The old cafeteria, a gloomy place that served unappetizing food at high prices, had been replaced by a well-lit and colorfully decorated new food court, featuring a variety of small kiosks. These included both local suppliers and brand-name fast-food chains, which offered choices of sandwiches, as well as health foods and a variety of desserts. Although she had wanted a sandwich, the line of waiting customers at the sandwich shop was rather long, so Susan joined her friends at Burger King and then splurged on a caffe latte from the adjacent Hav-a-Java coffee stand. The food court was unusually crowded today, perhaps because of the rain now pouring down outside. When they finally found a table, they had to clear off the dirty trays. "Lazy slobs!" commented her friend Mark, referring to the previous customers.

After lunch, Susan stopped at the automated teller machine, inserted her card, and withdrew some money. Remembering that she had a job interview at the end of the week, she telephoned

---

her hairdresser and counted herself lucky to be able to make an appointment for later in the day because of a cancellation by another client. Leaving the Student Union, she ran across the rain-soaked plaza to the Language Department. In preparation for her next class, Japanese for Business, she spent an hour in the language laboratory, watching an engaging video of customers making purchases at different types of stores, then repeating key phrases and listening to her own recorded voice. "My accent's definitely getting better!" she said to herself.

With Japanese phrases filling her head, Susan set off to visit the hairdresser. She liked the hair salon, which had a bright, trendy decor and well-groomed, friendly staff. Unfortunately, the cutter was running late and Susan had to wait 20 minutes. She used this time to review a chapter for the next day's human resources course. Some of the other waiting customers were reading magazines provided by the store. Eventually, it was time for a shampoo, after which the cutter proposed a slightly different cut. Susan agreed, although she drew the line at the suggestion to lighten her hair color. She sat very still, watching the process in the mirror and turning her head when requested. She was pleased with the result and complimented the cutter on her work. The process, including the shampoo, had lasted about 40 minutes. She tipped the cutter and paid at the reception desk.

The rain had stopped and the sun was shining as Susan left the store, so she walked home, stopping to pick up clothes from the cleaners.

This store was rather gloomy, smelled of cleaning solvents, and badly needed repainting. She was annoyed to find that although her silk blouse was ready as promised, the suit she would need for her interview was not. The assistant, who had dirty fingernails, mumbled an apology in an insincere tone without making eye contact. Although the store was convenient and the quality of work quite good, Susan considered the employees unfriendly and not very helpful.

Back at her apartment building, she opened the mailbox in the lobby and collected the mail for herself and her roommates. Her own mail, which was rather dull, included a quarterly bill from her insurance company, which required no action since she had signed an agreement to deduct the funds automatically from her bank account. There was also a postcard from her optometrist, reminding her that it was time to schedule a new eye examination. Susan made a mental note to call for an appointment, anticipating that she might need a revised prescription for her contact lenses. She was about to discard the junk mail when she noticed a flyer promoting a new dry-cleaning store and including a coupon for a discount. She decided to try the new firm and pocketed the coupon.

Since it was her turn to cook dinner, she wandered into the kitchen and started looking in the refrigerator and then the cupboards to see what was available. Susan sighed—there wasn't much in there. Maybe she would make a salad and call for home delivery of a large pizza.

Study Questions

1. Identify each of the services that Susan Lee has used or is planning to use.
2. What needs is she attempting to satisfy in each instance?
3. In each case, are there any alternative goods or services (including self-service) that could solve her need?
4. What similarities and differences are there between the dry-cleaning store and the hair salon? What could each learn from studying the other?

Four Customers in Search of Solutions

Segmenting Hong Kong's Telecommunications Market (A)

CHRISTOPHER LOVELOCK AND JOCHEN WIRTZ

Four residential line subscribers call their telephone company to complain about a variety of different problems. How should the company respond in each case?

Among the many residential customers of the telephone company are four individuals living in a middle-class suburb, Sha Tin, in Kowloon, Hong Kong. Each of them has a telephone-related problem and decides to call the company about it.

Leung Yew Wah

Leung grumbles constantly about the amount of his home telephone bill, which is, in fact, in the top two percent of all residential phone bills in Hong Kong. He makes many calls to the United States and Canada on weekday evenings, almost daily calls to Macau around mid-day, and calls to Shenzhen, Mainland China, on most weekends. One day, Leung receives a telephone bill, which is even higher than usual. On reviewing the bill, he is convinced that he has been overcharged, so he calls the telephone company's customer service department to complain and request an adjustment.

Sherry Tanaka

Tanaka has missed several important calls recently, because her line was busy. Her two teenage children surf the Internet for several hours almost every day. She phones the telephone company to determine possible solutions to this problem. Tanaka's telephone bill is at the median level for a household subscriber. Most of the calls from her house are local, but there are occasional international calls to Japan and the Philippines. She does not subscribe to any value-added services.

Chong Siew Lam

During the past several weeks, Chong has been distressed to receive a series of obscene telephone calls. It sounds like the same person each time. She calls the telephone company to see if they can put a stop to this harassment. Her phone bill is in the bottom ten percent of all household subscriber bills and virtually all her calls are local.

Victor Hung

For more than a week, the phone line at Hung's house has been making strange humming and crackling noises, making it difficult to hear what the other person is saying. After two of his friends comment on these distracting noises, Hung calls the telephone company and reports the problem. His guess is that it is being caused by the answer-ing machine, which is getting old and sometimes loses messages. Hung's phone bill is at the 75th percentile for a household subscriber. Most of the calls are local, usually on evenings and weekends, although there are a few calls to Shenzhen, too.

Study Questions

1. Based strictly on the information in the case, how many possibilities do you see to segment the residential telephone market?

2. As a customer service representative at the telephone company, how would you address each of the problems and complaints reported?

3. Review the product line of your local telephone company. Then, examine whether there would be any marketing opportunities for your telephone company relative to the types of complaints reported.

Segmenting Hong Kong's Telecommunications Market (B)

ADDITIONAL INFORMATION ON THE FOUR CUSTOMERS LIVING IN SHA TIN

LEUNG YEW WAH, 36, runs a small export-import business. Although he works out of his office in Kowloon City during the day, he often makes business calls to the United States and Canada from his home telephone in the evening. Leung also calls his brother in Shenzhen on a regular basis. His wife, who works part-time in the mornings, loves chatting on the phone and talks at length most days to her widowed mother in Macau. Despite grumbling about the amount of his home telephone bill, he has never taken a friend's advice to inquire about ways of cutting this bill.

SHERRY TANAKA, 42, is a divorced mother of two teenaged sons, both of whom spend hours surfing the Internet and talking with friends on the phone. Fluent in Japanese and Tagalog, Tanaka works as a freelance interpreter and translator, obtaining most of her assignments through an agency. She prepares translations at home, emailing or faxing them to the client when completed. More and more translations involve business clients, who want the work returned by email or fax. Tanaka spends between five and ten days each month as an interpreter at conferences or business meetings in different locations around Hong Kong. Some of her most profitable and interesting assignments as an interpreter come at very short notice.

This morning, the agency director telephoned to offer her some translation work on a technical brochure destined for Japan. "I tried to reach you a couple of times yesterday evening to see if you were free today to interpret for the president of a big Japanese company," he added.

"Their regular interpreter fell sick and they were willing to pay a premium rate to get a good replacement. Unfortunately, your line seemed to be constantly busy, so I ended up giving the job to somebody else." Tanaka reflects that this is the fourth time in the past six months that she had lost a good assignment—on three occasions, her phone was busy and on the fourth, she was in the bathroom and did not hear the phone ring. Last night, she recollects, her elder son was on the phone to his girlfriend for over an hour.

CHONG SIEW LAM, 74, is a widow in poor health who has not been very active since a heart attack last year. She has lived alone since her husband died several years ago. For her, the phone is a lifeline. Her son telephones her several days a week to check that all is well. It was he who advised her to call to report the obscene phone calls. Various friends and neighbors telephone to chat on a regular basis. However, Chong limits her own calls to friends with whom she plays mahjong; to local stores that will deliver food and other merchandise to her house; and to a home nursing service. Chong says she has reached the point where she is afraid to answer the phone, but does not want to miss a call from friends or family members, since these calls mean a lot to her.

VICTOR HUNG, 24, is a student at the business school at the University of Hong Kong. He lives in a house that his parents gave him last year when they retired to live in their vacation apartment in Vancouver, Canada. His only free time during the week is on Wednesday afternoons. He shares the house with three friends, Lee, Alvin, and Chan, fellow students who all pay him rent.

The telephone is listed in Hung's name, but everyone uses it. Alvin pays the most, since he often calls his fiancée in Shanghai, China. There are two extensions, one in the living room—where there is also an answering machine—and one in Hung's bedroom. (Unknown to him, the problem of poor reception on his telephone line is actually being caused by a faulty jack in the living room. The jack was damaged when a chair leg knocked into it in the course of a particularly rowdy party. There is, in fact, nothing wrong with the answering machine.)

Segmenting Hong Kong's Telecommunications Market (C)

PSYCHOLOGICAL PROFILES OF THE FOUR CUSTOMERS LIVING IN SHA TIN

LEUNG YEW WAH is meticulous to detail and regards accuracy and punctuality as great virtues. An intolerant man and easily angered, he despises bureaucracy, especially when it concerns the government. Somewhat paranoid, he is always afraid of being cheated and will go to great lengths to obtain restitution when he thinks he has been wronged.

SHERRY TANAKA is an articulate and self-confident woman who is good at communicating clearly what she needs. A pleasant individual with a direct manner, she sets high standards of performance in her own professional work, and expects the same of others. She is a modern Asian woman trying to manage her family, and provide for her children, particularly since she is also a single parent.

CHONG SIEW LAM is a charming old lady. Rather lonely, she used to enjoy a chance to chat on the phone, even with a complete stranger, but now she jumps and becomes fearful whenever the phone rings. She sometimes wonders if the problems she had been facing at home are associated with poor *feng shui* or geomancy, as she has recently changed the position of some of the furniture in her apartment.

VICTOR HUNG is a clever and ambitious young man who sometimes comes across to other people as arrogant and a "know-it-all," especially in situations where Chinese culture looks more favorably upon humility. (For example, success is usually attributed to one's diligence and perseverance rather than superior intelligence or abilities).

Segmenting Hong Kong's Telecommunications Market (D)

PROFILES OF FOUR EMPLOYEES OF THE TELEPHONE COMPANY

Customer Service Agents

Two customer service agents who work by telephone are Cheung Mui Kah and Tommy Kwok.

CHEUNG MUI KAH is fast, friendly, and accurate. Her voice inspires confidence on the part of customers. Cheung enjoys working by phone and likes being able to help people and to resolve their problems. Today, she is in her usual good mood.

TOMMY KWOK tries to deal with each customer call as quickly as possible. His supervisor notes that he ranks first among his coworkers in the number of customers handled per hour. After three years on the job, he is becoming increasingly bored with his work and is ready to move on, but does not know what he wants to do next. "I'm sick of spending all day on the telephone dealing with idiots and their stupid problems!" he tells his pals at the bar where he often hangs out in the evenings. Last night, Kwok had an argument with his girlfriend and got drunk. Today, he has a hangover.

Technicians

Two installation and repair technicians who visit customers' homes are Chan Kok Fai and Lam Yee Cheng.

CHAN KOK FAI has excellent technical skills and is very quick to diagnose and fix problems, but his manner is gruff. He wishes he could put his skills to more interesting use in a job that didn't involve dealing with other people all the time. "You wouldn't believe how dirty and untidy most people's homes are!" he tells his wife in their spotlessly clean apartment. Chan is convinced that most of the problems he has to resolve are the result of the customer's own stupidity or their abuse of the equipment. At the last call he made, the cause of the problem was totally obvious—the telephone instrument had been damaged by being dropped repeatedly on the floor. "Idiots!" Chan muttered to himself as he descended the stairs back to street level. "What a waste of my time!"

LAM YEE CHENG is a cheerful man who loves having a job that involves traveling around and meeting customers—he would hate to be stuck in an office or a factory all day. "Every visit is different," he tells his wife. Lam is technically proficient and enjoys problem solving. He also likes to explain to customers what caused the problem to occur and, if they show interest, how to minimize the chance that this same problem will happen again in the future. At the last call he made, the customer expressed warm appreciation for Lam's help and advice. His supervisor noted on his most recent evaluation that Lam's work was of good quality but that he needs to work faster.

Bouleau & Huntley

Cross-Selling Professional Services into the Philippines

CHRISTOPHER LOVELOCK AND JOCHEN WIRTZ

A professional firm specializing in pension fund audits seeks to extend the firm's relationships with existing clients in the Philippines by offering consulting services. But the first attempt at cross-selling is a flop. What has gone wrong and why?

Juan Miguel Duavit, a new partner and co-director in the Manila office of Bouleau & Huntley, pondered over what had gone wrong earlier in the day at his meeting with National Metals Corporation, a major metals manufacturer, where his carefully prepared consulting presentation had been greeted by a bewildered silence.

THE FIRM

Duavit, 42, had joined Bouleau & Huntley three months earlier, in March 2004. Bouleau & Huntley was a multinational corporation with headquarters in New York, that specialized in pension funds auditing and human resources management. Its Manila office had been serving clients in the Philippines for the past 15 years.

The firm was founded in 1923 by Robert Bouleau, a New York actuary, and William Huntley, an insurance executive, who had noted that American corporations were rapidly creating new pension funds for their executives. The two men recognized that this trend would create vast new opportunities for a professional firm that could advise firms properly and audit their plans every year, as required by the law.

Within ten years, Bouleau & Huntley had become the leader of a new profession, with a well-established presence in the United States. Subsequently, it began opening offices overseas. By 2004, Bouleau & Huntley was a worldwide firm with 42 offices, 325 partners, and revenues in excess of US$950 million. The firm continued to flourish with its combination of high-quality professionalism and aggressive marketing. New divisions had been launched in four areas closely related to pension funds: executive compensation, personnel management, insurance consulting, and reinsurance consulting.

Note: The authors gratefully acknowledge the assistance of Dr Leonardo R. Perez Jr., of De La Salle University, and Pressy Santos-Rowe, in preparing this case.

Expansion into the Philippines

The Philippines had a Retirement Act, the Republic Act No. 7641, which required that an employee facing compulsory retirement at 65 must receive from his employer a retirement benefit based on the final monthly salary and the number of years worked with the firm. Most companies turned to the private insurance industry for pension schemes.

Having repeatedly been sought out by various prestigious clients in the Philippines, Bouleau & Huntley opened its Manila office in 1989. By 2004, the firm had 11 partners and 120 employees in the Philippines, operating from its headquarters in Metro Manila, with small satellite offices in Cebu and Luzon. Total revenues in the Philippines were 545 million pesos (approximately US$10 million).[1]

The firm's mission, as stated by its director, Jose Arellano, was "to serve large international companies active in the Philippines and to develop a national clientele among leading Filipino companies." In addition, the Manila office had been assigned the task of experimenting with expansion into other types of professional activities that could be adopted worldwide throughout Bouleau & Huntley.

Duavit Changes Jobs

Juan Miguel Duavit had graduated from the prestigious University of Philippines (UP). After a two-year stint with Sun Corporation as a brand manager, he spent two years in the United States, obtaining an MBA from the Wharton School. On returning to the Philippines, he joined the glass division of Glasscore, holding several jobs in marketing and strategic planning over a four-year period. Through a UP classmate, he was recruited by the Manila office of Ascent Strategic Consultants (ASC), where he enjoyed a very successful career for 12 years, with the last seven as a partner. However, over time, he began to feel restless. His personal interest in the "soft" side of consulting problems, dealing with people rather than profits and efficiency alone, was not shared by the leadership in ASC.

It was through Jose Arellano, one of his neighbors in the plush Sangun district, that Duavit first became familiar with Bouleau & Huntley. Both men served on the board of the private school attended by their children and had come to know each other socially. Over dinner one evening, Arellano suggested that his friend think seriously about joining Bouleau & Huntley. "Our strategy committee in New York is constantly pushing me to develop new lines of professional activity," he told Duavit. "What you have done with ASC is of real interest to us, and I am sure that you would enjoy working with our personnel management and compensation partners." Warming to his theme, Arellano continued:

> We've been hugely successful in our major activity of pension fund auditing. Worldwide, we have 350 Fortune 500 companies as our steady clients. Historically, it's been a very profitable business, enjoying steady growth as the pension funds themselves grow in size. However, this has attracted new competition and the business is becoming more price-sensitive than in the past. In addition, it is heavily influenced either positively or negatively by regulatory and national political decisions totally beyond our control.
>
> In the Philippines, we're doing reasonably well, but we could certainly use additional revenues, if only to enhance our average revenue per partner and, of course our

---

[1] The peso is the Philippine currency. The exchange rate in mid-2004 was 1 peso = US$0.018.

bonuses. We should enter new professional areas, such as the strategy and general management consulting that you know so well. The synergies with our own main line of activity are obvious. With someone like you on board, and with the team we will help you build up, it should be possible to generate additional cash flow from existing clients, as well as gain new clients for the firm.

Further conversations during the subsequent months explored these opportunities and confirmed their mutual interest. Both men agreed that a vast potential existed in the Philippines among leading Filipino companies, as well as with the Asian affiliates of multinational groups headquartered in Manila. Arellano made several long-distance calls and exchanged confidential faxes with the managing director and most senior partners of the firm about hiring Duavit on a quasi-equal basis to himself, in recognition of his extensive experience and in anticipation of expected benefits.

Finally, over lunch at the Manila Hotel one day, Arellano offered Duavit an immediate directorship, a new departure for Bouleau & Huntley, plus a compensation package so generous that it was "impossible to refuse." Not only would Duavit receive a fixed compensation equal to his current total remuneration, but there was a provision for a large bonus (up to 30 percent of his salary) on incremental business from existing clients and up to 50 percent for the successful acquisition of new clients.

Working at Bouleau & Huntley

So Duavit joined the Manila office of Bouleau & Huntley in March 2004. His new colleagues welcomed him warmly, but he was surprised to find them somewhat reticent about discussing their own clients. Duavit ascribed this to professional respect for confidentiality. He set to work,

following up several leads of his own and within three months had brought in two new consulting clients. He was also involved in arranging for Bouleau & Huntley to audit a supplementary pension fund that one of his former employers was creating for its senior executives. He had started building up a team of four younger consultants, including one bright young man who, after spending two years in Bouleau & Huntley's compensation practice, had decided to move on to strategic work.

Duavit was already looking forward to the day when he could propose that this enthusiastic consultant should become the first junior partner of the new Manila practice. Despite these early successes, he was still concerned by the reserved attitude among his colleagues. One day when he was lunching with three of them, he answered their questions about his work at ASC. Describing a project that he had directed the previous year to reorganize a major oil company, he encountered a mixture of disbelief and incomprehension.

"Do you mean that you and your colleagues actually restructured this enormous company last year?" one of them asked.

"Yes," Duavit replied,

We helped them simplify their structure, reduce the number of levels from 11 to 6 and even helped them relocate 482 people, saving about 644 million peso (US$11.6 million) in overhead costs. Then, we streamlined their management information and planning system. Total fees amounted to 81 million peso (US$1.5 million) for 15 months of continued work by a team that ranged in size from four to seven consultants.

"Hey, what happened to their pension funds?" interjected another of his colleagues.

"Nothing, I believe," responded Duavit, slightly surprised. "Being nationalized, they only had the usual social security employee benefits. Do you want an introduction to their CEO to sell him one of your schemes?"

"No, I was just curious," the other replied.

"You might try to get the name of the guy who set up their last pension fund," another actuary partner suggested.

Duavit could see that his kind of work was not their "cup of tea," and he found it just as hard to understand the arcane workings of the assignments in which his actuarial colleagues were involved. He also marveled at the enormous fees the firm charged for what seemed to him was tedious and repetitive work. He was also deeply impressed by two things: their extensive use of "precooked" computer programs that seemed to be doing all the work, and the ease with which they obtained repeat business year after year without any need for the costly and time-consuming "developmental" work required in his own type of consulting. All they did was send a letter of renewal at the end of each year, with a prepared space for the company to sign. It seemed so easy! One Friday afternoon, just before 5 p.m., Duavit was beginning to check a 50-page report due at the client's the following Monday and he still had to write a proposal before going home for the weekend. Two of his partner colleagues poked their heads in at his open doorway. They were carrying raincoats and umbrellas and were evidently leaving for home. Quickly sizing up the situation, one of them, Victor Vasquez, remarked cheerily:

"My dear *pare* [the Filipino equivalent of "pal" or "chap"], you're obviously in the wrong business! You should have gotten an actuarial degree like us, instead of wasting your time at Wharton! See you on Monday! Cheers!"

A PRESENTATION AT NATIONAL METALS CORPORATION

Two weeks later, Duavit felt he was finally beginning to make progress. After much lobbying, Vasquez had agreed to open the door to his largest client, National Metals Corporation, a company involved in refining and marketing copper, chromium, and nickel. Since Duavit had led an ASC consulting team for Amix in Indonesia several years earlier, he knew the metals business and was certain that he could do something beneficial for Vasquez's client.

At National Metals Corporation's main administrative offices in Makati City, Vasquez led Duavit along a series of tortuous corridors to the office of Carlos Aseniero. Duavit was a bit surprised to find that his colleague's principal contact was a harassed-looking little man in a cluttered office. Aseniero greeted them politely and cleared several files off the chairs so that the two visitors could sit down. After the introductions were made and Vasquez had confirmed that the audit report would be ready on the promised date, Duavit launched into his presentation. He delivered a thorough but succinct analysis of five years of published figures, complete with diagrams he had prepared that very morning, comparing overall profitability, days of inventory, and asset rotation for National Metals Corporation and three of its Asian competitors. Duavit concluded what he considered to be a stimulating 15-minute presentation by inviting Aseniero to make use of Bouleau & Huntley's strategic consulting services to help National Metals Corporation carve out a market share and improve profitability.

Expecting an interested response, Duavit was amazed to be greeted by complete silence in the room. Not only Aseniero, but also Vasquez appeared somewhat bewildered by what they had just heard.

Seeking to regain the initiative, Duavit asked Aseniero, "Do you think that your boss would be interested in pursuing these issues further?"

Looking slightly ill at ease, the other replied:

You have to understand that my office reports to the assistant finance director, reflecting the immense amounts of money the company is investing in this pension fund. The fund is also used as collateral for some of the company's borrowings. I don't believe that my boss, Mr Perez, participates in strategy discussions with our board. Of course, I could ask him to arrange an appointment with our director general [CEO], but I'm told he's a very busy man.

"Thank you, Mr Aseniero," Vasquez said, rising to his feet and holding out his hand. "My colleague and I really appreciate your willingness to take time out of your busy schedule."

Duavit also shook hands with Aseniero and thanked him, but found it difficult to hide his disappointment. Then, the two partners left the office and retraced their way back to the reception area.

"What happened?" Duavit asked as the two of them climbed back into Vasquez's large new BMW. "I thought that I gave him a very convincing line. Wasn't he interested? Or did he simply not understand?"

Vasquez eased the BMW out of the parking lot and smiled wryly. "I think you scared him rather than impressed him, my friend. And you scared me, too. At one point, when you proposed raising the ante to the level of his superior, I thought that I was going to lose him as a client … Never again!"

Duavit remained silent for a long time. It was becoming clear to him that the actuarial partners appeared to be more interested in using him and his work to bring in new clients for their own practice, rather than the other way around. Yet, he liked what Jose Arellano had told him about Bouleau & Huntley's combination of professionalism and aggressive marketing. Obviously, a lot still needed to be done before the synergies he and Arellano had dreamed about could be achieved.

"Well, I won't give up that easily!" Duavit said eventually, as Vasquez accelerated onto Ayala Avenue. "Victor, let's think this experience through and decide, together with our other partners, what we should do differently if we want to succeed as a team. Have you ever heard of cross-selling?"

"No, as a matter of fact, I have not," Vasquez answered, "but Jose has given me the task of setting up the agenda for our yearly Manila Partners meeting in Makati City next month. I still have nothing for the morning of the third day. How much time do you need?"

Study Questions

1. What do you see as the key differences between pension fund auditing and management consulting? How good is the fit between the two?
2. Evaluate the visit to National Metals Corporation. What happened?
3. What are the lessons of this experience?
4. What actions should Bouleau & Huntley take now?

Appendix

The Auditing and Consulting World in 2004

Until the 1970s, auditing firms focused mostly on auditing activities. However, with the rise of information technology, many firms, including the Big Six (now Big Four) accounting firms branched into information technology (IT) and management consulting. Soon, revenues from consulting activities far exceeded their auditing revenues. Things came to a head after the collapse and bankruptcy of the energy giant, Enron, in December 2001 and the scandal involving the indictment of its auditor Arthur Andersen, by the U.S. Justice Department for document destruction. Arthur Andersen's dual role of auditor and consultant for Enron put it in the spotlight.

The issue of conflict of interest from serving corporate managers and auditing (i.e., protecting public interest) was soon highlighted. Critics argued that the provision of nonaudit services by audit firms could impair the independence of auditors, compromising the quality of their audits. In fact, a few academic studies found that there was more "creative accounting" among companies that also engaged their auditors in large consulting projects than in firms that made little use of their auditors for nonauditing related services. As a result, Ernst & Young's decision to sell off its consulting arm to Capgemini two years before the Enron collapse was hailed as a stroke of genius. After the Enron incident, PricewaterhouseCoopers sold its PwC Consulting unit to IBM Corp, while Andersen Worldwide sold its IT consulting practices on a piecemeal basis.

However, cross-selling of pension funds auditing and consultancy services appeared to present much less conflict of interest. Pension funds were generally managed separately from the other financial aspects of a business. Thus, unlike auditing of accounts, pension fund auditing was not concerned with the operations of a firm. Hence, it would be easier for pension fund auditors to maintain independence, even if their firm provided consultancy services to their audit clients. Nevertheless, Bouleau & Huntley would have to be sensitive to potential conflict of interest issues and how its activities were perceived in the market.

Giordano

International Expansion

Jochen Wirtz

As it looks to the future, a successful Asian retailer of casual apparel must decide whether to maintain its existing positioning strategy or not. Management wonders what factors will be critical to success and whether the firm's competitive strengths are readily transferable to new international markets.

To make people "feel good" and "look great."
GIORDANO'S CORPORATE MISSION

Giordano, a Hong Kong-based retailer of casual clothes in East Asia, was operating in some 30 territories by 2005. Its main markets were Mainland China, Hong Kong, Singapore, and Taiwan. Sales had grown to HK$3,389 million (US$435 million) by 2003 (see **Exhibit 1**). The company's board and top management team sought to maintain its success in existing markets and to enter new markets in Asia and beyond. Several issues were under discussion. The first concerned Giordano's positioning. In what ways, if at all,

should Giordano change its current positioning? The second concerned the critical factors that had contributed to Giordano's success. Would these factors remain critical over the coming years? Finally, as Giordano seeks to enter new markets around the world, there was debate over whether its competitive strengths were readily transferable to other markets.

COMPANY BACKGROUND

Giordano was founded in Hong Kong by Jimmy Lai in 1980. With a view to growing the business internationally, Lai picked an Italian name for his retail chain. In 1981, Giordano started selling casual clothes manufactured predominantly for the U.S. market by a Hong Kong-based manufacturer, the Comitex Group. In 1983, it scaled back on its wholesale operation and started to set up its own retail shops in Hong Kong. It also began to expand its market by distributing Giordano merchandise in Taiwan through a joint venture. In 1985, it opened its first retail outlet in Singapore.

The author gratefully acknowledges the assistance of Alison Law, Assistant to Chairman, Giordano International Ltd, and Elizabeth Xie Xunying, in preparing this case.

Exhibit 1 Giordano Financial Highlights

	2004 First Quarter*	2003	2002	2001	2000	1999	1998	1997	1996	1995	1994
Turnover (million HK$)	NA	3,389	3,588	3,479	3,431	3,092	2,609	3,014	3,522	3,482	2,864
Turnover increase (percent)	NA	(5.5)	3.1	1.4	11.0	18.5	(13.4)	(14.4)	1.1	21.5	22.7
Profit after tax and minority interests (million HK$)	194.0	266	328	377	416	360	76	68	261	250	195
Profit after tax and minority interests increase over previous year (percent)	NA	(18.9)	(13.0)	(9.4)	15.3	373.7	11.8	(73.9)	4.4	28.2	41.9
Shareholders' fund (million HK$)	NA	1,799	1,794	1,695	1,558	1,449	1,135	1,069	1,220	976	593
Working capital (million HK$)	NA	961	861	798	1,014	960	725	655	752	560	410
Total debt to equity ratio	NA	0.4	0.3	0.4	0.3	0.3	0.3	0.3	0.4	0.7	0.9
Bank borrowings to equity ratio	NA	NA	NA	NA	NA	0	0	0	0	0	0.1
Inventory turnover on sales (days)	NA	24	26	30	32	28	44	48	58	55	53
Return on total assets (percent)	NA	10.7	13.7	16.8	20.7	21.5	5.3	4.5	16.8	19.5	20.9
Return on average equity (percent)	NA	14.8	18.8	23.2	27.7	27.9	6.9	5.9	23.8	31.8	35.8
Return on sales (percent)	NA	7.8	9.1	10.8	12.1	11.6	2.9	2.3	7.4	7.2	6.8
Earning per share (cents)	NA	18.50	22.80	26.30	29.30	25.65	5.40	4.80	18.45	19.40	15.45
Cash dividend per share (cents)	NA	21.00	19.00	14.00	15.25	17.25	2.25	2.50	8.00	6.75	5.50

Note: "NA" indicates data were not available at time of print; *2004 figures are for the first quarter of Giordano's 2004 financial year, ended March 31, 2004.

Source: Annual Report 2003, Giordano International.

However, in 1987, sales were low and Lai realized that the pricey retail chain concept was unprofitable. Under a new management team, Giordano changed its strategy. Until 1987, it had sold exclusively men's casual apparel. When it realized that an increasing number of female customers were attracted to its stores, Giordano repositioned itself as a retailer of value-for-money merchandise, selling discounted casual unisex apparel, with the goal of maximizing unit sales instead of margins. Its shift in strategy was successful (see **Exhibit 1**). Lai left the company in 1994 to pursue other interests. In the same year, Peter Lau Kwok Kuen succeeded Lai and became Chairman of Giordano. A typical Giordano store is shown in **Exhibit 2**.

MANAGEMENT VALUES AND STYLE

The willingness to try new ways of doing things, not to do things in a conventional manner, and to learn from past errors was an integral part of Lai's management philosophy that has become an integral part of Giordano's culture until today. He saw the occasional failure as a current limitation that indirectly pointed management to the right decision in the future. To demonstrate his commitment to this philosophy, Lai took the lead by being a role model for his employees, adding, "… Like in a meeting, I say, look, I have made this mistake. I'm sorry for that. I hope everybody learns from this. If I can make mistakes, who … do you think you are that you can't make mistakes." He also believed strongly in empowerment—that if everyone was allowed to contribute and participate, mistakes could be minimized.

Another factor that contributed to the firm's success was its dedicated, ever-smiling sales force. Giordano considered front-line workers to be its customer-service heroes. Charles Fung,

Executive Director and Chief Operations Officer (Southeast Asia), remarked:

> Even the most sophisticated training program won't guarantee the best customer service. People are the key. They make exceptional service possible. Training is merely a skeleton of a customer service program. It's the people who deliver that give it form and meaning.

Giordano had stringent selection procedures to make sure that only those candidates who matched the desired employee profile were selected. Selection continued into its training workshops. Fung called the workshops "attitude training." The service orientation and character of a new employee were tested in these workshops. These situations, he added, were an appropriate screening tool for "weeding out those made of grit and mettle."

Giordano's philosophy of quality service can be observed in its overseas outlets as well as the numerous service awards its operations received over the years (see **Exhibit 3**). Its obsession with providing excellent customer service was described by Fung:

> The only way to keep abreast with stiff competition in the retail market is to know the customers' needs and serve them well. Customers pay our pay cheques; they are our bosses … Giordano considers service to be a very important element [in trying to draw customers] … service is in the blood of every member of our staff.

According to Fung, everyone who joined Giordano, even office employees, had to work in a store for at least one week as part of his or her training. "They must understand and appreciate every detail of the operations," he declared. "How can they offer proper customer assistance—internal and external—if they don't know what goes on in operations?"

Exhibit 2   Typical Giordano Storefronts

Exhibit 3   Recent Giordano Company Awards

Award	Awarding Organization	Category	Year(s)
ISO 9002*	SISIR	—	1994
American Service Excellence Award	American Express	Fashion/Apparel	1995
Ear Award	Radio Corporation of Singapore	Listeners' Choice and Creative Merits	1996
Excellent Service Award**	Singapore Productivity and Standards Board	—	1996, 1997, 1998
People Developer Award	Singapore Productivity and Standards Board	—	1998
HKRMA Customer Service Award	Hong Kong Retail Management Association	—	1999
The Fourth Hong Kong Awards for Services	Hong Kong Trade Development Council	Export Marketing and Customer Service	2000
Grand Award (Giordano International)	Hong Kong Trade Development Council	Export Marketing	2002
Grand Award (Giordano Ladies)	Hong Kong Retail Management Association	—	2002
Business-to-Consumer Service Supplier Award	Middle East Economic Digest (MEED)	—	2002
Dubai Services Excellence Scheme Award	Dubai Department of Economic Development	Customer Service	2003
Hong Kong Superbrands™ Award	Hong Kong Superbrands Council	—	2004

*ISO 9002 refers to the guidelines from the Geneva-based International Organization for Standardization for companies that produce and install products.

**To be nominated for the Excellent Service Award, a company must have had, among other things, significant training and other programs that ensured quality service. These include systems for recognizing employees and for gathering customer feedback.

Giordano invested heavily in training its employees. It had a training room complete with one-way mirrors, video cameras and other electronic paraphernalia. A training consultant and seven full-time line trainers conducted training sessions for every new sales staff and existing staff was required to take refresher courses. The company's commitment to training and developing its staff was recognized widely as can be seen by the awards it received, including the Hong Kong Management Association Certificate of Merit for Excellence in Training, and Singapore's People Developer Award among others (see **Exhibit 3**). Fung explained:

> Training is important. Every organization is providing its employees training. However, what is more important is the transfer of learning to the store. When there is a transfer of learning, each dollar invested in training yields a high return. We try to encourage this [transfer of learning] by cultivating a culture and by providing positive reinforcement, rewarding those who practice what they learned.

Giordano offered what Fung claimed was "an attractive package in an industry where employee turnover is high." Giordano was trying to motivate its people through a base salary that matched market rate, as well as additional performance-related bonuses. These initiatives and Giordano's emphasis on training had resulted in a lower staff turnover rate.

Managing its vital human resources (HR) became a challenge to Giordano when it decided to expand into global markets. To replicate its high-service-quality positioning, Giordano needed to consider the HR issues involved in setting up retail outlets on unfamiliar ground. For example, the recruitment, selection, and training of local employees could require modifications to its formula for success in its current markets owing to differences in the culture, education, and technology of the new countries. Labor regulations could also affect HR policies such as compensation and welfare benefits. Finally, expatriate policies for staff seconded to help run Giordano outside their home country and management practices needed to be considered.

FOCUSING GIORDANO'S ORGANIZATIONAL STRUCTURE ON SIMPLICITY AND SPEED

Giordano maintained a flat organizational structure. Fung believed that "this gives us the intensity to react to market changes on a day-to-day basis." The company had a decentralized management style which empowered line managers, while at the same time encouraging fast and close communication and coordination. For example, there were no separate offices for higher and top management; instead, their desks were located next to their staff's, separated only by shoulder-high panels. This closeness allowed easy communication, efficient project management, and speedy decision making, which were all seen as critical ingredients to success amid fast-changing consumer tastes and fashion trends. This kept Giordano's product development cycle short, and the firm made similar demands on its suppliers.

COMPETITION

Giordano's home base, Hong Kong, was flooded with retailers, both large and small. To beat what was often described as the "dog-eat-dog" competition prevalent in Asia—especially in Hong Kong—founder Jimmy Lai believed that Giordano must have developed a distinctive competitive advantage. Although many retail outlets in Hong Kong competed almost exclusively on price, Lai felt differently about Giordano. Citing successful Western retailers, Lai astutely observed that there were other key factors for success. He started to benchmark Giordano against best-practice organizations in four key areas: (1) computerization (from The Limited), (2) a tightly controlled menu (from McDonald's), (3) frugality (from Wal-Mart), and (4) value pricing (as implemented at the British retail chain Marks & Spencer).

The emphasis on service and the value-for-money concept had proven to be successful. Lai was convinced that service was the best way to make customers return to Giordano again and again. Lai declared, "We are not just a shirt retailer; we are not just an apparel retailer. We are also a service retailer because we sell feeling. Let's make the guy feel good about coming into here [our stores]."

SERVICE

Giordano's commitment to service began with the Customer Service Campaign in 1989. In that campaign, yellow badges bearing the words "Giordano Means Service" were worn by every Giordano employee. This philosophy had three tenets: "We welcome unlimited try-ons; we exchange—no questions asked; and we serve with a smile." The yellow badges reminded employees that they were there to deliver excellent customer service. The firm had received numerous service-related awards over the years (see **Exhibit 3**). It had also been ranked number one for eight consecutive years by the *Far Eastern Economic Review* for being innovative in responding to customers' needs.

Management had launched several creative, customer-focused campaigns and promotions to extend its service orientation. For instance, in Singapore, Giordano asked its customers what they thought would be the fairest price to charge for a pair of jeans and charged each customer the price that they were willing to pay. This one-month campaign was immensely successful, with some 3,000 pairs of jeans sold every day during the promotion. In another service-related campaign, customers were given a free T-shirt for criticizing Giordano's service. Over 10,000 T-shirts were given away. Far from only being another brand-building campaign, Giordano responded seriously to the feedback collected. For example, Giordano extended opening hours in some tourist-frequented shops by starting operations at 7.30 a.m. to cater for early birds, and closing only after the last customer had left the shop. Another example was Giordano's offer to tailor-make very large sized pants and shirts as it didn't carry products of extreme sizes.

To ensure that every store and individual employee provided excellent customer service, performance evaluations were conducted frequently at the store level, as well as for individual employees. The service standard of each store was evaluated twice every month, while individual employees were evaluated once every two months. Internal competitions were designed to motivate employees and store teams to do their best in serving customers. Every month, Giordano awarded the "Service Star" to individual employees, based on nominations provided by shoppers. In addition, every Giordano store was evaluated every month by mystery shoppers. Based on the combined results of these evaluations, the "Best Service Shop" award was given to the top store. Customer feedback cards were available at all stores, and were collected and posted at the office for further action, and increasingly customers provided feedback via its corporate Web site.

VALUE FOR MONEY

Lai explained the rationale for Giordano's value-for-money policy.

Consumers are learning a lot better about what value is. Out of ignorance, people chose the brand. But the label does not matter, so the business has become value-driven, because when people recognize value, that is the only game in town. So we always ask ourselves how can we sell it cheaper, make it more convenient for the consumer to buy and deliver faster today than [we did] yesterday. That is all value, because convenience is value for the consumer. Time is value for the customer.

Giordano was able to consistently sell value-for-money merchandise through careful selection of suppliers, strict cost control, and by resisting the temptation to increase retail prices unnecessarily. For instance, to provide greater shopping convenience to customers, Giordano started to open kiosks in subway and train stations in 2003. These outlets were aimed at providing their customers with a "grab and go" service.

INVENTORY CONTROL

In markets with expensive retail space, most retailers tried to maximize use of every square foot of the store for sales opportunities. Giordano was no different. Its strategy involved not having a back storeroom in each store. Instead, a central distribution center replaced the function of a back storeroom. Information technology (IT) was used to facilitate inventory management and demand forecasting. When an item was sold, the barcode information—identifying size, color, style, and price—was recorded by the point-of-sale cash register and transmitted to the company's main computer. At the end of each day, the information was compiled at the store level and sent to the sales department and the distribution center. The compiled sales information became the store's order for the following day. Orders were filled during the night and were

ready for delivery by early morning, ensuring that before a Giordano store opened for business, new inventory was already on the shelves.

Another advantage of its IT system was that information was disseminated to production facilities in real time. Such information allowed customers' purchase patterns to be understood, and this provided valuable input to its manufacturing operations, resulting in less problems and costs related to slow-moving inventory. As one manager noted, "If there is a slow-selling item, we will decide immediately how to sell it as quickly as possible. When the sales of an item hit a minimum momentum, we pull it out, instead of thinking of how to revitalize its [slow-selling] sales." As a result, Giordano stores were seldom out of stock of any item of merchandise.

The use of IT also afforded more efficient inventory holding. Giordano's inventory turnover on sales was reduced from 58 days in 1996 to 28 days in 1999, 30 days in 2001 and to merely 20 days by 2003. Its excellent inventory management reduced costs and allowed reasonable margins, while still allowing Giordano to reinforce its value-for-money philosophy. All in all, despite the relatively lower margins as compared to its peers, Giordano was still able to post healthy profits. Such efficiency became a crucial factor when periodic price wars were encountered. In recent years, the company was targeting more on gross profit and gross margin growth rather than on top-line growth and had managed to grow its gross margin amid a subdued retail market.

Besides the use of IT and real-time information generated from the information system, Giordano also owed its success in inventory control to close integration of the purchasing and selling functions. As Fung elaborated:

> There are two very common scenarios that many retailers encounter: slow-selling items

stuck in the warehouse and fast-selling popular items that are out of stock. Giordano tries to minimize the probability of the occurrence of these two scenarios, which requires close integration between the purchasing and selling departments.

In the early 1990s, when few retailers would use IT to manage their inventory, the use of IT gave Giordano a leading edge. However, today, when many retailers are using such technology, it is no longer our real distinctive competitive strength. In a time when there is information overload, it is the organizational culture in Giordano to intelligently use the information that sets us apart from the rest.

And this was further explained by Lai:

None of this is novel. Marks & Spencer in Britain, The Gap and Wal-Mart in America, and Seven-Eleven in Japan have used similar systems for years. Nowadays, information flows so fast that anybody can acquire or imitate ideas. What matters is how well the ideas are executed.

Thanks to rapid development in Internet and Intranet technologies, packaged solutions such as MS Office, point of sale (POS) and enterprise resource planning (ERP) software, and supporting telecommunications services (e.g., broadband Internet access), retailers could acquire integrated IT and logistics technology more easily and more cost-effectively than ever before.

PRODUCT POSITIONING

Fung recognized the importance of limiting the firm's expansion and focusing on one specific area. Simplicity and focus were reflected in the way Giordano merchandised its goods. Its stores featured no more than 100 variants of 17 core items, whereas competing retailers might feature 200 to 300 items. He believed that merchandis-

ing a wide range of products made it difficult to react quickly to market changes.

Giordano's willingness to experiment with new ideas and its perseverance despite past failures could also be seen in its introduction of new product lines. It ventured into mid-priced women's fashion with the label "Gio Ladies"—featuring a line of smart blouses, dress pants and skirts—targeted at executive women. "Gio Ladies" was aimed at helping pull up the brand image of Giordano's core product line. Furthermore, Giordano enjoyed higher margins, as margins in the market for upscale niches of women's clothing are in general higher—about 50 to 60 percent compared to 40 percent for casual wear.

Here, however, Giordano ran into some difficulties as it found itself competing in a market crowded with seasoned players. While there were no complaints about the look or quality of the new line, it had to compete with more than a dozen established brands already on the racks, including Theme and Esprit. Initially, the firm failed to differentiate its new clothing line from its mainstream product line, and even tried to sell both through the same outlets. In 1999, however, it took advantage of the financial troubles facing rivals such as Theme, as well as the post-Asian currency crisis boom in many parts of Asia, to aggressively relaunch its "Giordano Ladies" line, which met with great success. As of March 2004, the reinforced "Giordano Ladies" focused on a select segment, with 21 "Gio Ladies" shops in Hong Kong, Taiwan, and China offering personalized service (e.g., staff are trained to memorize names of regular customers and recall their past purchases).

During the late 1990s, Giordano had began to reposition its brand, by emphasizing differentiated, functionally value-added products and broadening its appeal by improving on visual merchandising and apparel. For instance, a large portion of its capital expenditure, totaling some HK$150 million in 2004, went into renovating its stores to enhance leasehold improvements, furniture, fixtures, and office equipment. Typical storefronts and store layout are shown in **Exhibit 2** and **Exhibit 4** respectively. Giordano's relatively mid-priced positioning worked well—inexpensive yet contemporary looking outfits appealed to Asia's frugal customers, especially during the Asian economic crisis. However, over time, this positioning became inconsistent with the brand image that Giordano tried hard to build over the years. As one senior executive remarked, "The feeling went from 'this is nice and good value' to 'this is cheap.' When you try to live off

selling 100-Hong Kong-dollar shirts, it catches up with you."

Nevertheless, while it gradually remarketed its core brand as a trendier label, Giordano continued to cater to the needs of customers who favored its value-for-money positioning. In 1999, it launched a new product line, Bluestar Exchange (BSE), to cater to the needs of its budget-conscious customers, after successful prototyping in Hong Kong and Taiwan. The good market response to this new line triggered plans to expand from the 14 Bluestar stores in Hong Kong and three in Taiwan, to 20 in Hong Kong, 15 in Taiwan, two in Singapore, and up to 100 in Mainland China (including franchised stores). By March 2004, Giordano had 19 BSE outlets in

Exhibit 4   A Typical Store Layout

Mainland China, 24 in Hong Kong, and 51 in Taiwan.

CREATIVE ADVERTISING AND PROMOTION

Giordano tended to spend relatively less on advertising and promotion than did its close competitors, preferring to adopt a more creative approach to spending such funds. In 2003, total advertising and promotional expenditure for the Giordano group amounted to HK$52 million, representing 1.5 percent of group retail turnover.

Among its successes was the "Simply Khakis" promotion, launched in April 1999, which emphasized basic, street-culture style that "mixed and matched," and thus fitted all occasions. Within days of its launch in Singapore, the new line sold out and had to be relaunched two weeks later. By October 1999, over a million pairs of khaki trousers and shorts had been sold. Garrett Bennett, Giordano's former Non-Executive Director, said, "We want to be the key provider of the basics: khakis, jeans, and the white shirt." The firm's skills in executing innovative and effective promotional strategies helped the retailer to reduce the impact of the Asian crisis on its sales and to take advantage of the slight recovery seen in early 1999.

In June 2003, right after the Severe Acute Respiratory Syndrome (SARS) crisis, Giordano launched the "Yoga Collection." They used a moisture-managed fabric, Dry-Tech™, for the line. It was an instant big hit. It allowed Giordano to recover nicely from the SARS crisis in Hong Kong. It also made Giordano's brand really stand out. While its competitors were still largely selling stocks that got accumulated during the SARS period and offering heavy discounts, Giordano's successful Dry-Tech™ campaign gave a fresh look to its stores.

THE ASIAN APPAREL RETAIL INDUSTRY

In the aftermath of the Asian crisis in the late 1990s, and the severe economic downturn as a result of SARS and the Iraq war in 2003, the Asian retail industry went through dramatic restructuring and consolidation. Many retailers reduced the number of shops in their chains, or closed down completely. Almost everyone in the industry implemented cost-cutting measures while, at the same time, cajoling reluctant customers with promotional strategies. Yet, there was a silver lining, as the more competitive firms were able to take advantage of lower rentals and the departure of weaker companies. Some firms, including Giordano, worked toward strengthening their positioning and brand image to compete better in the long run. Some retailers also explored opportunities, or accelerated their presence in markets that were less affected by the Asian crisis—mostly in markets outside Asia.

During the crisis and for the immediate future until a full recovery set in, industry analysts predicted that opportunities would continue to be driven by value. Thus, Giordano's value proposition appeared appropriate during these times. It was not surprising, then, that it won a place on *Forbes'* Global 2001 list of the "World's 200 Best Small Companies," indicative of world-class performance, together with eight other Hong Kong companies; and it was also chosen by the World Economic Forum as an Emerging Market Leader.

Giordano's performance was accredited to its responsiveness to market changes and customers' needs, as well as its management's swift cost-control strategies, in the areas of rents, outsourcing, inventory control, cash management, and overseas travel. The economic downturn had indeed revealed Giordano's flexibility and responsiveness in making decisive moves.

The retailing environment was becoming more dynamic, a change that was perhaps led by growing sophistication in tastes and rapid advancements in the media, communications, and logistics environment. Giordano's response to these trends would be the key to its ability to compete in the future, especially as these trends seem to commoditize its current competitive edge in IT, stock control, and logistics.

GIORDANO'S COMPETITION

Giordano's main competitors in the value-for-money segment had been Hang Ten, Bossini, and Baleno, and at the higher end, Esprit. **Exhibit 5** shows the relative positioning of Giordano and its competitors: The Gap, Bossini, Hang Ten, Baleno, and Esprit. Financial data for Giordano, The Gap, Esprit, Bossini, and Theme are shown in **Exhibit 6**. The geographic areas in which

Exhibit 5   Market Positioning of Giordano and Principal Competitors

Firms	Positioning	Target Market
Giordano (www.giordano.com.hk)	Value for money. Mid-priced but trendy fashion	Unisex casual wear for all ages (under different brands)
The Gap (www.gap.com)	Value for money. Mid-priced but trendy fashion	Unisex casual wear for all ages (under different brands)
Esprit (www.esprit-intl.com)	More up-market than Giordano. Stylish, trendy	Ladies' casual, but also other specialized lines for children and men
Bossini (www.bossini.com)	Low price (comparable to Giordano)	Unisex apparel, both young and old (above 30s)
Baleno (www.baleno.com.hk)	Value for money. Trendy, young age casual wear	Unisex appeal, young adults
Hang Ten (www.hangten.com)	Value for money. Sporty lifestyle	Casual wear and sports wear, teens and young adults

Exhibit 6   Competitive Financial Data for Giordano, The Gap, Esprit, Bossini, and Theme

	Giordano	The Gap	Esprit	Bossini	Theme
Turnover ('000,000)	3,389	123,344	12,381	1,691	172
Profit after tax and minority interests ('000,000)	266	8,013	1,186	(81)	(20)
Working capital ('000,000)	911	32,653	2,042	122	26
Return on total assets (percentage)	10.7	11.0	27.8	(7.2)	23.1
Return on average equity (percentage)	14.8	23.8	54.9	(31.4)	17.3
Return on sales (percentage)	7.8	6.5	9.6	(4.8)	11.8
Price/Sales ratio	NA	1.26	2.99	0.29	0.44
Sales growth (percentage)	(9.0)	9.7	34.3	6.5	(31.4)
Number of employees	7,900	153,000	NA	1,166	1,000
Sales per employee ('000,000)	0.29	0.78	NA	1.45	(0.02)

Note: Esprit reports its earnings in Euro and The Gap in US$. All reported figures have been converted into HK$ at the following exchange rate (as of March 2004): US$1 = HK$7.78.
Sources: Annual Report 2003, Giordano International; Annual Report 2003, The Gap; Financial Highlights 2003, Esprit International; Financial Report 2003, Bossini International Holdings Limited; Annual Report 2003, Theme Holdings.

Giordano, The Gap, Espirit, Bossini, Baleno, and Hang Ten operate are shown in **Exhibit 7**.

Hang Ten and Bossini were generally positioned as low-price retailers offering reasonable quality and service. The clothes emphasized versatility and simplicity. But while Hang Ten and Baleno were more popular among teenagers and young adults, Bossini had a more general appeal. Their distribution strategies were somewhat similar, but they focused on different markets. For instance, according to Fung, while Hang Ten was only strong in Taiwan, Baleno was increasingly strong in Mainland China and Taiwan. On the other hand, Bossini was very strong in Hong Kong and relatively strong in Singapore but had little presence in Taiwan and China.

Esprit was an international fashion lifestyle brand, engaged principally in the image and product design, sourcing, manufacturing, and retail and wholesale distribution of a wide range of women's, men's, and children's apparel, footwear, accessories, and other products under the Esprit brand name. Esprit promoted a "lifestyle" image and its products were strategically positioned as good quality and value for money—a position that Giordano was occupying. By 2000, Esprit had a distribution network of over 8,000 stores and outlets in 40 countries in Europe, Asia, Canada and Australia. The main markets were in Europe, which accounted for approximately 65 percent sales; and in Asia, which accounted for approximately 34 percent of sales in that year.

Exhibit 7   Geographic Presence of Giordano and Its Principal Competitors

Country	Giordano	The Gap	Esprit	Bossini	Baleno	Hang Ten
Asia						
Hong Kong/Macau	X	–	X	X	X	X
Singapore	X	–	X	X	X	X
South Korea	X	–	X	–	–	X
Taiwan	X	–	X	X	X	X
China	X	–	X	X	X	X
Malaysia	X	–	X	–	X	–
Indonesia	X	–	X	–	–	–
Philippines	X	–	X	–	–	X
Thailand	X	–	X	–	–	–
World						
U.S. and Canada	–	X	X	X	–	X
Europe	–	X	X	–	–	X
Japan	X	X	–	–	–	X
Australia	X	–	X	–	–	X
Total	750	3,016	6,580	436	971	NA

Note: "X" indicates presence in the country/region; "–" indicates no presence.

Sources: *Annual Report 2003*, Giordano International; Gap Inc., retrieved June 23, 2004 from http://www.gapinc.com/about/realestate/storecount.htm; Esprit, retrieved May 30, 2004 from http://www.esprit.com/shops/; *Financial Report 2003*, Bossini International Holdings Limited; Baleno, Retrieved May 30, 2004 from http://www.baleno.com.hk/EN/stores_list.asp?area=cn; Hang Ten, retrieved May 30, 2004 from http://www.hangten.com/contact/retail.cf.

The Esprit brand products were principally sold via directly managed retail outlets, wholesale customers (including department stores, specialty stores, and franchisees), and by licensees for products manufactured under licence, principally through the licensees' own distribution networks.

Theme International Holdings Limited was founded in Hong Kong in 1986 by Chairman and Chief Executive Officer Kenneth Lai. He identified a niche in the local market for high-quality, fashionable ladies' businesswear, although the firm subsequently expanded into casual wear. The Theme label and chain were in direct competition with "Giordano Ladies." From the first store in 1986 to a chain comprising over 200 outlets in Hong Kong, Mainland China, South Korea, Macau, Taiwan, Singapore, Malaysia, Indonesia, the Philippines, Japan, Thailand, Canada, and Holland, the phenomenal growth of Theme was built on a vertically integrated corporate structure and advanced management system. However, its ambitious expansion proved to be costly in view of the crisis, with interest soaring on high levels of debt. In 1999, the company announced a HK$106.1 million net loss for the six months up to September 30, 1998, and it closed 23 retail outlets in Hong Kong, which traded under its subsidiary The Clothing Shop. Theme International was subsequently acquired by High Fashion International, a Hong Kong-based fashion retailer specializing in up-market, trendy apparel.

Although each of these firms had slightly different positioning strategies and targeted dissimilar but overlapping segments, they all competed in a number of similar areas. For example, all firms heavily emphasized advertising and sales promotion—selling fashionable clothes at attractive prices. Almost all stores were also located primarily in good ground-floor areas, drawing high-volume traffic and facilitating shopping, browsing, and impulse buying. However, none had been able to match the great customer value offered by Giordano.

A recent survey by *Interbrand* of top Asian marque brands ranked Giordano number 20, making it Asia's highest-ranking general apparel retailer. The clothing names next in line were Australia's Quicksilver at number 45 and Country Road at number 47. However, a spokesman for advertising agency McCann-Erickson remarked, "It's a good brand, but not a great one. Compared to other international brands, it doesn't shape opinion." Giordano's take on this is that not only brands that can shape opinion are "great." Giordano believes that "Giordano means service" is very well stamped in the minds of people. Moreover, Giordano also means quality, which is backed by its worldwide no-questions-asked exchange policy. Giordano believes that a great brand is a brand that delivers consistently good quality, and this is what Giordano has been doing.

A threat from U.S.-based The Gap was also looming. Giordano was aware that the American retailer was invading Asia. The Gap had already entered Japan. After 2005, when garment quotas are likely to be abolished, imports into the region are expected to become more cost effective. With this in mind, the "Giordano Unisex" core line had upgraded its market position since the Asian crisis and launched the BSE brand in 1999 to cater to the value-for-money segment.

GIORDANO'S GROWTH STRATEGY

Early in its existence, Giordano's management had realized that it was difficult to achieve substantial growth and economies of scale as long as the firm operated only in Hong Kong, and saw the answer as lying in regional expansion. By 2002, Giordano had 1,398 Giordano stores in 26 markets (**Exhibits 8** and **9**).

Driven in part by its desire for growth and in part by the need to reduce its dependence on Asia in the wake of the 1998 economic meltdown, Giordano eventually set its sights on markets outside Asia. Australia was an early target and the number of retail outlets increased from four in 1999 to 34 in 2004. In Japan, Giordano opened 16 outlets from 2001 to 2004.

While the Asian financial crisis had caused Giordano to rethink its regional strategy, it was still determined to enter and further penetrate new Asian markets. This determination led to the successful expansion in Mainland China (see **Exhibit 10**), where the number of retail outlets grew from 253 in 1999 to 595 by March 2004. Giordano's management foresaw both challenges and opportunities arising from the People's Republic of China's accession to the World Trade Organization.

Giordano opened more stores in Indonesia, bringing its total in that country to 35 stores, located in Jakarta, Surabaya, and Bali. In Malaysia, Giordano planned to refurnish its outlets and intensify its local promotional campaigns to consolidate its leadership position in the Malaysian market. To improve store profitability, Giordano had already converted some of its franchised Malaysian stores into company-owned stores.

The senior management team knew that Giordano's future success in such markets would depend on a detailed understanding of consumer tastes and preferences for fabrics, colors, and advertising. In the past, the firm had relied on maintaining a consistent strategy across different countries, including such elements as positioning, service levels, information systems, logistics, and human resource policies. However, implementation of such tactical elements as promotional campaigns was usually left mostly to local managers. A country's overall performance in terms of sales, contribution, service levels, and customer feedback was monitored by regional headquarters (for instance, Singapore for Southeast Asia) and the head office in Hong Kong. Weekly performance reports were distributed to all managers.

As the organization expanded beyond Asia, it was becoming clear that different strategies had to be developed for different regions or countries. For instance, to enhance profitability in Mainland China, the company recognized that better sourcing was needed to enhance price competitiveness. Turning around the Taiwan operation required refocusing on basic designs, streamlining product portfolio, and implementing micromarketing strategy more aggressively. The company was continuing to explore the market in Japan and planned to open a few more stores in the second half of 2004. And in Europe, it was investigating a variety of distribution channels, including a wholesale-based business model.

THE FUTURE

Although Giordano had been extremely successful, the challenge facing top management was how it could maintain this success in the years ahead. A key issue on the agenda was how the Giordano brand should be positioned against the competition in both new and existing markets. Was a repositioning required in existing markets and would it be necessary to follow different positioning strategies for different markets (e.g., Hong Kong versus Southeast Asia)?

A second issue was the sustainability of Giordano's key success factors. It clearly under-

Exhibit 8   Operational Highlights for Giordano's Retail and Distribution Division

	2003	2002	2001	2000	1999	1998	1997	1996	1995	1994	1993
Number of retail outlets											
– directly managed by the Group	550	473	456	367	317	308	324	294	280	283	257
– franchised	813	783	703	553	423	370	316	221	171	77	481
Total number of retail outlets	1,363	1,256	1,159	920	740	678	640	515	451	360	738
Retail floor area directly managed by the Group (sq. ft.)	650,000	599,000	597,800	465,800	301,100	358,500	313,800	295,500	286,200	282,700	209,500
Sales per square foot (HK$)	4,200	4,500	5,100	7,400	8,400	6,800	8,000	9,900	10,500	10,600	12,600
Number of employees	7,900	8,000	8,287	7,166	6,237	6,319	8,175	10,004	10,348	6,863	2,330
Comparable store sales increase/ (decrease) (percentage)	(9)	(2)	(4)	4	21	(13)	(11)	(6)	8	(9)	15
Number of sales associates	3,200	2,900	2,603	2,417	2,026	1,681	1,929	1,958	2,069	1,928	1,502

Source: Annual Report 2003, Giordano International.

Exhibit 9   Key Regional Statistics for Giordano

	Taiwan	Hong Kong	China	Singapore	Malaysia
Net sales (million HK$)	604	697	815	348	114
Sales per sq. ft. (HK$)	2,600	6,200	3,000	7,700	NA
Change in retail sales (percentage) (comparing with same period in 2003)	13	(15)	(13)	(14)	0
Retail floor area (sq. ft.)	241,500	112,100	484,300	43,600	NA
Number of sales associates	794	486	703	279	NA
Total number of outlets March, 2004	200	80	595	45	46

Note: All data refer to the financial year ended 2003; "NA" indicates data were not available at time of print.
Source: Annual Report 2003, Giordano International.

stood its core competencies and the pillars of its success, but it had to carefully explore how they were likely to develop over the coming years. Which of its competitive advantages was likely to be sustainable and which ones were likely to be eroded?

A third issue was Giordano's growth strategy in Asia as well as across continents. Would Giordano's competitive strengths be readily transferable to other markets? Would strategic adaptations to IT strategy and marketing mix be required, or would tactical moves suffice?

Study Questions

1. Describe and evaluate Giordano's product, business, and corporate strategies.
2. Describe and evaluate Giordano's current positioning strategy. Should Giordano reposition itself against its competitors in its current and new markets, and should it have different positioning strategies for different geographic markets?
3. What are Giordano's key success factors and sources of competitive advantage? Are its competitive advantages sustainable, and how would they develop in the future?
4. Could Giordano transfer its key success factors to new markets as it expanded both in Asia and the other parts of the world?
5. How do you think Giordano had/would have to adapt its marketing and operations strategies and tactics when entering and penetrating your country?
6. What general lessons can be learnt from Giordano for other major clothing retailers in your country?

Exhibit 10 Giordano's Flagship Store in Shanghai

MakeMyTrip.com

DILIP SOMAN, ATUL WADHWA, AND BHAVNA HINDUJA

India's largest e-commerce company, an online travel services portal, has demonstrated spectacular results in the first few years of operation. However, the future brings new challenges in their quest for growth. Should they continue to be a niche player and develop new value-added services, or should they look to serve new market segments? Should they change the business model and look for new sources of revenue? It is obvious that they cannot grow by doing more of what they've been doing, the question is—what do they need to do next?

Deep Kalra, CEO of MakeMyTrip (India) Pvt Ltd (MMT) glanced contentedly at various newspaper stories about his fledgling company displayed on a bulletin board in his New Delhi office. MMT is an online travel company focused on the leisure and small-business traveler coming to India. In its very first year of operation in 2000, MMT had emerged as India's largest e-commerce company. Presently catering to the lucrative Non-Resident Indian[1] (NRI) market in the United States, the company aims to tap the potential of the huge US$1.5 billion NRI market worldwide. As Kalra looked back at the milestones that MMT had passed along the way, he stumbled on a headline that would catch any proactive businessman's attention:

> Online travel bookings up 250% in FY '03
> (*The Economic Times, May 15, 2003*).

As Kalra skimmed through the article, he thought about several strategic questions. Should MMT continue to target NRIs? Or, should they expand horizons and serve the foreign tourist market from the United States, the United Kingdom, and Australia? Should the company continue to be an India-focused company, or was it

---

This case was written by Dilip Soman, Professor of Marketing and Corus Entertainment Professor of Communication Strategy; and Atul Wadhwa and Bhavna Hinduja, Class of 2005 MBA students, Rotman School of Management, University of Toronto. It is meant to be used as a basis for classroom discussion, and is not designed to illustrate effective or ineffective management situations.

Copyright © 2005 Dilip Soman, Atul Wadhwa, and Bhavna Hinduja.

[1] NRI is an acronym for non-resident Indians, the term used to describe people who hold Indian passports, but are residents of other countries for tax and employment purposes. If these NRIs decide to take citizenship of their adopted countries, they cease to be NRIs. However, under a new Government of India scheme, they could apply for a PIO (Persons of Indian origin) status, which gives them many of the benefits available to NRIs.

time to start thinking about competing with global giants like Expedia and Travelocity?

THE TOURISM MARKET IN INDIA

Since 2001, India's tourism industry has been booming due to a rush of foreign tourists and increased travel by Indians to domestic and overseas destinations. Currently, it is a US$3 billion industry. In 2003, the number of Indians traveling abroad increased by 30 percent to 4.5 million. A recent surge in the Indian economy had raised middle-class incomes, prompting more households to spend on vacations abroad or at home. At the same time, India's emergence as a global information technology hub and an aggressive advertising campaign by the government are credited with changing India's image from that of a land of snake charmers to a modern economy, consequently sparking interest among overseas travelers. Moreover, domestic tourists are also fueling the industry's revival. In the recent past, domestic airfares in India had been substantially reduced by 10 to 15 percent. However, the industry is awaiting a revision to the dollar denominated airfare regulation applicable for inbound travels. As a form of price discrimination, Indians that travel abroad can purchase fares in Indian rupees, while NRIs and Persons of Indian Origin (PIOs) have to buy tickets in dollar denomination. This practice is widely seen as a constraint on further growth in the demand for travel.[2]

The distribution of travel services in India is fragmented and predominantly retailer based. Though there are a few national companies, most are small, independent businesses. While airlines, railways, hotels, and car rentals supply their travel services to the industry, consolidators, travel agents, and online travel portals distribute these services to the customers. The travel industry has experienced drastic alterations in the manner in which airlines sell their tickets. In the 1990s, airlines depended on consolidators (who sold to agents/dealers for retail sales) for most of their ticket sales. With all major international airlines reducing commissions, consolidators and travel agents across the country have tightened their belts. The fact that airlines have started undercutting fares on the Internet suggests that agents may soon become redundant. Currently, margins are being squeezed and airlines are using the Internet to reach travelers directly, thus eliminating the role of a consolidator. Airlines receive 15 percent of their business through Internet sales. As a result, retail margins have reduced to 2 percent for individual travelers. Travel agents sell airline tickets at cost to corporate travelers, charging a 1 to 2 percent service fee and have expanded their travel service offerings to hotel bookings, car rentals, and tour packages in order to earn profits from this segment.

A recent study suggests that India's Internet population is around ten million users and is expected to hit 46 million users by March 2005. However, these users predominantly use email applications, but don't conduct online transactions.[3] Even so, online travel bookings in India have witnessed more than a 250 percent jump to 50,000 bookings from 2002 to 2003. In 2003, online travel generated US$26 billion in sales and 12 percent of all

[2] Lola Nayar (January 23, 2004), "Travel, Tourism Industry Awaits Revision in Dollar Denominated Airfares" (http://desitalk.newsindia-times.com/2004/01/23/travel-top.html).

[3] "India's Net Population Will Be Second to China's by 2006," Courtesy: NASSCOM: Strategic 2003 Review, The IT Industry in India (http://www.financialexpress.com/fe_full_story.php?content_id=59545).

travel services were bought on the Internet. This percentage is expected to reach 30 percent by 2008. However, out of a total of over 20 million air bookings in India every year, online travel bookings constitute a very miniscule portion. High cost of e-commerce, lack of proper systems, and low awareness are the main obstacles to growth of online bookings. Equally so, the disintermediation of the travel industry is a double-edged sword for travel portals. While it leads to better deals on the Internet, something realized by most customers today, travel portals face stiff competition from travel service providers, such as hotels, that guarantee to match the discount received from intermediaries.

MAKE MY TRIP: THE COMPANY AND THE PRODUCT

MMT offered competitively priced travel products, supported by real-time booking capability, convenience, and stellar customer service, and had generated a turnover of Rs.23 million (US$0.5 million) in its first four months of operations. The portal (see **Exhibit 1**) provides its customers the entire gamut of travel services through the Internet by leveraging other technologies. In addition to airline tickets, MMT offers over 1,500 domestic and international hotels at negotiated rates, hundreds of attractive holiday packages, car rentals, trains, and cruises for Indian as well as international destinations. The unique feature of the portal is that it allows online booking and confirmations, round-the-clock customer support, online Web chat and a toll-free number. MMT is one of the few travel

service providers that acknowledges the fact that inbound travelers prefer an agent at the destination rather than the origin, which gives MMT the added advantage over other travel agencies. They have recently soft-launched www.indiaahoy.com, a business-to-business (B2B) site offering Indian hotels and tour packages for international travel agents in Australia.

MMT bundles its basic travel reservation offering with travel insurance, access to business lounges in India for all travelers, and valuable shopping discount booklets. Apart from these basic services, MMT believes that it offers an unsurpassed customer service experience through a variety of media. Their customer service representatives (CSRs) are accessible 24/7 throughout the year through their toll-free numbers in India as well as the United States. The CSRs are equipped to handle almost any customer questions, including questions about flight schedule changes, itineraries, hotel information, foreign currency exchange rates, and time zone differences. CSRs reconfirm all tickets 72 hours before departure.

The portal is a one-stop shop for all travel-related information. It offers information about travel-related issues like visas, passports, insurance, travel, and finance (in collaboration with a retail financial services company). MMT claims that it is different from other Indian travel portals as it provides value-added services like a free drop and pickup cab for its clients. The company goes the extra mile to add value to its customers' travel experience during their visit to India with its "Tripper Saver" promotional program.[4]

---

[4] Additionally, NetCarrots Loyalty Services (a service provider to MMT) has specially tied up with exclusive brand names and well-known establishments that provide discount coupons and freebies for MMT's customers.

Exhibit 1   The makemytrip.com Web Page

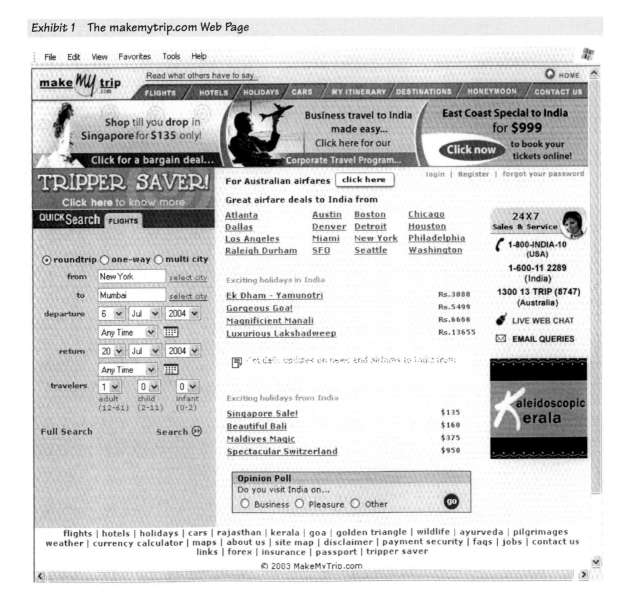

THE BUSINESS MODEL AND OPERATIONS

To tap the NRI and international market, MMT has created a network of offices in New Delhi, Mumbai, and New York. In addition, it has appointed franchise partners in all major cities in the United States, the United Kingdom, Australia, and India. MMT relies heavily on its network of leading tour operators to provide travel-related services in India and over 30 international countries. Moreover, the company exploits information technology, using India's natural cost advantage to service its customers based in high-cost economies. Kalra attributes MMT's success to the sound initial strategic decision to target NRI customers and subsequently supplementing it with in-depth knowledge of this target audience, coupled with rigorous processes and good trade relationships. MMT's operations are represented schematically in **Exhibit 2**.

Exhibit 2   MMT's Business Model and Operations

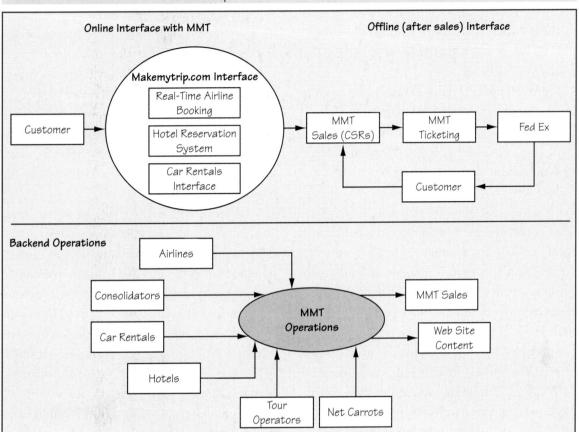

The sales team consists of three divisions—Internet sales, corporate sales, and general sales. MMT ensures a dedicated set of executives to service the sophisticated corporate and general sales business. In terms of human resources, Kalra believes in promoting from within to foster individual growth within the organization.

MMT believed in the "no-individual-sales-target" model to ensure high levels of customer service that may get neglected in a drive to compete for sales. Service calls (for schedule changes, following up on reconfirmations, itinerary confirmations, etc.) are estimated to form 40 percent of the total calls received. Instead of allocating individual sales targets to its sales staff, MMT sets a daily sales target for the entire team that is divided proportionately among the three

shifts. In general, the night shift achieves 55 to 60 percent of the daily sales target due to time zone differences. In order to encourage team performance, MMT rewards all its employees upon achievement of the company's sales target; such rewards form 10 to 15 percent of an employee's pay package.

MMT operates as two separate entities: MakeMyTrip-India and MakeMyTrip Inc. (U.S.A.). Due to cost and labor advantages, MMT-India offers call center facilities to MMT Inc. However, most airlines traveling from the United States to India do not permit tickets to be sold in India for travel originating outside the country—this requires MMT Inc. to source tickets from consolidators within the United States. A transfer pricing mechanism has been set in place that allows MMT-India to bill MMT Inc. for all the services rendered and tickets sourced in India (when permitted). Thus, both companies file their individual balance sheets in the respective countries.

Sumit Gupta (Head, Finance and Accounting) believes that MMT's profitability is directly linked to sales volumes. MMT's current revenue model depends heavily on its U.S. operations that generate about 90 percent of its sales, while the Indian operations contribute only 8 to 10 percent. MMT's Australian initiative is still in its infancy, contributing 2 percent of the company's turnover. MMT is funded primarily by private equity, with less than 5 percent of bank loans (usually overdraft associated with day-to-day operations). In order to minimize costs and ensure high levels of customer satisfaction, MMT is in the process of making key investment decisions. One of the critical investments considered by MMT is the setting up of an entity that will allow it to source tickets directly from airlines, thus eliminating consolidator fees. The initial investment required for this initiative is estimated to be in the region of US$300,000 to US$500,000, and it is expected to translate into savings of 2 percent on air tickets sourced from consolidators. Further, in order to address existing operational issues and increase the team's efficiencies, MMT is planning to make a series of investments in technological advancements in the region of US$200,000 in 2004 and US$300,000 in 2005.

Keyur Joshi (Chief Operating Officer) is particularly interested in the movement and fluctuations in the distribution costs of the airline industry. Due to increasing competition in the airline industry, the market has seen the airline ticket distribution costs plummet from 9 percent to almost 0 percent in the past decade. Direct sales to customers through the Internet contribute to 30 percent of an airlines' total revenue. The airline industry, even today, relies heavily on travel agents and other distributors for the bulk of their sales. On the same note, travel agents have come a long way, altering their revenue model from commissions earned from consolidators and airlines to charging service fees to customers for their ticketing services while investigating best fares and routes. Typically, a customer pays between US$10 and US$20 to the travel agent for his services.

Activities with various suppliers (e.g., consolidators and airlines for tickets, hotels for tourist guides and rooms, taxi operators for car rentals) need to be coordinated and sold as a package to customers. With the size of operations increasing manifold, there is a growing need for a software system that integrates various departments within MMT efficiently. Moreover, although MMT has serviced 30,000 NRIs in the United States in the last three years, it does not track repeat purchases. MMT is currently implementing a Customer Relationship Management (CRM) process that will allow it to track changes in its customers' buying and traveling habits.

MMT provides its customers with three modes of communication to reach MMT's sales/customer service team—emails, Web chats and toll-free numbers. Emails and chat sessions are saved in MMT's system for constant monitoring of the service quality given to the customers. All phone calls are recorded for quality control purposes. Each one of the four Assistant Sales Managers randomly listens to 15 to 20 calls serviced by every sales executive over a span of two weeks to provide them with critical feedback. Ashish Gautam (Deputy Manager, Quality) is cognizant of the fact that although this process helps address the quality of customer contact, MMT currently lacks a system to track timely customer follow-up. Another cause of concern for MMT is the turn-around-time taken by the sales executive to resolve a customer issue or query. This delay is due to the inaccessibility of relevant information required by the sales executive. This information typically needs to be gathered from various departments to ensure satisfactory customer service.

CUSTOMER SEGMENTS AND ADVERTISING

The Indian travel market can be classified into two broad categories—"international travelers" (those crossing international borders) and "domestic travelers" (those traveling within India). The international travelers can be further classified as "inbound travelers" (those who travel into India from overseas) and "outbound travelers" (residents of India who travel internationally). Domestic tourism is growing, and this seems to provide a good opportunity for technologically advanced travel portals like MMT to focus on customer loyalty and maximize the Internet's ability to drive repeat purchases by getting instant customer feedback. Convenience and good deals fueled by changes in lifestyles of Indians have changed consumer behavior toward transacting on the Internet. However, the Indian domestic traveler is susceptible to a number of constraints that makes this segment difficult for MMT to penetrate—namely, low PC penetration, poor quality of dial-up access coupled with increased competition among Internet service providers (ISPs) that lead to cramming a higher number of users with the same bandwidth at the backbone. Moreover, the absence of proper cyber legislation in line with international standards is inhibiting credit card usage on the Internet.

In the outbound segment, there are currently six million Indians traveling abroad from India (up from five million last year). Countries in Asia Pacific (e.g., Singapore, Malaysia, Hong Kong) along with a couple of Middle Eastern countries remain the preferred tourist destinations. However, one of the critical challenges faced by MMT in catering to this segment is that of extremely high price sensitivity and increasing competition from traditional brick-and-mortar travel agents. While the rate of Internet adoption in India is healthy, most people are still hesitant to make purchases on the Internet.

The inbound market in India in 2001–02 was 2.42 million arrivals. This market is further segmented into six broad categories—holiday and sightseeing, business travelers, conference attendees, students, visiting friends and relatives (VFRs), and others. **Exhibit 3** gives details on the NRI populations worldwide. Although residents in various parts of the Middle East (UAE, Oman, Bahrain, Saudi Arabia, Kuwait) make it to the top of the list of NRIs traveling to India, those residing in the United Kingdom and the United States are an important group for MMT. The fact that 90 percent of the NRI/VFR segment plans their trips in advance implies that sales from this segment are fairly stable and predictable. The remaining 10 percent are emergency cases. Kalra estimates that an NRI/VFR traveler spends approximately US$1,200 per person per trip, most of which is the cost of the air ticket. More recently, there has been an increasing trend among NRI/VFR travelers to explore India and take short vacations while visiting their family. This provides MMT with another opportunity to serve this segment within India. MMT estimates the average spends of this group of NRIs who choose to take short vaca-

Exhibit 3 NRI Populations and Arrivals

Country of Residence	NRI Population (in Millions)	NRIs Visiting India ('000)	% of NRI Visitors from Country
Middle East	1.5	308.81	45.57%
U.S.A.	2.5	63.50	9.37%
United Kingdom	1.5	57.76	8.52%
Far East and Southeast Asia	2	61.86	9.13%
Sri Lanka and Nepal	1	21.94	3.24%
Europe	1	18.63	2.75%
Africa	1	11.23	1.66%
Canada	1	8.82	1.30%
Australia	0.5	8.36	1.23%
Others	0.7	116.77	17.23%
Total	12.7	677.68	100

Sources: December 2003, Deep Kalra's presentation in TiEcon Indian 2003; and Tourist Statistics 2002, Ministry of Tourism and Culture, Government of India.

tions within India to be close to US$1,800 per person. Finally, they estimate that a non-NRI traveling to India would spend approximately US$2,200 per person. However, hotel quality and capacity in India remains an issue if MMT decides to target larger segments—it is estimated that Las Vegas has 130,000 room-nights, whereas India has only 120,000 room-nights, of four- or five-star hotel standard.

The NRI population in the United States has doubled in the past decade—currently, it is home to over two million NRIs, of which 67 percent have traveled at least once over the past two years. The population figure is expected to grow at 10 percent per year. Over the past few decades, NRIs residing in the United States have undergone an identity shift from "South Asians" to "Indian Americans" and thus, their buying behavior is strongly influenced by the Internet-savvy American culture. A U.S. survey done in 2003 indicated that 35 percent of travelers purchased tickets and packages online, which is projected to expand to 55 percent in the next two years. MMT has good reason to believe that NRIs

residing in the United States follow similar purchasing trends. It enjoys a 5 percent market share in the top 30 NRI-populated cities in the United States. According to a study conducted by Simmons Research in 2002, the earning capacity of these NRIs has increased, averaging US$88,000 as compared to the national average of US$51,900. Expedia and Travelocity are major players in the U.S. market.

In contrast to the situation in the United States, NRIs in the Middle East are primarily blue-collar workers or laborers, many of whose compensation package includes one paid trip to India per year. These tickets are arranged by employers who source them from a preferred set of vendors, making the Middle East a difficult market to penetrate into.

Initially MMT targeted all three markets—domestic travelers, inbound, and outbound Indian travelers. Kalra felt that if they had relied entirely on the foreign tourist market, they would have been hit very hard by the fluctuating international market conditions. But today, he is very clear about the strategic focus on the NRI/VFR segment since he believes this segment has tremendous growth potential. Moreover, MMT's infrastructure—fully integrated back-office function, business-to-consumer (B2C) sales model, lack of offices in India, service-oriented sales team, relationships with airlines and consolidators, technology, etc.—has been built around the needs and requirements of the NRI/VFR customer. Keyur Joshi indicates MMT's priorities in terms of customer segments as NRIs in the United States, the United Kingdom, and the Middle East, and American tourists/visitors traveling to India. Although MMT has ready access to the NRI segment in the United States, it is unclear if it should expand its offerings to NRIs traveling to destinations other than India. If they did, they would have to compete with Expedia, Travelocity, and Priceline, who already have a large customer base. Hence, these companies are able to purchase hotel nights and other travel services in bulk and retail the same to customers. MMT currently does not have the scale to bargain the same low prices with hotels and will, therefore, be expensive on these routes when compared to Expedia. Kalra wonders if it is feasible for MMT to move in this direction.

All the MMT advertising done in the United States is conceptualized in India. Devika Khosla (Head, Content) bases the company's advertising and communication strategy on three pillars—convenience of 24/7 service, reliability, and competitive pricing (see **Exhibit 4** for sample advertising).

In order to foster growth, MMT has formed strategic alliances with brands that are associated with the Indian consumer in a unique way. For example, its offline alliance with Coke is based on specific promotion schemes, like the cricket series played routinely in Sharjah. MMT also operates as the exclusive travel channel for Sify.com and provides weekend getaways for Maruti Udyog (a major Indian automobile manufacturer). Apart from these three prime alliances, MMT has also tied up with matrimonial and pilgrimage portals.

CONSUMER BEHAVIOR AND DECISION MAKING

A study carried out by PhoCusWright in November 2003 on "Exploring Internet Travelers" found that consumers use the Web early in the travel planning process, often immediately after deciding to take a vacation.[5] The most common topics for Web travel research are the vacation arrangements themselves (air ticket, hotel, etc.), followed by destination information. Approximately half of the respondents indicated that they start with flight arrangements first when assembling a vacation. Hotel and rentals are planned second and third, respectively. The study also revealed that flight and rental cars are the travel services most likely to be purchased online, while offline channels still dominate the travel activities category. Despite the availability of one-stop travel shopping, consumers still tend to purchase different travel services on different sites. Fewer than 30 percent of consumers have purchased a travel package of some sort. In summary, consumers in the U.S. market highly favor online travel agencies and destination Web sites for the purchase of vacation packages. A study conducted by AC Nielsen indicates that the reason why general sites like Travelocity and Expedia are so popular is because the air travel category is so driven by

---

[5] Vacation Packages: A Consumer Tracking and Discovery Study, November 2003, PhoCusWright Inc. and Vividence Corporation (www.phocuswright.com).

Exhibit 4   Sample MMT Advertising

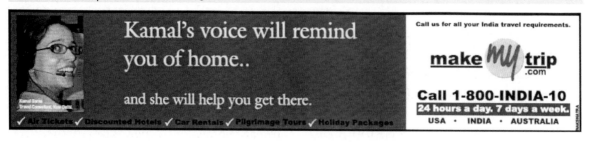

consumer awareness—thus, ad recall from continuous exposure to these brands is high, and their names are the first to come to the minds of people who seek information on airfares.[6]

COMPETITION

Ever since its inception, MMT has been the only travel portal focusing on the NRI market. This gives MMT a competitive edge over its international competitors such as Expedia, Travelocity, Orbit, and Priceline. MMT currently enjoys a 2.55 percent market share, and Mr Joshi is of the opinion that even if domestic competition replicates their model, they would find themselves on a learning curve in order to function efficiently. Moreover, MMT faces relatively less competition from U.S. travel agencies because the only agencies surviving there are bucket shops—small agents with specific markets—or mega portals like Travelocity and Expedia that have only online operations. Companies like Expedia rely heavily on buying tickets in bulk at discount prices and then reselling them at higher margins. The margins allow it to undercut its competitors, outspend them for product development, and drive hard bargains with struggling suppliers. Expedia is known for its aggressive advertising campaigns that run across online, TV, press, and outdoor media to convey to its customers that it has all the tools and ideas to let travelers book a perfect trip online.

MOVING ON

As Kalra contemplated his next move in this ever-evolving online travel business, he thinks of the various options available to him. Firstly, the inbound and outbound international travel market in India is growing at the rate of 20 percent annually. Currently, inbound travelers pay a very high price for travel services since intermediaries siphon off 50 percent of their charges. Kalra feels that MMT is in a good position to use the Internet to reduce these distribution layers while retaining a healthy 20 percent margin on travel services.

Secondly, MMT would like to move from a 90-10 percent split of revenues between air tickets and travel services to a 70-30 percent split. While only 20 percent of NRI/VFR travelers use additional travel services (e.g., car rentals), non-NRIs are more likely to consume additional high-margin services. In light of the rising trend toward exploring India besides visiting family and friends, MMT could expand the service offering to NRI travelers—by providing domestic tour packages in addition to their international travel-related needs, since the travel-related services offer higher margins than ticketing services. The

---

[6] AC Nielsen, Winning B(r)ands Brand Equity Model, 2004 (http://www.imscart.com/hotel_reservation_software_article_9.htm).

margins on domestic travel service vary across segments. While domestic travelers generate margins between 15 and 25 percent, the NRI/VFR tourists contribute margins as high as 50 percent. Kalra wondered what additional value-added products and services might be introduced into the product portfolio to extract more value from the NRI/VFR segment.

Thirdly, the outbound international traveler market is growing rapidly. Currently, MMT has its representatives in three other cities apart from their corporate headquarters in New Delhi, and tapping this growing market would require it to expand its operations within India. And, finally, Kalra contemplates the European market. MMT is most likely to face stiff competition from Expedia and Travelocity who are able to bargain deals with hotels and car rental companies based on their large customer bases. However, they have not penetrated into the Indian market as yet.

Study Questions

1. Can MMT sustain its business model by targeting only the inbound travelers, or does it need to look at other markets and segments? If yes, which segments would you recommend? If no, how can they grow within the inbound segment?

2. Ad revenues have never been core to MMT's business plan. However, MMT's role in promoting some leading NRI-focused brands suggests that this might be another avenue that Kalra could investigate. Does MMT need to look at advertising as a revenue generator?

3. Can MMT's business model work in other countries, in particular China, Singapore, and the Philippines? Are there any differences in consumers and segments in these countries that would render the model inadequate? What might need to be changed in other countries? Could MMT expand in a modular manner by replicating their business with overseas residents of other countries?

Primula Parkroyal Hotel

Marketing a Business and Resort Hotel in Malaysia

JOCHEN WIRTZ AND ALIAH HANIM M. SALLEH

Following a change of ownership, the general manager of a luxury hotel in Malaysia seeks to develop a new marketing plan to improve profitability at a time of increasing competition.

In August 2000, Mok Pin Chuan, PPR's new General Manager who was appointed in May 1999, worked on Primula's 2001 marketing plan. As input into this marketing plan, he needed to reexamine PPR's key target segments and its positioning. Uppermost in his mind was to reinstate the hotel's image as the premier quality hotel in Kuala Terengganu, increasing its occupancy rates and revenue and adopting cost savings measures with the overall objective of improving PPR's profitability.

MANAGEMENT TAKE-OVER AND REFURBISHMENT

The hotel was located on a beach off the South China Sea in Kuala Terengganu, the capital of Terengganu, a north-eastern state of peninsular Malaysia. Terengganu is an oil-rich state with a population of about 850,000, comprising mostly Malay Muslims. PPR was one of the first four-star hotels to be built along the eastern coast of peninsular Malaysia in the 1980s. However, under the previous ownership of a state government agency, it had incurred millions of ringgit (RM)[1] in accumulated losses and the state government's aim was to turn the hotel into a profit-making concern and help it to boost the state's tourism industry.

This case was written by Jochen Wirtz and Aliah Hanim M. Salleh, Associate Professor of Marketing, Faculty of Business Management, Universiti Kebangsaan Malaysia. The authors gratefully acknowledge the support and assistance provided by Mr Mok Pin Chuan, General Manager of Primula ParkRoyal Hotel, and Jasmine Ow Min Cheng, in preparing this case. This case was prepared as the basis for class discussion rather than to illustrate effective or ineffective handling of an administrative situation. PPR considered some data in the case as confidential, which was therefore disguised.

[1] Ringgit is Malaysia's currency. The exchange rate was US$1 = RM3.80 in April 2001.

The owner of the hotel was Lembaga Tabung Amanah Warisan Negeri Terengganu (LTAWNT). LTAWNT is an investment arm of the state government led by Parti Islam, which won the general election in December 1999. In 1996, LTAWNT's representative, PTB Resorts Sdn Bhd, engaged the Southern Pacific Hotels Corporation (SPHC) to manage the hotel. SPHC won a "12-plus-five-year contract," after successfully outbidding several other large hotel management operating companies from the Asia Pacific region. PPR's General Manager at that time, Rodney Hawker, asserted that the unique factors favoring SPHC's interest in PPR were Terengganu's unspoilt beaches, waterfalls, lakes, and untapped potential as an attractive tourist destination in Malaysia. This was seen relative to Penang and Langkawi, both of which were expected to reach saturation as tourist destinations. PPR was also the only hotel in Kuala Terengganu, which enjoyed both a resort image (with its beach location) as well as a business image, being so close to town.

In managing the strategic change of the hotel, SPHC focused on the following key priorities: upgrading the quality of the hotel's physical facilities, remarketing the hotel, training staff, and changing the work culture. Under the terms of a profit-sharing agreement, Permodalan Terengganu Berhad (PTB), the Terengganu government's investment arm and the new owner of PPR, financed an initial RM11 million to be used by SPHC for physically upgrading and refurbishing the hotel. Recognizing the need to motivate its staff to deliver quality services, SPHC saw to it that rebuilding a new staff canteen was the first renovation work undertaken. Other works included renovating 72 guestrooms in the double-story wing with access to the beach and refurbishing 150 deluxe rooms in the hotel's

11-story tower block. A new tea lounge was also opened adjoining the reception area and a coffee house facing the beach. The entire swimming pool area was also relandscaped, befitting a world-class business resort hotel.

However, in 1998, the hotel went through a difficult period during the economic meltdown. PPR posted a negative gross operating profit (GOP) of RM0.9 million for 1998. In 1999, changes in senior management and drastic measures were introduced to ensure the survival of the hotel. The efforts paid off and the hotel posted a small GOP of RM0.55 million for the year 2000.

In April 2000, Bass Hotels & Resorts (BHR) acquired SPHC. BHR is the world's largest global hotel company that owns, operates, and franchises more than 3,000 hotels and 490,000 guestrooms in some 100 countries and territories. With the ownership of brands like Inter-Continental, Crowne Plaza, Holiday Inn Hotels & Resorts, Holiday Inn Express, and Staybridge Suites by Holiday Inn and Centras, BHR plays hosts to more than 150 million guests every year. With the acquisition of Inter-Continental, BHR manages 59 Parkroyals and Centras in Asia Pacific, which Richard Hartman, MD for Asia Pacific, and his team were trying to reflag into BHR brands and integrate the disparate corporate cultures, owners, and staff. There were also negotiations going on with the respective owners to rebrand the Parkroyals and Centras to either Inter-Continental, Crowne Plaza, or Holiday Inn.

HOTEL COMPETITION ROOM SALES AND CUSTOMER SEGMENTS

Exhibit 1 compares physical facilities, services, room rates, and occupancy rates across competing hotels in Kuala Terengganu. Since rooms can be sold at steep discounts, SPHC used both oc-

Exhibit 1   Comparative Characteristics of Primula Parkroyal versus Competitors' Percentage

	Sutra Beach Resort	Seri Malaysia	Permai Park Inn	Primula Parkroyal	Grand Continental	Glenmarie Kenyir Hotels & Resorts
Location	38 km from town center; beach front	In town	5 km from town center	3 km from town center; beach front	2 km from town center; no direct access to beach	65 km from Kuala Terengganu's Sultan Mahmud Airport, beside Lake Kenyir
No. of rooms	120 chalets/ rooms	137 rooms	130 rooms	150 deluxe rooms, 27 suites, and 72 Garden Wing rooms	192 deluxe, family and suite rooms	130 deluxe chalets, seven executive suites, one presidential villa, 12 standard rooms
Affiliation/ Owner	SPR Management	Gateway Inn Management	Park Plaza International Hotel	Bass Hotels and Resorts (BHR)/Lembaga Tabung Amanah Warisan Negeri Terengganu	Grand Continental Group	DRB Hicom
Market segment mix	Private and government groups	Private and government groups	Corporate, government, travel agents/ tour groups	Corporate, government, travel agents/tour groups	Corporate, government, travel agents/tour groups	Leisure, travel agents, tour groups, incentive groups, corporate meeting groups
Service positioning	Three-star resort, mid-priced	Two-star "value-for-money" budget hotel chain	Three-star town hotel "bed and breakfast" image	Four-star beach cum business resort	Three-star mid-priced business hotel	Four-star up-market resort hotel
Occupancy rate (2001 est.)	40 percent	55 percent	50 percent	49 percent	47 percent	31.4 percent
Rooms sold (2001 est.)	16,790	30,113	23,908	44,805	32,937	14,899

Exhibit 1 (continued)

	Sutra Beach Resort	Seri Malaysia	Permai Park Inn	Primula Parkroyal	Grand Continental	Glenmarie Kenyir Hotels & Resorts
Avg room rate (RM – 2001 est.)	129.86	80.00	92.00	126.18	112.00	159.26
F&B Outlets/ Conference Facilities	• Merang Restaurant • R-U Tapai Lounge • Conference hall (350 pax) • Karaoke lounge	• Sekayu Café (À la carte menu except Friday and Sunday) • Meeting rooms	• Café-in-the-Park • Conference hall (250 pax) • Meeting rooms	• Rhusila Coffee House • One ballroom • Seven meeting rooms • Pelangi restaurant	• Jala Mas Coffee House • Two ballrooms • Six secondary meeting rooms	• Tembat Restaurant • Gawi Poolside Restaurant • Lobby Lounge • Peluang Room Karaoke Lounge • Banquet/Conference hall (220 pax)
Physical facilities and services	• Tennis court • Souvenir shop • Swimming pool	• Shopping arcade • Tea/Coffee-making facilities	• Retail stores • Tea/Coffee-making facilities • Swimming pool	• Business center • Swimming pool • Tennis and volleyball • Laundry • Iron and ironing board • Tea/Coffee-making facilities in rooms	• Swimming pool • Gift shop • Iron and ironing board • Tea/Coffee-making facilities	• Golf course • The Lake Store Souvenir Shop • Indoor gymnasium • Tennis and squash courts • Outdoor sea sports facilities • Lake tours • Individually controlled air-con • Tea/Coffee-making facilities in rooms • IDD telephone

Source: Primula Parkroyal's internal reports and authors' observations during site visits.

cupancy rates and average room rates to measure the yield of hotel rooms.

As of 2001, there were seven competing hotels in Kuala Terengganu. Of the total rooms market of 408,070 available rooms per year, PPR's business plan projected that for 2001, the hotel would be able to maintain its market leader position with 25.3 percent share of rooms sold and 31.4 percent share of revenue market. This was followed by the Grand Continental, a new competitor (with 16.1 percent and 14.9 percent of room and revenue market share, respectively), Permai Park Inn (12.1 percent and 9.2 percent, respectively) and Seri Malaysia (13.0 percent and 9.0 percent, respectively). In terms of average room rates, PPR projected that in 2001 it would be ranking third with an average rate of RM126.18, after Glenmarie Kenyir with RM159.26 and Sutra Beach Resort with RM129.86.

Room market segments targeted for 2001 comprised the corporate segment (26.2 percent), individuals (19 percent), government (9.4 percent), conference (25.4 percent) and sports and miscellaneous groups (6.6 percent) (see **Exhibit 2**). Out of RM10.8 million in total operating revenue planned for 2001, RM6.24 million was expected to come from room revenues (see **Exhibit 2**). It was expected that 76.8 percent of room revenues would be net contribution, which

Exhibit 2   Summary of Room Revenues for January–December 2001 (Planned)

2001 Budget	
No. of rooms available	90,885
No. of rooms occupied	47,532
Occupancy (percentage)	52.3
Average tariff (RM)	131.24

Customer Segment	Rooms Occupied		Average Tariff	Room Revenue
Commercial:		%	RM	RM
• Corporate	7,329	15.4	148.33	1,087,110
• Corporate conference	3,271	6.9	123.67	404,524
• Others	2,321	4.9	150.32	348,892
Total commercial	12,921	27.2	142.44	1,840,526
Private:				
• Rack	236	0.5	235.00	55,460
• FITs[a]	9,040	19.0	147.51	1,333,490
• Other discounts	5,608	11.8	122.32	685,970
Total private	14,884	31.3	139.40	2,074,920
Others				
• Govt – FITs Govt.	4,090	8.6	134.56	550,350
• Conference	12,070	25.4	110.36	1,332,045
• Sports	875	1.8	110.25	107,493
• Embassies and others	387	0.8	183.67	71,080
• Tour groups	2,305	4.8	113.66	261,986
Total others	19,727	41.5	117.75	2,322,954
Total	47,532	100.0	131.24	6,238,400

[a] F.I.T. stands for frequent independent travellers.

Source: Primula Parkroyal's internal reports.

compared to an actual net contribution of 79.5 percent for the time till December 2000 (see **Exhibit 3**). PPR's beach location fronting the South China Sea made it vulnerable to seasonal fluctuations of demand. During the peak holiday periods of June, July, and August, the occupancy rate was expected to reach 62 to 63 percent, (with average room rates of RM143), but demand could go as low as 31 to 34 percent (with average room rates dipping to RM125) in the off-peak monsoon season of December, January, and February.

HOTEL OPERATIONS

PPR's business was organized into the following three departments, which operated as separate profit centers: Room Division, Food and Beverage (F&B) Department, and Telephone Department. Furthermore, PPR had the following five cost centers: Sales and Marketing, the Kitchen, General Administration, Property Maintenance, and Energy.

Front Office Operations

Encik Radi managed the hotel's Front Office operations. This office was responsible for managing room reservations and determining room pricing, and for arranging every activity their guests engaged in throughout their stay. Its functions also included managing the reception counter and room services, porter and concierge services, and recreational support. Encik Radi was fully aware that personal interactions with his "front office" staff were the key drivers of guest satisfaction. He strongly felt that his staff needed to be trained to continually improve service levels.

Another key area of concern was to manage room capacity more effectively. In particular, the occupancy rate had to be increased throughout the year, but especially so during the low seasons (the monsoon months). Also, since Malaysians currently occupied 83 percent of the hotel's room nights, Encik Radi believed that more efforts should be made to attract Malaysian tour groups, rather than tying up high promotional expenses in an attempt to bring in more foreign tourists.

Exhibit 3	Income and Loss For Rooms Division up to December 2000 (Profit Center)		
P&L		**RM**	**Percentage**
Rooms income:		4,659,523	100.0
Expenses:			
• Salaries and wages	437,500		9.4
• Overtime	6,520		0.1
• Employee benefits	204,011		4.4
Subtotal		648,031	13.9
Other Expenses			
• Guest supplies	146,243		3.1
• Telephone and fax	17,849		0.4
• Replacements	33,725		0.7
• Cleaning supplies	31,669		0.7
• Miscellaneous	79,336		1.7
Subtotal		308,822	6.6
Total expense		956,853	20.5
Net contribution		3,702,670	79.5

HUMAN RESOURCES DEVELOPMENT

Encik Ahmad Shaari, the manager of the Human Resources Department (HRD), aimed at instilling a stronger customer-oriented culture among the staff and to continuously improve service quality and standards, and at the same time, to improve productivity. Consistent with the hotel's aim of increasing profitability through cost reduction, Encik Ahmad continued to freeze new appointments and replacements with the aim of reducing staffing costs (i.e., salaries, wages, and staff-related benefits), which stood at 39.2 percent of the hotel's revenue. PPR's staff strength was reduced from some 350 in 1996 to 212 by March 2001. To achieve dramatic improvements in productivity and improve service quality, morale, skills and work ethics, as well as processes and practices had to be improved.

To upgrade skills and advance career development, training programs were conducted at three levels. At the preliminary stage, knowledge of the hotel's service offerings was imparted to staff, and training targeted at instilling service orientation and a stronger work ethic was conducted. Next, customer-complaints handling and related skills training were improved. Lastly, for middle management and above, specific courses such as those on management accounting and industrial relations were conducted.

FOOD AND BEVERAGE DEPARTMENT

With 75 staff reporting to him, Encik Ahmad Zahid, the F&B manager, was responsible for the kitchen, four F&B outlets, conference facilities, and banquet services. In general, F&B contributed about 30 to 35 percent of a hotel's operating revenue. By introducing buffets for breakfast, lunch, tea, dinner, and supper, PPR managed to attract non-hotel guests; this pushed PPR's F&B contribution to almost 50 percent of total revenue.

Encik Ahmad Zahid continued to upgrade service quality, reposition jobs by promoting several staff to supervisory levels, enrich jobs by deploying staff for both room service and reception duty, and cut manpower and energy costs by merging the coffee house and bar operations and by finding ways to save electricity, fuel, and general maintenance.

Mok pondered over the formulation of the 2001 business plan. The need to improve PPR's profitability amid increased competition in Kuala Terengganu made it crucial for PPR to reexamine its key target market segments and its positioning, and to develop strategies to smoothen the severe seasonal demand fluctuations. As further cost-cutting measures had to be pushed through, marketing and communications expenditure had to be minimized and any marketing initiatives had to be designed in the most cost-effective manner.

Study Questions

1. What should PPR's positioning be to differentiate it from its competitors?
2. What should be its target markets for the coming year(s)? Should they be the same for peak and off-peak seasons?
3. How can PPR improve room revenue during all seasons?
4. What are PPR's key challenges to achieve its target positioning and improve room revenues?

5. What actions would you recommend PPR to take over the next 12 months?

    The following Web sites may provide useful information for the case analysis:

    • Asia Travel Hotels and Resorts Reservation Service — http://asiatravel.com/malaysia/primula/index.html
    • Introduction to Terengganu — http://terengganu.gov.my/intro.htm
    • Information on Tourism in Malaysia — http://tourism.gov.my/
    • Malaysia Home Page — http://www.visitmalaysia.com
    • SPHC Home Page — http://www.sphc.com.au
    • Grand Continental Reservation Service — http://asiatravel.com/malaysia/grandterengganu/
    • Glenmarie Kenyir Home Page — http://www.glenmarie.com

Managing an Advertising Agency in Myanmar

JointCom at the Crossroads

MAY LWIN AND JOCHEN WIRTZ

A local advertising agency has to make a deci-sion on whether to grow or contain costs against the background of a sluggish economic environ-ment after the SARS crisis.

It was January 2004, U[1] Mya Win, Managing Director of JointCom, an advertising agency in Myanmar, was reflecting on the company's re-cent performances. Latest news showed that Myanmar's economy, like those in the region, was still weak after the 2003 global Severe Acute Respiratory Syndrome (SARS) outbreak. Fore-casts pointed to a possible continuation of tough times ahead, especially with the expected down-turn in the United States. The advertising indus-try in the region had already seen drastic budget cuts and reduction in the amount of planned promotional activities, and it was too soon to tell if an up-trend would be seen.

U Mya Win met the management team to address how JointCom should respond to these challenges in planning for the next fiscal year. The recent spate of pitches saw some major ad-vertisers switch agencies. In particular, JointCom had been invited for a pitch by Yadana Airways, a large and complex account, which would re-quire JointCom to seek additional resources be-yond its present capabilities, if they did indeed win the account. The discussion saw the emer-gence of different viewpoints. On one hand, JointCom could continue to retain the cost-cut-ting measures that were implemented as a re-sponse to the Asian economic crisis in the late 1990s. On the other hand, some of the manag-ers felt that it was possible for JointCom to seize this opportunity and expand its operations. As U Mya Win wondered which approach to take, he asked the team to relook the market to assess the opportunities available.

JointCom is a medium-sized local advertis-ing agency based in Yangon, the capital of the Union of Myanmar. Its main business involves

---

This case was written by May Lwin, Assistant Professor of Marketing, NUS Business School, National University of Singapore, and Jochen Wirtz.

[1] The prefix used for males in Myanmar, equivalent to *Mr.*

providing marketing communication services. As one of the few locally owned and managed advertising agencies in Myanmar providing full-service marketing communications work, the company has been able to attract both local and foreign clientele. Among its clients are multinationals such as Canon and Toshiba, as well as local businesses.

The management team consisted of two directors and a general manager, all of whom were Myanmar nationals. The number of employees totalled 18. As with most small service organizations, the management was often involved in most aspects of the business, from planning to creative work to media placement. JointCom was particularly strong in developing Myanmar language advertisements. Not only was the creative team highly experienced, it had an in-house language expert who was able to conceptualize and write Myanmar and English copy simultaneously, whereas most agencies often had to rely on external translators.

THE ADVERTISING INDUSTRY IN MYANMAR

The advertising industry in Myanmar can be considered to be in its infancy. Before 1989, there were no major advertising players in the market. During this time, products were not marketed in a Western manner, and the little advertising for local and foreign products that did exist was on billboards and Myanmar magazines and newspapers. In the early 1990s, the opening of the economy saw the entrance of many Western brands into Myanmar. This was paralleled by the industry entry of foreign advertising agencies that set up businesses in Myanmar, mainly to service their pool of international clientele. In order to tap the knowledge of the local market, some of the foreign agencies also joined forces with local companies.

In the mid 1990s, a slowdown in the economy caused the withdrawal of various foreign brands from the Myanmar market. This slowed growth in the advertising business, leading some agencies to close down or trim their operations. Following the SARS epidemic in 2003, the business sector was wary of more economic difficulties ahead. Not only had marketing expenditures been reduced in the previous years, various promotional activities had been postponed or canceled to help cut costs.

With the pitch for Yadana Airways looming, JointCom executives contemplated the alternative courses of action.

U Mya Win: We have been reasonably profitable in spite of the downturn these past few years. Our client list has remained stable. Unfortunately, the economic situation continues to appear gloomy. We should plan our strategy for the next few years very carefully. Of utmost importance is our service and commitment to existing clients, keeping in mind possible opportunities for growth from both existing businesses and new ones. Yadana Airways is a sizable account that would make up almost half of our agency's total billings. We will definitely need a large budget to finance the pitch and hire additional staff if we gain this account.

U Myo Hlaing (Client Service Director): It does seem likely that clients will continue to hold or reduce advertising activities in the near future. I suggest we carefully budget and monitor our expenditure. For example, we can always use more freelance workers during busy periods instead of full-time staff. I am hesitant to hire new staff and face retrenchments if economic problems persist. We can still pitch for new accounts provided we have enough staff strength to manage them. Yadana Airways may be too large an account for us to take on at this point of time.

Daw[2] *Khin Khin (Creative Head)*: I feel that we should look for new businesses that suitably match our company's long-term objectives. The Yadana Airways account is large and would bring us much revenue. Perhaps it is timely to consider expanding this agency. I know it sounds like a risky move during these times, but I have heard that some agencies will be downsizing or even closing down soon. We should take the opportunity to gain a sizable market share by going for Yadana Airways.

COMPETITIVE ARENA AND MARKET OVERVIEW

The advertising scene was highly competitive, with over 50 agencies of various sizes vying for the advertising dollars. Foreign advertising agencies held the largest share of the market. While these foreign multinationals boasted of impressive international credentials and Western marketing know-how, they were at a disadvantage when dealing with the local market demands compared to local agencies like JointCom. Nevertheless, the foreign firms always charged premium rates, and enjoyed a high status among the agencies.

In general, advertising revenue was generated via the promotional efforts of international marketers, government joint ventures, and local firms. The majority of advertising spending came from foreign companies. With little restriction on the promotion of cigarettes and alcohol, Myanmar is a popular advertising ground for such companies, led by foreign brands such as 555 and Tiger Beer. Local advertisers tended to be from the dollar-earning service sector, such as the hotels and airlines.

During the past year, approximate billings for the industry were estimated to be between US$7 and US$10 million. Of this, JointCom's estimated share of the market was about 6 percent, while the top five agencies combined were thought to handle over 60 percent of the total advertising business in Myanmar.

BACKGROUND

Yangon is the capital and the largest city in Myanmar with a population of over three million people (see **Exhibit 1**). It is here in Yangon that most businesses are conducted, and where most foreign companies' headquarters are situated. In the 1990s, observers noted signs of increasing affluence in Yangon—new buildings and private houses in urban centers, new satellite towns, and stores stacked with imported goods were becoming common in Yangon.

The Myanmar consumer tends to be rather selective in his shopping habits, tending to prefer well-known labels over cheaper versions, and familiar makes over newer ones. However, because of tight budgets, the consumer often settles for a cheaper, less desirable brand. Myanmar shoppers tend to be very careful in selecting a product to meet their needs. In addition, close social ties create an environment where entire clans remain faithful to a brand. There is also a great deal of receptivity to foreign goods and advertising.

Various types of products are available to a typical consumer. Imported cooking aids, food, toiletries, electrical goods, and many other products are available not only at the central shopping areas, but also in small provision stores, even in the outskirts of Yangon. In Yangon and Mandalay (Myanmar's second largest city, see **Exhibit 2**), there are also large department stores carrying various types of foreign goods. A

---

[2] The prefix used for females in Myanmar, equivalent to *Ms*.

Exhibit 1   Aerial View of Yangon

Exhibit 2   Mandalay Scene

wide variety of local products are also available, a few of which are direct imitations of foreign goods, right down to the packaging. Lesser-known brands, imitations, and even totally unknown brands are also widely available. There has also been a great demand for electrical and high-technology products such as television sets, cameras, video recorders, and home computers.

PROMOTION AND ADVERTISING

The major media (e.g., TV, radio, and newspapers) are state-owned. There are a large number of print publications—mainly feature magazines, comics, cartoons, and novels. The local media, using the Myanmar language as the main vehicle, dominate the general communication scene in Myanmar. Television stations at present air approximately four to six hours of programs on weekdays and seven hours on weekends, reaching 80 percent of the country's households. It is estimated that 22 percent of the households in Myanmar own a television set, although this figure is much higher for cities like Yangon and Mandalay. A 30-second TV spot advertising can range from US$1,000 to US$2,300, with prime time slots commanding the highest rates. Myanmar television broadcasts both English and Chinese programs with Myanmar subtitles, and Myanmar programs.

The share of advertising expenditure for television in Myanmar is the highest, at 59 percent. Most of the commercials are locally produced, although some foreign advertisements are also broadcasted. Western television commercials are allowed as long as approval is obtained from the censorship board. The Myanmar Television and Radio Department also runs radio advertisements. These are mostly in the Myanmar language, with the range of products advertised being similar to that on television. Radio has a much higher reach of 95 percent, airing approximately ten hours a day in English and Myanmar.

Newspaper advertising seems to be the most cost-effective medium available in Myanmar at present. There are only three newspapers in the country, which have a wide readership. The approximate circulation is around 24,000 for *The New Light of Myanmar* (English), 180,000 for the *Kyemon* (Myanmar), and 220,000 for the *Myanma Alin* (Myanmar). There is also a wide range of local reading materials Myanmar people and visitors read, especially since TV viewing time is limited. There are about 40 monthly magazines, ranging from children's magazines to magazines devoted to selective translations of *Time, Newsweek* and *Asiaweek*.

Movies are a highly popular form of entertainment. There are over 20 cinemas in Yangon showing local films and a potpourri of Western and Asian movies. Billboards are a popular and effective advertising medium, especially in strategic locations in Myanmar. Other popular promotional activities include sports sponsorships (the most popular being soccer and golf), beauty contests, and festival participation.

Although the effects of the economic crisis,

which included a slowdown in the sales of consumer goods and divestment in certain sectors of the economy, seem to have stabilized, the business mood for the new millennium was one of extreme caution. Total advertising spending was estimated to have fallen to US$10 million in 2000 from US$12 million in 1996. Things picked up slightly in 2001 when the government turned to the private sector for its "Mystical Myanmar" advertisement campaign to attract tourists to visit Myanmar. However, the United States and the regional economies were thought to be facing further economic downturn, leading JointCom executives to map out the following options:

1. Retain Cost-cutting measures

This option would be directed at the variable components of future expenses (see **Exhibits 3** and **4**), and involve cost-control measures, including controlling staff strength. With the continued slowdown in advertising and promotional activities, this option would still be expected to meet the fluctuating service needs of clients. It was reasonable to assume that the agency could still be run at the present activity rate with about 10 percent less staff, with some of the work going to freelancers. The manpower buffer allowed

Exhibit 3 JointCom's Preliminary 12-Month Expense Budget for Forthcoming Year	
	Kyats
Fixed costs	
Lease	200,000
Amortization	22,000
Variable costs	
Personnel	360,000
Supplies	30,000
Utilities	15,000
Communication expenses	20,000
General expenses	15,000
Annual expenditure	**662,000**

Exhibit 4 Income Statement for JointCom in 2003 (in Kyats)	
	Kyats
Net sales	1,975,000
Less: Cost of sales	1,392,000
Gross profit	**583,000**
Operating expenses	
Staff expenses	363,200
Occupancy expenses	135,300
Sales expenses	21,000
Communication expenses	16,500
General and administrative expenses	11,300
Total expenses	**547,300**
Net operating profit (loss)	35,700

JointCom to take on additional jobs and small accounts without straining agency resources. JointCom's management was hesitant to retrench staff as its ethos was to provide staff with long-term job security, thereby instilling loyalty. They noted that in a small market like Myanmar's, it may be difficult to hire suitable staff again when the level of business activities picks up.

2. Increase sales activities

With many of the multinationals taking the short-term approach of cost cutting, JointCom has the opportunity to take a more aggressive stance by expending efforts to increase its market share. Expanding sales activities would require the agency to increase its manpower by at least one client service manager to source for new clients, and to seek additional business from existing clients. A competent manager could be employed for between K20,000 and K40,000[3] per annum. It was widely believed that, at any one time, approximately 5 percent of the total advertising market would be open to switching advertising agents. With the present economic situation, this figure could inflate to as much as 8 to 10 percent, thus making it opportune for sourcing new clients.

3. Bid for the Yadana Airways Account

The pressing question at this juncture was whether to embark on a pitch to become the appointed agency for Yadana Airways, a large and prestigious account. Pitching for this account would no doubt require much valuable time and finances from the agency. While actual manpower requirements have not been worked out, it is estimated that, at the minimum, three executives, a creative artist and a secretary will be needed. While the potential account billings were highly attractive, JointCom was aware that financial returns might not be immediate.

U Mya Win suggested that the team spend another two weeks reviewing the alternatives before meeting again to discuss a suitable course of action.

Study Questions

1. How would you characterize the consumer market in Myanmar?
2. How would you describe the advertising industry in Myanmar?
3. What are the alternatives facing JointCom, and the arguments for and against each option?
4. What actions should JointCom pursue and why?

---

[3] The official exchange rate is US$1 = K6. However, the (illegal) black market exchange rate was over K200 per US$ in October 2004.

Banyan Tree

Developing a Powerful Service Brand

JOCHEN WIRTZ AND MAISY KOH

Banyan Tree Hotels and Resorts had become a leading player in the luxury resorts and spa market in Asia. As part of its growth strategy, Banyan Tree had launched new brands and brand extensions that included resorts, spas, retail outlets, and even museum shops. Now, the company had to contemplate how to manage its brand portfolio and expand its business while preserving the distinctive identity and strong brand image of Banyan Tree, its flagship brand.

A brand synonymous with private villas, tropical garden spas, and galleries promoting traditional craft, Banyan Tree Hotels and Resorts received its first guest in 1994 in Phuket, Thailand. Since then, it had grown into a leading manager and developer of niche and premium resorts, hotels and spas in Asia Pacific. Despite having minimal advertising, Banyan Tree achieved global exposure and a high level of brand awareness through the company's public relations and global marketing programs. Much interest was also generated by the company's pro-environmental business practices. With a firm foothold in the luxury resorts market, the company introduced a new and contemporary brand, Angsana, to gain a wider customer base. As the resorts market become increasingly crowded with similar competitive offerings, lured by the success of Banyan Tree, the company had to contemplate how to expand its business and preserve its distinctive identity.

COMPANY BACKGROUND

By mid 2004, Banyan Tree Holdings Pte Ltd (BTHL) owned, managed and operated 15 resorts and hotels, 35 spas, and 38 retail shops in more than 40 locations in 20 countries. In the first ten years since its establishment in 1994, the company's flagship brand, Banyan Tree, had

---

This case was written by Jochen Wirtz and Maisy Koh, Corporate Director, Brand Management, at Banyan Tree Hotels and Resorts, and at Angsana Resorts and Spas. The authors gratefully acknowledge the assistance of Jeannette P. T. Ho, Corporate Director, Revenue Management of Banyan Tree Hotels and Resorts, and Sim Siew Lien, in preparing this case.

won over 100 international tourism, hospitality, and marketing awards, some of which included The "World's Best Spa" (Phuket) from *Conde Nast Traveler* 1998, "Best Resort Hotel in Asia-Pacific" (Phuket) for three consecutive years from *Business Traveller* since 2002 "Seychelles' Best Resort" and "Seychelles' Best Spa" from World Travel Awards (2003).[1] The Banyan Tree brand had also been compared to internationally established brands such as Harley Davison and Manchester United.

BTHL was founded by Ho Kwon Ping, a travel enthusiast and former journalist. Prior to entering the hotels and resorts business, Ho spent some 15 years managing the family business, which was into everything imaginable, such as commodities, food products, consumer electronics, and property development, competing mainly on cost, and was not dominant in any particular country or industry. The closing of a factory in Thailand one year after its opening–because it lost out to other low-cost producers in Indonesia–was the last straw for Ho, who then realized that a low-cost strategy was not only difficult to follow but would also lead him nowhere. Determined to craft out something proprietary that would allow the company to become a price maker rather than a price taker, Ho decided that building a strong brand was the only way for him to maintain a sustainable competitive advantage.

The idea of entering the luxury resorts market was inspired by the gap in the hotel industry that giant chains such as the Hilton and Shangri-La could not fill. There existed a market segment that wanted private and intimate accommodation without the expectation of glitzy chain hotels. This was fueled by the sharp price gap between the luxurious Aman Resorts and other resorts in the luxury resorts market. For example, the Amanpuri in Thailand, one of Aman's resorts, charged a rack rate for its villas ranging from US$650 to over US$7,000 a night, whereas the prices of other luxury resorts, such as the Shangri-La Hotel and Phuket Arcadia Beach Resort by Hilton in Thailand were priced below US$350.[2] Noticing the big difference in prices between Aman Resorts and the other resorts in the luxury resorts market, Ho saw potential for offering an innovative niche product that could also bridge the price gap in this market. A seasoned traveller himself, Ho backpacked throughout the world in his youth. His extensive experiences are evident in his nonconforming belief that resorts should provide more than just accommodation. Ho hit upon the idea of building a resort comprising individual villas, exotic in architectural design and positioned as a romantic and intimate escapade for guests. The rack rates are typically priced between US$500 and US$2,500 for the resort in Phuket, and between US$1,200 and US$4,400 for the resort in the Seychelles.[3] Such a value proposition had yet to be adopted by any hotel or resort then.

Operations at Banyan Tree began with only one resort in Phuket, situated on former mining land once deemed too severely ravaged to sus-

---

[1] The complete list of awards won by Banyan Tree can be found on the company's Web site at www.banyantree.com.

[2] Prices as of July 2004; obtained from the Web sites of Shangri-La Hotels and Resorts and Hilton Hotels at www.shangri-la.com and www.hilton.com, respectively.

[3] Prices as of July 2004; obtained from the Web site of Banyan Tree at www.banyantree.com. Prices of villas at Seychelles originally denominated in euros; converted to US$ at the exchange rate of €1=US$1.2.

tain any form of development by a United Nations Development Program planning unit. It was a bold decision, but the company, together with Ho and his brother Ho Kwon Cjan, restored it after extensive rehabilitation works costing a total of US$250 million. So successful was Banyan Tree Phuket when it was finally launched that the company worked quickly to build two other resorts, one at Bintan Island in Indonesia and the other at Vabbinfaru Island in the Maldives. The company had never looked back since. Even when the travel industry experienced a meltdown and was plagued by retrenchments after the September 11 attacks on the World Trade Center in 2001, room rates at Banyan Tree rose steadily, and no employee was retrenched.

BRAND ORIGINS

Known as Yung Shue Wan in the local dialect, Banyan Tree Bay was a fishing village on Lamma Island in Hong Kong, where Ho and his wife lived for three idyllic years before he joined the family business. Despite the village's modest and rustic setting, Ho remembered it to be a sanctuary of romance and intimacy. The large canopies of the Banyan Tree resembled the shelter afforded by Asia's tropical rainforests. Ho thus decided to name his resort Banyan Tree, and position it as a sanctuary for romance and intimacy.

THE SERVICE OFFERING

Unlike most other resorts then, Banyan Tree resorts comprised individual villas that came with a private pool, jacuzzi, or spa treatment room, each designed to offer guests exclusivity and utmost privacy. For example, a guest could skinny-dip in the private pool within his villa without being seen by other guests, putting him in a world of his own (see **Exhibit 1** for a private two-bedroom pool villa with Jacuzzi and spa treatment pavilion).

Exhibit 1   View from a Private Two-Bedroom Banyan Tree Pool Villa with Jacuzzi and Spa Treatment Pavilion

All Banyan Tree resorts and villas were designed around the concept of providing "a sense of place" to reflect and enhance the culture and heritage of the destination. This was reflected in the architecture, furnishings, landscape, vegetation, and the service offers. To create a sense of exotic sensuality and ensure the privacy of its guests, the resorts were designed to blend into the natural landscape of the surrounding environment and use the natural foliage and boulders as a privacy screen (see **Exhibit 2** showing Banyan Tree Seychelles). In Banyan Tree Phuket, for example, the bed was a square platform in the middle of the room, made similar to the Thai "dang", overlooking a lotus pond, and illuminated by soft lighting at night—in total contrast to the beds accompanied by strong reading lights that were found in most other hotels and resorts then.

The furnishings of Banyan Tree villas were deliberately native to convey the exoticism of the destination with its rich local flavor and luxurious feel. The spa pavilions in Seychelles were constructed around the large granite boulders and lush foliage to offer an outdoor spa experience in complete privacy. The resorts' local flavor was also reflected in the services offered, some of which were unique to certain resorts. Employees were allowed to vary the service delivery process according to local culture and practices, as long as these were consistent with the brand promise of romance and intimacy. Thus, in Phuket, for instance, a couple could enjoy dinner on a traditional Thai long tail boat accompanied by private Thai musicians while cruising instead of dining in a restaurant. Banyan Tree Phuket also offered wedding packages in which

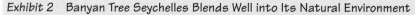

Exhibit 2   Banyan Tree Seychelles Blends Well into Its Natural Environment

couples were blessed by Buddhist monks. In the Maldives, wedding ceremonies could be conducted underwater among the corals. Guests could also choose to dine in a castaway sandbank with only their private chefs and a billion stars for company.

Service standards at Banyan Tree were determined in terms of customer satisfaction, rather than typical service standards in the industry. Products and services offered were also conceived with the desired customer experience in mind. One such product was the "Intimate Moments" package, specially created for couples. This is presented as a surprise when guests returned to find their villas decorated with candles, incense, flowers, satin sheets, a chilled bottle of wine or champagne, and at the outdoor bath with flowers and bath oils. The couple will be presented with a variety of aromatic massage oils to inspire those intimate moments.

Another draw of the resorts was the Banyan Tree Spa, found at every Banyan Tree property. The first tropical garden spas in the industry, Banyan Tree Spas offered a variety of aromatic oil massages, and face and body beauty treatments using traditional Asian therapies, with a choice of indoors or outdoors treatment. The spa products used were natural, indigenous products, made from local herbs and spices. Non-clinical in concept, Banyan Tree Spas relied mainly on the "human touch" instead of energy-consuming high-tech equipment. The spa experience was promoted as a sensorial, intimate experience that would rejuvenate one's "body, mind, and soul," and was mainly targeted at couples who could enjoy their treatments together.

To reinforce the Banyan Tree brand association with culture and heritage, and help promote cottage crafts, a retail outlet, known as the Banyan Tree Gallery, was set up in each resort. Items sold were made by local artisans, and included traditionally woven handmade fabrics, garments, jewellery, handicrafts, tribal art, and spa accessories, such as incense candles and massage oils, which guests could use at home to replicate the Banyan Tree Spa experience.

The result of Banyan Tree's efforts was "a very exclusive, private holiday feeling," as described by one guest. Another guest commented, "It's a treat for all the special occasions like honeymoons and wedding anniversaries. It's the architecture, the sense of place, and the promise of romance."

MARKETING BANYAN TREE

In the first two years when Banyan Tree was launched, the company's marketing communications was managed by an international advertising agency. The agency also designed the Banyan Tree logo shown in **Exhibit 3**, and together with the management came up with the marketing tagline "Sanctuary for the Senses."

Exhibit 3   Banyan Tree Logo

Though furnished luxuriously, Banyan Tree resorts were promoted as providing romantic and intimate "smallish" hotel experiences, rather than luxurious accommodation as touted by most competitors then. More than merely resort stays, "Banyan Tree Experiences" was marketed as those intimate private moments with loved ones at the Banyan Tree resorts. The resorts saw themselves as setting the stage for guests to create those unforgettable memories.

When Banyan Tree was first launched, extensive advertising was carried out for a short period of time to gain recognition in the industry. Subsequently, the company scaled down on advertising and kept it minimal, mainly in high-end travel magazines in key markets. The advertisements were visual in nature with succinct copy or showcase the awards and accolades won. **Exhibit 4** shows Banyan Tree advertisements highlighting the award-winning Banyan Tree resorts.

Brand awareness for Banyan Tree was generated largely through public relations and global marketing programs. For example, relationships with travel editors and writers were cultivated to encourage visits to the resorts. This helped increase editorial coverage on Banyan Tree, which management felt was more effective in conveying the "Banyan Tree Experience" from an impartial third-party perspective. A Banyan Tree Web site (www.banyantree.com) was

Exhibit 4   Advertisements Showcasing Awards Won by Banyan Tree Resorts

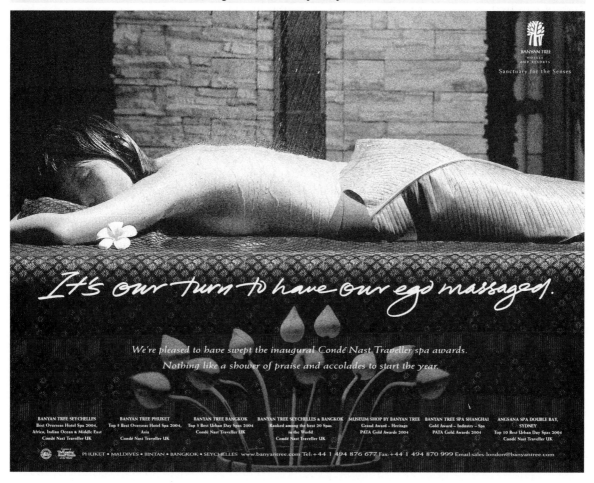

also set up to enable online reservations of rooms and spa services, and to provide information on Banyan Tree products and services.

The management of marketing activities was centralized at the Singapore headquarters for consistency in brand building. BTHL appointed a few key wholesalers in each targeted market, and worked closely with them to promote sales. Rather than selling through wholesale and retail agents that catered to the general market, BTHL chose to work only with agents specializing in exclusive luxury holidays targeted at wealthy customers. Global exposure was also achieved through Banyan Tree's membership in the Small Luxury Hotels and Leading Hotels of the World. Targeting high-end consumers, they represent various independent exclusive hotels and have sales offices in major cities around the world.

BRAND VALUES

Banyan Tree embraced such values as the active caring for the natural and human environment and revitalizing local communities, in turn creating pride and respect among staff. The company hoped to build the brand on values that employees and customers could identify with and support as part of their own life values. Thus, the company worked actively to preserve, protect, and promote the natural and human environments in which Banyan Tree resorts were located.

PRESERVING THE ENVIRONMENT

Resorts were built from scratch using local materials as far as possible, and at the same time minimizing the impact on the environment. At Banyan Tree Bintan, for example, the 70 villas located in a rainforest were constructed around existing trees, cutting down as few trees as possible, to minimize the impact the resort had on the natural environment. The villas were built on stilts and platforms to avoid cutting trees and possible soil erosion. At Banyan Tree Maldives Vabbinfaru and Banyan Tree Seychelles, fresh water supply was obtained by the more expensive method of desalination, instead of extracting water from the underground water-table, which risked disrupting the ecological system in the long run.

Toiletries, such as shampoo, hair conditioner, bath foam, and body lotion provided in the resorts were nontoxic and biodegradable, and filled in reusable containers made from celadon or ceramic. Refuse was recycled where possible and treated through an in-house incinerator system otherwise. Waste water was also treated and recycled in the irrigation of resort landscapes. Even the detergents and soap used in the resorts were biodegradable.

Through the retail arm Banyan Tree Gallery, the human environment efforts were evident in the active sourcing of furnishing from indigenous tribes to provide gainful employment. These employment opportunities provided a source of income for the tribes and, at the same time, preserved their unique heritage.

CREATING BRAND OWNERSHIP AMONG EMPLOYEES

All employees were trained in the basic elements of five-star service establishments, which included greeting guests, remembering their first names, and anticipating their needs. In addition, some employees got a taste of the "Banyan Tree Experience" as part of their training. Management believed that the stay would help employees understand better what guests will experience, and, in return, enhance their delivery of special experiences for the guests.

Although management imposed strict rules in the administration of the resorts, employees were given room to exercise creativity and sensitivity. For example, the housekeeping teams were not restricted by a standard bed decoration. Rather, they were given room for creativity although they had general guidelines for turning the bed to keep in line with the standards of a premium resort. Banyan Tree invested liberally in staff welfare: employees were taken to and from work in air-conditioned buses, and had access to various amenities, including good-quality canteens, and medical and child care facilities. Staff dormitories had televisions, telephones, refrigerators, and attached bathrooms.

The company's generous staff welfare policies apparently paid off. Ho said, "The most gratifying response is the sense of ownership that our staff began to have. It's not a sense of financial ownership, but they actually care about the property. In our business, service and service standards do not always mean the same thing as in a developed country, where standards are measured by efficiency and productivity, by people who are already quite well-versed in a service culture. We operate in places that, sometimes, have not seen hotels. People come from villages. What we need—more than exact standards—is for them to have a sense of hospitality, a sense that the guest is an honored person who, by virtue of being there, is able to give a decent livelihood to the people who work. This creates a culture in which everybody is friendly and helpful."

INVOLVING GUESTS IN ENVIRONMENTAL CONSERVATION

As part of the company's efforts to encourage environmental conservation and help save the en-

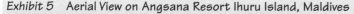

Exhibit 5   Aerial View on Angsana Resort Ihuru Island, Maldives

vironment, Banyan Tree organized activities that involved guests' participation to create more interest in environmental preservation. In the Maldives, for instance, guests were invited to take part in the coral transplantation program (see **Exhibit 5** for a picture of the island resort and its surrounding corral reefs). Guests who participated in the program were then encouraged to return several years later to see the progress of their efforts. Guests could also participate in marine biology sessions that allowed them to learn more about the conservation of marine life, and take part in reef cleaning projects. The response from guests had been tremendously positive.

Banyan Tree established The Green Imperative Fund to support community-based environmental action in the Asia Pacific region. Guests were billed US$1 per room night (of which they could opt out if they wished) and the company matched dollar for dollar. Details of the program were communicated to guests through various ways, such as environmental messages attached to in-villa turndown gifts.

Guests were often happy to know that their patronage contributed to meaningful causes, such as the building of schools for the local community, restoration of devastated coral reefs, and the survival of local village crafts.

INVOLVING THE LOCAL COMMUNITY

Banyan Tree also tried to involve the local community in all aspects of its business, even as the resorts were being built. Villas were constructed as far as possible from indigenous materials, most of which were supplied by local traders. Traditional art and handicraft that complemented the villas' aesthetics were also purchased from local artisans. In addition, the company engaged local craftsmen to produce indigenous art and handicrafts for sale at the resort's retail outlets, the Banyan Tree Gallery.

The company believed in building profitable resorts that would also benefit the local environment and contribute to the local economies through the creation of employment and various community projects. Thus, besides providing employment for the local community, the company also brought business to the local farmers and traders by making it a point to purchase fresh produce from them. Where possible, the company also supported local tourism ventures that would both benefit the wider local community and enhance the visitor's experience. In Phuket, for example, noting that the local hawkers tended to peddle food and gift items on the beachfront near Banyan Tree properties, the company constructed a food center with proper facilities for these hawkers, to promote proper hygiene standards and limit pollution from refuse and waste food scraps.

Recognizing that the disparity in lifestyles and living standards between guests and the local community might create a sense of alienation within the local community, a Community Relations Department was set up to develop and manage community outreach programs. Funding scholarships for needy children, building a school and child care center, hosting lunches and parties for the elderly, and supporting local cultural and religious activities were some of the community outreach programs introduced by the company.

GROWING THE BANYAN TREE

In 2002, BTHL took over the management of a city hotel in the heart of Bangkok from Westin Hotel Company. The hotel was rebranded as Banyan Tree Bangkok, after extensive renovation works were completed to upgrade the hotel's facilities, build new additional spa amenities and a Banyan Tree Gallery. This was the first Banyan Tree hotel to be located in the city area, unlike the other beachfront Banyan Tree properties.

As the Banyan Tree brand became established, the company began expanding its network of spas and retail outlets. Stand-alone Banyan Tree Spas and Banyan Tree Galleries were set up as separate ventures, independent of Banyan Tree hotels and resorts, in various cities such as Shanghai, Sydney, India, and Dubai, operating either in other hotels or as stand-alone outlets.

INTRODUCING NEW BRANDS

After establishing a foothold in the luxury resorts market, BTHL introduced the Angsana brand, in response to demand from hotel operators in Asia that were keen to introduce spa services in their hotels. As the positioning of these hotels did not fit that of Banyan Tree, the company decided to launch a new brand, Angsana, a more contemporary and affordable brand than Banyan Tree, to run as stand-alone spa businesses in other hotels.

The first Angsana Spa was opened in 1999 at Dusit Laguna, one of several hotels at Laguna Phuket, an integrated resort development with shared facilities located at Bang Tao Bay in Thailand. The Angsana Spa was so well received that the company quickly set up five other such spas in various hotels in Thailand. In 2000, BTHL opened its first Angsana Resort & Spa, complete with an Angsana Gallery, located less than one kilometer away from Banyan Tree Bintan.

In 2003, BTHL launched "Colours of Angsana" to penetrate the soft adventure and cultural tourism market, catering to the more adventurous segment of the market. "Colours of Angsana" was launched as a product line of Angsana, and comprised a collection of individual hotels and resorts, each with their own identity, situated at more offbeat and exotic locations, and priced more affordably than Banyan Tree. These hotels were acquired under management or revenue-sharing arrangements, and were "managed by" Angsana. The brand name was chosen, as Ho wanted them to "remain individual, each with their own color and name, like an artist's palette." As of 2004, two hotels were launched under the "Colours of Angsana" brand–the Gyalthang Dzong Hotel in Shangri-La, China's Yunnan province, and the Deer Park in Giritale, Sri Lanka.

THE ROAD AHEAD

To diversify its geographic spread, Ho planned to venture into locations in South America and Southern Europe, where he hoped to replicate Banyan Tree's success in Asia. However, given the higher costs of doing business in the Americas and Europe, would the same strategy that had brought fame and success to Banyan Tree in Asia be workable in the rest of the world? Ho's ultimate vision was "to string a necklace of Banyan Tree Resorts around the world; not quantity, but a number of jewels that form a chain around the world." A list of Banyan Tree's current and planned properties is shown in the Appendix at the end of the case.

Also, while expanding the company's network of hotels and resorts, spas, and retail outlets, Ho had to be mindful of the brands' focus and be careful not to dilute the brands. He also had to consider the strategic fit of the company's portfolio of brands, which comprised Banyan Tree, Angsana, and Colours of Angsana.

Banyan Tree certainly stood out among its competitors in the resorts industry when it was first launched. Since then, its success attracted various competitors which offered similar products and services. Thus, it was imperative that Banyan Tree retained its competitive advantage to prevent losing its distinctive position in the market.

Study Questions

1. What are the main factors that contributed to Banyan Tree's success?
2. Evaluate Banyan Tree's brand positioning and communications strategies. Can Banyan Tree maintain its unique positioning in an increasingly overcrowded resorts market?
3. Discuss whether the brand portfolio of Banyan Tree, Angsana and Colours of Angsana, as well as the product portfolio of beach resorts and city hotels, spas, galleries and museum shops fit as a family. What are your recommendations to Banyan Tree for managing these brands and products in future?

Appendix

Banyan Tree and Angsana Group Portfolio as of July 2004

(For details of individual hotels and spas, see www. banyantree.com.)

(A) HOTEL PORTFOLIO

(A-1) Banyan Tree Hotel and Resort

1. Banyan Tree Phuket, Thailand
2. Banyan Tree Bangkok, Thailand
3. Banyan Tree Bintan, Indonesia
4. Banyan Tree Vabbinfaru, Maldives
5. Banyan Tree Seychelles
6. Banyan Tree Marrakech, Morocco*
7. Banyan Tree Pylos, Greece*
8. Banyan Tree Lijiang, China*
9. Banyan Tree Mayakoba, Mexico*
10. Banyan Tree Acapulco, Mexico*
11. Banyan Tree Bali, Indonesia*
12. Banyan Tree Chiang Mai, Thailand*

(A-2) Angsana Resort and Spa

1. Angsana Resort Bintan, Indonesia
2. Angsana Resort Palm Cove, Australia
3. Angsana Resort Ihuru Island, Maldives
4. Angsana Oasis Resort Bangalore, India
5. Angsana Resort Hua Hin, Thailand*

(A-3) Colours of Angsana

6. Colours of Angsana Gyalthang Dzong Hotel, Yunnan, China
7. Colours of Angsana Deer Park, Sri Lanka
8. Colours of Angsana Maison Souvannaphoum, Luang Prabang, Laos*

9. Colours of Angsana Swannee Hotel, Sri Lanka*

(A-4) Angsana City Club

1. Angsana City Club and Spa at the Tiger City, Taiwan
2. Angsana City Club and Spa at Crescat City, Sri Lanka*
3. Angsana City Club and Spa Shanghai, China*

(A-5) Other Hotels

1. Sheraton Grande Laguna Phuket, Thailand
2. Dusit Laguna Phuket, Thailand
3. Laguna Beach Resort Phuket, Thailand

(A-6) Allamanda

1. Allamanda Phuket, Thailand

(B) SPA PORTFOLIO

(B-1) Banyan Tree Hotel Spa

1. Banyan Tree Spa at the Banyan Tree Phuket, Thailand
2. Banyan Tree Spa at the Banyan Tree Bangkok, Thailand
3. Banyan Tree Spa at the Banyan Tree Bintan, Indonesia
4. Banyan Tree Spa at the Banyan Tree Vabbinfaru, Maldives

---

* As of July 2004, this facility was currently under development.

5. Banyan Tree Spa at the Banyan Tree Seychelles

6. Banyan Tree Spa at the Banyan Tree Marrakech, Morocco*

(B-2) Banyan Tree Spa in Other Properties

1. Banyan Tree Spa at the Westin Shanghai, China

2. Banyan Tree Spa at the Sheraton Seagaria Phoenix Resort, Japan*

3. Banyan Tree Spa at the Laforet Gora, Hakone, Japan*

(B-3) Elements by Banyan Tree Spa

1. Elements by Banyan Tree Spa, Kuwait*

(B-4) Oberoi Spa by Banyan Tree

1. Oberoi Spa by Banyan Tree at the Oberoi Amarvilas, Agra, India

2. Oberoi Spa by Banyan Tree at the Oberoi Bangalore, India

3. Oberoi Spa by Banyan Tree at the Oberoi Calcutta, India

4. Oberoi Spa by Banyan Tree at the Oberoi Cecil, Shimla, India

5. Oberoi Spa by Banyan Tree at the Oberoi Mumbai, India

6. Oberoi Spa by Banyan Tree at the Oberoi New Delhi, India

7. Oberoi Spa by Banyan Tree at the Oberoi Rajvilas, Jaipur, India

8. Oberoi Spa by Banyan Tree at the Oberoi Udaivilas, Udaipur, India

9. Oberoi Spa by Banyan Tree at the Oberoi Vanyavilas, Ranthambhore, India

10. Oberoi Spa by Banyan Tree at the Oberoi Wildflower Hall, Shimla, India

11. Oberoi Spa by Banyan Tree at the Oberoi Bali, Indonesia

12. Oberoi Spa by Banyan Tree at the Oberoi Lombok, Indonesia

13. Oberoi Spa by Banyan Tree at the Oberoi Mauritius, Mauritius

14. Oberoi Spa by Banyan Tree at the Oberoi Hurgahda, Egypt

(B-5) Angsana Spa in Other Properties

1. Angsana Spa at the Angsana Resort Bintan, Indonesia

2. Angsana Spa at the Angsana Resort Palm Cove, Australia

3. Angsana Spa at the Angsana Resort Ihuru Island, Maldives

4. Angsana Spa at the Colours of Angsana Gyalthang Dzong Hotel, Yunnan, China

5. Angsana Spa at the Sheraton Grande Laguna Phuket, Thailand

6. Angsana Spa at the Dusit Laguna Phuket, Thailand

7. Angsana Spa at the Laguna Beach Resort Phuket, Thailand

8. Angsana Spa at the Allamanda Phuket, Thailand

9. Angsana Spa at the Green View Resort, Chiang Mai, Thailand

10. Angsana Spa at the Palm Island, Hong Kong

11. Angsana Spa at the Marriott Guam, USA

12. Angsana Spa Double Bay, Sydney, Australia

13. Angsana Spa Rydges Jamison, Sydney, Australia

14. Angsana Spa at the Angsana Resort Hua Hin, Thailand*

15. Angsana Spa at the Colours of Angsana Maison Souvannaphoum, Luang Prabang, Laos*

16. Angsana Spa at the Colours of Angsana Swanee Hotel, Sri Lanka*

17. Angsana Spa at the Colours of Angsana Deer Park, Sri Lanka

18. Angsana Spa at the Vineyard Hotel, Cape Town, South Africa*

19. Angsana Spa at Movenpick Resort & Spa, El Alamein, Egypt*

20. Angsana Spa at Brehon Hotel, Killarney, Ireland*

21. Angsana Spa at Baodao Garden Hotel, Suzhou, China*

22. Angsana Spa at the Movenpick El Gouna, Egypt*

23. Angsana Spa at the Steigenberger Golf Club House, El Gouna, Egypt*

24. Angsana Spa at Mutiara Hotel, Kuala Lumpur*

25. Angsana Spa at the Dubai Marina, UAE*

26. Angsana Spa at the Emirates Hills Golf, UAE*

27. Angsana Spa at the Emirates Hills Town, UAE*

28. Angsana Spa at the Arabian Ranches, UAE*

(C) SUMMARY

Total Number of Hotels Open = 15
Total Number of Hotels under Development = 10
Total Number of Spas Open = 35
Total Number of Spas under Development = 19
Total Number of Clubs Open = 1
Total Number of Clubs under Development = 2

Managing Word of Mouth

The Referral Incentive Program That Backfired

PATRICIA CHEW AND JOCHEN WIRTZ

A referral incentive program is introduced, but results in fewer referrals than expected, especially from the desired target segments!

INTRODUCTION

Ray Stevenson stared in dismay at the field-test reports on his desk. He was the sales and promotions manager at the Singapore subsidiary of AHL Insurance Corporation, the fifth-largest insurance company in the United States, and he had been the main driving force behind the company's new initiative to expand its customer base through the implementation of a "recommend-a-friend" incentive program, the first of its kind in the industry. Before the actual implementation of the program, the company had conducted a three-month field test and offered the incentive program to a small number of customers in each of the four segments it had identified in its database.

Based on the success of similar programs in the banking and mobile phone industries, he had thought that the initiative would be a runaway success. Results, however, were far below expectations, although the program was not a complete failure. There were referrals generated, but it was mainly from the low-yield segments of its customer base. Moreover, its higher-revenue customers, who had traditionally generated the highest number of referrals, seemed to have generated less rather than more referrals during the referral-program trial period.

BACKGROUND INFORMATION ON AHL

AHL Insurance Corporation had its humble beginnings as an automobile insurer in Madison, Wisconsin, in 1958. The founder, Rick Carlson, was an insurance salesman who decided to start his own business in a rural town in Madison, believing that it was a niche market with a lot of untapped potential. Since then, the company has grown by leaps

---

and bounds. Over the years, it expanded its markets and product lines to meet the changing needs of its customers. Today, it has offices in over 100 countries. In Asia, it had established 23 offices, and its Singapore office was the regional headquarters for Southeast Asia. There are currently more than 30,000 independent agents serving the needs of its customers.

The mission of AHL is to provide quality service and build relationships with its customers through mutual trust and integrity. AHL aims to be the customer's first and best choice and maintain its position of leadership as a comprehensive provider of insurance products, so it has a variety of insurance products to meet both the personal and business needs of its customers.

The main strengths of AHL lie not only in the diversity of its products, but also in the excellent customer service provided by its agents. On top of that, in an industry where some firms have gained a bad reputation by making it difficult for its customers to make insurance claims, AHL actually trains dedicated agents to explain the nitty-gritty details of claims to its customers and these agents also help customers to expedite the claims process. As a result, it has earned the trust and loyalty of its customers over the years.

CUSTOMER SEGMENTS

When the idea for the "recommend-a-friend" program was first mooted, the company used its sophisticated customer relationship management (CRM) system to segment its customers into four groups. The "Apostles" were customers who had been with the company for over ten years, and they had basically consolidated most of their insurance purchases with AHL. Besides themselves, their family members had also purchased various kinds of insurance products from AHL,

ranging from life insurance, investment-linked plans, retirement plans, and children's education plans to property liabilities, automobile insurance, etc. Those "Apostles" running their own businesses would also buy products like group insurance packages, commercial property liabilities, and disability packages from AHL. They were not price sensitive and were willing to pay a premium for a customized insurance plan to meet their individual needs. One distinguishing feature of the "Apostles" was the fact that they really helped to "sell" AHL to their family members, friends, and associates. This was the group of customers that had traditionally generated the most referrals for AHL to date. As is typical of most companies, this group of customers generated about 80 percent of the company's revenue.

The "Loyals" were customers who had been with AHL for more than seven years on average. Compared to the "Apostles," they bought fewer kinds of products, and generated fewer referrals. They generally consolidated their insurance purchases with a few companies and were reluctant to pay a premium for customized plans, preferring to buy the standardized ones. The "Leads" were termed such because of their seeming inertia. They usually bought only personal insurance products, and may have one or two insurance policies that are long-term in nature, like the life, health, endowment, or retirement insurance plans. When agents tried to sell them other kinds of plans, they were not open to the idea. Like the "Loyals," they also tended to use several insurance companies to meet their insurance needs based on price and coverage, but were not as price sensitive as the "Butterflies." In terms of referrals, this group would provide the occasional referral. Lastly, the "Butterflies" was the group of customers who bought the occasional short-term insurance policies like travel-related products, and might hold long-term policies from other insurance companies. This group of customers was highly price sensitive. They would flock to wherever there were any deals or promotional incentives on insurance plans.

THE "RECOMMEND-A-FRIEND" INCENTIVE PROGRAM

The program was based on a points system. Points were awarded on the basis of profitability and term of the insurance products sold. The higher the sum assured, and the longer the insurance coverage, the more points the referrer could collect. The points system was transparent as the referrer could check beforehand how many points they would get if their friends bought a certain kind of product or plan from AHL. Points could be accumulated and exchanged for a variety of gifts featured in a glossy and attractive catalog.

For example, with 100,000 points, which is the highest number of points one could accumulate for a single referral, one could exchange for a Tag Heuer watch costing US$1,500. Other products of lesser value in the catalog included Swatch watches; Samsonite travel luggage; Waterman and Parker pens; Nokia mobile phones; electrical goods like shavers, blenders, juicers, vacuum cleaners, microwave ovens, toasters and television sets; DVD and CD players; restaurant vouchers; spa vouchers, etc. In all, there were about 300 items in the catalog. The lowest number of points awarded was 50 points, for short-term travel insurance plans.

Referrals

Thus far, the "Butterflies" and "Leads" had generated the most referrals since the launch of the "recommend-a-friend" referral incentive program. However, since they themselves usually did not purchase the high-sum-assured policies, or long-term policies, their friends were also people who bought similar kinds of policies. As a result, short-term policies like travel policies that cover a few days, or up to one year, and child care policies that are typically no longer than two years, have been very popular. These policies typically did not produce high profit margins for the company, and the insured values tended to be lower.

What was alarming was the fact that the number of referrals from the "Apostles" had fallen since the start of the program. Ray had envisaged that this group would be motivated to refer even more friends to AHL. Their recommendations usually resulted in individuals buying policies that were long term, and of high sums assured, thus generating higher profits for the company. **Exhibit 1** details the results of the referrals in the three months of the field test. Five hundred customers from each of the four segments were selected to participate in the field test. For each segment, a control group consisting also of 500 customers was also selected and monitored during the market testing.

Initial Interview Results

Three months after the launch of the program, Stevenson had asked his marketing managers to conduct some interviews with customers from various segments, to cull their views about the program. As a result, about 30 in-depth individual interviews were conducted with customers from each of the four segments, in their homes. **Exhibit 2** shows some verbatim comments by the respondents.

Future Direction

Stevenson knew that before the next meeting with the marketing director, he had to come up with a

Exhibit 1   Referral Frequency and Value Index by Customer Segment

	Apostles	Control Group	Loyals	Control Group	Leads	Control Group	Butterflies	Control Group
Number of referrals over three months before the test	22	21	17	15	3	4	1	1
Number of referrals during the three test months	15	19	11	14	8	3	16	1
Conversion rate (i.e., customers who actually took up a policy)	32%	33%	27%	28%	18%	22%	12%	18%
Average policy value sold (US$'000)	223	235	193	198	109	115	83	91

Note: The index refers to the rebased number of referrals received per 1,000 customers per year. The average policy value closed by the referred customer is shown in thousand U.S. dollars ('000).

Exhibit 2 Verbatim Comments About the Incentive Program

Apostles	Loyals	Leads	Butterflies
"... I would only recommend if I thought it was good for the person. I would not do anything in a self-serving way ..." Marketing manager, 39	"... the gifts they offer. I have enough junk in my house already, I don't need anymore of it ..." Unemployed, 29	"... the kind of thing, I leave it to the individual, I don't push ..." Administrative assistant, 26	"... I will definitely be motivated to get in those customers because the incentive is very relevant to me ... I'll definitely do it fast—speak to anyone close to me and not so close to me ..." Student, 22
"... It's almost like a forced recommendation because, ultimately, you think there is something to benefit yourself. I do the recommendation out of helping somebody ..." Businesswoman, 64	"... I will not go out of my way to recommend just to obtain the incentive. That would be a waste of my time. I do have better things to do with my time." Home maker, 32	"... the reward that I have makes me want to tell others ..." Student, 18	"... When they started the program, I email everyone on my mailing list. I'm aiming to get the Tag Heuer. It would indeed be a dream for me!" Waitress, 20
"... I'm not the kind who looks at incentives. I look at ties. If the person is close to me ... and he needs an insurance, then I will want to help him out by giving him advice on what to buy ..." Banquet manager, 35	"... if the company was good, they wouldn't need an incentive program. When they do that, I start to have doubts about them, and am worried about my investment ..." IT executive, 35	I'm excited by incentives. I love the incentives in the catalog. I would definitely recommend it to anyone who is interested ..." Clerical assistant, 22	"... I'm saving a lot. I like the feeling of exchanging points for something that I don't have to pay money for." Home maker, 35
"... being a businessman who is time scarce, I never bother with it ..." Businessman, 56	"... I recommend my friends because the agents and customer service officers provide good service. I don't care if I get the incentive or not ..." Professional sportsman, 27	"... I've already gotten my friends and family to buy some insurance, and I got a Swatch watch in return. Isn't that wonderful?" Sales executive, 26	"... since it's free, why don't I take advantage of it right? It would be stupid not to." Security guard, 25
"... it's the service that the company has been providing that I like. It's not what they are offering ..." Management consultant, 41	"... the incentives that they are offering are just not worthwhile in the time that I would have to spend getting what they offer." Director, 46	"... if it wasn't for the rewards, I would not have told others about the company." Home maker, 40	"... whichever company is giving away freebies, I always try to take advantage of that ... it saves me a lot of money. I'll queue up overnight if I have to." Student, 19
"... I can buy those things with my own money. Why should I then be motivated to recommend based on the gifts?" Pilot, 44	"... I think the incentive is immaterial ... I will take it as an extra bonus. In the first place, we're doing word of mouth already all the time for people unknowingly ..." Teacher, 32		

report about the results of the field test, and also provide possible solutions to the problem. He was up for a promotion and did not want this project to affect his chances. What should he do next? Why were the results the way they were? Should he abandon the program even though about US$300,000 had been invested in it? Alternatively, should he change certain features of the program before relaunching it so that it is more targeted, because the different segments of customers seemed to react quite differently to the program? Was there a need for more market research to see what each group of customers would prefer in a referral incentive program?

Study Questions

1. Analyze the field test data and derive key managerial conclusions from them.
2. What course of action would you recommend to Stevenson? Determine his options, and assess the pros and cons for each option, and then recommend one course of action to him.

Revenue Management at Prego Italian Restaurant

JOCHEN WIRTZ AND SHERYL E. KIMES

Prego Italian Restaurant needs to decide how to best apply revenue management to improve profitability in both peak and off-peak periods. It is important for the company to consider potentially negative effects of revenue management strategies on customers and on staff, and to manage potential conflicts that may arise.

After the busy lunch hours on a weekday afternoon, Francesco Caponeri,[1] Prego's restaurant manager, was looking at the half-empty restaurant, feeling that it was in total contrast to the lunch and dinner hours, especially during the weekends, when they had to turn away customers. If seats were occupied during the off-peak hours, more revenue could be generated. During the peak periods, when customer demand exceeded the supply of tables and diners were unwilling to wait for long, Prego was losing revenue and perhaps even future business. Francesco thought that there should be better strategies in which the revenue could be increased, and was planning to develop a revenue management strategy that would increase revenues without jeopardizing diner satisfaction.

COMPANY BACKGROUND AND MARKET ENVIRONMENT

Prego is an upscale, trendy, and popular Italian restaurant in Singapore. It has repeatedly been rated as one of Singapore's best restaurants by the *Singapore Tatler*, an authoritative review guide to the local restaurant scene. Prego is located right at the heart of Singapore within the Raffles City complex. Part of the complex are Singapore's largest hotel, the Swissôtel The Stam-

This case was written by Jochen Wirtz and Sheryl E. Kimes, Professor at the School of Hotel Administration, Cornell University. The authors gratefully acknowledge the assistance of Jeannette P. T. Ho, Corporate Director of Revenue Management, Banyan Tree Hotels and Resorts, Singapore; Eric Blomeyer, F&B Manager; Giorgio Olivotti, Restaurant Manager, Prego; Shawn Tay Teck Heong, Goh Chwee Suan, Handy Amin, and Chua Hsiao Wei in preparing this case. Selected financial and market data have been disguised for confidentiality reasons. Copyright © 2005 Jochen Wirtz and Sheryl E. Kimes. An earlier version of this case was published in *Asian Case Research Journal* 7, no. 1 (2003): 67–87.

[1] The names of individuals have been disguised.

ford, a five-star hotel with 1,261 rooms; Raffles The Plaza, a $5^{1}/_{2}$-star deluxe hotel with 769 rooms; and the Raffles City Shopping Center. Prego enjoys a prime central location in the vicinity of Singapore's main shopping belt Orchard Road, and the Central Business District. The Raffles City complex is also conveniently accessible by public transport, and is located next to one of Singapore's three main subway train interchanges, the City Hall MRT Interchange.[2] Also, the three-level basement of the Raffles City complex provides ample parking space. Prego's prominent ground level location, at the busy intersection of Bras Basah Road and Beach Road, makes it highly visible to the large volume of passer-by traffic.

The restaurant industry in Singapore is fiercely competitive, with restaurants opening and closing on a regular basis. Singapore has a vibrant restaurant industry which accounts for US$3 billion per year (including sales at hawker stalls). The 799 full-service restaurants accounted for some US$900 million of the total market; the 245 fast-food restaurants for US$325 million; and the 198 hotel restaurants for US$650 million.[3]

Singaporeans eat out frequently. Nearly two-thirds (62.9 percent) eat at hawker centers (groups of local food stalls) at least once a week, while 56.9 percent patronize neighborhood coffee shops and 10.5 percent go to restaurants at least once a week.[4] Dining out expenditures increased from 46 percent of total average food expenditures some ten years ago to 55 percent of total average food expenditures in 2003.[5] The growth in dining-out expenditures is attributed to a number of factors, including (1) the increased affluence of Singaporeans, especially those under 40 years old, (2) lifestyle changes which have caused Singaporeans to prefer increased convenience, and (3) the increase in expatriate residents and tourists in Singapore.[6] A fact sheet on Singapore is provided in the Appendix at the end of the case.

Prego has been successful for over ten years, and maintained its reputation as a high-quality, authentic Italian restaurant. Prego's upscale positioning has contributed to its continuing success.

Prego serves Lunch (11.30 a.m.–2.30 p.m.), Snacks (2.30 p.m.–6.30 p.m.), Dinner (6.30 p.m.–10.30 p.m.), and Supper (10.30 p.m.–12.30 a.m.). The dining area consists of the Bar, Antipasto, Restaurante, Pizzaria, and Alfresco Dining sections, with a total capacity of 340 seats. **Exhibit 1** shows the floor plan of Prego, and **Exhibits 2 to 5** give an impression of the interior and design of the restaurant. The restaurant also includes a take-away Deli counter and a waiting area that can accommodate up to 12 diners.

The standard menu comprises approximately eight appetizers and salads, three soups, 27 entrees

---

[2] "MRT" is the acronym for the Mass Rapid Transit passenger service in Singapore. There are currently 67 train stations linking all areas of the island.

[3] Singapore Department of Statistics (2002), *Retail Sales Index and Catering Trade Index December 2002*; and Singapore Department of Statistics (2000), *Economic Surveys Series—Hotels & Catering 2000*.

[4] Kau Ah Keng, Tan Soo Jiuan, and Jochen Wirtz, *7 Faces of Singaporeans: Their Values, Aspirations and Lifestyles* (Singapore: Prentice Hall, 1998).

[5] Singapore Department of Statistics (2003), *Retail Sales Index and Catering Trade Index December 2003*; Singapore Department of Statistics (2000), *Economic Surveys Series—Hotel & Catering 2000*.

[6] Kau Ah Keng, Tan Soo Jiuan, and Jochen Wirtz, *7 Faces of Singaporeans: Their Values, Aspirations and Lifestyles* (Singapore: Prentice Hall, 1998).

Exhibit 1 Restaurant Layout

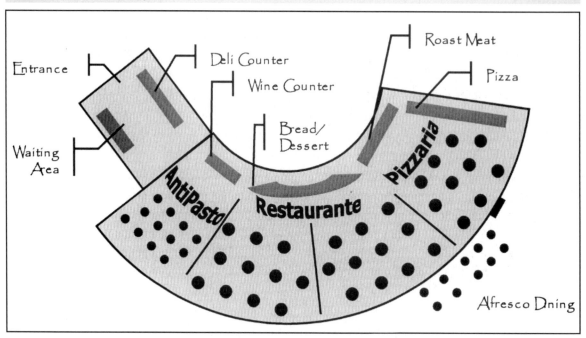

Exhibit 2 Entrance to Prego Italian Restaurant

Exhibit 3   Dining Area

Exhibit 4   Wine Counter and Bar in the Restaurant

Exhibit 5   Deli Counter at the Entrance to the Restaurant

including pasta, pizza, fish, and meat, and seven desserts. Prego also offers a wide selection of wines from Italy, France, Australia, California, and New Zealand. A manager is always on duty. Approximately 20 percent of the customers are hotel guests at Swissôtel The Stamford and Raffles The Plaza, 30 percent are tourists, and the remaining 50 percent are local diners.

REVENUE MANAGEMENT IN A RESTAURANT CONTEXT

Revenue management has been successfully applied to the airline and hotel industries for many years, but has only recently been applied to the restaurant industry.

Revenue management is a sophisticated form of supply and demand management. Its primary focus is managing customer demand through the use of variable pricing and capacity management to maximize profitability. The four

strategic levers for yield management are: calendar (reservations, bookings), clock (duration controls, turnover rates), capacity (demand smoothing), and pricing (price fences, discounts). Through the application of information technology, pricing strategy, and service product/process design, revenue management helps companies to sell the right product at the right time to the right customer for the right price.

Revenue management is particularly suited for the restaurant industry, with its relatively finite capacity of available tables, perishable inventory, microsegmented markets of restaurant guests, fluctuating demand, relatively low variable to fixed costs ratios, and services that can be sold in advance through bookings and reservations. Success in revenue management is typically measured in revenue per available time-based inventory unit. In the airline industry, this becomes revenue per available seat-mile; in the hotel industry, revenue per available room-night; and in the restaurant industry, revenue per available seat-hour (RevPASH). The revenue per available time-based inventory unit can be calculated by multiplying the capacity utilization by the average price.

For a restaurant to be able to apply revenue management, it should (1) establish its baseline performance, (2) understand the causes of performance, (3) develop a revenue management strategy, (4) implement the strategy, and (5) monitor performance.

PREGO DINERS

Guest Arrival Patterns

As Prego's arrival patterns differ significantly by half hours during the peak periods, the data was captured on a half-hourly basis. Guest arrivals were captured from the opening time of a check. This was an accurate measure of arrival times, since more than 95 percent of the checks were

opened within five minutes of guest arrival.

Lunch arrivals were heavily centered around 12.30 p.m. and attracted mainly diners on their lunch breaks or those on business lunches. Dinner arrivals were more widely spread between 6.30 and 8.00 p.m. (see **Exhibit 6**) and attracted mainly couples and working executives. On weekends, groups of friends and families were more prevalent. The restaurant received relatively few shoppers and in-house guests (i.e., guests that stayed in one of the two hotels located in the Raffles City complex).

A sample of the collected data on the pattern of dinner guest arrivals and revenues, per half-hour periods, for two weeks is provided in **Exhibit 7.**

Hostesses recorded the names of waiting diners who could not immediately be given a table. Prego found that approximately 15 to 30 customers could not be accommodated immediately for dinners from Tuesdays to Saturdays. Of those asked to wait, approximately 33 per-

Exhibit 6   Guest Arrival Patterns in a Typical Week

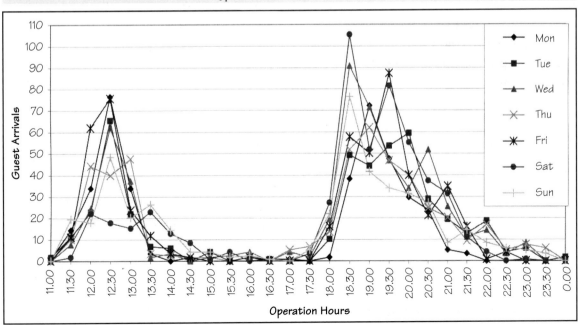

Exhibit 7 Sample Dinner Guest Arrivals

| Day of Week | Arrival Times | | | | | | | | Dinner Revenue |
	18.00	18.30	19.00	19.30	20.00	20.30	21.00	21.30	
Monday	3	59	88	37	36	24	10	7	$10,301.32
Tuesday	15	51	53	51	42	31	36	14	$11,470.39
Wednesday	14	90	73	42	39	73	25	19	$14,658.84
Thursday	24	59	61	53	42	17	8	15	$11,493.06
Friday	10	39	56	75	27	27	46	25	$10,501.53
Saturday	15	117	14	70	51	32	32	14	$13,543.46
Sunday	31	58	53	15	36	19	17	8	$8,052.16
Monday	0	17	56	58	24	24	0	0	$6,462.71
Tuesday	5	48	36	56	76	27	3	12	$13,085.65
Wednesday	25	92	70	51	29	31	25	3	$12,328.54
Thursday	3	44	63	41	37	32	32	3	$11,121.85
Friday	22	76	44	100	53	15	24	7	$12,702.21
Saturday	39	93	90	93	59	42	31	8	$14,398.04
Sunday	14	95	31	53	27	36	0	20	$10,230.51

cent did not wait and left for other restaurants. Diners with reservations were rarely turned away, as all reservations were accepted and honored.

minutes with a standard deviation of 37 minutes. Means and standard deviations varied by half-hour periods and by day of week.

Meal Duration

Both the mean and the standard deviation of meal duration for peak times were recorded and are shown in **Exhibits 8** and **9**. The average dining time was approximately one hour and 25

Course Timing

Measurement was carried out by conducting a detailed timing study of ten random tables (with fewer than six diners) per dinner sitting for each of the days from Wednesday to Saturday. Courses

Exhibit 8 Lunch Meal Duration. Mean and Standard Deviation

| Day of Week | Arrival Times | | | |
	12.00 Duration (STD)	12.30 Duration (STD)	13.00 Duration (STD)	13.30 Duration (STD)
Monday	1.14 (0.29)	1.01 (0.20)	0.51 (0.17)	0.22 (0.05)
Tuesday	1.23 (0.21)	1.19 (0.28)	1.15 (0.26)	0.49 (0.07)
Wednesday	1.12 (0.41)	1.05 (0.22)	0.53 (0.12)	0.30 (0.05)
Thursday	1.28 (0.30)	1.13 (0.44)	0.49 (0.15)	0.20 (0.05)
Friday	1.10 (0.34)	1.17 (0.23)	0.50 (0.19)	1.20 (0.11)
Saturday	1.04 (0.25)	1.19 (0.22)	0.50 (0.07)	1.22 (0.22)
Sunday	1.09 (0.18)	1.25 (0.34)	1.17 (0.19)	1.19 (0.27)

Exhibit 9 Dinner Meal Duration. Mean and Standard Deviation

	Arrival Times					
	18.00	18.30	19.00	19.30	20.00	20.30
Day of Week	Duration (STD)	Duration (STD)	Duration (STD)	Duration (STD)	Duration (STD)	Duration (STD)
Monday	–	1.22 (0.24)	1.13 (0.38)	1.08 (0.27)	1.11 (0.19)	0.46 (0.17)
Tuesday	1.58 (0.25)	1.09 (0.23)	1.10 (0.31)	1.27 (0.40)	1.34 (0.33)	1.14 (0.34)
Wednesday	1.23 (0.38)	1.15 (0.39)	1.13 (0.34)	1.08 (0.40)	1.21 (0.24)	1.09 (0.33)
Thursday	1.20 (0.08)	1.11 (0.33)	1.12 (0.43)	1.32 (0.41)	1.18 (0.37)	1.16 (0.23)
Friday	1.20 (0.27)	0.48 (0.29)	1.23 (0.31)	1.22 (0.43)	1.11 (0.40)	1.02 (1.10)
Saturday	1.20 (0.25)	1.20 (0.42)	1.10 (0.27)	1.07 (0.44)	1.25 (0.24)	1.18 (0.23)
Sunday	0.55 (0.22)	0.50 (0.30)	1.23 (0.45)	1.17 (0.28)	1.10 (0.30)	1.20 (0.17)

timed included (1) arrival to seating/drinks, (2) seating/drinks to food order, (3) food order to appetizer, (4) appetizer to entrée, (5) entrée to dessert/coffee, (6) dessert/coffee to check request, (7) check request to check clearance, (8) check clearance to leaving table, and (9) arrival to departure. During busy periods, the restaurant will take an average of nine minutes (with a standard deviation of six minutes) after guest departure before each table is being bussed. The average time needed to buss each table in order to be ready for new arriving guests is about five minutes. The findings are shown in **Exhibit 10**.

Revenue per Available Seat Hour

Not surprisingly, the RevPASH performance (see **Exhibit 11**) followed the arrival patterns, with the highest RevPASH being achieved between 12.30 and 1.30 p.m., and between 7.00 p.m. and 9.00 p.m. The afternoon period between 2.30 p.m. and 5.30 p.m. showed very little activity.

PREGO'S SERVICE BLUEPRINT

A service blueprint for Prego was developed (see **Exhibit 12**). It shows the individual steps of the whole dining process, starting from making reservations to customer departure.

Exhibit 10 Course Timing: Mean and Standard Deviation

	Day of Week			
Course Timing	Wednesday Duration (STD)	Thursday Duration (STD)	Friday Duration (STD)	Saturday Duration (STD)
Arrival to Seating/drinks	0.03 (0.01)	0.04 (0.02)	0.03 (0.02)	0.03 (0.01)
Seating/drinks to Food Order	0.05 (0.02)	0.04 (0.01)	0.04 (0.02)	0.04 (0.03)
Food Order to Appetizer	0.09 (0.02)	0.10 (0.04)	0.11 (0.03)	0.09 (0.03)
Appetizer to Entrée	0.15 (0.05)	0.14 (0.08)	0.16 (0.04)	0.14 (0.04)
Entrée to Dessert/coffee	0.30 (0.10)	0.31 (0.08)	0.28 (0.05)	0.32 (0.07)
Dessert/coffee to Check Request	0.14 (0.04)	0.15 (0.03)	0.18 (0.08)	0.16 (0.03)
Check Request to Check Clearance	0.03 (0.02)	0.03 (0.02)	0.03 (0.01)	0.04 (0.02)
Check Clearance to Departure	0.02 (0.01)	0.03 (0.02)	0.04 (0.03)	0.03 (0.01)
Arrival to Departure	1.21 (0.124)	1.24 (0.129)	1.27 (0.115)	1.25 (0.090)

Exhibit 11 Revenue per Available Seat-Hour (RevPASH) Patterns

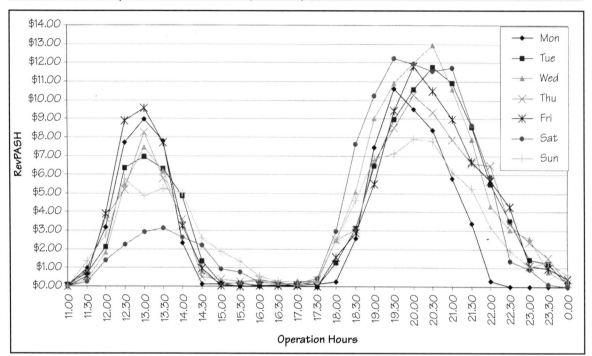

1. Advance Reservations

Phone reservations were taken as long as tables were still available, at the exact time requested by the customer. No credit card guarantees were asked, except for special occasions like Valentine's Day, Christmas Eve, New Year's Eve, and Chinese New Year.

2. Customer Arrival

Reservations generally accounted for about 50 to 60 percent of all arrivals, with an even higher proportion on peak days. When a table becomes available near the reserved time, the table was "held" even when other guests were waiting to be seated. If a customer with reservations was late or did not show up, the reserved table might have been sitting empty for some time even though other guests were waiting. Prego had approximately nine or ten no-show parties on a typical weekday, and around 13 no-show tables on a typical weekend.

3. Customer Greeting

This was handled by two or three hosts stationed at the entrance. These hosts were responsible for the flow of tables and must track when tables become available. However, Prego had no table management system and the large size of the restaurant often made it difficult for the hosts to know which ones were available. The hosts relied on servers to notify them about available tables and there sometimes was a significant time lag before a server was free to go to the entrance to pick up new diners. Often, the hosts had to leave the entrance to find available tables.

4. Customer Seating

Once a table became available, the host was notified and tried to find the next party on the waiting list. There were often lags between the time when the table was ready and when the host was notified, and until the waiting party was identified.

Exhibit 12   Service Blueprint

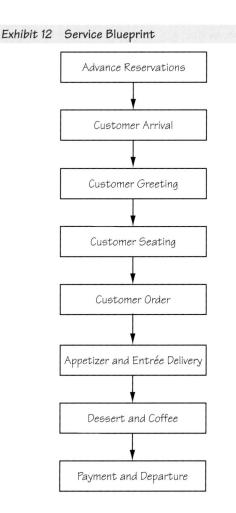

```
┌─────────────────────────────┐
│     Advance Reservations    │
└─────────────────────────────┘
              │
              ▼
┌─────────────────────────────┐
│       Customer Arrival      │
└─────────────────────────────┘
              │
              ▼
┌─────────────────────────────┐
│      Customer Greeting      │
└─────────────────────────────┘
              │
              ▼
┌─────────────────────────────┐
│       Customer Seating      │
└─────────────────────────────┘
              │
              ▼
┌─────────────────────────────┐
│       Customer Order        │
└─────────────────────────────┘
              │
              ▼
┌─────────────────────────────┐
│ Appetizer and Entrée Delivery│
└─────────────────────────────┘
              │
              ▼
┌─────────────────────────────┐
│      Dessert and Coffee     │
└─────────────────────────────┘
              │
              ▼
┌─────────────────────────────┐
│     Payment and Departure   │
└─────────────────────────────┘
```

5. Customer Order

Drink orders were taken first. Once the drinks were delivered, food orders were then taken. With the wide variety of wines and food available, customers may spend some time making their choices.

6. Appetizer and Entrée Delivery

The kitchen comprised three sections (Hot, Cold, and Dessert and Rotis), which made it difficult to coordinate common delivery times at the diners' tables. Two back runners and one or two front runners were deployed to run food to the serving stations. Courses which had become cold after being left waiting for too long on the counter had to be redone. The servers handled

ordering, serving, occasional food running, check clearance and bussing. This saved on overall labor requirements but was extremely challenging to operate during peak times. The high staff turnover prevalent in the restaurant industry made it difficult to adequately train all the new staff and part-timers on the variety of tasks. There were often times when the restaurant operated on 50 percent part-time staff.

7. Dessert and Coffee

The restaurant tried to use suggestive selling to increase the average check and guests were encouraged to order dessert and coffee, even during peak hours.

8. Payment and Departure

Most payments were done via credit card, which took longer to process than other payment methods. Delays could occur when customers could not attract the server's attention; when staff prepared the check and delivered it to the diner; and during payment processing. After payment, some customers chose to linger at their tables for a bit longer before departing.

DEVELOPING A STRATEGY TO MAXIMIZE REVENUE

Prego's Profit and Loss Statement for a typical month and financial status are shown in **Exhibit 13**. The Profit and Loss Statement shows that Prego had a contribution margin ratio of about 71.4 percent per dollar of revenue; fixed costs were at a monthly average of $250,126. The break-even point was at about $350,317 per month, or approximately 10,616 covers. Profit margins were approximately 14.2 percent of total revenues.

Francesco's main concern was to increase revenue and contribution by filling up the tables during off-peak periods and to reach higher turn-

Exhibit 13   Profit and Loss Statement for a Typical Month

PREGO

Revenues:		
Food	$322,718	73.8%
Beverage	$114,827	26.2%
Total revenues	$437,545	100.0%
Costs:		
Variable costs:	$96,882	22.1%
Cost of beverages	$28,232	6.5%
Total variable costs	$125,114	28.6%
Fixed Costs:		
Rental of premises	$104,528	23.9%
Depreciation of furniture, fittings, and equipment	$5,713	1.3%
Total labor costs	$121,111	27.7%
Laundry	$4,146	0.9%
Linen (table cloths and napkins)	$1,164	0.3%
Uniforms	$748	0.2%
Breakage and utensil replacement	$49	0.0%
Cleaning services and materials	$1,360	0.3%
Utilities (electricity, water, and gas)	$1,521	0.3%
Telecoms	$316	0.1%
Music and entertainment	$732	0.2%
Printing, stationery, and menus	$3,722	0.9%
Advertising and promotion	$2,512	0.6%
Miscellaneous	$2,502	0.6%
Total variable costs	$250,126	57.2%
Total costs	$375,240	85.8%
Gross operating profit	$62,305	14.2%
Food costs/food revenues	30.0%	
Beverage costs/beverage revenues	24.6%	
Total number of covers	13,259	
Average check	$33.00	

Note: The data are based on authors' estimates, and would be typical for an Italian restaurant of Prego's size and location.

over of tables without affecting customer satisfaction during peak periods. Francesco understood that to be able to achieve it not only required a well-planned and creative strategy, but also a careful implementation that does not alienate customers and staff.

Study Questions

1. Suppose Prego hired you as a consultant to help them develop and implement a strategy to increase revenue and contribution. Using the financial data given, assess the potential revenue and profit impact of potential revenue management measures Prego should consider, and make any logical assumptions needed for doing this.
2. Next, consider the potential customer and staff responses to these measures.

3. Finally, given the potential profit impact, and customer and staff responses, what revenue management measures would you recommend that Prego implement, and what should Prego do to minimize potential customer and employee conflicts resulting from these measures?

Appendix

Singapore Fact Sheet

Geographic Data

Location	South-eastern Asia, islands between Malaysia and Indonesia
Land area	692.7 sq. km.
Climate	Tropical; hot, humid, rainy; two distinct monsoon seasons— North-eastern monsoon from December to March and South-western monsoon from June to September; inter-monsoon— frequent afternoon and early evening thunderstorms

---

Singapore's People

Population	4,608,595 (July 2003 est.)
Age structure	0–14 years: 17.3 percent (male 411,656; female 385,575) 15–64 years: 75.5 percent (male 1,687,217; female 1,793,783) 65 years and over: 7.2 percent (male 144,277; female 186,087) (2003 est.)
Population growth rate	3.42 percent (2003 est.)
Life expectancy at birth	Total population: 80.42 years female: 83.6 years (2003 est.) male: 77.46 years
Ethnic groups	Chinese 76.7 percent, Malay 14 percent, Indian 7.9 percent, other 1.4 percent
Religions	Buddhist, Islam, Christian, Hindu, Sikh, Taoist, Confucianist
Languages	Chinese (official), Malay (official and national), Tamil (official), English (official)
Literacy rate (population 15 years and older)	93.2 percent

Economy

GDP at current market prices	Purchasing power parity—US$112.4 billion (2002 est.)
GDP—real growth rate	2.2 percent (2002 est.)
GDP—per capita at current market prices	Purchasing power parity—US$25,200 (2002 est.)
Inflation rate	−0.4 percent (2002 est.)
Labour force	2.19 million (2000 est.)
Unemployment rate	4.6 percent (2002 est.)

Sources and further information can be found at http://www.odci.gov/cia/publications/factbook/geos/sn.html

KFC and McDonald's in Shanghai

LU XIONGWEN AND CHRISTOPHER H. LOVELOCK

The fast-food market in Shanghai has become very competitive, featuring a variety of chains and a choice of both Western and Chinese cuisine. An independent study of KFC and McDonald's restaurants in Shanghai reveals some similarities between the two market leaders but also important differences.

The global fast-food brands, KFC and McDonald's, first entered China in 1987 and 1990 respectively. By 2003, after more than a decade of development, both had achieved a significant market presence in terms of number of restaurants, turnover, and market share. In cities such as Shanghai, even as new restaurants continued to open, one of the issues facing managers in these two chains was how to increase patronage and profits in their established restaurants.

THE FAST-FOOD INDUSTRY IN CHINA

China's fast-food industry had a late start. KFC introduced the concept of modern fast food when it entered the Beijing market in 1987. According to data from the National Bureau of Statistics, China's fast-food industry developed at a rate of over 20 percent annually in the 1990s, much faster than the 7.8 percent annual increase in China's gross domestic product (GDP). With a high annual margin of between 15 and 25 percent, quick-service restaurants became a driving force in the overall food service industry. By the year 2000, fast food had become the biggest and most attractive profit opportunity in China's commodity and labor markets with an annual turnover of over 200 billion yuan, accounting for over two-fifths of the overall food service industry. It was predicted that with the rapid development of China's economy, fast-food sales would continue to increase by over 10 percent annually during the next decade. **Exhibit 1** documents the structure of China's fast-food industry.

As an international metropolis with over 16

The authors gratefully acknowledge the assistance of Yu Wenjie and Wang Cheng, graduate students at the School of Management, Fudan University. This case is designed for class discussion rather than to illustrate either effective or ineffective handling of an administrative situation. Unless otherwise stated, all data are taken from a survey and field study of KFC and McDonald's operations in Shanghai, conducted by Wang Cheng, Xue Wenqian, Wang Yingwen, and Cen Ning of Fudan University. In 2003, 1 yuan = US$0.12.

Exhibit 1   The Structure of China's Fast-Food Industry, 2000

Factor	Structure
Cuisine	Chinese 78.9%, Western 21.1%
Ownership	Sino-foreign joint venture 36%, private 21%, foreign wholly-owned 16%, state-owned 16%, collective 11%
Business model	Chain restaurant 58%, single restaurant 42%
Operational pattern	Complete handwork 21%, mainly on handwork 57.9%, mainly on assembly line 15.8%, complete assembly line 5.3%
Regional distribution	South China 28%, Northeast China 27%, North China 18%, Middle China 18%, Northwest China 9%

Source: "Report on China's Fast-Food Industry," Beijing Huatongren Market Information Co., Ltd., 2001.

million people, Shanghai had seen its fast-food industry developing by leaps and bounds. By the end of 2001, there were 2,978 restaurants and 26,274 employees in the fast-food industry in the city. In 2002, Shanghai KFC ranked first among China's 500 catering companies with an annual turnover of 804 million yuan (see **Exhibit 2**).

The industry's rapid development led to fierce competition in Shanghai's fast-food market. According to a survey published in *IMI Consumer Behaviors and Life Patterns Yearbook 2002*, (see **Appendix Exhibits A–G**), the five most popular western fast-food brands were KFC (81.5 percent), McDonald's (67.6 percent), Pizza Hut (28.2 percent), American California King of Beef Noodle (1.9 percent) and Dicos (1.0 percent).

Meanwhile, domestic brands of Chinese fast food copied the Western service model while maintaining the taste of traditional cuisines. Ac-cording to a study of Shanghai consumers, the four most popular domestic fast-food brands in the city were Yonghe King (52 percent), New Asia Snack (27 percent), Grand Mother Dumpling (16 percent) and Malan Noodle (4 percent). The investigation also revealed that consumers evaluated fast-food restaurants against seven criteria. In order of importance, these factors were: food, service, environment, price, convenience, brand, and promotion.

KFC

KFC was affiliated to Tricon-Yum Global, the world's largest restaurant group that is responsible for managing such popular brands as KFC, Pizza Hut, and Taco Bell Grande. In 2003, KFC was the biggest fried chicken chain enterprise in the world, operating over 12,000 restaurants in more than 100 countries.

Since its arrival in China in 1987, KFC had

Exhibit 2   Top Ten Catering Companies in China, 2002

Rank	Company Name	Rank	Company Name
1	Shanghai KFC Co., Ltd.	6	Guangdong Sanyuan McDonald's Co., Ltd.
2	Beijing McDonald's Co., Ltd.	7	Tianjin KFC Co., Ltd.
3	Beijing KFC Co., Ltd.	8	Xi'an Catering Service (Group) Co., Ltd.
4	Hangzhou KFC Co., Ltd.	9	Shanghai Pizza Hut Co., Ltd.
5	Shenzhen McDonald's Co., Ltd.	10	Shenzhen KFC Co., Ltd.

set one record after another. On June 1, 1996, Shanghai People's Park KFC restaurant achieved a daily turnover of 400,000 yuan, breaking KFC's global historical record for turnover per restaurant per day. In 1999, KFC was ranked first among the top ten international brands, according to a poll of 16,677 consumers in 30 Chinese cities by AC Nielsen. On November 28, 2000, KFC became the first fast-food company in China to own more than 400 chain restaurants. Yet within little more than another two years, KFC had succeeded in doubling that number. By the end of 2003, KFC had set up 32 companies to run its more than 850 restaurants in some 200 cities.

McDonald's

McDonald's enjoyed the distinction of being the most recognized brand name in the world. The sentence "McDonald's is more than a restaurant" best describes this company's business concept. Management emphasized a credo of "quality, service, cleanliness, and value." It had made unremitting efforts to establish food supply networks in each country as well as a human resource management and training system that would enable the company to develop and progress jointly with the local market.

McDonald's selected Shenzhen as the site of its first restaurant in China in 1990. Shenzhen, the first economic special zone set up in China, was seen as a symbol of China's "open policy." The company then expanded its business to other areas in the country. The head office of McDonald's assigned its own employees to select locations, and supervised construction, decoration, and furnishing of each new restaurant prior to opening.

Relying on its high brand recognition, financial strength, and strong performance in other international markets, McDonald's sought to compete effectively with KFC, which enjoyed the advantage of having entered the Chinese market several years earlier. April 1992 saw the opening of the world's biggest McDonald's restaurant in Wangfujing, Beijing. Soon the golden arches appeared in such central city locations as Guangdong International Mansion in Guangzhou, Riverside Avenue in Tianjin, Huaihai Road in Shanghai, Confucian Temple in Nanjing, and Jianghan Road in Wuhan. Within a few years, McDonald's had opened more than 460 restaurants in 74 large- and medium-sized cities in 17 provinces.

COMPARISON OF KFC AND MCDONALD'S BUSINESSES

The similarities and differences between KFC and McDonald's in Shanghai were highlighted by the findings of independent research, based on observation, questionnaire surveys, and interviews at KFC and McDonald's restaurants in the Wujiaochang and Luxun Park areas of the city, where the large numbers of patrons represented a broad cross-section of Shanghai consumers.

Product

Generally, consumers evaluated the food itself against four criteria: taste, variety, nutrition, and cleanliness. In terms of taste, KFC and McDonald's both addressed quality from a production perspective, employing sophisticated, standardized operating systems to ensure that their foods maintained a consistent taste in each restaurant. In terms of variety, although KFC's main food was fried chicken and McDonald's was hamburger, consumers appeared to be satisfied with the variety of food provided in both restaurants. In terms of cleanliness, KFC and McDonald's achieved strong reputations of high-level sanitation. In contrast, where nutritional value was concerned, Western fast food had been widely portrayed by critics as "junk food" that contained excessive calories; consequently, consumers were not confident of its nutritional quality.

KFC and McDonald's both paid much attention to new product development. According to the study, KFC appeared to have the upper hand over McDonald's in terms of the rate of introducing new products. Most of KFC's new products were developed to suit the Chinese tastebuds such as breakfast items based on both Chinese and Western cuisines, Mexican chicken rolls, spicy double-layer hamburgers, and New Orleans wings. In addition, KFC had been introducing new products every two to three months—considered as high frequency—to attract consumer interest and stimulate consumption. In contrast, McDonald's new products were introduced at infrequent intervals, and were often merely variations in the sizes of hamburgers or the available components in the set meals.

The Shanghai survey showed that although more consumers reported they had tried KFC's new products (see **Exhibit 3**), McDonald's had achieved superior consumer satisfaction ratings (see **Exhibit 4**). In recent years, KFC and McDonald's had both tried to imitate each other,

to expand their business scopes, and to fill up the empty slots in their product lines. However, it was still their "classic products" that shaped customer loyalty.

Environment and Service

From the customer's point of view, the importance of service and environment was second only to that of product. Regarding restaurant decoration, KFC and McDonald's were rated as upper middle level compared with other restaurants in the industry. Customers could enjoy a bright and clean environment, soft lighting, and music in the restaurant even during peak hours. The décor of each KFC restaurant had a distinctive theme; examples include fitness, film posters, and animal images such as dinosaurs.

Entertainment facilities for children such as sliding boards could be seen in every KFC and McDonald's restaurant. These facilities were of different sizes and placed on different floors depending on the size of restaurant. Next to these entertainment areas were family style tables for seven to eight consumers or low tables for children. In some restaurants, certain employees were assigned to take care of the children in the entertainment area. In KFC's Wujiaochang restaurant, the staff member played with the chil-

Exhibit 3   Consumer Trial of New Products

	All (%)	Most (%)	Half (%)	Seldom (%)	None (%)
KFC	12.3	50.7	24.7	11.0	1.4
McDonald's	11.7	36.4	41.6	10.4	–

Exhibit 4   Consumer Satisfaction with New Products

	Very Satisfied (%)	Satisfied (%)	Average (%)	Not Satisfied (%)	Very Dissatisfied (%)
KFC	2.7	38.4	50.7	8.2	–
McDonald's	1.3	42.9	55.8	–	–

dren and encouraged them to return by saying, "Remember to come back here next time." Parents appreciated this service as their children were cared for in a secure environment.

70 percent of consumers were "satisfied" or "quite satisfied" with the sanitation in KFC and McDonald's. Almost every KFC and McDonald's restaurant provided free use of the toilets and assigned employees to keep them clean. In CBD areas, there were sometimes more KFC and McDonald's restaurants than public toilets.

Standardized service systems were designed to ensure the level of service quality and work performance of KFC or McDonald's employees. Among the consumers surveyed, only 2 percent were dissatisfied with the service, 23 percent considered it average, and the remaining 75 percent were "quite satisfied" or "very satisfied." Consumers could stay on at the restaurant to read or chat after the meal without worrying about being driven out by the staff. In China, KFC and McDonald's customers were not expected to clear their own tables. Instead, once consumers left their seats after a meal, employees cleaned the tables immediately. At the counter, employees greeted every customer with a cheerful "welcome." However, due to the larger volume of business, employees of KFC interacted less with customers than their counterparts at McDonald's.

Although KFC and McDonald's had purchased many point-of-sale (POS) machines, and McDonald's offered its "59-second quick service" (with a guarantee that if the wait exceeded one minute, the customer would get a free ice cream), the average waiting time still exceeded two minutes during the Shanghai survey period. Forty percent of customers surveyed considered waiting time "somewhat long" or "too long," especially at peak hours. **Exhibit 5** provides a sum-mary comparison of key elements at the two companies' restaurants in Luxun Park.

Price

On average, customers eating at KFC or McDonalds spent 24.07 yuan, but there were some variations by age group (see **Exhibit 6**). There was no distinctive difference between prices at KFC and McDonald's except for meal packages (see **Appendix Exhibit H**). For comparison purposes, the study classified all the products into one of the following categories: big hamburger set meals, small hamburger set meals (reflecting the size of the burger itself), chicken set meals, and other snacks; the results are shown in **Exhibit 7**. Consumers were asked how they rated the prices of food at KFC and McDonald's—the results are presented in **Exhibit 8**.

A comparison of the 2003 survey findings with those obtained in a survey of the same restaurants in 1997 shows an increase in the consumer's price sensitivity (see **Exhibits 9** and **10**).

Exhibit 11 shows how customer ratings of prices at McDonald's and KFC affect their brand choice behavior.

Promotional Activities

Advertising and coupons were two main promotional tools used by KFC and McDonald's. A majority of survey respondents reported that they were attracted to the restaurants by promotional activities (see **Exhibit 12**).

Demand Fluctuations

As service companies that were operating 16 hours a day, between 7.00 a.m. and 11.00 p.m., seven days a week, KFC and McDonald's could not avoid some fluctuations in demand. **Exhibits 13** and **14** document observed demand patterns at both restaurants. (In each of these charts,

Exhibit 5   Environment and Service in KFC and McDonald's Restaurants

	Restaurants	
Features	KFC Luxun Park Restaurant	McDonald's Luxun Park Restaurant
Number of tables and chairs	38 white square tables (ten on 1st floor and 28 on 2nd floor), about 140 chairs with specially designed chairs for babies	White tables, about 120 blue chairs, with specially designed chairs for babies
Lighting	About 40 ceiling lights and wall lamps, adequate and gentle lighting	In addition to standard lighting, also has decorative lamps with beige color
Texture of floor board	Brown, wooden	Natural wooden color
Number of POS machines and computers	6 POS terminals at work	2–3 POS terminals at work before 10 a.m., 4–5 POS during peak hours
Audio system	Yes	Yes, different types of music played at different times
Number of frescos and other decorations	5 frescos of KFC's history and 8 of its products, green decorations	Grass green and orange walls with big abstract pictures of human figures
Typical customer waiting time	2–5 minutes	1.5–2 minutes
Staff dress	Uniformed, clean	Uniformed, clean
Service attitude	Not particularly warm or kind, sometimes even impatient	Warm welcome to every customer, "Welcome to McDonald's"
Number of cleaning staff	8, with 1 security guard	6–7
Frequency of cleaning	Low frequency of floor mopping, every 3–4 hours	Always two employees mopping the floor

Exhibit 6   Average Expenditure at KFC and McDonald's by Age Group

	Under 18 Years	18–30 Years	31–55 Years	Over 55 Years	Total Sample
Average expenditure in yuan	25.56	23.53	25.13	17.50	24.07

Exhibit 7   Comparison of KFC and McDonald's Prices for Set Meals

	Average Price in Yuan			
	Big Hamburger Set Meals	Small Hamburger Set Meals	Chicken Set Meals	Snacks
KFC	17.50	20.50	21.50	4.00
McDonald's	18.33	17.50	19.25	4.50

the customer volumes were recorded for the 60 minutes beginning at the hour designated on the horizontal axis (for instance 22.00 designates the one-hour period ending at 23.00, when the restaurant closed for the night.)

Breakfast time (7.00 to 10.00) generated the smallest customer volume of the day. Students, clerical workers, young professionals, and old people accounted for most of the customers during this period. Students and office workers typi-

Exhibit 8   Consumer Ratings of the Cost of Eating at KFC and McDonald's by Age Group

Ratings of Food Prices	Under 18 Years (%)	18–30 Years (%)	31–55 Years (%)	Over 55 Years (%)	Total Sample (%)
Too high	7.4	14.4	0.0	0.0	10.7
Relatively high	66.7	50.5	58.3	100.0	55.3
Average	25.9	35.1	37.5	0.0	33.3
Relatively low	0.0	0.0	4.2	0.0	0.7
Total	100.0	100.0	100.0	100.0	100.0

Exhibit 9   Comparison of Price Perceptions of KFC and McDonald's: 1997 vs 2003

	1997 (%)	2003 (%)
KFC is more expensive	4.0	16.7
McDonald's is more expensive	8.0	10.7
KFC is as expensive as McDonald's	76.0	59.3
Not known	12.0	13.3
Total	100.0	100.0

Exhibit 10   Comparison of Price Influence on Consumers' Decision to Eat at KFC or McDonald's: 1997 vs 2003

	1997 (%)	2003 (%)
Choose the cheaper one	6.0	19.4
Not influenced by prices	86.0	33.0
No comparison conducted	8.0	46.6
Total	100.0	100.0

Exhibit 11   Relationship between Ratings of Price and Brand Choice Behavior

	Behavior			
Ratings of Price	Choose a Cheaper One (%)	Not Influenced by Prices (%)	No Comparison Conducted (%)	Total
Too high, not worthwhile	3.3	6.7	–	10.0
Relatively high, still willing to consume	3.3	56.7	3.3	63.3
Average, acceptable	6.7	20.0	–	26.7
Total	13.3	83.4	3.3	100.0

cally spent little time in the restaurant and some of them merely purchased food to take away. In contrast, older customers might remain in the restaurant for some time.

Lunch time (10.00 to 13.00) was the first peak of the day. Customer volume increased sharply at both McDonald's and KFC, peaking at 12.00, and then falling off moderately. During this pe-

Exhibit 12   Comparison of the Effects of Advertising and Coupons

	Attracted at Once (%)	Attracted (%)	No Impact (%)
Reported response to advertising	11.3	53.3	35.3
Reported response to coupons	20.7	54.0	25.3

Exhibit 13   Customer Volume at KFC by Time of Day and Weekdays vs Weekends

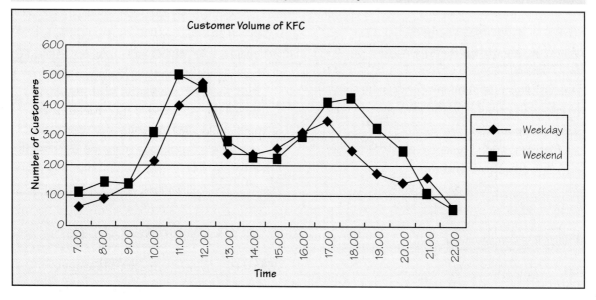

Exhibit 14   Customer Volume at McDonald's by Time of Day and Weekdays vs Weekends

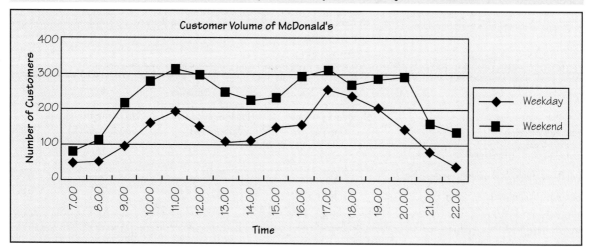

riod of time, the restaurant was crowded, customers waited longer, and the store was operating at full capacity. Customers who came for lunch stayed longer than those who ate break-fast at the restaurant.

Afternoon (13.00 to 16.00) mainly saw customers comprising teenagers, and young and middle-aged adults. They usually spent a long time in the restaurant but did not purchase much, reflecting the fact that they seemed to be there to socialize rather than to have a meal.

Dinner time (16.00 to 20.00) was the second peak of the day, and matched lunchtime in terms of customer volume. In contrast to lunch time, the proportion of children and customers over 55 was much lower during this period.

Evening (20.00 to 23.00) saw the second lowest customer volume of the day—the crowd was only slightly larger than that at breakfast time. The customers were mainly adults who came for dates or gatherings, and there were few children or senior people.

Customer volume on weekends was larger than on weekdays. **Exhibits 15** and **16** show the differences between patronage at the KFC and McDonald's restaurants for both weekends and weekdays.

On weekdays, the average daily customer volumes for KFC and McDonald's were 3,549 and 2,191 respectively. On weekends, these figures rose to 4,266 at KFC and 3,749 at McDonald's.

CHARACTERISTICS AND BEHAVIORS OF KFC AND MCDONALD'S CONSUMERS

Target Consumers

The age profile of KFC and McDonald's consumers in Shanghai changed somewhat between 1997 and 2003. Young adults became the largest consumer group and consumers aged 31 to 55 remained important, but the proportion of children decreased significantly (see **Exhibit 17**). In terms of the income profile of customers, KFC and McDonald's had become popular places for people with low and average incomes instead of being regarded as restaurants for white-collar workers. By 2003, a large proportion of KFC and McDonald's customers were individuals with low or average incomes, such as students and young clerical workers (see **Exhibit 18**).

Consumers' Preferences and Behaviors

In order to attract children, KFC and McDonald's had constantly paid much attention

Exhibit 15   Customer Volumes at KFC and McDonald's on Weekdays

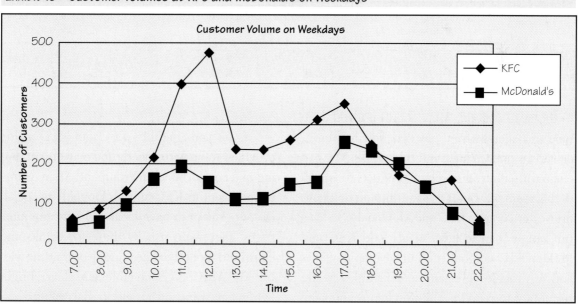

Exhibit 16   Customer Volumes at KFC and McDonald's on Weekends

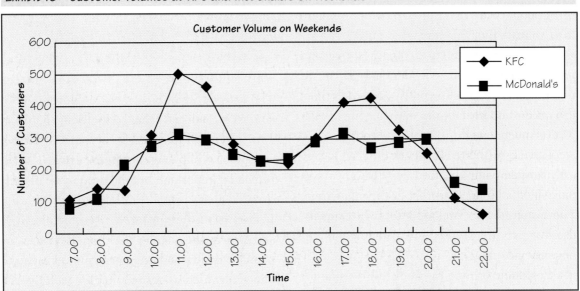

Exhibit 17   Age Distribution of KFC and McDonald's Customers: 2003 vs 1997

	Under 18 Years (%)	18–30 Years (%)	31–55 Years (%)	Over 55 Years (%)
KFC in 2003	14.5	47.8	34.1	3.6
McDonald's in 2003	12.6	52.9	31.6	2.9
1997 data for both restaurants	20.0	36.0	40.0	4.0

Exhibit 18   Income Distribution of KFC and McDonald's Customers

	Low Income (under 1,000 Yuan/Month) (%)	Average Income (1,000–3,000 Yuan/Month) (%)	High Income (over 3,000 Yuan/Month) (%)
KFC	67.9	28.6	3.6
McDonald's	63.3	33.3	3.3

to the taste of food. Most children loved such food as delicious fried chicken, soft hamburgers, crispy potato chips, and cold drinks. The two chains often introduced new products to appeal to this segment. But it is also common that children often came to KFC and McDonald's to have fun rather than to have meals, and KFC and McDonald's had both tried to develop new toys and to provide entertainment facilities in the restaurant to keep the children happy and keep

coming back.

As for young adults, KFC and McDonald's provided them with speedy and convenient dining in a comfortable environment. Many young people went to KFC and McDonald's to socialize rather than to have meals. In between meal times, they were usually there for drinks and chips, and spent the time relaxing or chatting with friends. With their clean tables and chairs, bright lighting, pleasing music, and special ceiling decorations, KFC and McDonald's were able to offer young people with a pleasant place for relaxation, dating, and parties. Of course, KFC and McDonald's were also good choices for busy people who wanted a quick meal.

In order to attract those between 35 and 45 years, KFC and McDonald's had established relevant standards and measures to ensure that the preparation of food was properly carried out, such as specifying the maximum usage life of cooking oil, and how long food might be stored before being discarded. Hygiene standards were also high, so the speed of cleaning tables, the frequency of checking toilets, etc. were also clearly specified.

Older customers formed a very small proportion of KFC and McDonald's consumers and they tended to spend more time in the restaurant than other segments of customers (see **Exhibit 19**). They seldom ate alone and were usually there with children or grandchildren as part of a family outing.

Surveys showed that frequency of patronage had risen significantly since 1997 (see **Exhibit 20**) and that there were some noteworthy variations in behavior among different age groups (see **Exhibit 21**).

OPPORTUNITIES FOR FUTURE DEVELOPMENT

Thus far, KFC and McDonald's had been successful in building up a good volume of business for their restaurants in Shanghai. Looking ahead, one of the issues management faced was how to

Exhibit 19   Average Time Spent in Restaurant by Age Group

	Under 18 Years (Min)	18–30 Years (Min)	31–55 Years (Min)	Over 55 Years (Min)	Average (Min)
Staying period	37.2	37.6	36.3	45.0	37.4

Exhibit 20   Frequency of Patronage in 1997 and 2003

	1997	2003
Once a week (%)	–	8. 2
Once every two weeks (%)	6.0	52.1
Once a month (%)	40.0	39.7
Seldom (%)	42.0	–
Not known (%)	12.0	–
Total (%)	100.0	100.0

Exhibit 21   Frequency of Patronage by Age Group

Frequency of Patronage	Under 18 Years (%)	18–30 Years (%)	31–55 Years (%)	Over 55 Years (%)	Total (%)
Once or less/month	22.2	46.4	20.8	50.0	38.0
2–3 times/month	63.0	49.5	62.5	50.0	54.0
4–7 times/month	14.8	4.1	16.7	0.0	8.0
Total	100.0	100.0	100.0	100.0	100.0

maximize the volume of customers at their existing restaurants even as the chains continued to open new ones. Two possibilities in the near future were to attract more older customers and to try to increase the demand for breakfast meals.

Older Consumers

Although customers over the age of 55 accounted for only 3 to 4 percent of the total, KFC and McDonald's no longer represented a "forbidden area" for them. Taking McDonald's Luxun Park Restaurant between 7.00 and 8.00 in the morning as an example, it was observed that most of its customers were old people who came for breakfast after their morning exercises in the nearby park. In between meal times in the afternoon, older people were also easily spotted in the restaurant. They did not usually consume a lot but spent much of the afternoon there chatting with friends. In explaining his choice, one old man stated, "The restaurant is nicely decorated. It has air-conditioning and music. The toilet here is very tidy. The food is clean as well, and the employees here are kind to us and [do not] drive us out. We all feel comfortable in the restaurant."

Shanghai has a huge population of old people, which makes it an attractive market for KFC and McDonald's. National statistics showed that there were some 132 million people over 60 in China, accounting for 10 percent of the Chinese population. Shanghai had the highest percentage of old people in the nation—by the end of 2001, the number of people over 60 had reached almost 2.5 million and the number continued to grow. The elderly people are also better off economically, due partly to improvements in the Shanghai social security system, and so have more disposable income to spend.

The Breakfast Business

Compared to the other meal times, the breakfast period attracted the smallest customer volume, resulting in excess capacity for the restaurants. There were several reasons for this: students and clerical workers were usually busy and so spent little time in the restaurant, and often only to purchase take-away meals. In contrast, older customers often stayed longer and preferred drinks and snacks such as mashed potato and congee to main dishes such as fried chicken and hamburgers. (Congee, a soft cooked food made by boiling rice or cereal in water, is a popular traditional breakfast among Chinese people.)

KFC and McDonald's had been testing new menu items and new promotional concepts in the breakfast business. In August 2002, McDonald's launched a promotional campaign for a "nutritional breakfast" in which customers were offered a hamburger for one yuan if they purchased any drink. During this period, between six and nine McDonald's restaurants advertised that they were offering a total of 88 free breakfasts (a lucky number in Chinese culture) every day except weekends and holidays. During the same period, KFC introduced two kinds of congee, together with egg hamburgers, cheese cakes, Hong Kong-style milk tea, fresh orange juice and milk, each priced from 3 to 6 yuan. To be more competitive, KFC equipped every restaurant with special facilities and advanced its opening time to 7.00 in the morning.

Study Questions

1. Who is running the more successful business in Shanghai—KFC or McDonald's? Why?
2. What is the appeal of KFC and McDonald's for different segments of the market? Why?
3. What can Chinese fast-food restaurants learn from KFC or McDonald's?
4. What actions should the management of KFC and McDonald's be taking for their respective companies' future in Shanghai? In particular, what strategies should be adopted in relation to older consumers and expanding the demand for breakfast?

Appendix

Exhibit A   Western Fast-Food Brands Ranked by Preference (N = 482)

Rank	Brand	Person/Time	Proportion
1	KFC	393	81.5%
2	McDonald's	326	67.6
3	Pizza Hut	136	28.2
4	American California King of Beef Noodle	9	1.9
5	Dicos	5	1.9
6	A&W	3	0.6

Note: As this question is multiple choice, the total proportion may exceed 100%.

Exhibit B   Patronage of Western Fast-Food Restaurants within Past Three Months by Age and Gender

	No. of Persons	Users	Nonusers
Total sample	1,027	46.9%	53.1%
All males	521	40.1	59.9
16–24	73	68.5	31.5
25–34	97	64.9	35.1
35–44	176	37.5	62.5
45–54	137	19.0	81.0
55–60	38	10.5	89.5
All females	506	54.0	46.0
16–24	74	77.0	23.0
25–34	92	72.8	27.2
35–44	176	56.3	43.8
45–54	125	29.6	70.4
55–60	39	33.3	66.7

Exhibit C   Frequency of Visiting Western Fast-Food Restaurants in the Last Three Months by Age and Gender

	No. of Persons	One or More Times a Week	Once Every Two Weeks	Once a Month	Once Every Two or Three Months or Less
Sample	482	10.4%	27.4%	41.1%	21.2%
All males	209	12.0	26.8	43.5	17.7
16–24	50	16.0	32.0	42.0	10.0
25–34	63	14.3	28.6	50.8	6.3
35–44	66	9.1	28.8	42.4	19.7
45–54	26	7.7	11.5	26.9	53.8
55–60	4	0.0	0.0	75.0	25.0
All females	273	9.2	27.8	39.2	23.8
16–24	57	19.3	38.6	29.8	12.3
25–34	67	9.0	31.3	40.3	19.4
35–44	99	6.1	17.2	47.5	29.3
45–54	37	5.4	32.4	29.7	32.4
55–60	13	0.0	30.8	38.5	30.8

Exhibit D   Value of Most Recent Purchase in a Western Fast-Food Restaurant by Males and Females of Different Ages

	No. of Persons	10 Yuan or Below	11–20 Yuan	21–30 Yuan	31–40 Yuan	41–50 Yuan	51–70 Yuan	71–100 Yuan	More Than 100 Yuan
Total sample	482	2.3%	30.1%	32.2%	7.5%	14.9%	4.6%	6.0%	2.5%
All males	209	1.4	29.2	30.6	6.7	18.7	6.2	4.8	2.4
16–24	50	0.0	32.0	36.0	6.0	18.0	4.0	2.0	2.0
25–34	63	1.6	27.0	28.6	7.9	20.6	6.3	6.3	1.6
35–44	66	3.0	27.3	30.3	6.1	18.2	9.1	4.5	1.5
45–54	26	0.0	34.6	23.1	7.7	15.4	3.8	7.7	7.7
55–60	4	0.0	25.0	50.0	0.0	25.0	0.0	0.0	0.0
All females	273	2.9	30.8	33.3	8.1	12.1	3.3	7.0	2.6
16–24	57	3.5	38.0	26.3	7.0	10.5	3.5	8.8	1.8
25–34	67	3.0	34.3	34.3	4.5	9.0	6.0	6.0	3.0
35–44	99	1.0	27.3	32.3	11.1	15.2	3.0	7.1	3.0
45–54	37	8.1	24.3	35.1	5.4	16.2	0.0	8.1	2.7
55–60	13	0.0	23.1	61.5	15.4	0.0	0.0	0.0	0.0

Exhibit E   Factors Considered When Choosing a Western Fast-Food Restaurant (N = 482)

Rank	Factor	Persons	Proportion
1	Good taste	299	62.0%
2	Cleanliness	223	46.3
3	Close location	202	41.9
4	Convenience and promptness	159	33.0
5	Good service attitude	141	29.0
6	Special decoration	101	21.0
7	Reasonable price	54	11.2
8	Special activities (e.g., birthday party)	17	3.5
9	Others	2	0.4

Note: As this question is multiple choice, the total proportion may exceed 100 percent.

Exhibit F   Age Distribution by Gender and Frequency of Visit (Frequent Patrons Only)

	No. of Persons	16–24 Years	25–34 Years	35–44 Years	45–54 Years	55–60 Years	N/A
Total sample	182	31.3%	29.7%	10.4%	10.4%	2.2%	16.0%
Male	81	29.6	33.3	6.2	6.2	0.0	24.7
One or more times per week	25	32.0	36.0	8.0	8.0	0.0	16.0
Once every two weeks	56	28.6	32.1	5.4	5.4	0.0	28.5
Female	101	32.7	26.7	13.9	13.9	4.0	8.8
One or more times per week	25	44.0	24.0	8.0	8.0	0.0	16.0
Once every two weeks	76	28.9	27.6	15.8	15.8	5.3	6.6

Exhibit G   Income Distribution of Frequent Patrons by Gender and Frequency of Visit (Yuan/Month)

	No. of Persons	Zero Income	500 or Below	501–1,000	1,001–1,500	1,501–2,000	2,001–3,000	3,000 or above
Total sample	181	19.3%	2.2%	14.9%	19.9%	14.9%	17.1%	11.6%
All Males	81	13.6	0.0	9.9	16.0	18.5	25.9	16.0
One or more times a week	25	16.0	0.0	0.0	8.0	24.0	40.0	12.0
Once every two weeks	56	12.5	0.0	14.3	19.6	16.1	19.6	17.9
All females	100	24.0	4.0	19.0	23.0	12.0	10.0	8.0
One or more times a week	25	36.0	0.0	12.0	16.0	4.0	24.0	8.0
Once every two weeks	75	20.0	5.3	21.3	25.3	14.7	5.3	8.0

Exhibit H   **Comparative Prices of KFC and McDonald's Products**

	Price of Food at KFC (in Yuan)		Price of Food at McDonald's (in Yuan)	
Set meal	Happy Children Meal A	13.50	Big Mac Meal	17.50
	Happy Children Meal B	15.50	Fish McDippers Meal	17.50
	Happy Children Meal C	15.50	McChicken Meal	17.50
	Original Recipe Chicken Meal	21.50	McCrispy Chicken Filet Burger Meal	17.50
	Garden Chicken Burger Meal	20.50	McPork Fillet Burger Meal	17.50
	Hot & Spicy Chicken Burger Meal	17.50	Chicken McNuggets Meal	17.50
	Mexico/Old Beijing Twister Meal	17.50	Baked Chicken Fillet Burger Meal	20.00
	Hot & Spicy Wing Meal	21.50	McWings Meal	21.00
	Family Bucket	55.00		
Hamburger	Garden Chicken Burger	7.00	Big Mac Burger	10.40
	Hot & Spicy Chicken Burger	10.00	McFish Burger	9.90
	Mexico/Old Beijing Twister	10.00	McChicken Burger	10.00
			McPork Burger	10.00
			McCrispy Chicken Filet Burger	10.00
			Baked Chicken Fillet Burger	12.00
Chicken	Original Recipe Chicken (1 pc)	7.00	McWings (2 pc)	7.00
	Colonel's Chicken	10.00	Chicken McNuggets (6 pc)	10.00
	Hot & Spicy Wings (2 pc)	7.00		
Snacks	Mashed Potato	3.00	French Fries	L 7.50 M 6.00 S 5.00
	French Fries	L 7.50 M 6.00 S 5.00	Vegetable and Seafood Soup	4.00
	Cobette	7.50		
	Carrot Muffin	1.50		
	Lotus Fresh Vegetable	4.00		
	Four Seasons Fresh Vegetable Soup	S 4.00 Family 12.00		
Drinks and desserts	Pepsi/7 Up/Mirinda	L 5.50 M 4.50 S 3.50	Coca-Cola/Sprite/Fanta	L 5.50 M 4.50 S 3.50
	Nestle Iced Black Tea	4.50	Orange Juice	7.00
	Nestle Orange Juice	Iced 4.50 Hot 4.00	Hot Black	L 4.50 S 4.00
	Sundae (Strawberry/ Chocolate /Blueberry)	6.00	Hot Coffee	L 4.50 S 4.00
	Hot Coffee/Black Tea/ Milk Tea/Milk/Milo	4.00	Hot Chocolate	4.50
	Dasheen/Milk Sweety	4.00	Strawberry/Chocolate/ Acidophilus Milk/ Mango Shakes	L 6.00 S 4.00
	Twist Cone	2.00	Apple/Pineapple/Herb Pie	3.50
			Strawberry/Pineapple/ Chocolate Sundae	6.00
			Twist Cone	2.00

Menton Bank Asia

CHRISTOPHER LOVELOCK, JOCHEN WIRTZ, AND PATRICIA CHEW

Problems arise when a large Hong Kong bank attempts to develop a stronger customer service orientation and widens the job scope of its tellers to include selling activities.

"I'm concerned about Cecilia," said Lau Siu Mei to Chan Chee Weng. The two bank managers were seated in the former's office at Menton Bank Asia. Lau was a vice-president of the bank and manager of the Queen's Road Central branch, the largest of Menton's 148-branch network in Hong Kong. She and Chan, the branch's customer service director, were having an employee appraisal meeting. Chan was responsible for the customer service department, which coordinated the activities of the customer service representatives (CSRs, formerly known as tellers) and the customer assistance representatives (CARs, formerly known as new accounts assistants).

Lau and Chan were discussing Cecilia Cheung, a 24-year-old CSR, who had applied for the soon-to-be-vacant position of head CSR. Cecilia had been with the bank for five-and-a-half years. She had applied for the position of what had then been called head teller a year earlier, but the post had been given to a candidate with more seniority. That individual was now leaving as his wife had been transferred to a new job at Kowloon City. The position was thus open once again. Two other candidates had also applied for the job.

Both Lau and Chan agreed that, against all criteria used in the past, Cecilia would have been the obvious choice for head CSR. She was fast and accurate in her work, presented a smart and professional appearance, and was well liked by customers and her fellow CSRs. However, the nature of the teller's job had been significantly revised nine months earlier to add a stronger marketing component (**Exhibit 1** shows the previous job description for teller; **Exhibit 2** shows the new job description for customer service representative.) CSRs were now expected to offer polite suggestions that customers use automated teller machines (ATMs) for simple transactions. They were also required to stimulate customer interest in the broadening array of financial services offered by the bank. "The prob-

---

This case was written by Christopher H. Lovelock, Jochen Wirtz, and Patricia Chew, a doctoral candidate at the National University of Singapore. This case, based on real-world research but featuring a fictitious bank, dramatizes a problem commonly faced by retail banks operating in a competitive environment.

Exhibit 1   Menton Bank: Previous Job Description for Teller

Function: Provides customer services by receiving, paying out, and keeping accurate records of all monies involved in paying and receiving transactions. Promotes the bank's services.

Responsibilities:

1. Serves customers.
— Accepts deposits, verifies cash and endorsements, and gives customers their receipts.
— Cashes checks within the limits assigned or refers customers to supervisor for authorization.
— Accepts savings deposits and withdrawals, verifies signatures, and posts interest and balances as necessary.
— Accepts loan, credit card, utility, and other payments.
— Issues money orders, cashier's checks, traveler's checks, and foreign currency.
— Reconciles customer statements and confers with bookkeeping personnel regarding discrepancies in balances or other problems.
— Issues credit card advances.

2. Prepares individual daily settlement of teller cash and proof transactions.

3. Prepares branch daily journal and general ledger.

4. Promotes the bank's services.
— Answers inquiries regarding bank matters.
— Directs customers to other departments for specialized services.

5. Assists with other branch duties.
— Receives night and mail deposits.
— Reconciles ATM transactions.
— Provides safe deposit services.
— Performs secretarial duties.

Exhibit 2   Menton Bank Asia: New Job Description for Customer Service Representative

Function: Provides customers with the highest-quality services, with special emphasis on recognizing customer need and cross-selling appropriate bank services. Plays an active role in developing and maintaining good relations.

Responsibilities:

1. Presents and communicates the best possible customer service.
— Greets all customers with a courteous, friendly attitude.
— Provides fast, accurate, friendly service.
— Uses customer's name whenever possible.

2. Sells bank services and maintains customer relations.
— Cross-sells retail services by identifying and referring valid prospects to a customer assistance representative or customer service director. When time permits (no other customers waiting in line), should actively cross-sell retail services.
— Develops new business by acquainting noncustomers with bank services and existing customers with additional services that they are not currently using.

3. Provides a prompt and efficient operation on a professional level.
— Receives cash and/or checks for checking accounts, savings accounts, taxes withheld, loan payments, Mastercard, Visa, mortgage payments, money orders, traveler's checks, cashier's checks.
— Verifies amount of cash and/or checks received, being alert to counterfeit or fraudulent items.
— Cashes checks in accordance with bank policy. Watches for stop payments and holds funds per bank policy.
— Receives payment of collection items, safe deposit rentals, and other miscellaneous items.
— Confers with head CSR or customer service director on nonroutine situations.
— Sells traveler's checks, money orders, monthly transit passes, and cashier's checks, and may redeem coupons and sell or redeem foreign currency.
— Prepares coin and currency orders as necessary.
— Ensures only minimum cash exposure necessary for efficient operation is kept in cash drawer; removes excess cash immediately to secured location.
— Prepares accurate and timely daily settlement of work.
— Performs bookkeeping and operational functions as assigned by customer service director.

lem with Cecilia," as Chan put it, "is that she simply refuses to sell."

THE NEW FOCUS ON CUSTOMER SERVICE AT MENTON BANK ASIA

Although it was the second-largest bank in Hong Kong, Menton had historically focused on corporate business and its share of the retail consumer banking business had declined in the face of aggressive competition from other financial institutions. Three years earlier, the Board of Directors had appointed a new chief executive (CE) and given him the mandate to develop a stronger consumer orientation at the retail level. The CE's strategy, after putting in a new management team, was to expand and speed up Menton's investment in electronic delivery systems, which had fallen behind the competition. To achieve this strategy, a new banking technology team had been created. He also initiated plans to develop a state-of-the-art retail banking environment.

During the past 18 months, the bank had doubled the number of ATMs located inside its branches, replacing older ATMs with new models featuring color touch screens, and capable of a broader array of transactions. Menton was already a member of several ATM networks, giving its customers access to freestanding 24-hour booths in shopping centers, mass transit railway (MTR) stations, and other high-traffic locations. The installation of new ATMs was coupled with a branch renovation program, designed to improve the cosmetic appearance of the branches, and a pilot program to test the impact of these "new look" branches was already underway. As more customers switched to electronic banking, the bank planned to consolidate its business by closing a number of its smaller branches.

Another important move had been to introduce telephone banking, which allowed customers to check account balances and to transfer funds from one account to another by touching specific keys on their telephones in response to the instructions of either a computerized voice or to commands displayed on the screens of their cellphones. This service was available 24 hours a day, every day of the year, and utilization was rising steadily. Customers could also call a central customer service office to speak with a bank representative concerning service questions or problems with their accounts, as well as to request new account applications or new check books, which would be sent by mail. This office currently operated from 8.00 a.m. to 8.00 p.m. on weekdays, and from 8.00 a.m. to 2.00 p.m. on Saturdays, but Menton was evaluating the possibility of expanding the operation to include a broad array of retail bank services offered on a 24-hour basis.

Finally, the technology team had just introduced home banking via the Internet. This service could be accessed through the bank's Web site, which also contained information about bank services, branch locations and service hours, location of ATMs, and answers to commonly asked questions. All these actions seemed to be bearing fruit. In the most recent six months, Menton had seen a significant increase in the number of new accounts opened, compared to the same period the previous year. Quarterly survey data also showed that Menton Bank Asia was steadily increasing its share of new deposits in the country.

CUSTOMER SERVICE ISSUES

New financial products were being introduced at a rapid rate, but the new accounts assistants were ill equipped to sell these services because of lack of product knowledge and inadequate training in selling skills. As Lau recalled:

The problem was that they were so used to sitting at their desks waiting for a customer to approach them with a specific request, such as a mortgage or car loan, that it was hard to get them to probe more actively for customer needs.

As the automation program proceeded, the mix of activities performed by the tellers started to change. A growing number of customers were using the ATMs and telephone banking for a broad array of transactions, including cash withdrawals from and deposits at the ATMs, transfer of funds between accounts, and checking account balances. The ATMs at the Queen's Road Central branch had the highest utilization of any of Menton's branches, reflecting the large number of young professionals served at that location. Lau noted that customers who were older or less educated seemed to prefer being served by "a real person, rather than a machine."

A year earlier, the head office had selected three branches, including Queen's Road Central, as test sites for a new customer service program, which included a radical redesign of the branch interior. The Queen's Road Central branch was in the heart of the financial district. The branch was surrounded by commercial and professional offices and government departments. It was also a stone's throw away from the Central MTR station. The other test branches were among the bank's larger suburban offices in two very different areas. One was located in Sha Tin Plaza, a busy shopping center that was near a stop of the Kowloon Canton Railway (KCR), while the other was located next to a hospital in a newly developed town called Shueng Shui.

As part of the branch renovation program, each of these three branches had previously been remodeled to include no fewer than four ATMs (Queen's Road Central had six), which could be closed off from the rest of the branch, so that they would remain accessible to customers 24 hours a day. Further remodeling was then undertaken to locate a customer service desk near the entrance. Close to each desk were two electronic information terminals featuring color touch screens that customers could activate, to obtain information on a variety of bank services. The CSR counters were redesigned to provide two levels of service: an express counter for simple deposits and for cashing of approved checks, and regular counters for the full array of services provided by the CSRs. The number of counters open at a given time was varied to reflect the anticipated volume of business, and staffing arrangements were changed to ensure that more CSRs were on hand to serve customers during the busiest periods. Finally, the platform area in each branch was reconstructed to create what the architect described as "a friendly, yet professional appearance."

HUMAN RESOURCES

With the new environment came new training programs for the staff of these three branches and new job descriptions and job titles: customer assistance representatives (for the platform staff), customer service representatives (for the tellers), and customer service director (instead of assistant branch manager). The head teller position was renamed "Head CSR." Position descriptions for all these jobs are reproduced in **Exhibits 2** to **5**. The training programs for each group included sessions designed to develop improved knowledge of both new and existing retail products. (CARs received more extensive training in this area than did CSRs.) CARs also attended a 15-hour course offered in three separate sessions, on basic selling skills. This program covered key steps in the sales process, including building a

---

Exhibit 3   Menton Bank Asia: New Job Description for Head Customer Service Representative

Function: Supervises all customer service representatives in the designated branch office, ensuring efficient operation and the highest-quality service to customers. Plays an active role in developing and maintaining good customer relations. Assists other branch personnel on request.

Responsibilities:

1. Supervises the CSRs in the branch.
— Allocates work, coordinates work flow, reviews and revises work procedures.
— Ensures counters are adequately and efficiently staffed with well-trained, qualified personnel. Assists CSRs with more complex transactions.
— Resolves routine personnel problems, referring more complex situations to customer service director.
— Participates in decisions concerning performance appraisal, promotions, wage changes, transfers, and termination of subordinate CSR staff.

2. Assumes responsibility for CSRs' money.
— Buys and sells money in the vault, ensuring adequacy of branch currency and coin supply.
— Ensures that CSRs and cash sheets are in balance.
— Maintains necessary records, including daily branch journal and general ledger.

3. Accepts deposits and withdrawals by business customers at the commercial window.

4. Operates counter to provide services to retail customers (see Responsibilities for CSRs in Exhibit 2).

Exhibit 4   Menton Bank Asia: New Job Description for Customer Assistance Representative

Function: Provides services and guidance to customers/prospects seeking banking relationships or related information. Promotes and sells needed products and responds to special requests by existing customers.

Responsibilities:

1. Provides prompt, efficient, and friendly service to all customers and prospective customers.
— Describes and sells bank services to customers/prospects who approach them directly or via referral from customer service representatives or other bank personnel.
— Answers customers' questions regarding bank services, hours, etc.

2. Identifies and responds to customers' needs.
— Promotes and sells retail services and identifies any existing cross-sell opportunities.
— Opens new accounts for individuals, businesses, and private organizations.
— Prepares temporary checks and deposit slips for new checking accounts.
— Orders check books and deposit slips printed with customer's name.
— Interviews and takes applications for and pays out on installment/charge card accounts and other credit-related products.
— Certifies checks.
— Handles stop-payment requests.
— Responds to telephone mail inquiries from customers or bank personnel.
— Receives notification of name or address changes and takes necessary action.
— Takes action on notification of lost passbooks, credit cards, ATM cards, collateral, and other lost or stolen items.
— Demonstrates ATMs to customers and assists with problems.
— Coordinates closing of accounts and ascertains reasons.

3. Sells and services all retail products.
— Advises customers and processes applications for all products covered in CAR training programs (and updates).
— Initiates referrals to the appropriate department when a trust or corporate business need is identified.

Exhibit 5   Menton Bank Asia: New Job Description for Customer Service Director

---

Function: Supervises customer service representatives, customer assistance representatives, and other staff as assigned to provide the most effective and profitable retail banking delivery system in the local marketplace. Supervises sales efforts and provides feedback to management concerning response to products and services by current and prospective banking customers. Communicates goals and results to those supervised and ensures operational standards are met in order to achieve outstanding customer service.

Responsibilities:

1. Supervises effective delivery of retail products.
— Selects, trains, and manages CSRs and CARs.
— Assigns duties and work schedules.
— Completes performance reviews.

2. Personally, and through those supervised, renders the highest level of professional and efficient customer service available in the local marketplace.
— Provides high level of service while implementing most-efficient and customer-sensitive staffing schedules.
— Supervises all on-the-job programs within office.
— Ensures that outstanding customer service standards are achieved.
— Directs remedial programs for CSRs and CARs as necessary.

3. Develops retail sales effectiveness to the degree necessary to achieve market share objectives.
— Ensures that all CSRs and CARs possess comprehensive product knowledge.
— Directs coordinated cross-sell program within office at all times.
— Reports staff training needs to branch manager and/or regional training director.

4. Ensures adherence to operational standards.
— Oversees preparation of daily and monthly operational and sales reports.
— Estimates, approves, and coordinates branch cash needs in advance.
— Oversees ATM processing function.
— Handles or consults with CSRs/CARs on more complex transactions.
— Ensures clean and businesslike appearance of the branch facility.

5. Informs branch manager of customer response to products.
— Reports customer complaints and types of sales resistance encountered.
— Describes and summarizes reasons for account closings.

6. Communicates effectively the goals and results of the bank to those under supervision.
— Reduces office goals into format which translates to goals for each CSR or CAR.
— Reports sales and cross-sell results to all CSRs and CARs.
— Conducts sales- and service-oriented staff meetings with CSRs and CARs on a regular basis.
— Attends all scheduled customer service management meetings organized by regional office.

---

relationship, exploring customer needs, determining a solution, and overcoming objections.

The sales training program for CSRs, in contrast, consisted of just two two-hour sessions designed to develop skills in recognizing and probing customer needs, presenting product features and benefits, overcoming objections, and referring customers to CARs. All staff members in customer service positions participated in sessions designed to improve their communication skills and professional image—clothing and personal grooming, and interactions with customers were all discussed.

Although Menton Bank Asia's management anticipated that the CARs would be responsible for most of the increased emphasis on selling, they also foresaw a limited selling role for the CSRs, who would be expected to mention various products and facilities offered by the bank as they served customers at the counters. For instance, if a customer happened to mention an upcoming vacation, the CSR was to recommend the purchase of traveler's checks. If the customer mentioned investments, the CSR was expected to refer him or her to a CAR who could provide information on money market accounts, or certificates of deposit. All CSRs were supplied with their own business cards. When making a referral, they were expected to write the customer's name and the product of interest on the back of a card, give it to the customer and send that individual to the customer assistance desks.

To motivate CSRs at the three branches to sell specific financial products, the bank experimented with various incentive programs. The first involved cash bonuses for referrals to CARs that resulted in the sale of specific products. The program was not renewed, since it was felt that there were other more cost-effective means of marketing the products. There were suspicions about CSRs colluding with CARs to claim referrals that had not actually been made, in order to receive the incentives.

A second promotion followed and was based on allocating credits to the CSRs for successful referrals. The value of the credit varied according to the nature of the product and accumulated credits could be exchanged for merchandise gifts. This program was discontinued after three months. The basic problem seemed to be that the value of the gifts was seen as too low in relation to the amount of effort required.

The bank next turned to an approach which, in Chan's words, "used the stick rather than the carrot." All CSRs had traditionally been evaluated half-yearly on a variety of criteria, including accuracy, speed, quality of interactions with customers, punctuality of arrival for work, job attitudes, cooperation with other employees, and professional image. The evaluation process assigned a number of points to each criterion, with accuracy and speed being the most heavily weighted. In addition to appraisals by the customer service director and the branch manager, with input from the head CSR, Menton had recently instituted a program of anonymous visits by what was popularly known as the "mystery client." Each CSR was visited at least once a quarter by a professional evaluator posing as a customer. This individual's appraisal of the CSR's appearance, performance, and attitude was included in the overall evaluation. The number of points scored by each CSR had a direct impact on merit pay raises and on selection for promotion to the head CSR position or to platform jobs.

To encourage improved product knowledge and "consultative selling" by CSRs, the evaluation process was revised to include points assigned for each individual's success in sales referrals. Under the new evaluation scheme, the maximum number of points assignable for effectiveness in making sales—directly or through referrals to CARs—amounted to 30 percent of the potential total score. Although CSR-initiated sales had risen significantly in the most recent half-year, Chan sensed that morale had dropped among this group, in contrast to the CARs, whose enthusiasm and commitment had risen significantly. He had also noticed an increase in CSR errors. One CSR had quit, complaining about too much pressure.

Cecilia Cheung

Under the old scoring system, Cecilia Cheung had been the highest-scoring teller/CSR for four-and-a-half consecutive years. However, after two half-years under the new system, her ranking had dropped to fourth out of the seven full-time tellers. The top-ranking CSR, Wong Tsui San, who had been with Menton Bank Asia for 16 years, had declined repeated invitations to apply for a head CSR position, saying that she was happy where she was, earning at the top of the CSR scale, and did not want "the extra worry and responsibility." Cecilia ranked first on all but one of the operationally related criteria (interactions with customers, where she ranked second), but sixth on selling effectiveness (see **Exhibit 6**).

Lau and Chan had spoken to Cecilia about her performance and expressed disappointment. Cecilia had informed them, respectfully, that she felt she was doing a good job, telling the two bank managers, "I feel that I have been doing a good job and the customers like me. That's why I applied for the head CSR post."

When pressed for an explanation as to why she was not doing any selling, she did not make any comments, and merely mumbled that she had nothing to say. Chan could not get her to speak her mind to him.

When queried by her friends, who thought that Cecilia should not be spoiling her own

chances for a promotion, she opened up and told them how she felt. To her, the most important aspect of the job was to give customers fast, accurate, and courteous service. Also, she had experienced a few negative instances when she tried to cross-sell products, following the approach that the trainer had taught them. For example, a few customers had expressed surprise when Cecilia brought up a different banking service from the one that they were currently using. Other customers were in such a hurry that they had no time to listen to her sales pitch. Finally, the last straw occurred when she noticed a woman with a lot of savings in her account and tried to recommend that the latter open a money market account so that she could earn more interest. The customer told Cecilia very rudely that "the money in my account is none of your business," and then stomped off in a huff. After these experiences, Cecilia would adopt a reactive ap-

Exhibit 6   Menton Bank Asia: Summary of Performance Evaluation Scores for Customer Service Representatives at Queen's Road Central Branch for Latest Two Half-Year Periods

CSR Name***	Length of Full-Time Bank Service	Operational Criteria* (Max.: 70 Points)		Selling Effectiveness** (Max.: 30 Points)		Total Score (Max.: 100 Points)	
		1st Half	2nd Half	1st Half	2nd Half	1st Half	2nd Half
Tsui San Wong	16 years, 10 months	65	64	16	20	81	84
Kwok Meng Li	2 years, 3 months	63	61	15	19	78	80
Tse Leung Lam	12 months	48	42	20	26	68	68
Cecilia Cheung	5 years, 7 months	67	67	13	12	80	79
Sharon Kok	1 year, 4 months	53	55	8	9	61	64
Chen Swee Hoon	7 months	50	–	22	–	72	–
Shirley Chow	1 year, 1 month	57	55	22	28	79	83

* Totals based on sum of ratings points against various criteria, including accuracy, work production, attendance and punctuality, personal appearance, organization of work, initiative, cooperation with others, problem-solving ability, and quality of interaction with customers.
** Points awarded for both direct sales by CSR (e.g., traveler's checks) and referral selling by CSR to CAR (e.g., debit card, certificates of deposit, personal line of credit).
*** 'Full-time CSRs only (part-time CSRs were evaluated separately).

proach and would only sell when customers themselves asked for advice or had questions about a certain product.

Selecting a New Head CSR

Two weeks after this meeting, it was announced that the head CSR was leaving. The vacancy had to be filled by someone who could supervise some of the work of the other CSRs, be available for consultation and, where possible, aid in the resolution of any problems occurring at the counters, and handle large cash deposits and withdrawals by local retailers (see position description in **Exhibit 3**). When not engaged in such tasks, the head CSR was expected to operate a regular counter.

The pay scale for a head CSR ranged from HK$9,500 to HK$16,000 per month, depending on qualifications, seniority, and branch size, as compared to a range of HK$7,350 to HK$12,200 per month for CSRs. The pay scale for CARs ranged from HK$8,400 to HK$14,200 per month. Lau indicated that the pay scales were typical for banks in the country, although the average CSR at Menton was better qualified than those at smaller banks, and therefore higher on the scale. Cecilia was currently earning HK$11,000 per month, reflecting her education, which included a diploma in business administration, five-and-a-half years' experience, and significant past merit increases. If promoted to head CSR, she would qualify for an initial rate of HK$13,500 per month. When applications for the positions closed, Cecilia was one of three candidates. The other two candidates were Shirley Chow, 42, another CSR at the Queen's Road Central branch, and Danny Law, 24, the head CSR at one of Menton Bank Asia's small suburban branches, who was seeking more responsibility.

Shirley was married with two sons in school. She had started working as a part-time teller at Queen's Road Central some four years previously, switching to full-time work a year ago in order to save for her boys' college education. Shirley was a cheerful and easy-going woman. She had a wonderful memory for people's names and Chan had often seen her greeting customers on the street or in a restaurant during her lunch hour. Reviewing her evaluations over the previous four years, Chan noted that she had initially performed poorly on accuracy and at one point, when she was still a part-timer, had been put on probation because of frequent inaccuracies in the balance in her cash drawer at the end of the day. Although Chan considered her much improved on this score, he still saw room for improvement. The customer service director had also had to reprimand her for tardiness during the past year. Shirley attributed this to health problems of her elder son, who, she said, was now responding to treatment.

Both Chan and Lau had observed Shirley at work and agreed that her interactions with customers were exceptionally good, although she tended to be overly chatty and was not as fast and efficient as Cecilia. She seemed to have a natural ability to size up customers and to decide which ones were good prospects for a quick sales pitch on a specific financial product. Although slightly untidy in her personal appearance, she was very well organized in her work and was quick to help her fellow CSRs, especially new hires. She was currently earning HK$9,700 per month as a CSR and would qualify for a salary of HK$12,400 per month as head CSR. In the most recent six months, Shirley had ranked ahead of Cecilia as a result of being very successful in consultative selling (see **Exhibit 6**).

Danny Law, the third candidate, was not working in one of the three test branches, so he had not been exposed to the consultative selling program and its corresponding evaluation scheme. However, he had received excellent evaluations for his work in Menton's small Tuen Mun branch, where he had been employed for three years. A move to Queen's Road Central would increase his earnings from HK$11,200 to HK$12,400 per month. Chan and Lau had interviewed Danny and considered him intelligent and personable. The Tuen Mun branch was located in the town center of an older, suburban area of Hong Kong , where commercial and retail activities were rather stagnant. This branch (which was rumored to be under consideration for closure) had not yet been renovated and had no ATMs, although there was an ATM accessible to Menton's customers one block away. Danny supervised three CSRs and reported directly to the branch manager, who spoke very highly of him. Since there were no CARs in this branch, Danny and another experienced CSR took turns to handle new accounts, and loan or mortgage applications.

Lau and Chan were troubled by the decision that faced them. Prior to the bank's shift in focus, Cecilia would have been the ideal candidate for the head CSR post. Cecilia had shown that she was dedicated to her job, and could be entrusted with further responsibilities. However, her sales record left much to be desired, compared to Shirley's. In addition, Danny came highly recommended for the post. Whom should they choose?

Study Questions

1. Identify the steps taken by Menton Bank Asia to develop a stronger customer orientation in its retail business.
2. Compare and contrast the jobs of a customer assistance representative (CAR) and a customer service representative (CSR). How important is each (a) to the bank operations, and (b) to customer satisfaction?
3. Evaluate the strengths and weaknesses of Cecilia Cheung and other candidates applying for the position of head CSR.
4. What action do you recommend for filling the head CSR position?

Customer Asset Management at DHL in Asia

JOCHEN WIRTZ, INDRANIL SEN, AND SANJAY SINGH

DHL serves a wide range of customers, from global enterprises to the occasional customer who ships the odd one or two documents a year. To be able to effectively manage such a diverse customer base, DHL implemented a sophisticated customer segmentation cum loyalty management system. The focus of this system is to assess the profitability from its customers, reduce customer churn, and increase DHL's share of shipments.

COMPANY BACKGROUND AND MARKET ENVIRONMENT

DHL, the international air express and logistics company, serves a wide range of customers, from global enterprises with sophisticated and high-volume supply-chain solutions shipping anything from spare parts to documents, to the occasional customer who ships the odd one or two documents a year. **Exhibits 1** and **2** show some of DHL's logistics operations. To be able to effectively manage such a diverse customer base, DHL implemented a sophisticated customer segmentation cum loyalty management system. The focus of this system is to assess the profitability from its customers, reduce customer churn, and increase DHL's share of shipments.

CUSTOMER SEGMENTATION

To achieve this, the first task was to segment its customers into actionable segments with distinct needs. DHL defined three main segments. First, "Strategic Customers" are extremely high-volume shippers with a full range of logistics solutions and express-shipment needs. This segment consists of approximately DHL's top 250 customers worldwide, which are mostly large multinationals. Second, the "Relationship Customers" segment consists of customers who use DHL to ship their products and documents regularly, but with a lower volume than the Strategic Customers segment and also not as sophisticated supply-chain needs. Finally, the "Direct Customers" segment ships infrequently with DHL. The cus-

This case was written by Jochen Wirtz; Indranil Sen, Research and Planning Manager Asia Pacific, DHL; and Sanjay Singh, an MBA student, NUS Business School, National University of Singapore.
Copyright © 2005 Jochen Wirtz, Indranil Sen, and Sanjay Singh.

Exhibit 1   DHL Logistics Hub in Singapore

Exhibit 2   DHL Logistics

tomer segmentation can be represented in the form of the familiar customer pyramid in **Exhibit 3**.

These segments are further divided into subsegments based on the kind of service required (see **Exhibit 4**). The needs of Direct Customers and many of the Relationship Customers often are fully met by DHL's *basic products*. For Relationship Customers with special needs, DHL also offers some *special programs* like direct distribution to its partners, test services, and parts distribution to fulfill these needs. Strategic Customers virtually always use *customized solutions*, like providing bulk-breaking facilities and planned production support for precision delivery schedules, and DHL aims to meet

their entire express delivery needs.

Customers using DHL's basic products find it easier to switch as switching costs are low and all key competitors also offer similar products. In contrast, the switching costs are significantly higher for customers with special programs, and highest for clients using customized solutions.

Exhibit 5 shows some output of DHL's segmentation analysis for one of its country markets. The majority of revenue and profits were derived from only 18 percent of the customers, its Relationship Customers. The Direct Customer segment consisted of 75 percent of the total customer base and contributed only 15 percent of revenues and 30 percent of profits. The Strategic Customer segment contributed only 6

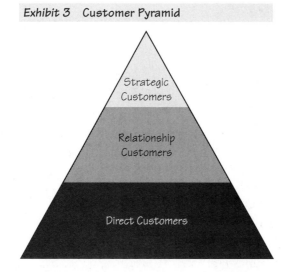

Exhibit 3   Customer Pyramid

Strategic Customers

Relationship Customers

Direct Customers

Exhibit 4   Customer Subsegmentation

	Strategic Customers	Relationship Customers	Direct Customers
Basic Product			
Special Programs			
Customized Solutions			

Exhibit 5   Segment Analysis

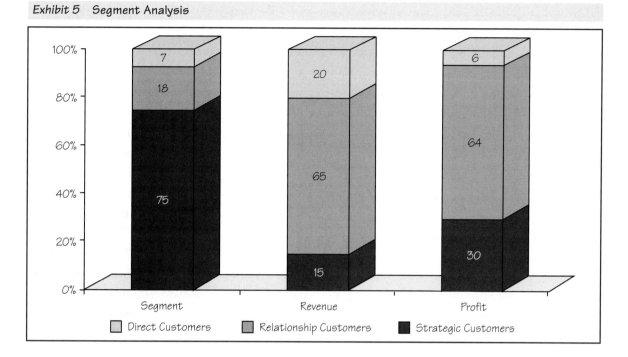

percent to profits. Similar patterns are observed for all countries where this analysis was conducted. The verdict seems clear: Focus on the Relationship Customers segment for maximum profitability. However, this does not mean that the other segments are neglected. The Strategic Customer segment, being the most loyal, needs deployment of leading edge technology and best practice infrastructure to maintain their loyalty as future business potential is high for this group. Extra effort is put into upgrading those Direct Customers who have high-volume potential and latent needs for special-program products.

LOYALTY MANAGEMENT SYSTEM: FURTHER CATEGORIZATION OF SEGMENTS

To focus service and sales staff on customer retention and development, it was necessary to get more information about these customers and hence, each of these segments was further classified into six categories and the data used to take corrective and proactive measures to enhance customer loyalty.

LOST   The customer in this category has stopped shipping with DHL, for external reasons like customer having gone into liquidation, or for internal reasons like service performance failure, or increase in prices, etc. Once the reason is identified, it is easier to control internal reasons and reduce customer churn. Sales and service staff then focus on regaining potentially profitable accounts.

DECREASED-PERFORMER   This category refers to customers who have shipped considerably less over a given period compared to a similar period in the past. Again, the reasons for down trading may be external or internal to DHL. The decreased-performer in each segment triggers an alarm bell to warn the sales staff of potential impending customer churn.

MAINTAINED   This category is for customers who continue to trade within a given bandwidth of shipment volume.

INCREASED-PERFORMER The customer in this category has shipped considerably more over a given period. Again, the reasons for increased performance may be external or internal. Follow-up work is done to identify the causes for increase in volumes and particularly whether the up trading is a result of a DHL initiative. The successful initiatives are further improved to gain better results.

NEW This category is for any customer who has shipped for the first time with DHL. Special efforts are made by the sales staff to make them permanent customers.

REGAINED This customer was previously "lost" but has recommenced shipping with DHL recently. The reasons for this renewed activity may be external (e.g., renewed business activity of a lapsed customer) or internal (e.g., the shipment was made as a result of reactive measures by DHL to regain the customer).

The data collected are graphically represented for each segment, as given in **Exhibit 6**, and reported to sales, marketing and customer service departments, and senior management. This makes it easy to understand the impact of the change in customer base and an increase in the percentage of decreased-performers should immediately cause the sales and customer service staff to take corrective action.

The classification and the data reported for each customer meant that the sales force was forewarned about potential customer defections. They could then take corrective actions, and identify service performance shortcomings and customer dissatisfaction, hence leading to more proactive measures in the future. The data also made it possible to calculate the defection rate of customers for each tier of the customer pyramid, and to calculate the lifetime value of each segment. The change in lifetime value of all customers gives the management an idea of the rev-

Exhibit 6   Direct Customers—Segment Analysis

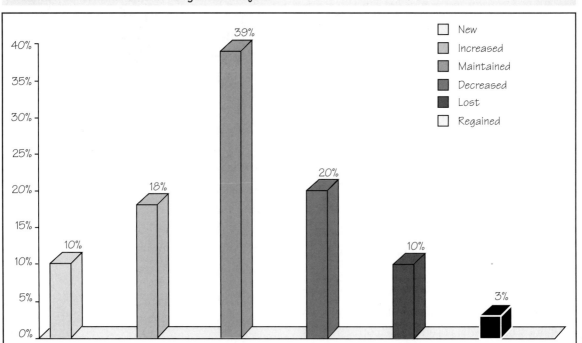

enue and profit implications of its marketing and service initiatives.

The expected increase or decrease in revenue for the month is also calculated and represented graphically, as shown in **Exhibit 7**, giving the impact of the change in the customer segment portfolio on DHL's revenues.

Similarly, the sales staff can study the reasons for up trading for each customer and tap the remaining potential for further up trading.

This program also helps the company send targeted communication to the customers based on the classification into segments, instead of general communication to all customers, thereby making communication cost effective.

After a short period of implementation, this initiative has already been yielding impressive results, and further modules are being developed and pilot tested for potential roll-out.

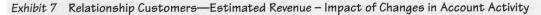

Exhibit 7   **Relationship Customers—Estimated Revenue – Impact of Changes in Account Activity**

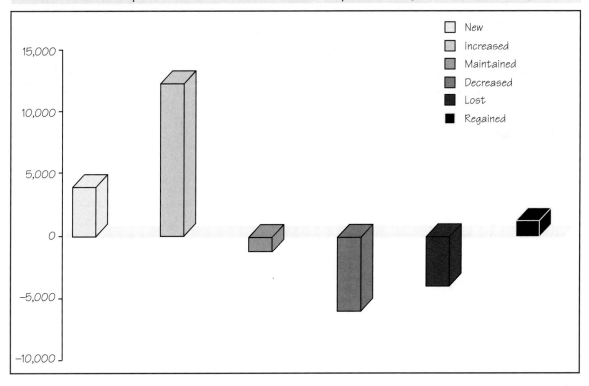

Exhibit 8   DHL Delivery Man

Study Questions

1. What do you see as the main challenges in implementing this segmentation in DHL's customer database?
2. How would you recommend DHL to address those challenges?
3. What are the various possible practical applications of this segmentation methodology by other functional department (e.g., sales, customer service, etc.)?

Bossard Asia Pacific

Can It Make Its CRM Strategy Work?

JOCHEN WIRTZ

Bossard Asia Pacific, an innovative manufacturer of fastening technology, is facing increasing competition from local and regional players. In a bold move, the CEO of Bossard AP embarks on a customer relationship management (CRM) strategy that requires its employees to embrace the CRM paradigm and become more customer-centric. He now needs to sell the idea of implementing a CRM system to his management team and staff in order to make the strategy work.

Scott MacMeekin, President of Bossard Asia Pacific, was about to enter the meeting room in his Singapore office. The room was filled with expectant faces of Team Leaders, Country Managers and General Managers from Bossard's offices from all over Asia. Ahead of him, Scott had a difficult task. He needed to sell the idea of implementing a customer relationship management (CRM) system for a medium-sized company with a highly distributed operation.

BACKGROUND TO BOSSARD'S CRM INITIATIVE

Some time ago, Scott had set up a task force to assess Bossard's current market position and find ways to accelerate growth in the Asia Pacific region. Bossard's core business of fastening technology was becoming increasingly competitive with many large local and regional players. The cost of customer acquisition was rising and hence, margins were eroding. The task force concluded their study with a strong recommendation for a CRM system to be implemented within the next 12 to 18 months.

His task force was driven by the Asia Pacific office and Bossard's headquarters in Switzerland did not show much appreciation for Scott's initiative. The resulting lack of support and funding further raised the doubts of a successful shift toward a CRM-centered strategy. Nonetheless, Scott and his team decided a year ago to push

The author gratefully acknowledges the assistance of Scott MacMeekin, President, Bossard Asia Pacific; Mark Mümenthaler, formerly the country manager of Bossard in China; and Tillman Fein, in preparing this case.

for a Dashboard CRM-driven (DCRM[1]) strategy and he was now chairing this meeting in order to obtain his manager's endorsement and a green light for the system roll-out.

IMPLEMENTATION RISK OF CRM STRATEGIES

Nonetheless, Scott was wary of the "miracle weapon" CRM. He had seen too many corporations committing enormous resources to the development and implementation of CRM technologies designed to capitalize on a deep, inside knowledge of a company's customer base. But promises of connecting companies and their customers for mutual benefit had been unsuccessful or even detrimental in many cases. Despite concerted efforts, many companies had failed to elevate their CRM performance to a satisfactory level.

BENEFITS AND CHALLENGES OF THE BOSSARD DCRM SOLUTION

After thorough discussions with his team—Scott went on to explain to his audience in the meeting room—he decided to build an internal solution, due to tremendous cost advantages, lack of support from Bossard's headquarters in Switzerland, as well as superior business knowledge that the Bossard IT team could utilize to accommodate business-specific requirements. According to his team's estimations, an internal Internet-based solution could be implemented for as little as US$100,000, whereas external providers were quoting US$800,000 and above. Scott showed a slide detailing the benefits and challenges of his decision (see **Exhibit 1**).

He said, "If you use 21st century technology to pave a goat path, you will end up with a really smooth goat path. But, it is still a goat path." In his belief, if a process is fundamentally flawed, technology may give it a boost, but more likely it will end up helping to do inefficient or ineffective things faster than before. The message that Scott wanted to send to Bossard's managers, employees, and customers was that it will use CRM technology to do things differently, not simply faster or cheaper. He stressed that Bossard's DCRM application could be seen as a sophisticated sales force management tool that facilitates both the sales person's knowledge generation and the management's need for a monitoring and decision-making instrument.

DCRM DEMONSTRATION

Scott realized that most of his audience had not seen any visual representation of the DCRM, so he had planned to show a few sample screenshots. He also referred his managers to an extensive training and user manual that was maintained online.

Explaining his online demonstration screens (see **Exhibit 2**), he said:

> The DCRM system's customer management screen provides a comprehensive customer profile view. From the contact details to the number of visits, and key profitability indicators, such as margin contribution charts as well as the competition proportion, can be analyzed at a glance.
>
> I want everyone from the country general manager downwards to use the DCRM system to present the company's performance to all members of the company. All

---

[1] DCRM describes a CRM implementation where customer-related information and key data points are organized in dashboards at a glance (i.e., one screen shows all the relevant information, and further drill-down into more detailed data can be performed from each dashboard for key data).

Exhibit 1   Benefits and Challenges of Bossard's DCRM Strategy Implementation

Benefits:

1. Cost of development is about 10 to 15 percent of an off-the-shelf DCRM software solution.

2. Documents such as existing Excel spreadsheets can be reused for ease of implementation.

3. Part of the DCRM development team are Bossard employees, who have a strong understanding of the business model. Flexibility for chance and adjustment are high.

4. The tool is built especially for Bossard and its requirements on customer data. This provides additional flexibility.

5. Minimal data entry and migration.

6. Compatibility to existing ERP systems.

7. Customized according to Bossard strategy; best fit.

Challenges:

1. Development process takes longer.

2. Bossard people who are involved in developing the tool have to be taken out of their regular duties. Employees are a scarce resource in a medium-sized company like Bossard Asia Pacific, which comes without extra IT support.

3. Inputs from the market—such as from sales people—are essential to continuously improve and upgrade the system and keep it on a very high standard.

Exhibit 2   DCRM Customer Management Screen

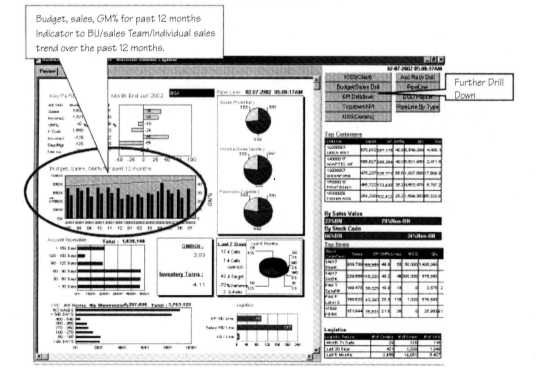

Budget, sales, GM% for past 12 months
Indicator to BU/sales Team/Individual sales
trend over the past 12 months.

Further Drill Down

the important indicators, such as the KPI (Key Performance Index), are captured in the DCRM system.

Referring to **Exhibit 3**, Scott said, "As you can see, the DCRM system's segmentation screen divides customers into different segments. This will help the sales force to stay in line with Bossard's target segmentation and not to move too far from a given strategy. If the focus changes, for instance after a strategy meeting, a new segmentation can be selected in the CRM system to reflect the new situation."

CRM IS BEING USED FOR MARKET IDENTIFICATION AND SEGMENTATION, AS WELL AS CUSTOMER TRACKING

Scott elaborated that the selection of target customers was done through several different analytical processes. First, it was important to look at the market segmentation. Once a segment was defined, the next step would be to select the most profitable customer in that segment. For this purpose, Bossard Asia Pacific had implemented a high yield margin contribution (HYMC) screen

Exhibit 3   DCRM Segment Screen

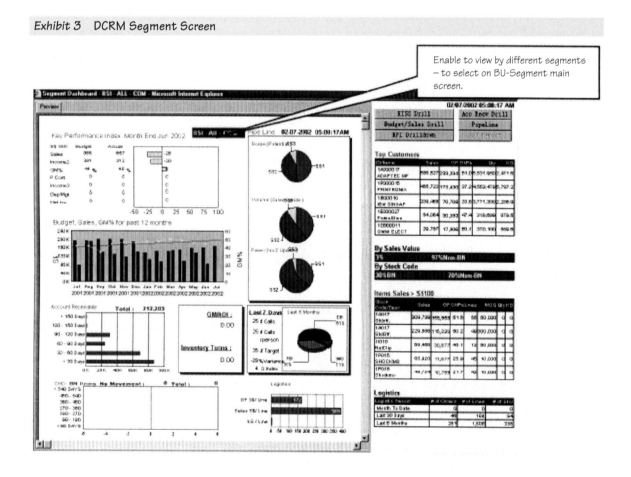

Enable to view by different segments – to select on BU-Segment main screen.

as part of the DCRM implementation. The HYMC included cost of sales, engineering support, cost of line items, 12 percent of annual revenue (AR) and inventory holding costs. After deducting the HYMC from the customer profit, what remained is the "true profit" that helped to decide whether the customer should be targeted.

A separate screen was used to analyze whether a company was growing or shrinking in conjunction with the margin trend (up or down). This was conceived as a very powerful tool to understand in which company Bossard shall invest. Scott explained:

> The DCRM system also includes a report about new working and market opportunity analyzing the pipeline trend. The pipeline report provides an excellent overview of whether the company has enough potential customers lined up as a back-up, which in return indicates the company's future growth potential.

TOP TO BOTTOM USAGE OF THE CRM SOLUTION FOR REVIEWS AND

MEETINGS

At Bossard Asia Pacific, the continuous use of the newly developed DCRM tool was to be ensured by scheduled management meetings. Scott presented the different meeting types to his audience, elaborating on each of the four different types of meetings that the DCRM implementation team had defined (see **Exhibit 4**).

TOP DOWN SUPPORT IS CRITICAL FOR SUCCESS

Scott was of the strong opinion that without him as a decisive top-management sponsor taking responsibility for the final sign-off on the completed system, the inevitable result would be that strong-willed steering committee members would shape the final implementation to reflect their desires for their departments or divisions. In an initial meeting with the regional GMs, Scott pushed:

> What you are dealing with is a whole set of new roles and responsibilities; you are moving toward a much more customer-focused

---

Exhibit 4   Planned Meeting Schedule Involving the DCRM Strategy Implementation

Bossard Asia Pacific Meeting Schedule

Meetings	Main Objectives	Attendees	Information Flow
Sales Team Review Meeting Weekly, 1 hour	Ensure team members' prospective choices fit the given market segmentation strategy	Team leader with team members	Bottom up
Financial/KPI Review Meeting Monthly, Half Day	Measure results to plans and prescribe corrective action as needed	GM and team leaders	Top down—led by finance
Strategic Planning Meeting Trimester, 1 Day	GM to ensure strategic alignment of team and members to business unit mission	CEO, GM, team leader, and team member	Bottom up and top down
General Staff Meeting	Prepare general staff and guide future expectations	GM, team leader, and all staff	Top down

organization. To implement CRM, you need people on your side to make change happen. This is what I need from you and that is what you need from your organization. Ask them to use the system and request their feedback. With the feedback, the system will constantly and quickly improve. For our DCRM system to be successful, every single person must support it. Using the DCRM system is not an option but a compulsory task for all people involved. The DCRM is a Bossard custom-made tool and none of the Bossard employees have experience. So, don't back off at the first sign of problems. No matter how much thought is put into the system, there will always be unanticipated problems to deal with.

The first CRM application is like a 15-watt light bulb in a dark room. It is not very bright, but can make a huge difference. The wattage can be turned up to 250 watts when relationships are viewed as a selected set of assets to be developed.

Across the company, each member of the sales team (Sales Executive, Sales Manager, and General Manager) was asked to use the DCRM system to present the latest activities in their accounts. Points to be presented were, for instance, how many visits were done during the week, what was discussed, and what kind of action would be undertaken in response.

Scott stressed that having every visit recorded would help sales team leaders to understand what each sales person was focusing on as well as whether there were any quality-control problems or other issues that required the team leader's attention.

CRM AS A KNOWLEDGE BASE AND SALES FORCE MANAGEMENT TOOL

While Scott was going through his slides, Mark Mümenthaler, Country Manager, China, was sit-ting in the meeting room, pondering a problem he had faced time and again. One of his Sales Managers, Loong Pong Pang, had just resigned. Pong Pang, being with Bossard in China for more than two years, had put in hard work and achieved tremendous success in client acquisition and account management. He had gained great knowledge of Bossard's business and the market segments that were identified as key industries to the company. Seeing him leave felt like an enormous waste to Mark. Mark knew that as a Sales Manager, Account Manager, or even as a Sales Executive, it was not easy to be up-to-date on each project and customer account. Without having the account's complete data and without capturing the customer-specific information, it was very hard to develop effective strategies to grow an account and increase revenue from the customer.

If a Bossard sales/account executive should leave the company, like Pong Pang, a tremendous customer-specific knowledge base would be lost with the departure of each staff. It occurred to Mark that with all data of a specific customer available any time through the DCRM, it was much easier for a new sales person to understand an account fast and anticipate the customer's behavior.

Furthermore, the DCRM would enable sales staff to provide the customer with better advice for mutual benefit. For instance, in the high yield margin contribution screen, the sales person could see that the customer ordered frequently, but in small quantities (meaning high order cost) or identify a potential for rationalization on the product range in use. Providing the customer with value-added services on possible improvement greatly helped to build a closer relationship while, at the same time, reducing costs and translating revenue opportunities.

Mark realized another strong advantage of the DCRM implementation, namely, its ability to provide an impartial source of information to his sales staff, which can be used to determine the optimal choice of which prospect to go after. This was critical, as each decision to engage a given prospect results in costs between US$20,000 and US$100,000.[2] Given that there were more potential prospects than resources at any given point in time, DCRM could be used by Mark and his team to direct the sales team more effectively.

By the time Scott had reached the end of his presentation, his audience seemed convinced that Bossard was embarking on a winning strategy. Nonetheless, Scott cautioned his managers and highlighted that a successful CRM strategy was an ongoing process. After developing the strategy, defining a project plan, involving all the right people, choosing appropriate technology, and implementing the program across the enterprise, the mission was not completed. In order to sustain a successful DCRM strategy and harness its benefits, continuous monitoring, improvements, and system maintenance were necessary.

Study Questions

1. What role can the CRM system potentially play in Bossard's marketing strategy? How will it help Bossard to segment existing markets and develop new ones?

2. What are the likely problems Scott will face with his CRM roll-out, and how should he address them? What are the main opportunities the CRM system will offer, and how can Bossard enhance its chances of realizing them?

3. Based on the information provided, how would you recommend Bossard to develop its marketing strategy and the CRM system to support it?

---

[2] This represents the average cost to bring in and develop a prospective account and includes expenses such as manpower, engineering work, travel, etc.

Appendix

Bossard's Research on Customer Relationship Management Strategies

Bossard's research had revealed that CRM systems are commonly used by major multinational companies around the globe. Its benefits are easily identified as enabling a business strategy that allows businesses to create and sustain long-term profitable customer relationships. However, CRM strategy implementations often did not succeed, and Scott knew that up to 75 percent of implementations did not deliver up to expectations. In addition, a substantial amount of funds could be tied up in a CRM system development, easily reaching up to several million dollars until implementation.

Speaking to other business leaders and academics, Scott had realized that successful CRM initiatives start with a business philosophy that aligns company activities around customer needs. Only then can CRM technology be used the way it should be—as an enabling tool of the processes required to turn customer-centric strategy into business results.

During the assessment and planning stage, he and his task force concluded that a successful CRM strategy implementation had to affect the entire corporation, from top to bottom. Not only did the company structure have to revolve around their customer, but the employees' customer-oriented skills needed to be fostered. Hence his initial claim that the business had to be disciplined in implementing the strategy change or else it would fail. He encouraged his team leaders and regional managers to communicate the value proposition of DCRM for its clients and to Bossard clearly to everyone in their teams. Employees at the sales executive or administrative level, especially, would not immediately see the benefits of CRM, but rather perceive it as an additional burden due to additional data entry.

Scott and his team had conducted extensive research and were approached by large consultancy firms and application development companies, all pledging to implement Bossard's customer-centric strategy with a customized CRM solution. Bossard's requirements were matched with the external offers and compared to a purely internal solution using Bossard's IT team and an external system development firm in Singapore.

The Accellion Service Guarantee

JOCHEN WIRTZ AND JILL KLEIN

A high-technology company introduces what it considers to be a bold service quality guarantee to communicate its commitment to service excellence to customers, prospects, and its own employees.

Accellion was a young high-technology firm with leading-edge technology in the distributed file storage, management, and delivery market space. Still new to the industry, the firm aimed to become the global backbone for the next generation of Internet-based applications.

Accellion's main value proposition to the world's largest enterprises ("the Global 2000"), as well as to Internet-based providers of premium content, was to allow them to serve their users faster, increase operational efficiencies, and lower total costs. Specifically, Accellion customers could improve the access time for downloading and uploading files by more than 200 percent. This performance improvement was achieved by locating an intelligent storage and file management system at the "edges of the Internet" and thereby delivering content from regions located closer to the end user. The typical time-consuming routing through many servers and hubs could be avoided using Accellion's infrastructure.

The need for an Internet infrastructure to deliver high bandwidth content to end users had never been greater. There was a trend toward multimedia and personalized Web content, all of which could not be delivered efficiently by existing infrastructure, which routed data through the congested network of servers that form the backbone of the Internet. This prompted Accellion to develop and launch a new service: distributed file storage, management, and delivery. Accellion provided an applications platform that resided on independent servers, which were directly connected to the users' Internet Service Providers (ISPs), thereby avoided the congested "centers" of the Internet. This decreased access time and allowed Accellion to distribute specialized content and applications more efficiently.

This case was written by Jochen Wirtz and Jill Klein, Associate Professor at INSEAD. The authors gratefully acknowledge the invaluable support by S. Mohan, Accellion's Chief Strategist, for his assistance and feedback to earlier versions of this case.

To effectively market Accellion's value proposition, Warren J. Kaplan, Accellion's CEO, and S. Mohan, its Chief Strategist, felt that in addition to its leading-edge technology, key success factors for Accellion's aggressive growth strategy were excellence in service delivery and high customer satisfaction. They envisioned that customers would prefer to leverage Accellion's technology and partnerships instead of having to manage the details of deploying, maintaining, and upgrading their own storage infrastructure for distributed Internet applications. To build a customer-driven culture and to communicate service excellence credibly to the market, Accellion aimed to harness the power of service guarantees.

Cost-effective services for improving performance and reliability were becoming critical, as the widespread use of multimedia and other large files increased exponentially. The value proposition was clearly attractive, but how could Accellion convince prospective clients that its technology and service actually could deliver what they promised?

Mohan felt that a Quality of Service (QoS) Guarantee would be a powerful tool to make its promises credible and, at the same time, push his team to deliver what has been promised.

Mark Ranford, Accellion's Director for Product Management, and Mohan spearheaded the development of the QoS Guarantee. They finally launched the QoS Guarantee (shown in **Exhibit 1**) stating that "it is a revolutionary statement of our commitment to the customer to do whatever it takes to ensure satisfaction." The official launch of the guarantee was announced to all staff by email (see **Exhibit 2**).

Their QoS Guarantee, however, was just part of Accellion's push for operational excellence. Many factors worked together to keep the company focused on their clients and providing the best possible service, so that they could create a large and loyal customer base for their innovative product. Thus, it was very important to raise awareness for Accellion's unique value proposition and convince the early adopters of the advantages.

Accellion's customers reacted positively. One customer stated, "Hey look at this. I haven't seen anything like it. No one offers 100 percent availability. That's tremendous." Another customer exclaimed, "You must really be confident in your service. This really is risk free now, isn't it?" Accellion was committed to its guarantee and strongly believed that having the best network and technology partners would enable it to deliver on its promise.

Study Questions

1. What is the marketing impact of a well-designed service guarantee?
2. Evaluate the design of Accellion's guarantee shown in Exhibit 1. How effective will it be in communicating service excellence to potential and current customers? Would you recommend any changes to its design or implementation?
3. Will the guarantee be successful in creating a culture for service excellence within Accellion? What else may be needed for achieving such a culture?
4. Do you think customers might take advantage of this guarantee and "stage" service failures to invoke the guarantee? If yes, how could Accellion minimize potential cheating on its guarantee?
5. Much of the research on service guarantees was conducted in North America. Do you think there are some Asia-specific aspects that need to be considered when implementing a service guarantee in Asia?

QUALITY OF SERVICE GUARANTEE

The Accellion Quality of Service Guarantee defines Accellion's assurance and commitment to providing the Customer with value-added Service and is incorporated into Accellion's Customer Contract. The definition of terms used herein is the same as those found in the Customer Contract.

1. Performance Guarantee

Accellion guarantees that the performance of the Network in uploading and downloading content, as a result of using the Accellion Service, will be no less than 200 percent of that which is achieved by a benchmark origin site being accessed from the edges of the Internet. For all purposes herein, performance measurement tests will be conducted by Accellion.

2. Availability Guarantee

Accellion guarantees 100 percent Service availability, excluding Force Majuere and Scheduled Maintenance for Customers who have opted for our replication services.

3. Customer Service Guarantee

Should Accellion fail to meet the service levels set out in Sections 1 and 2 above, Accellion will credit the Customer's account with one (1) month's service fee for the month affected when the failure(s) occurred, provided the Customer gives written notice to Accellion of such failure within five (5) days from the date such failure occurred. The Customer's failure to comply with this requirement will forfeit the Customer's right to receive such credit.

Accellion will notify the Customer no less than 48 hours (2 days) in advance of Scheduled Maintenance. If the Service becomes unavailable for any other reason, Accellion will promptly notify the Customer and take all necessary action to restore the Service.

Accellion maintains a 24-hour support center and will provide the Customer with a response to any inquiry in relation to the Service no more than 2 hours from the time of receipt of such query by customer service.

4. Security and Privacy Policy

Accellion has complete respect for the Customer's privacy and that of any Customer data stored in Accellion servers. The Accellion Service does not require Customers to provide any end-user private details for the data being stored on the servers. All information provided to Accellion by the Customer is stored for the Customer's sole benefit. Accellion will not share, disclose or sell any personally identifiable information to which it may have access and will ensure that the Customer's information and data [are] kept secure.

Disclosure of Customer's information or data in Accellion's possession shall only be made where such disclosure is necessary for compliance with a court order, to protect the rights or property of Accellion and to enforce the terms of use of the Service as provided in the Contract.

Accellion will ensure that the Customer's information and data [are] kept secure and protected from unauthorized access or improper use, which includes taking all reasonable steps to verify the Customer's identity before granting access.

Dear Team,

I am pleased to forward to everyone our industry's leading Quality of Service (QoS) Guarantee. Please read it over very carefully. You will find it to be very aggressive, and it puts the ownership on everyone in this company to deliver. Customers don't want a Service Level Agreement (SLA); they just want their network up and running all the time. That is why we have created this no questions asked guarantee. This type of guarantee has proven successful in other industries where service is key to success (e.g., Industry Leaders such as Gartner Group, LL Bean, Nordstrom, etc.).

As a member of the Accellion team, you are key to our client's satisfaction.

Thanks in advance for your support in making our clients and ourselves successful.

Wuxi Hospital for Women and Babies

LU XIONGWEN AND CHRISTOPHER LOVELOCK

A long-established hospital for women and babies in a big Chinese city has introduced a number of innovations in response to rising patient expectations and increasingly fierce competition in health care delivery. The management team is debating how best to differentiate the hospital and create core competitive advantages for the future.

Established in 1950, Wuxi Hospital for Women and Babies (WHWB) was a specialized hospital integrating the functions of obstetrics and gynecology treatment, health care science research, education, professional training, and family planning guidance. WHWB is located in the center of the city of Wuxi in the Yangtze River Delta area of China. As the only category IIIA[1] specialized hospital for maternal and children health care in the city, WHWB based its competitive advantages on its physical facilities, specialized equipment, and staff expertise. In 1994, it was named a "Baby Friendly Hospital" by China's National Ministry of Health.

Over the years, the hospital had introduced a variety of service innovations, including a personalized service concept, which had reinforced its leading position in Jiangsu Province. However, due to much higher expectations among patients and increasingly fierce competition among health care organizations, every hospital was trying to match service innovations introduced by others in order to attract more patients.

This case was prepared solely for use as a learning tool. It is not intended to serve as an endorsement, source of primary data, or illustration of effective or ineffective management. Financial data are in Chinese Yuan (exchange rate in 2003 was 1 yuan = US$0.12). The assistance of Cen Nin, Dong Zhuoyan, and Liu Ya, students at the School of Management, Fudan University, is gratefully acknowledged.

[1] In urban areas, hospitals in China are officially categorized into three levels: Level I are small-sized community hospitals providing local residents with basic health care and medical treatment; Level II are main hospitals in medium-sized cities or in districts of metropolitan cities, covering different communities, with advanced facilities and well-trained doctors; Level III are central hospitals in major cities, serving city people as well as treating patients from other areas. In each category, hospitals are labeled grade A, B, and C in terms of the scale and advancement of the facility and service. Grade A represents the highest grade in the category.

The management at WHWB was aware that if it failed to work on maintaining its lead, it could easily be overtaken by competitors. Yet the occupancy rates in the patient wards were almost always close to 100 percent and the medical treatment capacity had often proved insufficient to meet the demands placed upon it.

BACKGROUND

Located in the south of Jiangsu Province, Wuxi is known for its proximity to the beautiful Tai Lake. The city is located midway between Shanghai, China's international metropolis and economic and financial center, and Nanjing, the ancient capital of six dynasties (see **Exhibit 1**). Each city can be reached by train from Wuxi in less than two hours. Wuxi, which boasts a well-financed high-technology industrial park, is a

mid-sized city in the Yangtze River Delta city group, with a population of 4,380,000 in 2002. Its gross domestic product (GDP) and annual disposable income per capita were 160.17 billion yuan and 9,988 yuan respectively.[2]

The economic development of the Yangtze River Delta and the national reform of hospitals had stimulated both flourishing development and increasingly fierce competition among the hospitals in this area. In *The Instructions for Deepening the Trial Reform of the Cities' Hospital System* drafted by the National Ministry of Health in 2004, emphasis was placed on the need to attract outside investment, break the monopoly of state-owned hospitals, and boost healthy competition among medical organizations with different types of ownership. The *Instructions* classified hospitals into three catego-

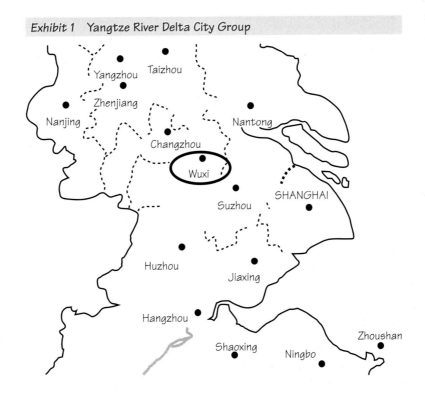

Exhibit 1   Yangtze River Delta City Group

---

[2] Data source: Key Economic Indices Comparison among 15 Cities in Yangtze River Delta in China (2002), Ningbo Statistical Yearbook (2003).

ries: (1) nonprofit hospitals directly under the government, which were wholly financed and controlled by the government, and enjoyed tax-free status; (2) nonprofit community hospitals, which were financed by market capital but required to reinvest their earnings in improving medical facilities; and (3) for-profit hospitals, financed by market capital, which could set their own prices but were required to pay taxes.

THE NATURE OF COMPETITION

The hospitals in the Yangtze River Delta region faced competition from both domestic and external sources.

Strong Rivals from Foreign Countries

The welcoming economic environment of the Yangtze River Delta attracted many foreign hospitals to enter this market. With their substantial management experience, foreign hospitals operated as for-profit businesses. Their advanced medical technology, modern equipment, and managerial orientation, reinforced by successful brand names, tended to leave their Chinese counterparts far behind. Before entering the Chinese market, most foreign hospital companies had undertaken significant studies of the entire Chinese medical market and used this information to make careful selection of hospital sites. In September 2003, with the approval of the National Ministry of Health and Ministry of Commerce, construction began in Suzhou on the first foreign hospital in Jiangsu Province—a 600-bed polyclinic. This hospital, containing multiple medical and surgical departments, and capable of treating a wide array of medical conditions, was financed by Hong Kong's Heng Sang Trade Company with an initial investment of 500 million yuan. Covering 130,800 sq. m., it would be the largest hospital in Jiangsu. For state-owned

hospitals that had never had to worry about competition in the past, the threat posed by the entry of such foreign hospitals into the Chinese health care market was deeply troubling.

Increasingly Severe Internal Pressures

The gradual implementation of medical system reform in China imposed new requirements on hospitals. Their ability to survive and grow would now depend on how well they could adapt to new policies and a radically changed environment.

As the only IIIA specialized hospital in Wuxi, WHWB included four major clinical departments: (1) Department of Gynecology (DG), (2) Department of Obstetrics (DO), (3) Department of Infants (DI), and (4) Technology Guiding Center for Family Planning (TGCFP). There were also two diagnostic centers for treating difficult and complex obstetrical and gynecological diseases. In 2002, a modern Ai Ying (meaning "cherishing babies" in Chinese) building was opened. Boasting advanced equipment and facilities, it had 19 floors, over 500 beds, and 580 employees (of whom 75 percent were professional personnel), making it the largest of the specialized maternal and children hospitals in the Yangtze River Delta region. In 2003, the clinical volume reached 273,613 persons and there were 14,500 in-patients. The annual revenue was almost 90 million yuan.

WHWB was seen as one of the trial hospitals for medical reform in the city and was also a pioneer in marketing hospital services. Under the leadership of its Director, Xue Wenqun, the management team continued to learn about advanced management theories, enhance the hospital's service concept, and promote a spirit of innovation that included launching an array of new services.

The evidence showed that people in Wuxi preferred WHWB to other gynecology or obstetrics clinics because of its advanced technology and good services. Although there were a number of hospitals in Wuxi and all those above Level II had gynecology and obstetrics departments, surveys showed that about one-third of pregnant women in the city would prefer to give birth in WHWB. The hospital's department of gynecology was not only the first choice of women living in Wuxi but also strongly preferred by those from the neighboring regions. Patients from outside the city accounted for 20 percent of the total in-patient volume in the Department of Gynecology.

INNOVATIVE SERVICES AT WHWB

On a rainy weekday in mid-June, a team of management researchers visited WHWB to explore the hospital and learn more about its services. The tour began in the comparatively shabby clinic building.

The Clinic

At the entrance to the clinic, the researchers saw that patients were immediately triaged according to the severity of their condition. When an ambulance arrived at the hospital, the primary emergency nurse would immediately evaluate the patient's condition. If deemed severe, the patient would receive "Special Green Card" service, which entitled him or her to priority examination and medical treatment, special nursing, and one consolidated bill. Other patients had to wait their turn.

Standing in the clinic's hall was a self-help information kiosk with a touch-screen display. Customers coming for the first time could obtain details of the process for using the clinic's services and other basic information about the hospital. However, the researchers found the touch screen somewhat difficult to operate and

concluded that this problem limited the kiosk's usefulness. Beside the kiosk was a directory of all the clinic's doctors, displaying each doctor's name, title, and area of specialization.

In the clinic hall, the sign displaying the slogan promoting the hospital as a "One-Stop Service Center" was quite impressive (see **Exhibit 2**). Patients coming to WHWB could expect the following:

1. *Hospital representatives in attendance.* They were ready to coordinate and resolve any conflicts between doctors and patients, and also to receive evaluations and suggestions from patients and their relatives.

2. *Clinic guidance service.* Staff would guide patients with appointments to their respective doctors and to examination areas, and render help to those needing physical assistance.

3. *Convenient service station.* At this station, equipment and amenities like wheelchairs, drinking water and cups, and free copies of *Jiangnan Health Post*, an influential local health newspaper, were obtainable. Staff would also be on hand to issue patients' examination sheets.

4. *Clinic reservations, medical consultation, and "Mother and Infant Hotline-271-3324."* A 50-yuan (US$6) fee was charged for each medical appointment made. The hospital would reconfirm appointments, thus serving as a reminder for patients to come on time for their medical appointments. If the patient failed to turn up for the appointment, the time slot, sufficient for a half-hour consultation, would be given to another person. Such appointments were limited to five per day for each doctor. According to the hospital, this reservation service was particularly useful for pa-

Exhibit 2   One-Stop Service Center

tients who had special concerns and were looking for close counsel from doctors.[3]

On this particular day, there were not many people in the clinic hall, perhaps reflecting the bad weather outside. Some people had gathered in front of the clinic guidance service station, and several nurses wearing green ribbons with the slogan "Green Bypass Will Help You" were helping them fill in the documents.

Crossing the hall, the researchers entered the clinic section which was shared by the different departments. In the nurses' station at the entrance, two nurses were busily searching through piles of case records. Behind them were two tall shelves filled with patient records. As the clinic section had not yet been fully computerized, information recording and transmitting still had to rely on traditional paper records.

---

[3] In China, clinics can be divided into two categories: common and special. Patients were not required to reserve appointments at common clinics, which operated on a walk-in basis. Registration costs only 2.5 yuan. However, the doctors working in common clinics tended to be relatively younger and less experienced, and to see a larger number of patients per day. Charges at special clinics were substantially higher, sometimes costing hundreds of yuan. The doctors at these clinics were usually specialists in difficult and complex diseases and had extensive clinical experience. In order to allow time for in-depth examination and diagnosis, special clinics could only accept a limited number of patients each day. WHWB's reservation service focused on its special clinic.

Maternity Training Courses

Next to the obstetrics clinic stood a classroom that served as the Maternity Training Center. This classroom was equipped with air-conditioning, color TV, and comfortable chairs. There were also several big exercise balls. On the wall hung some posters featuring the daily lives of pregnant women. A doctor explained that the training center targeted women who were more than four months into their pregnancy, and aimed to provide a warm, pleasant, and comfortable environment for them and their husbands to learn more about pregnancy, birth, and postnatal care. Experienced doctors would give interactive lectures on such topics as health knowledge, nutrition guidance, delivery skills, labor-pain-reducing methods, post-delivery issues for new mothers, care of newborn babies, and nursing skills. She emphasized that exercises and breathing techniques could stimulate blood circulation, help the women relax and hence reduce discomfort often experienced during pregnancy—generally to help women prepare for delivery and postpartum healing.

The training course was conducted for small classes of eight to ten couples, in order to ensure that each pregnant woman could have sufficient communication with the doctor. Among those who had taken this course, 70 to 80 percent enjoyed a trouble-free delivery and their babies were significantly stronger than others. The training course took place on weekday afternoons (see **Exhibit 3**) and consisted of eight lessons, each costing 50 yuan.

Despite the wet weather, there were still ten pregnant women who had turned up for the class, three accompanied by their supportive husbands. They were exercising under the supervision of a

Exhibit 3   Attendance at a Maternity Training Class

doctor (see **Exhibit 4**). One couple said that the wife's gynecologist had recommended this course to them. They felt that it was a good program for them and liked the way they could ask the doctor immediately if they had any questions. But because the class was held on a workday, the husband had had to apply for leave, which meant that he could only afford to come for the more important sessions. Some pregnant women commented that it was also inconvenient for them to come on working days. Moreover, the price seemed a little high for working-class participants, they observed.

In-Patient Services

Outside the clinic building, the rain was now coming down more heavily, but the researchers were pleased to find that the hospital had constructed an enclosed walkway to link the clinic building with the in-patient facility, which was divided into separate wards for obstetrics and gynecology.

Since March 2003, WHWB had launched many new services, including "Comfortable Waiting for Delivery," "Joyful Company and Guidance for Delivery," "Easing Labor," and "Pairing the Midwife and the Mother-to-Be." A new mother said that when she was paired with a nurse, she received a pink "Love Contact Card" containing contact information for the assigned doctor and the hotline telephone number. Whenever she had pregnancy-related problems or worries, she could contact the doctor who would patiently answer her questions.

"Comfortable Waiting for Delivery" meant that when the pregnant woman was waiting for delivery, a relative—usually her husband or mother—was allowed to accompany her in the delivery waiting room. The "guiding nurse" would massage her and teach her how to find relief from pain. For women giving birth for the first time, it was hard to avoid feeling tense and worried about the pain they might experience during labor. In order to address this problem,

Exhibit 4   Teaching Pregnant Women Appropriate Exercises That They Could Do on Their Own

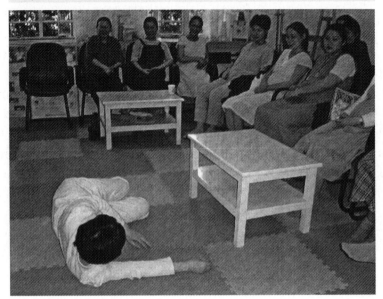

WHWB introduced a service called "Painless Delivery," which most new mothers said really did give them relief from labor pain.

In addition to addressing the needs of women during pregnancy and labor, WHWB had also launched some special services for their relatives. "Watching the Operation on TV" (80 yuan/time) enabled several relatives to watch the whole process on a monitor via a simultaneous video transmission, helping to relieve the relatives' own anxiety. "Accompanied Operation" (100 yuan/time) allowed one relative to enter the operating room and accompany the patient throughout the operation. Operations included all types of surgery relating to obstetrical and gynecological conditions. A hospital representative noted that a majority of women and their relatives took advantage of "Watching the Operation on TV" or "Accompanied Operation."

Furthermore, in order to help fathers participate in the child-birth experience and to enhance the love between father and child, WHWB launched its "Life Cut" service at the price of 180 yuan, which allowed the father to cut the newborn child's umbilical cord with a pair of specially-made scissors and thus mark the coming of a new life. Then, the special scissors, a lock of the baby's hair, and a part of the baby's umbilical cord were put into a special bottle as a souvenir. Details of this service had been widely publicized in the media and had been well-received.

In an obstetrics ward, the researchers met a woman who had completed "Painless Delivery" several days earlier. She looked well, and was willing to have a chat.

One of the researchers asked her, "Did you feel pain during delivery?"

"It was really painless," the new mother replied. "I had my baby two hours after entering the delivery waiting room. It was very smooth."

"Did you have the 'Life Cut' service?"

"What is 'Life Cut'? I don't know. No one told me about that."

The doctor accompanying the researchers explained, "Because she adopted Painless Delivery, and her delivery was very smooth and fast, we had no time to inform her about 'Life Cut.' Usually we get a nurse to introduce the services to patients while they are at the clinic. When a pregnant woman enters the delivery waiting room, the guiding nurse will let her know what kinds of special services can be provided. But as we have only just introduced these services recently, we don't try to push patients to adopt them. Take 'Painless Delivery' as an example: doctors generally make suggestions based on the patient's condition. Most of them are willing to choose this option."

"Then how many people are willing to select 'Life Cut'?" asked a researcher.

A midwife responded, "Since we launched this service last year, not many people have chosen it. In the first quarter of 2004, there were about 20, accounting only for 1 percent of all newborns. But many people want to keep the umbilical cords. If the father wants to cut the cord by himself, preventing the risk of infection is very important. He will be required to wear surgical clothing and have his hands disinfected. We find that many men feel sick at the sight of bleeding and are very nervous during the process. Sometimes they need special care themselves. Frankly, the whole process is too complicated, and we would prefer not to recommend it."

After the baby was born, the mother was usually quite weak and needed rest for some time in the hospital to recover. Recognizing that some new mothers might not get proper care at home, the hospital created some "Yue Zi Wards"[4] (350 yuan/day), which were suites with a bedroom and a sitting room. However, few patients seemed aware of this option. In addition to the central air conditioning system, color TV set, telephone, hi-fi system, and attached bathroom, Yue Zi Wards were even equipped with microwave ovens, refrigerators, and beds for one or two accompanying relatives, enabling the hospital to offer its patients the option of hotel-style service. Yue Zi Wards were staffed by experienced doctors and nurses who could provide postnatal health care, professional nutritionists who could carefully supervise the preparation of delicious meals around the clock, and maids who could attend to patients' other needs.

The most significant distinction between Yue Zi Wards and ordinary wards was that the former provided more scientific-recipe meals, helped the patients recover their physical figures, and significantly diminished the risk of such problems as postnatal adiposis[5] and lack of breast milk. The attending staff also taught scientifically-proven methods of feeding and bathing infants. According to a nurse in presence, postnatal patients usually remained in Yue Zi Wards for one or two weeks, but seldom for as much as a whole month. Since these wards were launched in 2003, only about ten women had stayed for a month. It depended on the family's economic situation and whether relatives were available to help, the nurse added.

One patient in the Yue Zi Ward told the researchers, "I got to know about Yue Zi Wards from the other patients. Most women can only have a baby once in their lives. The price here is 350 yuan a day, which seems a little expensive. Anyway, it is a suite ward. This ensures my rest without any interruptions. The guests can stay in the sitting room. What's more, there are some appliances such as a microwave. And my mother can also do some washing away from my rest area. It feels like a home." However, there was an additional charge for the specially-prepared meals and patients often found them unappetizing. Most patients would rather have their family send meals to the hospital (a common practice in China) than order those prepared by the hospital. Another service offered in the Yue Zi Wards, postpartum gym, was seldom patronized. The nurse explained that it was mainly due to Wuxi people's adherence to the old Yue Zi concept that women should lie in bed rather than undertake any exercise after labor.

Another special service for postpartum patients was the "Light Wave Bath" (20 yuan/time), which was safe, sanitary, and particularly suitable for women who had undergone a caesarean operation. It got rid of the bad habit of not taking a bath during the Yue Zi period. However, most of the postpartum patients were apparently unaware of this service.

The hospital had also set up "168" hotline service. Patients and their families could call this number anytime for non-medical assistance during their time in the hospital. The service center guaranteed arrival of personnel within 10 to 15 minutes of receiving the call to provide such ser-

---

[4] According to Chinese tradition, women are required to lie in bed for one month after labor, free of any work or other tiring activities, avoiding wind and bathing. They usually need some family members to help look after them. This month is called "Yue Zi".

[5] During the Yue Zi, the new mothers may easily gain weight as they are encouraged to eat well in order to rebuild their strength as well as to feed their babies.

vices as laundry, complimentary clothes mending, 24-hour meal delivery, and repairs of other personal possessions. It could also help patients find Yue Zi maids, book taxis, and make other transport arrangements when they needed to go for medical tests or examinations.

For newborn babies, WHWB offered services such as "Infant Massage" and "Infant Swimming." The former was introduced and sponsored by the Johnson & Johnson Company. A professional instructor, trained and certified by this company, gave new parents hands-on training on how to improve infants' adaptability to the environment and stimulate their growth—especially desirable for premature babies—by touching and massaging them as well as exercising them in a scientific way.

Babies could enjoy this exercise from as early as within three days after birth. At the beginning, they could only have this 20-minute treatment once a day, rising to twice daily after one month. Most parents liked to attend this class because they could perform the treatment at home once they had learned the skills involved. The table in the 20 sq. m. classroom could hold at most six babies each time and the course, which cost 50 yuan in total, sometimes attracted more than 50 infants a day (see **Exhibit 5**).

"Infant swimming" was designed for babies as young as one day old. The swimming room, where the air temperature was maintained at 26°C, contained five small, plastic-lined tubs, each at table-top height above the floor, so that a parent or nurse could comfortably reach the baby (see **Exhibit 6**). Simulated amniotic fluid was pumped into the tubs, which were always kept at 37°C—almost the same as the babies' own temperature. Before putting a baby into the water, a nurse replaced its normal clothing by water-proof fabrics around the umbilical area and

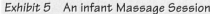
Exhibit 5   An infant Massage Session

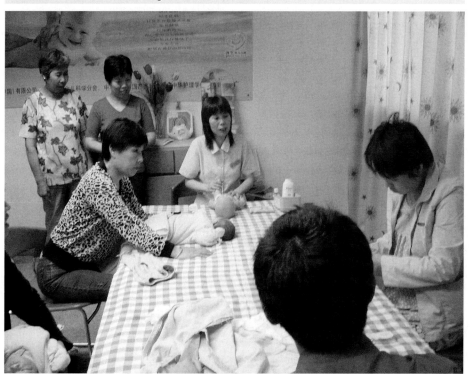

Exhibit 6   An Infant Swimming Session

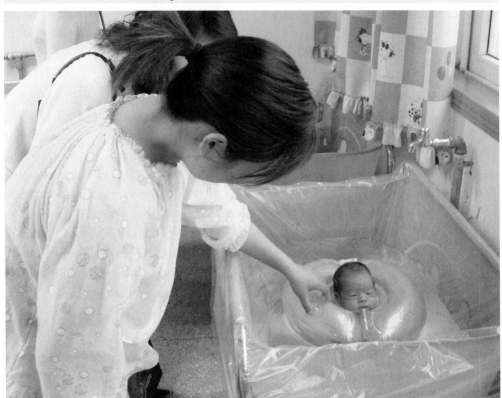

then put a swim ring around its neck. The new-born babies "swam" for 10 to 15 minutes each time. They could get good exercise by swimming once a week, which could establish a solid basis for their future health.

Because of the bad weather on the day of the researchers' visit, the nurses had thought that there would be no babies coming to swim that day. But, three babies did. The parents saw this service as a good opportunity for the babies to exercise, but most viewed 50 yuan per visit as relatively expensive. They said they would like to come once or twice, but not after leaving the hospital. These observations seemed at variance with the hospital's own data, which showed that 80 percent of new parents would return with their babies for the swimming sessions.

Patient Surveys

Before patients leave the hospital, they would complete a satisfaction questionnaire which had been placed beside their beds. The questions covered every aspect of a patient's hospital stay. However, some patients told the researchers that the questionnaire seemed a little superficial and formal, and that they were reluctant to record any dissatisfaction with the doctors and nurses whom they had interacted with during their hospital stay.

WHWB would also call their patients a week after they left the hospital to ask about the health of both mothers and babies. If there were any problems, doctors could be asked to immediately propose possible solutions over the phone. WHWB filed all the responses to the follow-up calls, with a view to building a long-term relationship with its patients. However, the file records contained only very brief information of the treatment received by each in-patient and simple feedback from the first follow-up call after a patient had returned home. No further record could be found in the file if the patient had any complaints or needed follow-up treatment. It was not apparent to the researchers whether the problems raised by the patients were actually resolved and, if so, how effectively it was done. Noting that the relationship usually lasted only for a few months, the researchers wondered if the data collected would form a useful basis for the future.

SERVICE MANAGEMENT

Although WHWB had introduced many innovative services, there had been few changes in the hospital's management structure, which was still organized around the design of the traditional planned economy system. In 2003, the hospital established a Marketing Department that executed such functions as promoting the innovative services to the public and conducting customer satisfaction surveys. However, this department had only one employee, who also worked for the Department of Staff Relationships.

Sources of Service Innovation

With patients becoming more demanding, and competition fiercer among health care organizations, WHWB was constantly seeking new ways to attract customers. Ideas for improvements and innovations came from two sources. One was through an annual innovation program and the other was from monitoring the activities of other hospitals through the newspapers or the Internet. WHWB had initiated an annual "Golden Ideas Collection" program in its search for good ideas and suggestions from employees and customers.

One way was to ask its patients to fill out a suggestions form before they left the hospital. The Department of Staff Relationships gathered all these suggestions and selected the most sensible and feasible ones. The hospital's management then discussed these suggestions and how to develop an appropriate plan to implement the good ones.

For example, one patient had recently proposed that the hospital should introduce a multiple-use ticket or membership pass for use of the infants' swimming service. WHWB viewed this as a good idea that might encourage more parents to return with their babies after the mother had left the hospital. So the Marketing Department was given the task of implementing this proposal, starting with calculating costs and trying to establish an appropriate pricing structure.

Among its many service innovations, the hospital was particularly optimistic about its "Female Health Examination Center." This program had been jointly launched by Wuxi General Labor Union, Wuxi Alliance of Women, and WHWB with the aim of safeguarding women's health. Recognizing that some poorly performing enterprises were unable to afford medical services for their female employees, WHWB initiated the "Health Safeguard Plan," under which female employees could enjoy a free health examination every year, obtain a discount if they were hospitalized, and receive corresponding medical insurance as long as their employers paid the hospital an annual fee of 30 yuan per woman. This program had helped the hospital build a good reputation in Wuxi. WHWB expected to enjoy a significant revenue stream in the long run as a result of future visits to the hospital by these women, reflecting the high rate of gynecological conditions requiring treatment.

Information Processing

The Ward Section at WHWB had computerized the processing of patient information, which encompassed an immense amount of data in the patient archives. In contrast, the Clinic Section had not yet been equipped with computers because of the relatively poor condition of the clinic building. As a result, most of the data collected at WHWB concerned mainly in-patients. At every quarter, the hospital summarized the statistics relating to the numbers of in-patients and clinic patients, average medical fee per bed, and so on. The data were then compared against those for previous quarters and trends were analyzed.

Surveying Customer Satisfaction

WHWB had conducted customer satisfaction surveys for some ten years and had achieved a more than 90 percent satisfaction level every year. The researchers were told that customer satisfaction levels had been around 95 percent five years ago but had dropped slightly to 92–93 percent in the last few years. The hospital explained that service quality had actually improved significantly, but patients' expectations had risen even more. Five years ago, all in-patients stayed in the old wards, which were much smaller than the new ones, but they were very satisfied with the skills and services of its doctors and nurses. After moving into the new building with improved facilities, patients' expectations for every aspect of their hospital stay had risen, thus resulting in these patients' somewhat lower satisfaction with skills and services.

Administration of customer satisfaction surveys involved the following four approaches: (1) giving each patient a questionnaire form when she was admitted and collecting it when she left the hospital; (2) conducting random personal surveys of patients in the wards; (3) mailing questionnaires to a sample of patients who had already left the hospital; and (4) personal visits to some patients at their homes.

The questionnaire form currently used at WHWB had been designed by the Jiangsu Health Bureau. The researchers concluded that, while easy to complete, the form only asked superficial questions about the service of each department of the hospital and failed to go into sufficient detail. Use of this survey was required in all hospitals in Jiangsu Province, and the results could influence the salaries that employees were paid.

In the case of certain special services, WHWB had received feedback that some patients had a poor opinion of them but the hospital ascribed their dissatisfaction to the fact that most patients could not afford them.

Commitment to Service Standards

Each department and team at WHWB had committed itself to meet certain standards in the services it provided and publicized them by framing a set of printed commitments and hanging them on the wall where they could be easily seen by patients. To avoid making empty promises, hospital management often checked doctors' and nurses' familiarity with these commitments. Certain staff members were assigned the task of monitoring performance to determine if the standards were actually being met. WHWB's principle was to "Never promise the moon." The hospital had once promised "No-more-than-half-an-hour-waiting." In practice, however, this promise could rarely be met because of the large number of patients, and so it was eventually withdrawn.

DETERMINING FUTURE STRATEGY

Facing severe competition among health care organizations, the WHWB management team realized that it would be quite easy for other providers to copy the innovative services that it had developed. They were debating how best to differentiate the hospital and create core competitive advantages for the future. Thanks to the hospital's growing reputation, the number of patients at WHWB had increased considerably; at times, demand even exceeded the hospital's capacity. A key issue was whether to position WHWB as serving a mass market and to expand its service capacity or, alternatively, to focus on elite customers and hence, transform it into a high-end hospital.

Study Questions

1. How has the marketing and competitive environment for hospital care changed in China in recent years and what are the implications for different types of hospitals?

2. Categorize WHWB's efforts to improve its competitive appeal into: Facility improvements, procedural changes, and value-added services.

3. In your view, how appropriate is each of WHWB's innovations? Why do some new services seem to be successful than others?

4. As a consultant to WHWB, which future strategy do you recommend the hospital should adopt: Serving a mass market or transforming itself into a high-end hospital? Why? What are the implications, including risks, associated with each stategy?

TLContact.com

CHRISTOPHER LOVELOCK

An Internet start-up company has successfully developed a Web-based service that enables hospital patients to stay in touch with family and friends through the medium of individualized home pages. Three years after launch, the company is finally becoming profitable and the founder and CEO is reviewing strategy for future growth.

Eric Langshur, CEO of TLContact, Inc. (TLC), was pleased as he drafted the company's quarterly activity update for April 2003. The news was encouraging on almost all fronts.

Utilization of TLContact.com, the company's Web-based service, was accelerating among existing customers, primarily acute care hospitals in the United States and Canada, and the company continued its record of 100 percent renewals. New sales were up dramatically, individual users continued to be delighted with the service, and new enhancements had been well received. Press coverage and word of mouth had been phenomenal; the latest Google search of "tlcontact" had yielded more than 400 entries. Meanwhile, competitors were stumbling, and one had just shut down. The firm had recently acquired a majority interest in Health Television

System, an in-hospital television programming service, and its sales also were doing well. Eric predicted that consolidated annual revenues would reach about US$3 million, up more than threefold over the previous year.

Then he shook his head as he looked again at the US$3 million figure. Fifteen years earlier, at age 25 and fresh out of an MBA program, he had been running a US$25 million business. And prior to launching TLC in 2000 with his wife, Sharon, a physician, he had been president of a large division of a multinational aerospace company. Were challenge and reward directly proportional to scale? He didn't think so.

The activity update on which he was working would make pleasant reading, he reflected, for the firm's board of directors in advance of their upcoming meeting. But Eric wanted to avoid any sense of complacency, because the firm's very success could still attract viable competition. Despite having some prestigious clients, TLC had penetrated only a small percentage of what was potentially a very large market. Both of the firm's products offered a trusted and valued access to hospital patients, with potential for hospitals and other sponsors to use them as customized communication channels. Yet TLC also offered access to a vastly larger audience of health-oriented consumers. Might other sponsors, in addition to hospitals, be interested in the potential synergies?

THE COMPANY

Located in Chicago, TLC was only three years old. Created at the height of the dot.com boom, it was among the small percentage of Internet start-ups that had survived after the bubble burst. The management team consisted of Eric Langshur, CEO; Charlyn Slade, RNC, president; Raul Vasquez, chief technical officer; Lindsay Paul, VP-business development-healthcare; JoAnne Resnic, VP-health care services; and Sharon Langshur, M.D., medical director. In addition, the company employed a technical team of four consisting of a graphic designer, a customer service manager, and two software engineers. Responsibility for the sales effort rested primarily with the Sales and Business Development team made up of Charlyn Slade, JoAnne Resnic, both former nurses and nurse administrators; and Lindsay Paul, a Harvard MBA with an extensive background in health care consulting.

TLC's primary product, the CarePage service, was a Web-based service that enabled patients to stay in touch with family members and friends through the medium of individualized home pages. In 2002, TLC had completed purchase of a majority share in the Health Television System, an in-hospital television network featuring two channels of original educational content delivered via closed circuit that patients could view on their bedside TVs.

During 2002, TLC had combined revenues of US$1 million and expenses of US$1.7 million. The company was privately held by the founders and 20 private investors. Financing had involved an initial investment in 2000 of US$3 million by

what Eric described as "angel" investors and an additional investment of US$900,000 and US$1.7 million of convertible loans, again from private investors, in 2002. At the end of the first quarter of 2003, monthly expenses were running at an average rate of US$100,000, and monthly revenues were meeting operational expenses.

The TLC Service Concept

TLContact.com was an interactive patient communications service available to hospitals and other in-patient health care facilities in North America. On behalf of sponsoring organizations, TLC created personalized home pages for patients to link them to their community of family and friends during hospitalization and extended care, including maternity. Typically, the home page, which TLC branded as a CarePage, was accessed through the organization's own Web site, but TLC also offered the option of access through the company's Web site. In both instances, all hosting took place on TLC's servers. The CarePage enabled family and friends to stay up to date on the patient's condition and to communicate messages of support (for an example, see **Exhibit 1**).

A CarePage was usually created when a patient was first admitted, although maternity patients often requested it be set up some time before their due dates. In most instances, a friend or family member agreed to act as CarePage manager and was provided with simple procedures for creating a page and updating content. The manager then informed the patient's family and friends of the address and the password required for access. Two levels of security were offered, with the higher level requiring additional screening to ensure that only specified visitors could gain access. Visitors, known as "members," could leave short messages on the site for all to read.

Exhibit 1   Sample CarePage

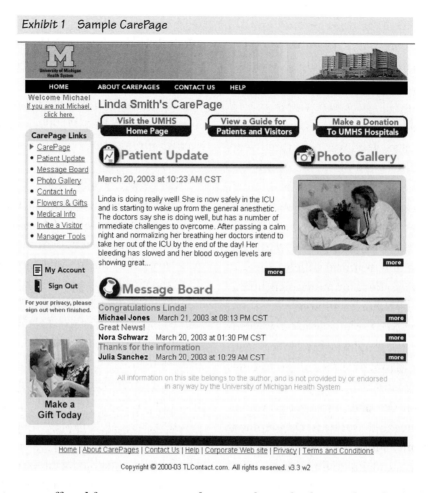

The service was offered free to patients and visitors, being presented as an added benefit of patronizing the sponsoring health care organization. The fee paid by the sponsor varied according to the size of the institution, level of use, and premium options selected, but in 2003 averaged about US$20,000 a year. TLC was exploring an alternative business model in which a third-party corporate sponsor paid the fee on behalf of the institution and received cobranding recognition on the CarePages.

The basic offering included such features as sending automatic email notification of an update on the patient's condition to all registered visitors to a specific CarePage, the ability to order gifts and flowers, and a guestbook tracking all visitors to the site. Options were posting photos and creating links to relevant background medical information.

TLC was currently testing a new feature that enabled visitors to make a donation to the health care institution serving the patient. For an additional fee, sponsors could also obtain feedback on use patterns, conduct surveys of visitors, post a hospital CEO welcome message, link to the hospital gift shop, and feature a customized inbox. Spanish-language CarePages were also available for an extra fee. The company had documented different patterns of CarePage use, showing that it varied according to the nature of the patient's situation. On average, a CarePage remained up for 85 days and attracted 50 members, each of whom visited 15 times. However, the average hospital stay in the United States, across all categories, was only 5.2 days.

TLC's procedures ensured privacy protection, meeting the provisions of the Health Information Privacy and Accountability Act (HIPAA). Its Web site displayed the TRUSTe Privacy Seal, a consumer branded symbol certifying that the site met stringent requirements of notice, choice, access, security, and redress.

Operations

TLC's service operated on three company-owned servers positioned at a remote facility, an arrangement termed colocation. These servers were connected to TLC's offices across a high-speed T1 line, which allowed almost all administrative and backup tasks to be achieved remotely.

TLC had invested heavily in technology, primarily its custom-built software, as part of a continuing effort to improve the usability of the service. This process benefited considerably from having a development team that, by necessity of the company's small size, spent part of their time providing customer support. Direct contact with users' problems and questions provided a constant stream of ideas for improvements to the site. In general, a new version of the software was released every six to eight weeks, incorporating newly developed ideas as well as the needs of new customers.

HISTORY: GENESIS OF AN IDEA

In February 1998, Eric and Sharon Langshur were looking forward to the birth of their first child. Like any young couple, they anticipated that this event would change their lives but had no inkling of the changes that would result in their careers, especially Eric's.

Eric, then 35, had enjoyed a meteoric career, developing an enviable record for his skills in both start-up and turnaround management. Born in Canada, he grew up in Montreal and

graduated from the University of New Brunswick with a degree in finance and information systems. Later, he obtained an MBA from Columbia and began a fast-paced progression through many different divisions of United Technologies Corporation (UTC) in the space of just nine years. As he later recalled:

> When I was 25, UTC gave me a chance to run a "little" [US]$25 million entity in southern California, which was my first opportunity to develop a quantifiable track record. I was fresh out of business school. I had to learn a great deal about managing people, which was definitely beneficial so early in my career.
>
> I did well in that job and was put in charge of a series of increasingly larger and more challenging businesses. Then I became vice president and general manager of UTC's Hamilton Standard propeller systems business that manufactures props for most of the commercial aircraft in the world. My last job was as president of ONSI, UTC's fuel cell business, the world's largest. In 1997, I received an offer to be president of the aerospace services division at Bombardier. It was a dream job.

Sharon, also a native of Canada, had graduated from McGill University in 1986 and entered the field of human genetics. Initially, she worked as a researcher and then, following completion of an M.S. at Sarah Lawrence College, as a genetic counselor in clinical human genetics. Deciding to pursue a career in medicine, she enrolled in medical school at the University of Connecticut and received her M.D. in 1997, achieving honors in all clinical rotations and serving as class valedictorian. During her pregnancy, she continued her one-year academic fellowship in anatomic pathology.

Eric's new job with Bombardier—a prominent Canadian manufacturer whose products included aircraft, rail transit systems, and recreational vehicles—involved a move from Connecticut to Chicago in September 1997. The plan was for him to commute for several months while Sharon remained in Hartford to await the birth of their baby.

On February 25, Sharon gave birth to a son, whom they named Matthew. But complications became evident almost immediately, and within days, a pediatric cardiologist had diagnosed the baby's heart as missing a left ventricle, a potentially fatal condition that would have been untreatable only a decade earlier. Facing the prospect of a series of complex operations on Matthew's heart, involving surgical procedures that only a handful of hospitals in the nation were qualified to perform, the Langshurs made the decision to complete their move to Chicago immediately and to have the baby treated at the University of Michigan Medical Center in Ann Arbor. The first surgery took place five days later.

It was a desperately worrying time for everyone. "When Sharon was pregnant," Eric remembered, "I wanted our child to be smart, handsome, athletic, outgoing, and with all the social graces. After he was diagnosed, I just wanted him to live." The couple's extended family and large circle of friends were deeply concerned and anxious for news.

Out on the West Coast, Sharon's younger brother, Mark Day, was completing his Ph.D. in mechanical engineering at Stanford. Feeling isolated, knowing nothing about the heart, and wanting to do something useful, Mark turned to the Internet, which was just beginning to hit its stride. His search turned up a lot of information from the American Heart Association and an array of medical sources. Within a few weeks, he had created a simple Web site that family and friends could access. He edited the information

he had gathered and loaded it on the site, together with bulletins on Matthew's condition and how the baby was responding to treatment. Sharon sent him regular updates on Matthew's progress and additional medical information. "It was a very simple site," Mark declared later. "If I had paid somebody else to do it for me, it probably wouldn't have cost more than a few hundred dollars." To minimize the need for emailing, Mark added a bulletin board so that people could send messages to Sharon and Eric.

To everyone's surprise, the site proved exceptionally popular. News spread by word of mouth, and the site recorded numerous daily visitors, with more than 200 people leaving messages for the family. People who confessed that they had never before used the Internet found a way to access the site, follow Matthew's progress, and send messages.

The Langshurs were overwhelmed by this outpouring of support but also deeply grateful for the way in which the Web site enabled them to avoid having to spend massive amounts of time responding to phone calls and repeating the same information time and time again. The site remained up for two years, during which time Matthew successfully underwent three surgeries to repair his heart and eventually developed into a happy, healthy toddler.

Creation of TLContact.com

The success of Matthew's Web site convinced the Langshurs that there was a market opportunity for an Internet-based company to deliver similar information services for patients and their families, potentially on a national basis. They were inspired not only by the business opportunities this venture presented but also by a desire to help other families enjoy the same benefits that they had received.

In late 1999, Eric and Sharon made the decision to quit their jobs (Sharon was a pediatric resident at Children's Memorial Hospital) and start their own company. "It was the height of the Internet boom," Eric recalled, "and a very heady time when millions of dollars could be raised on the basis of a short business plan." The Langshurs soon succeeded in raising US$3 million from several "angel" investors.

Meantime, Mark was enjoying a long-planned hiking and climbing tour of several countries in Asia and Africa. Having recently obtained his Ph.D., he had decided against pursuing an academic career and was debating what to do next. He and a group of friends celebrated New Year's Eve by climbing Mount Kilimanjaro, a dramatic extinct volcano in Kenya and, at 19,340 feet (5,896 m), the highest mountain in Africa. When the party returned to civilization, Mark found a message waiting for him from his sister and brother-in-law: Would he like to join their new start-up as chief technology officer?

Mark flew into Chicago on the day of the Super Bowl, the freezing temperatures of the upper Midwest contrasting sharply with the tropical heat of Kenya. But it was an intoxicating atmosphere for dot.com entrepreneurs and investors. Business news stories that day described the huge amounts of money that an array of Internet-based companies were spending on TV advertising during the Super Bowl broadcast.

The business model for the new venture followed the B2C approach that dominated most Internet start-ups. The goal was to market directly to patients' families and to prospective parents, charging a fee per page. The company needed a name and in keeping with its consumer orientation, the Langshurs wanted to call it 4U.com, which they saw as simple and memorable. However, a search revealed that this domain name, although not in use, was already registered. Eric laughed as he recalled what happened next:

> When we contacted the owner, he indicated that he was willing to sell the rights to the URL for US$2 million. The lunacy of the times was further highlighted when one of our early investors urged us to just go ahead and buy it! But we didn't think that was a prudent use of US$2 million.

Instead, they selected the name TLContact.com, a play on the common abbreviation of "tender loving care." Each patient site was named a "CarePage," and procedures were devised to control access and ensure patient confidentiality.

Initial Start-Up

In addition to Eric as CEO, Sharon as director of medical services, and Mark as CTO, the team was expanded to include a president with an extensive health care operations background, a VP-business development, and a VP-health care services, as well as administrative support staff. Mark began to build a technology team to create the Web site and its supporting systems. Meantime, an advisory board was formed to help shape the new company's strategy, monitor progress, and provide an objective perspective. TLC also benefited from advice provided by Sharon's father, George Day, an internationally recognized marketing professor at the Wharton School. She noted that he had taught them the importance of listening to the market, understanding the needs of target customers, and finding ways to avoid or circumvent strategic obstacles.

Eric found himself making a sharp transition in his professional lifestyle, moving from the president's office of a multimillion business to a second-floor office above a storefront in Chicago.

At Bombardier's aerospace division, and prior to that at UTC, he had had thousands of employees. After a few months, TLC's payroll (including himself, Sharon, Mark, and technical staff) was up to US$50,000 per month. However, he conceded that this situation did not prevent him from continuing to think big. There were 6,000 acute-care hospitals in the United States, 17,000 nursing homes, and more than 3,000 hospices. The number of patients treated each year was estimated at some 40 million. Everyone was convinced that huge rewards awaited the firm that could move quickly to penetrate this market.

Quickly recognizing the difficulties and expense of trying to market directly to individual patients, TLC soon shifted its sales focus to a hospital-based approach. With competition between hospitals becoming increasingly heated, enhancing patient satisfaction had become a strategic imperative at many institutions. Offering patients access to TLC seemed like a logical service enhancement to its proponents. But, despite early support from the pediatric cardiology group at the University of Michigan Medical Center (where Matthew had been treated), selling to hospitals proved much more difficult than expected.

TLC's original business model anticipated being in hundreds of hospitals within a year or so. The company was in a hurry to build a strong market base before competitors could do so. Already, there were a number of competing organizations, all of them quite small and each started by individuals who had created a Web site to keep family and friends informed of developments relating to somebody's health. They included Baby Press Conference, targeted at prospective parents; The Status, run as a sideline of a Web design company in Anchorage, Alaska; VisitingOurs, a rather basic service that outsourced the Web technology; and another rather basic service called CaringBridge, operated by a nonprofit organization.

To their dismay, the Langshurs and their colleagues soon realized that selling to hospitals was going to be a slow and difficult task. Sharon observed:

> We found the difficulties of selling to hospitals to be myriad. Based on my experience as a physician, we initially felt that we could sell to docs on the basis of helping them to enhance the quality of the patient experience. We knew they cared about patients and wanted to do the best for them. But after several months of barking up that tree, we realized that physicians didn't have the time to listen or the budget to purchase and were usually just too busy with delivery of medical care.
>
> So after six months or so, we shifted our efforts to PR and marketing departments, which did have a budget and were more likely to be able to see the advantages for their hospitals in terms of increased patient satisfaction.

However, hospital administrators didn't like the idea of having to ask their patients to pay for the service—after all, there were no charges for television and other nonmedical services designed to enhance satisfaction—so the discussion then shifted to the possibility of the hospital itself purchasing the basic service and making the option available to all patients who requested it. Yet many administrators failed to grasp the appeal of the service for patients or the advantages to the hospital of offering it. So TLC had to adopt a missionary approach, pointing out that advantages for the hospital included not only more satisfied patients but also fewer demands on hospital staff as families and friends replaced telephone requests for information by a simple search of the Web site.

In its sales efforts, TLC also cited the findings of a national study on patient satisfaction by the Picker Institute, which found that when asked about problems encountered during their hospital stays, 27 percent of the 23,763 patients surveyed reported lack of emotional support, 28 percent cited inadequate information and education, and 23 percent complained about insufficient involvement of family and friends. The survey data showed that patients receiving inadequate emotional support during their hospital stays were up to ten times more likely to say that they would not return to that hospital or recommend it.

Meantime, Mark and his technology team were hard at work on systems design. He emphasized that this task was vastly different in cost and complexity from the simple Web site that he had designed earlier for his nephew:

A key question at the outset had been whether to contract with someone to build the Web site or do it ourselves. It wasn't entirely clear whether it was worth the extra cost of outsourcing to gain the advantage of speed, although we were under tremendous pressure to move quickly since there was a level of paranoia about the risk that competitors might get a jump on us and dominate what was seen as a very lucrative market. On the other hand, if we did it ourselves, we would retain the intellectual capital and would find it easier to undertake future updates and expansions. Having had the experience of creating the initial Web site and seen its functionality, I had a very clear idea of how I wanted this thing built, which gave us a running start.

In February 2000, the dot.com boom was just about at its peak and outsourcing was wildly expensive—we were quoted US$400,000 for just a scoping study! So we hired some consultants who could really help us set up the initial architecture and help achieve some of our key goals, especially flexibility. During the same period, I hired several people full time. We took a deliberate approach to hire very skilled people. After a couple of months we had a technical team of about 10, including a programming group, a graphic design team, and a support group whose work included content design. The total cost was in the range of four to five hundred thousand dollars to achieve a functioning Web site.

It's very difficult to create a piece of software that's really user friendly. It takes an incredible amount of skill, effort, and time to develop something that's usable, functional, and scalable—meaning that it can be expanded and built upon without failing. For enterprise-wide applications you have to support the server with an operating system. We chose to go open source, which significantly reduced the cost because the source code is freely available. We launched in early August.

An additional round of "angel" financing was obtained during the summer of 2000, which enabled TLC to enhance the functionality of the service and add optional features. By late 2000, TLC had completed proof-of-concept prototype and alpha testing of the service. TLC had secured launch customers in three targeted market segments: acute care, long-term care, and hospice. Recognizing two distinct needs, it had created two distinct products, Acute CarePage and Baby CarePage. The latter was targeted at parents who were expecting a baby.

TLC's market strategy was evolving into a threefold thrust. The first strategic component was to continue offering a stand-alone service, positioned as an e-business patient satisfaction solution that offered important benefits for hospitals and health systems. Among patients and their families, TLC planned to rely on a "viral" marketing effect through word-of-mouth referrals, thus limiting the need for mass-media advertising. Although the number of users was still small, feedback had been exceptionally positive. The second component involved outsourcing direct sales to a national distribution partner that had established relationships with hospitals and health facilities. The third component involved licensing TLC software and its functionality to trusted third-party vendors and consultants. These partners could then bundle TLC's service as a "feature" to enhance their own product offerings, in return for royalties and other payments.

Progress in 2001 and 2002

By early 2001, sales discussions were in progress at more than two dozen hospitals and health systems. Despite validation of TLC service by a number of leading health care providers, the sales process was proving very slow. Hospital acceptance required the buy-in of numerous constituents, including administration, marketing, patient services, IT, legal, and physicians. But some still could not see the value of the service. As Sharon put it, "They had difficulty thinking outside the box." Budgetary constraints were a major reason for saying no. A few large hospitals with significant endowments declined on the grounds that they might want to develop their own in-house services.

However, TLC met its sales target for the first quarter by signing contracts with the University of Michigan Health System, New York Presbyterian Hospital, and Children's Memorial Hospital in Chicago. The first two hospitals specified that CarePages had to be fully branded under their own names and use their own distinctive color schemes, although the tag line "Pow-

ered by TLContact" would appear as a subscript.

Each branded product required the customization of more than 70 Web pages and 400 images, but TLC soon developed this capability, which it believed offered a significant competitive advantage. Other enhancements included an option for user feedback, addition of an email notification tool to announce updated news on a CarePage, and inclusion of software logic to automatically fix common mistakes that visitors might make in CarePage names, thereby reducing the volume of customer service enquires.

Eric had always been very cost conscious, so planning at TLC had emphasized the need to rush toward cash flow positive status. However, with the dot.com bubble now burst and sales progress proving sluggish, the Langshurs realized that TLC had to slow its burn rate by making significant cutbacks in staff numbers. It was a painful decision.

But slowing the burn rate was not sufficient. By fall 2001, Eric realized that TLC was running out of cash in an economy that was disintegrating. The environment for raising new capital was bleak. Attempting to raise further funds as a seed-stage Internet company without revenues was proving to be extremely difficult. Rather than close doors and wipe out shareholders' investment, Eric elected to refashion TLC as a health care media venture and acquired a controlling interest in Health Television System (HTS) through a mixture of cash and stock.

This Canadian-based company was a well-established hospital television network providing programming for patient education and hospital staff training. It already served 47 key hospitals across Canada, expected to serve 30 U.S. teaching hospitals by the end of the year, and had a positive cash flow. HTS featured two branded channels: the Parent Channel, aimed at women 18 to 35 in maternity and pediatric units; and Health TV, aimed at heart, cancer, and general medical units. Both channels featured original educational content delivered in a three-hour loop on patients' bedside TVs and achieved significant viewership.

During 2002, TLC continued to refine its sales approach so that it could address the specific concerns of the different decision makers at a hospital. TLC also refined its pricing policy, which Eric admitted had originally been rather unsophisticated, and began customizing it to the characteristics and needs of individual hospitals. On average, hospitals paid about US$20,000 a year for the service. One encouraging development was that the lead time for concluding a sales agreement with a hospital was getting shorter, dropping from an average of nine months in early 2001 to only three months by the end of 2002. Eric remarked:

> We've learned a great deal along the way about how to communicate our value proposition succinctly and to simplify our sales process. Most importantly, with every new account we sign, market acceptance of the product grows and the sales cycle shortens.

An important contributing factor was the exceptionally positive nature of the feedback received from CarePage users. Competitors, however, did not seem to be faring as well. BabyPressConference had shut down in 2002. TLC considered purchasing its assets but decided that this would not be a worthwhile investment. None of the remaining three appeared as active in the marketplace.

Although continuing to add individual hospitals to its client base and target new ones, TLC now recognized that prospects for significant sales growth centered on achieving distribution agreements with large systems. Its first success in what was seen as a long-lead-time sale came with a distribution agreement with CHCA, a buying consortium for 38 leading children's hospitals. A direct-to-hospice comarketing initiative was launched with the National Hospice and Palliative Care Organization, which represented 2,100 of the nation's 3,140 hospices. Subsequently, the firm began a paid pilot program with Tenet Corporation, operator of 116 acute-care hospitals.

Continued innovation in CarePage functionality included creation of a Spanish-language option, developed in collaboration with a Mexican hospital system, which would be offered to U.S. hospitals for an extra fee. Also under development was refinement of procedures for surveying members after they had completed a certain number of visits. Other new features in development included a Nurses Hall of Fame, allowing members to pay tribute to exceptional health care workers, thereby improving nursing hiring and retention; a Message Inbox, allowing hospitals to deliver targeted messages to members; and a "Send a Prayer" feature, which provided a functional link to a faith-based prayer group. Eric believed that each of these features demonstrated that the product had great acceptance as a trusted channel to the health care consumer.

In June 2002, Mark Day left the company to enroll in the MBA program at the Wharton School of the University of Pennsylvania. Having now transitioned from a technical role to one more deeply involved with marketing, sales, and fund raising, Mark sought to build a more fundamental understanding of these areas through his MBA studies.

Research Insights

Working with researchers and a sponsoring institution, TLC had conducted a survey of CarePage visitors and managers. In September 2002, it added a new feature to the Children's Hospital Boston site: an online survey capability. This was tested during a two-week period in the pediatric cardiology unit. One version was offered to CarePage managers, who were automatically presented with the survey at their fifth log-in, and another to CarePage visitors who first saw the survey at their third log-in. During a two-week period, 27 managers (90 percent) and 636 visitors (79 percent) responded. A majority (63 percent) of all respondents were female. The results, presented in **Exhibit 2** showed that the service was highly valued. The majority of users reported that the service improved their opinion of the Children's Hospital, made them more likely to recommend it, led them to visit the hospital's Web site, and increased their likelihood of donating to the hospital foundation.

A second project involved the launch of pilot donation programs at C. S. Mott Children's Hospital in Michigan and Children's Memorial Hospital in Chicago. When visitors were asked about their willingness to make a donation, 11 percent stated that they were willing to make a donation immediately, and a further 22 percent requested the opportunity to do so at a later date.

Eric was very excited about this finding, which suggested that TLC could be presented to nonprofit hospitals as a self-financing service. But he recognized the importance of continuing to use what some experts had described as "permission marketing":

> We're a mission-driven organization. We created this company to serve patients, their families, and their support networks. We understand the importance of the contract that we make with our members and we like to think of it as a moral contract.
>
> However, we recognize that the service we deliver to our members doesn't provide sufficient revenue to our customers, the hospitals. Added value items are what persuade hospitals to buy. So in certain respects we've commercialized the reach that we offer to the hospitals, but we try to do it in a way that we regard as "noble."
>
> We wouldn't do anything that would adversely impact the integrity of our service delivery. So we ask permission from our users to give their names to the hospital foundation for mailing—they can choose to opt in. If a hospital's CarePage service is sponsored by a third party, then a similar, permission-based approach might be used to give members the opportunity to receive information from that sponsor.

The Situation in Early 2003

The first quarter of 2003 saw a rapid acceleration of revenues as more hospitals signed up for TLC service, existing customers renewed their contracts, and the number of CarePages at each institution continued to grow. Unlike new sales, renewals involved almost no additional cost for TLC, and increasing utilization generated higher revenues from existing customers. TLC now served 40 hospitals; they were predominantly academic medical centers and included several of the most prestigious institutions in the United States and Canada. There were additional prospects in the sales pipeline. However, the company did not yet have any customers among nursing homes and hospices.

Existing competitors no longer seemed to pose a threat. VisitingOurs had recently shut down, and a comparison of the service features offered by TLC and the two remaining players—

Exhibit 2   Executive Summary: Children's Hospital Boston Online Survey Results

In September 2002, TLContact added a new feature to the Children's Hospital Boston (CHB) branded site: an online survey, with one version offered to CarePage Managers (who are first presented with the survey at their 5th log-in) and another to CarePage Visitors (who first see the survey after their 3rd log-in).

The TLContact Online Survey garnered an outstanding response rate. The initial test period ran from August 29 to September 13, 2002, and was targeted at patient families of the 50-bed cardiovascular unit of CHB. During the initial test period, surveys were completed by 27/30 (90 percent) of managers and 636/806 (79 percent) of visitors. There were a total of 663 respondents, most (63 percent) of whom were female. As detailed in the following section, virtually all managers and visitors highly value the CarePage service. Moreover, the majority of people who used the service report that it improved their opinion of the hospital, made them more likely to recommend the hospital, led them to visit the hospital's Web site, and increased their likelihood of donating to the hospital foundation.

Questions Asked of Both Managers and Visitors (27 managers + 636 visitors = 663 total)

	Number of Responses	Percent
1. How are you related to the patient?		
I am a friend	466	72
I am a family member or guardian	169	26
I am a caregiver or care provider	14	2
I am the patient	2	0
2. Would you recommend the CarePage service to other people?		
Yes	641	99
No	5	1
3. Do you think that CarePages are an important service for hospitals to offer?		
Yes	643	99
No	6	1

4. Did your experience with Children's Hospital Boston's CarePage service …	# Yes	% Yes
Improve your opinion of the hospital?	528	91
Make you more likely to recommend this hospital?	503	86
Cause you to visit Children's Hospital Boston's Web site?	319	55
Make you more likely to make a charitable gift to the hospital foundation?	298	53

The questions that were asked only of managers indicated that most learned of the CarePage service via hospital materials. The item in which managers rated hospital service (see #2, following) indicates the value of increasing adoption of the CarePage service, perhaps through personal messages from hospital staff. These "real-time" service ratings offer clear and significant opportunities for improving service and satisfaction.

Questions Asked Only of Managers (27 total)

1. How did you learn about the CarePage service?

	Number of Responses	Percent
Materials in the hospital	11	46
Hospital staff member	7	29
Friend or family member	6	25
Hospital physician	0	0
The Internet	0	0
Ad or story in the media	0	0

Exhibit 2 **(continued)**

2. Please rate the following ...

	Poor	Fair	Good	Very Good	Excellent
			(% based on 21 responses to this item)		
Overall quality of patient care	0	0	0	14	86
Doctor courtesy and attentiveness	0	5	5	19	71
Staff courtesy and attentiveness	0	0	0	33	67
Communication about patient care	0	0	5	43	52
Admissions process	5	5	20	30	40
Cleanliness of room	0	10	14	38	38
Food	5	10	29	38	19

Questions Asked Only of Visitors (442 responses of 636 total)

1. Please rate your overall impression of Children's Hospital Boston's ...

	%N/A	%Poor	%Good	%Excellent
Quality of care	55	0	9	36
Commitment to patient satisfaction	51	0	11	38
Staff courtesy and attention	60	0	9	31
		Valid percent (based on responses other than N/A)		
Quality of care		0	20	80
Commitment to patient satisfaction		0	22	78
Staff courtesy and attention		0	23	77

2. Which of the following areas of health education are of interest to you?

	Number of Responses	Percent of Respondents*
Heart disease	153	47
Cancer screening and treatment	120	37
Women's health issues	122	37
Health and fitness	121	37
Weight control and obesity	96	29
Common aging concerns	84	26
Allergies and asthma	77	24
Depression	75	23
Diabetes	69	21
Pain management	58	18
Growth and development	51	16
Behavioral problems	45	14
Common childhood illnesses	41	13
Clinical trials	21	6
Immunization	17	5
"Other"	28	9

*The total percentage for all items is greater than 100% because the 326 people who answered this question offered multiple responses (i.e., they were interested in more than one area).

Responses to the visitors' question regarding hospital service reflect what they hear from the CarePage managers, as well as general impressions and personal experience. The item regarding interest in health education provides a sense of topics about which respondents desire more information, suggesting an opportunity for TLContact's partners.

The Status, and CaringBridge—showed that TLC's CarePage service had substantial advantages (**Exhibit 3**). Moreover, the prospect that some hospitals might attempt to create their own service offerings appeared increasingly unlikely. A large, well-endowed children's hospital, which had previously declared its intention to develop a similar service in-house, had recently decided to adopt TLC instead, admitting that internal analysis had revealed that going it alone would not only be very time consuming but also prohibitively expensive.

The crisis created by the Severe Acute Respiratory Syndrome (SARS) epidemic had presented an unusual opportunity for TLC in Toronto, the only North American city to suffer significant infections and deaths. To contain the disease, the provincial government of Ontario had quarantined a number of hospitals, closing them to visitors. TLC announced that it would make CarePage service available immediately to such hospitals at a special price to facilitate patient/family communications, emphasizing that technical implementation was completely independent of a hospital's IT infrastructure and could be accomplished within 24 hours.

Exhibit 3   Patient Communication Service Feature Comparison

	TLContact	The Status	CaringBridge
Customer Service			
Toll-free phone support	✓	✓	
Email support	✓	✓	✓
Spanish-language support	✓		
Comprehensive online help	✓	✓	
Features for Health Care Facilities			
Custom Services			
Welcome message	✓		
Active survey system	✓		
Active donation system	✓		
Custom links to hospital's Web site	✓	✓	
Unit specification	✓		
Spanish-language version	✓		
Baby-specific version	✓	✓	✓
Detailed usage reports	✓	✓	
Branding			
Cobranded patient page	✓	✓	✓
Entire Web site cobranded		✓	
Customized colors and graphics	✓		
Features for Patients			
Patient Updates/News	✓	✓	✓
Email notification	✓		
Ability to edit	✓	✓	
Adjustable time zones	✓	✓	
Sorting and paging	✓		
Printer friendly version	✓	✓	
Message Board	✓	✓	✓
Ability to reply to messages	✓		
Printer friendly version	✓	✓	

PLANNING THE AGENDA FOR THE BOARD MEETING

Having completed the quarterly activity update, Eric turned to the task of creating an agenda for the upcoming board meeting. He started to rough out some thoughts. Under FUTURE GROWTH, he jotted down: "How fast? What directions? Key targets as selling priorities? Opportunities for revenues from new added-value services? Launch stripped-down version of TLC service at much lower price?"

The next heading was COMPETITION. He wrote "VisitingOurs folds. Comparison chart of TLC vs. The Status, Caring Bridge. Future threats?" Eric paused, holding his pen in the air. He recognized that at some point, a major player in the trillion-dollar health care market might be tempted to replicate TLC's CarePage technology and service features. However, he was reassured that it would require an extensive investment of money and time. A further barrier to competition was patent protection, although ultimately, strategic partnerships, continued growth, product enhancements, and maintenance of exceptional customer satisfaction levels constituted the most complete defense. Lowering the pen to paper, he added: "Would competition hurt us? Can we competition-proof TLC?"

Then he turned his attention to the Health Television Network. Should it continue to be run as a relatively independent service, he wondered, or should it be integrated more closely with TLC's core business? Under STRATEGY FOR HTN, he wrote: "Preferred target customers? Desired growth rate? Partnerships to develop expanded programming? Sponsors? If so, who? TLC as health care media venture—potential synergies between HTN and CarePages? New technologies?"

An important issue for the board to discuss concerned the role of future partnerships between TLC and other industry players. Recently, one large supplier of medical equipment and services had expressed interest in taking a minority financial stake in the company. POSSIBLE FINANCIAL PARTNERSHIP, he wrote, and below it: "Finance for accelerated growth? Market leverage? Pros and cons? Timing-now vs. later?"

Eric smiled. With an agenda like this, he anticipated a stimulating discussion at the board meeting. Then his face took on a more serious look. "WE ARE A MISSION-DRIVEN ORGANIZATION," he printed carefully, and underlined it twice.

Study Questions

1. Evaluate the evolution of TLC and identify key decisions that kept it afloat and underpinned its subsequent success.
2. How does TLC create value for (a) patients and their families, and (b) hospitals?
3. Review the five topics on Eric Langshur's rough draft of the agenda for the board meeting. As a board member, what position would you take on each, and why?

Appendix

Recent Feedback from Users

- "TLContact has been the lifeline of many of the families on my unit and keeps the support network of family and friends alive and thriving. I cannot stress enough how important this website is to families in crisis or enduring a chronic illness. Thank you Thank you Thank you!" (*Theresa, Child Life Specialist, C. S. Mott Children's Hospital*)

- "This is a prime example of why Children's has the world-class reputation it does. Thanks for caring enough about your patients and their families to continually strive to keep Children's 'a cut above.'"

- "What a wonderful service to provide to your patients and their families. …This can only help to enhance the patient's rate of recovery and help everyone cope with the hospitalization experience."

- "I cannot express what an incredible blessing this website was. We could update everyone at the same time without anything getting misconstrued. To go to the site and see so many folks sending well wishes and prayers and was so uplifting and helpful. We received so many comments from family and friends that the site was fabulous! Please keep this service!"

- "I want you to know that this is a brilliant idea. It helps immeasurably to humanize the difficulties of communication surrounding hospitalization."

- "What a great concept! For someone that is not a family member, but a close friend, this is a great way to communicate on the schedule of the patient's family. I'm really impressed. …I'm going to forward this link to my pastor, I'm sure he will find it useful."

- "My daughter's illness was sudden and life threatening. We were transferred from one hospital to a children's hospital. Everyone had thought the worst when they couldn't find us in our hometown hospital. Our only connection was your service. It saved me, mom, from intense stress as everyone wanted to know hour-by-hour updates. In some cases it was the ONLY information our families received. Your service is a godsend for the patients and the families. Because of your service, churches around the US gathered to pray for our little girl. Those prayers wouldn't have happened if we didn't have the internet connection that you and the hospital gave to us. Now we celebrate that our little girl made it and people like you helped us."

- "Excellent service, and such a help at such a stressful time in our lives. Not having to make multiple phone calls, and everyone hearing information "firsthand," is such a huge help. We've often logged on in the middle of the night, from the ICU, in the middle of our stressful life-and-death dance as the baby fights to live, to read all the kind words of encouragement our family and friends have left for us. The baby's been in and out of the hospital many times now in his short 6 months so far, and words cannot express what a difference it makes, to know that everyone's out there pulling for us, and praying for us. Thanks so much!"

- "This web service is perfect for our situation. My 19-year-old son suffered a severe head injury. The hospital he was transferred to is 3 hours from our home. We live in a very small, tight community. We have lots and lots of concerned family and friends. Our son will have ongoing treatment and progress that our family and friends want to stay informed of. It's a wonderful tool and I have had nothing but positive feedback from the users. Thank you."

- "You have truly done a wonderful thing with this CarePage, and the pictures, updates, and message board help friends and family all keep in contact, all at the same place—it's just remarkable! Thank you so much for providing this service. It's great for those of us who cannot afford to be there in person, but whose hearts are there to support our friends and family. It's people like you who make a difference in this world! May God Richly Bless You All in your continued efforts to help those in need!"

Name Index

Subject Index